BED & BREAKFAST
IN THE MID-ATLANTIC STATES

"A model for the guidebook industry."   —*Inn Business Review*

". . . the most detailed and extensively researched guidebooks available."
—*Country Almanac* magazine

"The best of its kind. A must . . ."   —**WPHL-TV, Philadelphia**

"It's one of those books you can't put down."
—**Phyllis Long, Hershey, Pennsylvania**

"Your guidebook was a very helpful tool for us, making our vacation in the U.S. very enjoyable."
—**Iris Ehgartner, Vienna, Austria**

"Answers to the kinds of questions you always forget to ask the innkeeper when making reservations."
—*Innsider* magazine

"Provides vicarious vacationing as well as being a good resource."
—**Sara E. Ward, Pittsburgh, Pennsylvania**

"Purchased four different B&B publications. . . . We found your guide to be outstanding and far superior to the other books. The information was wonderfully comprehensive, and the map format was invaluable."
—**Howard R. Katz, Chevy Chase, Maryland**

"In the world of publishing, she's a central point for the entire concept of Bed and Breakfast."
—*The Tab*, **Newton, Massachusetts**

"The Bed & Breakfast guru."   —*Travel Agent* magazine

"The travel philosopher. . . [whose] words I often recall."   —*Spy* magazine

"A legend in the B&B world."
—**Bed & Breakfast International, California**

"Unprecedented personal and logistical data about hosts and accommodations."
—**The American Bed & Breakfast Association**

"We have utilized your guide like a bible—and have never been steered wrong. Each time we leave, we swear to ourselves we're coming back next year—that this indeed was our best trip. But each year we wind up choosing another destination just to experience someplace new . . . with the sure knowledge of your book to guide us."
—**Patricia Caven, Ottawa, Canada**

Bed & Breakfast in the Mid-Atlantic States

Delaware, Maryland, New Jersey,
New York, North Carolina,
Pennsylvania, Virginia,
Washington, D.C., West Virginia

Third Edition

by Bernice Chesler

A Voyager Book

The Globe Pequot Press

Old Saybrook, Connecticut

Library of Congress Cataloging-in-Publication Data

Chesler, Bernice.
    Bed and breakfast in the mid-Atlantic States : Delaware, Maryland, New Jersey, New York, North Carolina, Pennsylvania, Virginia, Washington D.C., West Virginia / by Bernice Chesler. -- 3rd ed.
        p. cm.
    "A Voyager Book."
    Includes index.
    ISBN 1-56440-164-2
    1. Bed and breakfast accommodations--Middle Atlantic States--Guidebooks. I. Title.
TX907.3.M53C48   1993
647.947503--dc20
                                                                93-3429
                                                                CIP

Editorial and Production Services: Editorial Inc. of Rockport, Massachusetts
Cover design: Hannus Design Associates
Cover photo: Shelburne Museum, Shelburne, Vermont. Photograph by
    Ken Burris
Text design: Penny Darras-Maxwell
Composition in Meridien on the Ventura 3.0 system
    Manufactured in the United States of America
    Third Edition / Second Printing

To David

CONTENTS

Introduction   ix
Answers to Frequently Asked Questions   xi

B&B Reservation Services   1
Delaware   3
Maryland   11
New Jersey   53
New York   93
North Carolina   187
Pennsylvania   221
Virginia   313
Washington, D.C.   391
West Virginia   405

Index   421

INTRODUCTION

"Those hosts would be great for a documentary film," I said to my husband. We were leaving a Vermont bed and breakfast, a genuine farmhouse; the farmer had offered me cow salve to soothe leg muscles that ached from pedaling over the hilly terrain.

That was a dozen years ago. (I had been working as a documentary film researcher for public television.) Who would have guessed then that bed and breakfast was to become the hottest trend in American travel? The acceptance of B&Bs on this side of the ocean came at just the right time for us—just as our youngest left for college, just as we were to discover the joys of pedaling from B&B to B&B, and from one interesting experience to another in what is now a total of 14 states and 6 countries.

In the 1990s bed and breakfast has come to be recognized for its personalized style, for hosts who help to give a sense of place. Now many B&B hosts have plotted back-road routes for guests. With the advent of bed and breakfast reservation services, bed and breakfasts are in the city and suburbs as well as in rural areas. In addition, B&Bs have opened in restored everything—from churches to schoolhouses, from beach cottages to mansions.

To distinguish private homes from inns, this book has introduced a symbol (◢) for private homes that have one, two, or three guest rooms. B&B inns are likely to be larger, are a full-time profession, and in some cases have one or more hired staffers. Other symbols—in answer to travelers' requests—will lead you (quickly) to a romantic place, a spot that is great for kids, or a B&B where your group, family, or colleagues might book the entire place. See the key to symbols that appears at intervals throughout the book.

In documentary film style, *Bed & Breakfast in the Mid-Atlantic States* tries to focus as much on the memorable hosts as on their homes and B&B inns. In addition, each description aims to save travelers' time by anticipating questions: Located on a main road? What time is breakfast? Sample menu? Size of bed? What floors are rooms on? Shower *and* tub? Is smoking allowed? Any pets in residence? What's the difference between the $60 and the $90 room?

Research for my first B&B guide began in 1980. Eight B&B books and about 2,000 interviews later, this latest edition reflects the wide range of possibilities that fit into my original interpretation of bed and breakfast: a home setting with an owner in residence; a maximum of about 10 rooms; a common room; breakfast included in the rate, but no public restaurant or bar on the premises.

So what's changed? This edition has added one more state, North Carolina, in response to many requests. New owners are in residence. Lots of new places have opened. Many gazebos are on the outside. Many more private baths are on the inside. New layers of regulations have added to costs and rates. Old-timers (more than five years in business) find themselves adding a few rooms to keep B&B economically viable. Some move across the street or next door. They learn to hire an inn-sitter now and then. And always, there is a steady stream of dreamers who see B&B—after all, it's only breakfast, they say—as a fantasy lifestyle.

And what about you, the traveler? The art of letter writing is alive! Excerpts from some of the thousands of enthusiastic letters written to me are included in this book. There really is a letter of the day, usually one that reinforces the concept of a people-to-people program—and makes you feel good all over.

Accuracy is a hallmark of this book. Every detail was confirmed just before press time. But please keep in mind that successful hosts sometimes make *changes in rooms, beds, menu, or decor—and yes, in rates too.*

My thanks go to Lourdes Alvarez, who, with great cheer and efficiency, has handled more than 30,000 pieces of paper, deciphered floor plans, and decoded hieroglyphics. It is a pleasure to work with Jay Howland, my editor who remembers everything and everyone. Additional support and encouragement have come from my agent, Laura Fillmore, and the staff of Editorial Inc., including David Eales, Tim Evans, MaryEllen Oliver, and Mary Helen Gunn. Penny Darras-Maxwell, who created the design for this book, died before the book came out. We remember her with fondness and her work with gratitude and respect. And once again, David, my husband, has planned all our trips by plane, car, and bicycle. He listens, offers judgment when I solicit objectivity, and acts as my computer expert in residence.

Suggestions about people and places are welcome for consideration in the next edition. Please address them to me at The Globe Pequot Press, 6 Business Park Road, P.O. Box 833, Old Saybrook, CT 06475.

Bernice Chesler

Answers to Frequently
Asked Questions

What is bed and breakfast?

It is a package arrangement that includes overnight accommodations and breakfast. Although embellishments (amenities) are offered at many American B&Bs, the keynote is hospitality. Think of it as a people-to-people program.

Are baths shared?

Some are. But, depending on the number of guests, a shared bath could be private for you. Many American B&Bs have followed the trend to all private baths, sometimes with a shower but no tub, sometimes with a whirlpool bath and a sauna too.

How much do B&Bs cost?

Rates range from $45 to well over $100 (including breakfast) for two people. The season, location, amenities, food, length of ownership, maintenance costs, taxes—all affect the rate. Remember: Nothing is standardized at B&Bs. In this book, check under "Rates" to see what credit cards are accepted at a particular B&B. Many small places prefer cash or travelers' checks. And it's a good idea to check on deposit requirements; refund policies differ. Required local and/or state taxes vary from place to place, and are seldom in the listed rates. Suggestion: Consider paying upon arrival. Good-byes will be that much smoother, and you really do feel as if you have visited friends.

To tip or not?

In a private home, tipping is not a usual practice, *but* times may be changing. In a private home where B&B is rather constant, owners realize that extra help helps. Those B&B owners also know that some remembrance is appreciated by the part-time folks who contribute to your memorable stay.

In a B&B inn, treat staff as you would in a hotel. *Some inns, particularly those in resort areas, add gratuities to the tab*—or else they couldn't keep their help!

An interesting phenomenon: An amazing number of travelers write heartfelt thank-you notes to surprised and delighted hosts.

Is B&B like a hotel?

Not at all! It's not intended to be. You are greeted by a family member or an assistant, or occasionally by a note. Every room is different in size, layout, and decor. A B&B may not provide the privacy—or the loneliness—of a hotel. Because business travelers have discovered B&Bs, there may be a phone jack or even a private phone in the room. (Reminder: There is no desk clerk. Please call the B&B during reasonable hours.) If you must have things exactly as they are in the hotel you usually go to, go to the hotel!

Is B&B for everyone?

Many B&Bs are perfect for unwinding and a change of pace. However, if you seek anonymity, B&B probably isn't for you. As one host said, "Guests who come to B&Bs are outgoing; they want to be sociable and learn about you and the area." Among all the wonderful guests, a few hosts can recall an occasional "memorable" demanding guest (it's fun to see the change that frequently takes place overnight) or a first-timer who arrived with considerable luggage—cumbersome indeed on the narrow steep stairs to the third floor of a historic house. Tastes and interpretations differ. Take charm, for example. "Tell me," said the older guest, "what's so charming about a tub on legs? I was so glad when built-ins finally became the fashion." Recommendation: Tell the host if this is your first time at a B&B. When making the reservation, if privacy is a real concern, say that too. Hosts' listening skills are usually well tuned.

How do B&Bs on this side of the Atlantic differ from those in the British Isles or other countries?

The B&B-and-away-you-go is not necessarily the norm in North America. Although there are B&Bs with just one room and many where you are expected to leave for the day, guests are often invited to spend more time after breakfast "at home"—by the pool or fireplace, on the hiking trails or on borrowed bicycles. Even hosts are amazed at what they do when they get involved in others' lives! They worry about late arrivals. They have been known to drive someone to a job appointment or to do laundry for a businessman whose schedule changed or to prevail upon the local auto mechanic when the garage was closed.

Can I book through travel agents?

Many travel agents have caught on to the popularity of B&Bs. In this book B&Bs with the ♦ in the "Rates" section pay commissions to travel agents. And some agents will make arrangements for you, whether or not they receive a commission from the B&B.

Do B&Bs welcome children?

In this book B&Bs with the symbol 🎄 are always happy to host children. Some B&Bs without the symbol also welcome children, though not necessarily a houseful! Although there are B&Bs that provide everything from the sandbox to the high chair—and a babysitter too—some B&B hosts have been known to say (tactfully), "Children find us tiresome." Check the "Plus" section in the descriptions in this book. Consider the facilities, the room and bath arrangements, and the decor. Are your kids enticed by candlelit breakfasts? Are they used to being around "don't touch" antiques? Do they enjoy classical music? Are rooms limited to two persons? Is a crib provided? Are there lots of animals on the farm? Is there a built-in playmate, perhaps an innkeeper's child? Remember what you looked for B.C. (before children). If you do bring the kids and still wish for some private time at the B&B, please arrange for a sitter. Be fair to yourself and your children, to other guests, and the to host/chef/gardener/interior designer/historian—who really does love children.

Are there facilities for physically handicapped persons?

Some. Rooms that are handicapped accessible are noted in the detailed "Bed and bath" item of each B&B description in this book. In addition, each writeup mentions the floor locations of guest rooms.

Are there B&Bs that prohibit smoking?

Many do. (Note the ⚬ symbol in this book.) Among the B&Bs that do allow smoking, many limit it to certain areas or rooms.

If you like people and enjoy company and cooking, isn't that enough to make you a happy host?

It helps. But experienced hosts all comment on the time and work involved. Guests who ask, "Is this all you do?" would be surprised to realize that there is more to hosting than serving tea and meeting interesting people. Even I have fallen into the trap of multiplying a full house by the nightly rate, only to hear my husband say, "Never mind, that's 600 sheets!"

What do you recommend to those who dream about opening a B&B?

For starters, attend one of the workshops or seminars given by adult education centers, extension services, innkeepers, or B&B reservation services. Apprentice, even for a weekend, or sign up with a reservation service and host in your own home. Many prospective innkeepers attend Bill Oates and Heide Bredfeldt's seminar, "How to Purchase and Operate a Bed & Breakfast or Country Inn." Contact Oates & Bredfeldt, P.O. Box 1162, Brattleboro, VT 05302, 802/254–5931. For a free Aspiring Innkeepers' Kit that includes a list of innkeeping workshops conducted in various parts of the country, contact the Professional Association of Innkeepers International, P.O. Box 90710, Santa Barbara, CA 93190, 805/569–1853; fax 805/682–1016. Every host in this book enjoys what they call "the great emotional rewards of a stimulating occupation." Some remind couples who wish to make hosting a vocation that it helps to have a strong marriage. One who encourages prospective innkeepers to "Just do it!" adds, "but be aware that you have to be more gregarious than private. You have to learn to carve time out for yourself. Hosting requires a broad range of talents (knowledge of plumbing helps), a lot of flexibility, an incredible amount of stamina, and perseverance. And did I mention you might need some capital?"

Can a host or reservation service pay to be in this book?

No. All selections are made by the author. There are no application fees. And all descriptions are written by the author; no host or service proprietor can write his or her own description. A processing fee is paid after each selected B&B and reservation service reviews its writeup. The fee offsets the extensive research that results in highly detailed writeups reflecting the individual spirit of each B&B. The processing fee for an individual B&B is $125. (For those with one or two rooms and a top rate of $50, it is $100.) The fee for a fully described reservation service is $125; for a reservation service host, $40. The author pays for all her stays.

What are some of your favorite B&Bs?

Even when you stay in hundreds, you tend to remember the hosts of each B&B more than the place. We have arrived on bicycles and been greeted with the offer of a car to go to dinner. There's the horticulturist, a septuagenarian, whom we could hardly keep up with as she toured us through her spectacular gardens. There's the couple who built their own solar house. Multifaceted retirees. The history buffs who filled us in on the area and recommended back roads. The literary buffs who suggested good books. Hosts in a lovely residential section just minutes off the highway. Hosts we have laughed with. Yes, even some we have cried with too. Great chefs. People who are involved in their communities and trying to make this a better world. People whose home has been a labor of love and who love sharing it with others. We have enjoyed rather luxurious settings and some casual places too. It is true that each B&B is special in its own way. That's why the place to stay has become the reason to go. It's wonderful.

B&B RESERVATION SERVICES

A reservation service is in the business of matching screened hosts and guests. Although it can be a seasonal operation, in some areas the service is a full-time job for an individual, a couple, partners, or a small group. For hosts, it's a private way of going public, because the host remains anonymous until the service (agency) matches host and guest. This unique system allows hosts in private homes to have an off-and-on hosting schedule.

Listings may be in communities where there are no overnight lodging facilities, or they may provide an alternative to hotels or motels. Although most services feature private homes, others include B&B inns with 6–10 guest rooms. And some services now offer stays in unhosted homes.

Each service determines its own area and conducts its own inspections and interviews. A service may cover just one community, or a metropolitan area, or an entire region.

Advance notice is preferred and even, with many services, required. Length-of-stay requirements vary. Some services stipulate a one-night surcharge; some require a minimum of two nights.

Rates are usually much less than at area hotels and motels. The range may cover everything from "budget" to "luxury." Deposits are usually required. Refund policies, detailed with each reservation service description in this book, differ.

Fee arrangements vary. Many services include their commission in the quoted nightly rate. For public inns the services' quoted rate may be the same as what the inn charges, or it could be a total of the inn's rate plus a booking fee (about $5–$15).

Write for printed information or maybe, better yet, call. Before calling, think about bed and bath arrangements, parking, smoking, pets, children, air conditioning—whatever is important to you.

A reservation service acts as a clearinghouse and frequently provides an opportunity to stay at a B&B that would not be available any other way.

KEY TO SYMBOLS
♥ Lots of honeymooners come here.
♯ Families with children are very welcome. (Please see page xii.)
● "Please emphasize that we are a private home, not an inn."
♣ Groups or private parties sometimes book the entire B&B.
◆ Travel agents' commission paid. (Please see page xii.)
✖ Sorry, no guests' pets are allowed.
✕ No smoking inside *or* no smoking at all, even on porches.

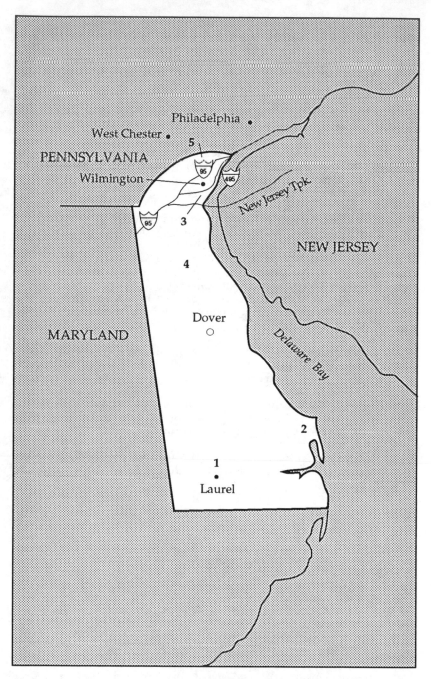

The numbers on this map indicate the locations of B&Bs described in detail in this chapter.

DELAWARE

1 **Laurel**
 Spring Garden Bed & Breakfast
 Inn, 5
2 **Lewes**
 Bed & Breakfast of Delaware
 Host #35, 6
3 **New Castle**
 Bed & Breakfast of Delaware
 Host #32, 7

4 **Odessa**
 Bed & Breakfast of Delaware
 Host #34, 7
5 **Wilmington**
 The Boulevard Bed &
 Breakfast, 8

___ Delaware Reservation Service ___

Bed & Breakfast of Delaware

Box 177, 3650 Silverside Road, Wilmington, DE 19810

Phone: 302/479–9500. Monday–Friday 9–5.

Listings: Over 40. Mostly hosted private residences. Some small inns. In Pennsylvania—in Brandywine Valley, Chadds Ford, West Chester, New Hope, Landenberg, Oxford, Kennett Square. In Delaware—Wilmington, Newark, New Castle, Odessa, Dover, Bridgeville, Laurel, Milford, Lewes, Dagsboro, and Selbyville. Some are near the University of Delaware in Newark and Del-Tech campuses in Wilmington. Others are on the Eastern Shore of Maryland and Virginia's Chesapeake Bay.

Reservations: 2–3 days' advance notice requested. Will try to accommodate last-minute requests.

Rates: $55 to $160 double occupancy. $5 less for singles. $5 surcharge for one-night stay. Reservations guaranteed by credit card required. Cancellations must be received 14 days prior to scheduled arrival date in order for deposit to be fully applied to any future visit within one year or for deposit to be refunded less a $25 per room processing fee. Deposits are on a per-night basis and cannot be credited against the balance due in the event of late arrival or early departure. MC, Visa. ◆

Millie D. Alford is an experienced host and reservation service owner who knows the area well. Some of her varied listings are on the National Register. "They are near beautiful museums, the beach, near a bus line, or in suburban locations. Some feature fireplaces, pools, and/or Jacuzzis. All feature hosts who enjoy making guests want to return soon!"

Plus: Short-term housing available.

KEY TO SYMBOLS

♥ Lots of honeymooners come here.

♯ Families with children are very welcome. (Please see page xii.)

◖ "Please emphasize that we are a private home, not an inn."

♣♣ Groups or private parties sometimes book the entire B&B.

◆ Travel agents' commission paid. (Please see page xii.)

✖ Sorry, no guests' pets are allowed.

✔ No smoking inside *or* no smoking at all, even on porches.

Delaware B&Bs

Spring Garden Bed & Breakfast Inn
Route 1, Box 283A, Laurel, DE 19956   302/875–7015

Host: Gwen North
Location: Hidden from road by pine trees. Bordered by three acres of lawn, fruit trees, herb and flower gardens, and boxwood. Minutes from Route 13. Within walking or biking distance of "our friendly unspoiled rural town," which is on the National Register of Historic Places. Four miles to state park; 30 minutes to Atlantic beaches and Chesapeake Bay.
Open: Year round.
Rates: Per room. $65 shared bath, $75 private. Suite $85. $5 one-night surcharge. Discounts for stays of five or more days.
♥ ⚔ ♣ ♦ ✈

"The house of two centuries," on the National Register, consists of a 1786 brick building and an 1800s clapboard Victorian addition. Most of the major work was done by Gwen's parents when they bought the house in the 1950s. In the 1980s Gwen completed the restoration, keeping the original wainscoting, dentil ceiling moldings, and latch-style locks and heart pine paneling too. Her interest in the family's collectibles and 18th-century furnishings will, someday, lead to an antiques shop in the barn. For her Eastern Shore inn-to-inn bicycling idea, she won Delaware's first tourism award for excellence in hospitality.

Gwen, a counselor and Realtor, had been associated with art galleries. A hit in Philadelphia's Bloomingdale's Meet-the-Hosts program and Manhattan's Bloomingdale's B&B photo essay (both based on this book), she greets guests with wine and cheese and has enough "to do" suggestions (see "Plus" below) to make you wish you were staying longer.

In residence: One dog, "Boo Too, a mixed-breed enthusiastic bilingual (English and Spanish) welcomer."
Bed and bath: Five rooms. A suite, next to garden, with a double four-poster bed, private shower bath, TV, sitting room. One room with canopied double bed, sitting area, private bath. Twin-bedded room and two double-bedded rooms (one with working fireplace) share two baths.
Breakfast: 8–9:30. Juice, seasonal fruits, cereals, yogurt; home-baked muffins, biscuits, or buns; Scotch eggs; coffee, tea, or milk. Served in country kitchen with wood stove or on porch overlooking garden.
Plus: Bedroom air conditioners. Fresh flowers. Fruit bowls. Fireplaced living room. TV. Library. Bicycles ($10 a day), badminton, croquet, horseshoes. Kitchen and laundry privileges (extra charge). Will meet guests at Salisbury airport (15 miles south). Among suggestions: "the best oysters"; a place where wild ponies roam free; auctions (Gwen goes too); flea markets; wilderness canoe trips; the last remaining free cable ferry in the state; canoes and rowboats for rent; "best bass fishing in the state."

Bed & Breakfast of Delaware Host #35

Lewes, Delaware

Location: Residential. On a treed corner lot along historic walking tour route. Two blocks from restaurants. Minutes from stores and antiques shops. A mile from bay beach; 2 miles from ocean beach.

Reservations: Available year round through Bed & Breakfast of Delaware, page 4.
Rates: $65 queen bed. $75 double bed. $85 double and single. $85 twin beds.
♥ ♯ ♠ ♣ ✂

High ceilings and lots of space, color, and art (a wonderful African collection) are features of this 1888 Victorian house that became a B&B when a retired salesman and his wife, a retired educator (plus—read on) converted it to a B&B seven years ago. They installed a Jacuzzi available to all, put rocking chairs on the front porch, an umbrella and tables on the back porch. There's a swing in the wisteria arbor, an orchard on the side, volleyball and badminton—and a hot/cold shower in the backyard.

Shoot pool. Or borrow one of the four bicycles. Read a book. (Some are in every room.) Or have interesting conversations with the energetic hostess, who was a teacher and counselor in Virginia; Washington, D.C.; Venezuela; and Afghanistan. Now she is very active with the American Association of University Women, the local women's club, political organizations, and a mentoring program for incarcerated women. At the University of Delaware she teaches applied economics (through Junior Achievement) and the history of women. She also teaches folk and square dancing and the history of African art to Elderhostelers. Guests can tell that the hosts love this area, the beaches, and B&B.

In residence: Four cats, in hosts' quarters only.
Foreign languages spoken: German, Spanish, French.
Bed and bath: Five rooms. On first floor—room with twin beds, private tub/shower bath; one double-bedded room with private tub/shower bath. On second floor—room with a double and a single bed and private shower bath. Room with queen bed, wicker furnishings shares "a purple passion shower/tub bath" with large queen-bedded room.
Breakfast: Juices. Fruit. Cinnamon hot bread with blueberries or raisins, sausage and bacon, plus cereal and pancakes, French toast, waffles or eggs any style. Swedish coffee.
Plus: Air conditioning and ceiling fans in each room, video movies, cable TV, stereo with classical, operatic, and jazz record collection. Off-street parking.

Unless otherwise stated, rates in this book are per room for two and include breakfast in addition to all the amenities in "Plus." As for taxes and gratuities, please see page xi.

Bed & Breakfast of Delaware Host #32

New Castle, Delaware

Location: On the market square facing the courthouse of town founded in 1651. In historic area with 17th-century village green and 18th- and 19th-century buildings. Near fine restaurants. Five miles from Wilmington; 20 to Winterthur and Longwood Gardens.

Reservations: Available year round through Bed & Breakfast of Delaware, page 4.
Rates: $60 single, $85 double.
♣ ♦ ⋊ ⤪

Sixteen-foot ceilings and red pine floors give this 1860s brick Federal-style townhouse a very spacious feeling. In 1991 the host, a former Marriott Corporation staffer, bought the B&B from the owners/restorers who had established it eight years earlier. She decorated the house with reproduction and antique furnishings and Laura Ashley linens and comforters. "Returnees ask for specific rooms—for the one with a four-poster rice bed or maybe the canopied bed. If they are celebrating a special occasion, they are greeted with flowers and a card. Relatives of local residents come here. And corporate travelers, too, seem to appreciate the wide back verandas that face Battery Park and the river beyond."

Bed and bath: Five air-conditioned rooms with private full baths. On second floor—two large rooms with queen beds, one small room with a single. On third floor, two large queen-bedded rooms.
Breakfast: Usually 8–9. Fresh fruit, juice, cereals, homemade baked goods, coffee. In dining room at table that seats 12.
Plus: Air-conditioned guest rooms. Mints on nightstands. Menus of New Castle and Wilmington restaurants.

Bed & Breakfast of Delaware Host #34

Odessa, Delaware

Location: Residential. Within minutes of historic houses open to the public for tours, exhibits, workshops. Twenty-six miles north of Dover, the state capital, which has walking tours of historic districts. Thirty minutes from New Castle. Four miles from the beautiful St. Andrews School campus (seen in the movie *Dead Poets*

Society). Within 30 miles of Winterthur, Brandywine Museum, and Longwood Gardens.
Reservations: Available year round through Bed & Breakfast of Delaware, page 4.
Rates: $65 double, $85 queen with whirlpool bath.
♣ ⤪

Picture perfect. As seen in *Mid-Atlantic Country* magazine. It's an 1840 house with narrow stairs, low ceilings, and four working fireplaces. There are antique quilts, clocks, ladder-back chairs, games, Chinese porcelain, samplers, kettles, brass, pewter—lots to look at and admire—all placed with care by the owner, an antiques dealer (and now auctioneer) who, as a Realtor in 1982, fell in love with the house that was a potential listing. By the time she had taken down the plaster and done brick work and most of the interior as well

(Please turn page.)

as exterior painting, the creative cook and student of interior design knew that she could never part with this marvelous place. B&B guests, too, are delighted with the decision.

Bed and bath: Three rooms. On second floor, room with double bed, working fireplace, and air conditioning shares a tub/shower bath with room that has canopied four-poster double bed. On third floor, suite with queen bed, private bath with whirlpool tub, air conditioning, TV, "hidden" refrigerator, window seat.
Breakfast: At guests' convenience. Repertoire includes ambrosia fruit cup, orange walnut muffins, baked apples, banana stuffed French toast, sticky buns. Served in fireplaced dining room or brick-floored screened porch.
Plus: Fireplaced sitting room. Fresh flowers. Clock radios. Robes. Books, magazines.

The Boulevard Bed & Breakfast   302/656–9700
1909 Baynard Boulevard, Wilmington, DE 19802-3915

Hosts: Judy and Charles Powell
Open: Year round.
Rates: $50–$55 shared bath. $65 double or queen bed, private bath. $70 suite. $5 rollaway. Singles $5 less. Amex, MC, Visa.
Location: On a tree-lined residential

street in the historic district. Two blocks from city park; 10 from the city center. Half mile east of I–95, exit 8. Within 30 minutes to museums, Longwood Gardens, many corporations.

From New York: "*Sumptuous breakfast . . . charming surroundings . . . my daily accounts of the B&B brought requests for Boulevard brochures from other Winterthur course participants.*" From Connecticut: "*Greeted with warmth and good cheer. . . . A majestic [red-carpeted] staircase that seems to draw you in. . . . Oh! And that porch, perfect for breakfast.*" From Maryland: "*We had our rehearsal, wedding ceremony and reception there . . . comfortable and elegant . . . graciousness of facility matched by graciousness of hosts.*"

What Judy imagined would be a someday New England country inn evolved as a big, gracious 1913 brick house in town with, as Chuck says, some neoclassical, some Federal, some turn-of-the-century architectural features. The furnishings, too, are eclectic—with some antiques and many family pieces. Several weddings have taken place on the landing at the top of the wide staircase. Many a cup of warm mulled cider is enjoyed by the medieval-style library fireplace.

The Powells became innkeepers (and restorers) after 30 years of suburban living, when Chuck, an avocational flier, took early retirement from AT&T in Wilmington in 1985. Judy, an accomplished needleworker, was a bank accounting officer.

Bed and bath: Six rooms with air conditioning, cable TV, desk. On second floor, three with double or queen bed, all private baths (one is tub and shower, two are shower only). On third floor, honeymoon suite with queen bed,

private bath with whirlpool; one twin-bedded and one single-bedded room share a tub and shower bath (robes provided). Rollaway.
Breakfast: Anytime through 9. Freshly squeezed orange juice. Fresh fruit dish. Homemade muffins or fruit bread. Entree made to order—eggs, three-cheese omelet, pecan waffles, apple or yogurt pancakes, cinnamon-swirl French toast. Sausage, ham, or bacon. Cereal. In dining room or through French doors on screened porch.
Plus: Ceiling fans and phones in some rooms. Fireplace and small organ in living room. Fresh flowers. Candy. Guest refrigerator. Transportation to/from train or airport.

Do you have to get up for breakfast?
There's no one rule. Check each description in this book for the various arrangements. More than one guest has been enticed by the aroma of fresh muffins. If you are on business or want to catch the morning ferry, eat-and-run is just fine. If, however, cuisine is a feature, plan on appearing at the specified time!
Vacationers find breakfast a very social time. One hostess says that even when guests say they want to be on the road early, they often linger over breakfast for hours. If hosts join you, please understand when they leave the table after a while.

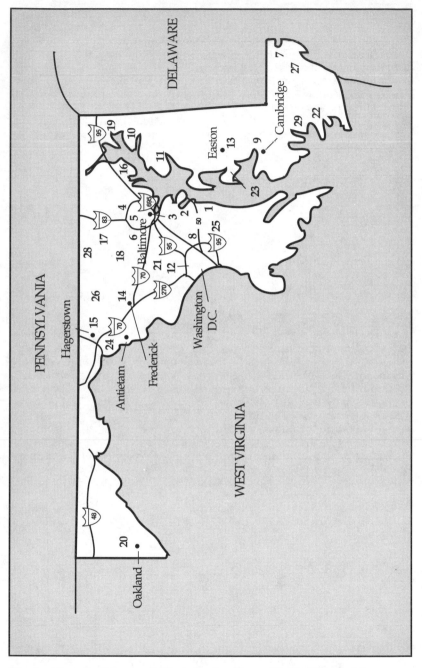

The numbers on this map indicate the locations of B&Bs described in detail in this chapter.

MARYLAND

1 **Annapolis**
   Amanda's Host #112, *14*
   Amanda's Host #259, *14*
   Bed and Breakfast of Maryland
      Host #129, *15*
   Bed and Breakfast of Maryland
      Host #139, *16*
   College House Suites, *17*
   The William Page Inn, *18*
2 **Annapolis: Edgewater**
   Riverwatch Bed & Breakfast, *19*
3 **Baltimore**
   Amanda's Host #110, *20*
   Amanda's Host #201, *20*
   Celie's Waterfront Bed & Break-
      fast, *21*
   Mr. Mole Bed & Breakfast, *22*
4 **Baltimore: Fallston**
   Broom Hall Bed & Breakfast, *23*
5 **Baltimore: Lutherville**
   Twin Gates B&B Inn, *24*
6 **Baltimore: Stevenson**
   Gramercy Bed & Breakfast, *25*
7 **Berlin**
   Holland House B&B, *26*
8 **Burtonsville**
   Bed and Breakfast of Maryland
      Host #189, *27*
9 **Cambridge**
   Glasgow Inn Bed & Breakfast, *28*
10 **Chesapeake City**
   Inn at the Canal, *29*
   Two Rivers Farm, *30*
11 **Chestertown**
   Brampton, *31*
12 **Chevy Chase**
   Chevy Chase Bed &
      Breakfast, *32*
13 **Easton**
   Amanda's Host #137, *33*
14 **Frederick**
   Middle Plantation Inn, *33*

15 **Hagerstown**
   Beaver Creek House Bed &
      Breakfast, *34*
   Lewrene Farm B&B, *35*
   Sunday's Bed & Breakfast, *36*
16 **Havre de Grace**
   Bed & Breakfast of Delaware
      Host #36, *37*
17 **Monkton**
   Amanda's Host #209, *38*
18 **New Market**
   National Pike Inn, *39*
19 **North East**
   The Mill House Bed & Break-
      fast, *40*
20 **Oakland**
   The Oak & Apple, *41*
21 **Olney**
   The Thoroughbred Bed & Break-
      fast, *42*
22 **Princess Anne**
   Elmwood c. 1770 B&B, *43*
23 **St. Michaels**
   Parsonage Inn, *44*
24 **Sharpsburg**
   The Inn at Antietam, *45*
25 **Silver Spring**
   Bed and Breakfast of Maryland
      Host #185, *46*
26 **Smithsburg**
   Blue Bear Bed & Breakfast, *46*
27 **Snow Hill**
   Chanceford Hall Bed & Break-
      fast Inn, *47*
   The River House Inn, *48*
28 **Taneytown**
   Antrim 1844, *49*
   Glenburn, *50*
29 **Vienna**
   Tavern House, *51*

___ Maryland Reservation Services ___

Amanda's Regional Reservation Service for Bed and Breakfast

1428 Park Avenue, Baltimore, MD 21217

Phone: 410/225–0001, Monday–Friday 8:30–5:30; Saturday 8:30–noon.

Fax: 410/728–8957.

Listings: 150. Private homes—historic, urban and rural; small inns (a few with restaurant); and yachts. Many are located throughout Maryland. In Baltimore, in addition to those in downtown row houses, there are some in large older homes and several within walking distance of the new baseball park or the new light rail line to the park. Others are in parts of surrounding states: Delaware; Washington, D.C.; New Jersey; Pennsylvania; Virginia; and West Virginia. Directory: $3.

Reservations: At least one week's advance notice preferred. Some hosts require a minimum stay of two nights.

Rates: $50–$125 single. $60–$295 double. Some family, senior citizen, and weekly rates available. Confirmed reservation cancellations with 10 days' notice receive refund less $25 service charge. Amex, Discover, MC, Visa; 5 percent surcharge. ◆

Betsy Grater is an experienced host as well as reservation service owner. Her listings, visited annually, vary in size, style, and location. Some feature fireplaces, pools, and/or Jacuzzis. Most have air conditioning and private baths. All are hosted by "wonderful and helpful people."

Bed and Breakfast of Maryland/The Traveller in Maryland, Inc.

P.O. Box 2277, Annapolis, MD 21404-2277

Phone: 410/269–6232, Monday–Thursday 9–5; Friday 9–1.

Fax: 410/263–4841.

Listings: 85 in Maryland—plus 115 in London/United Kingdom. In Maryland—in historic, urban, and rural private homes; small inns (a few with restaurant); and yachts. Located primarily in Annapolis, in Baltimore area, on the Eastern Shore, and in Civil War battlefield areas. Others are in Taneytown, Uniontown, and western Maryland. Directory: $5 Maryland; $3 United Kingdom.

Reservations: At least 24 hours' advance notice required. Last-minute reservations sometimes possible. Two-day minimum during holidays or special events.

Rates: $50–$80 single. $55–$90 double. Deposit of one night's stay plus $5 booking fee per location. If cancellation is received at least 10 days before arrival date, deposit less $20 refunded. Amex, MC, Visa. ◆

Founded in 1982, this service annually inspects its accommodations, which vary from "the practical and central to the historic and pastoral." Hosts are "kind, concerned, well-traveled and locally knowledgeable." The service is owned and operated by Greg Page and Rob Zuchelli, William Page Inn innkeepers (page 18), who are active with guided city tours and bed and breakfast organizations.

Plus: Entire itineraries can be arranged with B&B reservations. Short-term (a week or more) hosted and unhosted housing available. Membership (optional for reservations) in Traveler Society is a one-time fee of $15; benefits include Maryland travel information (guidebook and maps), national listing of B&B services, special mailings, and state B&B directory.

B&B guests respond to pampering and change (relax) from the time of arrival to departure. One observant host remarked to some executives: "Maybe when you get back to the big city, you'll be arrested for loitering."

Maryland B&Bs

Amanda's Host #112

Annapolis, MD

Location: On six acres of seclusion, quiet, lawn, gardens, and trees. On a high spot overlooking the cove that borders the sloping lawn. Three miles from historic Annapolis.
Reservations: Available year round through Amanda's Regional Reservation Service, page 12.
Rates: $55 single, $60 double. $15 each additional person.
♥ ♦ ♦ ♣ ♦ ✄

Country picture-perfect. The original cupola sits atop the converted 1850 horse barn. Inside, there are cathedral-ceilinged guest rooms, plenty of windows with water views, antique quilts, watercolors by the hostess, and crafts created by a daughter. It is just as the hosts, a Naval Academy faculty member and an artist, imagined—"the horse barn had the best view!"—during the seven years they lived in the farmhouse "up the hill." Now one married daughter lives in the farmhouse and another is in a newer house on the property. (Both weddings were held here.) Now guests come "to be away," to eat seafood in nearby villages, to walk down to the dock, and to paddle (for hours, if you'd like) up the creek. They comment on the tranquil setting, the food, and the hospitality—all just five minutes' drive from the shops and brick sidewalks of Annapolis.

Bed and bath: On guest (upper) floor, two rooms share two half baths and one shower/tub bath. One double-bedded room with ladder to loft that also has a double bed. One room with king/twins option.
Breakfast: 8:30. Choose from menu the night before. Eggs Benedict, cinnamon raisin bread as French toast with sauteed bananas, Belgian waffles, omelets, blueberry pancakes. One daughter's homemade (the old-fashioned way) herb, cinnamon raisin, or honey whole wheat bread.
Plus: Central air conditioning. A great Great Room. Use of canoe.

Amanda's Host #259

Annapolis, MD

Location: Secluded, quiet, private, and spacious. On two acres on a point with view of Chesapeake Bay. Ten minutes from downtown Annapolis, 30 from Baltimore.
Reservations: Available through Amanda's Regional Reservation Service, page 12.
Rates: Double occupancy $125. $75 each additional person.
♥ ♦ ♦ ✄

"I call the B&B loft a birdcage. It's so lovely! You can hear birds and see greenery. Built on top of our old farmhouse, it's an A-frame structure, a whole little house with living, dining, and sleeping areas. There are two skylights, big windows, and your own deck with umbrella table and chairs. Some guests come just to be here, to enjoy privacy and the grounds—the tall pine trees, the lawn, fish pond, and swimming pool."

The Dutch hosts—she sells jewelry and he is self-employed—have reason to be proud of their gardens. They enjoy sharing this cozy paradise.

Bed and bath: One double-bedded room. Plus a double sofa bed. Private tub/shower bath.

Breakfast: Flexible hours. Orange juice, fruit salad, eggs, muffins, coffee, tea. Brought to guests in loft. Or eat with hosts in first-floor living room overlooking the garden, pool, and (in winter) view of bay with boats.

Plus: Central air conditioning. Tennis court.

Guests wrote: *"A B&B lover's dream come true . . . a comfortable, relaxing retreat . . . delightful hosts . . . unassuming, quiet, perfect getaway place."*

Bed and Breakfast of Maryland Host #129
Annapolis, MD

Location: In the historic district, 1 block from main gate of Naval Academy.

Reservations: Available year round through Bed and Breakfast of Maryland, page 12.

Rates: $70 double bed, $75 king/twins, $85 suite plus $15 for each additional person.
🛋 🛏 🖾 🍽

Everyone asks about the age of this Greek Revival house. Surprise! It was built in the 1930s with brick and many inside doors and beams taken from the house that had been standing here since the 1740s. Furnishings are "eclectically traditional. Our guests, including many midshipmen's families, know that this is their home away from home. They use the screened porch, patio, and fireplaced living room. And we are the best place in town for children!" The experienced hosts (12 years) keep a geographic log and photo album of all guests. The hostess is a retired registered nurse. Her husband, a retired naval officer and corporate vice president, answers lots of questions about the Academy (take a map and tour yourself or take a guided tour); the town's history and architecture (he's a tour guide); restaurants, shops, antiquing, and festivities.

Bed and bath: On second floor—room with king/twins option, working fireplace, private shower bath. Another room with double bed, private tub/shower bath. Entire third floor has a double bed and four singles, private shower bath.

Breakfast: Flexible hours. "We like to be finished by 11; most guests want to be out earlier." Fresh fruit, juice, cereals, muffins and toast. Omelets, eggs Benedict, sausage casserole, pancakes, waffles, or French toast. Served in large dining room with Queen Anne furnishings or on garden patio that has a majestic magnolia tree. Host usually joins guests.

Bed and Breakfast of Maryland Host #139

Annapolis, MD

Location: In historic district. Two blocks from Naval Academy. One block from city dock. A half block from state capitol.
Reservations: Available year round

through Bed and Breakfast of Maryland, page 12.
Rates: Double bed $75, queen bed $85, king bed $90.

♥ ◀ ♣ ✖ ✄

Memorable. This 70-year-old store with tin ceiling and oak display case was converted into an unusual residence—there's not a square corner in any room—by the previous owners. It was purchased in 1990 by the hosts, native Californians (and former Napa Valley part-time B&B hosts), and furnished with turn-of-the-century furnishings and fascinating collections acquired in South America and Europe. Recently, with the assistance of an architect and the historic commission, the exterior has been changed to look more residential and historical.

The host, director of a college-level international language program, and his wife, vice-principal of an elementary school, "love the three centuries of history in Annapolis, the ambiance, events, water—we're among the 10 percent of residents who are not sailors!—the walk along the dock. We are steps from a theater, within 3 blocks of 15 great (and different) restaurants, within 15 minutes on foot from everything. It's exciting to share all of this with travelers from all over the world."

Foreign languages spoken: French, Spanish, Portuguese.
Bed and bath: Three rooms with private baths. On first floor, king bed and sofa suitable for third person, private en-suite shower bath. On second floor, queen bed, private en-suite tub/shower bath. Another room with double bed, private hall tub bath with hand-held shower.
Breakfast: Usually 7 or after. Buffet style. Freshly squeezed orange juice, fresh fruit, croissants, homemade nut bread, homemade granola and other cereals, coffees, teas.
Plus: Guest living and dining rooms. In every guest room, TV and coffee (and tea) maker. Two garage spaces ($5 each) available.

KEY TO SYMBOLS
♥ Lots of honeymooners come here.
◀ Families with children are very welcome. (Please see page xii.)
◀ "Please emphasize that we are a private home, not an inn."
♣ Groups or private parties sometimes book the entire B&B.
♦ Travel agents' commission paid. (Please see page xii.)
✖ Sorry, no guests' pets are allowed.
✄ No smoking inside *or* no smoking at all, even on porches.

College House Suites   410/263–6124

One College Avenue, Annapolis, MD 21401

Hosts: Don and Jo Anne Wolfrey
Location: Quiet, historic neighborhood. On a corner overlooking Naval Academy and 1 block from St. John's College. A short walk to everything—city dock, Paca House and Gardens, country's oldest state capitol building in continuous use, antiques galleries, theater, restaurants, shops.

Open: Year round. Two-night minimum at all times.
Rates: Double occupancy. $150 ($125 without breakfast). Third person $35 ($25 without breakfast). MC, Visa.

♥ 🖥 ♣ ♦ ✈ ✂

Unusual and beautiful collections gathered by the Wolfreys from all over the world are ingeniously displayed on the walls, mirror-finished antique softwood floors, shelves, and seating in this elegant Federal-style brick townhouse with crown moldings and wainscoting. There's a mask collection from three continents, a 1770s English grandfather clock, an extensive collection of antique, silk, and wool Oriental rugs—all blended with American antiques and contemporary pieces. The terraced deck is an urban oasis fashioned with heartwood cedar, an arbor, and seating surrounded by trees and planters, vines and blossoms.

During 15 years of living here, the Wolfreys have made all kinds of major—and wonderful—changes. Since 1988, when they "got into B&B by doing a favor for a friend," they have enjoyed sharing their lifestyle with first-timers and many returnees.

Jo Anne, a volunteer for the Historic Annapolis Foundation, was an accountant for the U.S. Navy. Don, a computer systems analyst with the Justice Department, commutes to Washington.

Bed and bath: Two suites. One on ground level has private ivy-covered courtyard entrance, small kitchen, antique brass double bed, desk, raised-hearth fireplace in sitting room that has double sofa bed, private shower bath. Third-level suite has a cherry four-poster double bed, window seats, double sofa bed in sitting room, private tub/shower bath with rose Italian marble floor, window seats, private deck, views of Naval Academy, and use of second-level deck.

Breakfast: 8–10. Fruit such as melon balls and raspberries with fresh mint and Grand Marnier. Strawberry-cheese croissants or iced carrot muffins. Freshly squeezed orange juice. Cereals. Perhaps yogurt. Coffee with cinnamon. Served in suite, in dining room, on deck, or in courtyard.

Plus: Window air conditioners. Bedroom ceiling fans. Individual heat thermostats. In each suite—phone (one with private line); remote color TV with cable (including HBO), desk. Down comforters. Fresh fruit, flowers, chocolates. Feather beds. Special occasions acknowledged.

Unless otherwise stated, rates in this book are per room for two and include breakfast in addition to all the amenities in "Plus." As for taxes and gratuities, please see page xi.

The William Page Inn
8 Martin Street, Annapolis, MD 21401-1716

410/626–1506
fax 410/263–4841

Hosts: Greg Page and Rob Zuchelli
Location: On a quiet, residential historic district street off of and 2 blocks from main downtown waterfront. Fifty yards from Naval Academy visitors' gate. Within minutes of restaurants and historic sites.
Open: Year round. Two-night minimum during special events.

Rates: December–March 15: $60 shared bath, $70 private bath, $95 suite. March 16–November 30: Sunday–Thursday, $65 shared, $80 private, $100 suite; weekends: $75 shared, $90 private, $120 suite. Amex (5 percent surcharge), MC, and Visa (3 percent surcharge).
♥ ♣ ✗ ⊁

They (almost) waved a magic wand. What was to be a five-year plan took one year. What, in 1986, was to be a B&B in Montreal, Boston, or Washington, D.C., appeared in an Annapolis (Rob's hometown) real estate column: a four-square 1908 cedar-shingled home, a Democratic Club for more than 50 years. The two young men, still in their twenties, gutted, redesigned, redecorated, and explored a tristate area for antiques. Within six months the Annapolis landmark was opened as a B&B. Soon after, Greg and Rob took on a bed and breakfast reservation service (page 12) and became B&B consultants and active community participants. Six years later, they and their guests are delighted with the results.

In residence: One well-behaved dog, Rascals, "seldom seen by guests."
Bed and bath: Five antiques-furnished rooms. First floor—Victorian furnishings, queen bed, private shower bath, access to wraparound porch. Second floor—queen bed, private bath with shower/whirlpool tub. Two rooms, each with queen four-poster rice carved bed, sitting area, and armoire, share (robes provided) a tub/shower bath. Third floor—skylit dormer-style room, twice the size of any other, with queen sleigh bed, sofa in sitting area, individual climate control system, private bath with shower, and separate whirlpool room.
Breakfast: 8–10. Buffet may include juice, fresh fruit, freshly baked breads and pastries, cheeses, quiche or egg casserole, cold cereals, coffee/tea.
Plus: Central air conditioning. Fireplaced living room. Refreshments. Wet bar setup. Off-street parking (one car per room).

From Wisconsin: *"Perfect . . . beautifully decorated . . . extremely friendly innkeepers. Highly recommended."*

Can't find a listing for the community you are going to? Check with a reservation service described at the beginning of this chapter. Through the service, you may be placed (matched) with a welcoming B&B that is near your destination.

Riverwatch Bed & Breakfast   410/974–8152

145 Edgewater Drive, Edgewater, MD 21037-1321

Hosts: Karen Dennis and Don Silawsky
Location: On the waterfront with spectacular river views. In a community with plenty of walkers and joggers. Ten minutes to historic Annapolis.

Open: Year round. Four-night minimum for Naval Academy commissioning week (late May) and during sailboat show (mid-October).
Rates: $65 king-bedded room; $75 queen; $90 suite (queen).
♥ ♦ ✂ ⚥

The crystal-chandeliered dining room with river view has a mirrored wall and sliding glass doors. Comfortable furnishings in the living room of the two-storied frame house are contemporary with Oriental accents. Each guest room has access to a waterfront balcony with chairs and table and a spiral staircase that leads to the outdoor (20-by-40-foot) pool and hot tub—"our favorite seasonal suggestion."

Karen is a scientist/researcher who specializes in obesity and weight loss. When she and Don, an engineer/lawyer (environmental law) bought this too-big-for-the-two-of-us property four years ago, "the extra bedrooms and baths along with the exceptional site and our sincere enjoyment of people 'clicked.' Guests enjoy relaxing on the patio after breakfast, watching the boats go by, and solving the problems of the world. Collectively, we've solved a lot of them . . . if someone would just ask us!"

In residence: Shadow and Rina, Siamese cats.
Bed and bath: On second floor, one room with king bed, one with queen; both with private full bath. On lower level, private entrance to suite with queen-bedded room, sitting area with double sleep sofa and TV, full bath, butler kitchen.
Breakfast: 8:30–9:30. Homemade muffins and breads. Pancakes or Belgian waffles. Juice and fresh fruits. Freshly ground coffee. Served in dining room or on patio.
Plus: Central air conditioning and heat. Fireplaced family room. Bedroom ceiling fans. Guest refrigerator. Turndown service. Mints on pillow. Forgotten items. Beach towels. Many suggestions for Annapolis attractions. Boat dock; no charge for tie-up. Ground transportation provided for guests who arrive by boat. Off-street parking.

> From Alaska: *"We were delighted . . . spacious, impeccably clean, and very comfortable. Hosts were warm and gracious."* From California: *"GREAT! . . . What a view! . . . manicured, beautiful grounds . . . outstanding breakfast. The Riverwatch deserves special attention as that is what you get from Don and Karen!"*

Innkeeping may be America's most envied profession. As one host mused, "Where else can you get a job where, every day, someone tells you how wonderful you are?"

Amanda's Host #110
Baltimore, MD

Location: In a quiet residential area bordered by two parks: one with a lake and a bike and jogging trail; the other with golf course, tennis courts, and ball park. Five-minute walk to 15-minute bus ride to Inner Harbor.

Reservations: Available year round through Amanda's Regional Reservation Service, page 12.
Rates: $65 single, $70 double ($65 shared bath).
⚓ ✗ ⚞

"Since our four children grew up and moved out, the house became too quiet! We enjoy hosting B&B in our European Tudor-style house, where we have lived for over 30 years. It has 'gemutlichkeit,' a German word that means comfort, an all-around good feeling."

The host, a retired chemist, plays clarinet in a band. The hostess teaches German and sometimes interprets for touring groups. Both are ardent sailors and classical music lovers.

In residence: Aja, a beautiful but shy cat who likes to be outdoors.
Bed and bath: "New, wonderful mattresses" in two second-floor rooms, one with twin beds and ceiling fan, the other with a queen bed and air conditioning. Private or shared modern full bath.
Breakfast: Flexible hours. Juice, fruits, hot and cold cereals, muffins with poached egg and hollandaise sauce, homemade croissants or breads—poppyseed, banana, or apricot. Maybe bread pudding with raisins marinated in brandy with fresh fruits. Option of German cold cuts and cheeses on German rye bread. "The best coffee in town." Served in breakfast room or on the secluded patio.
Plus: Beverages. Fresh flowers, fruits, chocolates in guest room. TV room. Parking.

From Vermont: *"Great cooking and conversation."*

Amanda's Host #201
Baltimore, MD

Location: On Middle River of Chesapeake Bay. Twenty minutes north of Baltimore's Inner Harbor; 10 minutes (8 miles) from I–95.
Reservations: Year round through

Amanda's Regional Reservation Service, page 12.
Rates: $65–$120 single, $75–$125 double.
♥ ⚓ ♣ ♦ ✗ ⚞

A jewel. Called The Manor House by locals. Now in an area of summer-turned-year-round cottages, the four-storied historic waterfront house was built with 12-foot ceilings in the early 1900s by a local brewmaster who, together with his wife, a musician, hosted summer parties here for the benefit of the Baltimore Opera. Since the B&B hosts, a CPA and his wife, a Realtor and an American Sign Language interpreter, purchased the "handyman's special" in 1987, rejuvenation has been an ongoing process. They added a large in-ground pool and retained the cupola, from which you get a spectacular view (binoculars provided) of Chesapeake Bay.

The spacious rooms are filled with antiques and collectibles. The dining room is Empire style with a 10-foot buffet. There are Tiffany-style lampshades, some Art Deco items, many paintings and prints, and pewter and egg cup collections. Many guests are en route along the interstate. Some are wedding guests. A few arrive by boat and moor at the adjacent pier. And then there are those who visit the city and love coming "home to the country," where they walk, jog, explore.

In residence: Two cats "absolutely forbidden in guest areas."
Bed and bath: Three centrally air-conditioned second-floor rooms (the smallest is 20 by 20 feet), each with private shower/tub bath. One is a suite with king bed, working fireplace, wicker-furnished room with wet bar and water view, Jacuzzi tub. Double-bedded room overlooks the pool. One king-bedded room has shower and 6-foot claw-footed tub "that everyone loves."
Breakfast: "Anytime." Featuring low-cholesterol recipes. Juice, fruit, egg/cheese casserole or French toast, turkey bacon, homemade muffins, coffee. In dining room or poolside.
Plus: At least eight local inexpensive restaurants recommended—with the support of guests' rave reviews.

> From Wilmington, Del: *"The house is gorgeous, beautifully decorated. . . . The host and hostess extremely friendly . . . Would like to visit again."*

Celie's Waterfront Bed & Breakfast

1714 Thames Street, Baltimore, MD 21231   410/522–2323

Host: Celie Ives
Location: Facing an active port. In Fell's Point Historic District. Minutes' walk to restaurants, shops, and galleries. One-quarter-block walk to water taxi ride to harbor attractions; Orioles Park; Johns Hopkins Medical Center; aquarium; science center; Little Italy; museums; antiques row.
Open: Year round. Advance reservations required. Two-night weekend minimum for rooms with whirlpool and/or fireplace.
Rates: Per room. King bed with whirlpool and fireplace $125–$140. Queen with whirlpool $110–$120. Queen without whirlpool $95–$105. Wheelchair-accessible room $85–$90. Amex, Discover, MC, Visa.
♥ ♣ ♦ ✕ ✄

(Please turn page.)

Amazing. An "instant landmark" built in 1989 with a historic-looking front, balconies, and flowering courtyards. The inviting interior features antique accents including a portrait of Celie's great-great-grandmother. In addition, there is every amenity (see "Bed and bath" below) sought by both business travelers and romantics. And then there's Celie, the Baltimore native who conceived this inn after renovating—with great imagination—a nearby 1870s townhouse. Her flair for design was recognized by Bloomingdale's when they chose her B&B as part of a *Bed & Breakfast in the Mid-Atlantic States* photo essay seen by a million people.

Bed and bath: Seven rooms (on three floors), each with private bath, desk, private phone line, modem capability, TV, refrigerator with setups and juices, coffeemaker (coffee, tea, cocoa). King-bedded rooms, facing harbor, have whirlpool tub, working fireplace, bar sink, microwave. Four queen-bedded rooms—two with whirlpool tub plus balcony overlooking rear garden; two with shower baths. First-floor handicapped-accessible unit with king/twin option, private courtyard.
Breakfast: 7–9 weekdays, 8–10 weekends. Freshly squeezed orange juice, fresh fruit, homemade breads, jams and jellies, brewed coffees and teas. Serve yourself. Eat in dining room, on private balcony or rooftop deck, in garden, or in your room.
Plus: First-floor room (for business retreats and meetings, small weddings, private parties) with fireplace and harbor view, two modem outlets, lounge area, conference table that seats 12. Central air conditioning. Ceiling fans. Flannel sheets. Bath sheets. Terry robes. Down comforters. Ironing facilities. Rooftop deck with built-in seating, view of harbor and skyline. Free off-street parking. Van service to and from convention center.

From Virginia: *"A gem."* From Pennsylvania: *"Heartwarming friendliness. . . . As we curled up to the living room fire, the sweet smell of that day's baked breads lingered on."* From Florida: *"Driving directions, full-length mirror, coffee in room, flowers . . . what more could you ask for?"*

Mr. Mole Bed & Breakfast   410/728–1179
1601 Bolton Street, Baltimore, MD 21217-4347   fax 410/728–3379

Hosts: "The staff"—Paul Bragaw and Collin Clarke
Location: On historic Bolton Hill. Within walking distance of subway and light rail system, Antique Row, Meyerhoff Symphony Hall, Lyric Opera, and Walters Art Gallery. Ten-minute drive to Johns Hopkins Hospital. Two miles to Johns Hopkins University and the Baltimore Museum of Art; 1 ½ miles from the Inner Harbor and Orioles Stadium. Across from bus stop.
Open: Year round. Two-night minimum on holiday weekends and during Preakness (Triple Crown thoroughbred race series) Week.
Rates: $75–$80 single, $80–90 double. Two-room suites $100–$140, depending on number of bedrooms used.

♥ ⁂ ♦ ✖ ✄

Decorated. Gracious. Beautiful. An urban B&B where guests invite Baltimorians, who are most anxious "to see"; where business travelers host clients; where getaway guests spend a lot of time; where one 73-year-old guest went up and down the three flights of steps 25 times a day for exercise.

The 1870 brick row house was on the League of Women Voters house tour even before the hosts' year-long restoration was finished in 1991. Paul is a former USAF colonel, and Collin is an antiques dealer who was a theatrical set designer in Australia, the United States, and England.

On the 14-foot-ceilinged first floor, there's a 9-foot concert grand piano in the music room, a converted 1870 gasolier, original plaster moldings and marble fireplaces, and drapes made by Collin with 150 yards of Madras plaid. Throughout the spacious rooms there are 18th- and 19th-century antiques, prints and portraits, antique snuff boxes, collections of ecclesiastical antiques, and New Guinea masks—all identified by date and country of origin on a list compiled for the Maryland House and Garden Pilgrimage.

Foreign languages spoken: French, German, and Dutch.
Bed and bath: On three floors, five queen-bedded suites (two have a second bedroom with a double bed) with sitting area, private tub/shower bath. One has private enclosed sun porch; some have canopied or four-poster bed. The street-level handicapped-accessible suite has private exterior entrance.
Breakfast: Usually 7:30–9. Their brown sugar/cream cheese pie or an Amish apple/walnut crumb cake are almost famous. (Recipes shared and exchanged.) Fresh fruit bowl, orange juice, assorted Swedish crispbreads, rum ginger raisin or other homemade breads, meats and cheeses. Freshly ground regular and decaf coffee, Earl Grey and herbal teas, Ovaltine, and milk. "We try never to repeat the same menu for any guest."
Plus: Central air conditioning. Garage with automatic door opener for each suite. Private telephones. Robes. Chocolates. Sherry. Fresh flowers. Forgotten items. Hair dryer. Use of refrigerator. High tea upon request. Transportation to and from Pennsylvania Station. Tips for everything—galleries, museums, a bicycle path, antiques shops, bars and eateries, even an all-night diner whose average meal cost is $6. Snack bag for guests traveling by car or train.

Broom Hall Bed & Breakfast

2425 Pocock Road
Fallston, MD 21047

410/557–7321
800/552–3965
fax 410/557–7321

Host: Laura Grace
Location: Tranquil. On a 40-acre estate surrounded by rolling hills and not another house in sight. Thirty-five minutes from Baltimore's Inner Harbor, 90 from Philadelphia and Washington, D.C. Less than a mile to Ladew Topiary Gardens (summer Sunday concerts). Minutes to excellent trout fishing. Near vineyards (summer Sunday picnics, spring wine tastings, tours) and restaurants.
Open: Year round. Two-day minimum stay on weekends in June, September, and October.
Rates: $95–$150 (vary according to furnishings and view). $15 third person in room. No charge for crib. Discover, MC, Visa.
♥ ♯ ⬛ ⁂ ♦ ✄

(Please turn page.)

"Portraits, antiques, medals, documents, all kinds of memorabilia. English history is everywhere in this country home, a red brick Georgian, built by my grandparents with seven baths, large rooms, many French doors—an open, airy feeling. My grandfather, a British general, was from a long line of British generals.

"Grandmother planted the berry bushes (guests are invited to pick and munch) and fruit trees. The house and patio overlook pond (fishing allowed), woods, and wildflower garden. Just beyond the English garden where weddings are held, there's a large swimming pool—good for laps, and for sitting and 'doing nothing'!

"After Grandmother died in 1978, my mother (Eileen Fisher), inspired by her brother who had a B&B in England, decided to do B&B here. And that's how my British husband, a shipping industry electrical engineer whom I met on the QE2, and I became innkeepers after living in Hong Kong, South Korea, and Canada. Now my mother, a travel agent, makes all the jams and jellies. Only those who come with children meet our sons (ages seven and nine), who usually take young guests to see the chickens. Spring through fall, there are cattle in the pasture. Some of the bedrooms have buzzers connected to the kitchen; honeymooners can ring and breakfast will appear.

"It feels good to know that there's a feeling of sharing, of continuity, of treating guests as Grandmother did—like royalty."

In residence: One female Labrador retriever.
Bed and bath: On first and second floors, six rooms, each with refrigerator. Five have private tub/shower bath; two are handicapped accessible. King, queen (one with snack area and microwave), double, or twin beds. Rollaway and crib.
Breakfast: 7–10. Full country meal with breakfast meats, eggs, breads, muffins, fruit, juice, and coffee and tea.
Plus: Fireplaced living room and library. Piano. Air-conditioned guest rooms; some ceiling fans. Individual thermostats. Private phone in some rooms. Coffee and tea service in each room. Turndown service. Volleyball and croquet. Discount passes to Baltimore Aquarium. Picnic baskets, $20 (includes wine) for two.

Twin Gates B&B Inn   410/252–3131
308 Morris Avenue, Lutherville, MD 21093   800/635–0370

Hosts: Gwen and Bob Vaughan
Location: In a quiet residential suburb north of Baltimore, 20 minutes by expressway to Harborplace and Aquarium. On an acre of land with mature pine trees and semicircular driveway framed by twin gates. Five-minute walk to light rail service to Penn Station, BWI Airport, Inner Harbor, and new Oriole Stadium. Fifteen minutes to Ladew Topiary Gardens and a free vineyard tour.
Open: Year round.
Rates: $95–$125 double occupancy. Amex, MC, Visa.
♥ ⁂ ◆ ✈ ⌣

This three-time "Best of Baltimore" winner was created in 1986 by native Baltimoreans who know how to welcome honeymooners, business travelers, college and prep school faculty and families—and the author of this book, who was in town for a B&B promotion in Macy's. (With her usual exuberance, Gwen gave samples of her marvelous cooking to hundreds of shoppers.)

The seventh Vaughan restoration, their first inn, is a mid-19th-century Victorian with "a secret room" (they show and tell) and 12-foot ceilings built by one of the ministers who founded the village. Gwen, a former corporate medical secretary, has shared her amazing heart-healthy food ideas at an international conference for innkeepers. Bob, a hospital management consultant, is president of the Lutherville Community Association. They are parents of grown twin daughters, West Coast residents.

Bed and bath: Seven rooms. Five second-floor rooms, each with a queen-sized bed; three rooms have private baths—two with showers, one with tub and shower; two rooms share bath with tub and shower. Two third-floor rooms, one with queen bed and one with king/twins option, share a hallway shower/tub bath. Each room is decorated with a geographical theme such as Maryland Hunt, Sanibel Shores, or California.
Breakfast: At 9. Entree, perhaps peach crepes or banana French toast, and a baked pear or apple such as you have never had before. Fresh fruit, homemade "muffins of the season," freshly brewed hazelnut coffee, herbal teas. Presented in candlelit dining room, in fireplaced greeting room, on front porch, or in gazebo in the garden.
Plus: Wine and cheese, usually 5–6. Room air conditioners. Bedroom ceiling fans. Fireplaced living room. Gazebo. Sometimes, bedtime surprises. Seasonal newsletter that includes B&B recommendations based on the Vaughans' travels.

> From New York: *"A loving home away from home, filled with cozy quilts, antique furniture, charming teddy bears, and the smells of home baking. Every convenience is available, including a stocked refrigerator, microwave, and iron all set up in the guest kitchen. Fluffy towels are changed as soon as they are used. The hosts are warm, caring, and thoughtful."*

Gramercy Bed & Breakfast   410/486-2405
1400 Greenspring Valley Road, Stevensen, MD 21153-0119

Host: Anne Pomykala; assistant: Annette Coy
Location: On 45 acres with trails, streams, organic gardens. In Greenspring Valley Historic District. One and a half miles from Route 83 and Baltimore Beltway (I–695); 20 minutes to Baltimore's Inner Harbor.

Open: Year round.
Rates: Double occupancy, $90–$125. Third person, $25 adult, $5 child; if extra single room required, $40 adult, $20 child. MC, Visa.
♥ ♦ ♣ ♠ ♦ ✈ ⚕

> From Philadelphia: *"Anne Pomykala has made this beautiful estate a welcome haven of warmth and comfort."* From Maryland: *"Breakfast is elegantly prepared, graciously served, and plentiful . . . makes me feel regal. The house is secluded, huge with winding staircase, highly polished and marvelously cared for . . . I love the place!"*

"The place" is a 26-room English Tudor mansion, built at the turn of the century with baronial first-floor recessed-paneled center hall and library and enormous
(Please turn page.)

fireplaces. Its fascinating history includes 35 years as the home of the Koinoina Foundation, which trained mature people in literacy methods and organic gardening for service on every continent. Restoration has been continuous ever since the Pomykala family purchased the property at auction in 1985. The house became a B&B shortly after it served as the 1986 Decorators' Showhouse. Now it is decorated with many antiques, window treatments, and sculpture and other art works. Guests are welcome to swim in the pool (towels provided, no lifeguard); enjoy the hot tub (spring through fall); play tennis; explore hiking trails (map available); go bird-watching (binoculars available); and visit the orchard as well as the shiitake mushroom laying yards and the herb gardens (pick some to take home) that supply many restaurants and gourmet shops. First-time guests learn what returnees know: Plan to spend the day right here.

In addition to B&B, Anne owns an educational video production studio and runs (elsewhere) high adventure programs for older Girl Scouts. Her husband "welcomes guests but devotes most of his time to his dental practice."

In residence: "Cookie is our six-year-old collie who likes to take guests on hikes and tours of the property. Yasser Aracat, a large alley cat, king of the house, resides at poolside all summer."
Bed and bath: Nine rooms. Four (three on second floor) have private bath; five decorated second-floor single rooms share two hall baths (one has claw-foot tub; one has tub/shower combination). Extra beds and crib available. King-bedded room with fireplace, whirlpool tub, dimmer lighting, chandelier. Double-bedded suite with antique Louis XIV furniture, chandeliered and fabric-covered ceiling, sun porch facing pool, sitting room with single antique sleigh bed, fireplace, game table, antique tub with legs (and shower). Room with double (modified canopied) bed, fireplace, bath with claw-footed tub (and shower). Third-floor room with double bed, bath with two shower heads, one hand-held.
Breakfast: 7–noon, guest's choice. Elaborate menu includes blackberries (year round); freshly squeezed orange juice; mushroom omelet with tomato, onion, and herbs; berry pancakes; fruit compote; vegetarian platter; maybe pierogi. Special diets accommodated. On porches or by dining room fireplace with fine china, silver, and stemware.
Plus: Grand piano in living room. Fireplaced living room, center hall, dining room, parlor, library. Bedroom air conditioning units. TV in most rooms. Bedroom beverage service. Bath sheets. Free passes to Baltimore Zoo.

Holland House B&B   410/641–1956
5 Bay Street, Berlin, MD 21811

Hosts: Jim and Jan Quick
Location: In historic downtown district. Seven miles from ocean beaches, Assateague Island and Ocean City. Seven championship area golf courses within 10-mile radius.
Open: Year round. Closed January 12–February 12.

Rates: Double occupancy. May 15–October 15, private bath $60 double bed, $70 queen bed. $95 second-floor suite. $10 less shared bath. $5 less singles. Rest of the year, $20 less. $10 cot or crib. Choice, MC, Visa.
♥ ♣ ♯ ♣ ✗ ✂

"Shortly after we purchased this house six years ago, we met the remaining Holland family members. It makes us feel good to know that this was a happy home. Everyone in town knew Doc Holland, as he was called in the 1920s and '30s. He was well loved and appreciated. There's been a lot of service to the community through this house. When we were doing it all over, saving it as a residence, the townspeople would look in on our progress. . . . Now I do all the baking and serving. Jim, an Eastern Shore native, is a hotel chef who makes all our breakfast specialties. Our busy time is the summer—when guests come for the beach, for clean, homey surroundings. The suite is very popular with families. For dinner, we recommend casual crab houses or we make dinner reservations for our guests at lovely intimate area restaurants."

The Quicks' immaculately kept turn-of-the-century frame house is freshly decorated with comfortable chairs and restored treasures. Jan works part time as a dental hygienist. Among the patients who encouraged her—"a perfect match"—to become an innkeeper: the Holland family! Her community participation varies; when we last spoke, she was wearing a vintage dress in preparation for a bridal-fashions-through-the-years show.

In residence: Henrietta, "Hattie," age eight.
Bed and bath: Five rooms. Private shower baths with three queen-bedded first-floor rooms. On second floor—two rooms that can be a suite connected by a shower bath. When booked alone, room with pineapple-post double bed shares a first-floor tub bath and queen-bedded room has private shower bath. Rollaway and crib available.
Breakfast: At 9. Freshly squeezed orange juice; homemade rolls, muffins, or breads. Plus one of Jim's creations—*pellichinta*, Hungarian crepes made with his grandmother's recipe; Belgian waffles with sauce; blueberry pancakes; French toast; or omelets.
Plus: Central air conditioning. Tea, soda, wine. TV lounge room. Front porch. Outdoor hot/cold shower. Babysitting available upon request. Sometimes in the winter, popcorn and VCR movies.

Bed and Breakfast of Maryland Host #189

Burtonsville, MD

Location: Serene. A working horse farm and equestrian center surrounded on three sides by 1,000-acre reservoir watershed. "Three very good restaurants within 2 miles; others in nearby (20–30) minutes) Columbia and Silver Spring." Near antiquing and dinner theaters. Via express bus, a half hour to Metro station plus a half hour on Metro into Washington, D.C. Five miles from I–95; 30 minutes to Baltimore and Annapolis.
Reservations: Available year round through Bed and Breakfast of Maryland, page 12.
Rates: $80 queen, $100 suite.
♥ ♦

Folks who come here want to get away from it all. (You can bring your horse for B&B too.) The lodgelike guest house is a rustic country home, built in 1975 with a great room that has a cathedral ceiling, exposed timbers from an old Baltimore warehouse, yellow pine paneling, an antiques-furnished living/dining area with

(Please turn page.)

wide-plank flooring, Oriental rugs, cushions by the fire. A floor-to-ceiling wall of glass overlooks the deck and the stallion pasture (about 25 horses).

Grounds are beautifully manicured and landscaped (many weddings are held here) by the owner, who is on the staff of a sleeping products trade association. His wife runs the farm. The resident innkeeper gives guests a tour of the flower and herb gardens, the three barns, and the first floor of the owners' residence—an 18th-century log cabin that has a fireplace constructed with soapstone quarried on the property.

When you hike through miles of wooded trails bordering the Rocky Gorge Reservoir, you might see deer and waterfowl.

Bed and bath: Two carpeted main-floor rooms. Room with queen bed, private tub/shower bath, botanical prints. Suite—Hunt Room decor with greens, red, and oranges—is one large room with king bed, double sleep sofa in sitting area, TV, private tub/shower bath. State-of-the-art beds are air mattresses with dual control (one on each side of bed) allowing for firmness adjustment.
Breakfast: Flexible hours. Fruit course. Entree such as cheese souffle with breakfast sausage. Homemade breads and muffins. Juice, coffee, tea.

Glasgow Inn Bed & Breakfast   301/228–0575
1500 Hambrooks Boulevard, Cambridge, MD 21613

Location: A parklike riverside setting with seven acres of lawn and century-old trees. Near summer river cruises, Blackwater National Wildlife Refuge, antiquing, outlet shopping, bird-watching, canoeing, country auctions, tennis, sailing, and hunting.
Hosts: Louise Lee Roche and Martha Ann Rayne

Open: Year round. Two-day minimum on weekdays, holidays, or dates of special events.
Rates: Per room. $90 semiprivate bath, $100 private bath. Fifteen to 25 percent discount Monday–Thursday.
♥ ✣ ◆ ✠ ✌

This is a wonderful National Register 18th-century brick and clapboard Georgian plantation manor with Palladian windows, spacious rooms, tall first- and second-floor ceilings, and deep window seats. It is furnished with 18th-century family heirlooms and reproductions. And still, guests often gather in the homey kitchen. One man who walked the grounds reported that he "saw more birds here than students during the college break in Fort Lauderdale."

After 25 years of hosting friends and relatives at their beach home in Ocean City, (outgoing) Louise Lee and (quiet) Martha Ann, college friends, former teachers and quilt-shop owners (who made a quilt that is hanging in the state house), decided in 1987 to pursue their dream of restoring a historic house and establishing a new career. Now they host cycling groups, wedding parties, hospital administrators and visitors, boaters, and many who come for "a birder's paradise where nature's voice can still be heard."

Bed and bath: Eight rooms on three floors; five have fireplaces. Private full bath for room with king bed and working fireplace and for three queen-bedded rooms (one is handicapped accessible). Two full baths for four queen-bedded rooms (two rooms per bath).
Breakfast: At 9, Monday–Saturday; 9:30 Sunday. Country style, with juice, cider, fruit. French toast, Amish omelet, or apple pancakes with scrapple and bacon.
Plus: Air conditioning everywhere, plus ceiling fans on second floor. Lemonade and iced tea on warm afternoons. Videos of musicals by the living room fire. Saturday winter weekend dinners. Pickup service at Cambridge marinas or Salisbury airport. Holiday dinners with hosts' families. Inn-to-inn biking arrangements. Innkeeping apprentice program.

From Virginia: *"Very attractively furnished . . . gracious hosts . . . delicious breakfast."*

Inn at the Canal

104 Bohemia Avenue, P.O. Box 187
Chesapeake City, MD 21915

410/885–5995
fax 410/885–3585

Hosts: Al and Mary Ioppolo
Location: On the world's busiest canal, the (lockless) Chesapeake and Delaware Canal. In historic district of village that has artists' workshops, canal museum, shops, restaurants. Within two hours of Washington, Baltimore, and Philadelphia. Ten miles from I–95.
Open: Year round. Two-night minimum stay on Memorial Day and Labor Day weekends.

Rates: Small double-bedded room, $70 or $75. Larger rooms, $95 queen; $95 king/twin water view; $105 queen with water view. Singles $5 less. Third person $25. December–March, excluding holidays, 50 percent less for second of two nights. Amex, Discover, MC, Visa.
♥ ✿ ✗ ⊱

During their two-year search for a country site to redo themselves, a fellow antiques dealer told the Ioppolos about this house, which was built in 1870 by a tugboat owner and restored as an inn in 1987. Since the Ioppolos took over in 1989, the inn and the town have been rediscovered. Al and Mary have placed antiques in every room. Extensive collections include oil lamps, coffee mills, baskets, and, on the fireplace wall of the "gather-round-kitchen-with-island," cast iron muffin pans. The parlor and dining room have original painted and stenciled ceiling, a parquet floor with rug insert, tall windows with imaginative curtains, and an interesting corner cupboard.

Al, a Philadelphia native who worked with the Department of Energy, has become a regular auctiongoer. (Hints shared.) Mary, an Alabama-born retired occupational therapist, is active in "this great town, which has canal cruises leaving from behind the inn, a tour that leads onto private horse farms in the area, and free summer Sunday concerts—with the best view from our porch!"

In residence: Three cats not allowed in guest rooms.

(Please turn page.)

Bed and bath: Six second-floor rooms with queen, double, twins, or king beds; some with four-posters. All private en-suite baths. One queen-bedded room with shower massage; all other rooms have tub/shower with shower massage.

Breakfast: 7–9 weekdays, 8–10 weekends and holidays. Freshly squeezed orange juice, breakfast meats, maybe poached pears with raspberry sauce or French toast stuffed with cream cheese and fresh peaches, hot beverages.

Plus: Individual air conditioning and heating controls. Welcoming refreshments. Wicker-furnished front and waterside porches. An antiques shop right here in restored milking room.

Two Rivers Farm

Chesapeake City, MD

Open: Year round.

Location: At the end of a boxwood-lined drive on a knoll of the Eastern Shore that overlooks the Bohemia River and Chesapeake Bay. On 23 acres with sweeping lawns and pastures that roll down to the water. An hour north of Annapolis and south of Philadelphia. Ninety minutes from Washington, D.C., 30 minutes from Wilmington, Delaware.

Reservations: Year round through Guesthouses, page 224.

Rates: $90–$110. Suite $100 for two, $135 for three, $170 for four.

♥ ⚐ ♣

The property is pretty dramatic. And so is the story of this fieldstone "whimsical Victorian Italianate"; it was built by descendants of Kitty Knight, "who saved the colonists during the Revolution" on "the finest land" found by a surveyor for Lord Baltimore. The Great Room's 25-by-30-foot Oriental rug has a mate in New York City's mayor's Gracie Mansion. The formal but comfortable furnishings—"not like a museum"—include wonderful antiques and some unusual items, such as a steward's bench from the now-defunct Coney Island race track, and a Racing Museum display case with halter and horseshoes from famous thoroughbred winners.

Guests walk to three marinas, passing by paddocks—there are a dozen thoroughbreds and one riding pony—and along the lawns with big old trees. They relax on the screened porch or wraparound veranda. They swim in the pool—and they enjoy meeting the innkeepers, two brothers who are still learning about the history of the farm purchased by their parents (Dad is a professional thoroughbred breeder/race horse owner) in 1988, two years after the parents adopted six Chilean siblings ranging in age from six months to 17 years. The location resulted in too much driving (for school and activities) for Mom, so they moved to their Saratoga, New York, farm and the two brothers became full-time innkeepers here.

The older brother, a trained chef "who can fix anything that moves," was in the Navy for 12 years. The younger one has a degree in hotel management and most recently was a Radisson general manager in North Carolina.

Bed and bath: Seven rooms, all private full baths. Five on second floor—one room has king in one bay and two twins in the other; other rooms have queen bed (two are canopied). One queen-bedded room on third floor. And one very popular room in annex with queen bed, Jacuzzi tub and shower, separate exterior entrance.

Breakfast: Usually 7–9. By 9:30 on Sunday. Oven pancake, cheese souffle or English toad-in-the-hole (egg-and-sausage dish). Juice, homemade breads and muffins, coffee and tea.

Brampton
410/778–1860

RR 2, Box 107, Chestertown, MD 21620

Hosts: Michael and Danielle Hanscom

Location: Surrounded by old trees on landscaped grounds. One mile southwest of Chestertown on 35 acres with pond and horses. Within two-hour drive of Baltimore, Philadelphia, and Washington, D.C.

Open: Year round. Two-night minimum on weekends.

Rates: $100 king bed, shower bath, private staircase. $110 double and twin beds, shower and tub bath, sun room. $120 queen (one is canopied) bed, shower bath, windows on three sides, working fireplace, third floor. $125 queen canopied bed or twins, shower bath, working fireplace, second floor. $150 two-level suite with king bed, tub/shower bath, huge cooking fireplace. $25 additional person. MC, Visa.

♥ ⁂ ✗

> From Massachusetts: *"A stately beauty that exudes peace and tranquillity. . . . Our room was beautifully decorated and very, very comfortable. We could not hear another sound in the house, despite the fact that the B&B was fully booked. Breakfast was delicious, imaginative, sustained us through the day. . . . Warm hospitality. Everything was perfect."*

"Everything"—the fireplaces, Michael's craftsmanship, the fine antiques, the amenities, and the hosts were extolled in great detail in other letters written by historians, young professionals, and retirees. Or, as acclaimed Connecticut innkeepers said in a word, "Fabulous."

Michael renovated houses in San Francisco before coming to the Eastern Shore in 1987. Danielle, a former Swissair flight attendant, always wanted to own a small hotel. Here in their 1860 Greek Revival brick plantation manor house, they too have warm memories of sharing, "drinking sherry or tea, rearranging the world."

In residence: In another building on the property, Sophie, age seven, and Simone, age one. Penny and Hershey are friendly Labradors.

Foreign languages spoken: Fluent German and French. Some Spanish.

Bed and bath: Four exceptionally large rooms on second (11-foot ceiling) and third (9-foot ceiling) floors. Plus a two-room suite on mezzanine. A two-level suite with 9-foot-wide fireplace in sitting room (the 1800s summer kitchen). One medium-sized room with its own stairway. All private en-suite baths. Trundle beds and crib available.

Breakfast: Weekdays 8–9:30, weekends 8:30–10. Guests' choice. Eggs "any style except poached!," French toast or pancakes with sausage and bacon from nearby Amish market. Homemade muffins, breads, and jams. Freshly squeezed orange juice or cranberry juice. Fresh fruit (homegrown melon and berries). In formal fireplaced dining room.

(Please turn page.)

Plus: Fireplaced living room with comfortable sofas. Bedroom air conditioners. TV/sun room. Veranda with wicker and swings. Down comforters. Sprinkler system.

Chevy Chase Bed & Breakfast   301/656–5867
6815 Connecticut Avenue, Chevy Chase, MD 20815

Host: S.C. Gotbaum
Location: In historic residential neighborhood. Eight miles from downtown Washington, D.C., and museums. Bus across street for 1-mile ride to Friendship Heights Metro; 20-minute subway to Washington, D.C. Less than a mile from Chevy Chase Circle/Washington, D.C. city limits. Ten-minute walk to Rock Creek Park and neighborhood restaurants. Three miles from Beltway, U.S. Route 495.
Open: Year round.
Rates: $50–$55 single, $60–$65 double.

♥ ♯ ☎ ⁂ ◆ ✖ ✔

Tapestries, carpets, indigenous art, and crafts from around the world are part of the reason for the international flavor in this beamed-ceilinged turn-of-the-century house. Guests from every continent find that there's a sharing of experiences, cultures, and values here. The host, a sociologist, is working on programs that promote and protect human rights in Africa.

Bed and bath: Two large second-floor rooms, each with adjoining private full bath. The spectacular treetop Garden Room has a double bed, cathedral ceiling, plants that flower year round. The Gabled Room has a single bed, a hi-riser for one or two, and many books on travel, sociology, political science, and women's studies "for welcome use by guests." Rollaway available.
Breakfast: Usually at 8. Variety of hot breads, homemade jams, cheeses, juice, fruit, cold cereals, "special coffee from New Orleans," tea.
Plus: Central air conditioning. TV and telephone in each room. Bedroom ceiling fans. Fireplaced living room. Piano in music room. Fresh flowers. Information and listings about theater, conferences, congressional hearings, events. Upon request, concert tickets purchased in advance.

> Guests wrote: *"Enjoyed the hospitality as much as my visits to various treasures in and around D.C.! . . . Talks each morning about Chile and U.S.A, their goods and misfortunes. . . . A peaceful, quiet home. . . . A beautiful breakfast. . . . The guest room was spectacular."*

KEY TO SYMBOLS
♥ Lots of honeymooners come here.
♯ Families with children are very welcome. (Please see page xii.)
☎ "Please emphasize that we are a private home, not an inn."
⁂ Groups or private parties sometimes book the entire B&B.
◆ Travel agents' commission paid. (Please see page xii.)
✖ Sorry, no guests' pets are allowed.
✔ No smoking inside *or* no smoking at all, even on porches.

Amanda's Host #137
Easton, MD

Location: In residential historic district. On a main street; 3 blocks to restaurants, boutiques, historical society, Academy of the Arts. Within 15-minute drive of Oxford (and ferry), St. Michaels (and Chesapeake Maritime Museum), cycling routes, cruises and sails.

Reservations: Available year round through Amanda's Regional Reservation Service, page 12.
Rates: $75–$120.
♥ ❀ ♦ ✄

Guests admire the restored 1880 Victorian, its 14-foot ceilings, the medallions in the drawing rooms, the wraparound porch—and the innkeepers' lifestyle. The hosts, visionaries who, five years ago, took on a house that relatives thought should be torn down, agree that they have the perfect arrangement!

The hostess was formerly employed in the financial world. Her husband is a systems analyst. The "nuts about detail who enjoy making every visit special for guests" furnished with 18th- and 19th-century oak, mahogany, and walnut pieces. Oriental and rag rugs are on the refinished Georgia pine floors. Lace curtains hang in every window.

In residence: Not allowed in guest rooms—"one long-haired dachshund who wandered in a couple of years ago and adopted us."
Bed and bath: Five rooms (seven for group events), all with antique beds. Two rooms (maximum) share tub/shower bath. (Robes provided.) On second floor—three double-bedded rooms, each with working fireplace and ceiling fan; the largest (17-by-28) room also has a trundle that converts to two twins. On third floor—double or two twin beds.
Breakfast: Usually at 8 or 9. Blueberry pancakes, two cereals (one homemade), fruit platter or bowl, fruit and nut breads, muffins, juice, coffee, tea, hot chocolate, milk.
Plus: Two fireplaced living rooms. Air-conditioned guest rooms. TV. Beverages. Porch rockers. Off-street parking. Secured overnight bicycle storage. Takeaway county cycling maps. Restaurant recommendations. Free (prearranged) transportation to and from marinas and Easton Airport.

Middle Plantation Inn   301/898–7128
9549 Liberty Road, Frederick, MD 21701-3246

Hosts: Shirley and Dwight Mullican
Location: In horse country, on 26 acres surrounded by woods and a stream. In the village of Mount Pleasant, 5 miles east of Frederick. Within 40 minutes of Gettysburg, Pennsylvania; Antietam Battlefield, Maryland; Harpers Ferry, West Virginia.

Ten minutes to New Market, the state's antiques capital.
Open: Year round.
Rates: Per room. $95 for one night. $90/night for two nights, $85/night for four or more nights. MC, Visa for security deposit only.
♥ ♦ ✄ ✁

One photo album shows the 1988 "coming down" of the 1810 stone and log house that was part of the 26-acre farm purchased by Dwight's grandparents

(Please turn page.)

in 1914. Another album shows the "going up" of the new house, which tries to capture the ambiance of the old with plaster between old wood on interior walls, remilled flooring, old chimney brick in the living room fireplace, old board and batten in the log gable ends. The breakfast/keeping room features a massive stone fireplace, skylights, and stained glass windows. Every room has some stenciling. For antique furnishings the Mullicans frequented Frederick County auctions and shops. ("We still do.") The vegetable garden thrives. Fresh eggs are gathered in the hen house.

Dwight is a bank vice president. Shirley works in the accounting department of a local power company.

Bed and bath: Four rooms, all overlooking yard, field, wooded area—and, at night, the lights of Frederick. All private full baths. First-floor room with private entrance, extra-long double iron bed, bath with footed tub and hand-held shower. Private access to three second-floor rooms. One with antique queen highback walnut bed, bath with claw-footed tub, stall shower; one with queen iron-and-brass bed; one with antique four-poster canopied double bed.
Breakfast: At 9. Orange juice. Seasonal fruit. Freshly baked breads, muffins, or pastries. Tea or coffee.
Plus: Air conditioning. Individual thermostats. Some ceiling fans. Phone jack. Beverages. Fresh flowers. Mints. TV.

> From Kansas: *"Accommodations were tops. Room was beautiful and delightfully private. Advice, particularly where to eat, was invaluable."*

Beaver Creek House Bed & Breakfast
20432 Beaver Creek Road, Hagerstown, MD 21740   301/797–4764

Hosts: Don and Shirley Day
Location: Country. Four miles east of town. One mile from I–70/U.S. 40 junction, 6 miles from I–81. Four miles to Appalachian Trail; 12 to Antietam; 22 to Harpers Ferry; 30 to Gettysburg. Close to many excellent restaurants.

Open: Year round.
Rates: $85 double bed, private bath. $80 twin beds, private full bath or double bed with private half bath. $75 double bed, shared bath. Singles $10 less. Midweek (except holidays) $10 less. Amex, MC, Visa.
♥ ♣ ♦ ✗ ✂

> From *Colonial Homes* magazine staffer: *"A gem. . . . Atop a hill surrounded by horses, lush green fields, and a gorgeous view of South Mountain . . . an inviting home with an eclectic mix of classic, elegant heirlooms. . . . Hospitality is the Days' specialty."* From California: *"Felt like special guests . . . even fresh lavender to take home."* From Indiana: *"Good food and conversation."*

Dozens of guests echoed those sentiments while recounting their visits "at home" with chef Don, a former CPA with the General Accounting Office in Washington, D.C., and Shirley, a docent at the local historical society.

When Don retired in 1986, the Days, Hagerstown natives, bought this turn-of-the-century country Victorian and filled it with family pictures and Victorian pieces, a clock collection, Oriental rugs, and many quilts. The popular porch swing is the very one Shirley used while growing up. Guests include history buffs, sports enthusiasts—and memorable sisters who arrived with a picture album showing this house (and themselves) as it was when they lived here in 1915.

Bed and bath: Five rooms; some with sitting areas. First-floor room with twin beds, private tub/shower bath. On second floor, private shower bath for room with four-poster canopied bed; private tub/shower bath for room with antique double brass bed. Two double-bedded rooms, one with en-suite half bath, share (robes provided) a full hall bath. Rollaway available.

Breakfast: Usually 8–9:30; coffee earlier. Locally grown fruits and berries. Cranberry-liqueured baked apples and buttermilk pecan pancakes with pure maple syrup, locally made sausage. Juices, homemade breads, freshly brewed coffee. With fine china, crystal, silver in crystal-chandeliered dining room or on screened porch overlooking garden.

Plus: Central air conditioning with individual bedroom thermostats and ceiling fans. Fresh fruit and flowers. Freshly brewed tea, home-baked cookies and/or tea breads at 4 p.m. Mints. Fireplaced parlor. TV, games, books, magazines. Outdoor grill. Horseshoes.

Lewrene Farm B&B   301/582–1735
9738 Downsville Pike, Hagerstown, MD 21740

Hosts: Irene and Lewis Lehman
Location: On a 125-acre crop farm surrounded by other farms. Four miles south of town on Route 632. Half a mile north of Maryland Route 68. Four miles to I–70 and I–81. Eight miles to Antietam Battlefield. Ninety minutes from Washington, D.C., and Baltimore.

Open: Year round.
Rates: Room with private full bath $65–$75 double, $60–$70 single; with whirlpool tub, $75–$80 double, $65–$75 single. $10 third person in room. Shared bath $50–$55 double, $40–$48 single.
♥ ⬛ ♣ ✖ ✂

With their six children grown (some of the 14 grandchildren help on the farm), the Lehmans added rooms in 1986 and opened a B&B in this turn-of-the-century house where they have lived for over 40 years. Candles glow in each window. Handmade quilts are everywhere; some are for sale. In season, you can see corn being harvested with tractors. Zeb, the dog, lives in the barn. There are some chickens and peacocks, and in the woods there are deer.

Visitors from Brazil, Guatemala, Switzerland, Honduras, Italy, Germany, Argentina, and Mexico have become "family" through several organizations including Mennonite Your Way and the Experiment in International Living. The Lehmans' own travels, often with homestays and B&Bs, have taken them to Guatemala, Kenya, Iceland, Czechoslovakia, and most recently to Germany.

Foreign languages spoken: Spanish and some German.
Bed and bath: Six second-floor Victorian/country antiques-furnished rooms. In 1900s part of house, one tub/shower bath shared by two double-bedded rooms and one room with a canopied queen bed. In newer part, one room with canopied queen bed, refrigerator, private bath with whirlpool tub.

(Please turn page.)

One room with two double beds (one canopied), private full bath. One very large room with a queen and a single, private full bath. Rollaway and crib available.

Breakfast: Flexible timing. Juice. Homemade breads and jelly, apple crisp, applesauce. Pancakes, eggs, bacon or sausage, casseroles. Special diets accommodated. Served family style at a big kitchen table.

Plus: Large fireplaced room with piano and TV. Bedside snacks. Air-conditioned bedrooms; some with ceiling fan, individual thermostat, phone jack. Plant identification book (for walks). Gazebo. A double platform swing, Irene's lifelong dream and a favorite with guests.

> From Washington, D.C.: *"Quiet and peaceful, lovely and immaculate. . . . A perfect experience topped off by the kindness and hospitality of the Lehmans."* From New Jersey: *"Vast property for quiet walks. . . . Breakfast is 'real country food.'. . . Not only was my two-year-old welcomed, she loved romping through the grounds."*

Sunday's Bed & Breakfast

39 Broadway, Hagerstown, MD 21740-4019

301/797-4331
800/221-4828

Host: Bob Ferrino
Location: Quiet residential area. Twenty minutes to Antietam Battlefield and Whitetail Ski Resort. Within five minutes of I–70 and I–81.

Open: Year round.
Rates: $65–$75 single. $75–$95 double. Package, corporate, and long-term rates available.
♥ ♣ ✄

Bob's dream of living in an old house with the hope of one day opening a bed and breakfast became a reality when he took an early retirement in 1992 after 22 years with IBM.

The pale pink paint on this 1890 brick Queen Anne Victorian has generated much interest. At last count, six former guests and/or area residents have inquired about it so that they could reproduce it on their own houses.

Return guests include one couple who became engaged here, wanted to return for their honeymoon, and then decided to have the wedding (50 guests) here. Another guest can't get over that Bob came to a theater at intermission with the glasses she left behind.

The B&B is named after Bob's mother. "In Italian, it is Dominica. And yes, we are open seven days a week." It's the same name he had given to his part-time antiques business, "the kind of business that makes you want to keep all the wonderful pieces you have purchased to sell."

The redecorated house is immaculate, bright, and airy, with tall windows, balloon shades, scatter rugs (some Orientals, some hooked), and antiques throughout.

Bed and bath: Three second-floor rooms. Private shower bath for room with a queen and a three-quarter bed. Two rooms, each with a double bed, share a tub/shower bath.
Breakfast: 7:30–9. Could be pumpkin raisin walnut bread; cantaloupe with fresh raspberry garnish, orange sauce with mint; sausage spinach quiche with potatoes on the side; French brioche bread. Juice, coffee, tea. In fireplaced tea

room; in breakfast room overlooking backyard; on back porch; in dining room; or in your own room.

Plus: Air conditioning, telephone jack, fruit basket, chocolates, and cordials in guest rooms. TV available. Fresh flowers. Tea (and cake) at 3 p.m.; wine and cheese at 6. Special soaps. Turndown service. Newspaper. Picnic baskets prepared. Babysitting arranged. Local airport pickup. Dinners by advance arrangement.

Guests wrote: *"A piece of heaven . . . felt incredibly pampered . . . comfortable . . . cozy . . . elegant . . . perfect."*

Bed and Breakfast of Delaware Host #36
Havre de Grace, Maryland

Location: In historic district, among 2,000 Victorian structures on the Chesapeake Bay at the Susquehanna River mouth. Two blocks from the water. Near fine restaurants, antiques shops, Concord Point Lighthouse, Havre de Grace Decoy Museum. Thirty minutes to Baltimore; 40 to Wilmington.

Reservations: Available year round through Bed & Breakfast of Delaware, page 4.
Rates: $55 single, $85 double. $10 third person.
♥ ⚄ ⚃ ⚅ ✗

"We were overwhelmed by its beauty," say the hosts, who had experience rejuvenating another old house "not nearly this size" in town. They could see through the disrepair and the apartments that had been carved out of the 19-room turreted Victorian stone mansion. In 1987 both dovetailed their jobs—as computer programmer analyst (he still is) and as manager of an international department of a Baltimore bank—with rebuilding and restoring absolutely everything inside and out. Now guests use the grand staircase with lighted newel post lamp at base and huge stained glass window at top. The central hall, wallpapered by the hosts with Bradbury and Bradbury paper, is flanked by two parlors (one with elaborate plaster ceiling) that have large pocket doors. There are 12-foot ceilings, intricate parquet floors, Oriental rugs, and many plants. Victorian antiques—a passion for the hostess since she was 14, are everywhere—except in the fireplaced family room, which has color TV, a stereo, games, and magazines. Outside, there are extensive flower gardens, a wraparound porch with glider and wrought iron furnishings, and even a fenced yard with swing and sandbox.

Bed and bath: Four large (two have five windows) second-floor rooms. One with queen brass bed, private tub/shower bath. Three (two unless it's all one party) double-bedded rooms share a full bath and a half bath. Extra twin bed available for any room.
Breakfast: At guests' convenience (within reason). Juices, fruit, yogurt, cereal, freshly baked breads or muffins. Entree might be apple pancakes or eggs Benedict. In dining room by working original gas fireplace.

(Please turn page.)

Plus: Room air conditioners. Two parlors with wood-burning fireplace, cable TV. Fruit basket, ice bucket, and mints in each room. Turndown service. Plenty of books and places to read them. Host-guided walking tour of historic district, by request.

> From Pennsylvania: *"Room was perfect . . . town delightful . . . breakfast delicious . . . enjoyed conversation with the hosts. Memorable."*

Amanda's Host #209
Monkton, MD

Location: On a 60-plus-acre working farm along a country road. Two miles to a popular country restaurant; 7 to The Milton Inn, a five-star restaurant; 5 to Ladew Topiary Gardens. Two miles to tubing on the Gunpowder River and 13-mile-long hike and bike trail (bike rentals available) along old railroad line. Forty minutes north of Baltimore, off I–83. **Reservations:** Year round. Available through Amanda's Regional Reservation Service, page 12. **Rate:** $85.
♥ ⛵ ✈ ⚒

City folk love this "escape to the country," a 150-year-old stone house on a farm with 11 cows, 2 draft horses, 1 pig, 3 dogs (not in guests' area, but "most guests beg to meet them"), and some cats. You might see deer—sometimes in the alfalfa field with a sunset backdrop—as well as beavers, hawks, and lots of colorful birds. Many guests walk the fields—with a dog as escort. They climb the hill for a wonderful view and then go down to the dock at the pond, where you are welcome to fish and release, swim, or skate.

The host is an avocational farmer, an investment advisor who makes haying time top priority—and answers many questions about balers. He and his wife, an early childhood teacher, enjoy having the world come to their door.

Bed and bath: In a 15-year-old addition, a private entrance to one second-floor room with canopied double bed, working fireplace, tub/shower bath. **Breakfast:** "Any time you'd like. It's kind of fun to spoil guests." Fresh seasonal fruit, juice, eggs, bacon or sausage; perhaps cheese omelet or French toast. Served on glassed-in porch overlooking the berry garden—and woodpile too; in winter, by kitchen fireplace. **Plus:** A tour of the farmhouse. TV/VCR in living room. Air conditioner in guest room. Beautiful countryside.

> From Maryland: *"Gracious hospitality. . . . Charming, delightful, warm and comfortable."*

If you've been to one B&B, you haven't been to them all. If you have met one B&B host, you haven't met them all.

National Pike Inn

301/865-5055

9-11 Main Street, P.O. Box 299, New Market, MD 21774

Hosts: Tom and Terry Rimel
Location: In historic district of a half-mile-long town known (especially on weekends) for its 30 antiques shops, old-fashioned general store, and restaurants (Mealey's is across the street). Just off I-70, exit 62. Seven miles east of historic Frederick. Near wineries, hiking, biking.
Open: Year round. Two-night minimum on New Market Days.

Rates: Monday-Thursday, $75 shared bath, $85 private bath; $65 singles. Weekends, per room: shared bath, $75 double bed, $85 queen; $95 queen canopied, private hall bath; $100 queen, private en-suite bath. $25 surcharge for Saturday-only bookings on holiday weekends, New Market Days, and Christmas in New Market.
♥ ♣ ✗ ✂

Fronted by a brick herringbone sidewalk and topped (in 1900) by a windowed widow's walk, this colonial house built between 1796 and 1804 (you can tell the stages) fulfilled Terry's idea of B&B. "During the 15 years that we lived a half mile from here, we often admired this beautiful old house, which deserves to be shared. There are eight fireplaces, each an architect's delight from the Federal period. Although the house had been restored 25 years before we bought it, we have strived to make it 'perfect,' keeping the worn wide-plank floors and old door hinges and locks. Room decor ranges from elegant to very country. We furnished with wonderful reproductions and some antiques."

Terry occasionally appears in period costume on Saturday evenings. Tom, a slate roof and tile specialist, joins her in hosting every evening. Their two youngest sons are in college. Their oldest is in business with Tom.

Bed and bath: Four second-floor rooms. Queen four-poster, private en-suite tub/shower bath. Queen canopied bed, high with step provided, private hall tub/shower bath. Room with queen brass bed and one with antique carved oak double bed share a connecting full bath.
Breakfast: 9. Full. Maybe pancakes or eggs. With muffins, breads (white, wheat, or chocolate dot pumpkin), shoofly coffee cake, apple pastry. Juice. Fresh fruit. Tea and coffee. Served in colonial dining room.
Plus: Bedroom air conditioners. Fireplace, wing chairs, and organ in living room. Complimentary Sunday paper. Bedside mints. Screened porch. Rear brick courtyard with gardens. An 1830s carriage house and smokehouse shown on request.

Innkeepers are sharers. One recalls the guest who arrived for a wedding only to find he'd left his dress pants at home. The innkeeper wore the same size. The guest appeared at the wedding properly dressed in borrowed pants.

The Mill House Bed & Breakfast   410/287–3532

102 Mill Lane, North East, MD 21901

Hosts: Lucia and Nick Demond
Location: Quiet. On a tidal creek, 2 miles south of I–95 exit 100. One block from the center of town, four antiques shops, and the nearby Day Basket Factory, where handwoven baskets have been made the same way since 1876. Short walk to waterfront town park and Upper Bay Museum. Less than an hour's drive to Baltimore's Inner Harbor, Pennsylvania Dutch country, Winterthur and Brandywine River museums. Ten minutes to designer factory outlet center.
Open: Year round.
Rates: $65 canopied bed. $55 Victorian double bed. Singles $5 less. Ten percent less for stays of three or more nights. MC, Visa.
◗ ◆ ✗

The sign is a millstone. An 18th-century tall-case clock ticks in the fireplaced living room. There are antiques throughout the rooms, which have white walls with trim painted in colonial blue, green, or gold. Along the banks of the tidal creek and the adjacent wooded area, up to 45 different wildflowers have been identified by the Demonds.

Lucia, a former docent at Winterthur Museum in Delaware and at the Valentine Museum in Richmond, Virginia, is curator for toys and dolls of the Historical Society Museum. Nick, a retired sales manager, is very active in several historical organizations, in scouting, and at the Fair Hill Nature Center. They have both had much experience in giving tours of the area.

Their 1710 house is really two houses, designed in an L-shape. One was built for the miller. The Dutch colonial, built for the mill owner, has accommodated B&B guests since 1988, when the Demonds returned to the family home that had been restored "from near collapse by another generation of our family in 1950."

Bed and bath: Two rooms, each with easy chairs and a desk, share a large tub/shower bath. Larger room with high canopied double bed (step provided) and walk-in closet. Room with Victorian furnishings has high double bed, walnut wardrobe.
Breakfast: 7–9:30. Bacon or sausage. Scrambled eggs or omelets. French toast. Orange juice. Seasonal fresh fruit compote. Biscuits, muffins, scones, or pecan sticky rolls. In dining room with fresh flowers, sterling silver, stemware.
Plus: Bedroom air conditioners. Use of canoe and two bikes. Plenty of off-street parking.

Unless otherwise stated, rates in this book are per room for two and include breakfast in addition to all the amenities in "Plus." As for taxes and gratuities, please see page xi.

The Oak & Apple   301/334–9265

208 North Second Street, Oakland, MD 21550

Hosts: Jana and Ed Kight
Location: In a residential/preservation district, within walking distance of shops and restaurants. Two hours from Pittsburgh, three from Baltimore and Washington, D.C. Ten minutes from Deep Creek Lake and Wisp Ski Resort, 40 to Canaan Valley. Within 25 miles of six state parks.

One hour from West Virginia University and Frostburg State University.
Open: Year round.
Rates: $50–$65. Ten percent less midweek, excluding Memorial Day through Labor Day. Singles $5 less. MC, Visa.

♥ ♣ ✗ ⚡

The Kights renovated the columned wide front porch to look like the original built around 1915. The grounds include old apple, oak, pine, cherry, and maple trees. Inside, there's a leaded-glass entrance foyer. And a big glass-enclosed sun porch. A wing chair and Sheraton sofa are by the living room fireplace. A TV/VCR/stereo is in the informal sitting room.

Jana, an audiologist who knows basic sign language, and Ed, a real estate sales associate, were introduced to B&Bs while bicycling in Vermont. They opened here "in this area we've known all our lives" in 1992, after restoring, painting, and papering this grand old house fronted by a large lawn, a sidewalk, "and small-town ambiance."

Bed and bath: Four rooms, modern baths. On second floor, queen-bedded room, private full bath, garden view. On third floor, "tucked under the eaves," two queen-bedded rooms, each with ceiling fan and pedestal sink, share a full bath; one room with a double and a twin bed has private full bath.
Breakfast: Flexible hours. Fresh fruits and juices. Homemade baked breads, muffins, scones, and cereals. Served in formal fireplaced dining room or on sun porch.
Plus: Beverages. Flannel sheets. Guest refrigerator. Fresh flowers.

From Maryland: *"The house is gorgeous . . . impeccable . . . breakfast was wonderful . . . Jana and Ed are the quintessential hosts . . . even windbreakers for our bike ride during an unexpectedly chilly weekend. . . . My only reservation with this glowing account is that it will become so popular that I might get preempted when I call for future stays."*

---

*A*ccording to many hosts:
*"Guests come with plans and discover
the joys of hammock sitting."*

The Thoroughbred Bed & Breakfast

16410 Batchellor's Forest Road, Olney, MD 20832   301/774-7649

Host: Helen Polinger
Location: A country road divides this 175-acre farm and its new (1993) 18-hole golf course. Minutes from restaurants. Twelve miles from Washington, D.C.; 6 miles to Metro (subway) station (with parking) and 40-minute ride to city; 40-minute drive to Baltimore's Inner Harbor.

Open: Year round. (Latest check-in: 8 p.m.)
Rates: Double occupancy. Main house, $70–$95. Farmhouse, $80. Carriage house, $95–120. Third person $35. MC, Visa.
♥ ◖ ♣ ♦ ✖ ✄

The Polingers built this country estate 32 years ago and had, at one time, up to 150 mares here. (Helen still breeds some horses.) In 1989, with five "empty nest" rooms, Helen opened her bed and breakfast in the main house, which has an English country feel—with fireplaced living room, upstairs sitting room with piano, a game room with championship-sized pool table, and many reproductions. Subsequently she gutted and redid the farmhouse, retaining interior wood trim and floors and furnishing with a mixture of new and old. Antiques are throughout the carriage guest house.

The pool, 20 steps from the main building, is complete with dressing room, bathroom, and lots of towels. There's an outdoor hot tub available year round. A gazebo. Opportunities for country walks. And views of the rolling countryside.

Helen is chef and hostess for guests who come for a getaway, for visitors of local residents and several nearby schools, and for Washington visitors who prefer to stay outside the city. In her earlier careers she has been a model, a fashion show commentator, a beauty salon owner and operator, and a retailer of ski and tennis hard- and software.

Bed and bath: Thirteen rooms, all with air conditioning, seven with private bath. King, queen, double, or twin beds. In main house—five rooms; three with full baths; two share a bath. Farmhouse—four rooms share two baths, each with whirlpool tub, shower, pedestal sink. Carriage house—four rooms, each with private bath and deck; two have working fireplace and double whirlpool tub.

Breakfast: 7–9 for main house rooms. Chef's choice. Fresh orange juice, fruits, French toast, eggs Benedict, pancakes, waffles, creamed chipped beef, corn beef hash, sausage, bacon, homemade breads and coffee cakes, coffee, tea, hot chocolate. Served in formal dining room. For farmhouse guests: serve yourself from stocked kitchen. Carriage house: continental served in your room.

Plus: TV in some rooms. You are welcome to visit the barns.

Looking for a getaway? Many B&Bs in this book offer "a secluded romantic interlude." Look for the ♥ symbol.

Elmwood c. 1770 B&B   410/651-1066

Locust Point Road, P.O. Box 220, Princess Anne, MD 21853

Hosts: Mr. Stephen F. and Mrs. Helen Monick
Location: Peaceful. A sense of discovery at the end of a mile-long entrance. A 160-acre site on the Manokin River with a mile of waterfront. Eight miles west of Princess Anne; 45 minutes to beaches, three hours from Washington, D.C. Short drive to Deal Island Wildlife area, antiques shops, restaurants, historic sites, golf, tennis.
Open: Year round. Two-night minimum on weekends.
Rates: Double occupancy. $85 shared bath. $95 private bath, water view. $105 guest house (no food provided); $10 each additional person over 12; $500 weekly. MC, Visa.
♥ ⚓ ♦ ✄ ✍

Returnees come for the commanding view of the Manokin River, the tranquillity, and the hosts. Writers and photographers have been inspired here. Guests comment on "artistic touches, gourmet food, a wonderful visit. . . ." History and architecture buffs, too, are delighted with the Federal brick residence built around 1770 by John Elzey, whose son, Arnold Elzey Jones, became a prominent Confederate Army general.

The Monicks' extensive restoration was a 1984 project when Steve retired from 35 years with United Airlines. Helen, a former teacher, once had a television cooking program while working as a Pennsylvania Power and Light Co. home economist.

Most of the rooms are painted in authentic colonial colors and furnished with period antiques and reproductions. Helen's needlework collection includes some of her own work. There's always something new to admire and enjoy: a rose garden, decor, changes in the menu. Currently, 90 acres of tillable farmland are being converted to a wildlife habitat with 33,000 trees and shrubs and a stocked pond.

In residence: Fifty mallards and some wood ducks come from the river to be fed twice daily.
Bed and bath: Four rooms, all with working fireplaces. Two with private tub/shower baths. A second-floor hall shower bath can be private or shared with third-floor room that has two twin beds. On second floor, two queen-bedded rooms and one with a double bed and screened porch.
Breakfast: 8:30–9:30. Includes fruits in season, home-baked pastries, homemade sausage (including chicken), crab or oyster entrees (in season). Served in dining room by fireplace or on screened porch.
Plus: Central air conditioning. fireplaced library, TV, wicker-furnished screened porch. Beverages. Books and games.

---

*I*s B&B like a hotel?
How many times have you hugged the doorman?

Parsonage Inn

210 North Talbot Street, St. Michaels, MD 21663

410/745–5519
800/394–5519

Host: Will Workman
Location: In the historic district. Two blocks from the harbor and Maritime Museum. Next door to widely acclaimed "208 Talbot" gourmet restaurant.
Open: Year round. May–November, two-night weekend minimum.
Rates: Double occupancy. Winter weekends: $114 fireplaced rooms, $102 king with deck, $82 queen, $94 two double beds, $86 king (handicapped accessible). Summer weekends: $102 fireplace, $108 king with deck, $92 queen, $108 two doubles, $96 king (handicapped accessible). Midweek, $10–$12 less. MC, Visa.
♥ ♪ ♣ ♦ ✄

You first notice the steeple, the intricate brickwork, and the gingerbread trim of the house built as a private residence in 1883 by Henry Clay Dodson, a brickyard owner. It was a parsonage from 1924 until 1984, when Will, a computer systems marketing director, and his father bought it as Dad's retirement project. (Dad was innkeeper until 1988.) They, together with skilled craftsmen and an expert on historic buildings, restored and rebuilt everything from moldings to fireplaces. Replicas of ceiling medallions were installed. Cherry Queen Anne reproductions and other fine furnishings were purchased. Comfortable sofas were placed by the living room fireplace.

Among guests: Members of the Dodson family, who remember visiting grandparents here. Some travelers come for business meetings (right here). "And many come just to be at the inn, to slow down, to enjoy the real beauty of Talbot County, the waterways and waterfowl, the quiet marshes, the outstanding bicycling, and the solitude of the area."

Bed and bath: Eight carpeted rooms (three have working fireplaces) with king or queen beds. Four in original building; four in rear addition with private entrances. Each with a different color scheme, Laura Ashley linens, private bath with Victorian pedestal sink and tiled shower stall. One first-floor handicapped-accessible room with king bed. Of the four second-floor rooms reached by narrow staircase in main house, two have direct access to deck.
Breakfast: 8:30–10. Belgian waffles, French toast, quiche, or pancakes and bacon. Orange and grapefruit juice, fresh fruit, yogurt, bagels, homemade muffins, and cold cereal. Freshly ground coffee, including decaf. Buffet style in dining room.
Plus: Air conditioning. Bedroom ceiling fans in all rooms. Two rooms have phone jack and TV. Library with books and magazines. Fresh flowers. Mints. Tea or lemonade at 4 p.m. Use of refrigerator. Second-floor deck with umbrella table and lounge chairs. Wicker-furnished front porch and patio with grill and picnic table. Four 12-speed bicycles (and route suggestions including ferry ride to Oxford). A before-and-after photo album.

> From North Carolina: *"A real find. . . . Enjoyed other guests around fireplace during one chilly evening. . . . Will is an energetic host . . . answers questions and steers you to a good restaurant. His enthusiasm about the inn is contagious."*

The Inn at Antietam

301/432–6601

220 East Main Street, P.O. Box 119, Sharpsburg, MD 21782

Hosts: Betty and Cal Fairbourn
Location: Rural. The perfect setting for walking. At the top of a long Main Street driveway. Surrounded by lawns with a buggy set against the horizon. Overlooking Sharpsburg, Antietam National Battlefield, and, sometimes, reenacters. Near Harpers Ferry; the C&O Canal; Shepherdstown, West Virginia; Crystal Grottoes Cavern; and hiking, canoeing, antiques shops, cottage industry craft shops, restaurants.
Open: Year round except two weeks at Christmas. Two-night minimum on weekends and holidays. Reservations required.
Rates: Double occupancy, $95 Sunday–Thursday; $105 Friday–Saturday and holidays. $25 extra person. Amex.
♥ ♣ ✈

Here's "homegrown hospitality with a sophisticated touch" as seen in a *Country Inns* cover feature and in *Victoria, Mid-Atlantic Country,* and many other publications; as seen in Macy's during a cooking demonstration—part of a Meet-the-Hosts program associated with this book; and as experienced by guests, who comment on the "relaxed style in a beautifully restored inn run by a charming couple."

It has been that way ever since the Salt Lake City, Utah, natives—Cal, a former General Motors (Detroit) executive, and Betty, a former hospice counselor—restored the rambling Victorian in 1984. They were so good at doing their own woodwork—including new moldings and kitchen cabinets—that they now restore other properties. They are so good at "touches" that they selected elegant period antiques with an emphasis on comfort.

What was to be a five-year plan is on its way to ten. As the Fairbourns say, "People are fabulous." Now grandsons are old enough to help/learn with the gorgeous flower gardens. In winter the wraparound porch is festooned with garlands.

In residence: Outdoor (only) pets allowed to sit with guests on porch— Annie, the dog; Mary, a calico cat; and Rebok, a Maine coon cat.
Bed and bath: Four air-conditioned suites. The first-floor suite has an 1800 queen-sized four-poster bed, sitting room, private tub/shower bath. Two second-floor suites, each with private tub/shower bath. One has a queen-bedded room plus a sitting room; the other, a queen bed and a dressing room. Adjoining Smoke House has loft with double bed, original massive fireplace in sitting room with beams and barnboard walls, wet bar, private tub-without-shower bath.
Breakfast: 8–9:30. Freshly squeezed orange juice. Fresh fruit with Belgian waffles, blueberry pancakes, French toast, or blintzes. Country bacon.
Plus: Wicker-furnished solarium. Formal parlor. Wraparound porch with swing and rockers. Brick patio overlooking Blue Ridge Mountains. Arrangements made for guided tours (rave reviews) of battlefield.

Bed and Breakfast of Maryland Host #185
Silver Spring, MD

Location: Secluded. Inside the Belt-way on an acre of landscaped grounds overlooking Sligo Creek and woods. Ten-minute bus ride to Metro station, 30-minute drive from White House.

Reservations: Available year round through Bed and Breakfast of Maryland, page 12.
Rates: Per room. $65 queen bed, $55 two single beds, $45 one single bed.
♦ ✈

"The coffee is always percolating. The paper is here. A harpsichord is in the fireplaced living room. The house is yours to enjoy." Guests are treated like family in this traditionally furnished "German-looking-with-steep-slate-roof" brick house, which is surrounded by woods on three sides.

The hostess, originally from England, is an elementary school art teacher. Her husband, who grew up in Europe, works for the government on So-viet/Russian affairs. He is also a violinist who sometimes plays here with a string quartet, trio, or chamber group.

Guests come from far (India and France) and near (overflow from local residents). They enjoy the quiet, the food, and conversations with the hosts—who provide a good orientation to Washington, D.C., maps, and suggestions for and menus of nearby ethnic restaurants.

In residence: One cat.
Foreign languages spoken: French, German, a little Russian.
Bed and bath: On second floor. Queen-bedded room has private tub/shower bath. Room with two single beds shares tub/shower bath with one room that has a single bed.
Breakfast: Flexible hours. "A lot of wholesome food." Juices, breads, cereals, fruit, granola, porridge, no meat, tea, coffee. If very late, help yourself. Sunday feature—waffles and maple syrup. In chandeliered dining room overlooking woods; on patio in warm weather.
Plus: Off-street parking. Two patios.

Blue Bear Bed & Breakfast   301/824–2292
22052 Holiday Drive, Smithsburg, MD 21783

Host: Ellen Panchula
Location: In apple and peach or-chard country, in a quiet residential neighborhood with a view of South Mountain. Thiry minutes' drive southwest to Antietam Battlefield or northeast to Gettysburg. Ten miles from Appalachian Trail, 25 to White-

tail Ski Resort. Six miles to Hagers-town restaurants. A little over an hour from Washington, D.C.
Open: Year round.
Rates: $40 single, $45 double. $8 child up to age 18.
♦ 🛏 ✈ ⚲

Ellen, an elementary school teacher, lives in a comfortable 25-year-old Cape Cod–style house that has many country crafts, some purchased from guests who have come to Smithburg's Steam & Craft Show in September. Every room has stenciling. On the handmade quilts in the guest rooms are many stuffed bears—and yes, some are blue!

In residence: Maggie is a 50-pound Border collie/husky/German shepherd.
Bed and bath: Two second-floor double-bedded rooms share a full bath. Rollaway available.
Breakfast: 7–9. Juice; fruit; Belgian waffles, quiche, baked French toast, or egg casserole; homemade rolls and breads; coffee. Served in the kitchen. Ellen joins guests.
Plus: Central air conditioning. Refreshments. Mints. Laundry facilities.

> From Maryland: *"Basket of fruit in the room . . . incredible breakfast at 7 a.m. . . . stimulating conversation. . . . Left with goodies in a 'Blue Bear' stenciled bag."* From Connecticut: *"Greeted us with hot tea and potato chip cookies. . . . At breakfast, keeps the food coming as long as you can eat it . . . teddy bears placed throughout the comfortable house."*

Chanceford Hall Bed & Breakfast Inn
209 West Federal Street, Snow Hill, MD 21863   **410/632-2231**

Hosts: Michael and Thelma C. Driscoll
Location: On landscaped grounds with English boxwood and 200-year-old walnut trees. In historic district of residential area. Five minutes' walk to town center. Near Pocomoke River and canoeing. Three hours from Washington, D.C., and Baltimore. Half an hour to ocean, to Crisfield and boats for Smith and Tangier Islands.
Open: Year round.
Rates: Per room. $105 second-floor double bed, $110 first-floor queen beds. Suite with queen and single bed, $125 for two, $135 for three.
♥ ⁂ ✕

Such detailed and enthusiastic guests' letters! They comment on the personal attention, the friendliness, the exquisite craftsmanship, the food—at this restored 1759 brick Greek/Georgian, declared "a gem" by the Maryland Historic Trust. Mid-Atlantic Country featured it. And Dan Rodricks of the Baltimore Evening Sun and WBAL-TV wrote, "Chanceford Hall has finally been brought back to greatness. . . . One wonders if George Washington slept there."

The Driscolls, parents of two grown daughters, had experience in graphics, real estate, market research, and sales in various parts of the country when, in 1986, they started to work on "the hulk." They scraped and sanded original crown moldings and 10 fireplace mantels; they installed a kitchen in the former ballroom, new bathrooms, and much more. Now Oriental rugs are on all the refinished floors. Throughout, there are handsome Queen Anne reproduction furnishings—some are for sale and some are made by Michael, a fine cabinetmaker (and groundskeeper). Decor done by Thelma is Williamsburg. The walls are 18 inches thick. And Chanceford Hall has been part of the Maryland House and Garden Pilgrimage.

Bed and bath: Five rooms, four with working fireplaces; all private (two full, three shower) baths. First-floor room, wheelchair accessible, has queen canopy bed, working fireplace, exceptional woodwork. Four rooms on second floor with canopied beds. Most are queen-sized; one is double.

(Please turn page.)

Breakfast: 7–11. Juice, eggs, bacon and sausage, potatoes O'Brian, home-made apple-cinnamon-raisin sticky ring (one for each couple). Served in crystal-chandeliered dining room with silver, cloth napkins, china.
Plus: Central air conditioning. Formal fireplaced living room. Down comfort-ers. Beverages and hors d'oeuvres. Bicycles. Sun room with puzzles, games, TV, overlooking covered outdoor lap pool. Dinner by prior arrangement ($105 for two).

The River House Inn

201 East Market Street, Snow Hill, MD 21863

410/632–2722
fax 410/632–2722

Hosts: Larry and Susanne Knudsen
Location: In the center of a 300-year-old village. Set back on two acres of lawns and gardens along the Pocomoke River. Surrounded by other architectural treasures. Across street from recommended restau-rant. Two doors from canoe and bike rentals. Half-hour drive to beaches.

Open: Year round. Two-night mini-mum on holiday weekends.
Rates: Double occupancy. $95 Me-morial Day–Labor Day. Off-season, $75 midweek, $95 weekends. $10 less singles. Extra person in room, $10 children under 12, $20 adults. MC, Visa.

Elegant. Gracious. And comfortable. An early retirement project for Larry, who was a CEO in Ohio. A change of career for Susanne, an interior designer (now) who was a political activist and needlework catalog buyer. In 1991 they converted this 1850 Victorian-with-Gothic-influence. They redecorated with striped and damask wallpapers and border treatments. Windows are draped, swagged, and lace-curtained. Furnishings are Chippendale, French, Sheraton, and Colonial. Colors are wonderful. And so are the wicker, rattan, and wrought iron–furnished porches.

And what about the guests? "Sports-oriented guests can hardly squeeze in all the activities they plan. Others intend to do more, but they find it so serene and relaxing, they just 'veg out.'"

In residence: Bonnie and Belle, black poodles, "our official greeters."
Bed and bath: Four main house carpeted rooms (three with working fireplaces); all with queen beds (some canopied) and private tub/shower baths; all baths attached except one across the hall (robes provided). One cottage with king/twins option and sitting room with daybed; two with queen bed, sitting room with daybed. Folding cot available.
Breakfast: 8–10. Coffee ready at 7. Fresh fruit. Home-baked goodies. Bacon and sausage. Eggs any style (Egg Beaters available). Omelet or French toast. Cereal. Toast. In back parlor and formal dining room at tables with summer garden flowers.
Plus: In main house, central air conditioning downstairs; window units and bedroom ceiling fans upstairs. Air conditioning in cottages. Fireplaced living room, dining room, front and back parlors. Beverages. Canoe launch area. Motorboats may tie up at inn bulkhead. Lawn chairs at the river's edge. Croquet. Badminton. Beach towels. "Guests may use our country club or eight other nearby courses for golfing." Picnic baskets ($7 per person). Dinners by advance reservation ($20 per person). Transportation to/from Salisbury airport.

Antrim 1844

30 Trevanion Road, Taneytown, MD 21787

410/756-6812
fax 410/756-6812

Hosts: Dorothy and Richard Mollett
Location: Secluded. Off the main street on 23 acres of gardens and orchards, with sunsets and mountain views. Forty miles west of Baltimore; 60 north of Washington, D.C.; 12 south of Gettysburg.
Open: Year round.
Rates: Double occupancy $175–

$275 weekends. $25 less Sunday–Thursday. $50 third or fourth person in suite or for trundle. Midweek corporate rates available. Five-course prix-fixe dinners by reservation, Thursday–Sunday, $50. Amex, MC, Visa.

♥ ♣ ♦ ✈

One of a kind. Soon to become a media darling. Already discovered for weddings and for getaways (getaway guests never leave the property). An antebellum working plantation that, as Dort says, "captivates historians. Civil War buffs find the whole property a treasure." Today it has a fireplaced dining room with cobalt-blue lacquered walls, crystal chandelier, and gold leaf plaster moldings and medallions. There are yards of gorgeous fabrics (arranged by Dort—she'll share secrets), murals and faux marbling, high canopied feather beds, magnificent antiques (the kind that Dort couldn't bear to part with as an antiques dealer), Oriental rugs, and a late-1800s Knabe grand piano. Each outbuilding—the smokehouse with three walk-in fireplaces, the distant converted barn with navy blue bath, and the former icehouse with working fireplace in bath—is extraordinary. May through November, day and night, guests enjoy the black-bottomed pool (it retains the sun's heat) that Richard designed to look like a reflecting pool. For your playing pleasure, there's a Nova Grass tournament tennis court and a tournament-sized croquet lawn.

In 1988, Richard, the preservationist, first entered the boarded-up (for 60 years) Greek Revival and saw the deep plaster crown molding, 14-foot ceilings, hand-blown glass panes, and original floor plan all intact. "It was like a museum with no facilities—no plumbing nor electricity." The Molletts (who went to a garage sale on their first date) wove their magic, living in the middle of their transformation—as they had with five Baltimore National Register houses. Now the interior designer–turned–innkeeper and the off-lease car broker turned co-innkeeper/groundskeeper/waffle king are living with teenage sons Brandon and Ryan (valet and busboy) on the property in a restored 1861 farmhouse that they moved through town. The acclaimed dinners, never part of the original four–guest room B&B plan, began in 1991 in response to guests' requests.

Bed and bath: Thirteen rooms (some are suites). In mansion, nine rooms (five with working fireplaces) on second and third floors with tub (some two-person)/shower baths; king, queen, or double bed; trundle for extra guest. Two fireplaced suites each in the very private converted barn by the stream and in the former icehouse by formal gardens.
Breakfast: Begins 8–8:30 with fresh fruit, warm muffins, coffee or tea, newspaper, and a fresh flower on silver wake-up tray outside your door. A full meal 9–10 in converted smokehouse, in formal dining room, or on canopied garden veranda—with fruit, maybe baked bosc pears; Belgian waffles or egg strata with veggies/bacon/cheeses.

(Please turn page.)

Plus: Central air conditioning. "James the butler" (a shaped wooden stand) outside your door brings you afternoon tea, phone messages, extra towels, and, in the evening, chocolates and a decanter of port. Fireplaced library, drawing rooms, and tavern room. Complimentary tea, wine, champagne, hors d'oeuvres and cheese. Phone jacks in rooms. View from widow's walk that was used as a Gettysburg battle lookout post. Picnic baskets prepared. Horse and carriage rides arranged to breathtaking working farms and mills.

Glenburn   301/751-1187

3515 Runnymede Road, Taneytown, MD 21787

Hosts: Robert and Elizabeth Neal
Location: In the country on a 200-acre farm on Route 140 between Westminster and Taneytown. Surrounded by spacious lawns and towering trees. Fifteen miles from Gettysburg. Within 15 minutes of Catoctin Mountain State Park, Carroll County Farm Museum. Antiques shops, winery, and golf course nearby. Sixty miles from Washington, D.C., 38 from Baltimore.
Open: Year round. Usual arrival time 4–6 p.m.; departure 10:30 a.m.
Rates: Main house: $55–$75 single, $65–$80 double. Guest house: $55–$85 single, $65–$90 double.
♥ ⚹ ⛵ ⚘ ✖ ✄

The unique setting arouses expectations that are fulfilled at this B&B—one that is reminiscent of British B&Bs in historic homes. Cross the iron bridge that stretches over a vigorous creek and proceed along the winding drive to an imposing 1840 country Georgian home with Victorian addition that has been in Robert's family for more than 55 years. (In the 19th century it housed a boys' private school; the Neals were married 15 years before Elizabeth learned that her grandfather was a student here.) Furnished elegantly with heirlooms and American and European antiques, it has been on several Maryland House and Garden Tours. And it has also served as a backdrop for a Quaker Oats commercial!

Now that all five Neal children are grown, Elizabeth, a seventh-generation area resident, and Robert, a former history professor who has always been involved with this farm, are continuing the tradition of hospitality by sharing Glenburn with travelers. It's a working farm. "Because of the farm machinery and cattle, please ask us about walking in the fields." Many guests rise early to see the deer by the creek, or to jog, bird-watch, or cycle, and then return for breakfast.

Bed and bath: Private guests' wing has three second-floor double-bedded rooms (with air conditioner and ceiling fan). Private bath for room with screened porch. Air-conditioned guest house has two large bedrooms—one with queen, the other with two twins—and a bath, large living room, and kitchen/dining area.
Breakfast: 7–9:30. Orange juice, fresh country eggs, country bacon or sausage, sweet rolls, toast, coffee and tea. Graciously served in dining room that has Grandmother's china displayed on wall plate racks.
Plus: Swimming pool. Fireplaced living room. Tea and coffee always available. Tour of house. Guests' refrigerator.

> Guests wrote: *"The busy world comes to a gentle stop as you approach the serene lawns of Glenburn, a haven for the weary world."*

Tavern House   410/376–3347
111 Water Street, P.O. Box 98, Vienna, MD 21869-0098

Hosts: Harvey and Elise Altergott
Location: On the Nanticoke River (much wildlife) in historic Eastern Shore town (with walking tour) between Salisbury and Cambridge. Near Routes 331/50 intersection, antiquing, and used bookstores. Flat cycling country. Few blocks from public tennis courts and boat ramp. Fifteen miles to Blackwater Wildlife Refuge, 100 from Washington, D.C.
Open: Year round.
Rates: Double occupancy. $65–$70. Choice, MC, Visa.
🛏 ✳ ♦ 🎠

> From Washington, D.C.: *"A five-star establishment . . . with charm of yesteryear and comforts of today . . . stimulating conversation. . . . Breakfasts, in themselves, worth the journey."* From New York: *"Delightful, talented couple."* From Maryland: *"Everything done with artistry and taste. . . . Their knowledge of local history added to our perfect stay."* From Spokane, Washington: *"Worn steps, sloping floors . . . a sense of history. . . . We felt pampered."*

Guests keep coming. And projects continue! The plane that Harvey has been building is almost ready for takeoff. And the Altergotts are helping their daughter restore an old house, just a few blocks away. Their own "hidden delight" (Baltimore magazine), built in the early 1700s, was pretty dilapidated in 1981 when the Altergotts, not in search of any property, decided to explore this "wonderful quiet town." Harvey, a former naval officer, was a manager at the postal services headquarters in Washington, D.C. He and Elise, a Salem, Massachusetts, native who was a Girl Scouts field executive, began restoring (it's ongoing) "to elegant simplicity"—including the staircase carvings, three massive chimneys, and many windowsills. Woodwork painted in authentic colors frames white lime-sand-and-hair plaster. Colonial antiques and reproductions fit just perfectly. And so does their hosting style, one that provides for privacy or company.

In residence: Phineas Calhoon is "a not very talkative parrot." A neighbor's cat, Cricket, drops in routinely.
Foreign languages spoken: "Basic" German and Spanish.
Bed and bath: On second floor, four rooms, two with working fireplace, share two full "next-door" hall baths. Double or twin beds. "One double-bedded room has what we like to think are rum barrel stains on the floor."
Breakfast: Social; 8–noon. Flower-garnished fresh fruit. Homemade muffins and rolls. French toast, a souffle, or "something new Elise dreams up." Overlooking the river with the morning sun.
Plus: Living room with fireplace at each end. Afternoon tea or wine with cheeses. Seasonal flowers in rooms. Air conditioners and ceiling fans in bedrooms.

*T*he place to stay has become the reason to go.

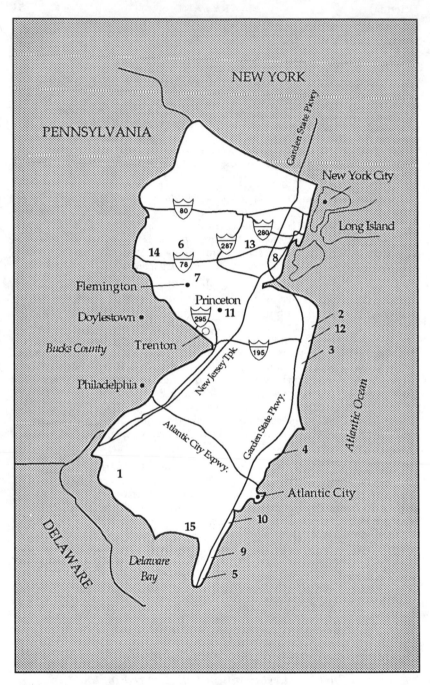

The numbers on this map indicate the locations of B&Bs described in detail in this chapter.

NEW JERSEY

1 Alloway
  Josiah Reeve House, 56
2 Avon-by-the-Sea
  Cashelmara Inn, 57
3 Bay Head
  Bay Head Gables, 58
  Conover's Bay Head Inn, 59
4 Beach Haven
  Pierrot by the Sea, 60
5 Cape May
  The Abbey Bed and
    Breakfast, 61
  Abigail Adams' Bed & Breakfast
    by the Sea, 62
  The Albert Stevens Inn, 63
  Barnard-Good House, 64
  The Brass Bed Inn, 65
  Captain Mey's Inn, 66
  COLVMNS by the Sea, 67
  The Duke of Windsor, 68
  The Gingerbread House, 69
  The Humphrey Hughes
    House, 70
  The Mainstay Inn & Cottage, 71
  Manor House, 72
  The Mason Cottage, 73
  The Queen Victoria, 74
  The Wooden Rabbit, 75
  Woodleigh House, 76

6 Clinton
  Leigh Way Bed and Breakfast
    Inn, 77
7 Flemington
  The Cabbage Rose Inn, 78
  Jerica Hill Inn, 79
8 Lyndhurst
  The Jeremiah H. Yereance
    House, 80
9 North Wildwood
  Bed & Breakfast Adventures
    Host #479, 81
10 Ocean City
  BarnaGate Bed & Breakfast, 82
  New Brighton Inn, 83
  Northwood Inn Bed &
    Breakfast, 84
  Top o' the Waves, 85
11 Princeton
  Red Maple Farm, 86
12 Spring Lake
  Ashling Cottage, 87
  Sea Crest by the Sea, 88
13 Stanhope
  The Whistling Swan Inn, 89
14 Stewartsville
  The Stewart Inn, 90
15 Woodbine
  The Henry Ludlam Inn, 91

__ New Jersey Reservation Services __

Bed & Breakfast Adventures
Bed & Breakfast of New Jersey, Inc.
103 Godwin Avenue, Suite 132, Midland Park, NJ 07432

Phone: For information: 201/444–7409 Monday–Friday 10–4. For reservations: 800/992–2632 (800–99BandB).

Listings: More than 200 hosts including more than 65 inns and 135 private hosted and unhosted accommodations. Located throughout New Jersey, in southern New York in Rockland and Westchester counties and New York City, and in eastern Pennsylvania (to Lancaster). Plus some in Florida from Orlando south to the Keys. Directory: $5.

Reservations: Two weeks' advance notice preferred. "Every effort is made to accommodate last-minute requests."

Rates: $40–$90 single, $55–$150 double. $5 one-night surcharge with some hosts. Package tours include accommodations together with discounts for restaurants and area attractions.

Aster Mould, founder of this 10-year-old reservation service, represents accommodations that range from modest to luxurious. "All hosts maintain the highest standards." Many hosts are bilingual. Some have computers and fax machines available for corporate and/or long-term guests. And some locations have appropriate space for corporate meetings and group functions.

One of the B&B industry's pioneers, Ms. Mould is a B&B speaker and writer, and a consultant to potential hosts. She has assisted state and local committees with regulations for B&B legislation.

Northern New Jersey Bed & Breakfast/ Temporary Lodgings for Transferees
11 Sunset Trail, Denville, NJ 07834

Phone: 201/625–5129. Year round Monday–Friday 9 a.m.–noon and 4–6 p.m.

Listings: 250. Mostly hosted private residences, some inns.

Reservations: Enough advance notice needed to allow for receipt of deposit by mail.

Rates: $40–$65 single, $50–$85 double. Weekly rates available. Deposit: for B&B, equivalent to one night's lodging; for transferees, one week's stay. If cancellation is made at least a week in advance, deposit less a $15 service charge is returned.

All of the hosts listed with Annette and Al Bergins are within 50 miles of New York City, in about 50 different northern New Jersey communities. Some are available for the traditional style of B&B, which includes breakfast. Most hosts accommodate corporate transferees and consultants for long-term (up to six months) stays, offering hospitality without the morning meal. Send self-addressed stamped envelope for listings.

KEY TO SYMBOLS
- ♥ Lots of honeymooners come here.
- ♣ Families with children are very welcome. (Please see page xii.)
- ♠ "Please emphasize that we are a private home, not an inn."
- ♣ Groups or private parties sometimes book the entire B&B.
- ♦ Travel agents' commission paid. (Please see page xii.)
- ✗ Sorry, no guests' pets are allowed.
- ✗ No smoking inside *or* no smoking at all, even on porches.

──────── New Jersey B&Bs ────────

Josiah Reeve House   609/935–5640

P.O. Box 501, North Greenwich Street, Alloway, NJ 08001

Hosts: Paul and Judith D'Esterre
Location: "In the state's last frontier, with a lot of farms, wildlife and marshland." On Route 540, 6 miles south of Woodstown. Two blocks to village center. Within 15 minutes of Delaware Memorial Bridge; New Jersey Turnpike; Mullica Hill, with over 30 antiques shops; restaurants, including country's second-oldest continuously run tavern. Twenty minutes from Wilmington; 40 from Philadelphia; 60 to Atlantic City.
Open: Year round.
Rates: Per room. Shared bath, $80. Private bath, $85 double bed, $95 queen bed. MC, Visa.
♥ ♣ ✕

Paul still can't believe that during 22 years of selling jeans (de rigueur attire for the hosts) in this territory, he never drove through this village of about 500 people. A 1989 supermarket newspaper ad mentioning "10 fireplaces, 4½ acres" attracted the D'Esterres to their third restoration (and first B&B), this spacious brick Greek Revival built by a shipbuilder in 1836. The long wide entrance hall features the original freestanding spiral staircase. Above wainscoting, recently painted murals depict early Alloway. Judith has experience as an Ethan Allen interior designer and antiques shop owner. Fine fabrics (decorating and shopping hints shared) are a passion. She furnished in "intentionally not museum-like" style with comfortable and interesting period pieces.

The grounds include a brick patio with fountain in addition to a bluestone patio, built by Paul for his daughter's wedding. For a peaceful walk, take the path through the woods to the creek where ships were built, to the millpond (ice skating in winter), or to the 112-acre lake where there is a dam, dock, float, rowboat, and paddleboat for two.

In residence: Two dogs—Helsa is a rottweiler; Horace "looks like a yellow Labrador." Truffles, "our black Vietnamese pig, loves to be petted; she turns out to be a major attraction!"
Foreign language spoken: Limited German.
Bed and bath: Four second-floor rooms, all with decorative fireplaces. French Room has coronet and drapes on queen bed; private bath with claw-foot tub, stall shower, and pedestal sink. Queen-bedded Empire Room shares tub/shower bath (robes provided) with double-bedded Victorian Room. Double-bedded room up narrow stairs has private shower bath.
Breakfast: Usually 8–9:30. Entree might be French toast with peach schnapps, fresh peaches, and maple syrup. Fresh local bacon and sausage; freshly squeezed orange juice; homemade breads and muffins. By dining room fireplace or patio fountain.
Plus: Central air conditioning. Fireplaced parlors. Square grand piano (c. 1860)—played by some guests. TV in living room. Wine and cheese. Bedtime

fruit or cookies. Bicycles to borrow. Directions to Wheaton Village (glass-blowing demonstrations) and a rodeo.

From New York: *"House and surroundings are lovely . . . food delicious . . . charming couple."*

Cashelmara Inn

22 Lakeside Avenue, Avon-by-the-Sea, NJ 07717

201/776–8727
800/821–2976

Host: Mary Wiernasz
Location: Facing a lake with swans and ducks. To the side, 100 yards away, is the Atlantic Ocean. In a non-commercial one-square-mile town. Near seafood restaurants; 50 miles from New York City; 60 miles from Philadelphia.
Open: Year round. Two-night minimum March–November weekends;

three nights for Memorial Day and July and August weekends; four nights July 4 and Labor Day.
Rates: Memorial Day–mid-September, $95 smaller rooms, $105 ocean view, $157 lakeside two-room suite. Off-season, $70 smaller rooms, $90 ocean view, $115 suite. Singles $10 less.
♥ ♯ ⛵ ♣ ✈

It was a blustery January afternoon in 1984 when Marty Mulligan, a technical representative for Eastman Kodak, stood on the veranda and saw the sunset over the lake and heard the ocean breaking on the beach. "After seeing the inside of this 1901 Colonial Revival home with an open center hall staircase and many fireplaces, it took me about five seconds to make an offer." Subsequently Marty had it all done over with wicker, Oriental rugs, Laura Ashley prints, and antiques that give an English country feeling—appreciated by vacationers, business travelers (for small conferences), and families (for reunions and weddings too).

In 1989 Mary, a well-traveled guest who had resort experience in her native Wisconsin, stayed in "this beautiful inn where one room is lovelier than the next" while she was working in the area for a Chicago market research company. She returned six months later to become resident inn-keeper. Now, when Marty visits from Pennsylvania (page 231), he meets some of Mary's many fans.

Bed and bath: On three floors, 11 rooms and 1 suite. Many with water (lake or ocean) view. All private baths; most tubless. King, queen, or double beds. First-floor suite with canopied double bed has working fireplace. A few rooms with two beds.
Breakfast: 8–10 in summer, 8:30–10 winter. Orange juice, home-baked muffins, coffee and tea. Choice of entree including omelets, French toast with challah, or house specialty of pork roll, fried egg, tomato, and melted cheese on English muffin. Served in dining room or on veranda.
Plus: Three parlors, one with working fireplace. Fresh flowers. Bedroom ceiling fans. Central air and heat in all common rooms. Individually controlled heat and air (window units) in each bedroom. That wraparound porch. Will meet guests at train or bus station. No parking problem. Bicycles, golf nearby. Lifeguarded ocean beach across the street.

Bay Head Gables   908/892-9844
200 Main Avenue, Bay Head, NJ 08742

Hosts: Don Haurie and Ed Laubusch
Location: Overlooking (across the road from) dunes and private ocean beach. At the head of the barrier island. About 75 miles from New York City and Philadelphia. One and a half blocks from train station (two hours from New York City's Penn Station). Short walk to restaurants and shops.
Open: Year round. Two-night minimum on weekends, May–October.

Three-night minimum on most holiday weekends.
Rates: Double occupancy. June–August, $95–$125 weekdays, $115–$160 weekends. April–May and September–November, $95–$125. December–March, $85–$95. Amex, MC, Visa.
♥ ♣ ✻ ✄

The community landmark is a pillared and cedar-shingled three-storied Georgian colonial built in 1913 as a private summer home in the architectural style of Stanford White. In 1983 Don, a retired teacher who is now a Bay Head planning board member, and Ed, a retired chemical industry lobbyist who has served as an environmental commissioner, "fell in love with this genteel, gracious but faded lady," which had at one time been a fine restaurant. They refurbished and redecorated (and then some), making each room quite different. Art Deco is featured in the inviting tall-ceilinged living room. A 6-foot impressionistic Mary Cassatt painting in the chandeliered, floral-papered Victorian bridal suite provided the perfect setting for a *Country Inns* magazine feature on a Bay Head hatmaker's workshop. Other rooms are done in country French or contemporary in colors inspired by an extensive collection of oil paintings, serigraphs, and textiles.

Bed and bath: Eleven rooms on three floors; some with private decks, each with at least two large windows. All private modern baths. King (one with private entrance on first floor), queen, double, or twin beds; some are canopied. Incredible ocean views from Main Avenue–facing rooms. Those facing waterfowl sanctuary are quieter.
Breakfast: 8:30–10. Pancakes, French toast, or strata with potatoes. Breakfast meats and pastries. Fresh fruit. Juices. Home-baked bread. In atriumlike glass-enclosed porch with ocean view or (off-season) in adjoining formal dining room.
Plus: Intentionally without TV; lots of good reading material. Bedroom air conditioners. Ceiling fans in common rooms and breakfast room. Spinet piano in fireplaced living room. Guest refrigerator. Ice machine. Beach towels. Wraparound porch. Self-serve cordials. Beach and tennis passes. Outside shower. Bike rack.

> From New Jersey: *"An oasis . . . peaceful . . . surrounded by good books, good artworks, and fun curios. The food is generous; plentiful and attractively served in a leisurely, unhurried fashion—and best of all, tasty. Bay Head Gables spells hospitality and elegance."*

*T*o tip or not? *(Please turn to page xi.)*

Conover's Bay Head Inn   908/892–4664

646 Main Avenue, Bay Head, NJ 08742

Hosts: Carl and Beverly Conover and son Timothy

Location: One block from the beach in this quiet one-square-mile town, which is still without parking meters or billboards but offers antiquing, boutiques, golf, tennis, swimming, fishing, crabbing. One hour north of Atlantic City. Seventy-five miles from New York City and east of Philadelphia.

Open: Year round. March–December 10, two-night minimum weekend stay; three or four nights on holiday weekends.

Rates: Second floor $130–$145; $165 private porch. Third floor $105–$145. Singles $10 less. $30 third person in room. Seventh night free. Off-season, as well as summer weekdays, much less.

♥ ♣ ✗ ⚭

Not just once, but all summer long, Joan Hamburg raved about Conover's on her radio program. The almost-legendary innkeepers have created a picture-perfect inn in this community, where they spent childhood summers. Now the 1905 residence that they bought in 1970 features a living room with Palladian window and, by the cut-stone fireplace, chintz-covered love seats. The entryway is trellised. Furnishings include turn-of-the-century pieces, family photographs, and original art. Under those matching comforters and bed ruffles are (do you remember?) line-dried and hand-ironed designer sheets. The most recent addition is an English garden.

Carl, a former structural steel erector, is an avocational steam engine restorer who recently completed work on his 1936 Elco wood boat. Timothy is now here full time. And Beverly shares her expertise with prospective innkeepers enrolled in Ocean County college courses.

In residence: One dog, Scotty. In summer, Beverly's parents and aunt and uncle.

Bed and bath: Twelve carpeted rooms (second and third floors) with double, queen, or king bed. All private baths (shower or tub/shower). View of ocean, bay, yacht club, marina, or gardens. One room with private porch has own hall, ocean view, Laura Ashley decor, oak furnishings, sitting area.

Breakfast: Freshly squeezed Florida orange juice in season. Fresh fruit. Their own biscuits, muffins, or coffee cake. Entree such as savory egg casserole, "decadent French toast," or blueberry oven pancake. Eat in intimate dining room with crystal chandelier and wall of many-paned windows, by fireplace, or on veranda.

Plus: Air-conditioned bedrooms. Afternoon tea November–April. Outdoor hot/cold showers. Porch rockers. Beach passes. Reserved private on-site parking.

*T*hink *of bed and breakfast as a people-to-people concept.*

Pierrot by the Sea

101 Centre Street
Beach Haven, NJ 08008
Winter address: 1611 Haworth Street
Philadelphia, PA 19124

609/492-4424
(winter phone) 215/743–9207

Hosts: Catherine Forrestal and Richard Burdo
Location: "Thirty seconds from the ocean." On a beach corner. One block from Surflight Theater and Museum. Close to shops and restaurants. Five minutes east of the Garden State Parkway. Seven miles south of Long Beach Island Causeway.

Open: May–October 15. Three-night minimum Memorial Day and July–Labor Day; four nights on holiday weekends.
Rates: Double occupancy. Shared bath $100. Private bath $125; $150 larger rooms. Weekend dinner, $35 per person.
♥ ⁂ ✗ ✄

"Completely Victorian down to the doorknobs!" Stained glass (much of it made by Catherine and Richard), gates, lamps, tall bedsteads, linens, cast iron urns. . . . It's all here, in the authentically restored "painted lady" summer cottage built as The Tea Cup Inn in 1876.

For Catherine, a former Saks Fifth Avenue fashion coordinator, and Richard, a professional house restorer (who entered a nursing program in 1992), opening a B&B was a natural progression from their antiques business and a five-star restaurant in Philadelphia. If you'd like to follow the restoration done here in 1984, there's a before-and-after album. Flowers are everywhere. Candy is on the pillow at night. Guests are served tea on the wraparound porch. The five-course breakfast is a feature. (And so are the five-course Northern Italian dinners offered as an option at least on weekends.) A gazebo in the garden completes the Victorian environment.

In residence: "Cassidy is our 23-year-old orange cat with green eyes."
Bed and bath: Nine rooms (most with ocean views) with queen or double bed. Two first-floor rooms with private shower baths and separate entrance. Five second-floor rooms with two private baths, one shared full bath. Two third-floor rooms with private full baths.
Breakfast: 8:30–10. Entree possibilities include eggs Benedict and French toast. Homemade breads and muffins.
Plus: Air conditioning in rooms with private bath; ceiling fans in others. Fireplaced living room. Afternoon tea with home-baked goodies. Outdoor showers. Beach tags. Free local papers delivered to your room.

Wedding guests love to stay at a B&B. One innkeeper tells of the bride who asked to have relatives booked on different floors. "Be forewarned, my aunts haven't spoken for 15 years."

Cape May

Known as the oldest seaside resort in America, Cape May might well be called the largest B&B community in the country. Homes, guest houses, and hotels, all with Victorian architectural detail, were built by the hundreds in the 19th century. Other resorts closer to home by way of "the machine" became more fashionable after the turn of the century. But early in the 1970s, Cape May, now a National Historic Landmark city, began to experience a renaissance. Today the streets are lined with restored Victorian homes (dozens are B&Bs) and beautiful gardens. During the summer months parking can be a problem.

The profiles of B&B owners on the following pages indicate how one has inspired another. Several hosts don appropriate hats and conduct walking tours of the historic district or of their own restored and refurbished B&Bs. There are trolley tours and horse-and-carriage tours, a boardwalk, and the main summer attraction, the beach. Some B&Bs provide bicycles, direct you to the restored Physick Estate, and note their proximity to the Washington Street Mall with its many art galleries, crafts shops, and antiques emporiums. Hiking and bird-watching opportunities are here too. Daffodils, tulips, and Victorian balls are among theme weekends in so-called off-season weekends. Christmas is celebrated—starting early in December—in glorious Victorian style with many special events, decorations, and B&B tours.

Innkeeping workshops, given periodically by a group of established B&Bs, are very popular with the enormous number of guests who dream of becoming innkeepers.

The Abbey Bed and Breakfast   609/884–4506

34 Gurney Street at Columbia Avenue, Cape May, NJ 08204

Hosts: Marianne and Jay Schatz
Location: One block from the ocean. One and a half blocks to main shopping area. Within walking distance of most restaurants and attractions.
Open: April–mid-December. Two-, three-, or four-night minimum stay in summer and on some weekends in other seasons. Longer minimum for some rooms.

Rates: Double occupancy. April–June and October through mid-December $80–$150. July–September $80–$175. Rates depend on room size and availability of site parking. Ten percent discount for seven or more consecutive nights.
♥ ❖ 🎿 ⅄

Guests wrote: "*A picture of graciousness. Attentive hosts who make a vacation a memorable occasion. A home filled with love and laughter. Guest rooms filled with beautiful Victorian furniture, lace curtains, flowers, lavender soaps, lace-trimmed pillows and sheets.*"

When Manhattan's Bloomingdale's had a photo essay based on *Bed & Breakfast in the Mid-Atlantic States*, a million people viewed the gorgeous picture of the harp in The Abbey's opulent front parlor. When ABC's *Home Show* came to Cape May, the back parlor was the set for a reading of *A Christmas Carol*.

(Please turn page.)

Throughout this Gothic Revival home, built in 1869 as a summer retreat for coal baron John B. McCreary, there are exquisite antiques, chandeliers, and window treatments. In 1979 it was the fourth Schatz house restoration (and second Cape May B&B). Seven years and many delicious breakfasts later, the cottage next door, originally built by Mr. McCreary for his son, came back "into the family" with the Schatz touch.

Before becoming innkeepers, Marianne and Jay, who also has an MBA, were in chemical research and marketing in Philadelphia. Now Marianne is also a Realtor. Jay is known for his 250 period hats—which are modeled (one at a time) in the morning (see "Breakfast" below) and again in the afternoon.

In residence: Four cats—Fergie, Bubba, Feather, Duke of Earl—restricted to first floor. (Sometimes guests coax one upstairs.)
Bed and bath: In two adjacent houses—14 rooms on three floors. All private baths. King, queen (one canopied), or double beds.
Breakfast: 8:30 and 9:30. Entree (perhaps casserole or quiches with fettuccine or fritters), muffins, fresh fruit, cereals, juice, coffee and tea. Chef Marianne and raconteur Jay (with chapeau) entertain in dining room or on veranda. "It's the best time of our day."
Plus: Air conditioning in 10 rooms; ceiling or portable fans in others. Late-afternoon refreshments. Monday, Wednesday, and Friday at 4 p.m., tour of house followed by tea and tidbits (free for guests, charge for public tours). Afternoon croquet while noncompetitors cheer from the veranda. On-site parking for Villa rooms; remote parking for next-door cottage. Beach chairs and passes in season.

Abigail Adams' Bed & Breakfast by the Sea
609/884–1371
12 Jackson Street, Cape May, NJ 08204

Host: Kate Emerson
Location: Just 100 feet from the beach. Half a block from Washington Street Mall. Short walk to restaurants.
Open: Year round. Two-night minimum except July–August and some holidays when it is three nights.

Rates: Double occupancy. July–August, $120–$140 private bath, $95–$110 shared bath. Off-season, $85–$95 private bath, $65–$75 shared. Rest of year, $110–$120 private bath, $85–$100 shared. Amex, MC, Visa.
♥ ♣ ♦ ✈ ✂

Almost a bed and breakfast pioneer. The thought of owning a B&B first came to Kate 12 years ago when she stayed in one of the then few Cape May B&Bs, at a time when she was restoring a house in Toronto, Canada. Then her position as marketing systems development director for American Express took her to London for several years. The next transfer was to New York, whence she rediscovered Cape May "and fell in love with the town all over again." In 1990 she bought the 1892 Italianate Renaissance Revival house from a couple who had established the B&B in 1983. So here she is, with a fulfilled dream and receiving rave reviews about the house, her hospitality, and breakfast. "And to think I never made a muffin until I came to Cape May!

My first day here, my country Victorian antiques, old wicker, and antique quilts were being moved in through the back door while my first guests appeared at the front door!"

In residence: In hosts' quarters—daughter Jillian, age seven. "Charley is our ginger tabby."
Foreign languages spoken: Some French and Spanish.
Bed and bath: Five rooms. On second floor—private tub/shower bath for queen-bedded room with bay window and ocean view and for double-bedded room overlooking garden. On third floor—queen bed, private tub/shower bath. Two double-bedded rooms share a shower bath. Rollaway and crib available.
Breakfast: 9:30. Hot entree—maybe quiche or souffle. Homemade muffins and coffee cakes. Fresh fruit. Juices. Served in fireplaced and hand-stenciled dining room.
Plus: Fresh flowers. Afternoon refreshments. Bedroom ceiling fans. Beach towels and tags. Babysitting. Fireplaced living room and dining room. Off-site permit parking May–October. Front street parking rest of year.

> From Maryland: *"Could see the ocean from the front porch—and even hear the sound of waves at night from our room."* From New York: *"A pretty house with lovely flowers, antiques, flowered wallpaper . . . helpful suggestions . . . scrumptious food . . . we hope there's a room if we go that way again!"* From New Jersey: *"Antiques created a warmth and romance that was exactly what we were looking for. . . . At the breakfast table, the relaxation in the air could be matched only by a week's vacation at a tropical island—even though most of us had only spent one night."*

The Albert Stevens Inn   609/884–4717
127 Myrtle Avenue, Cape May, NJ 08204

Hosts: Curt and Diane Rangen
Location: On a quiet street across from a park. Three blocks to Washington Street Mall, 4 to beaches. Within walking distance of major attractions.
Open: Year round. Two-night minimum on most weekends. Three-night minimum on holiday weekends.

Rates (dinner is included off-season): Double occupancy. $75, $85, $95, $115, depending on room size, decor, and bath. $135 suite; $15 third person. Ten percent discount for senior citizens and birders. Discover, MC, Visa; 4 percent surcharge.
♥ ♣ ♦ ✈ ✂

"A place we could handle ourselves. With space—for gardening, cats, and parking." That was The List when the Rangens, after researching noncorporate fields, decided to become innkeepers in their favorite vacation spot.

In 1989 they purchased this established B&B, originally built in 1890 by Dr. Albert Stevens for his bride. It still has a floating staircase, an oak mantel above a gas fireplace, and the Stevenses' mother-of-pearl inlay parlor set. "And there are loads of crystal and doodads collected by Diane over ten years." Now the exterior is painted in forest green and (Victorian) Perry Street

(Please turn page.)

Yellow, and trimmed in red. Landscaping includes a pond (complete with goldfish), a flower and herb garden, and a gazebo too. Guests sign up for the hot tub that is in a separate building in the backyard. And you are invited (without charge) to summer weekend public "Cats' Garden and Tea Tours" held to raise funds for animal welfare.

Before being won over to this lifestyle, Diane, the innkeeper/part-time counselor/cat fancier, had her own consulting business. Curt, an inn-keeper/part-time photographer, was in marketing in Philadelphia.

In residence: "The regular cast of nine Cape May felines."
Foreign language spoken: French.
Bed and bath: Six rooms and two suites, all with high Victorian feather beds, private baths, air conditioners. First floor—room with double bed, large sitting area, tub/shower bath. Room with canopied double bed, shower bath. Second floor—one with canopied queen bed, tub/shower bath; three double-bedded rooms with shower baths; two-room suite with a queen bed and a twin bed, tub/shower bath. Third floor is huge tower suite with queen bed in one room, twin and large sitting area in other, and tub/shower bath.
Breakfast: At 9. Perhaps Norwegian fruit, hot pumpkin bread, freshly squeezed juice, salmon strata, toasted muffins with homemade jam. Served in formal dining rooms on china and crystal.
Plus: Off-street parking. Fireplaced parlor. Beach towels and tags. In season, "afternoon tea in the Cats' Garden." Transportation to/from airport or bus station. Hot tub (September–June). Florida Room with TV, refrigerator, coffee and tea.

Barnard-Good House   609/884–5381
238 Perry Street, Cape May, NJ 08204

Hosts: Nan and Tom Hawkins
Location: Two blocks from main beach. Ten minutes' walk to town center.
Open: April to November. Two-night minimum April–June 15 and September 15–November 1. June 15–September 15, three- or four-night minimum.
Rates: Double occupancy. $86 double beds. $95 or $115 king beds. $118 suites. Ten percent less for singles and for seven-day stay. MC, Visa.
♥ ✈ ✄

From Pennsylvania: *"Everyone should have such a first B&B experience. . . . We felt lucky to find this gem."* From New Jersey: *"Perfect hosts: down to earth, cordial, interesting . . . extremely well-kept house. . . . Fantastic culinary experience. . . . Addicting!"*

We found that, indeed, the hosts love life and guests love the hosts—and their extraordinary breakfasts. It was early in the season when we visited, but it was a full house, with many in the 25 to 35 age range and others young at heart.

"I really do love Victorian," said Tom as he scraped the shutters scheduled to go on the lavender house.

Before coming here in 1980, the Hawkinses had lived in central New Jersey with early American decor "complete with hanging baskets in the kitchen." About the time of their 30th wedding anniversary, when Tom was a purchasing director for a plastics manufacturing firm and Nan was marketing director for a shopping center, they were searching for a career change and found this Second Empire mansard-roofed house—empty. They did (and continue to do) all the restoration themselves. The dining room has a gasolier made of iron, pewter, and brass. The 100-year-old organ in the living room really works if you pump hard. Each cozy guest room is quite different; the flamboyant pink, white, and green Hawkins Suite is a popular honeymooners' room. One of the bathrooms has a copper tub and pull-chain john.

Bed and bath: Five rooms on second and third floors; all private baths. Two double-bedded suites with sitting room, en-suite shower baths. One large king-bedded room, en-suite tub/shower bath. One other king-bedded room, keyed tub/shower bath across hall. One double-bedded room, en-suite half bath, assigned shower room next to room.

Breakfast: Their hallmark. Starts at 8:30. In dining room with fine china and silver. Maybe freshly extracted and blended juices, muffins, crepes, fruit soup, cheese bread, exotic chicken dish, chocolate chip banana cake. Menu never repeated regardless of your length of stay. (Special diets accommodated.) Can last two hours "depending on how much fun we are having." Cookbook— *Why Not For Breakfast*—released in 1993.

Plus: Bedroom air conditioners and ceiling fans. Living room with gas fireplace. Rockers and wicker furniture on wraparound porch. Afternoon refreshments. Off-street parking right here. Beach tags.

The Brass Bed Inn   609/884–8075

719 Columbia Avenue, Cape May, NJ 08204

Hosts: John and Donna Dunwoody; Angela Conran, assistant innkeeper
Location: In the historic district, 2 blocks from the ocean.
Open: Year round. Two- or three-night minimum (depending on accommodations) on all weekends plus July and August.
Rates: Double occupancy. January 1–March 31, shared bath $55 midweek, $65 weekends; private bath $80 midweek, $95 weekends; pri-vate hall bath $70 midweek, $80 weekends. April 1–June 15, $65/$70, $95/$105, $85/$92. June 16–September 15, shared bath $97; private bath $120, $125, $140; private hall bath $105 or $110. September 16–December 31, shared bath $55 midweek, $82 weekends; private bath $80 midweek, $115 weekends; private hall bath $80 midweek, $95 weekends.
♥ ✖ ⅄

Personal touches are everywhere—family heirlooms, old photos of relatives, the 1895 upright piano that may be a gathering spot for singing, and daughter Mary's dollhouse in the foyer. (The Christmas display of the family's toy collection is almost famous.) It's like grandma's—John's grandma did take summer boarders in her Victorian shore house—where everything is touchable and guests are treated like family. Part of the wicker-furnished veranda is screened in summer, glass-enclosed and heated in winter.

(Please turn page.)

There were only two B&Bs in Cape May when the Dunwoodys—without a thought about innkeeping—were in search of a new place. In 1980 they "fell in love with Cape May and a 'need everything' house"; moved from Voorhees, New Jersey; and "jumped into a new lifestyle" while John, a graphic designer, continued to commute at dawn to Philadelphia. (Now the Dunwoodys participate in innkeeping workshops.)

Polished period brass beds are in every room. Many restored furnishings in the 120-year-old house are original—armoires, marble-topped tables, washstands, and dressers. There are lace curtains, period wallcoverings, and patterned Oriental carpets. Early recordings are heard on the 19th-century Graphonola, purchased in 1962 and restored by John. As the guest from Maryland wrote, "Magical."

In residence: Not allowed in guest rooms—Clancy, the dog; felines Clarice and Clouseau.
Bed and bath: Eight rooms (largest is 14 by 16 feet; smallest 10 by 12 feet) with king or double bed, on second and third floors. All baths are with shower, no tub. Four rooms with private adjoining baths. Two with private hall baths, and two on third floor share a bath; robes provided.
Breakfast: At 9 and 9:45. Fresh fruit, cereal, homemade baked goods, beverages. Eggs, pancakes, or other hot entrees. By gas fireplace in parlor.
Plus: Bedroom air conditioners and ceiling fans. Afternoon tea, lemonade, or cider. Front porch rockers. Outside hot/cold shower, dressing room. Hair dryers. Bicycle rack. Beach passes. Guests' restaurant recommendations and hints in guest room logs.

From Pennsylvania: *"Cozy . . . romantic . . . quaint . . . entirely delightful."*

Captain Mey's Inn
202 Ocean Street, Cape May, NJ 08204

609/884–7793
609/884–9637

Hosts: Carin Fedderman and Milly LaCanfora
Location: Two blocks from the beach. A half block from the Victorian shopping mall. Within walking distance of all restaurants.
Open: Year round. Two-night minimum on weekends off season. Three-night minimum in season.

Rates: Vary according to room location and bath arrangement. Double occupancy, $125–$155 private bath, $75–$85 shared bath, July–Labor Day. $20 additional guest in room. Less off-season. Singles $5 less.
♥ ♣ ✖ ✄

For a national television feature on Dutch Christmas, the cameras came here, to an inn where there's a delightful mix of Dutch and Victorian—with lots of brass, copper, and pewter, a Delft Blue Collection, Tiffany glass, and Victorian furniture. The fastidiously maintained and comfortable inn—where guests awake to the strains of classical music—is hosted by the creators of Cape May's Tulip Fest. Their own grounds have a show of 400 bulbs as well as an herb garden with eight varieties.

Once a doctor's residence, then a tearoom and later a rooming house, Captain Mey's, named after the Dutch founder of Cape May, was converted to a B&B in 1979. That was when Milly, a travel coordinator, and Carin, a computer programmer (who is from Holland), stripped and refinished all that woodwork—all the way to the third floor. Now handmade quilts, fresh flowers (mostly from the garden), and imported Dutch lace curtains are in the rooms. The exterior is painted in authentic custom-mixed tones of purple, wheat sheaf, and fawn. And there's plenty of what-to-do information here; for three years, Milly has served as chamber of commerce president.

Foreign languages spoken: Dutch and Italian.
Bed and bath: Nine rooms on three floors. Six with private baths. First-floor suite has queen bed and private entrance. Five second-floor double-bedded rooms. On third floor, two rooms, each with a double and a single bed, and one double-bedded room share a large tub/shower bath.
Breakfast: 8:30–9:30. Fresh fruit, homemade breads and cakes. Dutch cheeses. Breakfast meats. Hot entree such as cheese strata, quiche, or French toast. Beach plum jelly. Enjoyed buffet style in the dramatic foyer, in candlelit dining room, or on the wraparound veranda with privacy afforded by Victorian wind curtains.
Plus: Air-conditioned bedrooms. Bedroom ceiling fans. Iced tea (with mint from the garden) and homemade goodies on the veranda in summer; sherry by fire in winter. Beach passes, chairs, and towels. Turndown service with pillow mints. Landscaped courtyard with bistro setting for picnic lunch. Off-street parking.

From New Jersey: *"From handmade quilts to delicious Dutch gourmet breakfasts . . . an oasis. . . . A step back to a period when gracious living was a way of life."*

COLVMNS by the Sea   609/884–2228
1513 Beach Drive, Cape May, NJ 08204

Hosts: Barry and Cathy Rein
Location: On the ocean. Across the street from fishing. One block from a not-so-crowded protected swimming beach. About a mile to mall, main beach, restaurants.
Open: February–December. Two-night minimum stay at all times; three nights June–October weekends.

Rates: Double occupancy. $110–$150 private bath, ocean view. $145–$175 private bath, oceanfront. $35 extra person in room. Singles $10 less. Off-season (before June and after October) midweek discounts.
♥ ✖ ✂

"Fall asleep to the sound of the ocean. Wake up to a breathtaking view." That's exactly what attracted this couple, who went from being tourists to summer house owners to innkeepers in just four years. When Barry decided to make a career change from managing new business development, the Reins (and help) brought this turn-of-the-century "great cottage" from its then apartment status "back to the original splendor, as they say." They restored coffered ceilings, wainscoting, and the three-storied staircase; and they furnished with Victorian antiques, reproduction beds, and a collection of Chinese ivory carvings. The highback bed that reaches the ceiling in one room is part of a three-piece suite from the Blair House in Washington, D.C.

(Please turn page.)

Built for the 1878 Centennial, the bed was purchased in 1988 after being exhibited at the Smithsonian. For a personal touch, Cathy has written notes about the history or the fashion of the times.

The hosts spend winters in New York City and Arizona. Six months of the year, Barry is in Cape May while Cathy, a lawyer who is executive vice president of Metropolitan Life, flies in from Manhattan for weekends.

Foreign language spoken: German.

Bed and bath: Eleven rooms on second and third floors, all private full baths. Five are oceanfront. King, queen, or twin beds. Three rooms with trundles sleep up to four.

Breakfast: A feature at 9:30. (Coffee is ready at 8.) Fruit, juice, homemade breads and coffee cakes, blintz souffle, Barry's scrambled eggs with country smoked bacon, caramelized French toast, cheese bread, and "any other great recipe we come across." Served in bay-windowed dining room with marble-tiled fireplace.

Plus: Tea at 5. Evening sherry. Bedroom ceiling fans. Hot tub (spring and fall) on L-shaped veranda that overlooks the ocean. Living room with fireplace, nickelodeon. Upstairs parlor and large foyer for reading or writing. Downstairs parlor with TV. Ice. Bicycles. Beach badges, towels, and chairs. Victorian Holmes weekend for Sherlockians in November. Coachman's Christmas House Tour in December. On-site off-street parking.

The Duke of Windsor

609/884–1355
817 Washington Street
Cape May, NJ 08204
(reservations only) **800/826–8973**

Hosts: Bruce and Fran Prichard
Location: In historic area. Four blocks from beach, "close enough, but quiet too."
Open: Year round. Three-night minimum stay, July–September. Other months, two-night minimum.
Rates: Double occupancy; vary according to room size, bath arrangement, weekdays or weekends, air conditioning. $68–$95 shared bath, $85–$125 private bath. Off-season, $65–$75 shared bath, $80–$95 private bath. $10 extra person.

♥ 🛏 ♣ ✗ ⚲

Although the Prichards instantly took to Cape May in 1980, they weren't quite sure about the abrupt change in lifestyle made by their friends from home (Voorhees, New Jersey); "but when we came to help them open The Brass Bed, it was neat to see the restoration progress. We soon bought this grand (in every way) 1896 house with its dramatic 45-foot tower and extended our entertaining style to new friends. We love our guests!"

The classic Queen Anne detailing includes Tiffany stained glass; a restored dining room with replica wallpaper of Queen Victoria's throne room, ornate plaster ceiling, and 1871 chandelier; original natural oak woodwork; and a three-story cantilevered stairway. Research and restoration—a labor of love by the three (the fourth is growing up) generations—are ongoing. Grandmother made the curtains. Son Bruce wallpapered. Furnishings are antiques and period pieces. A Victorian garden is in process. There are plans for restoring the exterior too.

Fran, a library/media specialist, and Bruce, a teacher of chemistry and physics, still divide their time between Voorhees and Cape May. When they are not able to be in Cape May, daughter Barbara hosts with the "assistance" of junior innkeepers, daughter Maria Frances and son Michael.

Bed and bath: Nine rooms—on second and third floors—with private baths. One with queen bed; one with queen and a single; one with double and a single; rest with double bed (including octagonal tower rooms that each have five windows). Eight baths are en suite, one bath (robes provided) is across the hall. One double-bedded room has tub and shower bath; other baths are shower only.

Breakfast: 8:30–10, but late sleepers won't go hungry. Fresh fruits, juice, freshly baked items, cereal, and an entree of the day—pancakes, scrambled eggs, or French toast, with sausage or bacon.

Plus: Afternoon tea. Beach passes. Hot/cold outside showers. Fireplaced foyer and parlor. Air conditioners (removed in mid-September) in five bedrooms. First-floor tower game room for cards, chess, and checkers. On-site off-street parking. Participant in month-long Christmas grand tour.

A guest wrote: "Personal touches everywhere, from the sheets hung in the sunshine to the candies by the door. I arrived tense and tired and drove home singing."

The Gingerbread House   609/884–0211
28 Gurney Street, Cape May, NJ 08204

Hosts: Joan and Fred Echevarria
Location: In the historic district, half a block from the beach. Within walking distance of restaurants, shops, and homes open for tours.
Open: Year round. Four-night minimum weekend stay during summer and holidays. Two- or three-night minimum weekend stay other times.

Rates: Shared bath: $75 single, $85 or $95 double. Private bath: $115 or $125 single, $130 or $140 double. $15 additional person. Six percent discount for week-long stays. Midweek discounts October–May.
♥ ✹

To begin with, Fred's fine craftsmanship shows in the arches and porch railing. In 1992 he made his own pattern for these missing features, which had been part of the original 1869 house. The teakwood double front doors with ornate beveled glass as well as the arched transom are also his creations—as are the teak bathroom cabinets topped with Corian counters. The parlor and dining room medallions are various shades of rose. All the wonderful watercolors—with the exception of the one of the house done by the first paying guest—were painted by Fred's mother, Jane Echevarria, an artist featured in her own book, *Victorian Interiors*. (When a guest buys a painting, Jane creates a replacement!) Antique furnishings are walnut, rosewood, wicker, and oak. There are collections—cranberry glass, animal teapots, paperweights, shells, and vases. Classical music plays all day. There's a warm, bright, airy feeling in this impeccably maintained B&B.

(Please turn page.)

When the Echevarrias bought the house in 1979, many family members helped with the restoration. Until 1992 Joan commuted on weekdays to a Philadelphia investment advisory firm where she was manager of data processing. Fred is a clinical psychologist/award-winning photographer turned wood- and metalworker and cohost.

In residence: Moby, the cat.
Bed and bath: Six double-bedded rooms. Three second-floor rooms (one with two double beds and private porch) have private baths. Three third-floor rooms (one with skylight, one with cathedral ceiling) share one large shower bath plus a first-floor half bath.
Breakfast: 8:30–10. Buffet includes fresh fruit, homemade coffee cake or muffins, homemade cereal, juice, coffee, tea.
Plus: Fireplaced living room. Bedroom ceiling fans. Outside enclosed shower with changing area. Wicker-furnished front porch. Afternoon tea with lemonade, tea, and sweets. Guest refrigerator. Bicycle storage (bring lock). Garden. Beach tags.

> From New Jersey: *"Beautiful rooms and friendly people—all the ingredients for a wonderful stay. Highly recommended!"*

The Humphrey Hughes House   609/884-4428
29 Ocean Street, Cape May, NJ 08204   800/582-3634

Hosts: Lorraine and Terry Schmidt
Location: One block (five houses) from the ocean. One and a half blocks from Washington Street Mall. In historic area. On corner of Columbia Avenue.
Open: Year round. Three-night minimum May–October weekends.
Rates: Double occupancy: May–October $110–$135 king, $105–$140 queen, $90–$120 double; November–April $90–$110 king, $85–$130 queen, $80–$105 double. Suites: May–October $165–$210; November–April $125–$150. Singles $10 less. MC, Visa.
♥ ✖ ✶

It's big and beautiful. It's a Shingle Style Colonial Revival with a huge, awninged wraparound porch, wicker-furnished sun room, stained glass windows, and, between the parlor and living room, solid carved chestnut columns. Weddings are held here. So are Christmas house tours. Returnees come to visit the Schmidts, who changed careers in 1986. Previously, Lorraine was with Merrill Lynch as vice president of banking; Terry was New Jersey Casino Control commissioner.

Built in 1903 for Dr. Humphrey Hughes, "The Doctor's House" was home to the Hughes family until 1980, when it was converted to an inn. In addition to the Hugheses' grandfather clock, dining room sideboard and table, and much silver, the inn is furnished with many museum-quality Victorian pieces, with a light touch, with peaches and blues and florals, with Lorraine's attention to detail.

In residence: "The girls"—Maggie, a standard poodle, and Elizabeth, a miniature poodle.

Bed and bath: Ten rooms (nine are extremely large and have ceiling fans) on four levels. Three are suites (two with ocean view) that have TV, air conditioner, bed for a third guest. All private baths with tub and/or shower (en suite except for two original full baths that are a step away from room). King, queen, or double bed. Ground-level suite with king bed is handicapped accessible. One double-bedded room is air conditioned.
Breakfast: At 9. Fruit plate. Juice. Entree such as apple and potato frittata or cheese and bacon puff. Sour cream coffee cake, strawberry bread, bran muffins. (Newsletter includes recipes.) In candlelit dining room.
Plus: Fireplaced living and dining rooms. Grand piano in parlor. Afternoon tea with home-baked goodies. Fresh flowers. Guest refrigerator. Beach towels.

The Mainstay Inn & Cottage   609/884-8690
635 Columbia Avenue, Cape May, NJ 08204-2305

Hosts: Tom and Sue Carroll
Location: On historic, tree-lined street, within walking distance of everything.
Open: Mid-March until mid-December. Three- and four-day minimum stay June–October. Some two-night package weekends available in spring and fall. First-time guests, in particular, should call so that the rooms and amenities can be described.
Rates: Spring/fall $95–$145. Weekends/summer $125–$175. A little more for two-night weekend packages in spring and fall.
♥ ✽ ♦ ✈

Elegance. Attention to detail. A visual feast that is enjoyed by "both those who want to be alone and others who seek friendship." But hardly a hidden treasure. Many major publications picture the long walnut dining room table, gas chandeliers, and ceiling-high mirrors in addition to the beautiful exterior of what was built in 1872 as an exclusive clubhouse for gamblers.

The Carrolls loved old houses, even when Tom was a Coast Guardsman (he's now a captain in the reserves) in Cape May. For postservice living, they bought their first Mainstay, which had a few rooms for summer guests. Tom worked with the planning board. Sue taught. In 1976 they acquired the current Mainstay with many of the original furnishings and fixtures. Ahead of the renewed interest in Victoriana, Sue created swag patterns (she still makes the window treatments) and wallpaper borders. Now Oriental rugs are in the 14-foot-high parlors, which feature Bradbury and Bradbury silk-screened papers. The cottage next door, where we stayed, is also furnished with choice Victorian antiques.

In many ways this is considered a model of the evolution of a B&B business, all the way from the hosts' struggle to overcome local opposition to the dramatic (positive) impact of B&Bs on an entire community—and the innkeepers' community involvement (Mid-Atlantic Center for the Arts, Cape May Music Festival, Cape May Point Lighthouse restoration). To this day, the Carrolls enjoy wallpapering and painting. They join guests for breakfast and tea. Tom, text writer for *Cape May: Images of a Seaside Resort*, narrates the

(Please turn page.)

thrice-weekly Mainstay tours. This is a business run with joy, style, and personalization.

Bed and bath: Twelve large rooms with private baths on three floors (one with steep staircase). One first-floor room. Two with private porches. King, queen, double, or twin beds.
Breakfast: 8:15–9:45. In season, light meal with homemade breads. Off-season, a full meal could include corn quiche, chicken pie with bacon, and homemade sticky buns. Served on the veranda or in the dining room.
Plus: Afternoon tea. Drawing room with coal stove. Three parlors. Veranda with rockers and swing; private porches with some guest rooms. Garden for sunbathing. Ladder to cupola for ocean view. Beach passes. Outside shower. Three rooms have private parking.

Manor House   609/884–4710
612 Hughes Street, Cape May, NJ 08204-2318

Hosts: Mary and Tom Snyder
Location: On a quiet side street in historic district, 1½ blocks from the ocean. One block from shops, restaurants, and pedestrian street mall.
Open: Year round except January. Two-night minimum on weekends; three nights on holiday weekends.

Rates: Double occupancy. Shared bath $65–$95. Private shower bath $75–$125. Private tub/shower bath $85–$138. Suite with whirlpool bath $95–$158. Higher rates in July and August, lowest on winter weekends.
✖ ✄

Your host/barbershop quartet singer/golfer serves breakfast in bow tie, starched shirt, and colored suspenders. Mary's made-from-scratch sticky buns are signature food—a hit, too, with hundreds of Macy's shoppers who attended cooking demonstrations given by innkeepers in this book. Flash! Just published: *Mary's Buns and Tom's Puns.*

When the mid-life career changers bought this 1906 house, they acquired a homey place that had been completely redone in 1983 by a wood-carver who had a special appreciation for the chestnut and oak staircase, the floors and moldings. Originally a summer home, the house (without gingerbread) has bay windows, ornate radiators, a great living room fireplace, and some original as well as new stained glass. Furnishings are of the period, with each room being quite different in size and decor. Tom's postbreakfast information (performance) about doings past and present is spiced with facts and humor.

Between both hosts, there's experience in college administration, potato chip manufacturing (their own), and (for a short time) the corporate world.

Foreign language spoken: Pennsylvania Dutch.
Bed and bath: Nine rooms (some are air conditioned; ceiling fans in all) with king, queen, or double bed. On second and third floors. Seven with private baths include third-floor suite with queen bed, whirlpool tub, corner glass shower; others with shower only or tub and shower. Room with double bed and private half bath shares (robes provided) full hall bath with queen-bedded room that has sink en suite.

Breakfast: 8:30 and 9:30 seatings. Two entrees (you choose one) prepared from a repertoire of "more than 68." Maybe asparagus on homemade English muffin toast, poached eggs and sauce Mornay, apple-cheese pancakes, Mexican quiche, strawberry crepes, or Manor House French toast.

Plus: Punch, cider, tea, or sherry. Theme weekends include one for runners in May, a December Dickens program, and a cooking seminar. Off-premises valet parking. Garden. Beach towels and tags. Hot/cold outdoor shower. Information about an area championship golf course where Mary and Tom have renewed an old interest.

> From New Jersey: *"Special touches make us feel warm and welcome. No small detail ever overlooked for our comfort. Good food and good fun."*

The Mason Cottage   609/884–3358

625 Columbia Avenue, Cape May, NJ 08204

Hosts: Dave and Joan Mason
Location: On a quiet tree-lined street in historic district. One block from beach; on horse-carriage and trolley tours route.
Open: May–November. Two-night minimum stay on weekends, three nights on holidays.
Rates: Double occupancy; vary according to room size, location, weekday or weekend, and season. Rooms:

summer $85–$125; spring and fall $75–$100 weekends, $65–$80 weekdays. Suites: summer $135–$165; spring and fall $110–$140 weekends, $90–$115 weekdays. Ten percent less for four to six consecutive nights, plus seventh night free—excluding holidays. Five percent AARP discount. Some packages available.
♥ ♣ ♦ ✈ ⅄

Everyone remembers the hospitality in this B&B, which has been in the Mason family since 1946. Returnees of the 1980s saw constant changes made by Joan, a registered nurse and clinical editor, and husband Dave, an electrical engineer and licensed contractor, who took over in 1981. The parlor restoration—complete with Victorian brass chandelier, plaster medallion and moldings, and floor-to-ceiling windows—has been outdone by their 1993 project: the interior connecting of the twin houses (which look like one from outside) and the addition of suites. Most of the furnishings are restored antiques that are original to the mansard-roofed house, built in 1871 as a summer residence by the Warne family of Philadelphia. To complete the picture, there are Victorian wallcoverings, refinished floors, Oriental rugs, and watercolors done by local artists.

Honeymooners receive special attention. Some weddings are held here. And, sometimes, Joan conducts tours of the inn for the Mid-Atlantic Center for the Arts.

In residence: Dave is here on all weekends; Joan, May–October weekends. Staffers are May–November weekday hosts.
Bed and bath: In original B&B, five rooms on three floors, all private baths (some tub and shower, some shower only). In twin house, four new suites on second and third floors (one room with ocean view); all private baths, some with whirlpool tub. Queen or double beds.

(Please turn page.)

Breakfast: 8:30–10:30. Fresh fruit. French toast, baked apples, ham-and-egg quiche, or omelet. Homemade breads, muffins, coffee cakes. Granola and dry cereals. Juice, coffee, teas. Hosts join guests in dining room or on wraparound veranda.

Plus: Suites are air conditioned. Rooms have ceiling fan or air conditioner. Afternoon tea. Private outside hot/cold shower and dressing area available to guests after checkout. Restaurant menus. Beach passes. Bike rack. Wicker and cane porch rockers with boardwalk view.

> A guest wrote: *"The rooms and the surrounding neighborhood are almost like a scene out of a movie. A prime example of the charm and hospitality this historic town has to offer."*

The Queen Victoria   609/884–8702
102 Ocean Street, Cape May, NJ 08204

Hosts: Joan and Dane Wells
Location: In the historic district, 1 block from the beach and 1½ blocks from Washington Street shopping.
Open: Year round. "We never close." Holidays and weekends may require much advance notice. Weekend minimums—two nights in winter, three in spring/fall, four in summer. Two- or three-night midweek minimum stay in summer and some spring and fall periods.
Rates: Double occupancy; vary according to season (lowest on winter weekdays; highest on summer weekends). $125–$250 quad suite. $110–$195 double suite. $95–$150 large double. $75–$130 small double. $20 extra person. Singles $10 less. MC, Visa.
♥ ♦ ✗ ✕

Fit for a queen (and king), for romantics, and for families (see suite descriptions below). With classical music and handmade quilts. With period antiques, chocolates on the pillow, and innkeepers who enjoy spending time (breakfast and tea and then some) with guests. And guests who ask about Cape May (Dane was chamber of commerce president); Victoriana (Joan was executive director of the Victorian Society in America); restoration (their first building opened in 1981 after two years of researching, demolishing, and chair caning); paint colors (guests bring photos of their own home); beer judging (for American Home Brewers' Association) and barbershop quartet singing (Dane); outdoor activities and Victorian gardens (Joan); Christmas decorations (workshops are an annual feature); benefits (the Mid-Atlantic Center for the Arts and public television)—*and* the growth of a home-based occupation. Now the inn is located in three neighboring restored 1880s houses. Among the 15 year-round staffers is one full-time professional painter. Before becoming an innkeeper, Dane was in neighborhood commercial revitalization and economic development in Philadelphia.

In residence: Daughter Elizabeth, age 10. Two cats—Spats and Mugsy.
Foreign languages spoken: Fluent French (Dane). Some Spanish (Joan).
Bed and bath: Twenty-three rooms with queen or double beds, all private baths (three are shower only). Seven are suites with whirlpool tub, TV, refrigerator. One suite has two bedrooms (one with gas log fireplace), each with queen bed; private bath with two-person whirlpool tub, TV; bedrooms

share a parlor, pantry with refrigerator, coffeemaker, microwave, popcorn machine, sink with "hot tap." The barrier-free suite has a porch and working fireplace.

Breakfast: 8–10. Homemade granola and breads such as peach yogurt or poppyseed; Wolferman English muffins; a different egg dish each day. Baked apple or hot curried fruit compote. Eat in one of two dining rooms, in bay window of parlor, or on porch.

Plus: Air conditioners and refrigerators in all rooms; ceiling fans in many. Afternoon tea with homemade cookies, pates, and cheese spreads. Two parlors, one with fireplace and player piano, the other with TV and games. Library. Setups, mixers, coffee, tea, popcorn maker. Dozens of porch rockers. Bicycles (free). Beach tags. Bathhouse with changing room and showers. Annotated take-away maps. Concierge and bell services. Newsletter including handyman tips and recipes.

From New Jersey: *"We have stayed at 85 inns from Maine to Florida to California. Our overall favorite is The Queen Victoria."* From Pennsylvania: *"Joan and Dane make it feel like home."*

The Wooden Rabbit   609/884–7293

609 Hughes Street, Cape May, NJ 08204

Hosts: Greg and Debby Burow
Location: In historic district "on what we consider the prettiest gaslit street in town." Two blocks from beaches. One block from shops. Within easy walking distance of restaurants.
Open: Year round. Usually, three-night minimum in July and August, two nights rest of year.
Rates: Double occupancy. June–September $165 suite, $145 other rooms. Less off-season. $15 extra person. MC, Visa for deposit only.

The country decor, very different from Cape May's featured Victoriana, follows the lead taken from the original cooking hook still in the fireplace of the house built in 1838. The rabbit theme—stuffed, painted, ceramic, and stitched rabbits—started with Debby's Beatrix Potter collection. This is a B&B where children are comfortable, where adults with or without children feel relaxed. There's stenciling, baskets, comfortable seating by the fire, and interesting folk art.

The Burows stayed in B&Bs for seven years before opening here in Cape May in 1988. For a few years Debby commuted to her full-time job as art director/graphic designer in Philadelphia—while Greg was the full-time innkeeper/photographer/sticky bun baker. Recently they switched arrangements; Greg is a full-time carpenter and Debby is the primary innkeeper, greeting guests who seek a family environment.

In residence: Two school-aged sons. "Our cat, Oscar, who is not supposed to visit guest rooms, loves the fireplaces and guests' laps—and is a regular in many local shops!"

(Please turn page.)

Bed and bath: Three second-floor rooms; all with private baths, TV, and air conditioning. Suite with king/twins bed option, sitting room, shower bath. Room with king/twins, shower bath. Queen-bedded room with tub/shower bath. Cots (but no crib) available. Please bring your own portacrib.
Breakfast: 8:30–9:30. Fruit or fruit dish. Quiche, egg casserole, blueberry waffles or pancakes. Homemade cinnamon buns, bread, or muffins. Greg's "famous homemade granola." Teas and coffee. Buffet style in dining room.
Plus: Home-baked goodies at 4 p.m. tea. Chocolate treats. Guest refrigerator. Small basket of toys in common room. Outside hot/cold shower. Beach tags and chairs. Clothesline for bathing suits. Enclosed backyard with flower garden. Wicker-furnished sun porch. Free parking in driveway next to inn. Nanny service recommendation (please call ahead).

Woodleigh House   609/884–7123
808 Washington Street, Cape May, NJ 08204

Hosts: Buddy and Jan Wood
Location: Centrally located in the quiet historic district.
Open: Year round. Two-night minimum on June–October weekends.
Rates: Double occupancy. All rooms the same rate; vary according to season. $95–$130 June–October; $75–$95 November–May except holiday weekends. $30 additional person.
♥ ♨ ♣ ✕ ⅄

> From New Jersey, Pennsylvania, and New York City: *"The decor is authentic without being cloying. . . . Other Cape May B&Bs are fancier, but none can match the Woodleigh House when it comes to hominess and hospitality. . . . Particularly like their informal and flexible approach to breakfast. . . . It is obvious that they enjoy the collecting and restoring that is part of innkeeping in Cape May. . . . A house for all seasons!"*

That's it, folks, a home away from home offered by the consummate hosts, who were "in and out" as assistants through all the years that Buddy's mother ran the guest house until she died in 1983. Since taking over, they have added their own touches (Victorian furniture, collections of glass and Royal Copenhagen), renovated (latest: all private baths), and completely redecorated. From the moment you call for a reservation, you can tell that they enjoy their role—a real balance to their other positions, where they work with "other wonderful people." In neighboring communities, Buddy is an elementary school principal and Jan is a kindergarten teacher.

Bed and bath: Four rooms, all private full baths. Double-bedded room on first floor. On second floor, two double-bedded rooms and one with a double and a single. Plus a one-bedroom apartment with sleep sofa.
Breakfast: 9–10. Fruit, cheese, granola, juice, three or four homemade pastries, bread sticks, coffee, tea. Self-serve in dining room during winter, on porch in summer. Hosts join guests.
Plus: Bedroom ceiling fans. Porches. Use of refrigerator. TV and VCR. Unscheduled—champagne sherbet, wine, or lemonade. Picnic table in garden. Courtyard lounge area. Bicycles. Beach tags. Outside shower. Off-street on-site parking.

Leigh Way Bed and Breakfast Inn

66 Leigh Street, Clinton, NJ 08809   908/735–4311

Host: Terry Schlegel
Location: In an old residential neighborhood. Six hundred feet from Raritan River, which "meanders through this Victorian town where motorists stop to allow geese and ducks to cross the street." Minutes to shops, restaurants, art center, mill with working waterwheel. Close to countryside with wineries. Fifteen minutes to Flemington and outlets; 30 to New Hope.
Open: Year round.
Rates: Weeknights, $65 single, $75 double. Weekly rates available. Amex, MC, Visa.
♣ ✖ ⅄

> From Connecticut: *"Breakfasts are bountiful, varied, and hot. Terry is friendly and energetic."* From Mississippi: *"Stayed while attending a weaving workshop . . . fell in love with the charm of Leigh Way . . . furnished in keeping with Victorian style so that it has a rightful place among other period houses in the dear picturesque town of Clinton."*

The mansard-roofed 1862 slate Second Empire house was restored by the previous owners, who researched the exterior colors for authenticity and gave the interior a light and airy feeling. In 1989 Terry purchased the property "after raising a large family (10 years were in Clinton), and having had careers in interior design and, most recently, in sales and marketing in New York City. Bed and breakfast combines my love of antiques, entertaining, and decorating."

Bed and bath: Four air-conditioned rooms. On second floor, one room with two twin beds, private shower. One queen-bedded room with private shower bath, and one with tub/shower bath. On third floor, queen-bedded room with private shower bath. Rollaway available.
Breakfast: Weekdays 7–9:30; weekends 8:30–10:30. Juice, fresh fruit, homemade baked goods, bagels and cream cheese, freshly brewed coffee. In dining room at table set with "our best china."
Plus: Bedroom ceiling fans. Fireplaced living room with upright piano. Welcoming and evening refreshments. Sherry. Fresh flowers. Robes. Toiletries. Off-street parking.

KEY TO SYMBOLS
♥ Lots of honeymooners come here.
♯ Families with children are very welcome. (Please see page xii.)
♩ "Please emphasize that we are a private home, not an inn."
♣ Groups or private parties sometimes book the entire B&B.
♦ Travel agents' commission paid. (Please see page xii.)
✖ Sorry, no guests' pets are allowed.
⅄ No smoking inside *or* no smoking at all, even on porches.

The Cabbage Rose Inn   908/788–0247

162 Main Street, Flemington, NJ 08822

Hosts: Pam Venosa and Al Scott
Location: "Typical Main Street USA" in active historic district. Five-minute walk to outlet shopping. Within 15-minute drive of countryside wineries, New Hope, and Lambertville.
Open: Year round. Two-night minimum for weekend reservations that include Saturday.

Rates: Double occupancy. $80–$98; $98 with fireplace. ($7 surcharge for use of fireplace.) Romance-and-roses packages; midweek and corporate rates available. Amex, MC, Visa.
♥ ♠ ✗ ✄

With turret and third-floor open gazebo, this century-old Victorian with gingerbread has a wedding cake appearance and has recently become a painted lady with five colors, including pink, white, maroon, and a touch of gold leaf. This is where Al and Pam were married in 1988, the day before they opened the inn, and just a few months after they discovered the house "with potential"—and with a few surprises, such as a gorgeous oak parquet entry floor and, embedded in a wall, a 1920 will (now framed for all to see).

The career changers—both were AT&T managers—based the floral decor on Pam's Aunt Rose's "cabbage rose–theme" china collection. They furnished eclectically—with family photographs, many Victorian pieces, Oriental and hooked rugs, and wicker. And they learned about the history of the house, the town (its architecture and the courthouse where the Lindbergh kidnapping trial was held), and the area—"New Jersey's last and only covered bridge is nearby."

What's new? Their very own line of handmade chocolates shaped as cameos, butterflies, or fans topped with pink roses.

In residence: Two West Highland terriers, Rosie, "who sings for our guests—honest!," and Daisy.
Bed and bath: Five second-floor rooms, all private baths. One fireplaced room with four-poster queen bed, attached shower bath. Three more queen-bedded rooms; one with attached tub and shower bath, one with attached shower/no tub bath, one with shower stall in bath plus antique claw-footed tub in the bedroom. One double-bedded room with shower bath down the hall. Rollaways available.
Breakfast: 8:30–10 weekends with full menu; cinnamon-raisin French toast a specialty. (Earlier on weekdays with fresh fruit salad topped with yogurt or homemade granola.) In winter, warm applesauce. Hot or cold cereals. Homemade muffins, breads, scones, and/or coffee cake (plum a specialty). Juice, coffee, tea, cocoa. In dining room, on sun porch, or, by request, on tray delivered to your room.
Plus: Central air conditioning. Bedroom ceiling fans. Fireplaced living room. Baby grand piano; sometimes musicales or sing-alongs. Robes. Private phones; some rooms with desks. Late-afternoon lemonade, hot or cold cider or tea, "and strains of Mozart." Daily *New York Times*. Picnic basket ($40 for two). Guest refrigerator. Sherry at bedtime. Transportation to/from bus stop. A before-during-after-restoration photo album.

Jerica Hill Inn   908/782–8234

96 Broad Street, Flemington, NJ 08822-1604

Host: Judith S. Studer
Location: On a quiet corner in residential area of historic district. Two blocks from Main Street, near shops, outlets, restaurants. Sixty miles west of Manhattan and northeast of Philadelphia; 14 miles from New Hope, Pennsylvania.

Open: Year round. Two-night minimum on most weekends.
Rates: Double occupancy. $75–$95 weekends, $10 less midweek. Corporate rates available. $20 additional guest. Amex, MC, Visa.
♣ ◆ ✗ ✂

Classical music. A glowing fire. Antiques without fussiness. Impeccable housekeeping. And a welcoming hostess.

"My childhood memories of this house are special. Often, I came here to visit the grandfather of a best friend. My parents ran the local hotel and I would dream of opening my own place. After buying this in 1984, I supervised the work done by a restoration firm."

Judy's creative ideas are everywhere in the antiques-filled 1901 Victorian, which features a graceful center hall staircase and individually decorated guest rooms. (Repeat guests seem to have their favorite rooms.) As you tour the house, you can tell that she enjoys books (there are baskets of them), auctions (cherry, pine, and wicker pieces), theater, gardening (plants everywhere), and hot-air ballooning (featured in *Country Inns* magazine).

Corporate and business travelers comment on the "quiet, efficient, personal service and the right price." Some guests request decorating advice. Some come to shop at the factory outlets or for antiquing or the Delaware River sports. "They discover the architecture in this beautiful, historic town, and the area wineries."

In residence: Sometimes adult children, Jessica and Eric, visit. Two cats— Binky and Mookie, "who look almost exactly alike."
Bed and bath: Five rooms with en-suite private baths. One first-floor room with queen-sized canopied four-poster, shower bath. Upstairs, three double-bedded rooms: two with tub/shower bath; one with shower bath. One room with twins/king option with shower bath. All antique beds—pineapple, pine, iron-and-brass. Rollaway available.
Breakfast: 8:30–9:30 weekends, at guests' convenience on weekdays. Juice, assorted teas and coffees, fresh fruit, homemade breads (pear a specialty), local jams, cereal, yogurt, warm pastry. Served in dining room or on screened wicker- and plant-filled porch.
Plus: Bedroom air conditioning and ceiling fans. Fireplaced living room. Flowers and fruit in rooms. Beverages including hot cider or iced tea. Guests' pantry open "all the time" with mixers, cookies, fruit, and more. The *New York Times*. Plenty of local information. Cable TV. Limited kitchen privileges. Yard. Off-street parking. B&B&B (and ballooning or bicycling) packages. Winery tour with picnic arranged.

B&Bs offer the ultimate concierge service.

The Jeremiah H. Yereance House   201/438–9457

410 Riverside Avenue, Lyndhurst, NJ 07071   fax 201/939–5801

Hosts: Evelyn and Frank Pezzolla
Location: Across from a riverside park with walking and jogging path, bicycle trails, picnic areas, tennis. Three miles from New Jersey Turnpike; 1 mile from Fairleigh Dickinson University; 5 minutes to Giants' football stadium in Meadowlands sports complex. *To New York City:* 12 miles; 15–45 minutes by car; 25 minutes by bus that leaves 4 blocks from house. Twenty-minute ride to 4-minute ferry ($9 round trip—less for senior citizens—includes bus service to Manhattan's theater district as well as commuters' destinations); $4.50 for New Jersey parking. *From airports:* 10 miles to Newark; 25 to LaGuardia; 35 to JFK.

Open: Year round except holiday weekends, Easter, first two weeks in August, Thanksgiving, Christmas.
Rates: Per room. $75 suite. $55 double bed. $50 twin bed. $15 each additional child over age 12. Weekly rates available.
♥ ⊁ ⊬

The friendly hosts are enthusiastic and energetic. As Evelyn says, "We just love old buildings and hands-on experiences. Having been born and raised in this community, where I was an elected official for six years, I had a special interest in what was a very dilapidated house in 1984. It's now on the state and national registries, has a new cedar roof, and is completely restored with original floors, moldings, and doors. The older wing was built by a ship joiner in the late 1700s, the later one in 1840. We have furnished with some antiques. It's 'home' (loved by guests) and most of all, private."

More: The Pezzollas led the one-year restoration—and hosted the official restorers—of the next-door one-room schoolhouse, an 1892 Queen Anne–style school building with bell tower. (Special tours given to B&B guests.) They are also active with a former vaudeville theater restored as a center for the performing arts. "Our primary business is a family truck dealership, but our labor of love results in historic preservation along with meeting wonderful people."

Still more: Evelyn is working toward a degree in humanities. Her senior honors thesis is about bed and breakfast for the corporate traveler.

Bed and bath: Four rooms. First-floor south wing suite has private exterior entrance, double-bedded room, private shower bath, parlor with wood-burning stove, double sofa bed, breakfast area. In north wing on second floor, two rooms with double bed and one with a twin bed share a tub/shower bath. Rollaway available.
Breakfast: Self-serve. Juices. Homemade muffins or breads or cakes, jellies, fresh fruits, dry cereals. Coffee, tea, or cocoa.
Plus: Air-conditioned bedrooms except for twin-bedded room. Italian dessert and wine upon arrival. Fireplaced parlor. Fresh flowers. Wisteria-covered outside sitting area. Special occasions acknowledged.

From New Jersey: *"The charm of yesterday with the convenience of today."*
From New York: *"A wonderful base for showing the area to visitors from Japan."*

Bed & Breakfast Adventures Host #479

North Wildwood, NJ

Location: Residential. On a corner of a street with landscaped islands in the middle. Three blocks from beach and 2½-mile boardwalk. Also within walking distance of shops, restaurants, and tourist information center located in a Victorian lighthouse (on land now). Forty-five minutes south of Atlantic City; 7 miles north of Cape May.

Reservations: February–December through Bed & Breakfast Adventures, page 54. Two- or three-night minimum on July, August, and holiday weekends.
Rates: $75–$90 winter, $90–$110 summer. Rates vary according to room and bed size.
♥ ♣ ♦ ✈ ⅙

The outdoor hot tub is a feature all year long for "romantic getaway" guests. (Many are returnees.) In summer, porch sitters enjoy a breeze. New Year's Eve is booked the previous summer. There are murder mystery weekends here. And always, plenty of what-to-do information provided by the hostess, who prepares the annual chamber of commerce guidebook, and by the host, who is active with the zoning board and the lighthouse commission.

The enthusiastic hosts, high school sweethearts, converted this turn-of-the-century Queen Anne house to a B&B in 1985. It still has some original gas lighting fixtures, pocket doors, and a built-in dining room breakfront. Lace curtains are on all the windows. Antiques include many Eastlake pieces and some from the Arts and Crafts period, Oriental rugs, an 1855 sofa, and a 1927 Estee baby grand piano (patented in 1897).

In residence: In hosts' quarters, many cats and one dog.
Foreign language spoken: French.
Bed and bath: Nine rooms on ground, third, and fourth floors; seven with private baths. On fourth floor, room with queen bed and one with double bed share a bath that has whirlpool tub and a shower. Other rooms have king, queen, or double bed with shower baths. On first floor, king-bedded room with tub and shower and double-bedded room with shower bath share an air-conditioned and fireplaced parlor that has TV. All rooms have ceiling fans. Top floor has central air conditioning.
Breakfast: At 8:15 and 9:30. Fruit, hot or cold cereal, home-baked breads or muffins. A choice of two entrees—maybe eggs Benedict, waffles, pancakes, casseroles, or quiche. The host cooks; the hostess bakes; both join guests in the dining room.
Plus: Afternoon refreshments. Wicker-furnished wraparound porch with hammocks and swing. Sun deck and that hot tub. Beach towels. Fresh flowers. Complimentary sherry and chocolates. Gourmet dinners upon request. Special occasions acknowledged. Dinner reservations made. On-site parking.

B*ed and breakfast gives a sense of place.*

BarnaGate Bed & Breakfast   609/391–9366
637 Wesley Avenue, Ocean City, NJ 08226

Hosts: Frank and Lois Barna, Donna Barna
Location: On a corner, 3½ blocks from beach and boardwalk, 2 blocks to shopping. Seven minutes from the Garden State Parkway. Ten miles south of Atlantic City, 40 minutes north of Cape May. Ninety minutes from Philadelphia.

Open: Year round. Two-night minimum on holiday weekends.
Rates: Double occupancy. July 1–Labor Day $120 suite, $70 private bath, $65 with powder room, $60 shared bath. Fall and spring $10 less. $10 extra person. Midweek discounts. MC, Visa.
♣ ✻ ⊭

B&B has made the hosts local history buffs and antiques collectors. It's all part of the fun for Lois, who often planned social functions and business seminars while assistant to a bank president, and Frank, an avid sports fan who had his own TV repair shop. Now he creates stained glass lamps. (The one in the front hall is his.) Together they host guests who come for showers, celebrations, family reunions, vacations, crafts shows—"people from all over who come for the B&B experience."

When looking for a career change, the Barnas took a B&B seminar, stayed at B&Bs, and then bought this 1895 Victorian that was a guest house. In time to redecorate the guest rooms completely for the 1988 season, they moved from Somerville, New Jersey, to "America's greatest family resort, a town with a friendly atmosphere." All the beds have quilts. The furnishings are country Victorian. For special treats on holidays, the Barnas make their own ice cream.

Bed and bath: Five rooms. On second floor, private full bath for one double-bedded room. One twin-bedded room with powder room shares a tub bath with a double room. Two third-floor corner double-bedded dormer rooms (a suite when booked together) share a tub bath and a private sitting room. Rollaway available.
Breakfast: 8–9:30. Juice; fruit; sweet rolls, muffins, and breakfast cakes; coffees and teas. Extended menu in the winter—stuffed French toast or pumpkin pancakes with homemade applesauce. Buffet style in dining room that has a ceiling fan and period antiques.
Plus: Bedroom ceiling fans. Enclosed outside shower. Refrigerator privileges. Backyard with table and chairs. Clothesline for wet beach clothing. Free beach tags provided with two-night stay.

From Pennsylvania (and echoed by several guests): *"Lois and Frank made us feel like we were old friends coming to visit. . . . Animated conversations. . . . A visit with them is good for the spirit. . . . Their home is cozy, very clean, and the breakfast is delicious. . . . Our simple pleasures are all within minutes. . . . The only thing we didn't like about BarnaGate was leaving."*

Unless otherwise stated, rates in this book are per room for two and include breakfast in addition to all the amenities in "Plus." As for taxes and gratuities, please see page xi.

New Brighton Inn   609/399–2829

519 Fifth Street, Ocean City, NJ 08226

Hosts: Dan and Donna Hand
Location: Facing a church and the
Tabernacle grounds. Three blocks to
beach, boardwalk, and bay. Within
10 minutes' walk of shops and restaurants.

Open: Year round. Two-night minimum on weekends.
Rates: Double occupancy. $75–$85
private bath. $10 additional guest.
Amex, MC, Visa.

♥ ⚑ ✿ ✕ ⅍

With memories of childhood vacations in Ocean City and adult vacations at
B&Bs, cabinetmaker Dan, who studied art, and quilt maker Donna, former
computer programmer, transformed the turreted Queen Anne into a B&B in
1988. Along the way they made a video of this major project, which included
stripping the hall woodwork (all three floors) and adding baths. Oriental rugs,
brass beds, lots of rockers, and light colors give a warm ambiance. Recently,
when Dan redid the library, he made oak bookshelves and painted the ceiling
with clouds, moon, and stars. During summer sunsets the hosts often join
guests on the porch. Year round, the breakfast is remembered.

Foreign language spoken: Limited French.
Bed and bath: Six rooms. On second floor, two with queen bed (one with
eight windows) and private shower bath. One double-bedded room has bath
with claw-foot tub and shower. On third floor—same arrangement. Rollaway
available.
Breakfast: 8–10. *Bon Appétit* recipes including fruited cheese pizza, honey
lemon walnut tart, spinach frittata, quiche lorraine, strawberry tart with
almond cream. Homemade sticky buns, coffee cake, or bread. Juices. Fresh
fruit. Plenty of tea and coffee. On sun porch or terrace. Newspaper provided.
Plus: Air conditioner, ceiling fan, and TV in each guest room. Beverages
served on arbor-covered slate patio. Ceiling fans on sun porch. Babysitting.
Airport (10 minutes away) pickup. Hot/cold outside shower, changing stalls;
available after checkout. Bicycles. Beach tags. Directions to a nearby state
park that has dunes.

> From Pennsylvania: *"Bedrooms with country charm feature 20th-century com-*
> *fort (wonderful mattresses) in a setting Grandmother would have recognized. . . .*
> *Breakfasts are copious and delicious. . . . Housekeeping met high standards of our*
> *fussy parents. . . . Front porch with wooden glider. . . . The Hands' friendly*
> *unaffected manner makes for a truly relaxing visit!"*

✺

Can't find a listing for the community you are going to? Check with a
reservation service described at the beginning of this chapter. Through
the service, you may be placed (matched) with a welcoming B&B that
is near your destination.

Northwood Inn Bed & Breakfast   609/399–6071

401 Wesley Avenue, Ocean City, NJ 08226

Hosts: Marj and John Loeper
Location: In a neighborhood of older homes. Three and a half blocks to beach (recently restored) and boardwalk, 4 to town, shops, restaurants. Eight miles south of Atlantic City, 30 miles north of Cape May, 15 to wildlife refuge.
Open: Year round except January 2–15. Two-night minimum stay on summer and holiday weekends.

Rates: Double occupancy. $80 shared bath. $85 twin beds, private detached bath. $90 or $95 queen, private en-suite bath. $105 tower room, $140 suite. $10 less post–Labor Day until Memorial Day. $15 third person in room. MC, Visa.
♥ ❖ ✖ ✂

An award-winning restoration. An 1894 Queen Anne turreted Victorian that was abandoned after being gutted by the previous owner, the house was rescued just two weeks before its scheduled demolition. All thanks to John, a builder of custom homes (and ship half models) who specializes in historic restoration. To boot, he is the chairman of the town's historic preservation commission. And in 1977–78 he studied wooden boat building—"a family adventure"—in Lubec, Maine.

Under the graceful main staircase, John built an English phone booth (with working phone). Intentionally, decor is uncluttered, light and airy. The entire project was documented with photographs and video by Marj, who also wears the official chef's hat. Among the first guests: "One who turned out to be a long-lost cousin!"

In residence: Summers, daughter Rebeca, a college student.
Bed and bath: Eight rooms on second and third floors. All baths have tub and shower. On second floor—one queen-bedded room and one with two twin beds have detached private baths; sink in room. Two queen-bedded rooms with private en-suite baths. Plus suite with queen bed, double sofa bed in sitting room, TV, private bath. On third floor—two queen-bedded rooms, each with sink in room, share a bath. Tower room has queen bed, private bath with dressing room. Extra bed available.
Breakfast: Usually 8–10. Repertoire (recipes shared) includes French toast with apple syrup, raspberry and blueberry pancakes, three-cheese egg puff, baked apples, Chelsea buns, apple strudel, Heath Bar crunch coffee cake (John's mother's specialty), orange or banana/sour cream muffins, cream scones. Juice, fruit, yogurt, cereal, and breads.
Plus: Central air conditioning. Bedroom ceiling fans. Fresh flowers. Upright piano. Hot cider or iced tea. Guest refrigerator. Outdoor hot/cold shower. Mints on pillow. Rockers on wraparound porch. Back and rooftop decks. Beach tags. Bike storage area. Newspapers. Transportation to/from Ocean City bus station or Atlantic City Amtrak station. Murder mystery weekends in October, November, February, March.

> From Pennsylvania: *"We would like to go on believing that Northwood is our secret and the Loepers our extended family. . . . It was a cold blustery February day when we discovered warm and welcoming Victorian charm . . . immaculate . . . excellent food . . . pampered us."* From Ohio: *"Five star."*

Top o' the Waves

609/399–0477
5447 Central Avenue, Ocean City, NJ 06228

fax 609/399–6984

Hosts: Dolly and Des Nunan
Location: On the beach. "In an elite, upscale, quiet residential neighborhood." Five minutes from Garden State Parkway (I–80) exit 25 (Ocean City/Marmora); 65 from Philadelphia, 30 from Cape May, 10 from Atlantic City.
Open: Year round. Three-night minimum June–Labor Day weekends; two nights on off-season weekends.
Rates: $110–$185. $250 anniversary suite. $18.50 additional person. Off-season, $81–$145 double, 10 percent less for singles. Ten percent discount for three days or more. Amex, Discover, MC, Visa.
♥ ♯ ⬛ ♣ ♦ ✈

When the Nunans were looking for property way back in 1971, their children—four boys and a girl—chose this place out of five properties. Through the years they have redone, torn down, and added to. Now there is one simple cedar building with completely updated suites and contemporary furnishings. The wide decks are shared by all. Business executives meet here. Many guests come for a getaway. Families are greeted with a weather report and lots of suggestions—beach, zoo, lighthouse, wildlife refuge. Entertainment ideas include pops concerts. Restaurants? The Nunans "test them for food and service" before giving recommendations.

Dolly is a former art teacher and guidance counselor. Since Des retired in 1992 from his administrative position with the New York State Education Department, he is full-time cohost.

Foreign languages spoken: Italian, Spanish, and French.
Bed and bath: On three floors, a total of eight suites, each with private entrance, phone, and bath. Six with queen bed, private shower bath; two are handicapped accessible. One two-bedroom unit with large tub/shower bath. One very large wedding/anniversary suite with living/dining area, large bath with double Jacuzzi and separate angle shower, remote-control TV/VCR/stereo and CD player, fully equipped galley kitchen. Rollaways available.
Breakfast: In summer, anything from the menu in the Nunans' son's 25-seat restaurant right here. Eat inside or outside with ocean view. Off-season, welcome basket with fruit, crackers and dip, bagels or English muffins, jam and butter or margarine, coffee and tea.
Plus: Air conditioning. Individual thermostats. Beach towels. Private courtyard. Summer turndown service and bedtime treat. Babysitting. Barbecues. Free beach tags. Fax and copier available.

> From Pennsylvania: *"Ideally located. . . . The beauty of Ocean City is the family atmosphere, and T.O.W. adds to that family flavor. . . . The primary reason we return so often is the hospitality of Dolly Nunan, a warm, loving, generous woman who takes a personal role in seeing to the comfort of each guest."*

Looking for a B&B with a crib? Find a description with the ♯ symbol and then check under the "bed and bath" section.

Red Maple Farm
908/329–3821

203 Raymond Road, Princeton, NJ 08540

Host: Roberta Churchill
Location: On 2½ acres. Four miles from Princeton University. Near Route 1 business corridor. "Road is busy during the day but quiet at night." One hour from Philadelphia or New York City.

Open: Year round.
Rates: $55 king/twin option. $65 queen, $75 with fireplace. Singles $10 less.
♦ ✖ ✁

This National Register property, the food, and the hosts are all remembered by guests. Roberta is a former chef who had "one of the five best restaurants in New Jersey" (*New York Times*). Now she's "a passionate gardener, theater-goer, reader, and political activist." Lindsey, her husband, is a sociology professor who also teaches an adult education center wine-tasting course.

The house, built between 1740 and 1820 and owned by the Churchills for two years, is complete with latched doors that have strapped hinges. All guest rooms are freshly wallpapered. One bath is stenciled. Restoration is ongoing. Furnishings are comfortable "without valuable antiques to worry about harming." As for the grounds with birds, deer, rabbits, and woodchucks: "It's like having a park of your own," said one guest. Roberta tends many flower beds and cooks with her own organic fruit, berries, and vegetables. There's a 1740 stone smokehouse; the remains of the 1740 stone barn form a great backdrop for the swimming pool, which is available to guests; and an 1850 barn built with hand-hewn beams is still in use. "Hessian soldiers were stabled here during the Revolution, and the house was an underground railroad stop during the Civil War. Hosting B&B guests is a natural outgrowth of my restaurant and local catering business."

In residence: One barn cat. "And one friendly German shepherd allowed in kitchen only."
Foreign language spoken: Limited French.
Bed and bath: Three second-floor rooms, two shared baths. Fireplaced room with queen bed connected by bath with shower stall to room with extra-long king/twins option. One room with queen four-poster shares tub/shower bath with hosts.
Breakfast: Usually 8:30. Repertoire includes johnnycakes, fruit slump, buck-wheat pancakes, raised waffles, shirred eggs with asparagus, vegetable garden frittata. Local smokehouse bacon or Amish sausages. Homemade sweet breads and preserves. Served in 1820 fireplaced dining room or on patio of 1740 stone smokehouse.
Plus: Air-conditioned bedrooms. Late-afternoon tea with baked goods. Fire-placed front parlor. Fireplaced back parlor with television. Antique upright piano. Barbecue. Lawn games. Tennis nearby. Picnic baskets ($8–$25). Din-ner, with advance notice ($10–$30). Pickup at Princeton or Princeton Junc-tion train station.

If you've been to one B&B, you haven't been to them all.

Ashling Cottage

106 Sussex Avenue, Spring Lake, NJ 07762

908/449-3553
800/237-1877

Hosts: Goodi and Jack Stewart
Location: On a sycamore-shaded residential street, 1 block from ocean, 2-mile-long boardwalk, and lake. Two blocks from downtown shops. One hour from Philadelphia or New York, 1½ hours to Atlantic City.
Open: April–December. Two-night minimum on weekends in July and August.

Rates: Double occupancy. Mid-June–mid-September: weekdays $75 shared bath, $95 private; weekends $90 shared bath, $135 private. Off-season: weekdays $65 shared, $75 private; weekends $70 shared, $80 private. Singles $5 less. Discounts for third night.
♥ ♣ ✗ ✄

"We wanted to live in Spring Lake, a storybook wedding town, a most surprising shore community with none of the frenzy often associated with beach locations. Ashling Cottage fell right in line with our desire to work together and enjoy people. [Jack was a sales executive in Los Angeles and New York; Goodi was in the barter business in New York.] We have seen neighbors meet here. We have hosted a fashion film crew, and have seen guests who have been our inn-sitters become innkeepers.

"Our house was built in 1877 with lumber from the Philadelphia Bicentennial agricultural exhibit. We have blended tasteful antiques with comfort, leaning toward the 'genteel mood of yesterday' rather than formal Victorian and total authenticity. White wicker fills our screened (and glassed) solarium, which gives a peek at the ocean to the east and, to the west, the spring-fed lake with surrounding park, migrating waterfowl, and wooden bridges."

In residence: Lady Latimer, the cat, "the real mistress of Ashling Cottage," and "her nemesis Princess Graci," an adopted stray cat.
Foreign language spoken: A little German.
Bed and bath: Ten queen-bedded rooms on three floors, each with ceiling fan and cross-ventilation. (One on first floor with private porch.) Eight with private baths; some have shower or tub only, one bathroom is sunken. Two rooms, each with sink in room, share a hall tub bath.
Breakfast: 8:30–10. Freshly ground coffee or brewed tea, two fruit juices, cold cereals, seasonal fruits, eggs (maybe in a casserole). At least two home-baked goods; might be muffins (about a dozen varieties in repertoire), Irish soda bread, sour cream pound cake, nut braid, or brioche. Served buffet style in the parlor or solarium, on porches, or in living room.
Plus: Year round, fresh flowers. Living room with TV and VCR. Books and board games. Grill and picnic table on the patio. Books. Impromptu wine gatherings. Labor Day Creative Black Tie Weenie Roast. Transportation to/from Spring Lake train or bus station.

Some executives who book a meeting at an inn return on a weekend for a getaway. Some on a getaway return with colleagues for a meeting.

Sea Crest by the Sea 908/449-9031

19 Tuttle Avenue, Spring Lake, NJ 07762

Hosts: John and Carol Kirby
Location: Set back from street among other Victorian homes. Half block from ocean and noncommercial boardwalk. Five-minute walk to village center and its 50 small shops. One-hour drive or 90-minute train ride from Manhattan.
Open: Year round. Two-night minimum July–August and on March–November weekends.
Rates: Per room. May 16–September: $105 hall bath, $126 attached bath, $147 feather bed. Off-season, October–May 15: $84 hall bath, $102 attached bath, $110 feather bed. MC, Visa.
♥ ✖ ✂

This turreted Queen Anne Victorian, furnished with French and English antiques and period reproduction lighting, has fantasy-bent innkeepers, romantics who admit to being "more whimsical than rigid in our Victoriana." Lots of light comes through 75 big windows. Croquet and bicycles await. So does classical music, lace-trimmed Egyptian cotton sheets, and afternoon tea (mulled cider in winter) with player piano "entertainment."

Carol was a real estate agent and John, president of a medical equipment manufacturing company. In 1989, shortly after John, at age 45, decided to leave the company, "the dream happened" (a good match!). You'll probably meet many returnees. Many unwinders. Or honeymooners. Or maybe two nuns "who taught us lessons in charity, conversation, humility, and fun."

In residence: "Family members—Sneakers and Princess, affectionate cats, and Daisy, a sheltie collie mix."
Bed and bath: Twelve queen-bedded rooms on second and third floors. Eight with ocean views; two with working fireplace; three with feather beds. Each with private shower bath (four also have tubs). One with private porch. Room names include George Washington, Sleigh Ride, and Yankee Clipper (with John's sailing logs from merchant marine days).
Breakfast: Buffet on carved sideboard "starts at the civilized hour of 9." Fresh fruit salad; their own granola; yogurt; muffins; Carol's buttermilk scones and John's honey walnut bread (and "when the spirit moves" maybe white chocolate cheesecake, cheeses, or fresh berries from the garden); featherbed eggs or quiche; freshly squeezed orange juice; Sea Crest's coffee blend (Scandinavian, half decaf), teas. Table set with family china and silver; by candlelight in winter.
Plus: Central air conditioning. Fireplaced living room and library. TV in library. Rockers on wraparound and awninged porches. Fresh flowers. Handmade chocolate mints on silver tray. Beach towels. Tennis court passes. Down comforters. Flannel sheets. Transportation to/from train station. For those who drive—fabulous orchard stop suggestion.

Is B&B like a hotel?
How many times have you hugged the doorman?

The Whistling Swan Inn   201/347–6369

P.O. Box 791, Stanhope, NJ 07874-0791

Hosts: Paula Williams and Joe Mulay
Location: A quiet main street of a small rural northwest New Jersey town. Near fine dining and casual restaurants. One mile north of I–80 (exit 27), off Route 183/206. Forty-five miles west of George Washington Bridge; 25 miles east of Pocono Mountains.

Open: Year round. Two-night minimum on holiday weekends.
Rates: Double occupancy. $75 small (cozy and often chosen) room, $85 medium, $95 large. $105 suite. $5 senior and corporate discount. Special romantic weekend and winter midweek rates. Amex, Discover, MC, Visa.

♥ ✿ ◆ ✕ ⊱

From a Maryland architect who specializes in "design and build": *"A totally renovated, stunning Victorian home, full of charm and character . . . decorated with wonderful Victorian accents and details . . . not too much, just enough to be refined but warm . . . inviting, cozy, and so comfortable . . . also immaculately clean, which is vital to me as I am allergic to dust! . . . A delicious, homemade full breakfast . . . hosts who are welcoming, helpful, relaxed and quite simply delightful."*

The governor of New Jersey and his wife are among those who have been won over to B&B after staying in this turreted Queen Anne, which has a stone-pillared wraparound porch (with swings and hammocks). International travelers, too, enjoy meeting Paula, a former speech therapist, consultant, and corporate manager, and Joe, who was also an AT&T manager, marketeer, and corporate planner. They opened in 1986 after doing most of the restoration themselves, "after watching big New Jersey homes being torn down," at a time when Paula was thinking about early retirement and when they had inherited her grandmother's furniture.

"Many of our guests are business travelers. Others come for antiquing; rural-village living; Waterloo Festival of The Arts (inquire about picnic dinners here and discounts on tickets); history; scenery; water (boat rentals on Lake Musconetcong) and winter (including tobogganing) sports; wineries; and just plain 'laying back.' Our youngest bride and groom were teenagers; the oldest, in their late 70s."

Bed and bath: Ten queen-bedded rooms furnished in period themes such as Victorian, Twenties, Oriental antiques, Forties. All private baths. Second-floor rooms have shower baths. Third-floor rooms, including two-room suite, have baths with claw-footed tubs and hand-held shower. A two-tub bathroom, "our Victorian Jacuzzi," is available for all guests; robes provided. Rollaway available.
Breakfast: 6:30–8:30 weekdays, 8:30–10:30 weekends and holidays. Buffet style. Egg/fruit/cheese dishes, quiche, baked omelet, frittata, whole kernel corn pancakes (a specialty), or waffles. Hot biscuits or muffins; toaster breads. Juices, fruit, yogurt, dry cereal, oatmeal, granola bars. Hosts join guests for coffee. In lace-curtained dining room or on front porch.
Plus: Central air conditioning. Bedroom ceiling fans. In parlor, player piano, cable TV, and cookie jar. Antique radios in each room. Fireplaced dining room and foyer. Beverages. Loaner bicycles. Picnic tables. Picnic baskets ($15).

(Please turn page.)

Before-and-after restoration photo album. Discount on Waterloo Festival of The Arts tickets. Innkeeping apprentice program. Small business conferences.

The Stewart Inn   908/479–6060

Box 571, RD 1, South Main Street, Stewartsville, NJ 08886

Hosts: Brian and Lynne McGarry
Location: Pastoral. On 16 wooded acres with trout stream. Minutes from I–78. Five miles from Easton, Pennsylvania; 10 from Bethlehem. Near many corporate headquarters, Bucks County, historic and agricultural Warren and Hunterdon counties in New Jersey, wineries, shopping, fine restaurants. One hour from Manhattan, 75 minutes from Philadelphia.
Open: Year round.
Rates: Double occupancy: $85 or $95; $105 with fireplace (and private hall bath). $130 larger fireplaced suite. Corporate rates available Sunday–Thursday, MC, Visa.
♣ ♦ ⚞ ⚟

Although many of the McGarrys' guests are business travelers from all over the world, weekend romantics, too, appreciate this gracious 1770s fieldstone manor house, which has been featured in *Country Inns* magazine. It is complete with Palladian window, working fireplaces, Oriental rugs, and early American and English antiques. Arranged flowers are throughout. The landscaped grounds include a free-form swimming pool, gardens (iris, daylilies, herbs), horseshoes, and badminton. And then there are all those animals.

With B&B in mind, the multifaceted McGarrys—who met during a Sierra Club trail cleanup—opted for rural living in 1986, choosing a historic estate that needed "decorating only." Lynne, a licensed wildlife caretaker, has been a small-town mayor, tax collector, and kennel owner. Now she and Brian, a lawyer, design, manufacture, and market needlework kits. In spring they feature a sheep-shearing weekend. In fall they suggest nearby pick-your-own apples and vegetable and pumpkin places. Year round, they offer "peace and solitude of our rural world."

In residence (mostly in the barns): One dog, 5 cats, 30 sheep, 3 goats, 2 peacocks, geese, chickens, ducks, raccoons, rabbits, a parrot, doves, and parakeets.
Bed and bath: Eight rooms including two suites. All with four-posters, TV, private phone. First-floor poolside room has a queen bed, private bath. All second-floor rooms have a queen bed, most with tub/shower baths. Larger suite has separate tub and shower bath, sitting area with sofa, two wing chairs, working fireplace, TV, desk.
Breakfast: 7–9:30. Farm-fresh eggs, country smoked bacon, pancakes, French toast, fruits, granolas. Served in dining room with a corner fireplace. Hosts join guests.
Plus: Bedroom air conditioners and oscillating fans. Fireplaced living room. Tour of house and farm. Use of barbecue. For sale: needlework kits and unprocessed or processed-to-order wool. Guests' comments:

From New York: *"The tangible pleasures and comforts speak for themselves . . . warmth, charm, and hospitality in everything [they] say or do assures the well-being of guests."*

The Henry Ludlam Inn   609/861–5847

Cape May County, 1336 Route 47, Woodbine, NJ 08270

Hosts: Ann and Marty Thurlow
Location: In a rural area on Route 47 overlooking a 55-acre lake. Close to Stone Harbor Bird Sanctuary, zoo, museums, Belle Plain State Park, and "great antiquing." Ten miles from Garden State Parkway; 20 minutes northwest of Cape May; 25 miles to Atlantic City.

Open: Year round. Two-night minimum on weekends April–November. Three-day minimum on holiday weekends.
Rates: Double occupancy. $75–$85 shared bath, $85–$95 private. $20 extra person. Amex, MC, Visa.
♥ ♣ ♦ ✈ ⊱

"Is this the inn that has a ghost?" Year round, calls start that way because of *Cape May Ghost Stories,* the very book that brings long lines to a Cape May restaurant. Ghost stories that revolve around this 1760 house (with 1804 addition) make for fascinating and endless breakfasts. Marty doesn't believe a word. Ann does.

Romantics, too, appreciate this award-winning "best-kept shore secret" (*Atlantic City* magazine), which has also been featured in *Mid-Atlantic Country.* In 1982 it was a "fixer-upper" that satisfied Ann's desire for a New England house by the water. She decorated with stenciling, handmade quilts, and antiques from the shop she had and from auctions. Marty, a master cabinetmaker, duplicated an old stairway. And he modeled the "right" front door after a picture Ann found. Now the Thurlows have fans who write about the "warmth of this old house and hospitality [that] gives me a hug. . . . As if the world stopped and the inn was there just for the two of us."

Bed and bath: Five rooms, all with feather beds in winter, on three floors. Three with private baths. First-floor room (overlooks lake) with double bed, fireplace, private bath with shower only. On second floor, one room with working fireplace and both a single and a double bed has a bath with tub. Overlooking lake, one double-bedded room (circa 1760) with working fireplace, large bath with shower. Two lofted double-bedded rooms share a shower bath.
Breakfast: At 9. "Unforgettable." Freshly squeezed orange juice. Entree could be French toast with bananas and walnuts, pear or mushroom omelets, baked French toast with kir sauce, or gingerbread pancakes. Homemade breads, popovers, or corn bread; freshly ground coffee. By dining room fireplace (candlelit in winter) or on enclosed porch overlooking the lake.
Plus: Room air conditioners. Bedroom fans. Afternoon wine or tea. Mints on pillow. Player piano. Kitchen privileges. For dreaming—gazebo and swing on lake shore. Beach tags. Use of canoe, tubes, fishing equipment.

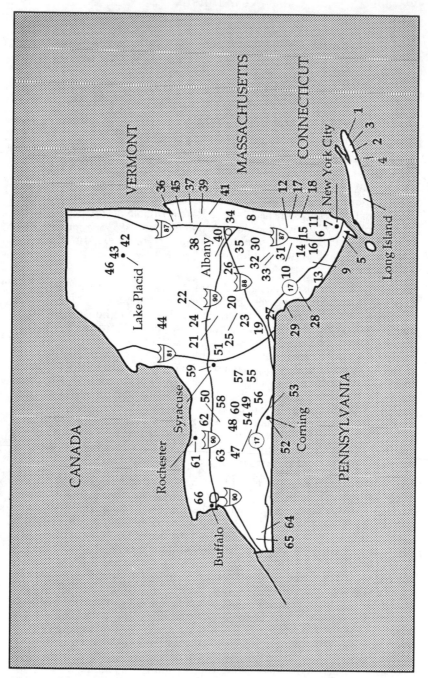

The numbers on this map indicate the locations of B&Bs described in detail in this chapter.

NEW YORK

EASTERN NEW YORK

(Regions in eastern New York are arranged from south to north.)

Long Island
1 East Hampton
   Centennial House, 97
   Mill House Inn, 98
2 Hampton Bays
   House on the Water, 99
3 Southampton
   The Old Post House Inn, 100
4 Westhampton Beach
   Seafield House, 101

New York City Area
5 Brooklyn
   Bed & Breakfast on the Park, 107
6 Croton-on-Hudson
   Alexander Hamilton House, 108
7 New York
   Abode Bed & Breakfast Host #77, 109
   Urban Ventures Host #HAR111, 109
   Urban Ventures Host #CON200, 110

Hudson Valley
8 Ghent
   The American Country Collection Host #082, 112
9 Goshen: Campbell Hall
   Tara Farm Bed & Breakfast, 113
10 High Falls
   Captain Schoonmaker's Bed & Breakfast, 114
11 Katonah
   The American Country Collection Host #155, 115
12 Kingston
   Rondout Bed & Breakfast, 116

13 Middletown/Goshen: Slate Hill
   The American Country Collection Host #064, 117
14 New Paltz
   Ujjala's Bed & Breakfast, 118
15 New Paltz: Clintondale
   Orchard House, 119
16 New Paltz: Wallkill
   Audrey's Farmhouse B&B, 120
17 Rhinebeck
   Village Victorian Inn, 121
18 Rhinebeck: Stanfordville
   The Lakehouse Inn . . . On Golden Pond, 121

Leatherstocking/Central New York
19 Bainbridge
   Berry Hill Farm B&B, 124
20 Cooperstown
   Creekside Bed & Breakfast, 125
   The Inn at Brook Willow, 126
   Litco Farms Bed & Breakfast, 127
   Thistlebrook, 128
21 Cooperstown: Richfield Springs
   Summerwood, 129
22 Dolgeville
   Adrianna Bed & Breakfast, 130
23 Guilford
   The Village Green Bed & Breakfast, 131
24 Ilion
   Chesham Place, 132
25 New Berlin
   Sunrise Farm, 133
26 Stamford: Hobart
   Breezy Acres Farm Bed & Breakfast, 133

Catskills
27 Deposit
   The White Pillars Inn, 135

28 Jeffersonville
The Griffin House Bed &
Breakfast, *136*
29 Long Eddy
The Rolling Marble Guest
House, *137*
30 Tannersville
The Eggery Inn, *138*
31 West Shokan
Haus Elissa Bed & Breakfast, *139*
32 Woodstock: Chichester
Maplewood Bed & Breakfast,
139
33 Woodstock: Mt. Tremper
Mount Tremper Inn, *140*

Albany Area to Lake George
34 Albany
The American Country
Collection Host #097, *143*
35 Altamont
Appel Inn, *143*
36 Bolton Landing
Hilltop Cottage B&B, *144*
37 Lake George: Lake Luzerne
The Lamplight Inn Bed &
Breakfast, *145*
38 Saratoga Springs
Saratoga Bed and Breakfast, *146*
The Six Sisters Bed and
Breakfast, *147*
Union Gables, *148*
The Westchester House B&B, *149*
39 Saratoga Springs: Schuylerville
The Inn on Bacon Hill, *150*
40 Schenectady
The Widow Kendall House, *151*
41 Stillwater
The American Country
Collection Host #005, *152*

Adirondacks
42 Keene Valley
Trail's End, *154*
43 Lake Placid
Stagecoach Inn, *155*
44 Lowville
Hinchings Pond B&B Inn, *156*
45 Queensbury
Crislip's Bed & Breakfast, *157*

46 Saranac Lake
Adirondack Bed & Breakfasts
Host #10, *157*

WESTERN NEW YORK

Syracuse/Finger Lakes Area
47 Avoca
Patchwork Peace Bed &
Breakfast, *160*
48 Branchport
Four Seasons Bed &
Breakfast, *161*
49 Burdett
The Red House Country Inn, *162*
50 Canandaigua: Rushville
Lakeview Farm Bed n'
Breakfast, *163*
51 Cazenovia
The American Country
Collection Host #162, *164*
52 Corning
1865 White Birch B&B, *164*
Rosewood Inn, *165*
53 Elmira: Chemung
Halcyon Place Bed &
Breakfast, *166*
54 Hammondsport
The Blushing Rosé B&B, *167*
The Bowman House, a bed and
breakfast, *168*
55 Ithaca
Buttermilk Falls Bed & Break-
fast, *169*
Hanshaw House B&B, *170*
Rose Inn, *171*
56 Ithaca: Alpine
The Fountainebleau Inn, *172*
57 Ithaca: Groton
Gale House Bed & Breakfast, *173*
58 Penn Yan
The Wagener Estate Bed &
Breakfast, *174*
59 Syracuse
The Russell-Farrenkopf House,
175
60 Watkins Glen: Rock Stream
Reading House, *176*

Rochester Area
61 Rochester
   428 Mt. Vernon—a bed and
    breakfast inn, *177*
62 **Rochester: Fairport**
   Woods-Edge Bed &
   Breakfast, *178*
63 **Rochester: Mumford**
   Genesee Country Inn, *179*

Niagara/Buffalo/Chautauqua Area
64 **Chautauqua**
   Plumbush at Chautauqua, *181*
65 **Chautauqua: Westfield**
   Westfield House, *182*
   The William Seward Inn, *183*
66 **Niagara Falls: Lewiston**
   The Cameo Inns, *184*

___ Long Island Reservation Service ___

A Reasonable Alternative, Inc.

117 Spring Street, Port Jefferson, NY 11777

Phone: 516/928–4034, Monday–Friday noon–5.

Fax: 516/331–7641.

Listings: About 50 (number varies according to season) hosted private residences in Nassau and Suffolk counties, mostly along the north and south shores. Among the communities represented in Suffolk County are all of the Hamptons, South Fork, Port Jefferson, Stony Brook, and the North Fork villages (winery country). B&Bs are colonials, Victorians, and contemporaries, and a few apartments. "Long Island is about 15 miles (north to south) by 120 miles (east to west), so almost every place is close to the water."

Reservations: Most hosts accept one-night reservations except those in the Hamptons during summer months, when there is a two-night minimum, three nights on holidays.

Rates: $40–$75 singles, $44–$75 doubles. In July and August, $48–$99 singles, $52–$99 doubles. Reservations for homes in the East End (North Fork and South Fork) must be prepaid and are nonrefundable. Some weekly rates. Deposit required—at least one night's lodging. If cancellation (East End excepted) received three days before scheduled arrival, all but a $10 service charge returned; no refund if received later. MC, Visa. ◀ ✖

Kathleen Dexter started her reservation service in February 1981 and to this day has many of her original hosts, friendly people who enjoy sharing their homes with others. "The only reason they stop hosting is if their kids come home or they sell their house. As our guests say, 'They are wonderful people.' We take pride in operating a quality service."

Do you have to get up for breakfast?
There's no one rule. Check each description in this book for the various arrangements. More than one guest has been enticed by the aroma of fresh muffins. If you are on business or want to catch the morning ferry, eat-and-run is just fine. If, however, cuisine is a feature, plan on appearing at the specified time!

Vacationers find breakfast a very social time. One hostess says that even when guests say they want to be on the road early, they often linger over breakfast for hours. If hosts join you, please understand when they leave the table after a while.

Long Island B&Bs

Centennial House

(N.Y. Metro area) **800/479–3396**

13 Woods Lane, East Hampton, NY 11937

516/324–9414

fax 516/324–2681

Hosts: David Oxford and Harry Chancey, Jr.
Location: On a parklike acre with beautiful gardens, lawns, and trees. In historic district of country/summer estates. Within walking distance of village and beach. Along the main road; 100 yards from "Currier and Ives pond" just as you enter village.
Open: Year round. Four-night minimum Memorial Day, July 4, and Labor Day; three nights on weekends, July–mid-September. Cottage: one-week minimum Memorial Day–Labor Day.
Rates: (Vary according to size of room and bed) May–October $175–$275, November–April $100–$200. Cottage (three bedrooms) $450 high season; $300 off-season. Holiday packages and corporate retreat rates. Amex, MC, Visa.

♥ 🛏 ❀ ◆ ✈ ⚭

Pictured in a wonderful six-page *Country Inns* spread, this is a "passion that became a venture" only because a neighboring inn called in need of "one more room."

Built in 1876 as a family residence, the shingled Victorian had changed hands only once before David and Harry bought it in 1987. Originally from Alabama, David is a lawyer who has lived in Paris, Washington, D.C., and Manhattan. Harry is an executive with public television station WNET.

During restoration the signature of the noted builder, Thomas E. Babcock, was uncovered. Now the hosts often share anecdotes about the acquisition of the many fine antiques and traditional furnishings. In addition to hospitality, they offer a sense of peace and quiet, privacy, and contentment.

In residence: Earl and Edwinna, two fawn-colored Lhasa apsos.
Foreign language spoken: French.
Bed and bath: Six air-conditioned rooms with king, queen (canopied or four-poster), or double beds; all with adjoining luxurious baths. Plus a three-bedroom, two-bath "fairytale cottage" (without breakfast).
Breakfast: 8:30–10. Juice. Fruit. Muffins made with homegrown herbs or scones, breads, cakes, coffees. Buttermilk pancakes, French toast, or omelets. Buffet in Georgian dining room.
Plus: Grand piano in marble-fireplaced parlor. Beverages. Bedside phones. Chocolate truffles. The Sunday *New York Times*. Terry robes. Potpourri from inn's garden. Front porch. Swim at beach or in pool right here.

From Pennsylvania: *"We have tried almost all the inns in the Hamptons in search of the perfect spot. We will look no further!"*

Mill House Inn   516/324–9766

33 North Main Street, East Hampton, NY 11937

Hosts: Barbara and Kevin Flynn
Location: Seven houses from the shopping district, on a fork off Main Street. Opposite the village green and Old Hook Windmill. One mile to "New York's most pristine beaches." Short drive to North and South Fork wineries and to whale watch excursions.

Open: Year round. Three-night minimum on summmer weekends; four nights on holiday weekends; two nights on fall weekends.
Rates: June–September, $95–$135 weekdays, $115–$165 weekends. Rest of ycar, $75–$95 weekdays, $95–$135 weekends.

Original hand-hewn ceiling beams are in the living and dining rooms of the 1790 colonial house, which was expanded in 1898. When the Flynns bought the then guest house in 1987, they decorated with chintzes and designer fabrics, coordinating wallpaper or stenciling, some country pieces, antiques, Orientals, and botanical prints. Thus began the fulfillment of their decade-old New England college days' dream of becoming innkeepers.

Talk about a good match for a changed lifestyle: Since the last edition of this book, the Mill House Inn's Christmas decorations have been described in *Parade. Country Inns* featured the inn and, in a subsequent edition, a tie-quilt that Barbara made of Waverly prints. Many guests ask about Barbara's window treatments (every room has a different style). Kevin has become executive director of the East Hampton Chamber of Commerce. Guests continue to comment on the hospitality.

"Before": Barbara was a software engineer and Kevin a steamship executive. They had at least one stint at inn-sitting and spent months "looking" in the mountains. It was a *New York Times* ad that brought the Nassau County natives back to Long Island.

In residence: In hosts' quarters, Caitlin, a red-haired five-year-old. Maggie is a blonde two-year-old. Beamer, the cat, is "playful but elusive."
Bed and bath: Eight rooms, most with sloping ceilings. Private baths (most with shower and without tub) for first- and second-floor rooms. On third floor, two air-conditioned rooms share bath that has claw-footed tub and shower. Queen (one is canopied, one a four-poster), double, twins, and a pair of three-quarter beds. Rollaway available.
Breakfast: 8:30–10. Entree might be French toast stuffed with cream cheese and apricot preserves or pumpkin pancakes. Juice, fruit, homemade muffins, coffee. Served at dining room table with lace tablecloth, Depression glass, and china teacups.
Plus: Lemonade, hot tea, or apple cider. Bedroom ceiling fans for second floor. Fireplaced living room. Porch. Backyard with lawn furniture. Two hammocks. Parking. Will meet guests at train or bus. Bicycles with baskets. On some off-season weekends, complimentary theater tickets with two-night reservation. "Simple" quilting seminars.

House on the Water   516/728–3560
Box 106, Hampton Bays, NY 11946

Host: Ute
Location: On Shinnecock Bay. On two acres in a friendly neighborhood good for jogging. One mile from the village center and train. Two miles from bus and to ocean beaches. Seven miles from Southampton.
Open: May–December 1. Two-night minimum on weekends except July and August (three nights); four nights for July 4 and Labor Day weekends.
Rates: Memorial Day–October 1, $70–$90 single, $75–$95 double. Adjoining room $40 single, $50 double. $20 extra (folding) bed. $20 less off-season. Weekly and monthly rates available.
🛥 ♦ ✈

"My home seems to appeal both to those who want to rest, relax, and hardly leave the premises, and to those who try to take in everything from discos to restaurants."

The location is one major attraction. The hostess, who definitely has a home and not an inn, is another. It's a B&B in the traditional sense. The large ranch house has a part shade/part sun 50-foot terrace where you can lounge and watch the boats go by. You are welcome to borrow a bicycle (there are four), the pedal boat, or the Windsurfers or small sailboat, all without charge.

After 20 years of owning a boutique in Acapulco for custom-made resort wear (for all ages), Ute sails, plays tennis and golf, and pursues her interests in health food, diet, and exercise. From January 15 until April she continues hosting in her Acapulco condominium, which is on a lovely beach, has two pools, and is within walking distance of restaurants.

Foreign languages spoken: German, Spanish, and French.
Bed and bath: Three simply furnished rooms (water views from two) with two twin beds in each. All private full baths. One room with private entrance can connect with another room (available only with first room). Two folding beds.
Breakfast: Generally 8–12. Fried, boiled, poached, scrambled, or Mexican eggs. French toast, Spanish tortilla, various breads, hot and cold cereals. Special diets accommodated. In kitchen, in living room, or on the terrace.
Plus: Coffee, tea, hot chocolate always available. Kitchen privileges. Beach lounge chairs and umbrellas. Laundry facilities. Portable fans. Transportation provided from bus or train stations and to beaches.

Guests wrote: *"Very European style. Custom breakfasts, interesting conversations. A oneness with nature. A memorable visit."*

The Old Post House Inn   516/283-1717

136 Main Street, Southampton, NY 11968

Hosts: Cecile and Ed Courville, and son Mark, manager.

Location: In the village. One block from Jobs Lane Boutiques, Parrish Art Museum, and Southampton Cultural Center. Two doors from Saks Fifth Avenue. Next door to Post House Restaurant. One mile to miles of ocean beaches.

Open: Year round except December 20 through January. In season, two-day weekend minimum; three days on summer holiday weekends.

Rates: Per room. May $85 weekday, $100 weekend, $160 Memorial Day weekend. June $95 weekday, $120 weekend. July–August $120 weekday, $160 weekend, $170 special event weekends. September $85 weekday, $115 weekend. October–April $80 weekday, $90 weekend. $5–$10 one-night surcharge on in-season or holiday weekends. $50 late checkout (between 11 a.m. and 4 p.m.). All major credit cards accepted.

♥ ⚜ ✈

Antiques, floral prints, and charm; fireplaces, private baths, and air conditioning. All wrapped up in the fantasy life of an innkeeper surrounded by history in this seaside resort just two hours from Manhattan. The ceiling beams of the common room date back to the 17th century. English soldiers were quartered here during the Revolutionary War. An archaeological dig in the basement (Ed's idea) indicated that this, the oldest privately owned and occupied English wood frame house in New York State, was part of the Underground Railroad.

When Ed retired early, in 1984, from his AT&T executive position, he and Cecile, a former department store buyer, searched for a New England–type inn where they could work together. What they found was a run-down boardinghouse for summer help. The added-on-to 1684 farmhouse was a guest house when the railroad came to town in 1870. "As you can well imagine, a house at this age did not have a straight wall or a level floor in it. We left them that way, of course," says Ed, a frequent visitor to the local library and historical society and a former president of the Southampton Chamber of Commerce. In addition to hostessing, Cecile has found a new career in interior design. Their "oldest bed and breakfast country inn on Long Island" is listed on the National Register of Historic Places.

Bed and bath: On three floors, seven air-conditioned rooms named for "our country's founders and famous local residents." Double or twin beds; all private shower baths.

Breakfast: 9–10:30. Juice, croissant, coffee, tea, decaf. Buffet style in fireplaced common room.

Plus: Wicker-furnished and lattice-enclosed porch. Two contiguous fireplaced living rooms.

Seafield House

2 Seafield Lane, P.O. Box 648
Westhampton Beach, NY 11978

516/288–1559
800/346–3290

Host: Elsie Collins
Location: "In a small village atmosphere" on a quiet lane, 2 blocks from Main Street shops; 15-minute brisk walk to ocean beach; 90 minutes' ride from Manhattan.
Open: Year round. Two-day minimum on weekends; three-day on holiday weekends.
Rates: Per suite. Memorial Day–Labor Day: weekends $200 per night with two-day minimum; three-day on holiday weekends. Three-night weekends $175 per night. Weekdays $175 per night, two-day minimum. Four days $650, Monday–Thursday. Seven days $1,200, Friday through Friday. September–May: $100 per suite per night, two-night minimum. $60 third or fourth person in suite.
♥ ♣ ♦ ✈ ⅍

From Vermont: *"I have spent most of my life on the road, traveling in every state except Alaska. I've been to England, Europe, and Japan. . . . The accommodations and food that Elsie offers are Number One on my list. Her warm personality only adds to the charm of the house."* From Michigan: *"All the warm fuzzies she sent our way made our visit memorable . . . flower arrangements, apples and mints, the thirsty towels, the special shampoo and soap and the* New York Times.*"*

Elsie's low-keyed approach is appreciated by guests who come to her comfortable century-old estate. The dining features a 1907 Modern Glenwood potbellied stove, "the hurricane hero." Victorian, primitive, English, and Chinese antiques and Oriental rugs all blend into the ambiance of a country retreat that is complete with a swimming pool and a tennis court. And all year round Elsie, an early childhood educator who retired early, comes up with interesting ideas—Saturday teas, senior citizens' luncheons, and local bird-watching places. A B&B since 1982 and featured in *Country Accents* in 1993, Seafield House is considered a "hidden treasure" by many.

Bed and bath: Three suites, private baths. Two upstairs suites, each with double brass bed and sitting room; one with shower bath, one with claw-foot tub and shower. Third suite, in a rustic converted 100-year-old barn with a floor-to-ceiling window, has a double brass bed, hi-rise that sleeps one, a shower bath, microwave oven, refrigerator, and, for decoration, handmade quilts on rafters.
Breakfast: 9:30–10:30. Freshly squeezed juice. Homemade muffins (rave reviews), breads, and jams. Bacon and eggs, pancakes, or French toast. Teas, freshly brewed coffee. Barn suite has option of breakfast there or in main house.
Plus: Welcoming beverage. Piano. Fireplaced parlor. Complimentary "take-home goodies that extend the vacation." Off-street parking.

New York City Area
_____Reservation Services_____

Abode Bed & Breakfast Ltd.
P.O. Box 20022, New York, NY 10028

Phone: 212/472–2000. (New York, New Jersey, Connecticut, or Pennsylvania) 800/835–8880. Year round, Monday–Friday 9–5, Saturdays 11–2. Answering machine at other times.

Listings: Over 100 hosted and unhosted private residences in New York City area. All accommodations have air conditioning, and most have private baths. All are within a $5 cab ride of the center of Manhattan and have good access to public transportation. Short-term (one to three months) hosted and unhosted housing available at monthly rates.

Reservations: Two-night minimum for all hosts. Advance reservations advisable. Last-minute reservations accepted, according to availability.

Rates: $65–$80 single. $80–$100 double. $90–$275 unhosted studios to three-bedroom apartments. Discounts for extended stays. Deposit required is 25 percent of total stay. Deposit minus a $20 booking fee is refundable if cancellation notice is received at least two weeks prior to scheduled arrival date. Amex.

Shelli Leifer knows B&B from the inside out. After being a host herself for several years, she opened a personalized service, selecting hosts who "put out the welcome mat," meet guests (in both hosted and unhosted arrangements), and maintain clean residences with a warm ambiance.

At Home in New York
P.O. Box 407, New York, NY 10185

Phone: 212/956–3125; (outside New York state) 800/NYC–4BNB (692–4262). 9:30–5 weekdays, 9:30–noon weekends.

Fax: 212/247–3294.

Listings: 300. Mostly hosted private residences in large attended apartment buildings as well as in private brownstones and townhouses. Some unhosted pied-a-terres ranging from studios to three-bedroom flats. Most listings are in Manhattan; a few are in Bridgehampton, Brooklyn, Bronxville, Queens, Roosevelt, and Staten Island. For a sample listing of accommodations, send a self-addressed stamped business-size envelope.

Reservations: At least two-week notice suggested for best availability. Minimum two-night stay required by most hosts; some one-night reservations accepted 48 hours before arrival. Two-night minimum for all unhosted accommodations.

Rates: $50–$80 single, $75–$100 double. $80–$260 unhosted apartments. One-night surcharge of $10 for single, $15 for double. Deposit required: 25 percent on four-night (or more) stay, or one night's rate on up to three-night stay. Deposit refunded, minus $15 cancellation fee, if cancellation notice received at least 10 days prior to arrival date; otherwise no refund made.

Lois Rooks offers a personalized service that caters to out-of-towners' needs and preferences. Accommodations range from modest with a shared bath to luxury with private bath, maid service, and gourmet breakfast. Her hosts, "screened for cleanliness, convenience, security, and comfort," share their knowledge of the city's cultural events, restaurants, and shopping. (And many have told me that they appreciate the care that goes into appropriate placements.) Lois, a former professional actress and singer, often has free and discounted concert, theater, and museum tickets available to guests.

Bed & Breakfast (& Books)

35 West 92nd Street, New York, NY 10025

Phone: 212/865–8740. Year round, Monday–Friday 10–5.

Listings: 100. Mostly hosted private residences, some unhosted. All are in Manhattan. Most have air conditioning and are near public transportation. Short-term (up to a year) hosted and unhosted housing available. Send self-addressed stamped business-size envelope for directory.

Reservations: Two-night minimum stay.

Rates: $60–$75 single. $75–$85 double. $85–$130 for two in unhosted residences. $15 one-night surcharge. Some weekly rates. Deposit of one night's stay required. With 14 days' notice of cancellation, deposit minus $15 service fee refunded. ♦

"Your hosts become your guides," is the way Judith Goldberg describes her B&Bs. The range of accommodations includes an Upper West Side residence overlooking Central Park, a renovated Victorian brownstone near the Museum of Natural History, and an artist's loft in Soho.

The service began when Judith's husband, a former bookseller who was also in the travel business, saw the need to offer Manhattan vistors a more personalized style of traveling. Now the list includes many arts-oriented hosts, several of whom have libraries in their homes.

---

*H*ospitality is the keynote of B&B.

Bed & Breakfast Network of New York

134 West 32nd Street, Suite 602, New York, NY 10001

Phone: 212/645–8134, Monday–Friday 8–6.

Listings: 200. Most are in Manhattan. Some are in Brooklyn and Queens.

Reservations: A few weeks' notice preferred. One-night bookings made a maximum of seven nights before scheduled arrival.

Rates: $50–$60 single. $80–$90 double. $10 one-night surcharge. Family, weekly, and monthly rates available. Unhosted apartments $80–$300. Deposit of 25 percent of entire amount required. For cancellations received at least 10 days before scheduled arrival, deposit less a $20 booking fee is refunded; with less than 10 days' notice, deposit is nonrefundable. Unhosted stays of seven nights or more are nontaxable. ◆

Founded in 1986, this reservation service takes pride in making suitable matches between guest and host. The wide range of B&Bs represented by Mr. Leslie Goldberg includes lofts, brownstones, and high-rise condominiums. Most are near public transportation, shopping, and theaters.

City Lights Bed & Breakfast, Ltd.

P.O. Box 20355, Cherokee Station, New York, NY 10028

Phone: 212/737–7049, Monday–Friday 9–5, Saturday 9–12.

Fax: 212/535–2755.

Listings: 400 hosted (simple to opulent) and unhosted (studio to four-bedroom) private residences. Most are in Manhattan. Some are in Park Slope, Brooklyn Heights, and Westchester, and on Long Island in the Hamptons. Major European cities represented include London, Paris, Rome, and Florence. For a sample listing, send a self-addressed stamped envelope.

Reservations: A minimum of two to three weeks' advance notice preferred. Bookings, if available, may be made within 24 hours. Generally there is a two-night minimum stay; three nights in the Hamptons on holidays.

Rates: Hosted: $45–$70 single, $65–$95 double. Unhosted: $90–$350. $10 one-night surcharge. Some weekly rates for 10 or more nights. Weekly billing service. Deposit required: 25 percent of entire stay. Refunds minus $20 booking fee for cancellations received at least 14 days prior to arrival date. One month's cancellation notice required for bookings made six months in advance. Amex, Carte Blanche, Diners Club, MC, Visa. ◆

Since 1985, when Yedida Nielsen began matching Manhattan hosts—many in theater and the arts—with travelers, she has considered the guests' needs for "the best room in the house," for hospitality, and for privacy. Together with her staff, she books a wide range of accommodations for guests who "fall somewhere between honored visitors and cherished family members." All hosts' residences are inspected. All guests are invited to submit an evaluation form. All unhosted properties—"increasingly popular"—provide dairy products and staples for several days together with much detailed information about resources in the neighborhood and city. Upon request, arrangements are made for theater tickets, walking tours, shopping, and car services.

Urban Ventures

38 West 32nd Street, Suite 1412, New York, NY 10001

Phone: 212/594–5650, Monday–Friday 8–5.

Fax: 212/947–9320.

Listings: At least 700. Residences, both hosted and unhosted, are in Manhattan, Brooklyn, and Queens. Short-term housing is available for up to three months.

Reservations: Two to three weeks' advance notice preferred. Will try to accommodate last-minute requests. Two-night minimum stay for hosted listings; three-night minimum for unhosted.

Rates: $50–75 single. $70–$125 double. $125–$160 for three or four people. Under age four, $15 per child. For two-night reservations, $5 per night booking charge. Deposit equal to cost of one night's stay (or credit card number, charged a week before arrival) is required. Deposit less $20 booking fee refunded for cancellations made at least five days before expected arrival date; with less notice, one night's fee is charged. Amex, Carte Blanche, Diners. Discover, MC, Visa. ◆

This well-established service represents a wide range of accommodations, from quite simple to luxurious; all are inspected. Mary McAulay's staff books you with "achieving New Yorkers, our main stock in trade. They chat and give advice. And for business travelers as well as travelers who feel at home in New York, the apartments with no host offer the privacy of a hotel room combined with the comforts of home. Our apartments, throughout the city, range from studios to three-bedroom, two-bath homes."

All the B&Bs with this ◀ symbol want you to know that they are a private home set up for paying guests and that they are not an inn. Although definitions vary, these private home B&Bs tend to have one to three guest rooms. For the owners, people who enjoy meeting people, B&B is usually a part-time occupation.

New York City Area

B&Bs are located just about everywhere, near any place you want to be. They are in townhouses, brownstones, apartments, penthouses, lofts, and other possible city spaces. Among the hosts are legal secretaries, lawyers, interior designers, social workers, executives, craftspeople, actors, teachers, writers, caterers, antiques shop owners, and scientists. And some (many) places are hostless, entirely for you. Here, as in all major cities, depending on location, parking can be an added expense.

Not always, of course, but often B&B in New York City can be quite different from any other large city in the country. It is a place where guests may be looking for a particular location at a particular rate and personal interaction may not be the top priority. But among the hundreds of Manhattan hosts there are many interesting, busy, and caring people who have comfortable to luxurious residences that they are happy to share. B&B in New York can be a home-away-from-home arrangement; and when the chemistry is right, some find that they have made new friendships and/or become repeat guests.

KEY TO SYMBOLS
♥ Lots of honeymooners come here.
♣ Families with children are very welcome. (Please see page xii.)
♠ "Please emphasize that we are a private home, not an inn."
♣ Groups or private parties sometimes book the entire B&B.
♦ Travel agents' commission paid. (Please see page xii.)
✖ Sorry, no guests' pets are allowed.
✄ No smoking inside *or* no smoking at all, even on porches.

New York City Area B&Bs

Please see pages 96–101 for Long Island B&Bs.

Please see page 80 for the Jeremiah H. Yereance House in Lyndhurst, New Jersey, just 15 minutes from Manhattan.

Bed & Breakfast on the Park   718/499–6115
113 Prospect Park West, Brooklyn, NY 11215   fax 718/499–1385

Host: Liana Paolella
Location: Across from Prospect Park in Brooklyn's historic Park Slope district. Two miles from Manhattan. Two blocks from the F train subway line. Ten-minute walk to Brooklyn Museum and the Botanic Garden.
Open: Year round. Two-day minimum on weekends.

Rates: Double occupancy. Shared bath $100 or $115. Private bath $135 weekday, $150 weekend. Suite $150 weekday, $175 weekend. Seven nights or more, weekday rates. $35 each additional person in room. $15 for breakfast (only) for guests' guests. $10 one-night surcharge. MC, Visa.
♥ ♨ ⬛ ✿ ✗ ✕

From Georgia: *"One room is more beautiful than the next. . . . I was amazed and in awe to find out that Ms. Paolella did all the decorating herself. . . . At breakfast there was a South African couple visiting their son, a judge. We chatted like old friends. . . . None of us wanted to leave the table . . . felt that we were very special guests in her home."* From New York City: *"I just needed to get away from the frenetic pace of Manhattan. . . . This B&B is a step back into a more relaxed, elegant, and gracious period and only a short cab ride from my apartment . . . fine silver, china, crystal goblets holding freshly squeezed orange juice . . . freshly baked quiche . . . tiny French porcelain pitcher with cream for aromatic coffee . . . music of Vivaldi filled the high-ceilinged room . . . beautiful paintings . . . and Shiva, who could make even a Zombie feel welcome."*

Liana, a Realtor and former antiques shop owner, grew up in France and Switzerland in a family of artisans. She traveled with her mother, an impresario, throughout Europe. While attending the Sorbonne in France, she lived in a pension. When in 1984 she moved with her college-age children into this 1892 four-story landmark brownstone, she realized that there was no nearby place for her visiting parents to stay. So when tenants moved out, she did "what I always wanted to do"—restored; polished floors; retained the birds-eye maple, chestnut, and oak woodwork; refurbished with Victoriana; and began her dream B&B in 1987. Just as this book went to press, *Victoria* magazine arrived for a photographic feature.

In residence: Shiva, "a loving miniature shepherd."
Foreign languages spoken: French and Finnish.
Bed and bath: Six rooms (two are large suites with sofa beds) on three floors; four rooms have private full baths; two share a full bath. Three rooms on garden level have private entrance. King, double, and twin beds; some are canopied.

(Please turn page.)

Breakfast: 8:30–9:30. Elaborate fruit platter. Home-baked yeast bread. German pancakes, crepes, souffles, Irish oatmeal, and frittatas. In dining room "bathed with panorama of stained glass and original woodwork."
Plus: In each guest room, air conditioning in summer; ceiling fan, color TV, private phone, down comforters, bedside treats, baked goods. Guest kitchen. Laundry facilities. Use of bikes.

Alexander Hamilton House   914/271–6737
49 Van Wyck Street, Croton-on-Hudson, NY 10520

Host: Barbara Notarius
Location: In a friendly neighborhood on a cliff with view of Hudson River. A 10-minute walk to the center of town. $2.50 (2-mile) cab ride to 50-minute train to New York City. Twelve miles from West Point; 35 from midtown Manhattan; 20 minutes to Westchester Corporate Center along I–287. Ten-minute drive to Rockefeller Museum, opening in 1994 in Pocantico Hills.

Open: Year round. Two-night minimum on weekends.
Rates: Small room $50 single, $60 double. Large room $60 single, $75 double. First-floor suite $100 single, $125 double, $25 each additional person. Bridal suite $250 one night, $200 two or more nights. One-bedroom apartment $60 single, $75 double. Weekly rates available. Amex, MC, Visa.
♥ ♨ ♣ ♦ ✖ ⅄

All in one—everything from a comfortable, well-maintained home away from home to a luxurious skylit suite with Jacuzzi and pink marble fireplace. Discovered by corporate executives, transferees, tourists, and romantics.

In the early 1980s, English B&B experiences were the inspiration for this family's host activities. Since, B&B has become a full-time occupation for Barbara, a psychologist and world traveler who has authored *Open Your Own Bed and Breakfast.* The large Victorian residence is furnished eclectically with Oriental rugs and antiques. Guests take walks in nearby woodlands and bird sanctuaries; bicycle (it's hilly); visit Hudson Valley historic houses; swim (right here); and sometimes use the home as a base for touring New York City.

In residence: Brenda, an assistant. Cydney, teenage daughter. Patti-cakes, a Shih Tzu.
Foreign language spoken: A little French.
Bed and bath: Seven rooms. A first-floor suite with queen bed and fireplaced sitting room with queen sofa bed, private shower bath. Four second-floor rooms share two full baths; two have double beds (one with sitting room and daybed), one has twin beds, and one has queen bed. Third-floor bridal suite with king bed, Jacuzzi tub for two, five skylights, pink marble working fireplace, microwave, refrigerator, and an entertainment center. Plus one-bedroom apartment.
Breakfast: Flexible timing. Full menu with homegrown raspberries, apples, or peaches. Served on patio beside pool, in 35-foot sun room, or in bridal suite.
Plus: Air conditioning. Bedroom ceiling fans. Thirty-five-foot in-ground pool, Memorial Day–Labor Day. Free loan of bicycles. Large fireplaced living room

with piano. TV in four rooms, plus one on huge sunporch that also has VCR and views of orchard and, in winter, river. Transportation provided from train.

Abode Bed & Breakfast Host #77

New York, NY

Location: Upper West Side residential block. Just off Broadway. Close to Dutch church (oldest congregation in this country) with magnificent Tiffany windows; neighborhood shops—even a shoemaker; subway and buses; restaurants; Lincoln Center (10-minute walk); Museum of Natural History; internationally famous food emporium Zabar's (4 blocks). One block from Riverside Park, Hudson River, jogging and walking paths.

Reservations: Year round through Abode Bed & Breakfast, page 102.

Rates: $120 single. $120 double.

♥ ⬛ ✕

Two years in England inspired this popular host, an architect, to convert apartments to private B&Bs that have a country feeling in decor and setting. Since 1990 he has been meeting travelers—he lives right here—who appreciate these quiet rear units with views of the trees and gardens of contiguous townhouses. Forgot an umbrella? Need directions? Would you like restaurant suggestions? "I'm always trying new ones," says the host, who often hears guests comment about the friendly neighborhood.

Bed and bath: Two studios with separate entrances off restored oak-paneled, wallpapered, and carpeted hallway. Third floor: queen four-poster plus single sofa bed, wood-burning fireplace, full bath, kitchenette, sitting area by window, armoire, antique dresser, books, treasures from host's trips. Fourth floor: French antique queen sleigh bed, full bath, camelback sofa, decorative fireplace, kitchenette, small round table with ice-cream chairs, French doors leading to terrace gazebo with hanging plants and flower boxes.
Breakfast: Fruit bowl. Cereals. Milk and half-and-half. Jams. Margarine. Tea and fresh coffee. Travelers usually buy freshly baked goods at Zabar's or at bakeries that are open late and/or early.
Plus: Air conditioning, cable TV, private phone with answering machine. Current *New York* magazine. Maps.

Urban Ventures Host #HAR111

New York, NY

Location: On the east side. A couple of blocks to center city with its many corporate headquarters, including Citycorp, where there's a theater, church, and frequent noontime performances. Near Bloomingdale's.

Reservations: Year round through Urban Ventures, page 105.

Rates: Studios $100 for two, $130 for three. One-bedroom apartments $125 for two; $150 for three or four; $165 for five.

⬛ ♦

(Please turn page.)

Deceiving! The outside of this six-story 1920s building is not as attractive as the inside. Completely done over, it is freshly painted and furnished with modern pieces. The host, a Southerner, who has decorated the entire building, lives in one of the units and has a first-floor office. A staff keeps everything shipshape, while the the host is your concierge. She welcomes you (until a reasonable hour), shares maps, and has all kinds of helpful information about her adopted city. Because of the number of units, this is a good place for groups as well as others who wish to be based in this area.

Bed and bath: Ten air-conditioned studios (all with queen bed and queen sofa bed) and 10 one-bedroom apartments. All with kitchenettes and full modern baths.
Breakfast: Provide and make your own.

Urban Ventures Host #CON200

New York, NY

Location: Residential tree-lined block of brownstones with flowering plants. Between Columbus and Amsterdam Avenues. Fifteen-minute walk across Central Park to Metropolitan and other museums.

Reservations: Year round through Urban Ventures, page 105.
Rates: $50 single. $60 double.
♥ 🛏 ⚹

Many publications have pictured this handsome brownstone, which cost $12,000 to build in 1887. The lovely garden features trickling water in a pond that has goldfish. There's a fireplace in the gracious living room. And throughout the five stories, there are traditional furnishings, magnificent Oriental rugs, fine arts, and lots and lots of books. Still, this is one of those B&Bs where the conversations with the warm, friendly hosts—a publisher and his wife, an urban activist—are often the most remembered part of the visit.

In residence: One cat—but not on guests' floor.
Bed and bath: Three third-floor rooms; all with ceiling fans. Two rooms with a double bed (one is a four-poster that photographers love) and one with a single share a large full bath that has a washer and dryer (available to guests).
Breakfast: Juice, fresh fruit, bagels or muffins, hot beverages. Served in formal dining room.

Hudson Valley Reservation Service

Some B&Bs in Hudson Valley are represented by:
The American Country Collection, page 142.

From the country: " Rural living is great. Did I tell you about the night the cows came? A farmer neighbor up the road had left a gate unlatched. About 10 p.m. I had 22 holsteins and one bull milling around the back yard, peering in the windows, mooing and munching! The guests loved it. (The garden didn't.)"

─────── Hudson Valley B&Bs ───────

The American Country Collection
Host #082
Ghent, NY

Location: On 10 rural acres with pond. Across from a hay field. Next to a miniature horse farm. One-quarter mile from dairy farm, cows, silos. Against a backdrop of rolling hills. Five miles from Taconic Parkway, 10 to Shaker Museum in Old Chatham, 20 to Hancock Village in Massachusetts; 9 to Olana Restoration; 24.7 miles on back roads (no stop lights) to Tanglewood in Lenox. Three miles to Mac-Haydn, summer stock musical theater.

Reservations: Year round through The American Country Collection, page 142.

Rates: $45 single. $60–$70 double. $15 extra person in room.
🛠 ♣ ✈ ⚜

Guests come for homemade bread. An escape from the city. An easy drive to museums, Tanglewood, antiquing, auctions. Everything from roller skating to "cabin fever concerts" in the winter. Or the opportunity to sit outside for a good read.

Years of weekend trips from Westchester convinced the hosts, a former antiques shop owner and a manufacturing company controller, that this would be a lovely area for a growing family. Following a trip to B&Bs in Ireland, the college-age children's rooms became B&B rooms for one of the most enthusiastic hostesses you'll ever find. "I came from a big family so I'm used to having lots of people around."

The 1850 farmhouse, built into a hill, has wide floor boards, hand-hewn beams, antiques, and—everywhere—stenciling. "If it doesn't move, you can stencil it." New this ninth year of hosting: how-to stenciling and faux-finish weekends (for six) held in an area studio.

Bed and bath: Second-floor queen room with shower bath; down two steps to room with double bed, big private hall bath with tub and shower, common sitting room with stocked refrigerator—juices, soft drinks, cheese and crackers. Up very steep steps to third floor—open sitting room with daybed (two twin mattresses) and room with two twin beds, private shower bath.
Breakfast: 7:30–9:30. Homemade bread, muffins, coffee cake. Bacon and eggs or waffles and sausage. Cereals. Hot beverages. Low-fat, vegetarian, or other special diets accommodated. Served in fireplaced dining room.
Plus: Air conditioning. Large-mouth bass on one-acre spring-fed pond. Picnic table. Lawn chairs. Swimming in local parks.

───────────

*D**id you hear the one about the salesman who
left a B&B breakfast with five good leads?*

Tara Farm Bed & Breakfast   914/294-6482
RD 2, Box 290, Kiernon Road, Campbell Hall, Goshen, NY 10916

Hosts: Fred and Meghan Hughes
Location: One of four houses on a half-mile-long dead end road. About a mile from village (Campbell Hall) with general store and train station. Near three wineries, outlet stores, Sunday flea market, fine dining and home cooking. Twenty-five minutes from I–84 and I–87. Four miles northeast of Goshen; 65 north of New York City.

Open: Year round. Two-day minimum on holiday weekends. (Booked a year in advance for West Point weekends and graduation.)
Rates: May 15–November 15 and holiday weekends: $45 single, $60 double. Rest of year: $40 single, $50 double.
🛏 ♦

Food, friendship, and hospitality are keynotes here in what the hosts call an old-fashioned personalized B&B. They speak from experience. Both Irish-born, they met in Australia, ran hotels and inns there, and emigrated to the United States in 1977, when they became innkeepers in Boothbay, Maine. In 1980, when Fred took his job as customer relations manager for a major airline (he commutes 60 miles each way), Meghan wanted to live on a farm, a lifestyle she knew from childhood. Since their move to this 50-year-old Cape Cod–style house, their children have grown (their son recently graduated from West Point), and "it just seemed natural to have B&B in their rooms." The centerpiece of the cathedral-ceilinged dining room, added in 1986, is Meghan's full-sized harp. Although a beginner, she sometimes will play for guests. Twice a year there are couples, "regulars by now," who stay overnight on their way to and from Florida and Maine. There are many international travelers. And then there are city folk who arrive by train (pickup provided), "just to relax in the country."

In residence: Often, a visiting seven-year-old granddaughter. On the farm: Shimaul, a horse; Sweet William and McGinty, goats; Vodka and Tonic, ducks; Thanksgiving and Christmas, Henrietta and Rambo, geese; Ben and Cara, dogs; Wombat and Ashley, cats; six hens.
Foreign languages spoken: French and Irish.
Bed and bath: On second floor, two queen-bedded air-conditioned rooms (with TV) connected by a shared shower bath, "our loo with a view." (Tub available in downstairs bath.) Rollaway available.
Breakfast: 8–10. "Proper. British style." Fresh fruit, juices, cereals, preserves, breads. Imported bacon; sausages; grilled tomatoes or pan-fried onions; sauteed mushrooms or potatoes; puddings. Served in dining room overlooking the valley.
Plus: Fireplaced living room with TV. Wood stove in dining room. Deck. Beverages. Down comforters with English coverlets. Babysitting. Pets are welcome.

If you have met one B&B host, you haven't met them all.

Captain Schoonmaker's Bed & Breakfast

RD 2, Box 37, High Falls, NY 12440   914/687–7946

Hosts: Sam and Julia Krieg
Location: On Route 213, a state highway but a country-style road. On sloping land with grass and gardens by a trout stream, waterfall, woodlands. Half a mile from tiny High Falls village. Ten miles south of Kingston; 20 minutes to Woodstock.

Open: Year round. Two-night minimum on weekends mid-September–Thanksgiving.
Rates: $45 single. $75 double. $80 canopied bed, private porch. $85 double with private bath. $85 double with fireplace, October–March.
♥ ♣

When the Poughkeepsie Mall held its grand opening, there was Julia, merrily cooking while introducing the B&B concept to hundreds who stopped to taste her specialities. Such joie! You don't forget this effervescent grandmother and just-retired elementary school teacher, who cohosts with friendly Sam, a biology professor. For a huge number of guests, one visit to this B&B is hardly enough; many return several times a year.

Woman's Day magazine, among others, has used the setting for photographs. One guest sent notepaper with a sketch of the inn, which was created by the Krieg family when their children were in college. In 1981 they bought "renovation project #8," the 1760 historically registered stone cottage with its 1800 eyebrow colonial Greek Revival addition, which was without plumbing, electricity, water, heat, or cosmetics. Within 10 months they opened as a B&B "without fussiness" and filled with quilts, antique toys, stenciling, and collections of Americana. Soon after, the 1810 barn/carriage house was renovated to accommodate more guests. Then came the lock-tender's house on the Delaware-Hudson Canal, a pleasant half-mile jog or cycle to the sumptuous "expanded family" breakfast table. Suites in an 1876 Victorian house are the most recent project.

In residence: Babo, a Maine coon cat.
Bed and bath: Fourteen rooms in four guest houses. Twin, double, or single beds. Some with private bath, canopied bed, working fireplace, private veranda, or porch overlooking stream. Suites have large rooms, canopied beds, carpeted tub and shower baths, private porch. Cots and a cradle available.
Breakfast: At 9. Home-baked bread, juices, honey-poached apple, souffles or crepes, sausage, blueberry-walnut strudel with phyllo, rocky road fudge cake, or lemon-poppyseed cake. Almond mocha coffee. By candlelight in front of original working fireplace.
Plus: Beverages and snacks at 6 p.m. in wicker-furnished solarium. Living room with Hudson Valley Dutch fireplace (6 feet high, 5½ feet wide).

From New York: *"Nicer than we could have imagined."*

Many guests write: "I hesitate to rave too much for fear of finding no place at the inn next time I call."

The American Country Collection Host #155

Katonah, NY

Location: On four acres of woods, gardens, maple sugarbush. Opposite 100-acre farm. In an upper Westchester County village, part of Bedford township. Two miles down a dirt road (or accessed from a major county road). Three miles from I–684 or Sawmill River Parkway. Near IBM and Pepsico, Caramoor Music Festival (June–August), fine art museums, gardens, historic sites (same period as B&B). Within 3–10 miles of "wonderful variety of restaurants, from very casual to elegant." Fifty miles from center of New York City, "but once you get here, it seems much farther than that."

Reservations: Year round through The American Country Collection, page 142.

Rates: $45 and $50 single. $50 and $75 double.

♥ ⚐ ⚑ ⚘ ✗ ⚌

One neighbor discovered the area by staying in this 1723 farmhouse, which was renovated—"while maintaining its integrity"—by the hosts in the early 1970s. It has wide-board floors, exposed beams, and eclectic furnishings— "touchable kinds of antiques, comfortable sofas to lounge on, window seat by the kitchen fire."

Warm hospitality and memorable breakfasts are offered by the hosts, an actor whom some guests recognize and his wife, an actress who made homemaking a full-time job when the children were growing up. They delight in sharing their home with many honeymooners, who come here "on their way out of the city," and with business travelers, wedding guests, and people from all over the world who have joined the ranks of discoverers.

In residence: One cat, not allowed in guest rooms.

Foreign languages spoken: French, Greek, Russian.

Bed and bath: Up five steps to master bedroom with double bed, freestanding wood-burning Franklin fireplace/stove, en-suite private tub/shower bath. On third floor, room with double bed and one with two twin beds share tub/shower bath.

Breakfast: Flexible hours. Different every morning of your stay. Waffles, crepes, or pancakes with homemade maple syrup, homemade muffins, fruit, juice, coffee or tea. In kitchen by fire, in formal dining room, or on patio.

Plus: Fireplace in second-floor sitting room. Swimming and trout fishing in pond across the street. Benches and picnic tables.

From Bernice's mailbag: "And then there was the classmate from 1935, whom I hadn't seen in 50 years, who read about us in your book. He's been here twice."

Rondout Bed & Breakfast
88 West Chester Street, Kingston, NY 12401

914/331–2369
fax 914/331–9049

Hosts: Ralph, Adele, and Donna Calcavecchio
Location: On two acres in an old residential neighborhood. On a hill with views of Catskills. Near Hudson River, antiquing, historic sites, hiking; 25 minutes to Bard College, Vassar, and New Paltz. Ten minutes from New York State Thruway; 40 minutes to Hunter and Bellayre Mountains.
Open: Year round.
Rates: Shared bath, $50 single, $60 double. Private bath, $60 single, $75 double. $10 additional person.
🏠 🛏 ✈ ✄

> Guests wrote: *"Welcoming, elegant, relaxing home. . . . The rooms are fresh, airy, and pretty—and big; the breakfasts are delicious—and big! The house itself is wonderfully pleasant to sit about in, as are the porches and grounds . . . heard crickets at night. . . . An island of charm and peace."*

When theater friends asked the Calcavecchios, both thespians, to accommodate actors in 1985, they started a whole new "pleasurable lifestyle" for the hosts, whose five older children were working or in college. Daughter Donna added her artistic touches and in the early 1990s dovetailed full-time hosting with tutoring at a school for emotionally disturbed adolescents. In 1992 her well-traveled parents and teenage brother, Daniel, returned from two years in England, where Ralph was working for IBM.

Built on a grand scale with a 33-foot living room, a 20-foot dining room, and many big windows, their 1905 Federal Revival house had seen several uses when the Calcavecchios bought it in 1980. Now "loved" once again, it is furnished eclectically, with paintings and prints everywhere. Adele, a writer and teacher, and Ralph, an engineer and pilot, share many sightseeing suggestions, including a "magnificent-in-any-weather" place that they compare to Lake Como in Italy.

In residence: Sammy, a friendly springer spaniel, not allowed in guest rooms, and What-a-Trill, "a tirelessly singing canary."
Bed and bath: Four rooms. On second floor, one very large queen-bedded room with private full bath. On third floor, a full bath is shared by three double-bedded carpeted rooms that have a view of the Catskills.
Breakfast: Usually at 9. Lots of fresh fruit, frittata, pastry, waffles, French toast with their own maple syrup. Endless coffee or tea. Served with crystal and silver in dining room or on porch.
Plus: Fireplaced living room. Wood stove in living room and kitchen. Wicker- and rattan-furnished glassed-in porch. Evening refreshments. Electrically operated player and baby grand pianos. TV. Books. Lawn furniture. Outdoor and indoor games.

---

*If you've been to one B&B, you haven't been to them all.
If you have met one B&B host, you haven't met them all.*

The American Country Collection
Host #064

Slate Hill, NY

Location: High in scenic country-side on a 90-acre horse farm. Ten minutes to Delaware River; 20 to Hudson River; 2½ miles from Routes 6 and 84; 75 minutes from Manhattan. Near antiquing, wineries, crafts shops, canoeing, historic homes, orchards, museums. Eight miles north of New Jersey's Sussex County.

Reservations: Year round through The American Country Collection, page 142.
Rates: $60 single, $75 double. $85 king. $110 suites with triple, $130 quad. $10 extra child in room, $15 adult.
♥ ♯ ♣ ♦ ✗

Rise early on a hunt day and you might see the gathering and start of the horses and hounds. Walk to the other side of the pond and sit under the trees, listen to the trickling water and the peepers, and enjoy the country view. Cross-country ski, fish, and hike right here. Relax in the six-person Jacuzzi at this spacious hunt club decorated with an English country flavor. What started out as one room in 1730 later became a dairy farm, part of the Underground Railroad during the Civil War, and a summer resort.

The hostess, an artist and skilled seamstress, breeds international sport horses and Jack Russell terriers—"a big hit with guests"; has a tack shop; and also sells antiques, gifts, and secondhand items (by demand) on the premises. Her husband, a retired engineer, works with her on this farm they bought in 1986 "for its beauty, size, and location." Guests are happy they did.

In residence: Three Jack Russell terriers. Six horses.
Foreign languages spoken: Some German and French.
Bed and bath: Private hall bath for first-floor room with double plus another twin. On second floor, five carpeted rooms including two suites (which have sink in room) share two shower baths. Rooms have king or a double. One suite has queen in one room, twin in the other; other suite, double and two twins.
Breakfast: 7:30–9:30. Fresh fruit. Entree possibilities: Mexican eggs, challah bread French toast with currant sauce, pecan waffles. Home-baked breads and homemade preserves.
Plus: Bedroom air conditioners and window fans. Tea, cheese, and crackers. Pickup at local bus or train station for a fee. Tour of house and farm. Hot-air balloon rides launched right here. Game room with billiard table under construction. Picnic lunches and dinners by prior arrangement.

From a father's account of a B&B stay: "Before falling asleep, my son read a few pages of a book he found downstairs in the living room. He put the book down on his chest, sighed, looked up at the ceiling and said, 'This is the life.'"

Ujjala's Bed & Breakfast   914/255–6360
2 Forest Glen, New Paltz, NY 12561

Host: Ujjala Schwartz
Location: Ten minutes from the New York State Thruway. On a corner lot, set back from the main road, among apple, pear, and quince trees. Three and a half miles from the village. Antiquing country. Minutes from hiking and cross-country skiing in Shawangmunk Mountains.

Open: Year round. Two-night minimum May–October.
Rates: (Depend on length of stay.) Shared bath $60–$65 single, $70–$90 double. Private bath $80 and $90. Children 7–12, $15. Over age 12, $20 extra person.
♥ ♨ ⏸ ⁂

All in one: a former dancer, model, and cooking instructor; a rock climber who practices on her own personal barn wall; mother of an actor and a college student; a therapist in stress management and body awareness; a hostess who believes in healthy foods and a sense of humor; and, as of 1992, an interfaith minister who conducted her first wedding right here. For over a decade Ujjala has been hosting in her 1910 Victorian cottage. The house is decorated in casual country style with hanging baskets and herbs, and with many plants and flowers. Dozens of varieties of herbs, flowers, and vegetables flourish in the garden, which is complete with paths, a bench, and, of course, wonderful aromas. Guests appreciate the relaxed, serene ambiance of this B&B.

Bed and bath: Four air-conditioned rooms. On first floor are two rooms with Murphy beds, private shower baths. One has a queen bed, sitting area, and hat collection; the other a double bed, skylight, barn siding on one wall, wood-burning fireplace. Two second-floor rooms: One with a double feather bed, and one with a double feather bed and a single bed, share a shower bath.
Breakfast: 8:30–9:30, Sunday until 10. All natural ingredients. Fresh fruits, eggs, homemade breads, freshly ground coffee, and teas. Special diets accommodated. Served in country kitchen surrounded by large windows overlooking the orchard and herb garden.
Plus: Living room with TV. "A common space to read, relax, meditate, or exercise." Welcoming refreshments. Fireplaced skylit common room. Deck. Tepee (kids love it), a sweat lodge used for monthly Native American purification ceremonies. Workshops on alternative lifestyles. Coming: a cookbook with instructions for preparing and garnishing foods with edible flowers.

> From Canada: *"I enjoyed everything—the surroundings, the house, the decor, the food, and especially the landlady!"*

---

*G*uests arrive as strangers, leave as friends.

Orchard House   914/883–6136

Route 44/55 at Eckert Place, P.O. Box 413, Clintondale, NY 12515

Host: Carol Surovick
Location: On two terraced acres of partially wooded land with extensive flower gardens and a Victorian three-holer painted to match the house. In a tiny village on a two-lane country highway that leads to area orchards. Ten minutes from New York State Thruway (exit 18) and SUNY at New Paltz. Two hours from New York City; one from Albany; 30 minutes to Hyde Park, Vanderbilt Mansion, and Culinary Institute of America.
Open: Year round. Two-night minimum on weekends in October and on holiday weekends.
Rates: Per room, $75. Private bath $10 extra per night.

♥ 🛍 ♣ ✗ ⚊

> From New York: *"The best choice for 50 miles around! . . . Tasteful, attractive, comfortable, warm feeling. . . . As for breakfasts—superb! . . . Surroundings were quiet, peaceful, and gorgeous . . . able to do morning yoga and tai chi exercises in back."* From Massachusetts: *"Wonderful B&B. . . . Never expected our hostess to be a tourism bureau unto herself. Our mountain hike, winery visit, and restaurant were all selected from her information. . . . Directly across the road from front porch is a postcard-size farmhouse complete with pond, ducks, horse, pony, barn, vegetable garden, and rolling hill."*

While Carol was an IBM staff communications specialist, she fell in love with this restored 1866 Queen Anne Victorian. In preparation for her 1992 early retirement—she's now a free-lance technical writer and editor—she saw B&B "as an excuse to live in a big beautiful house and decorate it to her heart's content—with needlework [many pieces are her own], art, and antiques," with a European rather than a Victorian touch. Romantics appreciate the room that is complete with enclosed balcony overlooking the plant-filled first-floor solarium. Wedding attendants like to book the entire place. Hikers, too, are among those who thank Carol for doing what she does.

In residence: Two cats, Squeaker and Lizzy.
Bed and bath: Three second-floor queen-bedded rooms. One has private shower bath. Two share a full bath.
Breakfast: Usually at 9. Full, varied menu with fruit, homemade breads or muffins, whole wheat or Belgian waffles, French toast, sausage strata, or other egg dish. Served in formal dining room.
Plus: Flowering plants in solarium year round. Bedroom window fans. Rockers on front porch. Fresh fruit. Mints. Access to nearby pool and golf course.

Many B&Bs that allow smoking restrict it to certain rooms and/or public areas. Although some of those B&Bs that have the ✗ symbol allow smoking on the porch and/or patio, others do not allow smoking anywhere on the property.

Audrey's Farmhouse B&B   914/895–3440

2188 Brunswyck Road, RD 1   fax 914/895–3440
Box 268A, Wallkill, NY 12589

Hosts: Don and Audrey Leff
Location: Romantic. Site of many tent weddings. On 35 acres with "golf course-like" lawns, gardens, and panoramic mountain views— "breathtaking scenery that inspires photographers." Ten miles south of New Paltz. Fifteen minutes' drive to Minnewaska Mountain trails, Mohonk, and cross-country ski rent-als. Near restaurants and auctions. One hour and forty-five minutes from New York City.
Open: Year round. Two-day minimum on weekends, three-day on holiday weekends.
Rates: Double occupancy. $85 shared bath. $95 private bath. MC, Visa.
♥ 🛏 ♣ ♦

"How will anyone ever find us?" Don asked Audrey in 1989 when they looked at this restored 1840 farmhouse. Audrey just knew. It's pegged, without a nail. Ceilings are beamed. There are wide-board floors and white plaster walls. Throughout, there's a lifetime collection of country antiques that blends with the recently acquired Southwestern art (from Colorado living in the 1980s). There are fireplaces. An inviting library. An in-ground swimming pool. And a hostess who has entertained all her life—for her father, who had a freeze-drying corporation; for family; for the six kids' friends. What started in a smaller (New Paltz) house as "a lark" for Audrey, who has worked with relatives of intensive care patients, has become a lifestyle with an enormous extended family. On weekends Don, who has parking garages in Manhattan, becomes co-chef, part of a team who love doing what they do.

In residence: Tigger and Ben Jur, "very ancient" Shih Tzus. Two cats.
Bed and bath: Five rooms; three with private bath. All with feather beds. Private exterior extrance for first-floor room (pets allowed) with queen bed, large tub and shower bath. Second floor: Double four-poster with private tub and shower bath, wood stove, TV, VCR overlooks pool. Double bed and a single bed, cathedral ceiling, private stall shower bath. In a wing up steep stairs, two smaller double-bedded rooms share a stall shower bath.
Breakfast: 9:30–10. Five-course meal. Crepes, waffles, pancakes, omelets, breakfast meats, vegetable and fruit juices, homemade breads and muffins. Served with sterling silver and china by huge fireplace.
Plus: The house is yours as long as you are here. Fresh flowers. Turndown service. Mints on pillow. Library with electronic piano, TV, CD, games, lots of books, and late-1740s working fireplace. Window fans in bedrooms.

*A*ccording to many hosts:
*"Guests come with plans and discover
the joys of hammock sitting."*

Village Victorian Inn   914/876–8345
31 Center Street, Rhinebeck, NY 12572

Hosts: Judy and Rich Kohler, owners
Location: One block from village main street, Beekman Arms, restaurants. Two miles from Hudson River; 10 miles north of historic mansions, including Franklin D. Roosevelt National Historic Site and Vanderbilt Mansion, and Culinary Institute of America; 90 minutes north of New York City.

Open: Year round. Two-night minimum on weekends.
Rates: Double occupancy. Queen bed $175. King bed $225, $250 with working fireplace. $40 extra person. Package rates for murder mystery, chocolate lovers', and tree-trimming weekends. Amex.
♥ ♣ ♦ ✗ ⊬

All done up, but not overdone. To the nines. With French wallpapers, Oriental carpets, period antiques, armoires, laces, fine linens. Intentionally romantic.

It's as Judy envisioned it—for other buyers! Just as the buyers were about to purchase the Italianate Victorian house and her planned restoration work, she realized that this was the perfect place to fulfill a long-held dream of creating a fantasy B&B. In 1986 this can-do woman—through her three-year-old construction company (reproduction colonial houses)—replumbed, rewired, and decorated. For hands-on innkeeping experience—"I love it"—she had the company office in the kitchen the first year!

Now, when the resident innkeeper serves tea and cookies on the wicker-furnished side porch, neighbors sometimes join guests. Judy, an art major who was a Manhattan advertising account executive, is in and out of here and the other very different lavish B&B (below) she created by the lake in the nearby countryside.

Bed and bath: Five rooms with ceiling fans. All private baths; some shower only, others with tub and shower. First floor: room with antique king brass bed, sitting area, bay windows. Second floor: four rooms, each with antique queen oak or king canopied bed (one also has working fireplace) and sitting area. Rollaway available.
Breakfast: 8–10. Fresh fruit and homemade sweet breads. Eggs Benedict, pecan-stuffed French toast, sausage-and-egg casseroles, baked apple pancakes. In fireplaced dining room (featured on *Victorian Accents* cover) with old English bar.

The Lakehouse . . . On Golden Pond
Shelley Hill Road, Stanfordville, NY 12581   914/266–8093

Hosts: Judy and Rich Kohler
Location: Secluded. Without a sign. Overlooking private lake on a 22-acre wooded estate. Six miles east of Rhinebeck. Ninety minutes from New York City. Within 20 minutes' drive of Hudson River mansions, wineries, antiquing, Rhinebeck Aerodrome, restaurants.

Open: Year round. Two-night minimum on weekends.
Rates: Double occupancy. $150 double bed. $175 queen bed. $225 king with working fireplace. $250–$350 queen or king with working fireplace, two-person Jacuzzi, private deck, color TV. $40 extra person. Amex.
♥ ♣ ♦ ✗ ⊬

(Please turn page.)

Talk about getting away from it all. Here on the lake, surrounded by natural beauty, peace and quiet, sunsets, blue heron and deer, Judy and Rich Kohler built their own house. Judy's innkeeping experience with the Village Victorian Inn (page 121) encouraged her to design a luxurious bed and breakfast that takes advantage of this idyllic hillside site. In 1990, with the assistance of manager Julie Mueller, she opened this contemporary inn. It has a cedar exterior, huge redwood walkway, cathedral ceilings, several levels, and plenty of glass. Furnishings are a blend of original art, antiques, and modern pieces. Those decks with views await. Fireplaces do too. Boats tied up at a covered dock can be rowed to a private island. Getaway guests love this very private place. So do executives who come for meetings. Gorgeous small weddings are held here. And murder mystery parties are, too.

Many guests ask Judy how she happened to get into the construction business. "It was a passion, so I just did it." Rich is an engineer who is in the satellite television business.

Bed and bath: Eight rooms with views (of lake or woods) in three buildings—lake house, boathouse, and guest house. All private full baths, several with two-person Jacuzzi and oversized shower. King, queen, or double beds. Some with wood-burning fireplace, TV, refrigerator, private deck. Rollaway available.

Breakfast: 8–10. Fresh fruit. Homemade sweet breads. Belgian waffles with sauteed apples, strawberry-stuffed French toast, omelets, or sausage-and-egg casseroles. Served in dining room overlooking the lake.

Plus: Central air conditioning. Ceiling fans throughout. Late-afternoooon appetizers and pastries. Swimming right here—off dock.

B&B guests respond to pampering and change (relax) from the time of arrival to departure. One observant host remarked to some executives: "Maybe when you get back to the big city, you'll be arrested for loitering."

Leatherstocking/Central New York
———— Reservation Service ————

Some B&Bs in this region are represented by:
The American Country Collection, page 142.

KEY TO SYMBOLS
♥ Lots of honeymooners come here.
♯ Families with children are very welcome. (Please see page xii.)
♠ "Please emphasize that we are a private home, not an inn."
♣ Groups or private parties sometimes book the entire B&B.
♦ Travel agents' commission paid. (Please see page xii.)
✖ Sorry, no guests' pets are allowed.
✕ No smoking inside *or* no smoking at all, even on porches.

Leatherstocking/Central New York
B&Bs

Berry Hill Farm B&B

RD 1, Box 128, Bainbridge, NY 13733

607/967-8745
fax 607/967-8745

Hosts: Jean Fowler and Cecilio Rios
Location: On a winding country road, high on a hill overlooking miles of rural scenery and 180 acres of woods and meadows. Forty-five minutes to downhill ski areas. Seven miles from I-88, Bainbridge, and Afton; 30 from Binghamton, 35 from Oneonta, 2⅓ miles from Route 206.

Open: Year round.
Rates: $45-$50 single. $55-$65 double. Package weekends for horse-drawn foliage tour, winter wonderland, cut-your-own Christmas tree by sleigh, and Mexican theme. MC, Visa.

Away from it all. A treat. A friendly informal atmosphere. Sunrises. Sunsets. Stargazing. Fresh air. Views. Peace and quiet. Everywhere—space! All offered by ex-Brooklynites who came for all those good things in 1982. They restored an 1820s farmhouse and filled it with primitive and European antiques. In 1986 they started to share this large comfortable house with B&B guests. Now they also greet travelers who come from miles around just to see their herb and flower gardens, laid out in a daisy design that has 16 petals, each with its own variety of herbs and dryable flowers.

Cis, originally from Mexico, grew up in Texas, and earned one master's degree in Oriental studies and another in history. He is a former teacher and Brooklyn antiques shop owner. Jean, a Realtor and former textile designer, makes cloth dolls and braided rugs. They both grow and sell plants, flowers, and dried arrangements. Their guests unwind, cross-country ski, ice skate, or go sledding right here. During warmer months they hike, pick berries, enjoy the extensive perennial and vegetable gardens, swim in the pond, go to auctions. And with advance arrangements they take an old-fashioned horse-drawn buggy or sleigh ride through meadows and woods.

In residence: Outdoor pets: two dogs, several cats.
Foreign languages spoken: Spanish, French, Italian, German, Latin.
Bed and bath: Three second-floor rooms. One with queen bed and two with double beds share two full baths.
Breakfast: Until 9. (Very early for hunters.) Juice, cereals, fresh fruit, eggs/pancakes/French toast with ham, sausage, or bacon; homemade muffins, jellies, jams, sausage/cheese grits; baked herbed garden tomatoes.
Plus: Garden flowers. Bedroom ceiling fans. Tea, coffee, juice always available. Flannel sheets. Terry robes. Down comforters. Wraparound porch. Wood stove in living room. Grill, picnic table. Some ice-skating and ski equipment (no charge) available. Workshops—gardening, fresh and dried flower arrangements, wreath making.

Creekside Bed & Breakfast   607/547-8203

RD #1, Box 206, Forkshop Road, Cooperstown, NY 13326

Hosts: Fred and Gwen Ermlich
Location: On an old stagecoach route off County Route 26. Surrounded by huge manicured lawns. Bordered by creek (for swimming and fishing). Three miles southwest of Baseball Hall of Fame in Cooperstown center, 12 miles to Glimmerglass Opera.

Open: Year round. Two-day minimum, May–November weekends; three days some holiday weekends, four on Baseball Hall of Fame weekend.
Rates: Double occupancy. $70–$85 queen. $85 suite. $99 cottage. $10 additional person, cot or crib.

♥ ⛷ ⛵ ✿ ♦ ✈

A perfect setting for a Victorian dessert buffet, an opera fund-raiser with Renaissance singers. This colonial house, discovered by *Country Inns* and *Travel & Leisure*, has atrium lights that twinkle all year round. While this B&B has grown from 9 to 18 rooms, the goats' house has become a honeymoon cottage. Weddings take place in the huge living room and on the grounds.

Still, in true B&B style, the Ermlichs are the reason that Creekside is so popular. Even though they've been hosting—and making changes—since 1983, Gwen still gets just as excited about house decor as she did about all the opera costumes she used to make for the company she and Fred founded in 1975. During the summer you might see the multifaceted hosts perform—as they have in over 200 productions—at the acclaimed Glimmerglass Opera built on Otsego Lake in 1987.

Before coming to Cooperstown in 1970, Gwen was an actress and singer in Manhattan. Fred, a former Roman Catholic priest and arts consultant, is assistant dean of continuing education at SUNY Oneonta. As hosts they offer privacy and company, warmth and joy to "Buddhists, Christians, Jews, Baha'i, Moslems, actors, artists, baseball luminaries, international travelers, balloonists, cyclists [we were there], and all-American families."

In residence: Paul, a college student. Patrick is 17. Several outdoor cats.
Foreign languages spoken: French and German.
Bed and bath: Four queen-bedded rooms; all private shower baths, some skylit. On second floor, one bridal chamber with canopied bed, ceiling fan, private entrance, and deck. One double-bedded room. Third-floor suite has dining and sitting area. In three-room cottage, queen bed, shower bath, living room, wet bar, deck. Rollaway and crib available.
Breakfast: 8–9:30. Fred's menu varies. Maybe scrambled eggs with dill, cinnamon French toast, or pancakes. Juice, bacon or ham or sausage, fruit, coffee, tea, hot chocolate. Or "scrumptious low-cholesterol menu." Served in the elegant dining room.
Plus: Cable TV/HBO in each room. Two fireplaces in living room. At Christmastime, five decorated trees in the house. Beverages. Refrigerator space. Bedroom ceiling fans. Restaurant suggestions and reservations. Opera and theater tickets. Babysitting.

The Inn at Brook Willow
607/547–9700
RD 2, Box 514, Cooperstown, NY 13326

Hosts: Joan and Jack Grimes
Location: Quiet. Up a tree-shaded drive, over a creek, onto 14 acres with views of meadows, cows, deer, and mountains. Five minutes to Glimmerglass Opera, Leatherstocking Summer Theatre, Baseball Hall of Fame, Victorian homes, antiquing, swimming and boating at Otsego Lake.
Open: Year round. Two-night minimum on weekends Memorial Day–Columbus Day.
Rates: Double occupancy. $55–$75. $20 cot. Crib free.

♥ ⚓ ♣ ♨ ✄

Guests have arrived on Thursday and announced that they would like to be married this Saturday, right here. (It happened.) Some young parents—many are returning guests—have their "first night out since baby arrived" with Joan and Jack, grandparents of four, as babysitters. The Grimeses declare, "What a joy with a new extended family. After 10 years as hosts, we still consider B&B a dream come true. When we moved from Long Island to this former hops farm 16 years ago, we redid the 1900s Victorian cottage house and our 1880s barn—the last of the big barns—keeping the exposed beams in one room and decorating with antiques, wicker, collectibles, and lots of plants. Each spring the creek—on what we call our pastoral retreat—is stocked. Thanks to our thousands of guests from all over the world, we have warm memories of travelers who share hopes, dreams, and experiences."

Joan, a former nurse/teacher, is New York State coordinator of Vocational Industrial Clubs of America.

Bed and bath: Four rooms, all with queen beds and country and Victorian antiques. Three, each with private shower bath, in reborn barn. Suite in main house has a large full bath with twin sinks, tub, and shower. Cot and crib available.
Breakfast: 7:30–9. Juices, fresh fruit, homemade muffins, eggs, cereal, toast, jam. French toast, pancakes, or waffles; coffee, tea, milk. Served by candlelight on china in the dining room. "We judge breakfast success by how far down the candles burn."
Plus: A Great Room with fireplace, books, puzzles. Fireplaced parlor. Beverages. Fresh flowers, fruit, and candy. Bedroom ceiling fans. French toiletries. Decks. Paths through woods. A glen to climb. Barbecue. Badminton.

> Guests wrote: *"Time to be alone together. Time to plan ahead. Time to set priorities, to make some decisions for a change in our lives and for our family. . . . Beautiful location. Lovely decor. Great food. Super clean. . . . Restaurant menus and suggestions. . . . Made theater reservations for us. A fantastic experience."*

---

*B*reakfast is where the magic happens.

Litco Farms Bed & Breakfast   607/547-2501

P.O. Box 1048, Cooperstown, NY 13326-1048

Hosts: Margaret and Jim Wolff
Location: On 70 acres with plenty to do right here. On New York Route 28, 3 miles north of Cooperstown. Restaurants within walking distance.
Open: Year round. Two-night minimum on weekends Memorial Day–Columbus Day.

Rates: $59 single. $69 double. $79 triple. $99 quad family suite. $109 five in suite. Ten percent less November–March. Package rates for quilting (workshop) weekends.
♠ ♠ ❖ ♦ ✳ ✂

Quilts are everywhere in this B&B, one of Cooperstown's originals. Two of the Wolffs' guests, an Italian sculptor and an English art critic who fell in love with the area, "bought a home around the corner and were married by Jim in our living room!" Some guests walk the dog with Margaret and Jim at sunset to the eight-acre beaver pond, which also has ducks and geese. Some just relax, tour the area, or even get tips about refinishing floors or rearranging furniture every time a new auction treasure is acquired. Always, there's a warm welcome here.

Before Jim became Otsego town justice, he had his own imported lumber and plywood business and helped to organize the local natural food co-op. Margaret, a former home economics teacher and co-owner of a restaurant, is placement director for vocational/technical students. "And my dream has come true with Heartworks, right here at the B&B; it's a unique shop featuring fabrics and quilting supplies as well as handmade quilts that are shipped all over the country and to merry old England and Japan too."

In residence: Miss P., a pussycat, and Ruby, "the wonder dog, who is very tricky."
Bed and bath: Four rooms, all with Margaret's quilts. Two first-floor rooms (one with a double bed; one with two double beds, nonworking fireplace, and cable TV) share a bath. Upstairs suite has one room with a double bed and a double sofa bed, adjoining room with two twin beds, private full bath. Very private carriage house with double bed, bunk beds, shower bath, kitchenette, cable TV.
Breakfast: Usually 8:30 or 9. Whole-grain freshly baked breads, homemade fruit preserves and granola, farm-fresh eggs, bacon, French toast or hotcakes with pure maple syrup, freshly brewed coffee. At tables set with hand-quilted placemats and runners.
Plus: In-ground 20-by-40-foot pool. Hiking, nature, and cross-country ski trails. Deck overlooking meadows. Common room with books, magazines, and board games. Trout fishing. Bedroom ceiling fans. Picnic baskets by advance arrangement.

From New Jersey: *"Appreciated advice on touring the town. Home is lovely and breakfasts are delicious."*

Thistlebrook   607/547-6093
RD 1, Box 26, Cooperstown, NY 13326

Hosts: Paula and Jim Bugonian
Location: Peaceful. On a country road with gorgeous views of valley; farm fields; meadows; and the two-acre natural pond with ducks, herons, red-winged blackbirds, deer in the evening, bullfrogs at night. Three miles from center of town.

Open: May through October. Two-night minimum on weekends during July and August and on holiday weekends.
Rates: $85–$95 per room. $110 master suite. Extended stay discount rates available.
♥ 🏠 ⚜ 🎿 🍴

One of a kind. It still looks like an old (1866) red barn from the outside. Inside, there are elegant and comfortable spaces (find your own) on several levels—with soaring ceilings, fluted columns made by Jim, welcoming fireplace, Oriental rugs over carpeting, and antique furnishings from several periods. Windows are many-paned, arched, and Gothic (from a local estate).

The Bugonians, who spent eight years renovating a 150-year-old farmhouse, saw the potential that the previous barn owners had barely begun to realize. In 1992, just two years after this four–guest room B&B opened, it was the "Inn of the Month" feature in *Country Inns*. Subsequently Thistlebrook was placed on the magazine's annual "top 12" list.

Jim was a financial aid director (and golf coach) at a community college before beginning a cabinetry and carpentry business in 1986. Now he does faux finishes on interior walls, floors, and furniture. His passion for gardening and landscaping shows in the lovely lawns and gardens he is developing on the former barn grounds. Here he and Paula, who worked at IBM in the development and test areas before resigning in 1990, continue their joy of entertaining at home in a B&B that Paula calls "my absolute love!" Guests can tell.

In residence: "Kashka, our cat, is loving and friendly; imposes only when asked!"
Bed and bath: Four spacious and very private rooms; all with private full baths. On main floor, twin beds, handicapped accessible. From library, separate stairways to rooms with a queen or a double bed plus twin-size daybed. Master suite on two levels (three steps) has queen bed, desk, bath with double shower stall, large tub, vanity with two sinks. Rollaway and crib available.
Breakfast: 8–9:30. Served in crystal-chandeliered dining room, it typically includes juice, fresh fruits, breakfast breads, home-baked muffins or biscuits (assorted jams and jellies), a variety of cold cereals, granola and yogurt, coffees, teas, and hot chocolate.
Plus: Bedroom ceiling fans and individual thermostats. Small indoor pool "good for a dip" (summer months only) in sun room overlooking pond and 150 acres of farm fields and meadows. Outdoor chairs and tables with those views. Laundry facilities for extended stay guests.

Summerwood   315/858–2024

P.O. Box 388, 72 East Main Street, Richfield Springs, NY 13439

Hosts: Lona and George Smith
Location: On three acres surrounded by lawns and trees. On Route 20, midway between Albany and Syracuse; 12 miles from New York State Thruway, exit 30 I–90. Fifteen miles north of Cooperstown, 7 miles to Glimmerglass Opera.
Open: Year round. Two-night minimum on Baseball Hall of Fame weekend.

Rates: $55–$60 shared bath, $70 private. Rollaway $15 adult, $10 child. Singles $10–$15 less per room. Discount for booking of more than one room, for stays longer than three days, or for families (except July–August). MC, Visa.
♥ ♫ ☄ ♣ ✕ ✂

Drive up to the portico, alight from your motor-driven "carriage" and enter the Queen Anne Victorian, which is on the National Register of Historic Places. There are fireplaces in the parlor and dining room—and, as Lona says, "always, when I'm cooking, a chair at the kitchen table." Many gables and stained glass windows command your attention, but the real hit is the authentic turn-of-the-century carousel horse in the dining room.

When the Smiths lived on the West Coast, Lona was a microbiologist and George was in computer sales and management. They came east several years ago to take over George's family dairy farms. In 1984 they bought and redecorated this big 1890 house "with 86 windows, acres of lawn, and a barn with wainscoting that fascinates many guests." Lona became president of the Glimmerglass Opera and a sought-after caterer. George tours guests through the farm (no cows), on hikes (acres of woods), and up to hilltops with magnificent views. Together they host weddings, play readings, family reunions, opera and theater benefits—and visiting heads of state.

In residence: Joe, a black Lab, performs tricks (kids love them) with George.
Bed and bath: Five rooms. Second floor: two queen bedded rooms, each with a private full bath (one has old-fashioned deep tub). Third floor: queen-bedded room and one with two twins share a full hall bath. One room with brass double bed, private tub/shower bath tucked under eaves.
Breakfast: 7:30–9:30. Seasonal fruit; quiche; eggs from local farms; bacon, sausage, and ham (also local); homemade coffee cakes, rolls, and muffins; sourdough pancakes with maple syrup and homemade jams. Low-cholesterol or natural-food menus available.
Plus: Air-conditioned first floor. Beverages. Sitting room with TV. Wicker-furnished porches. Yard games. Refrigerator and ice. Assistance to guests who are seeking ancestors. Picnic lunches ($5–$10). By advance arrangement, opera tickets purchased and dinner ($10–$20) here.

From New York, Michigan, Maryland, Delaware: *"Breakfasts are outstanding. . . . Everything is beautiful, the atmosphere is informal, thanks to Lona and George. . . . Treated royally. . . . So large, you hardly know others are there. . . . Five stars."*

Adrianna Bed & Breakfast   315/429–3249
44 Stewart Street, Dolgeville, NY 13329

Host: Adrianna Naizby
Location: Five minutes from center of "quiet inviting village that has African violet greenhouses, a wildlife sanctuary, Daniel Green Slipper outlet, and unusual restaurants and shops." With panoramic views of Adirondacks. Six miles north of New York State Thruway exit 29A; 28 miles northeast of Utica.
Open: Year round except December 24 and 25.
Rates: Shared bath $45 single, $50 double. Private bath $45 single, $55 double. $10 extra person. MC.
♣ ✗

One guest liked the town so much he moved here. A couple found the B&B so appealing that they were inspired to open their own. Adrianna remembers guests in their nineties who were living history, honeymooners who later returned with family, and annual returnees on their way to vacation destinations. "Today I am waiting for 6 guests who are among 400 coming to work together to build an entire church in three days. Imagine!"

This contemporary house looks smaller from the outside than it is. One of the very first B&Bs in the region, it is the home of a Dolgeville sixth-grade teacher who was inspired by her own B&B travels.

In residence: Barney, a friendly cat.
Foreign language spoken: Limited Italian.
Bed and bath: On air-conditioned second floor, three large rooms (only two booked at a time) with double bed, high queen bed, or two twins share a shower bath. Plus first-floor room with canopied double bed, private tub bath, ceiling fan.
Breakfast: Usually 8–10. Orange juice, fresh fruit, or baked apple. Peaches and cream French toast and ham or pancakes and sausage. Pure local maple syrup. Homemade pumpkin bread. Cold cereals always available. Hot beverages. Served by candlelight with crystal and china in dining area.
Plus: Welcoming refreshments. Fireplaced living room with TV, VCR. Piano. Bedroom air conditioners and ceiling fans. Babysitting with prior arrangements. Kitchen privileges. Laundry. Picnic table. Terry robes, toiletries, hair dryers. Guest refrigerator with juices. Books, magazines, newspapers. Original art for sale.

From Ohio: "Perfect. Like staying in a friend's home . . . immaculate with those nice extra touches that make a house a home . . . blueberry pancakes that melt in your mouth . . . best of all was the warmth of Adrianna." From New York: "A beautiful house with a woman who is very loving and caring and will make you feel like you are staying at some fancy resort."

To tip or not? (Please turn to page xi.)

The Village Green Bed & Breakfast

P.O. Box 169 607/895–6211
Guilford, NY 13780 fax 607/895–6211

Hosts: Doug Taylor and John Lynch
Location: In historic village (population: 150) with no commerce. (Well, there is one one gas pump.) With deer in the meadow and, from neighboring farms, sounds of mooing cows and gobbling wild turkeys. Thirty minutes west of Binghamton; 40 minutes to Hamilton and Colgate colleges and Cooperstown. Within 7 miles of canoeing, fishing, and hiking (several state parks). Five-minute walk to 70-acre spring-fed, lifeguarded (in summer) lake.

Open: Year round.
Rates: Per room. $60–$100. Singles $10 less.
❖ ♦ ✄ ⅊

Clanggg. Cl-aangg. Your (daytime) arrival is announced to the world as Doug pulls with all his might on the rope of the 36-inch, 450-pound bronze steeple bell. It's in the stone church set in the former town park across the street from this large 1840s Greek Revival house, a landmark complete with pillars, huge windows, and fabulous perennial and herb gardens. Doug bought the facing properties in 1991 and has converted the church to Praiseworthy Antiques— "Heaven knows you'll find it at Praiseworthy"—a shop designed with a Madison Avenue (floor is trompe l'oeil marble) rather than country-style interior. The "never-been-botched" house, less formal than the shop, is a visual treat, filled eclectically with fine antiques—all for sale—and with many Oriental rugs that John acquired during Peace Corps days in Libya, Iran, and Egypt.

Doug, who moved here from a farm, is an illustrator who has done editorial art for dozens of major magazines, including *Time* and *Newsweek* covers. "In this wonderful unspoiled hamlet," he runs his shop "after almost 20 years of buying and selling antiques as a sideline in Manhattan." He also feeds miniature horses, breeds affenpinscher and papillon dogs for shows, and plants espalier pear trees as well as hundreds of varieties of lilies and other magnificent flowering plants. John, who managed La Louisiana, a Manhattan restaurant, for 10 years, is full-time B&B host to guests who feel like discoverers.

In residence: Seven miniature horses; four were pregnant when this book went to press.
Foreign languages spoken: Arabic and Persian.
Bed and bath: All with park view. Four second-floor rooms (could be a suite) with double or twin beds; one new full bath. On first floor, bath and very large custom tile shower; one guest room.
Breakfast: 8–9:30. A picture. Colonial recipes baked by local residents. Huge candlelit buffet arranged by Doug might include gingerbread and raspberry cheese coffee cakes, cranberry and banana date muffins, custard-filled corn bread, and fruit bowl. Always, freshly baked bread—maybe dill or cinnamon. Local goat cheeses. Special diets accommodated with advance notice.
Plus: Three living rooms; two with working fireplaces. Floral arrangements. Window fans in summer. Flannel sheets. Down comforters. House, park, and gardens available for private catered parties of up to 100 people.

Chesham Place   315/894-3552

317 West Main Street, Ilion, NY 13357

Hosts: Bob and Ann Dreizler
Location: On a rise of four wooded acres within walking distance of village center. Halfway between Albany and Syracuse, 1 mile south of I-90. Within 10 miles of Herkimer County, Mohawk Valley, and Utica colleges; about 30 minutes to Hamilton and Colgate colleges and Cooperstown.

Twelve miles to country's highest lift lock and Russian Orthodox monastery; 15 miles to hands-on Musical Museum.
Open: Year round.
Rates: Private bath $45 single, $50 double. Shared bath $5 less. MC, Visa.
🦆 ♦ ✂

This is one of those places to stay that has become the reason to go. It's an elegant 27-room living museum—and very low-key. I felt as if I were visiting friends in their antiques-filled home decorated with many original velvets, silks, Oriental rugs, and extensive collections of china, glass, and books. History comes alive as the Dreizlers share historical anecdotes, some ghost stories, and fascinating information gathered from the original owner's grandson, who died at age 92 in 1992.

In 1983 Bob was retiring from 40 years as an executive with Aerospace Corporation of Los Angeles. Ann agreed to live in Bob's hometown if they could buy this imposing five-storied 1866 brick Italianate/Second Empire mansion, which had been unoccupied for 17 years. In 1984 the Dreizlers began by framing paintings found in the tower. They cleaned eight Italian marble fireplaces; put the butcher table used by Bob's grandfather in the kitchen (and installed a new parquet floor); planted hundreds of bulbs; placed the home on the National Register of Historic Places; and saved the carriage house, another gorgeous structure that is also on the National Register.

Chesham Place gives a sense of place—right up to today. Ann works with preschool handicapped children. Bob is chairman of the hospital foundation. They both work with hospice; the arts; and historical, preservation, and recreational groups. They crew for the local balloonist—and find joy in meeting travelers from all over the world.

In residence: Francis, a 20-pound indoor tomcat. Mama, a small outdoor cat.

Bed and bath: Three rooms. Room with queen brass bed has sink in room, large shower bath. Honeymooners often request room with century-old double feather bed; working fireplace; hand-painted bird frieze; attached Venetian tub and shower bath (the county's first) with porcelain ceiling, walls, and floors. One large room with queen canopied bed, single sleigh bed, sink, and fireplace. For families or couples traveling together, two or more rooms may share the Venetian bath.

Breakfast: At guests' convenience. Fresh fruit, juice, egg dish, meat, potatoes, dry cereals. Sometimes waffles, hot oatmeal, or popovers. In kitchen or formal dining room. Ann and Bob join guests.

Plus: Tour includes formal parlor with extraordinary Austrian crystal chandelier. Library with hundreds of first editions that captivate some guests until the wee hours. TV in den and sitting rooms. Down comforters and flannel sheets. Candy by bedside. Spontaneous evening treats—popcorn, cider, hot chocolate, or root beer floats.

Sunrise Farm   607/847–9380
RD 3, Box 95, New Berlin, NY 13411-9614

Hosts: Janet and Fred Schmelzer
Location: On a 65-acre farm. Near antiquing, several state parks for hiking, swimming, boating. Five miles to restaurants, 20 west of Cooperstown and Oneonta; 70 west of Albany.

Open: Year round.
Rates: $35 single. $45 double. $20 third adult. Children prorated by age.
🏕 🏠 ✈ ✂

The Schmelzers needed more acreage for their "photogenic and friendly" Scotch Highland cattle, so in 1992 they moved to this new Cape Cod–style energy-efficient house, modeled after the one they had built in Pine Bush, New York. Here, too, there's a wood stove in the living room and an attached solar greenhouse. Their organic garden includes garlic and potato cash crops. Guests are welcome to stroll around the farm or in the adjoining woods. In winter, bring cross-country skis. "Only the docile cattle will see you fall down."

Fred was an office supply salesman, and Janet, a native of England, did office work before "retiring." At least half a dozen guests wrote to tell me how thankful they are that the Schmelzers are hosting in traditional B&B style.

In residence: Two cats, "never in guest room."
Bed and bath: One second-floor paneled room with twins/king bed option, double sofa bed, skylight, ceiling fan, adjoining private shower bath.
Breakfast: Preferably by 9. Eggs with bacon or sausage. Pancakes. Cereals, toast, English muffins, juice, fruit. If available, homegrown berries, home-baked goods, preserves, and "their own" honey.
Plus: Evening tea and cookies. Dinner by special arrangement. Lawn chairs.

> From Ohio: *"Good food and conversation."* From New York: *"Hearty breakfast with everything from their farm . . . a warm welcome . . . spacious comfortable room . . . nice to feel like part of the family."* From North Carolina: *"Flexible, caring, congenial."*

Breezy Acres Farm Bed & Breakfast
RD 1, Box 191, Hobart, NY 13788   607/538–9338

Hosts: Joyce and David Barber
Location: On 300 acres of farmland and rolling hills. Five minutes from Scotch Valley ski area. Half hour to Windham and Hunter ski areas. Two miles south of Stamford.

Open: Year round. Two-night minimum on holiday and special weekends.
Rates: $50 weekdays, $60 weekend. Singles $10 less. $10 child. MC, Visa.
♥ ⚘ ✈ ✂

(Please turn page.)

Guests wrote: *"You feel as if you're visiting friends. . . . So close to country fairs, antiquing, and hiking. . . . Fresh air and scenic views are right there and through the woods. . . . A wealth of knowledge about Delaware County. . . . Joyce keeps track of what she serves, so returnees never have a repeat menu. . . . A good soak in hot tub warms and relaxes the body after a day in the outdoors. . . . Relaxed by candlelight on front porch overlooking the mountains. . . . Gave us a tour and showed how they make maple syrup from the 8,500 trees they tap. . . . Pampered. . . . Cozy country style, but it's the warm hospitality that makes the difference."*

A blend of antiques (many family pieces), crafts, and contemporary furnishings are in this impeccably kept 18-room, 150-year-old rambling farmhouse. Guests relax on the wide curved leather sofa in the den. Or by the fieldstone fireplace in the living room. Maple sugaring takes place in March and April. Homegrown blueberries are served in the summer. Ninety varieties of perennials flourish. In the woods there's a private pond for swimming and fishing. Come pick your own pumpkins (from 4,000) in the fall. Cross-country ski and snowshoe here in the winter.

As for the popular hosts: Joyce, a former teacher, is a professional home economist who attended Cornell's School of Hotel Administration. For many years Dave continued the family tradition of dairy farming. Now he farms, hunts (and guides), taps those maple trees, sells real estate (lots right here), and sometimes builds log houses.

Bed and bath: Three second-floor rooms, all private tub/shower baths. King bed, attached bath. Double bed and daybed, attached bath. One double-bedded room with unattached bath.

Breakfast: 8–9:30. A highlight. Menu changes daily. Juice. Maybe baked apple or fresh fruit. Warm homemade muffins—apple/raisin/walnut or bran with cream cheese filling. Pumpkin (homegrown) pancakes with "our own" maple syrup. Hot beverages.

Plus: Joyce bakes often. Ping-Pong table. TV in den. Fireplaced living room. Treats in each room. Garden flowers. Wicker-furnished porches with rockers. Deck with umbrella table.

"I'll just sleep in the morning," said one college-age son, until the next day when he smelled the muffins.

Catskills B&Bs

The White Pillars Inn
82 Second Street, Deposit, NY 13754

607/467–4191
607/467–4189
fax 607/467–4191

Host: Najla R. Aswad
Location: Quiet. Among 18th-century Federal and Greek Revival homes in a lumbering and farming community (with well-known Americana antiques shop on old Route 17). In the Catskill Mountains; 25 minutes east of Binghamton; under three hours from Manhattan.

Open: Year round.
Rates: May–October, $50 single; $60 double with shared bath, $70–95 private bath; $110 suite; $20 third person. Rest of year, $45 single; $55 double/shared bath; $65–89 private bath; $110 suite. Amex, Carte Blanche, Diners, Discover, MC, Visa.
♥ ♣ ✈ ✄

What a success story! At age 22, Najla decided, after college, after much experience in the food and hotel industries, and after managing a hometown (Binghamton) restaurant, that the nonstandardized world of innkeeping would allow her "to make a huge impact on a small scale." That's when she opened here, in April 1987, in the 1820 Federal Greek Revival house that had been built by the founder of the town. Najla knows how to cook (meals are created and presented here as well as at other sites) and how to bake (wedding cakes, fruit pies, and chocolate chip cookies marketed in the area), and has established an inn apprenticeship program for dreamers. ("There's a time for hosting and a time to let go.") Some guests seek her consultation on their own home decor. Always, the inn kitchen seems to be a popular gathering place. Corporate guests love this inn. "But weekends belong to the romantics who start breakfast after 10, read the *Times*, and relax."

Bed and bath: Four air-conditioned second-floor rooms. Suite with private entrance has a king-bedded room and one with a twin bed, full bath, TV, phone. Room with double bed, private bath with door shower, sofa and love seat, desk. Two rooms, each with a double and a twin bed, share hall full bath.
Breakfast: 8–10. "As early as 6:30, with coffee at 6, on weekdays." Guests' choice—French Toast Sampler, including Grand Marnier, Flaky, and Pecan Stuffed; overstuffed Greek, vegetarian, or make-your-own omelets; eggs Benedict; baked apple wrapped in pastry with warm caramel sauce. Blended juices, fresh fruit. Homemade muffins. Specialty coffees. In dining room with heirloom Haviland Limoges, gold flatware, Waterford crystal, fresh flowers, and soft jazz. Or brought to your room.
Plus: Central air conditioning. Evening refreshments by the fire. Coffees and teas always available. *New York Times*, plus *Wall Street Journal* and CNN programming on weekdays. Fine toiletries. Pima cotton bath sheets. Bottomless cookie jar. Dinner by reservation ($17.95–$22.95 for entrees); with two-day notice, for public too. Directions (in spring) to a spectacular waterfall "where the mist can be seen for half a mile," plus local hiking, bicycling, swimming, canoeing, cross-country skiing.

(Please turn page.)

From New York: *"Delightful. . . . An energetic gracious proprietor whose inn is in a sleepy, rural, quaint town . . . but comfortable. The rooms should be featured in* Better Homes and Gardens. *Guests are pampered."*

The Griffin House Bed & Breakfast

RD 1, Box 178 Maple Avenue, Jeffersonville, NY 12748   914/482-3371

Hosts: Irene and Paul Griffin
Location: Surrounded by tall pines on almost two acres on a residential side street in a "step-back-in-time" Catskills village. Across from a church. Quarter mile from restaurants. Ten minutes to Delaware River. Three miles to horse trails. Ten miles from Liberty; 20 from Monti-cello. Two hours from New York City.
Open: Year round. Two-night minimum on weekends in season or holidays.
Rates: Per room. $75 shared bath, $95 private.
🛥 ✳ ♦ ✘ ⅏

Ten master carpenters spent five years building this Victorian house with chestnut paneling, intricate fretwork, stained glass windows, and herringbone oak floors. Original gaslights, now electrified, are in the house, which was occupied by three generations of the original (Scheidell) family until the Griffins bought it in 1990. As a B&B, it's the perfect place for family reunions, getaway New Yorkers, and guests of local residents, too.

Each room tells a story—the history of the Scheidells; of Fred Waring (of Pennsylvanians fame), who introduced his trumpeter (Paul) to a singer (Irene) he had met in England; and of Paul's father (who lives in nearby Liberty), a trumpeter who played with Jackie Gleason and Benny Goodman. The Lancastrian Room honors Irene's English roots.

For their early retirement "for a different kind of show business," the Griffins found the house of their dreams in what they knew only as a pass-through town on their way to performances. Irene still sings in theaters and resorts—and occasionally in her own parlor. She sews more than her own gowns. The dolls that she dresses, as well as other area-made crafts, are sold in the original settlement home that became a chicken coop—"the place where the kids used to smoke," according to grandnephews who have come by to share some oral history with the Griffins.

In residence: Three cats: two 1-year-olds and one 17-year-old.
Bed and bath: Four large second-floor rooms. Antique double bed, private shower bath. Antique double brass bed, shower bath with seats. Room with two antique cannonball twin beds shares a full hall bath (robes provided) plus a downstairs half bath with carved antique double bed.
Breakfast: Around 9. Juice. Fresh fruit. Cereals. Homemade muffins and preserves. Egg strata or oven-baked French toast with fruit; sausage or bacon. Tea. Gourmet coffees.
Plus: One bedroom has ceiling fan. Grand piano. Fireplaced parlor and receiving room. Reading area in bay window of library. Beverages. Turndown service. Dinner by arrangement.

The Rolling Marble Guest House   914/887–6016

P.O. Box 33, Long Eddy, NY 12760-0033

Hosts: Karen Gibbons and Peter Reich
Location: "On an acre and a half along the shore of the wild and scenic Upper Delaware River, which goes on forever." Off Route 97 in a little hamlet with historical society, freight trains passing through a couple of times a day, nearby antiquing.

Twelve miles north of Callicoon, "the dining capital of the Delaware"; 100 miles northwest of New York City.
Open: Usually year round; advance reservations required in winter. In 1993, opening in July.
Rates: Tax included. $50 single. $65 double, $10 cot. MC, Visa.

♥ ☎ ♣ ✈ ⊁

> From New York: *"Great place and wonderful people . . . easy-going spirit. . . . Feel as if you're in another time . . . attention to detail . . . wraparound gingerbread porches . . . beautiful grounds with breathtaking views . . . a family canine born in Brooklyn by chance but living in God's country by choice . . . flowers . . . clean air . . . peace . . . romantic walks . . . homemade and homegrown food . . . homemade chocolate chip cookies atop the 1930s white-enameled refrigerator . . . the perfect hideaway. . . . Felt rejuvenated. . . . Like being at grandmother's house in the country. . . . The closest you will come to unconditional love of life here on Earth. . . . P.S. Ask to see album of restoration process."*

Urban dwellers are passionate about the hosts and their home, a five-year restoration done by Karen, a sculptor and painter, and Peter, an industrial designer. Most guests find no reason to leave—except for a 12-minute ride to dinner. Although first-timers inquire about canoeing, hiking, horseback riding (all available), they often just enjoy the backyard, birds in the mulberry, the porches with river view, wading and swimming from the stone beach. As Peter says, "It's why *we* are here!"

In 1985, "by luck," Karen and Peter found this "used and abused" Italianate Victorian built by a local lumberman in 1888. Opened in 1989 as a B&B, it has a grand staircase, French doors, tall windows, curved walls, wainscoting, and—outside—flower and vegetable gardens, fruit trees, and paths through the woods to the river.

In residence: Hector is a friendly blond shepherd mutt. Scuro is an aloof, elderly cat; Ruth, a shy black cat.
Bed and bath: Five second-floor rooms with queen, double, or single bed share one full and one half bath upstairs and one full (with hand-held shower) downstairs bath.
Breakfast: 9–11. Buffet style. Homemade breads—French, oatmeal, zucchini, pumpkin. Muffins with homegrown cherries, berries, peaches. Tart apple or potato and cheese quiche. Fresh fruits, juices, cheeses. All kept warm until you get to it in upstairs common room that has antique refrigerator and outdoor deck.
Plus: Wood stove in living room. Intentionally without TV. Beach chairs to take to river. Lawn games.

The Eggery Inn   518/589-5363

County Road 16, Tannersville, NY 12485

Hosts: Abe and Julie Abramczyk
Location: At 2,200-foot elevation; minutes to Hunter (snowmaking and innovative summer festival), Cortina Valley, and Windham alpine ski areas, and to hiking trails in Catskill Forest Preserve; 1½ miles from the village. Forty miles south of Albany; 14 northwest of I–87; 18 miles north of Woodstock; 125 from Manhattan.
Open: Year round. Two-night minimum on winter, summer, and fall weekends; three nights on holiday weekends. No meals served in April, early May, or early November.
Rates: Midweek $55–$60 single, $75–$85 double. Weekend $90–$100 per room. Additional adult $20 midweek, $25–$30 weekends. Holiday rates a little higher. Family rates when children sleep in adults' room. Amex, MC, Visa.
♣ ♦ ✇

The idea of having a ski slope in their backyard is what attracted two Long Island health care administrators (who are also jazz fans) to the then 23-room summer lodging house in 1979. "We landscaped. We refinished wainscoting, added baths and antique finds. We have redecorated several times over! And still we make changes. The parlor has a wood-burning Franklin stove, an antique player piano, and mission oak furniture. Recently we added French doors (great views!) that lead to the wraparound porch. And the dining room now has a gas fireplace. This is the casual, friendly country inn we hoped to have."

In residence: Two cats, Tootsie and BoBo, "unavailable for home-taking." Babe is a black Labrador.
Bed and bath: Fifteen rooms; six rooms are handicapped accessible. All private baths: most are shower only, some are tub/shower baths. Queen, one double, two double beds, or a double and a twin bed. Cot available.
Breakfast: About 8:30. (8–11 on full-house days.) Juice, fruit, hot and cold cereals, local jams and maple syrup, coffee, herbal teas, and hot cocoa. Eggs or omelets, French toast or pancakes, bacon, sausage, home fries. Plus heart-healthy selections. Served in the plant-filled dining room with picture windows that face mountain range.
Plus: Parlor games. Cable TV and table fans in each guest room. Wraparound porch. Ceiling fans in living and dining rooms. Volleyball. Dinner by prior arrangement for groups, family reunions, small weddings. Small fully licensed bar (for guests only) faces Hunter Mountain slopes.

> From New York City: *"Greeted with warmth and care. Serene at night. Huge delicious hot breakfasts. Great dining and excursion suggestions. Two thumbs up!"*

Unless otherwise stated, rates in this book are per room for two and include breakfast in addition to all the amenities in "Plus." As for taxes and gratuities, please see page xi.

Haus Elissa Bed & Breakfast   914/657-6277

P.O. Box 95, West Shokan, NY 12494-0095

Hosts: Helen and Gretchen Behl
Location: In a small Catskills village across the road from the Ashokan Reservoir. Surrounded on three sides by forests. Twenty minutes from Woodstock; 30 from Kingston, "5–30 from a veritable United Nations of restaurants," 30 to Hunter and Belleayre skiing. Two hours from New York City.

Open: February–December. Two-night minimum required over holidays and preferred during the month of October.
Rates: Per room. $55 or $60 shared bath. $85 private bath. $5 less for shared bath bookings made at least two weeks in advance.
♠ ✈

From California: *"Genuine German hospitality and friendliness, a cozy welcoming room (fresh flowers and all), breakfasts complete with homemade German pastries that still make our mouths water whenever they come to mind.... A glimpse of deer ... or chickadees."* From New York: *"Beautiful sky without light pollution. Extensive file on restaurants ... printed directions to various hikes and towns.... When I went home with a nature question unanswered, they researched it and wrote the answer to me! ... impeccably clean ... home-baked goodies grander than we can dream ... good mattresses ... even though house is small, plenty of privacy."*

Those excerpts are from a stack of long letters from guests who enjoyed this almost-century-old home, brought back to life by Helen, who was a USO director, and her daughter, Gretchen, a librarian. They decorated with local and German themes and their own handwork and opened as a B&B in 1988. Gemutlichkeit. It's here.

In residence: Rip Van Winkle, "feline host, diplomat par excellence."
Foreign languages spoken: Fluent German; a little Dutch and French.
Bed and bath: Two second-floor rooms, each with queen bed and sloping ceilings, share a full bath. Private bath arranged if room booked at least two weeks in advance.
Breakfast: Usually at 9. Fruit cup. Bacon and eggs or fruit-filled German *pfannkuchen* (pancakes). Home-baked German coffee cakes and pastries. In dining room or on enclosed back sun porch overlooking back garden, spruces, wildlife.
Plus: Spinet piano. Fresh flowers. Ice water carafe and homemade German cookies in each room. Window fans. Three-minute walk to town pool.

Maplewood Bed & Breakfast   914/688-5433

6 Park Road, P.O. Box 40, Chichester, NY 12416

Hosts: Nancy and Albert Parsons
Location: On a quiet country lane in a beautiful valley. On more than an acre of grass, trees, and gardens. Two miles north of Phoenicia; 12 miles northwest of Woodstock; 28 miles northwest of Kingston; 12 miles from

four ski slopes. Near major hiking trails.
Open: Year round. Same-day response to reservation messages left on answering machine.
Rates: $40 single, $55 double.
♠ ✈ ✂

(Please turn page.)

From Connecticut: *"A good introduction to B&Bs . . . outstanding breakfasts . . . sightseeing ideas off the beaten track . . . interesting history of the area . . . roaring fire in the evening."* From New Jersey: *"A magnificent piece of property complete with towering pine trees, a backyard mountain, and an in-ground swimming pool. . . . Delicious breakfasts. Welcoming, well-appointed, and clean. Our five-year-old daughter thinks it is charmed. A back staircase, an under-the-stairs bathroom, a secret passageway leading to the bedroom—what more could a city kid ask for!"*

Many guests are surprised at the size. Built in 1923, it was formerly the manor home of Beryl Swartzwalder, owner of Chichester Wood Products, who owned the entire village. This spacious colonial, home to the Parsonses for almost 35 years, became their B&B once their family was grown. Skiers, tourists, fishermen, and getaway weekend travelers appreciate the hospitality here. One family that gathered from all over the country found it a perfect reunion spot.

Nancy, an accountant, and Albert, a sales manager, are active in civic organizations and politics, sports and gardening.

Bed and bath: Four second-floor rooms with semiprivate full (tub and shower) baths plus a half bath downstairs. One king bed, one canopied double, one queen bed, and one single.
Breakfast: Starts at 8:30. (At 7 for skiers.) Albert's omelets, crepes, pancakes, or fruit French toast with homemade maple syrup "tapped from our own trees." Freshly squeezed juices, grapefruit or fruit salad, home-baked breads, freshly ground coffee. Low-cholesterol diets accommodated. Served in fire-placed dining room or on porch overlooking gardens. Leisurely (except for skiers), with hosts often joining guests.
Plus: Beverages, cheese, and crackers. Family room with fireplace, color TV. Library with piano. Toiletries. Thick towels. Croquet, badminton. Sun porch. Hiking trails right here.

Mount Tremper Inn   914/688–5329
P.O. Box 51, Route 212 and Wittenberg Road, Mount Tremper, NY 12457

Hosts: Lou Caselli and Peter LaScala
Location: In the Catskill Mountain Forest Preserve; 20 miles west of Kingston; 10 miles west of Woodstock. Across from one well-known French restaurant and near others.
Open: Year round. Two-night mini-

mum on weekends, three nights on holiday weekends. Reservations required.
Rates: $65 shared bath. $80 private bath. $95 suite. MC, Visa.
♥ ⬛ ♣ ⋊

Discovered! By dreamers in 1984. By the *New York Times* in 1986. By *Ski* magazine in 1987, *Victorian Homes* in 1989. Now—with velvet parlor walls, French lace curtains, and ornate prismed lamps—it is just what the two New Yorkers, Lou, a former marketing coordinator, and Peter, a fabric importer, envisioned while they collected museum-quality antiques—everything from armoires to bedsteads—for eight years. They found the 1850 23-room summer guest house, last used as an orphanage, all boarded up and in need of everything. In five and one-half months, the two men did everything all themselves. Ever since, they have been pampering guests. The innkeepers, too, love this business.

Bed and bath: Twelve rooms; every one with a sink. Private tub bath for first-floor suite that has two double beds. Private shower bath for first-floor room with two twin beds. Ten second-floor rooms (each about 10 by 12 feet) with a double or twin beds share three full hall baths.

Breakfast: 8–10. Juice, cereals (including homemade granola), "their own" baked quick breads, baked eggs with cheese and vegetable, hot beverages. Buffet style with crystal and silver in elegant dining room with classical music playing. On veranda in summer.

Plus: Bluestone fireplace in grand parlor. Full game room and library. An old music box that plays beautifully; an old organ that plays reluctantly. Croquet, badminton, shuffleboard.

> From Connecticut: *"A lovely, quiet, restful country location. Owners hospitable . . . well-deserved pride in authentic Victorian ambiance they created."* From New York: *"Breakfast was superb. Room was comfortable and homey."*

KEY TO SYMBOLS
♥ Lots of honeymooners come here.
⚓ Families with children are very welcome. (Please see page xii.)
⛵ "Please emphasize that we are a private home, not an inn."
♣ Groups or private parties sometimes book the entire B&B.
♦ Travel agents' commission paid. (Please see page xii.)
✖ Sorry, no guests' pets are allowed.
✄ No smoking inside *or* no smoking at all, even on porches.

Albany Area to Lake George
─────── Reservation Service ───────

The American Country Collection
4 Greenwood Lane, Delmar, NY 12054

Phone: 518/439–7001, Monday–Friday 10–5.

Fax: 518/439–4301.

Listings: Over 110. Mostly hosted private residences, many inns and some unhosted residences. Many on the National Register. Communities represented in New York State are in the Albany/Saratoga, Hudson Valley (upper and lower), Catskill, Central Leatherstocking (west to Utica and Syracuse), Adirondack, and Lake George regions. In New England—throughout Vermont, in Berkshires of western Massachusetts, and in northern New Hampshire. Also—several B&Bs on St. Thomas, Virgin Islands. Directory, 100 illustrated pages, $6.50.

Reservations: Two weeks in advance preferred. Last-minute accepted when possible. During busy seasons, some B&Bs have a two- or three-day minimum.

Rates: $35–$75 single, $40–$130 double. Weekly and family rates at some locations. Senior citizen discounts for multinight weekday stays, excluding foliage season and Saratoga in August. Deposit of one night's lodging or one-half of total stay required, whichever is greater. Deposit refunded less a $20 service fee if reservation is cancelled no less than 14 days (30 days August–October) prior to scheduled arrival; for later cancellations, same refund made if room is filled. Administration charge $5–$10 on first booking; none for any bookings within next six months. Amex, MC, Visa. ◆

"When a guest walks in and says, 'This is just the way The American Country Collection described it,' we know we have done our job well," says Arthur Copeland, a reservation service owner whose annual inspection includes mattress testing. As one who lists customer service and satisfaction as top priorities, he selects hosts who present homemade foods, know their area, and are attentive to guests' needs while being aware of their desire for privacy.

Plus: "Ski 'n' B&B," romance packages, and short-term (up to several months) hosted and unhosted housing available. Pickup at transportation points provided by some hosts. Gift certificates available.

Albany Area to Lake George B&Bs

The American Country Collection Host #097
Albany, NY

Location: In residential area on a main street with bus transportation in every direction. Within 2 blocks of movies, restaurants, library. Minutes' ride to colleges, state office buildings. Fifteen minutes from airport. Two miles from New York State Thruway.

Reservations: Year round through The American Country Collection, page 142.
Rates: $49 single, $64 double.
♥ ⬛ ♣ ♦ ✕ ⚲

After staying at a Vermont B&B, the host, a nurse administrator, returned to look for property that would be her very own B&B. She found this "grand old house," which is now very Victorian inside—with many antiques and lots of lace and flowery prints. From auctions and estate sales came a china cabinet, a side server, iron-and-brass beds, oak dressers. "Now that I am all furnished, buys are limited to wineglasses and candlesticks!" Guests comment on the hominess, the feeling of what many call "Grandmother's house."

Bed and bath: Four second-floor rooms share two baths; one with tub and shower, one shower only. Two rooms with double bed; two with a double and a single in each.
Breakfast: 9–10 weekends, earlier on weekdays. Juice. Fruit cup. Bagels, muffins, rolls. Cereals. Hot beverages.
Plus: Air conditioning and phone in each guest room. Fireplaced living and dining rooms. Special occasions acknowledged. TV in living room. Wicker-furnished front porch. Back porch with swing. Off-street parking.

> Guests wrote: *"We loved the Victorian atmosphere . . . I would recommend it for both personal and business trips. . . . A wonderful hostess."*

Appel Inn   518/861–6557
Route 146, RD #3, Box 18, Altamont, NY 12009

Hosts: Gerd and Laurie Beckmann
Location: Twelve miles southwest of Albany and Schenectady. Near SUNY and Union College. Two miles from Altamont. Thirty miles south of Saratoga. Across the street from Hendrick Appel's cemetery.

Open: Year round.
Rates: $45–$60 single, $60–$75 double. $10 third person. $10 child in room with adult. Infants free. MC, Visa.
♥ ♯ ⬛ ♣ ✕

Getaway guests, business travelers, and returnees who feel like family appreciate the large (15-by-25-foot) rooms in this house, which was built as a

(Please turn page.)

tavern in 1765. The pillars and solarium were added in 1900. When the hosts, not yet 25, bought this property in 1981, it was a private home on both the State and National registers.

To innkeeping, Laurie brought considerable food service experience. Gerd, a metallurgist who is now an RPI research manager, earned his PhD in 1992. The hosts, friends since they were 12, started collecting antiques (pocket watches and silver) in college days. At one point, Laurie had an antiques shop here. Now she offers bridal planning services as well as "simple to elegant" bridal gowns. For weddings or guests who want to go out to dinner in style, Gerd rents three antique autos.

In residence: In hosts' quarters, David, 10; Christopher, 6; and Jason, 4. Oreo, a Swiss mountain dog.
Foreign language spoken: German.
Breakfast: 7–9:30. Fruit, juices, homemade muffins or croissants, eggs, French toast, phyllo pastries, coffee and assorted teas. In oval solarium with wraparound windows overlooking grounds, flowing stream, and wishing well.
Bed and bath: Four rooms. On second floor, one with canopied brass double and pullout queen sofa shares claw-foot tub bath with room that has queen and a twin daybed; a fireplace with gas logs in each room. Two third-floor rooms, each with a double and a single bed, share a bath with claw-foot tub and shower. Cot and crib.
Plus: Third-floor bedroom ceiling fans. Evening beverages. Fireplaced living room. Games and TV. Guest refrigerator. Volleyball, croquet, badminton. Cross-country and downhill skiing (rentals nearby) and ice skating (on creek) on grounds.

From New Jersey: *"We loved the antiques, special linens, friendly hosts, and delicious food."*

Hilltop Cottage B&B   518/644–2492
P.O. Box 186, 6883 Lakeshore Drive, Bolton Landing, NY 12814

Hosts: Anita and Charlie Richards
Location: Quiet. Eastern Adirondack region, a half mile from village center on Route 9N. On two acres across the road from Lake George. Minutes from beaches, marinas, and the Sagamore luxury resort hotel. Eight miles from I–87 exit 22.
Open: Year round.
Rates: Shared bath, $35 single, $45 double. $55 private bath. $10 extra person. $65 cabin.
🛏 🍴 ♣ ✖ ⅙

From Pennsylvania: *"Make you feel like part of the family . . . share wealth of information about this charming area . . . a breakfast beyond compare.* From New York: *"A charming comfortable home. . . . Perfect location away from touristy area—yet walking distance to swimming, restaurants, and town. . . . Remarkable ability to be around when we needed something and out of sight when we wanted quiet and privacy."*

The retired educators—Charlie was a guidance counselor and Anita taught German—appreciate the cycling, hiking, and cross-country ski possibilities here. Since they acquired this house in 1985, they have redecorated and updated. Now they're restoring the greenhouse and working on the 110-year-old post-and-beam barn. Pictures reflect the estate area as it once was and the hosts' German background.

Anita had lived here with her family from the age of 8 until she was 25; at that time, this was the caretaker's house belonging to one of the estates along Millionaires' Row. (Anita's parents ran this house as a tourist home from 1950 to 1980.) For what to do or see, you couldn't find a better resource than Hilltop, a B&B since 1986. The Richardses' favorite little-known place is the Marcella Sembrich Opera Museum (open summers) just 150 yards down the road. Because Anita is now executive director, out-of-season guests, too, often have the opportunity to see the memorabilia from the golden age of opera and to have a guided tour of the parklike grounds bordering the lake.

In residence: Max the dog and cats Toby and Mietze "live mostly outdoors."
Foreign language spoken: Anita is fluent in German.
Bed and bath: Three second-floor rooms. One room has two twin beds (with the option of king size) and private shower bath. Two rooms share a bath with shower; one has a queen bed, the other two twin beds. Family bath available on first floor. Cabin has queen bed, TV, private shower bath, refrigerator.
Breakfast: 8–9:30. Fruits, homemade breads and coffee cakes, jams, jellies, plus standard fare, if requested; but Anita prefers to offer quiches, sausage-egg-cheese bake, German apple-and-potato pancakes, or French toast with locally produced maple syrup. In dining room or kitchen; or on screened porch shaded by lush Dutchman's-pipe vines.
Plus: Piano. Picnic table. Lawn chairs. Ample parking for boat trailers and RVs. Bedroom ceiling fans. Wood stove in living room.

The Lamplight Inn Bed & Breakfast

2129 Lake Avenue, P.O. Box 70   518/696–5294
Lake Luzerne, NY 12846-0070   800/262–4668

Hosts: Gene and Linda Merlino
Location: On Route 9N, surrounded by lawn and tall pines. Half a block to Lake Luzerne (swimming; winter ice skating and ice fishing). Minutes to antiques shops, restaurants, outlets, horseback riding (year round), two-hour hiking trail to mountaintop, hayrides, snowmobiles (tours for beginners), skiing. Ten miles from Lake George village; 17 north of Saratoga.
Open: Year round except Christmas Eve and Christmas Day. Three-night minimum on holiday weekends and during Saratoga Race Course season. Two-night minimum on other special events weekends.
Rates: May–July and September–October $110–$125 weekends, $80–$95 weekdays. November–April $80–$95 weekends, $75–$90 weekdays. August (Saratoga Race Course season) $125–$140 weekends, $95–110 weekdays. $25 third person. Dinner packages available. Amex, MC, Visa.
♥ ♣ ♦ ✖

(Please turn page.)

From New Jersey and Massachusetts: "I never wanted to leave! . . . Even though our room was one of the least expensive, it was nicely furnished with antiques and quilts and had a skylight that opened. . . . Extremely clean . . . amenities galore . . . a sewing basket too. . . . Plentiful, absolutely delicious, beautifully presented breakfasts . . . how they do it is beyond me. . . . Although on a main road, has a quiet, peaceful ambiance. . . . We were so impressed with the innkeepers and the inn that we returned with eight couples."

Some whim of a purchase in 1984! A Great Room with 12-foot beamed ceiling and chestnut wainscoting. A keyhole staircase also crafted in England. Back-to-back fireplaces. Eight-foot doors that lead out to a wraparound porch and lawns. And one bathroom (then). In New Jersey Gene, an electrician, carpenter, and plumber, was manager of a textile engraving business. Linda, the "comfortable Victorian" antiques expert/decorator/seamstress, was a textile artist. Since restoring the massive Victorian that had been built by a wealthy lumberman in 1890 as a summer Adirondack retreat, the Merlinos have added rooms, baths, and fireplaces. And a long list of enthusiastic fans.

In residence: Never upstairs: Toto, a husky/shepherd with an almost-famous howl heard if Merlinos aren't nearby.

Bed and bath: Ten centrally air-conditioned second-floor rooms; five with gas fireplaces. All with individual heat thermostat. All private baths; one with tub and shower, others shower only; eight en suite, two with bath across hall (robes provided). Queen (two are canopied), double, or double and a twin bed. Rollaway available.

Breakfast: 8:30–9:30. A highlight. Begin with buffet of homemade granola, fruit, cake or muffins. Gene's entree repertoire includes crepes, Belgian waffles, French toast, three-egg omelets, home fries and sausage; served by Linda in sun porch dining room with mountain view.

Plus: Ceiling fans in bedrooms and Great Room. Candy. Guest refrigerator. Perennial garden. Croquet. Badminton. Wicker- furnished wraparound porch with swing. Hammock suspended from pine trees. Flannel sheets. Picnic baskets. Reservations for you-name-it. March candlelit dinners. November murder mystery weekends. Linda's granola for sale. Wine and beer license.

Saratoga Bed and Breakfast   518/584–0920

434 Church Street, Saratoga Springs, NY 12866

Hosts: Noel and Kathleen Smith
Location: On a main road with rural characteristics on the outskirts of town. Within 2 miles of Saratoga Performing Arts Center, racetrack, shops; 200 yards to acclaimed restaurant. On seven acres with tall trees, lawn, gardens, and three buildings "including motel that came with the farmhouse." Near country lane for walkers and joggers.

Open: Year round. Two-night minimum on most weekends.
Rates: Double occupancy. Farmhouse $65–$95; $75 June and July, $110–$125 racing season and weekends. 1850 House suites $95–$125; $150–$195 racing season. Winter and arts center packages. Amex, MC, Visa.
♥ ♣ ♦

Zest! Love for "this fabulous town." For guests (lots from Ireland and Manhattan). For family (you'll probably meet relatives). For food. And for keeping up with the times.

"Whatever has become of this fine native that she wants to take in roomers?" wondered town fathers in 1984 when Kathleen and Noel, local restaurateurs, decided to open the town's first B&B in an 1860 farmhouse. In 1991 the Smiths—who still travel to Ireland several times a year—added a tower, private baths, and some fireplaces. They also bought the adjacent 1850 Federal brick house for more upscale accommodations. Nocl has a degree in hotel administration and is chef extraordinaire. Kathleen, "the social engineer," sometimes takes guests on tours that focus on architecture, culture, and history complete with stories of who married whom 40 years ago.

In residence: Assistants—daughters Ann, 14; Sheila, 20; Amy 23. Bates, a 100-pound yellow Labrador, "the best dog in America." Sam is Bates's cat.
Foreign language spoken: Canadian French.
Bed and bath: Eight air-conditioned rooms; all private baths. In Farmhouse—four second-floor rooms; two with working fireplace. Queen, double, or twin beds. In 1850 House—four suites (king bed in most) with fireplace, remote-control TV, private phone. Very private suite has two queen beds, two love seats, claw-foot tub and shower in bath.
Breakfast: 8:30–10. "A party." Juice. Fruit course. Blueberry-walnut pancakes or ratatouille omelets. Irish scones or corn muffins.
Plus: "Almost any request fulfilled." Upright piano in farmhouse. Babysitting. Guest refrigerator. Fresh flowers. Bathrobes. Transportation to/from local airport, train and bus stations; taxi is $2.50 anywhere in town.

> From New York: *"Romantic. Private. Beautiful. Extremely clean. Knowledge of town was entertaining and helpful. A very special place."*

The Six Sisters Bed and Breakfast   518/583–1173

149 Union Avenue   fax 518/587–2470
Saratoga Springs, NY 12866-3518

Hosts: Kate Benton and Steve Ramirez
Location: Across from racetrack and National Museum of Racing. Within walking distance of downtown shopping, antiques, museums, restaurants.
Open: Year round. Four-night minimum in racing season. Three nights during special events.

Rates: Double occupancy. January–March and November–December $65–$80. April–July and September–October $85–$100. Racing season (August) $195–$215. $20 extra person. Discounts to seniors and to extended stay and business travelers. Package rates with arts center, spa, restaurant.
♥ ⬛ ⁂ ◆ ✗ ✂

> From New Jersey: *"Traditional decor . . . great home- away-from-home atmosphere . . . innkeepers who are sensitive to guests' needs. . . . Used to go out for brunch in Saratoga before we found the Six Sisters . . . coffee and fruit available when we go out for early golf. . . . Watch the action from porch rockers with tasty*

(Please turn page.)

snacks served. . . . The best part is when Kate opens the door and says, 'Welcome home.'"

The Victorian "built around 1880 with scallop-edged roof and basket weave porch added about 20 years later" was just what Kate was dreaming about in 1989 when she decided to return to her roots. For 14 years she had been in Hawaii, where she attended college, worked as a guidance counselor, and met Steve, her husband, an audiovisual teacher who has become a breakfast cook acclaimed by *Gourmet* magazine. Kate, daughter of a former mayor—and daughter and granddaughter of Saratoga Springs hoteliers (Grand Union Hotel)—grew up in a family of six sisters (hence the B&B name) and six brothers who "are waiting." Now she is involved with historic preservation. Steve, president of the New York State B&B association, is a tour guide "in this wonderful walking city."

In residence: Astor and Kela, wire-haired fox terriers, "love guests and guests love them."
Bed and bath: Four large rooms, each furnished in a different style; all private baths. First floor—king bed, full bath. Upstairs—two rooms with king bed, shower bath; one has nonworking fireplace and private balcony. Suite has two double beds, living room with TV, eating area, private patio, shower and tub bath.
Breakfast: Usually 8:00–9:30. Fresh fruit. Thickly sliced honey oat bread French toast. Homemade apple crisp. Maple sausage. Or vegetable/cheese quiche with bacon and apple biscuits. Macadamia nut coffee. In candlelit dining room.
Plus: Air conditioners and ceiling fans in bedrooms. Late-afternoon beverages. Candy and cookies in rooms. Fresh flowers. Guest refrigerator. Off-street parking. Pickup service at train station.

Union Gables   518/584–1558
55 Union Avenue, Saratoga Springs, NY 12866   800/398–1558

Hosts: Jody and Tom Roohan
Location: On a main street with other Victorian houses and B&Bs. Short walk to shopping, restaurants, convention center, Saratoga Race Course, and National Museum of Racing. One and a half miles from the New York Northway (I–87) exit 14.
Open: Year round. Closed Christmas week.
Rates: $80–90 per room; $180 in August. Amex, MC, Visa.
♦ ♣

"It was like Christmas watching all the furnishings come in. They finished wallpapering the dining room ceiling at 3:30 and the grand opening began at 5 [in June 1992]."

    And that's when the Jody first saw the work done by a team of interior designers who, in just four months, had transformed all 10,000 square feet of this 1901 Queen Anne Victorian that is complete with octagonal tower rooms. Originally a summer home, for 30 years a Skidmore College dormitory (Furness House), and for another 17 years a home for adults with developmental disabilities (who now reside in smaller group homes), it's now a popular "tour home," a B&B where guests often ask for the designer's name, for a resource, or for a method (for reproducing a glaze or lincrusta).

Tom, a Realtor whose office is across the street, oversaw the restoration and the installation of five furnaces and air-conditioning and sprinkler systems. Jody, too, is a master juggler. When Mary was an only child, this flexible couple ran a local ski area together.

In residence: Mary, 11, "assistant innkeeper." Trey, 8; Danny, 6; Kevin, 5.
Foreign language spoken: Minimal French.
Bed and bath: Ten spacious corner rooms (two are suites) with king or queen beds (suites have a queen and two twin beds) on second and third floors; all with private baths (four full, six shower only). Rollaway and crib available.
Breakfast: 8–10. Intentionally unstructured. Juice, cereals, freshly baked goods from local shops, fruit, yogurt, hot beverages. Eat on porch, in dining room, or in your own room.
Plus: Central air conditioning. Television, private phone, and refrigerator in each room. Thick bath sheets. Babysitting. Snacks. Coffee, tea, ice always available. Several bicycles (with helmets) for loan. Huge wicker-furnished porch with glider too. Restaurant recommendations and reservations.

The Westchester House B&B   518/587–7613

102 Lincoln Avenue, P.O. Box 944, Saratoga Springs, NY 12866

Hosts: Bob and Stephanie Melvin
Location: A quiet neighborhood with tree-lined streets and Victorian homes. Two blocks behind Congress Park and Broadway; 3 blocks from racetrack. Within walking distance of Skidmore College, Performing Arts Center, Museum of Dance, town walking tours, state park with groomed cross-country trails.

Open: Year round except January. Two-night minimum in July; three-night minimum on August weekends.
Rates: Per room, $70–$100. Jazz Festival–Labor Day, $15 more. Racing season, $175–$200.

♥ ❖ ♦ ✗ ✄

From Maryland: *"A warm home rather than a museum . . . and plumbing, wiring, and heating that is up to snuff with the newest hotels!"* From California: *"It wasn't the beautiful home, the careful lighting next to the beds for reading and at the washbasin, or the Victorian lace curtains that made me want to return. Bob and Stephanie's personal touch made my stay all the more enjoyable."*

Stephanie still finds time to sing opera and classical music. Bob, a former computer analyst, is also delighted with their carefully selected location, which offers rich cultural and recreational opportunities. In 1987 this personable couple transformed a well-built 1885 Queen Anne Victorian that had been a rooming house for 50 years. From Washington, D.C., they brought their collections—ranging from pre–Civil War antiques to contemporary art glass. After the inn became a "painted lady" in 1991, it received local and state preservation awards. "We, too, are delighted with the interaction here. Some guests, designers, gave a personalized museum tour of their display in

(Please turn page.)

progress. Others have suggested garden ideas (hence the name of each garden) or given impromptu seminars on antique jewelry or carousel restoration. Guests discuss a concert or the Saratoga baths, or they solve the problems of the world."

In residence: Tiger Lily, "a 35-pound, mostly Labrador retriever who shares the social responsibilities with us."

Bed and bath: Seven air-conditioned rooms with ceiling fans, all private tiled baths. On first floor, ornate brass Victorian queen bed, shower bath, signed hand-hooked rug. Second floor—corner room with Victorian queen bed, tub/shower bath. Queen brass bed, bay window, shower bath. Corner room with two Louis XVI beds, oversized shower, balcony. High Eastlake Gothic queen bed, shower bath. Double bed, shower bath. Corner room with double bed, oversized shower.

Breakfast: 8–9:30. Freshly squeezed orange juice. Fresh fruit. Local freshly baked goods, tea, "our own blend of freshly ground imported coffee." A lively family-style affair in formal dining room with china and crystal by arched window overlooking century-old maple tree.

Plus: Afternoon social hour with beverages in parlor or garden or on wraparound porch. Baby grand piano. Stereo system. Extensive library. Chocolates and fresh flowers in rooms. Old-fashioned gardens.

The Inn on Bacon Hill   518/695–3693

200 Wall Street, Schuylerville, NY
Mailing address: P.O. Box 1462, Saratoga Springs, NY 12866

Host: Andrea Collins-Breslin
Location: Surrounded by dairy and horse farms, 12 minutes east of restaurants, Saratoga's racetracks, Performing Arts Center, Battlefield. Eight miles from I–87 (Northway); 45 minutes to Albany, Lake George, and Vermont.
Open: Year round. Two-day mini-

mum on weekends during August thoroughbred racing season only.
Rates: June–July, and September–October, $65 double shared bath, $75 private bath, $85 suite. August racing season, $50 more. November–March, 10 percent less. MC, Visa (for balance after deposit).
♦ �>< ✔

From New York, Rhode Island, Virginia, California, Connecticut: *"Breakfasts are best meals we've had in the area. . . . Lovingly restored and beautifully maintained. . . . Greeted by two enthusiastic women, a mother and daughter team with boundless energy and good humor. . . . Quiet and peaceful. . . . Well-loved herb and flower garden wrapped around the historic, elegant gentleman farmhouse. . . . Comfortably furnished rooms with fresh flowers, basket of toiletries, robes. . . . Enjoyed distinct absence of television. . . . Called to the dining room by classical music echoing up the stairs. . . . Felt as if we had known other guests for years. . . . From the bedroom window, the peaceful sight of waving corn stretching down the hill. . . . It was the experience more than anything that made this visit remarkable."*

The fans rave on and on about this personalized B&B. It's an 1862 Victorian mansion restored and redecorated in four months by Andrea and her mother, an artist, while Mark, Andrea's husband, a consulting engineer, was out of town. It has original moldings and border paper, bay windows, a kerosene chandelier converted to electricity, and marble fireplaces. For Andrea, the career change made in 1987 is such a perfect fit that she has transferred her 18 years of corporate world (career counseling at General Electric) experience to off-season getaway/innkeeping workshop weekends held for just three couples.

A baby grand piano is in the Victorian parlor suite. The Queen Anne guest living room is less formal. There are books galore. A stereo. A wicker-furnished porch. And a screened gazebo overlooking farmland and the distant Vermont hills.

In residence: "Vicki, a gentle golden retriever. Muffin, a friendly cock-a-poo "similar to Benji," lives with Andrea's mother, Millie Rekdal, in the carriage house next door.
Bed and bath: Four rooms. First floor, queen-bedded room with tub and shower bath. Private adjoining shower bath for suite with spacious parlor and 10-by-10 double-bedded room. On second floor, room with two twin beds shares a shower bath with room that has a queen four-poster bed.
Breakfast: Usually at 8:45. Different entree daily; maybe French toast and bacon, blueberry pancakes and sausage, or egg souffle with meats. Juice, fruit, homemade muffins and jams, cold cereals, coffee, tea. "Can last up to two hours!"
Plus: Central air conditioning. Welcoming refreshments.

The Widow Kendall House
518/370–5511

10 North Ferry Street   (New York state only) **800/244–0925**
Schenectady, NY 12305   fax **518/382–2640**

Host: Richard Brown
Location: On quiet street in "stockade" historic district. Near Union College, General Electric, Mohawk River parks and bike path; antiquing; 23 miles south of Saratoga Springs.

Open: Year round.
Rates: Per room. $95 May–October. $90 November–April.
♥ ♨ ✿ ◆

> From Washington, D.C., and New York: *"The house is very old and wonderfully renovated and decorated. Subtly updated . . . Rich Brown is a warm and gracious fellow. . . . Delicious breakfasts are attractively presented. . . . Very comfortable, relaxing, quaint, and romantic. The bathrooms and kitchen are as beautiful as you would see in a magazine."*

"One room at a time" is Rich's secret to restoration. After 10 restoring years, friends suggested B&B to the host, an attorney whose partner is in theater arts. "Modernized" in 1836 with interior Greek Revival moldings, the brick-front colonial saltbox still has "a charmingly tipsy front door and, in the back, beautiful gardens." When the house was built in 1790, Widow Annie Kendall served cakes and ale here. Richard has furnished with antiques and reproductions. He lends bicycles. He directs guests to walking tours, the gardens at Union College, or the historical society. Many write about "the perfect host."

(Please turn page.)

Bed and bath: Three rooms. Two second-floor queen-bedded rooms (one with wood-burning fireplace) share a bath with Jacuzzi and walk-in shower plus a half bath. Across the garden to next-door house (home of Rich's office too) for double-bedded room with a connecting shower/tub bath to room with three-quarter bed.

Breakfast: 6:30–10:30. Fresh muffins, croissants, or bagels. Fresh fruit cup and juice. Hot or cold cereal. Cheese or mushroom omelets; sometimes pancakes or French toast. Bacon, yogurt, low-fat cottage cheese, raisins. Served in large kitchen or in dining room.

Plus: Air-conditioned bedrooms. Tea. Fresh flowers in rooms. Fireplaced parlor. Guest pickup at nearby Amtrak or bus station. Babysitting arranged. Kitchen and laundry facilities. Often, cuttings from herb garden.

The American Country Collection
Host #005

Stillwater, NY

Location: Quiet. In the country on 100 acres with mountain views. Nine miles from Skidmore College. Fifteen minutes from Saratoga Springs, one-quarter mile from Saratoga National Historical Park with cross-country trails. Four miles from Saratoga Lake, 25 to Lake George.

Reservations: Year round through The American Country Collection, page 142.

Rates: September–June, $75 suites and first-floor queen; $65 second-floor queen; $10 one-night surcharge. July until two days before racing season, $95 and $85, $15 one-night surcharge. August (racing season), Jazz Festival, and Christmas–New Year's, $105 and $95, with three-night minimum stay.

♥ ⛵ ♣ ♦ ✗ ⚹

Such foresight! It's almost 25 years since the hosts decided to leave the city for the peaceful countryside. That's when they converted a barn built in 1800 to an exquisite home, a blend of old and new with original beams on angled ceilings. When the children were grown, the hosts, both in finance and real estate, opened one room for B&B guests. The match was right. Now more travelers enjoy good food and conversation surrounded by country decor in this quiet retreat.

In residence: One German shepherd.

Bed and bath: Four rooms (two are suites) with private attached baths. First floor—queen bed, shower and tub bath. Second floor—room with queen bed, shower bath; two king-bedded suites with shower and tub baths.

Breakfast: About 9. Menu decided ahead of time, according to guests' choice. Could include fresh fruit (homegrown raspberries in season) and pancakes or eggs. In dining room or on deck.

Plus: Flowers, Candy. Fruit. Bedroom ceiling fans. Brick patio. Countryside for jogging, cycling, walking.

__ Adirondacks Reservation Service __

Adirondack Bed & Breakfasts

10 Park Place, Saranac Lake, NY 12983-1837

Phone: 518/891–1632 or 800/552–2627 (daily).

Listings: 25 and growing. Mostly B&Bs; some inns and a few private residences. Located throughout Adirondack Park including Bolton Landing, Blue Mountain Lake, Elizabethtown, Essex, Gore Mountain, Keene Valley, Lake Clear, Lake George, Lake Placid, Lake Pleasant, Long Lake, Malone, Old Forge, North Hudson, Plattsburgh, Saranac Lake, Warrensburg. For directory send self-addressed stamped envelope.

Reservations: Minimum of two weeks' notice preferred, but "spur-of-moment calls" often accommodated. Two-night minimum required.

Rates: $35–$85 single, $46–$95 double. Family and weekly rates available. One night's rate required as deposit. If cancellation is received at least seven days prior to scheduled arrival, deposit refunded minus $15 processing fee. MC, Visa. ◆

Nadia Korths established this service in early 1992 to provide a central booking number for a region she knows well. "This is a 100-year-old, 9,000-square-mile state park where each B&B is within minutes' drive of canoeing, hiking, or cross-country skiing. The diversity among the 130,000 park residents is well represented by hosts." An Adirondack resident for almost 20 years, Nadia has been a local chamber of commerce staffer for 6. She is fluent in French.

Unless otherwise stated, rates in this book are per room for two and include breakfast in addition to all the amenities in "Plus." As for taxes and gratuities, please see page xi.

——————— Adirondacks B&Bs ———————

Trail's End
518/576–9860
Trail's End Road, P.O. Box 793, Keene Valley, NY 12943   800/281–9860

Hosts: Laura and Ray Nardell
Location: Secluded. At base of hiking and cross-country ski trails. On three acres with big lawn and mountain views. "Near all the highest peaks." Eighteen miles south of Lake Placid. Within walking distance of two restaurants.

Open: Year round.
Rates: $35 single. $65–$80 double. $110 suite. $10–$12.50 extra person. Fifteen percent less in April, May, November, and December 1–19. MC, Visa.
🚶 ♣ ♦ 🛬 ⚓

"It's homey and rustic, with plenty of space inside and out. We are definitely not the crystal and silver kind of place. Our guests love the outdoors regardless of the weather. Some even hike up Marcy in mud season! There's lots of conversation about hiking and skiing trails, and rock and ice climbing too. This B&B, the oldest (1962) in Keene Valley, was built in the 1900s with big brick fireplaces, French doors, Palladian windows, hardwood floors, and screened porches. When we came here in 1991, it fulfilled our dream of bringing up a family in the area where we met during ski season. We've done a lot of work, keeping the pedestal sinks and claw-foot tubs, and have started on wallpapering. Ray, a computer teacher at a private boarding school, is the talented carpenter-in-residence. By the time your book is out, we'll be painting the outside. Our country antiques are enhanced with my mother's crafts—dried wreaths and flower arrangements, little dolls, quilts, and pillows."

Laura was head track and cross-country coach at West Virginia University. Ray is from Philadelphia.

In residence: Nicholas is two years old. Sibling expected just as book went to press. Marty, the cat, is not allowed in guests' area. Bo, a Labrador retriever.
Bed and bath: Eight large rooms; five have private screened porch (sometimes enjoyed for sleeping). Seven share three large full baths; several have sink in bedroom. Private full bath for two-room suite (sleeps 2–6) with porch. Room with working fireplace has double four-poster, sink in room, porch. Other rooms (most sleep 3–5) have king/twins option, double, and/or single beds. Plus a bunkhouse with kitchen and fireplace that sleeps 10.
Breakfast: 7–9. (It's usually over by 9.) Intentionally hearty. Blueberry pancakes with sausage or scrambled eggs with broccoli, ham, or cheese; home fries, freshly baked biscuits, and fruit. Oatmeal and cold cereals. On glassed-in porch; parents linger while watching kids play soccer and volleyball.
Plus: Two fireplaced living rooms; fireplaced dining room; very wide front porch. Electric piano. TV, VCR, stereo. Winterized sun porch with toys and games. Guest refrigerator and microwave. Trail lunches $5. Weekend dinners by reservation $12.95/person for minimum of 10. Babysitting with advance notice.

From New York: *"A welcome antidote to New York City's normal hyper pace."*

Stagecoach Inn

518/523-9474

Old Military Road, Lake Placid, NY 12946

Host: Lyn Witte
Location: On a side road in wooded residential neighborhood between Routes 73 and 86. One mile from Lake Placid Village.
Open: Year round. Two or three nights minimum on weekends and holidays; four nights during Christmas holiday week.

Rates: Double occupancy. Shared bath $55. Private bath $65 twins, $75-$80 double, $90 double bed and working fireplace. Singles $10 less. Triple $10 more. Deposit required.
♥ ✻ ◆

When you relax in the rustic two-storied Adirondack living room complete with balcony made of birch logs, you know you're in a former stagecoach stop filled with legend and history. Revived as an inn in 1977, the farmhouse-style clapboarded building with a long front porch still has wainscoting throughout, bark on the main support beams, and two fireplace mantels fashioned from half a log. But the hard jigsaw puzzle has gone—home with the family that worked on it during visits over a three-year period. Lyn's most recent changes include new slipcovers for the sofas, a porcelain doll collection, and handmade quilts for some of the beds. Before becoming innkeeper here in 1982, she was a host in her own home and executive secretary to the president of the 1980 Olympics Committee. She also has experience in the ski business. An application has been filed for listing on the National Register of Historic Places.

In residence: Baroness Theodora, an Old English sheepdog, "loved and spoiled by all."
Foreign language spoken: A little French.
Bed and bath: Nine rooms, no two alike, on first and second floors. Baths—most are private—are full, some with claw-footed tub and hand-held shower. Twin, double or antique three-quarter (many brass) beds. Suite possibility. Two rooms with working fireplace; one with cable TV. Two have ceiling fans. One room with private entrance for pets. Rollaway bed.
Breakfast: 8–9:30. Waffles with ham, cream cheese, and pineapple; scrambled eggs, sausage, and bread; Danish pancakes or French toast; or "sammies"—egg/ham/cheese on English muffins. Fruits, juice, coffee, tea, milk. Served in breakfast room with fireplace and garden view.
Plus: Fireplaced living room with color cable TV. Front porch rockers. Picnic table in back yard. Babysitting arranged. Guest pick-up at bus station.

From England: *"The nicest place we've stayed in in New York state."* From Canada: *"Quiet, charming, lovely antiques everywhere."* From New York: *"Probably our tenth stay. Continues to be the best."*

---

*T*hink *of bed and breakfast as a people-to-people concept.*

Hinchings Pond B&B Inn   315/376–8296
P.O. Box 426, Lowville, NY 13367

Hosts: Skip and Connie Phelps
Location: Overlooking a private 18-acre, 50-foot-deep glacial pond. One hour north of Rome; under two hours from Syracuse; 1½ miles east of Chases Lake; 20 minutes east of Lowville; 45 southeast of Watertown/Fort Drum. "A wide range of excellent restaurants within 20–30 minutes' drive."

Open: Year round except during April "spring thaw."
Rates: $45–$65 weekdays. $60–65 weekends and holidays. No charge for crib. Family, business, and clergy rates available. MC, Visa.
♥ ♣ ✗ ⅄

"No neighborhood" was the translation of the perfect description one Japanese exchange student gave to another when talking about this Adirondack-style rustic house. Designed and built in 1990 by Skip, who is in the construction business, and his family, it's on 125 private acres surrounded by "millions in state park land." Guests explore some of the 45 miles of horse trails that mountain bikers consider one of the Northeast's best-kept secrets. They skate by day and night, play hockey, snowshoe, cross-country ski, and get pulled by a snow scoot on ice. During the summer there's that crystal-clear blue spring-fed pond, from which water was once bottled and sold. Swim, snorkel, fish, or canoe. Enjoy the sandy beach. A panoramic view of the pond is available from the living room, cathedral-ceilinged dining room, screened porches, and deck.

Here the Phelpses have combined their desire to bring up a family in a backcountry environment, their love for Adirondack Park (where they lived in a winterized camp for five years), and their memories of wonderful European pensions.

In residence: Hunter, age 15, knows the woods, marks trails, and plots routes according to guests' ability and desire. Austin, age 12, knows the art of hospitality "and has a way of making each guest feel 'special.'" Logan, age 10, is known as the resident social director who matches guests to appropriate board and card games.
Bed and bath: Five second-level rooms. Two rooms with queen beds and private shower baths. One two-bedroom family suite with connecting shower bath. Other rooms have two twin beds, private shower baths.
Breakfast: 8–9:30. Most-requested recipes—Skip's bread pudding and Connie's baked oatmeal with warm berry sauce. Other possibilities—coddled eggs, fried bread, French toast, bacon or ham, baked apples, local Mennonite breads and pastries. Juice, fruit, hot beverages.
Plus: Huge open soapstone wood stove in dining room. Dinners ($8–$15 per person) with prior reservation. Babysitting if arranged in advance. Outdoor campfire ring. Kitchen privileges—often enjoyed by groups who book entire B&B. Driving or skiing directions to local craftsmen who practice the almost-lost art of Adirondack guide boat building.

Crislip's Bed & Breakfast   518/793-6869

RD 1, Box 57, Ridge Road, Queensbury, NY 12804

Hosts: Ned and Joyce Crislip
Location: On Route 9L, 4 miles from I-87 exit 19. Midway (about 15 minutes) north of Saratoga and south of Lake George's recreation area. An hour to Albany or Killington, Vermont. Near Glens Falls summer opera performances. Ten minutes to West Mountain; 45 minutes south of Gore Mountain. Half mile from Warren County airport.
Open: Year round.
Rates: $55 September–June. $65 July, $75 August. Singles $10 less. $10 per child. MC, Visa.
♥ 🏡 🛏 ♣ ✄

A hitching post and carriage mount are in front of the early 19th-century Federal-style house. (At one time the surrounding land was the largest working farm in the county.) Williamsburg decor is featured in the guest rooms of this third restoration done by Ned, a vocal music teacher, and his wife, Joyce, a former teacher.

Originally the residence of the town's first doctor, the Quaker-built home was used for many years as a training center for young medical interns. The Crislips bought the property from a family that had owned it for over a century. Since opening as a B&B in 1984, the enthusiastic hosts find that business travelers appreciate the home atmosphere. Vacationing guests are interested in antiques, music, eating, and skiing. Some of them follow the hosts' suggestion and visit the Hyde Collection in Glens Falls.

In residence: Britta, a Shih Tzu. Amber is a cat.
Bed and bath: Four rooms. On first floor, one large efficiency with double four-poster bed, private shower bath. On second floor, a room with king-sized four-poster, private shower bath. One double room with canopied double bed, private full bath. One room with three-quarter Jenny Lind bed, shared bath, for children or other family member.
Breakfast: Until 10. Juice, sausage, eggs, English muffins, or pancakes and syrup. Prepared by both hosts and served on linens in dining room, which adjoins keeping room with massive stone cooking fireplace and sun room with view of lawn, stone walls, and mountains.
Plus: Living room with grand piano. Tour of the large and interesting house. Bedroom fans. Bedroom air conditioners (rarely needed) available. Front porch with view of mountains and, in late September, the balloon festival.

Adirondack Bed & Breakfasts Host #10

Saranac Lake, NY

Location: Way up on a hill in historic neighborhood overlooking the village "and the mountains that ring all around us." Within minutes' walk of everything—a mile-long walk around pond; a mountain hike (great view of Saranac Lakes); boat trips through locks; concerts; restaurants; shops. Near winter cross-country skiing, dogsled races and winter carnival. Ten miles west of Lake Placid.
Reservations: Year round through Adirondack Bed & Breakfasts, page 153.
Rates: $45 single. $55 double.
♥ 🛏 ♣ ✈ ✄

(Please turn page.)

Country Living photographed and published Susan's touch—potpourri, a greenhouse porch, a drying room. Magazine staffers wrote, "We love your house—lots of magic and flowers!" in the guest book. Then, in 1989, Susan and Glenn opened their turn-of-the-century Queen Anne house as a B&B. Fans from all over the world appreciate the peaceful ambiance—not fancy, not cutesy, but filled with original furnishings, Aunt Josie's down sofa, Susan's creative dried arrangements, books, carved cherry woodwork, refinished floors, all those added-on cure porches—"a little bit like being in the clouds"—and even a ceiling with pattern recreated by squeezing plaster through a cookie cutter mold. The restoration—"15 years and still more to go"—has been done by the acclaimed B&B chef, Glenn, an electrical contractor, a Saranac Lake native who knows every trail around. Outside he built cobblestone-walled beds that are filled with perennials and herbs. Susan, the local youth center director who met Glenn when he had the natural food store, loves sharing this house, this "magical town," Adirondack history, driving routes, and museum suggestions. By request, she'll tell the story of early guests, cyclists in search of a wedding site, who got married in this National Register house "within an hour!" Guests *and* hosts refer to this B&B as a retreat, a place for rejuvenation.

In residence: One cat "who captures guests' hearts."
Foreign language spoken: "Speak French slowly and, with the aid of translation book, it will work."
Bed and bath: Four third-floor rooms. One with double bed, private tub/shower bath. Three share third-floor tub/shower bath and second-floor tub/shower bath. One room has queen poster bed, sun porch with sofa and rocking chair; one room has double bed, sun porch, sofa, and rocking chair; one room has single bed.
Breakfast: 8–9. Orange juice, fresh fruit, homemade raspberry streusel muffins. Entree might be bread pudding with blueberry sauce, French toast with orange sauce or pineapple souffle. Coffee and herbal teas. With music— maybe American Indian flute or Irish Celtic harp. In dining room.

---

*One out of five guests leaves with
the dream of opening a B&B.*

Syracuse Area Reservation Service

Elaine's Bed & Breakfast Reservation Service

4987 Kingston Road, Elbridge, NY 13060

Phone: 315/689–2082 after 10 a.m.

Listings: 50 hosted private residences located in about 25 different communities—from Syracuse east to Rome, west to Geneva, south to Homer, and north to Watertown. For directory send self-addressed stamped envelope.

Reservations: At least two weeks' notice preferred; at least two months' for major college weekends. Last-minute reservations sometimes accommodated.

Rates: $40–$70 single. $50–$150 double. Senior citizen discounts for stays of five days or more. Weekly rates available. Refund minus $10 processing if cancellation is received at least two weeks before scheduled arrival date. ♦

Elaine, who hosted Syracuse's very first B&B in a private home, developed this reservation service to fill a need. Her listings—everything from contemporary to historic, from urban to lakeside, cover an ever-expanding area. Most do not allow smoking. Breakfasts range from full to serve-yourself. Both private and shared baths are available. A warm welcome is the keynote with all hosts.

Many B&Bs that allow smoking restrict it to certain rooms and/or public areas. Although some of those B&Bs that have the ✕ symbol allow smoking on the porch and/or patio, others do not allow smoking anywhere on the property.

___Syracuse/Finger Lakes Area B&Bs___

Patchwork Peace Bed & Breakfast 607/566–2443
4279 Waterbury Hill Road, Avoca, NY 14809

Hosts: Bill and Betty Mitchell
Location: Quiet. In the middle of 300 acres of woods, barns, and farmland, 1 mile up hill from Route 415. Four and a half miles from I–390/Route 17. About 30 miles to SUNY Alfred, Keuka College, Alfred University; 40 to SUNY Geneseo; 30 to Corning; 20 to Keuka Lake; 40 to Canandaigua Lake. Near a small pottery and a miniature horse farm.
Open: Year round.
Rates: Shared bath $30 twin bed, $40 double bed, $45 queen. Private bath $60. Singles $5 less. $10 rollaway. No charge for portacrib.
♥ 🛏 ⚛ ✗ ⚲

> From New York: *"The most comfortable and immaculate accommodations possible in the most beautiful countryside this side of Eden . . . genuinely warm hosts . . . daughter just finished freshman year at Geneseo SUNY—please God, we'll spend many visits with Betty and Bill."* From Texas: *"Truly wonderful . . . about 100 cows up on the hill, about a quarter mile from the house . . . huge barns and silos with the most gorgeous scenery you can imagine . . . most helpful in advising places of interest . . . enjoyed playing the piano and singing together."* From New Mexico: *"Hospitality went beyond the call."* From Pennsylvania: *"Nicely decorated . . . a special place . . . eating with the hosts makes breakfast an event."* From New York: *"We stayed one week . . . delightful . . . books and toys to keep our three-year-old happy."* From New Jersey: *"More like visiting family. . . . Visited barn and petted new calf. . . . My dad was hesitant, but now he is as anxious to return as the rest of us."*

Guests from all over the country want the world to know that this is what many seasoned travelers call "a real B&B." It's a neat 1925 clapboard farmhouse purchased in 1983 by the Mitchells from the great-grandson of the original family. The floors and woodwork are refinished. Old-fashioned quilting parties are held here in the winter. Bill, who farms, as he has for 50 years, "next door," likes the idea of "traveling by having the world come to us!" Betty, who happily shares recipes, has experience as town clerk, bookkeeper, sales clerk, and tutor for Literacy Volunteers.

In residence: "Whiskers is a kind, vocal terrier who warms up to guests quickly."
Bed and bath: Four second-floor rooms. Private full bath for queen-bedded room that has ceiling fan and balcony. Three rooms—with twin, double, or queen bed—share hall bath that has claw-foot tub and hand-held shower. Rollaway and portacrib available.
Breakfast: Usually 8–9. (As early as 5:30 for hunters.) Juice. Fresh fruit cup. Quiche, French toast, or pancakes with homegrown pork sausage or bacon. Homemade breads, muffins, and jams. Plenty of hot beverages.

Plus: Sun-dried linens. Soft drinks. Mints on pillow. Individual heat thermostat. Picnic baskets for two (with wine) $15. In season, opportunities to observe planting and harvesting.

Four Seasons Bed & Breakfast

470 West Lake Road	(June–October) **607/868–4686**
Route 54A, Branchport, NY 14418	(November–May) **607/732–5581**

Hosts: Brent and Martha Olmstead
Location: On 2½ acres along a scenic road that follows Keuka Lake's west shoreline. Five miles south of Branchport. Nine miles north of Hammondsport. Minutes' drive to six wineries, four lakefront restaurants. Three-minute walk to private beach. Half hour to Corning Glass Center or Watkins Glen Raceway.
Open: Daily May 15–October 15. Weekends, rest of year, by reservation only. Two-night minimum on weekends, holidays, and special events.
Rates: $60–$85 per room.
♥ ⬛ ⁂ ✈ ⚅

I wanted to move right into this century-old jewel with its vaulted living room ceiling and walls done with old barn siding. Quilts, collectibles, lots of wicker, and treasures from the Olmsteads' world travels are everywhere. Martha's magic touch extends to culinary arts too.

To this setting the Elmira natives bring many interests. Brent, a practicing physician, is an accomplished violinist. Martha, a registered nurse, has served as wine chairman for a regional cookbook. When Martha says, "We go with the flow," she really means it. Sometimes the house is filled with cyclists. Then along come a bride and groom who have just been married in a hot-air balloon. Visitors from all over Europe, regatta participants, family reunions, and church groups have found it too. Go and experience.

In residence: "Muffin, our non-meowing cat, is not allowed in guest rooms."
Bed and bath: Four carpeted and wallpapered bedrooms, with either double or twin beds. First floor: double bed, private shower bath. Second floor: three rooms (two open onto hallway balcony overlooking barn-sided living room) share a tub/shower bath.
Breakfast: 8–9 weekdays; 9–10 weekends. Different entree daily. Could be puffed apple pancake, cheese strata, French toast, or eggs Mornay. Homemade coffee cakes, muffins, bread puddings, seasonal fruits. In dining room, by windowed wall with views of evergreens and bird feeders. Sometimes on decks.
Plus: Large rear decks. Chaises longues and chairs on expansive lawn. Open front porch. Fireplaced living room. Den with color TV. Private beach. Beach towels. Boat trailer parking. Bicycle storage.

---

*T*hink *of bed and breakfast as a people-to-people concept.*

The Red House Country Inn　　607/546–8566

Finger Lakes National Forest
4586 Picnic Area Road, Burdett, NY 14818-9716

Hosts: Sandy Schmanke and Joan Martin
Location: In New York State's only national forest, with 28 miles of maintained (year round) trails at the door. On the east side of Seneca Lake. Short drives to Glen Gorge, Corning Glass Center, swimming, wineries.
Open: Year round except Thanksgiving and Christmas Day. Two-night minimum on weekends and holidays.
Rates: $39 single bed. $70 double and twin bed or double bed with working fireplace. $85 queen bed. $10 extra person. Amex, Discover, MC, Visa.
♥ ✕ ✂

> Guests wrote (and wrote): *"Serene. . . . Surpassed all our expectations. . . . Thirteen satisfied middle-age adults feel we discovered this delightful place. . . . Comfortable country atmosphere. . . . Many interesting items, each with a story. . . . Breakfast is a celebration. . . . Plenty of hot water, fresh thick towels daily, even a supply of shampoo. . . . We walked, talked, played the piano and pump organ, joked, snoozed. . . . Perfect for hiking, fishing, bird-watching, berry picking, cycling, cross-country skiing, and peace of mind. . . . Gracious hostesses who share their corner of paradise."*

One of a kind. The only private property in the forest. (The only farm not purchased by the federal government during the Great Depression.) Built in 1844, restored by owners in the 1970s, and purchased in 1981 by Sandy and Joan, who opened it as a freshly wallpapered inn in 1983. Since, they have built an addition and landscaped five acres of lawns and gardens. They have been featured in *New York Alive* and *New York* magazine and have been etched in the hearts of guests and their friends and relatives. Before becoming innkeepers (once they discovered the shortage of guest rooms in the area) Sandy owned a media buying service and Joan, also in Rochester, New York, was in TV and radio production and business management.

In residence: In hosts' quarters only, Samoyeds Tucker, Susie, and Muffin. The goats—Nellie, Annie, Sarah, Andy, and Tina—have their own quarters.
Bed and bath: Five second-floor rooms share four full baths. One room has a single bed. One with double bed, working fireplace. Two with a double and a single bed in each. Master bedroom has a queen four-poster bed plus a queen hide-a-bed. Rollaway available.
Breakfast: 8–9:30. Fresh fruit, freshly squeezed orange juice, or local grape juice. Homemade popovers or scones and jams. Fresh eggs with slab bacon or honey-glazed ham. Homemade Pilgrim's bread, apple flaps, or cinnamon crisp French toast. Freshly ground coffees, fine teas. In two dining rooms with sterling and crystal.
Plus: Afternoon tea. Candy. Bedroom fans. Huge in-ground pool with deck, cabana, and kitchen with grill. Flower-bedecked veranda. Horseshoes, darts. Picnic area. Cross-country skiing. Gift shop. November–April, option of dinner ($20 per person) with reservations.

Lakeview Farm Bed n' Breakfast   716/554-6973

4761 Route 364, Rushville, NY 14544

Hosts: Elizabeth and Howard Freese
Location: Rural. On 170 acres on both sides of the road, overlooking the east side of Canandaigua Lake. Between (5 miles from) tiny Rushville and (6 miles south of) Canandaigua's Sonnenburg Gardens. One mile to restaurants, public beach; 20 minutes to Naples and Widmers Winery; 45 to Rochester.
Open: Year round.
Rates: Include tax. $35–$40 single. $50–$55 double.
🐾 ♦ ✗ ⅍

"The view. That's what this place is all about. When we first got here 17 years ago, it was the only thing that didn't need fixing! Now it's a country home furnished with many interesting family antiques from the South, circa 1850s or '60s, together with other pieces that blend well. We added a family/dining room with 20 feet of windows overlooking the lake, the pond, birds and wildlife. We love it and so do our guests. Some of our visitors walk down the ravine, a beautiful spot with a little waterfall and loads of fossils. Or they go fishing, antiquing, and wine tasting. Yes, I'm still pickling Jerusalem artichokes with our secret recipe and making jelly."

Betty, a former newspaper journalist, is a retired high school librarian. Howard is a retired engineer working with their son in his machinery business located in the red barn. The hosts, Elderhostel fans, live in what some travelers call "a real B&B."

In residence: Outdoors: Tobey, a mostly Gordon setter, loves to be petted. Ashley, "a friendly, fat male dog," announces arrivals.
Bed and bath: Two second-floor double-bedded rooms, both with lake views, share full bath across the hall. Cot available.
Breakfast: Early-morning coffee and tea in upstairs sitting room. Juice, homegrown fruit, eggs; bacon or sausage. Buns or interesting breads, homemade jellies. French toast or blueberry pancakes on request. Cereal available.
Plus: Central air conditioning. Welcoming beverage. Wood stove in that great family room. TV. Trails through woods and fields for cross-country skiing. A half-hour area drive complete with history and Indian legends. The gift of a jar of jelly or Jerusalem artichoke pickle.

> Guests wrote: "Showed us Spook Hill. We'll talk about it for years to come. . . . Trusted us with Tobey for an early morning walk. . . . Pressed cider together. . . . Superb breakfast at a lovely table. . . . Excellent books. . . . So clean. . . . Wonderful memories."

From a father's account of a B&B stay: "Before falling asleep, my son read a few pages of a book he found downstairs in the living room. He put the book down on his chest, sighed, looked up at the ceiling and said, 'This is the life.'"

The American Country Collection Host #162

Cazenovia, NY

Location: Secluded. At end of winding driveway. Surrounded by wildflower gardens, trees, and a lawn that slopes to dock at shores of Cazenovia Lake. Two miles to Cazenovia village and college, 19 to Syracuse, 20 to Colgate University, 22 to Hamilton College, 15 to Erie Canal Museum.

Reservations: Year round through The American Country Collection, page 142.
Rates: Per room. May–October $90 queen, $80 two single beds. Rest of year $80 queen, $60 single beds.
♥ ⬛ ✗

Lakeside. Contemporary. With stairways going up to both sides of the balcony that overlooks the spacious living room with its huge fireplace, cathedral ceiling, large curved sectional sofa, sculpture and prints from India, and that water view. Year round, this makes a good getaway destination or small meeting site. During the school year, parents visiting colleges appreciate the serenity and change of pace.

In residence: One dog who provides a "show" as he swims in circles.
Bed and bath: Three carpeted rooms; all with private tub/shower baths. On first floor, ramp and one step to room with queen bed, dressing area, private deck overlooking lake. On second level, off balcony, room with queen bed and one with two single beds.
Breakfast: 8:30–10:30. Juice. Fruit. Homemade bread and baked goods, coffee or tea. In winter, by fire in living area; in summer, on patio.
Plus: TV. "Plenty of unique shops, restaurants, and things to do in the town." Cross-country skiing on lake or at Lorenzo (1 mile).

1865 White Birch B&B   607/962–6355

69 East First Street, Corning, NY 14830

Hosts: Kathy and Joe Donahue
Location: In a quiet residential neighborhood. One block from the Rockwell Museum, 2 from downtown, and 6 from the Corning Glass Center.
Open: Year round.

Rates: Tax included. Double $65.40 shared bath, $70.85 private. Single $49.95 shared bath, $54.50 private. $15 extra person over age 10 in room. Amex, MC, Visa.
♥ ⬛ ⬛ ✣ ✂

Recipes, including one for lemon yogurt poppyseed bread, have traveled with guests to countries all over the world. The Donahues have been caterers for 18 years. Before becoming a full-time innkeeper, Kathy was a registered nurse for 24 years. Joe has been with the Corning Glass Works' food service department for over 30 years. So "it just made sense to combine our enjoyment of people and cooking, and our love of architecture, and an old home." In 1989 they bought this 1865 house, which has a Federal-looking exterior and Victorian moldings and trim on the inside. A B&B since 1984, it was a rectory for 25 years before that. Furnishings are country pine, oak, and wicker pieces. Williamsburg blue with cream and soft mauve colors predominate. Among the more than 3,000 contented Donahue guests are a glass artist who comes from Holland four times a year, a retiree who grew up in the house, a Berkeley sociology professor who comes for six weeks every summer, and many first-timers too.

In residence: "Guests who express an interest in Abby, our three-year-old basset hound, fall in love with her!"
Bed and bath: Up a wide winding staircase to four large second-floor rooms. Twin-bedded room has private en-suite tub and shower bath. One queen-bedded room with private shower bath. Two queen-bedded rooms share a large shower bath that has a double-sinked counter. Rollaway and crib.
Breakfast: Usually 8–9. Hot entree repertoire includes baked apple puff pancakes, fruit-filled French toast, egg-and-cheese souffle, three-layer omelet on croissants, Dutch babies. Juice. Fruit—compote, strawberry parfait, home-made applesauce. Cereals and homemade granola. Homemade muffins and bread. Served on long oak dining room table by large window overlooking yard. Hosts join guests.
Plus: Fireplaced living room with TV, VCR, tapes, radio. Babysitting. Garden flowers. Bedroom window fans. Picnic tables, umbrella tables, chairs, gas grill. Restaurant suggestions. Special holiday weekends.

Rosewood Inn   607/962–3253
134 East First Street, Corning, NY 14830

Hosts: Suzanne and Stewart Sanders
Location: On a tree-lined residential street, 1 block south of Route 17. Within walking distance of Corning Glass Center, museums, downtown historic district.

Open: Year round.
Rates: Single $70–$90. Double $75–$99. Suites $90–$115. $20 extra person. Amex, Carte Blanche, Diners, Discover, MC, Visa.
♥ ❖ ✗ ⅍

Transferred—from their New Jersey printing business to innkeeping in Corning, "and we're never going to leave!" From, as Suzanne says, "corporate America's suit-and-briefcase world to Victorian blouses and shawls." At home, Stewart was always the official cook; here he does all the baking and cooking.

In 1992, following a two-year search "all over," they bought the Finger Lakes' first and almost-famous bed and breakfast. Appointed with fine Victorian antiques, Oriental rugs, and lace curtains, this 1853 Greek Revival was renovated in 1915 into an English Tudor. Now glass blowers' tools are in the Fred Carder (originator of Steuben Glass) Room. And there's a photographic "homage to the house" collection that portrays previous residents dating back to the early 1900s. The marvelous blend of guests—including corporate transferees—agree that the Sanderses made the right decision.

Bed and bath: Seven rooms, all private baths. Queen, double, or twin beds. Two large first-floor suites with private full bath, private entrance, color TV, air conditioning; queen canopied bed and working fireplace in one suite, twin

(Please turn page.)

beds and a kitchen in the other. Second-floor queen-bedded rooms have tub and shower baths; shower baths in other rooms.

Breakfast: Usually 8:30–9:30. (Coffee available at 7:30.) Juice, fruit. Home-made banana or zucchini bread with Rosewood brandy/honey butter. Cereals, granola, yogurt. Entree might be challah French toast or omelet. A very sociable time in candlelit dining room.

Plus: Bedroom air conditioners. Fruit basket in room. Late-afternoon tea and cookies by the fire or lemonade and cookies on porch. In winter, flannel sheets. Sitting room with TV.

> From North Carolina: *"Elegant . . . welcomed us as if we were old friends . . . breakfast was a feast. A must for B&B aficionados!"* From Pennsylvania: *"Stewart and Suzanne truly are the definition of hospitality . . . made us feel at home . . . provided for our every need . . . allowed for privacy as well . . . a great experience."* From Arizona: *"All six couples on our bicycling trip have stayed at many B&Bs. All agreed Rosewood was the best ever. Fantastic!"*

Halcyon Place Bed & Breakfast   607/529–3544

197 Washington Street, P.O. Box 244, Chemung, NY 14825-0244

Hosts: Yvonne and Doug Sloan
Location: In a tiny town dubbed "the Northeast's most English-like village" by young English guests. Quiet streets with a range of architectural styles. Former blacksmith shop two doors away. "Just down the street," area's oldest one-room schoolhouse, now a private residence.

One mile off Route 17, 12 east of Elmira. Forty minutes to Ithaca, 45 to Binghamton and international racing at Watkins Glen.
Open: Year round.
Rates: Private bath $55. Shared bath $45, $50 with working fireplace. $15 extra person.
🛏 ✗ ⅙

"We felt we had discovered a secret when we stayed in B&Bs! In 1990 we bought this restored circa 1825 Greek Revival house with its wide-plank floors and six-over-six hand-blown glass windows, and furnished it with our collection of late 18th- and early 19th-century furnishings. Sometimes guests visit our favorite antiques dealers, especially our 85-year-old mentor. Upon departure, everyone receives a lavender wand (for a linen closet or lingerie drawer) that I make from Doug's herb garden. The name Halcyon is from the Greek myths, signifying peacefulness, tranquillity, and a healing richness. It's all part of sharing our dream come true."

Yvonne, a tympanist with the Corning Philharmonic, teaches middle school instrumental music. Doug, a trained musician/avid gardener/antique furniture restorer, is an employment counselor who works with disadvantaged youths. Their B& B has an extensive backyard lawn with fruit-bearing trees, mature bushes, perennial beds with hummingbirds and butterflies, a formal herb garden, and a rose trellis with seat for stargazing.

In residence: "Tucson is our affectionate, laid-back, and well-traveled chocolate Labrador."
Foreign language spoken: Some German.

Bed and bath: Three second-floor rooms. Room with canopied double bed has private en-suite shower bath. Room with tall double four-poster and working fireplace shares a full hall bath with room that has "a stunning antique tiger maple double bed."

Breakfast: Usually 8–10. Juice, freshly ground coffee, seasonal fruits. Raspberry streusel muffins with homegrown berries or popular rum sticky buns. Blueberry waffles with locally made maple syrup, omelets with herbs, quiche, or crepes. Bacon or sausages. Table set with heirloom silver on wicker-furnished screened porch overlooking garden or by candlelight in fireplaced dining room with classical music.

Plus: June–August, free tickets for 90-minute Mark Twain Country trolley tour. Afternoon tea with lemon tea bread, rose geranium cake, or lemon balm cookies; evening beverages with crackers and herb cheese. Piano. Window fans for guest rooms. Turndown service. Mints. Bicycles for guests' use. Extensive LP and CD collection of jazz and classical music. "Narrated" herb garden tour.

The Blushing Rosé B&B
11 William Street, Hammondsport, NY 14840

607/569–3402
607/569–3483
800/982–8818

Hosts: Ellen and Bucky Laufersweiler
Location: Minutes' walk to village park bandstand, historic area, Glen Curtis Museum, shops, and free beach on Keuka Lake. Thirty minutes west of Corning; 10 minutes from Bath; two hours from Rochester, Syracuse, and Binghamton; four from Toronto. Near wineries, waterfalls, and gorges.
Open: Year round. Two-night minimum holiday weekends, July, August, October foliage season, and local special events.
Rates: Per room. $85 May–October, $75 off season. $10 third person.

Quite a combination. A hostess who loves decorating, sewing, and cooking. A host who is a wood-floor specialist/refinisher. Together, a couple who, since 1986, have offered warm hospitality to grateful travelers.

Ellen and Bucky—skiers, cyclists, and boaters—"loved every minute of restoring and redecorating the entire Victorian Italianate," which was built in 1843 with a cupola, recently identified as "original air conditioning" by the local historical society. The exterior, painted a blushing rose color, is trimmed with a deep burgundy. Inside, ruffled (Priscilla) curtains are on all the windows. The country decor is complete with handmade quilts, a spinning wheel, grapevine wreaths, and Oriental-style rug under the dining room oak table. For Ellen, who has appeared as a B&B host on the ABC-TV "Home" show and is active with regional and national B&B organizations, it is all a dream come true.

In residence: Bolt, a friendly 13-year-old golden retriever, loved by guests.
Bed and bath: Four spacious second-floor rooms; three with queen bed, one with king. All private baths; two en suite, two in hall.

(Please turn page.)

Breakfast: One seating at 9. (Early-bird coffee at 8:15.) June 15–September 15, "copious continental plus," with gourmet coffees and teas, juice, fruit dishes, homemade granola and muesli, homemade multigrain bread, yogurt. Rest of year, hot entree might be French toast, omelet, or feather-bed eggs.
Plus: Air-conditioned bedrooms; two have ceiling fans. Guest refrigerator. A sitting room with TV, stereo, VCR, much reading material. Traditional music. Wicker-furnished porch. Guest pickup at bus station.

> Guests wrote: *"Fond memories of friendliness, large breakfasts, country antiques. . . . Beautifully decorated. Gave me some new ideas. . . . Good advice on places to visit and to eat. . . . Clean, clean, clean! . . . Every detail was perfect."*

The Bowman House, a bed and breakfast

61 Lake Street, P.O. Box 586   607/569–2516
Hammondsport, NY 14840

Hosts: Manita and Jack Bowman
Location: Two-block walk to village shops, restaurants. In a picturesque village; free summer jazz concerts. Ninety minutes south of Rochester, 30 to Corning and Watkins Glen.

Open: Year round.
Rates: $70 shared bath, $80 private bath. Singles $5 less.
♥ ⬛ ⁂ ✖ ⅊

> Guests wrote: *"A fantastic experience. . . . From all my travels, one of the most comfortable and appealing B&Bs in the U.S. and Europe. . . . Bowmans seem to sense just how much privacy and how much help the guests need. . . . Wonderful food. . . . Very clean. . . . Hated to leave. . . . We first heard about it through friends, very fussy ones. . . . A treasured find. . . . Their personal charm extends to their surroundings."*

And the accolades go on and on—from cycling groups and business meetings too—about the hosts who moved in 1988 from a smaller nearby residence to this turn-of-the century house. The Bowmans started hosting in 1983, "just about the time our youngest left the nest." Jack is a personnel manager at Corning Incorporated. And you can tell that Manita enjoys interior decorating "in a comfortably elegant style, using several shades of blue." Most furnishings are antique. Recently they put a "fresh face" on the exterior in tones of grays and blues. On the sunset side, they added a large screened porch off the library. "Select a book on your way out." Welcome home.

Bed and bath: Four large second-floor bedrooms with double or queen bed. Three full baths; two private, one shared.
Breakfast: 7:30–9. Abundant fruit, homemade breads and jellies, butter, coffee, tea, milk, local grape juice. "Close to two hours sometimes!" In dining room with linen, silver, china, and crystal.
Plus: Fireplaced first-floor sitting room. TV in second-floor sitting room. Beverages. Flowers. Mints. Bedroom ceiling fans.

Buttermilk Falls Bed & Breakfast   607/272-6767

110 East Buttermilk Falls Road, Ithaca, NY 14850-8741

Host: Margie Rumsey
Location: Just off Route 13, at the foot of waterfalls in adjoining Buttermilk Falls State Park; 3½ miles south of Cornell University and Ithaca College.
Open: Year round. Two-night minimum on some weekends and college graduations.

Rates: Vary according to season. $150–$195 king bed with Jacuzzi, fireplace. Second floor, $65–$110 extra-long double; $81–$115 double; $92–$125 king. $10 less for singles. MC, Visa (for holding reservations only).
♥ ♣ ✗ ⅙

We won't ever forget our before-breakfast dip in those magnificent waterfalls—followed by Margie's dramatic presentation of juice blended from fresh fruits. Her 1820 painted brick house with wide pine floorboards is decorated with antiques, family heirlooms, old Persian carpets (even on the porch), and a son's handcrafted tables and Windsor chairs. In the fireplaced gathering room there are reproduction wing chairs and an early American sofa, 1800s country pieces, books, magazines and CD music, and many antique games.

"The idea of having B&B in our family home of five generations started with a 1983 trip to England," says Margie, the innkeeper in residence—except when she sleeps in the maple tree or takes a quick getaway (always with inn brochures to exchange). A Class of 1947 Cornellian, native Ithacan, and private pilot, she flies to Florida to pick calamondins for making jam. From trips to Turkey, Africa, India, Japan, New Zealand, and Australia, she brings back spices and seasonings for taste treats. All five grandchildren, ages 5–18, help when they can. Their parents (one is a Cornell hotel school graduate), who were raised here, also assist.

Bed and bath: Four air-conditioned rooms; all private baths. "Unless there's a draft or a deep freeze, the falls can be heard from all bedrooms." On first floor, king bed, double Jacuzzi bath, shower, wood-burning fireplace, ceiling fan, TV, VCR, big comfortable chairs. On second floor, room with king bed, antique day-bed, shower bath, refrigerator, windows on three walls. Room with double bed, antique daybed, shower bath, windows on three walls. Room with extra-long double hydraulic (vibrating) bed has hall tub and shower bath immediately next to bedroom door.
Breakfast: 8:30–9:30. Full. Menu changes with the seasons. Features fresh fruits, hot whole-grain cereals with a variety of toppings such as raisins, dates, walnuts, maple syrup, honey, yogurt, or cream. Bacon and eggs with fresh breads, "oven surprises," and apple fritters. Buffet style on busy weekends. In kitchen, in formal dining room, on screened porch with thriving plants, or under trees at picnic table at foot of waterfall.
Plus: Fireplaced living room. Yard swing. Beverages. Cross-country skiing from the door. Hiking and biking suggestions.

From Pennsylvania: *"A breakfast that could almost make a morning person out of me."* From New York: *"A treat to walk up the park slope before breakfast. . . . A place full of peace."*

Hanshaw House B&B   607/273–8034

15 Sapsucker Wood Road, Ithaca, NY 14850

Host: Helen Scoones
Location: Tranquil. A country setting overlooking pond (created by former owner, a Cornell-based ornithologist), woods, and a century-old apple tree. Within 10 minutes of downtown, fine restaurants, state parks, Cayuga Lake. Half a mile from Cornell's Sapsucker Woods Ornithology Laboratory and Bird Sanctuary. Less than half an hour to Greek Peak ski slopes.

Open: Year round. Two-day minimum on college graduation and parents' weekends, and on some major holidays.
Rates: Double occupancy. $70–$105. Off-season $65–$84. $5 less for singles. Slightly higher on major holiday weekends. $20–$25 extra person in room. $10 crib. Corporate and educational discounts available. Amex, MC, Visa.
♥ ♺ ⚘ ✗ ⚮

> From Massachusetts and New York: *"I can't think of a place that would have been as romantic for our honeymoon. Every detail was perfect! . . . Our relatives recommended this B&B for our Thanksgiving visit. We have been to many B&Bs and couldn't recommend any more highly. . . . Saw two pileated woodpeckers—simultaneously—right there in her backyard. Beautifully appointed rooms . . . spotless . . . lovely gardens . . . breakfasts are scrumptious enough to make you want to kidnap the cook . . . couldn't ask for a more gracious or helpful hostess . . . directions to a vineyard and MacKenzie-Childs pottery studios . . . suggestions for places we never had been to in four years as students."*

What was, in 1988, to be a decorating studio in the 1830s Federal-style farmhouse "with a few rooms to rent occasionally" became a full-time B&B for Helen—"maybe you can tell, I am somewhat of a naturalist." Her husband, Bill, is dean at Ithaca College. The 1989 B&B addition, a perfect architectural match, was constructed from Helen's own plans drawn on graph paper. She decorated in light and cheery country English style with antiques, wicker, dhurries, chintzes, and plants. Guests from all over the world appreciate this gracious hostess.

Foreign language spoken: "French partially understood."
Bed and bath: Four rooms with private full baths that have pedestal sink, cosmetic stand, hair dryer. One on first floor; three on second. One room with antique double bed; three with queen bed (one is a four-poster). Rollaway and crib available.
Breakfast: Flexible timing. Menu varies. Fresh fruit, baked apples, or poached pears. Juice, homemade breads and granola, bacon or sausage from local butcher, unusual coffees and teas. House specialty—Swedish pancakes with creme fraiche. Cooked before your eyes in open kitchen/dining room. Served in dining room or on garden patio.
Plus: Bedroom air conditioning and ceiling fans. Goose-down comforters and pillows. TV room. Mints on pillows. Fresh flowers. Late-afternoon lemonade or mulled cider with homemade brownies, cookies (gingerbread at Christmas), or cakes. Adirondack chairs—and, in fall, deer too—by the pond. Bluebirds at the feeder.

Rose Inn

607/533–7905
813 Auburn Road, Route 34N   fax (call first) **607/533–4202**
P.O. Box 6576, Ithaca NY 14851-6576

Hosts: Charles and Sherry Rosemann
Location: Rural. On 20 landscaped acres with lawns, gardens, terraces, and orchard. Twelve minutes from the center of Ithaca and Cornell University.
Open: Year round. Two-night minimum if stay includes Saturday night.

Three nights for holiday and special university weekends.
Rates: $110 double bed, $140 queen, $150 king or twin beds. Suites with Jacuzzi $175–$250. $25 additional person.
♥ ⁂ ♦ ✈ ✂

The ultimate. An architectural gem. For most guests, not just like home. An elegant showplace with period furnishings, artworks, flowers, attention to every detail, and service. It's personalized by professionals who began a decade ago with five guest rooms and some shared baths. With the option of dinner, this acclaimed inn has become a destination for romantics, and with the transformed carriage house, a meeting site for groups. Weddings and receptions are held here too.

There's a fascinating story to the magnificent freestanding, self-supporting Honduran mahogany spiral staircase that extends from the main entrance hall up to the cupola with skylight in this 1851 mansion. And then there's the story of the Rosemanns, parents of two college-age children.

Since Charles started his career in his native Germany in the 1950s, he has opened major Hyatt hotels in this country and managed Washington, D.C.'s Sheraton and the hotel school at Cornell. Sherry, who has lectured on American furniture, has considerable experience as an interior designer. She mastered the arts of cooking, catering, and administration after receiving an undergraduate degree in microbiology and her master's in social work. Here she supervised the construction of you-can-hardly-tell additions, duplicating the 10-foot ceilings and 8-foot French doors. The latest project: an addition to the conference center (accommodates 60)—wide-screen TV and comfortable seating available to all inn guests.

In residence: Brandi, a Labrador/Samoyed. Elizabeth (Lizzy) Arden, a calico cat.
Foreign languages spoken: German and Spanish.
Bed and bath: Sixteen no-two-alike rooms (all private tub/shower baths), including four suites that have wood-burning fireplace and Jacuzzi for two. On first and second floors. King, queen, double, or twin beds. Three rooms can be connected with a parlor that has two sleep sofas.
Breakfast: 8–9:30; 8:30–10 Sundays. Coffee available at 7. In season, fresh apple cider from Rosemanns' orchard. German apple pancakes with apple butter, French toast, and a special house blend of coffee. Artistically presented on china, crystal, and silver in dining room.
Plus: Fireplaced parlors with ornate crystal chandeliers. Air conditioners in guest rooms and dining room. Bedroom ceiling fans and individual thermostats. In season, apples (a dozen varieties) from the inn's orchard. Turndown service with style. Candlelit dinner, Tuesday–Saturday, with advance notice ($50/person).

The Fountainebleau Inn   607/594-2008
2800 State Route 228, Alpine, NY 14805

Hosts: Terri and John VanSoest
Location: Serene. On Lake Kayutah (canoeing, fishing, cross-country skiing, and swimming) with 10 acres of lawns sloping to shore, mature trees, perennial gardens, and a gazebo too. Along a rural highway, minutes' drive to Finger Lakes hiking and cross-country skiing trails. Nine miles from Watkins Glen; 15 to Seneca Lake wineries; 17 to Ithaca; 20 to Corning. Next door to county historical society–owned chapel, available for weddings.
Open: Year round. Two-night minimum on weekends April–November.
Rates: $70 king or queen bed; $60 double bed. Singles $10 less. $15 cot. Discounts for stays over four days.
♥ ♠ ♣ ♦ ✿ ✄

> From award-winning Maryland innkeepers (page 24): *"What a beautiful setting for a beautiful inn . . . spotless . . . fine innkeepers . . . breakfast was wonderful."* From New York: *"Setting reminds me of Mount Vernon . . . have never been treated so royally . . . relaxed atmosphere . . . old-fashioned charm. . . . Simply but beautifully decorated. . . . Genuinely happy to share their home with us."* From North Carolina: *"Perfect in every way."*

This ideal union of place and people began in 1990, just weeks after a chance conversation when the VanSoests, Ithaca natives, asked to use the inn's phone because of car trouble. Terri, who handles weddings with "ease and perfection," had experience as a chef and caterer, and as assistant innkeeper at her mother's B&B. John is a contractor who has experience as a chef and boat builder. Obviously, guests sense their love of spontaneity, food, and this old house. The oldest section, a former summer residence, was built in 1814 with handsome crown and dentil moldings. The dormered bed and breakfast wing, added about 1860, is decorated with a country theme. The fireplaced banquet hall, added in the 1920s, was built with beams from the original barn.

In residence: "Sushi and Savannah, two wonderfully affectionate cats."
Bed and bath: Three second-floor rooms; one with slanted ceilings, two with lake view. King-bedded room shares connecting tub and shower bath with double-bedded bath. Room with queen bed (which has space for cot) has a private tub and shower bath. Crib available.
Breakfast: Memorable. Flexible hours. Raspberry streusel muffins or blueberry sour cream coffee cake. Fresh fruit sundaes with yogurt and granola, stuffed French toast, eggs Benedict, or Mexican omelets. Fresh pork sausage or custom-smoked and -cut bacon. On porch overlooking lake, in dining room, or in kitchen.
Plus: Fireplaced living room and library. Piano. Bedroom ceiling fans. Plush bathrobes. Wicker-furnished porch. Iced tea or hot cider. Garden flowers. Babysitting. Guest refrigerator. Canoe. Barbecue. Sleds. Picnic baskets prepared. Dinners by advance reservation.

---

*B*ed and breakfast gives a sense of place.

Gale House Bed & Breakfast   607/898–4904

114 Williams Street, Groton, NY 13073-1136

Hosts: Ray and Barbara Ingraham
Location: On a quiet village street, within walking distance of restaurants. Thirteen miles north of Ithaca; 9 miles west of Cortland. "A base for a country drive to skiing, boating, lake cruises, wineries, summer theater."
Open: Year round. June–October, two-night minimum for Saturday night reservations.

Rates: Tax included. Shared bath $61.05 twin, $72.15 queen. Private bath $83.25 queen. Ten percent less Sunday–Thursday. Higher on special weekends. Package rates arranged. MC, Visa.
♥ ⌨ ♣ ♦ ✈ ⌇

From China: *"Through three countries and a number of cities, the most comfortable hotel (or inn) we found."* From Connecticut: *"Beautiful . . . immaculate . . . delicious food."* From New York: *"As soon as they have built a much-deserved reputation there will be waiting lists to get in . . . impressed with attention to every little detail . . . certainly five-star."*

The Ingrahams' daughter, who works for Best Western, suggested that the family home (of a dozen years) become a B&B. Opened in 1991 after a two-year restoration, the Queen Anne Victorian is furnished in period antiques and decorated with light-patterned wallcoverings, crisp window treatments, pressed white linens, and ferns on plant stands. Robes are folded just so. Godiva chocolates are placed on pillows. Special occasions are acknowledged.

Ray is a principal consultant with New York State Electric and Gas Information Systems. Before innkeeping, Barbara was a department store purchasing agent. They sell antiques at Gale House, named for the prominent banking family that owned the property for 100 years.

In residence: A friendly golden Labrador, "kept away from guests' area."
Foreign language spoken: Japanese. (While Ray was in the air force, he studied the language and spent much time with local residents during 18 months on Okinawa.)
Bed and bath: Four second-floor rooms (three with antique queen brass beds, one with a twin) along one side of hall share two large full baths (one with two sinks) on other side. Private baths sometimes available. Rollaway.
Breakfast: 8:30. "All you can eat." Weekdays, homemade breads, muffins, and coffee cakes. Cereals and yogurt. Fresh fruit, juice, teas, freshly ground coffees. Weekends, a hot egg dish, waffles, pancakes, or French toast. In dining room or on porches.
Plus: Air-conditioned rooms. Fruit and crackers in rooms. Turndown service. Guest refrigerator on second floor. Down comforters. Lace-trimmed bed linens. Synthetic and down pillows. Spa slippers. Late-afternoon lemonade. Evening decaf in parlor. Picnic baskets ($14–$21).

B&Bs offer the ultimate concierge service.

The Wagener Estate Bed & Breakfast

351 Elm Street, Penn Yan, NY 14527   315/536–4591

Hosts: Evie and Norm Worth
Location: "Away from city traffic and hustle and bustle." On a hillside surrounded by four acres of lawns, apple trees, stone walls. Five minutes' walk to village. About an hour from Corning, Syracuse, and Rochester. Near many wineries, restaurants, festivals.

Open: Year round. Two-night minimum May–October.
Rates: Shared bath $50 single, $60 double. $15 cot. Private bath $60 single, $70 double. Amex, MC, Visa.
♥ ♣ ✈ ✄

"People are a constant wonder to us. One couple flew into Penn Yan Airport, set up their collapsible bikes, and found us. A Californian was inspired to sketch the dining room her first morning at breakfast. . . . After our guests settle in, we usually invite them for tea. Later we sometimes join them in their living room or our family room, the one that has wainscoting done by Norm from attic floorboards. The large pillared porch (with wicker furniture), part of the 1830 addition to the house, is a great gathering spot too. We gladly answer all sorts of questions about the town founder who first owned our property and built the 1790 rooms, one of which still has the fireplace and oven. And guests express amazement that we lived through the upbringing of 10 children! (There are now 16 grandchildren, ages six months to 25). When Norm retired as director of Keuka College's physical plant and I retired from teaching, we did some traveling and realized we weren't ready for retiring. We love this house, which is filled with the country look, many crafts, and usable and comfortable antiques. Our latest project was the redecoration of one room—all with old-flavor roses. After eight years, we don't know whether the hosts or guests have more fun!"

It's a natural. It's home. A hideaway. It is recommended for a place on the National Register of Historic Places. It is recommended as a B&B.

Bed and bath: Five second-floor rooms. King bed, private shower bath, air conditioning. Queen bed, private tub and shower bath, window fan. Queen bed, private shower bath, ceiling fan. Room with two twin beds and window fan shares a shower bath with air-conditioned "small, cute" double-bedded room.
Breakfast: At 9. Juice (maybe a white grape juice blended from local vineyards), lots of seasonal fruits, homemade sticky buns, toast, or muffins. Cheese, tomato, and mushroom omelet with ham or bacon; or buckwheat (Penn Yan is the world capital) and corn pancakes; crepes with blueberries and sausages; French toast or quiche and featherbed eggs.
Plus: Fresh flowers. TV in rooms with private baths as well as in the guest living room. A great story about huge front hall mirror.

> From New York: *"It's like an inn from 200 years ago, where people would stop their journeys, sit down, eat, and talk together."*

The Russell-Farrenkopf House   315/472-8001

209 Green Street, Syracuse, NY 13203

Hosts: Joan Farrenkopf, owner/innkeeper, and Peggy LaRue, co-innkeeper
Location: Residential. In the Hawley–Green Street historic district. Five blocks from downtown, 9 to the campus, Carrier Dome, Up-

state Medical Center, and Carousel Center Shopping Center. Within minutes of several restaurants.
Open: April–November.
Rates: $65 shared bath, $75 private. Singles $10 less.
🌸 🛥 ✂

> From Washington, D.C.: *"A gem, with its beautiful chestnut-and-mahogany staircase; high ceilings with plaster cornices; large, sunny rooms; plants everywhere; and fine Victorian pieces. . . . Proprietress who offers a homelike environment . . . tours of the city. . . . A wonderful house with warm spirits within."*

"This 1865 French Second Empire/Italianate house taught me how to restore," says Joan, the fine arts major (and ski instructor) whose interest in historic preservation led to her restoring several other houses on the block as well as six in Wilmington, North Carolina. Some floors and doors in the eclectically furnished B&B, opened in 1988, may look like walnut or mahogany, but they are grained through a process that Joan figured out. Joan's latest project: a research and plaque program for Syracuse historic district property owners. Meanwhile, Peggy, a management school graduate who has become a creative caterer (right here for special occasions), wows guests with her baked creations.

Bed and bath: Four rooms. First-floor room has king/twins option, private full bath, and private entrance. On second floor, large full bath is shared by one double-bedded room, one with a queen bed, and one with a king.
Breakfast: 7:30–9:30. Fresh fruit. Juice. Gourmet coffee. Stuffed apple dumplings, oven-baked French toast with cranberry/maple syrup, or vegetable frittata. Blueberry muffins with strawberry butter or coffee hazelnut scones. Served in bay-windowed red breakfast room.
Plus: Wicker-furnished skylit solarium. Welcoming beverage. Bedroom ceiling fans. Chocolate mints. Parlor reed organ in music room. Piano in formal dining room. If you'd like, a tour. (Can you find the artist's intials in the graining?) Swing on side porch. Open front piazza. Some off-street parking. Afternoon tea by request. Perennial gardens.

The tradition of paying to stay in a private home—with breakfast included in the overnight lodging rate—was revived in time to save wonderful old houses, schools, churches, and barns all over country from the wrecking ball or commercial development.

Reading House   607/535-9785
4610 Route 14, Rock Stream, NY 14878

Hosts: Rita and Bill Newell
Location: On a rural main road, with gardens and lawns and expansive view of ponds, woods, and Seneca Lake in back. Across from farmland. Within walking distance of a "fried-food tavern." Five miles north of Watkins Glen; 5½ miles to town center; 30 miles south of Geneva. Within 5 miles of gorge, International Auto Raceway, four wineries, golf, swimming, boating, fishing, cross-country skiing. Within 30 miles of Corning (southwest) and Ithaca (southeast).
Open: Year round. Two-night minimum on major holiday and Watkins Glen Raceway weekends.
Rates: $45–$50 single. $50–$55 double. $10 third person. January–March, package rates with restaurant dinner, discounts at wineries.
♥ ⌂ ♣ ✗ ✄

From Connecticut: *"Our accommodations were so pleasant and the Newells' company so engaging that we stayed an extra night . . . beautifully and comfortably furnished . . . memorable breakfasts . . . chatting with them on spacious back lawn was delightful."* From New York: *"Friendly conversation outdoors by fish ponds . . . by fire in winter . . . helpful with restaurant recommendations . . . a 'must stop' for us."*

In New York City and western New Jersey, Scottish-born Rita was a Head Start director, Bill an exporter. They moved to this rambling restored 1820 Federal house in 1989 and furnished without clutter and with a mix of antiques, period pieces and reproductions, many books, prints, and works by local artists. Rita, a League of Women Voters board member, has become an avid bird-watcher. "A bluebird colony is nesting in one of our boxes." Bill, active with the cooperative extension service and the town planning board, is the gardener. The Newells grow vegetables, herbs, many perennials, and fruit. In one of the ponds there are water lilies. In another there are fish that eat from your hand. Current plans call for a flowering meadow, a rock garden, and a maze.

In residence: In hosts' quarters, two cats.
Bed and bath: Four second-floor rooms, all private baths. In front of house, large room with queen bed, attached full bath; smaller room with double bed, Indian shutters, detached full bath. In rear with lake view, king/twins option, attached shower bath; room with a double bed and a twin bed, attached shower bath.
Breakfast: 7:30–9. Buckwheat or puffed pancakes with fruit. Or French toast made with French bread. Or omelets and other main courses. Juice, fresh fruit, cereal, homemade muffins. All kinds of special diets accommodated.
Plus: Handmade quilts on beds. Beverages and cookies. Guest refrigerator. Bedroom ceiling and window fans. Picnic table, lawn chairs. Skating right here. Sometimes, great blue heron in morning, deer and rabbits at night.

Rochester Area B&Bs

428 Mt. Vernon—a bed & breakfast inn

428 Mount Vernon Avenue, Rochester, NY 14620   716/271–0792
                                                      800/836–3159

Hosts: Philip and Claire Lanzatella
Location: On two acres of trees, wildflowers, and birds in a residential neighborhood at entrance of Highland Park (annual Lilac Festival). One mile from University of Rochester Medical School Campus and I–390/I–490 intersection.
Open: Year round.
Rates: Tax included. $100.35 single. $110.39 double. Amex, MC, Visa.
♥ ♣ ♦ ✗

An elegant Irish manor house. Discovered by many business and international travelers, by wedding planners, and by Rochesterians who told me that it was "a getaway without the driving, a fulfillment of our fantasy of what a B&B should be." The heirloom-filled 40-foot-long living room has fine art, Oriental rugs, an 1859 Knabe grand piano, and huge windows that look out onto magnificent copper beech trees. I found Max, the lovable mixed Lab, on the cushioned window seat with a choice view, the place he established as his very own during the 17-month restoration period. Thanks to Claire's patience, the elaborately carved mantel no longer has layers of paint in its crevices. And all the exquisite moldings, having been marked on the back piece by piece, have been reassembled by Phil, a contractor who specializes in historic preservation. In the former chapel, added when the Sisters of St. Joseph lived here (1952–86), there's a telescope. The ambiance throughout all 10,000 square feet is comfortable and welcoming.

The Lanzatellas lived three houses away for 17 years and bought this estate—which "needed everything"—for a B&B when their children were grown. They segued quite naturally into innkeeping. I enjoyed my stay. Highly recommended!

In residence: Max, the dog, and a crow named Joe.
Bed and bath: Seven very large rooms on second and third floors with antique queen, double, or twin beds. All private en-suite baths, all with showers, some with tubs. One room is handicapped accessible; elevator available.
Breakfast: 7–9. Six courses selected from menu the night before. Claire makes the jams and bakes the breads (including whole wheat raisin), muffins, and scones. Presented by candlelight in fireplaced dining room with 12-foot expanse of windows and bird feeders.
Plus: Homemade cookies await your arrival. Guest rooms have individual thermostats, ceiling fans, and phones. A desk in several. TV available. Turndown service. Down comforters. Fresh fruit. Homemade candy. Beverages. Restaurant suggestions. Dinner for groups by reservation only.

Woods-Edge Bed & Breakfast   716/223-8877

151 Bluhm Road, P.O. Box 444, Fairport, NY 14450

Hosts: Betty and Bill Kinsman
Location: Up and away. Quiet and beautiful in a heavily wooded setting. Twenty minutes southeast of downtown Rochester and museums. Short drive to restaurants. Five minutes to one winery tour; half hour to Sonnenberg Gardens; 12 miles to Lake Ontario; 3 from exit 45, New York State Thruway (I–90).

Open: Year round except during selected times in January, July, and August. Two-night minimum in May. Cottage available year round.
Rates: $60–$65 double occupancy. Guest cottage $80 ($10 one-night surcharge). No charge for crib.
♥ � ♣ ♦ ✗ ✄

What one guest describes as "a perfect refuge from reality" is a discovery for Rochester residents too. I met honeymooners who were delighted with Bill's hiking suggestion (on the property). And there were some fishermen—who had risen at 4 a.m.—here for their tenth time.

Just thinking about this place gives me a sense of peace. Geraniums bloom year round in the contemporary house that Betty, an artist, and Bill, a recently retired mechanical engineering professor, designed and built in 1975 when the two youngest of their five children were still at home. It has old barn beams; a chimney of gray lake stones and brick; an open skylit kitchen—great for cooking and entertaining simultaneously; rough-hewn shelves to hold Betty's duck decoy collection; and a screened porch that feels like a tree house—with views of deer, foxes, chipmunks, and tall pines too. Antique pine furniture and comfortable sofas enhance the at-home feeling.

In residence: Scramble, "an easygoing 17-year-old cat."
Bed and bath: Two main-house rooms plus a fully equipped "hideaway" guest house; all private baths. One room with queen bed, full bath; one with king/twins option, bath with hand-held shower. Charming 650-square-foot guest house has a queen-bedded room (with a marvelous Kinsman-created white birch headboard), queen sleep sofa in fireplaced living room, kitchen, full bath.
Breakfast: Flexible; time established the night before. Always early on Thursdays (garage sale day). Fruit. Homemade muffins. Eggs, raisin bread French toast, strawberry crepes, broccoli quiche, pancakes, or oatmeal with grated apples and raisins. In dining room or on screened porch. For guest cottage, eat there or in main house.
Plus: Central air conditioning. Beverages and snacks. Fresh flowers. Refrigerator storage. Laundry facilities. Bicycles. Piano. Guitars. Dulcimer. An invitation to accompany Betty on weekly garage sale trips that result in fabulous finds.

Guests wrote: *"What a great feeling to have a friend in Rochester. . . . Delicious breakfast. . . . Cottage is the most perfect B&B we have found."*

The place to stay has become the reason to go.

Genesee Country Inn
948 George Street, Box 340
Mumford, NY 14511-0340

716/538-2500
fax 716/538-4565

Hosts: Glenda Barcklow (proprietor) and Kim Rasmussen
Location: On 8½ idyllic acres. Thirty minutes south of downtown Rochester; 20 from University of Rochester, Strong Medical Center, Rochester Institute of Technology. Fifteen minutes to Kodak's Emgrove plant, 10 from I–90 exit 47. Ninety minutes to Niagara Falls. Three hours from Toronto.

Open: Year round. Closed Sunday noon–Tuesday noon, November through March and Christmas week. Two-night minimum on several May–October weekends.
Rates: $80 double bed, $98 two beds, $98 queen. $116–120 with sitting room or private patio and gas fireplace. $10 additional person.
♥ ♣ ♦ ✗

"We're really an island surrounded by water," says Glenda when describing this "escape." Built in 1833, it was a mill for one hundred years. Then a private residence. Since 1982, a haven for getaway travelers and business guests who appreciate "all the creature comforts" along with history and natural beauty.

When Glenda, a Kodak accountant for many years, and her late husband established the inn, they were experienced restorers of several Rochester area 19th-century houses. An extension of Glenda's interest in painting, needlework, and nature, the limestone inn is picture perfect inside and out. On *Country Inns'* 1991–1992 top 12 list, the inn has antique and reproduction pine and maple, colonial colors, and marvelous stenciling painted by Glenda and local folk artist Ruth Flowers. The grounds, often compared to a Southern bayou, are complete with millponds (for trout fishing), 16-foot waterfalls (for dreaming), gazebo, fountain, gardens, and woodlands.

Kim, a Rochester Institute of Technology Hotel School graduate, is a Corning (nearby Finger Lakes) native. She and Glenda direct guests to wineries; Letchworth State Park, "the Grand Canyon of the East"; back roads for cycling; outlets and antiques shops. Some spend the day less than a mile away at the fascinating Genesee Country Village Museum, which has 50 buildings plus events. Before dinner at nearby (less than a mile away) fine restaurants, guests relax here with tea and cheese and crackers.

In residence: Three cats: Sylvester, Pepper, and Kati.
Bed and bath: Eight rooms (with background sound of gurgling stream) on three levels have a queen, a double, or two beds (a queen or double with a single). Some with gas fireplace. All private baths; some full, some shower only. Garden-level rooms have canopied beds and gas fireplaces; one has French doors onto private patio.
Breakfast: 7:30–8:30 weekdays, 8:30–9:30 weekends. Daily choices vary and include fresh fruit, cheese omelets, pancakes with vanilla-cinnamon sauce, and scrambled eggs. Homemade breads and muffins. Cereals. In wood-ceilinged breakfast room with water view, gas fireplace, and morning newspaper.
Plus: Air conditioning, desks, private phone (conference-call capability), and TV in each guest room. Mints on pillows. Deck by pond, gazebo, grill.

From California: *"Beautiful pond, woods, ducks. . . . Great breakfast orchestrated with a wonderful snowfall. . . . It's a good thing Hollywood hasn't discovered this inn. We'll be back before they do."*

Niagara/Buffalo/Chautauqua Area
—————— Reservation Service ——————

Rainbow Hospitality, Inc.
Bed and Breakfast Reservation Service
for Western New York

504 Amherst Street, Buffalo, NY 14207-2844

Phone: 716/874–8797. For reservations: 800/373–8797, Monday–Friday 9–4.

Fax: 716/873–4462.

Listings: Over 70. Many private residences; some guest homes and country inns. Areas covered include Niagara Falls, Buffalo, Rochester, Toronto, and Lake Ontario to Northern Pennsylvania. Directory $5.

Reservations: At least 24 hours' advance notice if possible.

Rates: $45–$150. $35 single, $150 double. Weekly and family rates available. One night's rate required as deposit on less than three nights; three or more nights require one-half of the total in advance. Deposits, less $25 cancellation fee, are refundable if cancellation is made at least seven days prior to scheduled arrival; no refund with less than seven days' notice. ◆

The experience of B&B hospitality has been offered through this service for five years. The wide range of listings includes a lakefront home, an Italianate Victorian, a former gristmill, a bungalow, an urban B&B, a ranch-style home, a century-old farmhouse, and a mansion near Chautauqua. Listings range from modest to luxurious. Many are restored historic properties. In addition, owner Georgia Brannan, active in the B&B industry, offers corporate B&B stays, short- and long-term stays, gift certificates, and B&B travel planning. Karen Ruckinger is reservation manager.

KEY TO SYMBOLS
♥ Lots of honeymooners come here.
♠ Families with children are very welcome. (Please see page xii.)
♠ "Please emphasize that we are a private home, not an inn."
♣ Groups or private parties sometimes book the entire B&B.
◆ Travel agents' commission paid. (Please see page xii.)
✽ Sorry, no guests' pets are allowed.
✂ No smoking inside *or* no smoking at all, even on porches.

Niagara/Buffalo/Chautauqua Area
———— B&Bs ————

Plumbush at Chautauqua   716/789–5309
Chautauqua-Stedman Road, P.O. Box 864, Chautauqua, NY 14722

Hosts: Sandy and George Green
Location: On 125 acres, set back from the country road. One mile from Chautauqua Institution. Opposite 36-hole golf course. One mile to lake, swimming, boating, skating; 20 minutes to wineries and antiques shops; 30 to downhill skiing. On Route 33, 3 miles from Route 17, less than 1 mile from Route 394.

Open: Year round; reservations preferred. Two-night minimum stay, sometimes three, during peak seasons and on some weekends.
Rates: Double occupancy. $75 double bed, $85 king/twins option or queen. MC, Visa.
♥ ✥ ♦ ✈ ✰

> From New York: *"Everything about Plumbush is wonderful . . . from the choice of colors to the breakfasts, from the architecture to the hosts."* From North Carolina: *"A perfect 10."*

Maybe you saw this B&B in *Victorian Homes*. Or *Victoria* or *Innsider* magazines. Or even on a Benjamin Moore paint chart!

Sandy knew this 1860s Italian villa–style house from the schoolbus window as a child. She grew up on a nearby dairy farm, 3 miles from where George was raised in a family that has been in the lumber industry for five generations. So when the Greens felt it was time to come back home, they sold their acclaimed Hudson Valley B&B and took on this challenge, which became a two-year restoration project. George wired throughout, installed five bathrooms, and designed a sun room with arches that echo the windows of the 11-foot-ceilinged rooms. Sandy substituted painting and papering for church organ playing. Because of the views from each window, she chose shutters rather than curtains. By the summer of 1988, the first guests climbed the beautiful circular staircase to the tower for its commanding panoramic view. Ever since, the hosts have been greeting guests, who enjoy the music room with its piano and organ, the almost-famous Green hospitality, and the country Victorian decor.

Bed and bath: Four second-floor rooms, all private shower baths. One with a double bed. One with king/twins option. Two with queen beds.
Breakfast: 8:30–9:30. Coffee ready at 7. Juice, fresh fruit, homemade muffins and breads, home-blended granola, cheese and crackers, yogurt, hot beverages. Often, extra treats on Sunday. Guests usually take breakfast into wicker-furnished enclosed sun room overlooking gardens and woods.
Plus: A real cookie jar—filled. Self-serve hot or cold drinks. Sun room with Franklin wood stove and ceiling fans. Bedroom ceiling fans. Rockers on veranda. Two-mile wooded trail for hiking, cross-country skiing, and birding right here. Bicycles available for guests' use.

Westfield House

716/326–6262

East Main Road, Route 20, P.O. Box 505, Westfield, NY 14787

Hosts: Betty and Jud Wilson
Location: Two miles east of town, between Buffalo and Erie. Near I–90 exit 60. Way back from road behind large trees. Surrounded by grape vineyards. Five minutes to Lake Erie, 15 to Lake Chautauqua, 30 to cross-country and downhill skiing. Close to wineries and antiques shops.

Open: Year round. Two-night minimum July and August weekends.
Rates: $55 single. $60–$75 double. $85 suite. $15 additional person in room. Midweek senior citizen discount. MC, Visa.
♥ ⁂ ♦ ✗ ✂

Guests can tell: The Wilsons love B&B. And they love their red brick Gothic Revival house, beautifully furnished with some museum-quality antiques and family heirlooms and portraits. There's a cherry staircase, lots of beveled glass, crystal-chandeliered front hall, and, in the common rooms, Gothic woodwork and windows. The house, restored by the Wilsons in 1987 following years of searching for the "right place," was at one time the home of *Antiques Journal.*

Betty, who has a needlepoint shop here, and Jud, a salesman, have "entertained together"—as Betty says—for 42 years. As hosts they are delighted with guests who relax and enjoy their home, this wonderful area, and all the area has to offer.

In residence: Grandchildren may visit during the month of August.
Bed and bath: Six rooms (two are suites); all private baths. All custom-made mattresses. Two adjoining first-floor rooms with shower bath; large room with queen four-poster bed and fireplace, other room with pull-out sofa bed and telephone. On second floor, queen beds, shower bath; king, shower bath; double bed, full bath. Suite has two double beds, full bath, living room with TV and telephone. Rollaway.
Breakfast: 9–10. Fresh fruit, homemade breads and muffins, coffee, teas, and juices. Crepes, pancakes, or French toast. By candlelight in fireplaced dining room set with linen, cloth napkins, silver, fine china.
Plus: In season, bowls of grapes from the surrounding vineyards; grape juice in rooms. Evening refreshments. Fresh flowers. Down comforters. Air conditioning in three second-floor rooms. Ceiling fans in some. Upright organ in parlor. Guest refrigerator. Picnic tables. Lawn furniture. Walking/jogging trails in vineyards. Bicycles.

---

*If you've been to one B&B, you haven't been to them all.
If you have met one B&B host, you haven't met them all.*

The William Seward Inn

716/326–4151
800/338–4151

RD 2, South Portage Road (Route 394)
Westfield, NY 14787

Hosts: Jim and Debbie Dahlberg
Location: On a high knoll overlooking Lake Erie. Minutes from the village, 20 antiques shops, five wineries. Four miles to Lake Chautauqua, 7 to Chautauqua Institution. Adjacent to cross-country skiing. Half hour to downhill ski resorts; 65 miles south of Buffalo.

Open: Year round. Two-night minimum on July, August, October weekends.
Rates: Main house $80–99. Singles $10 less. $25 extra person. Carriage house $135. Mystery, antiquing, and some holiday packages available. MC, Visa.
♥ ♣ ♦ ✈ ⅄

Although Chautauqua Institution is a major draw, many travelers come specifically to stay at this antiques-filled 1821 inn, which has become almost famous for Jim's cooking. (Recipes are shared—sometimes right in the kitchen.) The comfortable ambiance, created with period antiques (mid-1800s–early 1900s), wallpapers, and decor, has been acknowledged in a full-page *New York Times* travel article. Yet, as skiers, honeymooners, business guests, and antiques lovers attest, Jim and Debbie make the difference. If you'd like, they'll share the history of the inn, which was given its mansion appearance when William Seward (later governor of New York and Lincoln's secretary of state) added pillars in the 1840s. Full restoration took place in 1982, and the inn opened for business in 1983. The Dahlbergs made their career change in 1990 when they moved from Buffalo. Jim "retired" from a major commercial bank as vice president in operations. For two years Debbie continued working for a fair housing organization before becoming full-time innkeeper in 1992.

In residence: In hosts' quarters, four cats whom you might meet on the patio.
Bed and bath: Fourteen rooms, all private baths. On first and second floors in mansion, ten rooms with king, queen (some four-posters), double, or twin beds; some baths are tub/shower, some shower only. In carriage house, king or queen beds, Jacuzzis for two.
Breakfast: 7:45–9:30, earlier for businesss guests and skiers. Juice, homemade muffins, fruit. Garnished hot entree choices include scrambled eggs with tarragon and four cheeses, French toast, apple cinnamon pancakes. In dining room with view of birds at feeder.
Plus: Air conditioning throughout. Fireplaced common areas. Wet bar. Grounds with gardens, benches, chairs, trails. Option of dinner, Thursday–Sunday, $36 per person including tax.

> From Indiana: *"A native . . . returned to Westfield after 50 years . . . delighted to find such fine accommodations at the historic inn . . . friendliness makes it a must for a return visit."* From Pennsylvania: *"Superb."* From Ohio: *"Fabulous food. . . . The library with Vivaldi was a delight. . . . A wonderful hideaway."*

The Cameo Inns

716/754–2075

4710 Lower River Road, Lewiston, NY 14092

Hosts: Gregory and Carolyn Fisher
Location: Two properties, three minutes' drive apart. Both on the Seaway Trail, Route 18F. Victorian house, 5 miles north of Niagara Falls, is on 60-foot bluff overlooking the Niagara River and Canadian shore. Manor house, 2½ miles farther north on same road at number 3881, is on three secluded acres. Within a half hour of 14 wineries. Five minutes to Canada.

Open: Victorian house in Lewiston is open spring through fall. Manor house in Youngstown is open year round.
Rates: In Victorian house $80 queen, $99 suite, $65 double or twins with shared bath. In manor house $95, $115; suites $125 or $175; $75 shared bath. Singles $5 less. $15 cot. No charge for crib. MC, Visa.
♥ ♣ ♦ ✈ ⊱

Guests other than romantics are welcomed by the Fishers, but romance is surely a feature of their "two-part" B&B. The 27-room manor house has a 45-foot-long living room; there's a stone fireplace at each end. And another in the hunter green–colored library. Decorated in English country style, the mansion was "brought back to life" by the Fishers, native Buffalonians, in 1990, three years after they opened the original Cameo Inn, a sizable Victorian house complete with period wallpapers, antiques, and Oriental rugs. (The Victorian exterior has become a traffic stopper in shades of taupe, green, burgundy, and cream.)

Carolyn, a registered nurse who also has a degree in fine arts, is color consultant for Greg, a professional painting and decorating contractor who recently revived his interest in vintage sports cards.

In residence: Son Aaron, a college student, is assistant innkeeper. A Gordon setter, Beauregard, "captivates guests with his beauty." Heidi is an Airedale/shepherd mix.
Foreign language spoken: A little French.
Bed and bath: In Victorian house, four second-floor rooms with ceiling fans. Private full bath for room with brass queen bed. Private shower bath for suite with queen bed, sitting room, view of Niagara. Full hall bath shared by room with antique double oak bed and one with view of river, two twin white iron beds. In manor house, three suites (one has four rooms and one is a bridal suite) with private tub and shower baths, private sun rooms, cable TV, and private phones. Plus two rooms—one with two twin beds and one with a queen bed—that share a connecting full bath.

Breakfast: 8:30–9. Guests at both houses eat in manor house dining room. Buffet with fresh orange or grapefruit juice. Crepes, omelets, "Greg's eggs," or Dutch babies (oven pancakes). Homemade pastries. Hot beverages.

From Ohio: *"Private . . . romantic . . . elegant room with breathtaking view. . . . breakfast was incredible . . . feeling of visiting dear friends."*

Do you have to get up for breakfast?
There's no one rule. Check each description in this book for the various arrangements. More than one guest has been enticed by the aroma of fresh muffins. If you are on business or want to catch the morning ferry, eat-and-run is just fine. If, however, cuisine is a feature, plan on appearing at the specified time!
Vacationers (not skiers) find breakfast a very social time. One hostess says that even when guests say they want to be on the road early, they often linger over breakfast for hours. If hosts join you, please understand when they leave the table after a while.

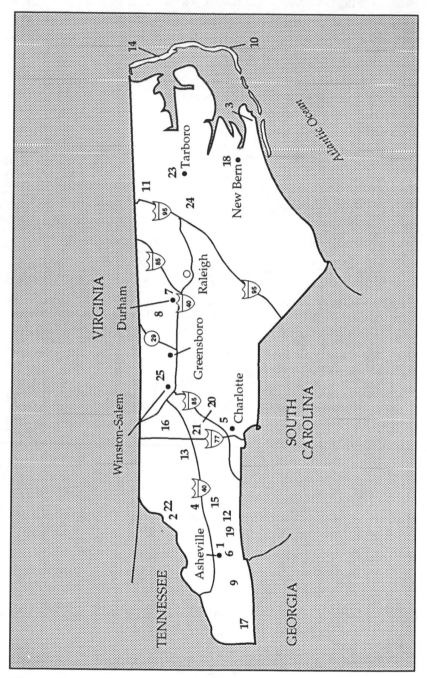

The numbers on this map indicate the locations of B&Bs described in detail in this chapter.

NORTH CAROLINA

1 **Asheville**
   Applewood Manor, *188*
   Black Walnut Inn, *189*
   Cairn Brae, *190*
   The Inn on Montford, *191*
2 **Banner Elk**
   The Banner Elk Inn B&B, *192*
3 **Beaufort**
   Pecan Tree Inn, *193*
4 **Black Mountain**
   Bed and Breakfast Over
      Yonder, *194*
5 **Charlotte**
   The Homeplace Bed &
      Breakfast, *195*
   The Inn on Providence, *196*
6 **Clyde**
   Windsong: A Mountain Inn
      (and llama farm), *197*
7 **Durham**
   Arrowhead Inn, c. 1775, *198*
   Old North Durham Inn, *199*
8 **Durham: Hillsborough**
   The Hillsborough House Inn, *200*
9 **Franklin**
   Buttonwood Inn, *201*
10 **Hatteras**
   Outer Banks Bed & Breakfast,
      202
11 **Henderson**
   La Grange Plantation Inn, *203*
12 **Hendersonville**
   The Waverly Inn, *204*
13 **Hiddenite**
   Hidden Crystal Inn, *205*

14 **Kill Devil Hills**
   The Figurehead, *206*
15 **Lake Lure**
   The Lodge on Lake Lure, *206*
16 **Mount Airy**
   Pine Ridge Inn, *207*
17 **Murphy**
   Huntington Hall Bed &
   Breakfast, *208*
18 **New Bern**
   The Aerie, *209*
   Harmony House Inn, *210*
19 **Rutherfordton**
   Pinebrae Manor, *211*
20 **Salisbury**
   The 1868 Stewart-Marsh
      House, *212*
   Rowan Oak House, *213*
21 **Statesville**
   Aunt Mae's Bed & Breakfast,
      214
22 **Sugar Grove**
   Rivendell Lodge, *215*
23 **Tarboro**
   Little Warren Bed and
      Breakfast, *216*
24 **Wilson**
   Miss Betty's Bed & Breakfast
      Inn, *217*
25 **Winston-Salem**
   Lady Anne's Victorian Bed &
      Breakfast, *218*

North Carolina B&Bs

Applewood Manor

704/254–2244

62 Cumberland Circle, Asheville, NC 28801-1718

Hosts: Susan Poole and Maryanne Young

Location: A quiet residential area of Montford Historic District. On two acres with trees and wildflower gardens; ¾ mile north of downtown Asheville; 3 miles from Biltmore Estate. Two blocks from Botanical Gardens.

Open: Year round. Two-night minimum on weekends.

Rates: $75 per room, $85 with balcony and fireplace. $95 with fireplace and sitting area with daybed. $100 cottage with living room and kitchen. Singles $5 less. Discover, MC, Visa.

♥ ⁂ ♦ ✗ ⚡

As guests, they were two cytotechnologists from State College, Pennsylvania, when they learned that the inn was for sale. In 1991 Maryanne, a bluegrass/traditional musician, and Susan, a basketry and fitness enthusiast, exchanged their microscopes for innkeeping hats. Now they host many guests who come for the nearby Biltmore Estate, the Blue Ridge Parkway, and Connemara (Carl Sandburg's house) too. Their turn-of-the-century Colonial Revival house, an inn since 1987, is furnished with antiques, Oriental rugs, and linens and lace.

In residence: Lucy, a calico cat, usually in hosts' quarters.

Bed and bath: Four queen-bedded second-floor rooms. Three with working fireplace and a balcony. All with private baths; two shower only, two tub and shower. Rollaway bed. Cottage has queen bed, queen sofa bed, living room, kitchen area, bath with oversized shower.

Breakfast: 8–9:30. "Susan cooks, Maryanne serves." Blueberry sour cream pancakes, orange pecan waffles, herbed egg bake, apple brie omelets, English muffin or pear bread, cranberry orange nut or pineapple muffins. Served on wicker-furnished porch or in fireplaced dining room.

Plus: No TV. Fireplaced common areas. Air-conditioned guest rooms with ceiling fans. Afternoon beverage. Fresh fruit and flowers. Mints on pillow. Badminton and croquet right here. Complimentary use of nearby sports club facilities including Nautilus, racquetball courts, sauna, whirlpool, and outdoor pool. Picnic baskets, $8.50 per person. Three- and 10-speed bikes (no charge).

Unless otherwise stated, rates in this book are per room for two and include breakfast in addition to all the amenities in "Plus." As for taxes and gratuities, please see page xi.

Black Walnut Inn   704/254–3878

288 Montford Avenue, Asheville, NC 28801

Host: Jeanette Syprzak
Location: In the Montford Historic District. Within a 15-minute drive of Biltmore Estate, restaurants, Blue Ridge Parkway. Two-minute walk to nearest park.

Open: Year round.
Rates: $55 double bed, $75–$95 queen bed. $5 less singles, $10 extra person (in queen rooms only). Discover, MC, Visa.
♥ ♦ ♣ ♦ ✖ ⅍

The house, influenced by the Biltmore Estate and built in 1899 for a woman from Chicago, is once again owned by a native Chicagoan. Jeanette was a Realtor and marketing company art director who had already restored and decorated three houses when she decided to become an innkeeper. She bid on this Shingle Style house even before having the opportunity to see the big foyer, the eight fireplaces, the heart of pine flooring, the window seats, and the many-windowed tower linen room, which has become a favorite bedroom for many guests.

In the fall of 1992, Jeanette opened with a combination of antique and traditional furniture, comfortable sofas and chairs, and sound insulation in many walls, and with plans to have faux mahogany finish restored on all the interior doors. The huge century-old backyard walnut tree, for which the inn is named, provides a lovely canopy for the planned terrace and plantings.

In residence: In hosts' quarters, Adam, age seven. Mr. Kitty the cat. Mr. Snow is a small American Eskimo dog.
Foreign languages spoken: "Some Polish, and a tiny amount of French, German, and Spanish."
Bed and bath: Four second-floor rooms; three with fireplaces. One with double bed, three queen (one in turret room with cloud-painted ceiling). All private baths—one with whirlpool, one with a steam/shower room, two with original claw-footed tubs. Rollaway available.
Breakfast: 8:30–9:30 continental buffet; 8–9 full and family style with French crepes, homemade waffles, or eggs, breakfast meats. Jeanette's own peach preserves.
Plus: Air conditioning. Fireplaced common rooms. Grand piano in living room. Welcoming refreshments. Bedtime chocolates or cookies. Down comforters. Turndown service. Fresh flowers.

KEY TO SYMBOLS
♥ Lots of honeymooners come here.
♦ Families with children are very welcome. (Please see page xii.)
♦ "Please emphasize that we are a private home, not an inn."
♣ Groups or private parties sometimes book the entire B&B.
♦ Travel agents' commission paid. (Please see page xii.)
✖ Sorry, no guests' pets are allowed.
⅍ No smoking inside *or* no smoking at all, even on porches.

Cairn Brae

704/252–9219

217 Patton Mountain Road, Asheville, NC 28804

Hosts: Milli and Ed Adams

Location: Secluded and quiet. On three wooded acres with trails, a pond, and views of Blue Ridge Mountains. Fifteen minutes from downtown.

Open: April–November. Two-day minimum in October and on holiday weekends.

Rates: Double occupancy. $80 room with queen or room with double and single bed; $95 king with sitting room; $15 extra person. $120 family suite (maximum of four guests). MC, Visa.

♥ ⅋ ♣ ◆ ✗ ⅄

As Milli and Ed say, "We were only halfway up the driveway when we fell in love with this wonderful big three-storied house," which has paneling, hardwood floors, and many floor-to-ceiling windows.

In Florida they were in retailing and advertising—and used to entertaining. Since 1987 their guests (many repeats and referrals) can tell that the Adamses "love every minute" of B&B in this mountain retreat furnished with wicker, antiques, and traditional pieces.

Bed and bath: Four rooms—all with floor-to-ceiling or large picture windows. All with private baths. King bed, sitting room with queen sofa bed; queen bed; or room with a double and a single bed. Family suite has queen-bedded room connecting with room with bunk beds, rocking horse, toys, and games.

Breakfast: Usually 8–9. Homemade rolls or special breads. Casseroles, waffles, or quiche. Local fruits in season. Juice. Served at table set with fine china and crystal in dining room overlooking treetops.

Plus: Living room with stone fireplace. Phone jacks, window fans, individual thermostats in each room. Fresh fruit and flowers. Afternoon refreshments on terrace or by fire. Bedside homemade goodies. Picnic baskets.

> From Michigan: *"I came for the Biltmore Estate. . . . [The Adamses'] gracious hospitality makes us want to return. . . . Suzie [daughter, age 14] discovered that an appreciation of antiques and a bygone way of life has a place in our hurry-scurry way of life."* From Virginia: *"The highlight of our trip."* From Florida: *"We could live there!"*

※

From the country: " Rural living is great. Did I tell you about the night the cows came? A farmer neighbor up the road had left a gate unlatched. About 10 p.m. I had 22 holsteins and one bull milling around the back yard, peering in the windows, mooing and munching! The guests loved it. (The garden didn't.)"

The Inn on Montford

704/254–9569

296 Montford Avenue, Asheville, NC 28801

Hosts: Ripley Hotch and Owen Sullivan

Location: On a rise, set back from a wide street that has arched old oak trees. In Montford Historic District, surrounded by grand old homes (most are being restored). "We're in a comfortably sized city that seems to have a festival every other weekend—unusual botanical gardens, antiques, crafts, folk arts, foliage, Christmas . . . it goes on and on."

Open: Year round.

Rates: Per room, $90–$110 according to size of room. MC, Visa.

❀ ◆ ✕ ⅃

When the innkeepers sold Boydville, their mansion B&B in Martinsburg, West Virginia, they bought this more informal "Arts and Crafts interpretation of a gabled English cottage." The house was designed by the supervising Biltmore Estate architect with exterior shingles and pebble-dash stucco.

Ripley and Owen added soundproofing and Jacuzzis, furnished with their extraordinary antiques and art collections, and opened in the fall of 1992. A corner stone fireplace and window seat are in the entry hall. Marine paintings and ship models, a wonderful old leather sofa, and blue and white porcelain are in the fireplaced den. French doors lead to the semicircular sun room, where a door opens to the big wide front porch.

Ripley talks about his dream combination: collecting antiques, running an old-fashioned business, and writing about technology. He is coauthor of the recently released *How to Start and Run Your Own Bed and Breakfast Inn* and technology editor of *Nation's Business* magazine. Owen is a raconteur who is thinking of having an antiques shop in town. Returnees know that he enjoys taking guests to auctions "to keep them from spending too much money or from passing up a great buy."

In residence: Two dogs: Jefferson Davis, a collie/shepherd, "has had more offers of homes than you can imagine." Dolley Madison is an American Eskimo.

Foreign language spoken: French.

Breakfast: About 9. Continental if earlier. Entree possibilities include puffed apple pancakes, stuffed raspberry French toast, orange croissants, frittatas, stratas. Sometimes, "Caribbean pear" in orange sauce with cinnamon stick (as a stem) and kiwi cut as the leaf. In dining room at inlaid table surrounded by collections of porcelain and china.

Bed and bath: Four second-floor queen-bedded rooms; each with gas fireplace. All private en-suite baths; three with Jacuzzis, one with claw-foot tub and full shower.

Plus: Air-conditioned bedrooms. Refreshments. Down comforters. Flannel sheets. Off-street parking. Porch rockers. Wonderful garden furniture in backyard, where a fountain is planned.

The Banner Elk Inn B&B   704/898–6223

Route 3, Box 1134 or P.O. Box 1953, Banner Elk, NC 28604

Host: Beverly Lait
Location: In a mountain valley village setting on Highway 194 north, .2 mile from town's only traffic light. Minutes to Sugar and Beech ski resorts and Grandfather Mountain. Walking distance to fine restaurants. Six miles from Blue Ridge Parkway.

Open: Year round. Two-night minimum on weekends.
Rates: Per room. Shared bath $60. Private bath $65 weekdays, $75 weekends. Families (total of four people) midweek, $90 for two rooms. MC, Visa.
♥ ⛄ ♣ ✂

The innkeeper is a tapestry maker, portrait artist, real estate broker, and foreign exchange student counselor. She lives in a raspberry-pink expanded 1912 farmhouse that has been a church, an inn, and a residence. Once abandoned, now it has been restored. When Beverly, a native of Charleston, South Carolina, opened her "casual, elegant, friendly, spontaneous" B&B two years ago, she filled it with carved woods, stained glass, and antiques—many collected during 14 years of living in Peru, England, Uruguay, and Germany. One of her first guests was an Uruguayan architect who was amazed to find Uruguayan architectural books in her library. Many guests who come "to get away from it all" utilize the hand-drawn fun map with selected highlights including a famous general store (est. 1833), hiking and ski areas, and shops.

Foreign languages spoken: Spanish and German.
In residence: "Princess, a 14-year-old overly sensitive and pampered German shepherd."
Bed and bath: Four soundproofed second-floor rooms. Two rooms, each with Victorian double bed, have large private tub/shower bath. One queen bedded room and one with two twin beds share a tub/shower bath plus an extra hall half bath.
Breakfast: 8–10. Cottage cheese pancakes or baked cinnamon apples stuffed with granola or Belgian waffles with fresh-cooked cinnamon apples, whipped cream, syrup, and sausages. Or fruit salad and scrambled eggs. Homemade whole wheat or banana nut bread. Orange juice and freshly ground coffee. Served in wonderful Great Room at large table set with fine china, crystal, and silver—or at individual tables in small dining room.
Plus: European down comforters. Fireplaced Great Room with cable TV. Cordless phones. Fresh fruit. Wildflowers. Handmade sweater shop on premises.

> From North Carolina: *"Perfect . . . art, antiques, and food . . . wonderful sense of color and texture. . . . For an English assignment on the topic of a memorable meal, our 16-year-old wrote about Beverly's breakfast."*

*H*ospitality *is the keynote of B&B.*

Pecan Tree Inn   919/728–6733
116 Queen Street, Beaufort, NC 28516

Hosts: Susan and Joe Johnson
Location: In historic district with restored period homes; half a block to waterfront. A short walk to fine restaurants, shopping, North Carolina Maritime Museum, old burying grounds. Close to two-minute boat ride to Carrot Island, where wild ponies graze. Near ferry for Shackleford Island. Fifty minutes' drive to Outer Banks ferry.
Open: Year round.

Rates: Mid-April to mid-September: weekdays, $80 twin, $80–$95 queen, $95 king or canopy bed, $105 bridal suite; weekends, $10 more. $15 third person in room. Mid-September to mid-April: weekdays, $65 twin, $65–$80 queen, $80 king or canopy bed, $90 bridal suite; weekends, $5 more. $15 third person in room. MC, Visa.
♥ ⚜ ♦ ✗ ⚰

A perfect match. Joe was a New Jersey hardware store owner (a third-generation one) and was used to spending time looking for—and usually finding—all kinds of five-cent widgets requested by customers. He and Susan, who worked with the AAA's insurance department, "enjoyed staying at B&Bs, enjoy people, had plans for about five years down the road. We found this house for sale, loved the town—once you're here for a few days, you're on Beaufort time—changed our plans, spent six months renovating, planted herb and wildflower gardens, and opened in 1992. When 92-year-old Howard Jones, a local resident, had breakfast with his granddaughter in our dining room, he recalled planting the two pecan trees for which the inn is named."

At the turn of the century, additional rooms, turrets, and gingerbread were added to the 1866 Masonic Lodge, which has seen use as a teahouse, school, doctor's office, and apartments. Now the freshly decorated inn has refinished pine floors, patterned carpets and some Orientals, antiques, and an uncluttered look; it is sought after by business travelers, honeymooners, and tourists. Just as this book went to press, the inn was photographed for *Condé Nast Traveler.*

Bed and bath: Seven rooms, all private shower baths. On first floor, room with brass queen bed. Rooms on second floor (two open onto a porch) have twin, queen (one canopied), or canopied king beds. Bridal suite has king bed, two-person Jacuzzi. All rooms with canopied beds have private entrance onto porches. Rollaway available.
Breakfast: Usually 7:30–9. Homemade muffins, breads, and cakes. Fresh fruits, cereal, juices, freshly ground coffee. In dining room or on front porch.
Plus: Central air conditioning. Bedroom and living room ceiling fans. Fresh flowers. Freshly made pecan candy. Guest refrigerator with soda, juice, ice, cold water. Beach towels and chairs. Books and games in library. Bicycles (no charge). Picnic baskets prepared. Transportation to/from local marina and Beaufort Airport.

From Pennsylvania: *"Enchanting."* From North Carolina: *"After visiting B&Bs far and wide, I give Pecan Tree Inn a five-star rating in all respects."*

Bed and Breakfast Over Yonder　704/669–6762

431 North Fork Road　　　　　　(winter phone) **919/945–9958**
Black Mountain, NC 28711
Winter address: 5930 Robinhood Road
Pfafftown, NC 27040

Host: Willie Headley
Location: "On a hillside on 18 very private acres, in a town filled with antiques shops and surrounded by views of the Black Mountains." Two miles north of I–20; 9 from Blue Ridge Parkway, 17 from Asheville's Biltmore Estate, ¼ mile from golf course. Within an hour's drive of gem mining, white-water rafting, hot-air balloon rides, and Mount Mitchell.
Open: May 15–November 15.
Rates: $40–$55 single. $45–$60 double. $10 extra person in room.
♥ ⅏ ⁂ ◆ ✠ ✂

"I was raised here and have come back after 40 years to run this B&B (with added baths and new beds) in quiet, restful surroundings. It's great fun to share this lovely house with guests from all over the world, and to restore my mother's gardens and wildflowers back to their glory! So far I haven't been stumped in suggesting a neat place for an activity, a place of interest, or just a perfect spot to relax or picnic."

Willie, a psychiatric nurse, and her husband Bob (cohost on weekends), a professor of cardiology at the Wake Forest Medical Center, are grandparents of seven. Their 1920s American Craftsman house has lots of comfortable seating in the large fireplaced, paneled living room. There are some French and English antiques and some family pass-me-downs dating back to Grandmother's boardinghouse in the 1800s.

In residence: Puff, the cat, sometimes "joins guests on the porch."
Bed and bath: Five rooms on two floors with attached private baths (three full, two shower only). Rooms furnished with canopied double bed plus trundle bed, queen bed (wicker or high-post), or white iron king bed. Rollaway and crib available.
Breakfast: 8:30. Homemade breads, fresh fruit, juice. Served on mountain-view porch overlooking wildflower garden or by candlelight in paneled dining room.
Plus: Fresh flowers "always." Each guest room has ceiling or window fan and hot pot with tea, coffee, and cocoa. Some rooms with desks. Down comforters. Fireplaced living and dining rooms. Forgotten-items basket. Guest refrigerator. Complimentary champagne or wine for honeymooners and anniversaries. Gazebo. Mountain hiking right here.

Guests wrote: *"Lovely. . . . We felt right at home. And I loved the breakfast."*

Wedding guests love to stay at a B&B. One innkeeper tells of the bride who asked to have relatives booked on different floors. "Be forewarned, my aunts haven't spoken for 15 years."

The Homeplace Bed & Breakfast 704/365-1936

5901 Sardis Road, Charlotte, NC 28270

Hosts: Peggy and Frank Dearien
Location: A country setting in a residential neighborhood on a corner 2½ acre property. Five miles from uptown, in southeast Charlotte. Within 15 minutes of I–77/I–85 intersection, restaurants, shopping malls; 20 to coliseum, merchandise mart, and Mint Museum.

Open: Year round. Two-night minimum on holidays and special event weekends.
Rates: $68 single, $78 and $88 double, $15 daybed (third person). Amex, MC, Visa.
♥ ♣ ♦ ✗ ✂

In true American B&B style, this place to stay has become the reason to go. And all because, in 1984, the Deariens, a legal secretary and an accountant/treasurer in Charlotte, purchased "on impulse" the 1902 country Victorian house they had often admired. It has a tin roof—with that special sound when it rains. There are rocking chairs on the popular wraparound porch, wooded grounds, walkways and wonderful gardens, a gazebo, and a restored barn. It is home—and now the Deariens' full-time occupation, where breakfast was made on a grill after Hurricane Hugo, and where one North Carolina resident observes: "Peggy's personality is everywhere. The Deariens give the entire B&B industry a special luster." Throughout, there are family treasures, including primitive paintings that are collectors' items done in the 1980s by John Gentry, Peggy's father, who lived to be 91.

Bed and bath: Three queen-bedded rooms with private baths and nonworking fireplaces. First-floor room with attached tub/shower bath has private entrance to wraparound porch. One second-floor room with bay windows, attached tub/shower bath. Other second-floor room with poster bed, daybed, shower bath one step outside room, privacy hall screen.
Breakfast: 7–9. Fresh fruit. Homemade breads. Egg dishes and breakfast meats. Served in intimate Victorian dining room, on screened or wraparound porch, or—for honeymooners—in room (extra charge).
Plus: Central air conditioning. Fresh fruit and flowers. Bedroom ceiling fans. TV in study. Guest refrigerator. Homemade cookies or cake in evening. Coffee, tea, soft drinks, juices, and ice available until 11 p.m. Forgotten-items basket. Mints. Bathrobes.

> From Louisiana: *"THE place to stay in Charlotte. I appreciate the ambiance, the Deariens, and the breakfasts.... Oh those breakfasts! Have traveled extensively ... don't know if they can be equaled anywhere. An unforgettable experience which I recommend to all who appreciate the best in accommodations."* From North Carolina: *"We feel spoiled ... rooms that make you feel romantic and at home ... met guests we still keep in touch with."* From Georgia: *"We wish The Homeplace was in many places."*

---

*B*ed and Breakfast gives a sense of place.

The Inn on Providence   704/366–6700

6700 Providence Road, Charlotte, NC 28266

Hosts: Daniel and Darlene McNeill
Location: A residential neighborhood on two-lane Highway 16, which
becomes four lanes within a mile as it
reaches the business center and malls.
Eight miles from downtown Charlotte; 1 mile north of Highway 51.

Open: Year round. Two-night minimum on holiday weekends.
Rates: Per room. Shared bath $59.
Private bath $69 queen bed, $85
king. MC, Visa.
♥ ♣ ✗ ✂

The brick Federal-style colonial is "home" to friends and relatives of Charlotte residents, to business travelers (many returnees), to wedding guests and honeymooners too. Freshly decorated, it is filled with Darlene's collection of quilts and early American antiques, including her own cannonball bed and her grandmother's mahogany twin beds. Classical music is played all day.

Darlene and Dan, the gardener and "Mr. Fix-it" who is a manufacturer's rep for large electrical industrial supplies, had several summers of resort experience by the time they married in their last year of college. Eight years later, in 1985, they fulfilled their dream by converting this gracious private residence to an inn.

Bed and bath: Five rooms, three with private baths. One very private queen-bedded room, under eaves, over garage, with en-suite shower/tub bath. First-floor walnut-paneled queen-bedded room with private bath across the hall. On second floor, one very large fireplaced room has canopied king bed, shower/tub bath, French doors to private veranda; one room with queen four-poster shares a tub/shower bath (robes provided) with room that has two twin beds.

Breakfast: Usually 8, Monday–Friday; 9 on weekends. Freshly squeezed orange juice. Fruit such as poached pears, baked pineapple, or broiled grape-fruit. Chili cheese egg puff, croissants l'orange, or raspberry-filled French toast. Sausage balls, bacon bow ties, or curly ham. Homemade breads—coffee date, pear, cranberry/pumpkin—or muffins. Served in dining room or on screened, slate-floored, wicker-furnished veranda overlooking swimming pool.

Plus: Central air conditioning. Bedroom ceiling fans in all but paneled room, which has brass chandelier. Fireplaced living room. Fruit bowl. Chocolates. Lounge chairs on pool deck.

---

*B*reakfast is where the magic happens.

Windsong: A Mountain Inn (and llama farm)

120 Ferguson Ridge, Clyde, NC 28721

704/627-6111
fax 704/627-8080

Hosts: Donna and Gale Livengood
Location: Away. At 3,000-foot elevation on a mountainside with panoramic view of Smoky Mountains and green valley. Eight miles from U.S. Route 40. Within 40 minutes of Biltmore Estate, regional airport, Great Smoky Mountain National Park, Cherokee Indian Reservation, Appalachian Trail. Twenty minutes to antiquing and restaurants.
Open: February–December. Two-night minimum in guest house.
Rates: $95 main floor, $90 lower level. $20 each additional person. Ten percent less for singles or for five or more nights.
♥ ♣ ♦ ✻ ✄

Romantic. Spectacular inside and out. Peaceful. Inviting. With high-beamed ceilings, Mexican tile floors, and windowed walls. Native American and Eskimo artifacts accent the spacious contemporary light-pine log home designed by Donna's architect brother. There's a heated outdoor pool (what a setting); a tennis court; grounds with ornamental grasses, flowers, huge boulders, and hemlock hedge; and a hiking trail. The lovable llamas (the youngest was weeks old when I was there) are available for treks led by daughter Sarah.

For 35 years Gale was a Chicago-based educational film company executive. Now he imports French feature films, dreams up other exciting projects, and cohosts with chef and llama farmer Donna, who had a Round-the-World boutique in Illinois. When you visit, maybe there will be a tape of the local octogenarian explaining how "those woods up there used to be all cornfields." (If not, ask Gale to tell the story.) Maybe you too will be mesmerized by the fog and mist over the mountains and enchanted by Gale's poem, "The Legend of Windsong."

In residence: Katie, "the wonder dog, who deems it a pleasure and duty to accompany guests on our hiking trail." Seventeen llamas.
Bed and bath: Five rooms, each with phone jack, VCR player, deck or patio. Each with vanity in a separate niche. On main floor—king/twins option plus cot-sized Jenny Lind bed plus loft with twin bed; bath with deep tub, separate shower; fireplace. Fireplaced queen-bedded room has loft with twin bed, sunken tub for two, separate shower and toilet. Queen-bedded room has bath with tub and shower. On lower floor—queen bed, tub for two facing fireplace, separate room with shower and toilet. Queen bed, deep tub, fireplace, separate room with shower and toilet.
Breakfast: 8–9:30. Juice, breads, and coffee available earlier. Fresh fruit; juices; home-baked sweet breads, coffee cakes, croissants. Grand Marnier orange French toast, blueberry buckwheat pancakes, omelets, quiches, egg-sausage casserole or German apple pancake. (Recipes shared.) Livengoods join guests.
Plus: Huge stone fireplace in cathedral-ceilinged living room. Upright piano, TV, refrigerator/wet bar, and hundreds of videocassettes (fine and performing arts and feature films) in guest lounge.

From North Carolina: *"Tears welled in my eyes. Quite simply, I did not want to leave."*

Arrowhead Inn, c. 1775

106 Mason Road
Durham, NC 27712

919/477–8430
800/528–2207
fax 919/417–8430

Hosts: Jerry, Barbara, and Cathy Ryan
Location: On four acres with 150-year-old magnolias, 32 varieties of birds. Seven miles north of I-85. Within 20 minutes of Duke University, Stagville Preservation Center, North Carolina Museum of Life and Science, Duke Tobacco Museum, and Research Triangle Park.
Open: Year round.
Rates: Per room. $65 shared bath. $85 private bath. $110 suite with canopy bed, private bath, patio. $135 two-room log cabin. $10 third person. Amex, Diners, MC, Visa.
♥ ♣ ✤ ♦ ✈

This family-run B&B, known for its warm welcome, is the source of a story that everyone loves to hear: The Ryans, mentors to many innkeepers, may be the only B&B owners in the country who were introduced to their new careers through a gift of an innkeeping seminar from two of their eight adult children. Subsequently, in 1985, Jerry, a Manhattan publisher, and Barb, a writer and needlewoman, bought and restored this historic, comfortable, inviting property. They furnished the rooms in various periods—from colonial through Tidewater—and were written up in *USA Today, Food & Wine, House & Garden,* and *Mid-Atlantic Country.* Eventually their daughter Cathy left the world of retailing and the New York–to–Hong Kong lifestyle to assist in welcoming relocators, Duke parents, museumgoers, and sheepherders (from Utah) . . . and to help with corporate meetings, family reunions, and weddings held here. Go and experience.

In residence: Three outdoor cats. "The one in the black tux is Fred Astaire. The other two are Bartles and Jaymes."
Bed and bath: Seven rooms (plus the cabin). Two have working fireplaces. Private baths are en suite. Rollaway and crib available. *In manor house,* on first floor, two queen-bedded rooms, one with private tub/shower bath, one with private shower bath; one with working fireplace and private patio. On second floor, queen, double, or twin-bedded rooms (two share a bath). *Carriage house* has two queen-bedded rooms, private full baths. *Cabin* (handicapped accessible) has king bed in sleeping loft; queen hide-a-bed in fireplaced sitting room, large full bath, porch with rockers.
Breakfast: Full served 8–9. Continental 7:30–9:30. Freshly squeezed orange juice, fruit, homemade baked goods. Chef's choice of entree could be ham, eggs, broiled tomatoes; French toast and bacon; banana pancakes; or chicken crepes. "Our own" preserved figs. Served in dining room and keeping room.
Plus: Robes provided in all rooms; private phones in some. Central air conditioning. Fireplaced living room and keeping room. Piano. Afternoon or evening refreshments. Guest refrigerator. Forgotten-items basket. Hammock. Picnic baskets.

> Guests wrote: *"A great example of what a B&B should be. . . . Just like being at Grandma's house, but we didn't have to do the dishes."*

Old North Durham Inn   919/683-1885
922 North Mangum Street, Durham, NC 27701-2229

Hosts: Jim and Debbie Vickery
Location: In historic district, an older suburb where many homes have been restored. Five minutes from I–85, Duke University, Durham Civic Center, Durham Bulls Baseball Park (two reserved seats for Bulls' games available for guests). Twenty minutes from I–40, Raleigh/Durham airport, UNC–Chapel Hill.
Open: Year round.
Rates: $65–$80 private bath. $100 suite. Singles $5 less. MC, Visa.

♥ ♯ ♣ ♣♣ ♦ ✈ ⅀

Although you missed the "as is" January 1990 open house held for 75 neighbors, you can see the results of the award-winning renovation—everything from major projects to the removal of 100 telephone lines. Two hundred admiring people came to the grand B&B opening of this early 19th-century Colonial Revival house.

In Washington, D.C., Debbie was a family and youth services specialist. Jim, a Bulls fan, worked with the Environmental Protection Agency. The parents of two grown children found Durham; the Ryans' innkeeping course (Arrowhead Inn, page (198); alocal EPA agency position for Jim; the house with 10-foot coffered ceilings; and capable used-to-replacing-with-new Vern Medlin—"we'll probably name a room after him someday"—who took on his first historic renovation job. When it came to decor, Vern would look at the tinted base for a rose-colored living room or the lavender sunroom and tell Debbie, "Jimmy's going to kill you." Period wallpapers were hung. Furnishings are a mix of traditional and antiques. Debbie, now a full-time innkeeper, is very involved in the community. The Vickerys and guests, too, are delighted.

In residence: "Sophie, a 14-year-old part golden retriever, part sheep dog."
Bed and bath: Four second-floor rooms. Queen-bedded room with daybed and private bath with whirlpool. Queen high-poster bed with fireplace, private bath. Suite has one room with queen bed and fireplace connected by a full bath to room with double bed and TV. Rollaway and crib available.
Breakfast: Usually 8–9:30. (Busy schedules accommodated.) Fresh juice and fruit, variety of egg dishes, fruit-filled pancakes or thick homemade French toast with sausage, bacon, or ham. Muffins. Served to daily rave reviews in fireplaced dining room.
Plus: Central air conditioning. Bedroom ceiling fans. Fireplaced living room with piano. Fresh flowers. Extensive North Carolina reference library. Guest phone. Veranda with wicker rockers. Late-afternoon or evening refreshments. Turndown service. Bathrobes. Mints on pillow. Forgotten-items basket. Guest refrigerator.

From Missouri: *"A real haven . . . fresh towels as fast as you can use them, friendly and ultrasolicitous hosts."* From Maryland: *"Loved the charm, hospitality, many thoughtful touches, delicious breakfast."* From New Jersey: *"Homey."* From Virginia: *"The ultimate . . . what a value."*

The Hillsborough House Inn   919/644-1600

209 East Tryon Street, P.O. Box 880, Hillsborough, NC 27278

Host: Katherine Webb
Location: Set back from road, on seven acres of woods, gardens, and ponds. In historic district of the state's colonial capital (population today: 4,500) where there are historic homes, churches, public buildings, antiques shops, and restaurants. Minutes from I–85 and I–40. Within 15 minutes of Duke University (Dur-ham) and University of North Carolina at Chapel Hill; 30 minutes from Raleigh International Airport, 20 to Burlington's factory outlets.
Open: Year round except Christmas–New Year's.
Rates: Double occupancy. $95, $105 with porch, $140 honeymoon suite. $25 trundle. MC, Visa.
♥ ♣ ♦ ✗ ⊁

Altogether, the local landmark with sweeping lawn and huge trees, with landscaped swimming pool and fish pond, is "comfortable and beautiful, elegant and gracious, casual and warm, eclectic and funky"—with family antiques, original art, and draped beds. The oldest part of the house was built about 1790. It became Italianate in 1853 (with columned 80-foot porch added around 1900). Almost 140 years later, artist Katherine, her lawyer husband Bev, and three sons moved from Charlotte to this home, which has been in Bev's family for 150 years.

Foreign languages spoken: "Un peu francais and Southern."
In residence: Katherine and Bev, her husband, live in family's quarters built in 1990. Outside, two dogs and three cats.
Bed and bath: Five large bedrooms in main house with queen (two with trundles) or king/twin option. All private baths; four full, the fifth with shower only. First-floor room has private outside entrance. Two second-floor rooms have porch overlooking pool and 1790s brick kitchen. The renovated brick kitchen has fireplaced queen-bedded room, plus fireplaced sitting room, and full bath with fireplace and whirlpool.
Breakfast: At guests' convenience. Cereals include a special mix. Fresh fruit. Homemade baked goods. Cheeses. Juices. Custom-blended coffees. Teas. Homemade jams, preserves, and other spreads. From cookbook-in-progress: Pecan Fool, Really Sticky Affairs, or equally "sinfully delicious" Willie's Apple Dapple. Buffet style.
Plus: Central air conditioning. Fresh flowers. Fireplaces in living room, dining room, and library. Original paintings by Katherine. Complimentary soft and hot drinks and snacks always available in guest kitchen. Electric blankets, down comforters and pillows. Bedroom ceiling fans. Porch rockers. Hammock. Jogging and walking routes in historic district and countryside.

Innkeepers are sharers. One recalls the guest who arrived for a wedding only to find he'd left his dress pants at home. The innkeeper wore the same size. The guest appeared at the wedding properly dressed in borrowed pants.

Buttonwood Inn   704/369–8985
190 Georgia Road, Franklin, NC 28734

Host: Liz Oehser
Location: In a cul-de-sac, surrounded by tall pine woods. On the county/city line, just off of 441 Business South. "Not totally quiet, but lots of cricket noises." Next to the Franklin Public Golf Course (hidden by trees in summer). One mile south of town (pop. 2,000), 76 miles southwest of Asheville. Forty-five minutes to the Nantahala Gorge, Forest, and rafting; 20 minutes to steam trains.
Open: April–November. Two-day minimum on holidays and on October and holiday weekends.
Rates: Include tax. $55 shared bath. $70 private bath. $10 third person. $10 rollaway.
♥ ✄

"Many guests come, as I did in 1984 (from Florida), to get away from the heat, to be in the mountains. I decorated this established B&B, a rustic cottage that was built in the 1920s and added on to in the 1950s, with country collectibles. In the past I sold my crafts—cross-stitching, stenciled items, decorated baskets and wreaths, and painted miniatures, but cooking gets more of my attention these days. Guests go gem mining and hiking. They book water rafting day trips where some of the Olympic kayakers trained, and they shop in two wonderful craft coops. The steam train excursions (three or four hours) through the mountains are very popular. It is beautiful here. Hummingbirds love the feeders. Foliage season is spectacular."

In residence: "Buttons, a dog that belongs to the former innkeepers, is here all the time. She never got used to the idea that they moved to the new house in back of Buttonwood."
Bed and bath: Four rooms with ceiling fans. On first floor, two rooms with private shower bath; one with double bed, one with a double and a twin. On second floor, double-bedded room and (smaller) room with two twin beds share a shower bath. Rollaway available.
Breakfast: At 8:30 or 9. One sitting at one large table. Stuffed French toast, artichoke quiche, puffy scrambled eggs or eggs Benedict, Dutch babies and peach and sausage bake, sausage ring, or crunchy baked bananas. Homemade scones with lemon butter, breads, muffins, or coffee cakes.

> From Kentucky: *"A place that makes you smile and feel good all over. Gracious hostess. . . . Loved the decor, scenery, and attention to detail."* From North Carolina: *"Very clean and comfortable. Great place for bird watching. Sat on deck with binoculars for much of two days."* From Florida: *"A delightful B&B experience . . . breakfasts are extraordinary."*

---

*If you've been to one B&B, you haven't been to them all.
If you have met one B&B host, you haven't met them all.*

Outer Banks Bed & Breakfast   919/986–2776

P.O. Box 610, Hatteras, NC 27943

Hosts: Diane Doyle-Phoenix and Ed Phoenix, Kathryn Phoenix
Location: In a small island village that until about 30 years ago was accessible by ferry only. Next to a pond on one side, a high privacy fence on other. On the ocean side of Route 12. Two-block walk to ocean along a quiet back street. Many restaurants within 10 miles (some within walking distance). Ten miles southwest of Cape Hatteras. "About six hours from Washington, D.C."
Open: March–December. Two-night minimum on weekends.
Rates: $70; $75 for large room. $10 third person. MC, Visa, Discover.
♥ ⛺ ♣ ✈

Wanted: A simple old fishing village house on the Outer Banks, where a marina sign reads, "If the world came to an end, it would take Hatteras three days to find out about it." Found in 1987 by Diane, who had been coming "for serenity of the soul" for about 20 years: This turn-of-the-century residence that was in the same family for four generations. She furnished in "Hatteras style—Grandma's house at the beach" with a mixture of antiques and comfortable contemporary pieces. Blue herons are everywhere—they're a logo, they appear in prints and carvings, and there's one antique taxidermied version. "Those on the pond are live."

Guests are curious about the island's history, the names, the Elizabethan accent still used by some old-timers, the lighthouses, the weekly community fish fries Diane assists with—and what one *Washington Post* staffer described as "Diane's dream life."

By the time you read this, Ed, a college administrator and county youth board chairman in upstate New York, may be retired. Until now he and Kathryn, age 12, have been summer hosts, with Kathryn taking the role of social director—sharing favorite places and playing Trivial Pursuit "till all hours." Off-season Diane has been teaching financial planning and consumer economics in New York on behalf of her consulting business clients.

Bed and bath: Three rooms. One first-floor double-bedded room shares a full bath with owner. On second floor, one large room with a double and a single brass bed shares a shower bath with a double-bedded room. Crib available.
Breakfast: 9. Fresh fruit, maybe in sherry/ginger drizzle. Quiche or souffle; fresh vegetables with a dip or dressing; homemade bread or muffins; bacon, sausage, ham, or chicken livers; coffee, tea, juice. Special diets accommodated. Served at antique Jacobean dining room table.
Plus: Central air conditioning plus individual guest room units. Ceiling fans everywhere. Coffee, iced tea, and lemonade always available. Cable TV in living room. Picnic baskets prepared. Deck with table and chairs overlooking secluded yard. Grill and crabpot for boiling; nutcrackers and paper goods too. Beach towels. Beach chairs and umbrella loaned. Boogie board. Canoe for rent. Outdoor hot/cold shower, toiletries, dressing room. Guest refrigerator. "Fifty-six continuous miles of sand."

La Grange Plantation Inn   919/438-2421
Route 3, Box 610, Nutbush Road, Henderson, NC 27536

Hosts: Jean and Dick Cornell
Location: Country setting. On eight acres with path through woods to Kerr Lake's southern shore. Six miles north of Henderson. Five miles from I–85, midway between Petersburg, Virginia, and Durham, North Carolina. Close to many restaurants. Two miles from public golf course and 1 mile to state recreation area (boat ramps).
Open: Year round.
Rates: $85 first night, $65 each consecutive following night. Singles, $75 first night, then $60. Amex, MC, Visa.
♥ ♣ ♦ ✗ ✂

Guests enter the covered and latticed breezeway for peace, quiet, and relaxation. The National Historic Preservation award-winning restoration of the inn incorporated the addition of seven baths, a kitchen, and a glassed-in dining room. Charleston, South Carolina, B&Bs were the inspiration for the Cornells' 1986 purchase of this "retirement project," which came without plumbing or landscaping, with Historic Register designation, and with pre–opening weekend pup tent living. The earliest part of the house was built in 1770. An extensive remodeling, which included Greek Revival features, was carried out in 1858. The property was owned by the same family—a cemetery is on the grounds—from 1825 until 1985.

In "contemporary California," Dick was in the paper industry; Jean, in Napa Valley wine public relations. Most recently Dick, the floor refinisher and gardener (with new greenhouse), was a professor at North Carolina State University. Jean, a native of England, became the inn's chef, interior designer, and—for all those window treatments and bedspreads—seamstress. The English antiques are from Dick's family and auctions—"one of our favorite forms of entertainment."

In residence: In hosts' quarters, Mai-Tai, a seal point Siamese cat.
Foreign languages spoken: "Broken French and Spanish."
Bed and bath: Five rooms with private baths. Four are queen-bedded; one on first floor has handicapped-accesible tub/shower. One room has two double beds.
Breakfast: 8–9. (Fresh coffee and tea await early risers.) Souffle, crepes, or casserole. Homemade muffins and breads. Special diets accommodated. In dining room overlooking rose garden.
Plus: No TV. Pool, beach towels. Individual bedroom air conditioning/heat control. Turndown service. Guest refrigerator. Fishing equipment. Horseshoes. Croquet. Hammock. Rental boats at local marina.

> From North Carolina: *"Pampered. . . . It was as if we entered another time period."* From D.C.: *"Exquisite gourmet breakfast."* From Virginia: *"Charm outdone only by that of its host and hostess, whose hospitality is generous beyond compare."*

The Waverly Inn
704/693–9193

783 North Main Street, Hendersonville, NC 28792-3622   800/537–8195

Hosts: John and Diane Sheiry (pronounced Shire-ey); Darla Olmstead (Diane's sister)
Location: In town on a main street, across from tennis courts and a church. Nineteen miles south of Biltmore Estate. Two miles west of I–26. Three-minute walk to historic area, antiques shops, restaurants; 3 miles to Flat Rock Playhouse (state theater)

and Carl Sandburg Natl. Historic Site.
Open: Year round. Two-night minimum on all major holidays.
Rates: $75 double. $85 queen. $95 king. $149 two-room suite with canopied king bed. $65 singles. $10 third person. Crib free. Theme weekend package rates include dinner. Amex, Discover, MC, Visa.
♥ ♯ ♣ ♦ ✄

Unwind. Eat. Sleep. Enjoy the mystique of the mountains and all that (or some of what) there is to do in the area. Select a book from the inn's library. Watch a holiday parade from the porch with former guests, now local residents, invited for the vantage point. Or come for a wine lovers' weekend. Or a mystery weekend. (One participant spent four hours under a table waiting for the "suspect" to make a move.) If you want a snowy scene, call to see if a particular three-times-a-year guest is expected. ("It always snows shortly after she arrives.")

This "direct people business" is just what the Sheirys sought in 1988 when they left Atlanta and 18 years (each) in the hotel and restaurant business— shortly after John, who grew up in the neighborhood of three Franconia, New Hampshire, inns, wrote a thesis on country inns for his MBA.

An outstanding Eastlake staircase, the original registration desk, period furnishings, and family photographs are among the features of this National Register white wood-framed structure built as an inn in 1898.

In residence: "Christie" (Emily Christine), nine-year-old daughter.
Bed and bath: Fourteen tall-ceilinged rooms (some canopied beds; one two-room top-floor suite) on three floors with king, queen, double, or two twin beds. All private shower baths; some with claw-footed tub. One crib and rollaway.
Breakfast: Usually 8–9. All-you-can-eat. Cooked to order. Hot or cold all-natural cereal. Eggs. Pancakes or French toast. Fresh fruit. Home fries or grits. Bacon or sausage. Wheat or white toast. Juice. Perked coffee and decaf.
Plus: Air-conditioned guest rooms; some ceiling fans. Phones in some rooms. Social hour with refreshments, 5–6 p.m. Veranda with rocking chairs. Guest refrigerator. AT&T Language Line available. Suggestions for hikes, panoramic views, photogenic waterfalls. Innkeeping internships.

From North Carolina: *"Warm greeting . . . felt at home right away."* From New York: *"Help in relocation was invaluable."* From Georgia: *"Beautiful place and delightful hosts . . . attention to detail . . . fantastic breakfasts. . . . When we get our new/old home fixed, we'll decorate the bed and bath the same."*

Guests arrive as strangers, leave as friends.

Hidden Crystal Inn   704/632–0063
Sulphur Springs Road, P.O. Box 58, Hiddenite, NC 28636

Hosts: Richard and Jeanne Pleasants
Location: In a Brushy Mountains hamlet known for emeralds as well as for hiddenite, a mineral found (rarely, these days) only in North Carolina. Behind the Hiddenite Center for Folklife and Cultural Arts (performances and classes) and Lucas Mansion Museum (antique doll and toy collections in restored Victorian mansion). An hour from Boone, Charlotte, Greensboro, and Winston-Salem; 17 miles from I–40 and I–77 at Statesville; half mile from "digging and sluicing" at emerald and crystal mines. Near a cornfield used by one helicopter-flying guest.
Open: Year round.
Rates: $80 per room; $90 with fireplace and Jacuzzi. $15 third person in room. Singles $5 less. Dinner $16 per person. MC, Visa.
♥ ♣ ♦ ✈ ⅃

From North Carolina: *"It's a best-kept secret that belongs in your book."*

Gems and minerals are displayed throughout the inn, a restored columned manor house and adjacent garden cottage. Rooms, each quite different and elegant, are gem-named. There are antique armoires, paintings, murals, sculptures, and crafts. The carved antique self-playing European grand piano still has many of its original rolls. A gazebo garden provides a magical setting for proposals—one experienced a perfectly timed snowfall—and many weddings.

The ambiance is embellished by the personable innkeepers. Richard, a former executive chef, harvests herbs, describes the menu when taking your order, and creates incredible dishes. (A cookbook is planned.) Jeanne, a former hotel staffer/country innkeeper, credits Zsa Zsa Gabor's mother, for whom she worked during several summers, "for convincing me to go into the hospitality business."

In 1981 Eileen Lackey Sharpe and her husband, the late R. Y. Sharpe, president of Pilot Freight Co., founded the cultural center and museum in their native Hiddenite. In 1989, to provide the first public lodging in town since fire destroyed the famous Sulphur Springs Hotel and Spa in the 1920s, Mrs. Sharpe and family members created this small, wonderful B&B inn.

In residence: In innkeepers' quarters, Ryan, age 10, and Ross, age 7, who attend school across the street. "Sam is our four-year-old golden retriever."
Bed and bath: Ten rooms on first and second floors. Five in manor house; five in cottage. All private baths; all with shower, two without tubs. King, queen, double, or two twin beds. Two handicapped-accessible rooms, each with a queen and two twin beds. Working fireplace and queen bed in room with Jacuzzi. Rollaway available.
Breakfast: 8–10. (Coffee ready in the kitchen at 5:30 when Richard starts bread making.) Country ham, grits, scrambled eggs, buttermilk biscuits, fresh fruit, granola. Surprises. Special diets accommodated. Served by Jeanne on glassed-in porch overlooking pool and patio.
Plus: Central air conditioning. Swimming pool. Fireplaced living room in manor house and in cottage. Fresh flowers. Turndown service. Mints. Coffee and tea always available. TV in rooms; desks in many. Videotapes and games in library. Badminton, volleyball, croquet. Extensive gardens. Picnic baskets, $10 per person.

The Figurehead

417 Helga Street, Kill Devil Hills, NC 27948-9626

919/441-6929
800/221-6929

Host: Ann Ianni
Location: In a residential area of 2-by-5-mile town on a barrier island, off U.S. 158. A 10-minute walk to the ocean. Restaurants from 2 minutes to 30 minutes' drive. Three miles north of Wright Brothers Monument.
Open: Year round. Three-day mini-

mum stay on holiday weekends Memorial Day–Labor Day.
Rates: Double occupancy (includes tax). $95–$105 May–Labor Day. $85–$95 spring and fall. $65–$75 winter. Extra person: $15.
♣ ♦ 🦌

"Today [mid-March] we went down to Oregon Inlet, a beautiful spot. In that marvelous air and early spring sun, we went shelling while the tide was out. We went wading up to our knees and saw dolphins basking in the sun. . . . Guests who come for the beach often wish that they had reserved another day so they could visit the sites such as the tallest lighthouse (Hatteras) in the country, some museums, or forests. Some discover that a simple game or sport like kite flying can be quite complicated, especially with trick kites that may require another person to hold you down. . . . Atlantic Coast life-saving stations inspired my design of this comfortable light-filled house, which has panoramic views of the sound, a large deck for sunset viewing, and hammocks too."

Here she is—the well-traveled Alexandria, Virginia, B&B host, an active League of Women Voters member, a mother of five grown children who loves to sail, swim, cross-country ski, and ice dance—who was in my very first B&B book. She dreamed of opening a B&B on the Outer Banks of North Carolina—and did it!

In residence: One cat.
Bed and bath: Three rooms, each quite different. All private baths. Queen-bedded room with private balcony, shower, and Jacuzzi tub. One double-bedded room with handicapped-accessible shower stall with seat. One smaller first-level room with two twin beds, tub/shower bath.
Breakfast: 8:30. Juice and fresh fruits. Buns, muffins, breads. Plenty of coffee, tea, milk. In fireplaced common area. "Lasts for up to two hours."
Plus: Central air conditioning. Bedroom TVs and ceiling fans. Late-afternoon or evening tea. Beach towels. Outside shower. Transportation to/from local airport. One tandem, some beach bikes, and kites for borrowing. Grill and picnic table.

The Lodge on Lake Lure

Route 1, Box 529A, Lake Lure, NC 28746

704/625-2789
800/733-2785

Hosts: Jack and Robin Stanier
Location: On a lakeside hill with a view that reminds Europeans of fjords. East side of Lake Lure, at the end of a wooded drive. Off Highway 64/74; 22 miles southeast of Asheville; 80 miles west of Charlotte.
Open: February 14–New Year's.

Two-day minimum on weekends.
Rates: Per room. April–October, $79.50 weekdays, $95 weekends. Suite $95 weekdays, $105 weekends. $15 third person in room. Ten percent less off-season except holidays. Amex, MC, Visa.
♥ 🏠 ♣ ♦ 🦌

What a combination! The only inn—built in the 1930s as a North Carolina Highway Patrol retreat—on what the National Geographic Society called "one of the ten most beautiful lakes in the country." A great room with vaulted ceiling, hand-hewn beams, wormy chestnut walls, and a 20-foot-tall stone fireplace. A hostess who, during 17 years abroad, collected "quantities of unusual items" for her someday inn. A (wealthy) former owner who was enamored with interesting antiques. (Guests take pictures.) An equipped boathouse with rooftop deck.

A B&B since 1985, the World War II officers' club/boarding school/foreign missionaries' retreat/private home was "found in 1990 and we have lived happily ever after" by the jeans-wearing, enthusiastic Staniers. Jack was in steel sales. Robin, a "pioneer woman in the oil industry," worked in drilling and production equipment marketing and sales. Here they offer peace, privacy, and camaraderie too.

In residence: (Blackberry) Muffin, a very friendly black Labrador.
Foreign language spoken: Spanish.
Bed and bath: Eleven rooms including a honeymoon suite. All with private baths (some with shower; others with tub and shower). King, queen, double, or twin beds; some four-posters. Rollaway and portacrib available. Ceiling fans. Air conditioning in some rooms.
Breakfast: 8–9:30. An event. Juice made of blended fruits "plus." Home-made muffins, apple dumplings, or breads. Entree could be grilled peaches flambe with fresh blueberries, French toast with cardamom and currant jelly sauce, or puff pancakes with sauteed plums. On Sundays, eggs Benedict "from our New Orleans days." At round tables for four in room with The View.
Plus: Sunset lake cruise. A 6 p.m. social hour. Library with wood stove, books, games, videotapes, magazines. Guest refrigerator. Beach towels and robes. Rocking chairs and hammocks on veranda. Dock for sunning, swimming, fishing, barbecuing. Canoes and johnboat. Babysitting. Restaurant menus.

Pine Ridge Inn

919/789–5034
2893 West Pine Street, Mount Airy, NC 27030   fax 919/786–9039

Hosts: Ellen and Manford Haxton
Location: In the foothills, on eight acres (four are grass-covered) with panoramic views. Set way back from Highway 89. Five miles west of Mount Airy; 1½ miles from I–77, exit 100; 45 miles north of Winston-Salem; 75 minutes to High Point. Near golf course, tennis, country's largest open-faced granite quarry, Pilot

Mountain, and Blue Ridge Parkway.
Open: Year round.
Rates: $60 twins, $75 double, $85 queen or room with two double beds, $100 king. $10 extra person. Ten percent less for singles and senior citizens. Ten percent off all rates in December, January, and February. Amex, MC, Visa.
♥ ♯ ✿ ♦ ✈

This is one of those "surprise" stories. Seven years ago, when a Realtor friend invited Ellen, a retired piano teacher, and Manford, a patent attorney with R. J. Reynolds, to visit the English manor B&B built in 1949 as a private home, the Haxtons had never thought of becoming innkeepers or caterers (right here). The grandparents of nine had hosted foreign exchange students—and

(Please turn page.)

through Friendship Force they have traveled to several continents, most recently to New Zealand.

The large rooms with crown moldings are furnished with antiques and traditional pieces. In the living room is an early 1900s Steinway concert grand piano made for Mary Curtis of the Curtis Institute of Music family. Weddings are sometimes held on the terrace. Many overnight guests are on their way to the coasts of North or South Carolina. Others come for a two-night package that includes dinner. Some stay to enjoy the pool and extensive grounds.

Bed and bath: Six second-floor rooms with private baths. (Five have both shower and tub.) Twins, one or two doubles (one with private balcony), queen (one with Jacuzzi), and king-size beds. Rollaway and portacrib.
Breakfast: 7:30–9:30. Juice, entree such as sausage bake, fruit, muffins, coffee and tea. Served at table for 12 in crystal-chandeliered and fireplaced dining room or in a smaller dining room at tables for four.
Plus: Central air conditioning. Phone and cable TV in each room. Fireplaces in living room, library, and lower-level common room. Late-afternoon refreshments. Mints on pillows. Fresh flowers. Robes. Electric blankets. Pool with sun deck, beach towels.

Huntington Hall Bed & Breakfast 704/837–9567
500 Valley River Avenue, Murphy, NC 28906   800/824–6189

Hosts: Bob and Kate DeLong
Location: Between home of a late senator and a church—and near another church with carillon bells that chime twice daily. Wonderful hills behind the house, which faces a small barbecue restaurant and a historic house used for public school offices. Within two hours of Atlanta, Georgia, and Asheville, North Carolina. Within 30 miles of two major white-water rafting rivers.
Open: Year round.
Rates: $49 single, $65 double. Twenty percent less December–April. $10 third person. Family rates for two rooms. Amex, Diners, Discover, MC, Visa.

This is the kind of comfortable place, an 1881 two-storied country Victorian, where guests, upon leaving, often ask, "Can we take you home?" Sometimes neighbors stop in to chat with the DeLongs, avid backpackers and runners who are excited about the possibility of 1996 Olympic white-water rafting on the nearby Ocoee River. Bob has 14 years of experience in the hotel industry—as pastry chef, baker, manager, and chief engineer. Katie, an aspiring writer of children's books, worked in the corporate world and did theatrical lighting. Two years ago, when they heard that this inn was for sale, they made an offer on the first visit and became innkeepers a month later. They uncovered fireplaces and refinished heart of pine floors. Frequently they direct guests to Joyce Kilmer Forest—"45 miles away and worth it," to a black bear sanctuary, or to the Appalachian Trail (30 miles). "And some, even those with an agenda, just unwind and do nothing."

In residence: In hosts' quarters, Elizabeth Ashley, age 18 months.
Foreign language spoken: "Un peu French!"

Bed and bath: Five rooms with private baths. Two queen-bedded rooms on first floor. One is handicapped accessible with hallway shower bath (robes provided); the other has bath with tub and shower. On second floor, one queen-bedded room and one four-poster double bed have attached baths—with shower and claw-footed tubs. Room with two twin beds has shower bath. Rollaway and crib.

Breakfast: 6–9:30. "Choose your own time." Crepes with peaches and apricot sauce; banana French toast with bran bread, strawberries, and whipped cream; sausages poached in apple juice; or bacon. Raspberry coffee cake or bran muffins with raisins and walnuts. Served in glassed-in porch at round tables seating two to four.

Plus: In each guest room—heat and air-conditioning control, ceiling fan, cable TV. Desk in most rooms. Refreshments. Turndown service with hand-made chocolate truffles.

The Aerie

509 Pollock Street, New Bern, NC 28560

919/636–5553
800/849–5553

Hosts: Lois and Rick Cleveland
Location: Downtown. In the historic district, "on the Williamsburg to Savannah route, surrounded by museums and a couple of professional buildings." One block from Tryon Palace. "Within 4 blocks of everything—antiques and wonderful gift shops, museums, restaurants." Forty minutes to the beach.

Open: Year round.
Rates: $60 one person. $85 for two. Ten percent AAA discount. Corporate and government rates offered Sunday–Thursday nights. December dinner package (first four courses here followed by Tryon Palace tour and dessert back at inn).
♣ ♦ ✻

"I made a cheesecake. Can I talk you into it?" Spontaneity is the order of the day in this turreted two-story 1882 Victorian owned by an almost-famous (in the innkeeping world) family. Five years ago the Clevelands, a computer programmer and a chemical engineer who had lived in New Jersey for 12 years, took a vacation to look for a lifestyle change.

As Lois, a craftswoman (smocking) who is president of the New Bern PTA, the North Carolina Bed & Breakfast Association, and a few other organizations, says, "Everyone asks how we got into this. When we were shown this B&B in good condition but in need of redecorating (now it has all been done inside and out), we had never stayed in a bed and breakfast. We could have ended up with a pizza parlor! Rick [who recently returned to engineering] loves to do things with his hands. I love to cook. [She caters luncheons.] We are fussy eaters and like options. Here we seem to have an ongoing social hour in the late afternoon and evening. Many of our guests like the idea of parking their car here and having the opportunity to wander for three or four days."

In residence: Cynthia, age eight, and Sarah, age four. "Tigger is a fat cat."
Bed and bath: Seven rooms furnished mostly with antiques. All reproduction beds except for an 1840s pair of twin beds. All private baths—six with tub and shower, one queen on second floor with shower only. On first floor,

(Please turn page.)

room with twin beds or queen bed. On second floor, one room with two twins, three with queen bed, including one "hidden room" (off by itself) "surrounded with windows."

Breakfast: 8 9. Choice of three entrees cooked to order. Repertoire includes big thick Belgian waffles, omelets, French toast, pancakes. Fresh fruit, hot beverage. Lois usually joins guests for conversation.

Plus: Central air conditioning. All bedrooms have telephones, cable TV, and desks, and all but one have a ceiling fan. Beverages always available. Living room player piano —with about 50 rolls. Back patio shaded by 150-year-old pecan tree. Plenty of parking. Forgotten items provided. Mints. Airport pickup and drop-off.

Harmony House Inn   919/636–3810
215 Pollock Street, New Bern, NC 28560

Hosts: A. E. (Buzz) and Diane Hansen
Location: In historic district of about 100 homes, museums, and sites. Four blocks from Tryon Palace, 1½ from Neuse and Trent rivers. "Within 3 blocks of everything from a deli to fancy restaurants." Seven minutes from airport.
Open: Year round.
Rates: $55 single. $80 double. $20 third person. Amex, MC, Visa.
❖ ◆ ✶ ⅄

Is Benny here? One travel agent tells Diane that Harmony House is the only place she can call and say simply "Benny's coming!"

Other returnees—and their friends and relatives—also come to visit the Hansens, who, eight years ago, fell in love with this small town (about 20,000) with water (two rivers) and attractions. As Diane tells it, "The building wasn't exactly what we wanted, so we added 10 bathrooms, rewired, and furnished with comfortable and elegant antiques to reflect New Bern—with much Empire that fits in with these spacious rooms. What we couldn't find locally— a dining room trestle table, beds, nightstands, some wardrobes—we had reproduced in the area. . . . We have a good time with cyclists, honeymooners, retirees (several move or build here), and business travelers. They walk everywhere and appreciate the historic district, the lack of crowds, the community (lots of young families), quiet evenings, and—sometimes I think most of all—our front porch rockers."

The most interesting expansion of the 1850 house occurred in 1900, when two sons moved one half of it 9 feet and filled in the space with more rooms for their "separate" residences. Hence today's two front doors and extensive hallways.

In Illinois Buzz, "the maintenance man," was controller for a multinational packaging company. Diane is chef and gardener.

Bed and bath: Nine rooms, two with connecting door. All private full baths. Three rooms on first floor, six on second. Queen four-posters or twin beds. Rollaway and crib.

Breakfast: 7:30–9 weekdays, 8–9:30 weekends. Hot egg and meat dish, homemade coffee cakes and granola, fruit, coffee and tea, juice. Buffet style in dining room and parlor.

Plus: Central air conditioning. In each bedroom—ceiling fan, two comfortable chairs, cable TV, electric blankets in winter. Guest refrigerator with complimentary juices and soft drinks. Private phone available. Backyard with garden. Garage for bicycles. "Plenty of maps and advice about what to do and see."

Pinebrae Manor   704/286-1543

RR 5 (Highway 108), Box 479-A, Rutherfordton, NC 28139-9805

Hosts: Allen and Charlotte Perry
Location: On 10 acres with deer (sometimes) and a panoramic view (always) of woods. Three miles west of town. In foothills of the Blue Ridge Mountains. Within 30 minutes' drive of Chimney Rock Park, Carl Sandburg Home, and Biltmore Estate.

Open: March through November.
Rates: Per room. May–October: shared bath $49 double bed; private bath $59 double four-poster, $69 king bed. $7 less March, April, November. Group and corporate discounts available. MC, Visa.
♥ 🛏 ⚓ ♦ 🪶 🖊

> From Florida: " . . . *Absolutely the best experience I've ever had as a guest while away from home . . . a Southern plantation–like house . . . gorgeous rooms, as comfortable and cozy as is possible to imagine. The hosts were very gracious and accommodating. I wish I could live there!"* From Texas: "*Marvelous, historic . . . wonderful breakfast at beautifully set table. . . . Rooms were so attractive I took pictures."*

Now it's a Georgian colonial furnished with family heirlooms and antiques. A local builder transformed the Rutherford County Home administration building, salvaging brick and doors from other buildings on the property for walkways, retaining walls, and wainscoting. He added crown molding and broken pediments.

The well-traveled Perrys bought this "ideal for B&B" house when Allen, a chemical engineer, retired from the corporate world in 1991. Charlotte, an art instructor and craftswoman who was editor and illustrator for the Hannibal, Missouri, Bicentennial cookbook, is writing a family cookbook and a "Sailing Wife's Handbook." (Off-season allows time for Al to sail and Charlotte to cook their sea bounty—conch being a favorite.)

Bed and bath: A wide stairway leads to four second-floor rooms. Two double-bedded rooms share a full hall bath (robes provided). One room has king/two twin beds option, working fireplace, full bath. One has four-poster bed, private shower bath.
Breakfast: "Flexible. Have served as early as 5:30 and as late as 10:30." Juices. Hot or cold cereal. Muffins, bagels, toast. Eggs to order. Sausage casserole, French toast, eggs Benedict, or pancakes; Canadian bacon, ham, bacon, sausage. For full house, could be buffet. Just one or two couples? You might design the menu. Or it could be chef's choice with "Bon appetit" greeting. Served with fine china and heirloom silver in fireplaced and brass-chandeliered dining room.
Plus: Fireplaced living room with piano. Phone and TV in each room.

(Please turn page.)

Refreshments. Candy. Guest refrigerator in gathering room. Porch rockers Horseshoes. Croquet. Game tables. Fresh flowers. Hiking right here. Half-mile nature trail with, if you would like, an audiotape made by a friend with commentary about flora and fauna. Airport pickup arranged. For corporate guests, use of private office.

The 1868 Stewart-Marsh House   704/633–6841
220 South Ellis Street, Salisbury, NC 28144

Hosts: Chuck and Gerry Webster
Location: On a quiet tree-lined historic district street "with a resident mockingbird." Four blocks from town center; 1.5 miles from I–85. Within walking distance of restaurants, shops, and historic sites. Forty miles north of Charlotte.

Halfway between Washington and Atlanta.
Open: Year round.
Rates: $50 twin beds, $55 queen. Singles $5 less. $15 extra person in room. Discounts for stays over three nights. MC, Visa.
◆ ✶ ✂

A planned retirement lifestyle for the hosts, a history buff and an artist. With just two guest rooms, a hard-to-find kind of B&B for the guest. In 1987, two years after the Websters bought the 1868 Federal-style house, they moved here from western Pennsylvania, where Chuck was a production engineer and Gerry had a consignment shop. They renovated (80 percent of the windows still have original glass); became historic house docents; and, in their own backyard, discovered a brick walkway under 4 inches of sod. Furnishings include period pieces, Gerry's paintings and cross-stitch work, and family treasures including a trunk Chuck's grandfather brought to America from Sweden.

Some guests kick off their shoes in the pine-paneled library. Some have memories of a reenactment held here. One husband and wife—who arrived stressed and left unwound—asked the Websters if they would adopt them!

Bed and bath: Two second-floor rooms, separated by hallway. Heart pine floors, private baths with garden view. One room has queen four-poster, tub and shower bath. One has two antique twin beds and bath with tub and hand-held shower. Rollaway available.
Breakfast: 7–10. Juice. Fresh fruit—maybe baked pineapple with raisins and pecans or poached spiced peaches in winter. Homemade breads, muffins, or coffee cakes. A hot entree such as corn fritters or puffed eggs and ham topped with cheddar cheese. Garnished with fresh garden herbs or flowers. Served on china with crystal and silver in dining room.
Plus: Air conditioner and ceiling fan in bedrooms. Afternoon lemonade or soft drinks. Evening tea. Homemade cookies. Mints. Wicker-furnished screened porch.

From Ohio: *"Every detail thought of—fruit in room, flowers on table, fresh muffins and bread, and on and on. I felt so cared for . . . truly gracious hosts."* From Missouri: *"One of the highlights of our two-week trip."*

Rowan Oak House

208 South Fulton Street, Salisbury, NC 28144-4418

704/633–2086
800/786–0437

Hosts: Bill and Ruth Ann Coffey
Location: Surrounded by other elegant homes in historic district. Three blocks from "turn-of-the-century business district, good restaurants, genealogical library." One mile off I–85, 35 miles to High Point, 39 to Winston-Salem, 42 to Charlotte.

Open: Year round.
Rates: $65 double-bedded room, shared hall bath; $85 twin beds; $95 honeymoon suite. $10 less for singles. Ten percent less for senior citizens or stays over four days. $15 rollaway or crib. Discover, MC, Visa. ♥ ♦ ✗

> From New York: *"A touch of class. . . . Elegance of the Victorian period, sumptuous breakfasts, warm Southern hospitality."* From South Carolina: *"An incredible experience . . . I was able to drop the normal stress associated with work, wander from one creative, historic room to another, and marvel at the precise detail in each. . . . Retired in true comfort, woke up 'somewhere in time' as though I had always lived there . . . hosts who absolutely made each guest feel totally at home."*

One of the Coffeys' sons was right. This is the perfect business for the former Austin, Texas, residents. Bill, a retired AAA general manager, and Ruth Ann, mother/Realtor/florist, are very involved in this "town that looks back in time, with its old houses that have volunteer guides, old cemeteries to browse through, an old country store, and a modern-day potter to visit." The avid antiques collectors ended their two-year coast-to-coast search in 1987 when they bought (in one day) this house-tour Queen Anne with wraparound porch (swings and rockers frequently occupied), elaborate woodwork, and original ornate electric and gas light fixtures. A guest from Florida summed it up: "Exceptional and delightful."

Foreign language spoken: Some Spanish.
Bed and bath: Wide ornate staircase leads to upstairs sitting room and porch accessible from the three 17-by-17-foot double-bedded rooms. All private up-to-date baths. One room with carved high-back mahogany bed, huge hall bath (robes provided) with tub and hand-held brass shower. Another mahogany bed in honeymoon suite; attached bath has double-sized Jacuzzi, French flowered pedestal sink, working gas log fireplace. Third room has two twin-sized sleigh beds, attached shower bath. Rollaway and crib.
Breakfast: Usually 8–9. Repertoire includes baked cheese souffle, Dutch baby puff pancakes, stuffed French toast. Meats. Fresh fruit, juice, homemade breads, gourmet coffee. At table set with linen, silver, and china in dining room with original hand-painted wallpaper and large oil painting of Queen Louise of Mecklenberg/Prussia. Coffeys join guests.
Plus: Fireplaced living and dining rooms. Air conditioning, ceiling fan, desk, phone jack, down comforter in each guest room. Fresh fruit, flowers, and candy. Refreshments—cookies, cheese, homemade dips, veggies.

The place to stay has become the reason to go.

Aunt Mae's Bed & Breakfast   704/873–9525

532 East Broad Street, Statesville, NC 28677-5331

Hosts: Richard and Sue Rowland
Location: On nearly an acre in the middle of town. Surrounded by lawn and plantings. One mile off intersection of I–40/I–77. A short walk from historic downtown and shops. Forty-

five miles north of Charlotte; 40 west of Winston-Salem.
Open: Year round.
Rates: $50 per room. $10 third person in room. MC, Visa.
♥ ♨ ♦ ♣ ♦ ✖ ✄

> From Texas: *"Two wonderful people . . . made me feel like part of their family . . . breakfast was a treat every morning." From Ohio: "Evening ice cream with homemade caramel sauce and nuts from their trees . . . memorabilia everywhere. . . . Spotless, quiet, comfortable rooms. . . . We awoke to coffee on a tray outside our door. Breakfast included banana-orange juice that Sue blended (I watched her) and marvelous stuffed French toast. The best part though, was the conversation. You know, a house is just a house. The people in it make it a home."*

According to Sue, "In the 51 years that (great) Aunt Mae lived in this Victorian house, she kept everything—books, magazines, articles, love letters, children's clothes and toys, dishes and linens—many with notes telling of their origin or use. There were many scraping, painting, and decorating parties with family and friends before we opened in 1991. B&B, the best job I've ever had, is a fun way to share the collections. . . . We've met people from all over the world. One Halloween we learned from a French guest—who stood up many times that evening—that our doorbell plays the French national anthem. Many people come with extensive plans—or just for a getaway. Lots of laughter is heard from our guests enjoying one another. All this goes back to my prior vocation (mothering eight children). What a training ground!"

The house, commissioned by a cabinetmaker, was built by workers who moonlighted while Statesville's beautiful city hall was under construction. Richard, husband and cohost, works with a heavy equipment manufacturing company.

Bed and bath: Two second-floor rooms, each with attached private shower bath. One Victorian with double four-poster bed and single Jenny Lind daybed. One cozy country room with antique double iron bed. Rollaway and crib available.

Breakfast: Anytime until 9:30 a.m. "Homemade juice concoctions." Hot or cold fruit soup, fruit sundaes, and even Swedish cream. Souffles, casseroles, omelets, or stuffed French toast. "Ends on a sweet note with homemade goodies." By candlelight. Often, complete with history of Aunt Mae's crystal, china, or linen being used.

Plus: Central air conditioning. Bedroom ceiling fans. Upstairs gathering room with homemade snacks always available. Lemonade or hot chocolate and tea.

Mints on pillow. Babysitting. Kitchen and laundry privileges. Weather report and list of local events with morning coffee brought to door. TV in common room.

Rivendell Lodge   704/297–1685
P.O. Box 211, Sugar Grove, NC 28679

Hosts: Sarah and Loren Williams
Location: Spectacular. "Nearest visible neighbor is 1.5 miles away." Overlooking Watauga River rapids (250 yards to river by easy downhill trail). At the end of a half-mile wooded country lane and .3-mile-long gravel driveway. Twelve miles west of Boone; 3.1 miles off U.S. 321; within 25 miles of five ski slopes; 30 minutes to restaurants and shops.
Open: Year round.
Rates: $60 per room. $10 third person in room. Suite (two rooms, one bath; up to four people), $110.
♥ ⚐ ⁂ ◆ ✕ ⅄

Framed quotations from *The Lord of the Rings* include "Time doesn't seem to pass here; it just is. A remarkable place altogether." The B&B name was also taken from J.R.R. Tolkien's book.

You, too, will probably ask, "How did you ever find this place?" After Loren, a consultant in the field of multicultural awareness, retired from an academic career in Richmond, Virginia, and Sarah, a social worker/massage therapist/weaver/resident star expert, bought the contemporary residence in 1988 through a Realtor, they "rebuilt it from inside out." They opened in 1990 with 2,000 square feet of multilevel decks, a large and inviting kitchen, a great room with wood stove and huge stone fireplace, and an extensive library. Decor is "Scandinavian rustic" with a mix of contemporary and antique pieces and original art.

Foreign language spoken: "Halting Spanish."
Bed and bath: Four rooms (including one two-room suite) on various levels. Two large rooms with double four-poster bed. Suite has queen water bed in smaller room, two twin four-poster beds in large room. All private full (tub and shower) baths. Crib available.
Breakfast: Guests choose the hour. Coffee ready by 7. Fresh fruit and freshly made scones. Entree possibilities—egg/cheese/sausage casserole, baked apple or cornmeal blueberry pancakes. Served on deck or in dining area.
Plus: Individual bedroom thermostats. Down comforters. Hammocks and deck chairs. Star gazing. Guest pantry with refrigerator, snacks, picnicware. Guests' restaurant reviews. Grills at far end of woodshed (built by Loren). Massage ($35/hour).

(Please turn page.)

From North Carolina: *"Breathtaking view of neighboring valley and surrounding mountains . . . plenty of information without playing tour guide or activities director . . . Loren and Sarah provide a peaceful quiet that is easily punctuated with laughter or conversation."* From Florida: *"We felt as guests in their home rather than paying guests . . . a very comfortable, relaxing environment."*

Little Warren Bed and Breakfast   919/823-1314
304 East Park Avenue, Tarboro, NC 27886

Hosts: Patsy and Tom Miller
Location: Quiet, residential part of historic district, facing the town common. Nineteen miles off I–95, exit 138 (Rocky Mount).

Open: Year round.
Rates: Per room. $65 double, $58 single. $20 cot. Amex, Discover, MC, Visa.

Twists and turns and lots of cubbies within the National Register house inspired the name of this B&B, which was built in 1913 with spacious rooms, 13-foot ceilings, and wraparound porch. Restored twice (most recently by Patsy and Tom), it has elaborate dentil work, crown molding, beams, and several knotty pine–paneled rooms. Since 1984 it has been home to the Millers, following their 24 years of living in Africa, England, the Orient, and many parts of the United States.

Kitchenalia by the thousands (much displayed on walls) represent a lifetime of collecting, dating back to the days when Tom ran a country store in his youth. Other collections include clocks, tea covers, baskets, miniatures, glassware, and furnishings—"eclectic, mostly antique, all livable and touchable, some for sale."

The official B&B chef, Tom, is a retired Marine colonel. Cohost Patsy, who teaches Spanish at the local high school, was raised in her family's small Virginia Beach hotel.

"Our guests are often surprised by the friendliness of this colonial town of 11,000 people. Several guests—including a couple who ran the B&B one summer while we went to Europe—have returned to live here."

In residence: "Duffy, our friendly 'Westie,' is kept away from allergic guests and inside for dog lovers."
Bed and bath: Three second-floor rooms; each with desk, all with private bath. One double-bedded room with hall shower bath (robes provided). One with twin beds, adjoining shower bath. One with three-quarter bed, shower bath. Rollaway available.
Breakfast: Any time until 8:30. Full English, expanded continental, or American Southern with fried apples (a favorite). Juice, cereal with fruit, eggs, soft bacon, sausage, toast, marmalade, grilled tomatoes, tea or coffee. Special diets accommodated. In dining room with English silver and china, crystal, and linens.
Plus: Fireplaced living room. Central zoned air conditioning. Late-afternoon

beverage and snack before fire or on porch. Forgotten-items basket. Fresh flowers. Mints. Turndown service. Historic district walking tour map. Arrangements made for Y gym and workout facilities.

Miss Betty's Bed & Breakfast Inn 919/243–4447
600 West Nash Street, Wilson, NC 27893-3045   800/258–2058

Hosts: Betty and Fred Spitz
Location: On an acre and a half, on main street in downtown historic section, with big old trees, a large lawn, and gardens. About 2 miles to "antiques capital of North Carolina." Three miles to auction house (which schedules antiques auctions no more than two weeks in advance). Less than 6 miles from I–95. Midway between New York and Florida. Across street from Rib Room, a major restaurant. Near four well-manicured golf courses, many tennis courts, Olympic-sized pool.
Open: Year round.
Rates: Per room $60–$65, suite $70. Singles $10 less. Honeymoon, anniversary, or birthday package rates. Amex, Discover, MC, Visa.

"Pictures are always being taken here. Today 'CNN Headline News,' local edition, did a segment in this National Register Italianate house, which is furnished with all locally purchased American Victorian antiques. When we came from New Jersey, looking for a historic house for the two of us, we were introduced to the idea of B&B. Since doing this wonderful place over in 1989, we have also restored an early 1900s house (very popular with business travelers) that we moved, by splitting it in half, from the Barton College campus 2 blocks away. Now we are about to add a new building that will look like an old country store with a big open porch, an antiques shop (Miss Betty's), a tin roof to hear the pitter-patter of rain, and three more executive suites with fireplaces and gas logs."

Husband Fred, sometimes called "Mr. Betty" by first-time guests, is an engineer who was with General Dynamics. Both Betty and Fred are getting a kick out of growing 200 hybrid cotton plants—green, brown and white— and 29 tobacco plants, "so that guests can see what these major crops look like."

Bed and bath: Eight rooms, including one executive suite; seven with working fireplace; all with private phone, cable TV with remote control, electric blankets, and alarm clock. All private baths (robes provided for two hall baths); some shower only, some tub and shower baths. One room is handicapped accessible. Four rooms are in main inn, four in Riley House. King, double, or twin beds. Some four-poster, antique, brass, Jenny Lind, or canopied beds.
Breakfast: At 7 and 8; on weekends at 8 or 9. Homemade blueberry and peach muffins; pumpkin bread or everyone's favorite, cinnamon nut cake (pecans grown on site). "North Carolina's finest 'bacon-pressed' bacon,"

(Please turn page.)

locally made sausage links. English muffins. Sometimes grits. Fresh fruit. Freshly squeezed orange and grapefruit juice. Eggs or pancakes. Served family style in dining room of main inn by the chef, Miss Betty, in period dress. **Plus:** Fireplaces in three parlors. Central air conditioning. Ceiling fans. Games. Playing cards. Snack crackers. Candy. Guest refrigerator with ice and cold soft drinks. Transportation to and from airport, train, or bus station.

From a California innkeeper: *"The highlight of my trip."*

Lady Anne's Victorian Bed & Breakfast
612 Summit Street, Winston-Salem, NC 27101   919/724–1074

Hosts: Shelley Kirley and Steve Wishon
Location: On top of a hill in the West End, a residential historic neighborhood "with beautiful sunsets." Less than a mile from Old Salem Historic Village, Baptist Hospital/Bowman Gray Medical School, Wake Forest University, and Salem College. A few blocks to restaurants, antiques shops, Benton Convention Center. Three hours to coast; 45 minutes to Blue Ridge Parkway; 30 to Pilot Mountain for picnicking, hiking, and views.
Open: Year round.
Rates: Per room. Suite with whirlpool $105. Ground-level suites $95. Queen room with private bath $55, or $65 (for three people) with twin-bedded room.
♥ ⬤ ⁂ ✕ ✂

The 1890 Queen Anne, on the National Register of Historic Places, was restored in the 1980s by Steve, a contractor who renovates old homes, and Shelley, a recreation therapist who was first introduced to B&Bs in California's Napa Valley. Throughout, there are antiques—mostly Victorian—and Oriental rugs, swags, and some stained glass windows.

It's a haven for business guests, and a favorite for getaways. One couple, celebrating their tenth anniversary, both booked the same suite as a surprise (it worked) for each other! One Illinois family wrote a rave review about everything from the cleanliness to the cheerful hostess. Other guests were impressed with "this delightful Victorian home, its history as well as that of the surrounding area. We enjoyed the old-world charm, quiet atmosphere, gracious service . . . a pleasant change from the usual hotel scene."

In residence: "Chee Chee is a small, gentle Lhasa apso."
Bed and bath: Five rooms; updated baths. Two ground-level suites with private entrances. One has private porch, elaborate Victorian double bed, private tub/shower bath, private parlor with cablevision, VCR, and stereo. The other has a queen bed, queen sofa bed, room refrigerator, kitchenette with microwave, private parlor, and two-person shower. On second floor, large suite with canopied queen bed, two-person whirlpool, private balcony. One queen-bedded room sometimes shares full hall bath with small room that has one twin bed.

Breakfast: 6–10:30. Juice. Homemade breads; bagels and muffins. Fresh fruit or apple dumplings. Yogurts. Cereals. Main dish could be waffles, French toast, omelets, or quiche. In dining room or on porch. Room service is an option for suite guests.

Plus: In each bedroom—central air conditioning, ceiling fan, cable TV/HBO, poetry books, music tapes and stereo. A desk in some. Victorian pump organ in main parlor. Fresh flowers. Tea with dessert.

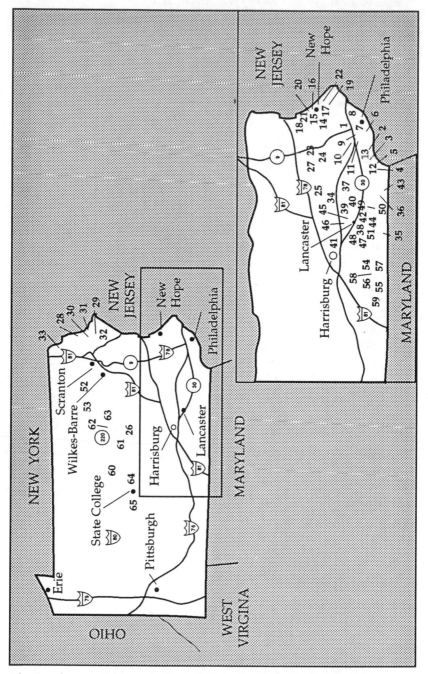

The numbers on this map indicate the locations of B&Bs described in detail in this chapter.

PENNSYLVANIA

Philadelphia and Brandywine Valley
1 Blue Bell
   Blue Heron B&B, *225*
2 Chadds Ford
   Bed & Breakfast of Delaware
      Host #3, *226*
3 Kennett Square
   B&B at The Lighted Holly, *227*
   Meadow Spring Farm, *227*
   Scarlett House, *228*
4 Kennett Square: Avondale
   Bed & Breakfast at
      Walnut Hill, *230*
5 Landenberg
   Cornerstone Bed and
      Breakfast, *231*
6 Lima
   Hamanassett, *232*
7 Philadelphia
   Antique Row Bed &
      Breakfast, *233*
   Center City Retreat, *233*
   Cromwell House, *234*
   New Market Surprise, *235*
   Shippen Way Inn, *236*
8 Philadelphia: Huntington
   Valley
   Shirl's Shed, *237*
9 Radnor
   The Barn at Gulph Mills, *238*
10 Valley Forge
   Amsterdam B&B, *238*
11 Valley Forge: Malvern
   The Great Valley House of
      Valley Forge, *239*
12 West Chester
   The Bankhouse Bed &
      Breakfast, *240*
   Lenape Springs Farm, *241*
   The Valentine, *242*
13 West Chester: Dilworthtown
   Monument House, *243*

Bucks County
14 Doylestown
   The Inn at Fordhook Farm, *246*

15 Gardenville
   Maplewood Farm Bed &
      Breakfast, *247*
16 New Hope
   The Wedgwood Collection of
      Historic Inns, *248*
   The Whitehall Inn, *249*
17 New Hope: Holicong
   Ash Mill Farm, *250*
   Barley Sheaf Farm, *251*
18 New Hope: Kintnersville
   The Bucksville House, *252*
19 New Hope: Wrightstown
   Hollileif Bed & Breakfast
      Establishment, *253*
20 Point Pleasant
   Tattersall Inn, *254*
21 Upper Black Eddy
   Bridgeton House on the
      Delaware, *255*
22 Washington Crossing
   Woodhill Farms Inn, *256*

Lehigh Valley/Reading Area
23 Allentown: Macungie
   Sycamore Inn Bed &
      Breakfast, *259*
24 Boyertown
   The Enchanted Cottage, *260*
25 Leesport
   The Loom Room, *261*
26 Lewisburg
   The Pineapple Inn, *262*
27 Mertztown
   Longswamp Bed and
      Breakfast, *263*

Poconos
28 Beach Lake
   The Beach Lake Hotel, *264*
29 Canadensis
   Brookview Manor Bed &
      Breakfast Inn, *265*
30 Hawley
   Academy Street Bed &
      Breakfast, *266*

31 **Lackawaxen**
Roebling Inn on the
Delaware, *267*
32 **Mount Pocono**
Farmhouse Bed & Breakfast, *268*
33 **Starrucca**
The Nethercott Inn, *269*

Pennsylvania Dutch Country
34 **Adamstown**
Adamstown Inn, *271*
35 **Airville**
Spring House, *272*
36 **Christiana**
Winding Glen Farm Tourist
Home, *273*
37 **Churchtown**
Churchtown Inn, *274*
38 **Columbia**
The Columbian, *275*
39 **Ephrata**
Clearview Farm Bed &
Breakfast, *276*
Historic Smithton, *277*
40 **Gordonville**
The Osceola Mill House, *278*
41 **Hershey**
Pinehurst Inn Hershey, *279*
42 **Lancaster**
Buona Notte Bed &
Breakfast, *280*
Lincoln Haus Inn Bed &
Breakfast, *280*
O'Flaherty's Dingeldein
House, *281*
Patchwork Inn, *282*
43 **Lancaster: Oxford**
Bed & Breakfast of Delaware
Host #31, *283*
44 **Lancaster: Willow Street**
The Apple Bin Inn, *284*
45 **Lititz**
Swiss Woods Bed &
Breakfast, *285*
46 **Manheim**
Herr Farmhouse Inn, *286*
47 **Marietta**
The Noble House, *287*
Vogt Farm Bed & Breakfast, *288*

48 **Mount Joy**
Cedar Hill Farm, *289*
The Country Stay, *290*
Hillside Farm Bed &
Breakfast, *291*
49 **Paradise**
Maple Lane Guest House, *292*
50 **Strasburg**
Limestone Inn, *292*
51 **Wrightsville**
1854 House, *293*

**Central and Western
Pennsylvania**
52 **Beaumont**
Ponda-Rowland Bed &
Breakfast, *296*
53 **Eagles Mere**
Shady Lane, A Bed & Breakfast
Inn, *297*
54 **East Berlin**
The Bechtel Mansion Inn, *298*
55 **Gettysburg**
Baladerry Inn, *299*
The Brafferton Inn, *300*
Keystone Inn, *301*
56 **Gettysburg: Gardners**
Goose Chase Bed &
Breakfast, *302*
57 **Gettysburg: Hanover**
Beechmont Inn, *303*
58 **Gettysburg: New Oxford**
Conewago House, *304*
59 **Gettysburg: Orrtanna**
Hickory Bridge Farm, *305*
60 **Howard**
Curtinview, *306*
61 **Loganton**
Webb Farm Bed &
Breakfast, *306*
62 **Montoursville**
The Carriage House at
Stonegate, *307*
63 **Muncy**
The Bodine House, *308*
64 **Potters Mills**
General Potter Farm, *309*
65 **Stormstown**
The John Thompson House
B&B, *310*

Philadelphia and Brandywine Valley ——— Reservation Services ———

Bed & Breakfast Connections

P.O. Box 21, Devon, PA 19333

Phone: 215/687–3565 or (outside Pennsylvania) 800/448–3619, Monday–Saturday 9–9. (Sundays—respond to message.) Closed major holidays and Sundays.

Listings: 60. Most are private homes; 6 are inns. Located in the extended Philadelphia area including the Center City and University, Society Hill, and Main Line suburbs. Many are located near historic sites and are convenient to public transportation. Nearby areas with listings include Valley Forge, Brandywine Valley and Pennsylvania Dutch country, and Poconos. Free directory available.

Rates: $30–$190 single, $45–$190 double. Family and weekly rates available. $2–$5 booking fee. $5 one-night surcharge. One night or 20 percent deposit required. Deposit refunded, less a $15 service charge, if cancellation is received at least seven days prior to arrival date. No refund with less than seven days' notice. Guest can avoid deposit forfeiture by booking and staying with same host within three months from time of cancellation. ◆

This personalized reservation service is owned and operated by Peggy Gregg and Lucy Scribner, who have had experience as travel agent, educator, and social worker. They know their helpful and hospitable hosts well and conduct annual inspections. While booking first-time and experienced B&B guests, they explain the geography of the area and arrange for an appropriate host and location.

Bed & Breakfast of Philadelphia

1616 Walnut Street, Suite 1120, Philadelphia, PA 19103-5311

Phone: 215/735–1917 or 800/220–1917, Monday–Friday 9–5.

Fax: 215/735–1909.

Listings: 60. Most are hosted private residences in and around Philadelphia and include historic Philadelphia, Main Line suburbs, Chestnut Hill, Bucks County, Valley Forge, Montgomery County, Brandywine Valley, and Chester, Delaware, and Lancaster counties.

Reservations: At least a week's notice is preferred.

Rates: $25–$140 single. $35–$150 double. Booking fee is 2.5 percent. Ten percent discount for weekly stays. One night's lodging or credit card guarantee required as deposit. One night's tariff charged for cancellations made within seven days of expected arrival date. Amex, MC, Visa. ◆

(Please turn page.)

This reservation service, the oldest in the region, was purchased in 1991 by John Miller, one of Philadelphia's original B&B hosts. "We have all types of buildings in many locations and in a wide price range. What they all share is wonderful, warm hosts who understand the special bond between host and guest that makes every B&B visit a unique experience."

Debra Wiggins, who has seen all the listings and met the hosts, makes all the bookings for this service.

Guesthouses

Box 2137, West Chester, PA 19380

Phone: 215/692–4575, Monday–Friday noon–4.

Fax: 215/692–4451.

Listings: Over 200. Mostly hosted private residences. Some inns.

Reservations: At least 10 days' advance notice preferred. Last minute accommodated if guest can receive fax.

Rates: $65–$200 double occupancy. $5 less for singles. Deposits (received within five days of request) or guarantees by credit card for the first and last nights' lodging (including tax) are required. For cancellations received five days prior to scheduled visit, full credit given as a deposit applied to any future visit within one year. To be eligible for a refund, less 5 percent bank processing fee if charged to credit card, guest must apply for cancellation insurance at the time of reservation or on receipt of confirmation. As a member of B&B World-Wide, Guesthouses guarantees its accommodations; if a guest arrives but does not take occupancy, for any reason, there is no charge and any monies received are refunded in full. Amex, MC, Visa. ◆

Although many Brandywine Valley hosts are part of Janice Archbold's personalized service, her widespread listings—mostly historic—are in Philadelphia and the Main Line (Wynnewood to Paoli), Valley Forge, Lancaster, Reading, Longwood, Chadds Ford, West Chester, Gettysburg, New Hope—all in Pennsylvania. Some others are in Delaware and New Jersey and on Maryland's Chesapeake Bay.

"We best serve those guests who want to savor the experience of being a guest and want more than a bed to sleep in. All of our hosts want to share their part of the world and give their hospitality in return for meeting, however briefly, new friends."

Unless otherwise stated, rates in this book are per room for two and include breakfast in addition to all the amenities in "Plus." As for taxes and gratuities, please see page xi.

Philadelphia and Brandywine Valley
B&Bs

Blue Heron B&B
Blue Bell, PA

Location: Country. On three acres with neighboring sheep, horses, Sicilian donkeys (that come to you when you call), and pond. Fifteen minutes to King of Prussia and Valley Forge; 35 minutes northwest of Philadelphia. Five-minute drive to many corporate headquarters, seven to Washington State Park. Close to antiquing, fine dining, farmstead museum, country shopping, Valley Forge National Park.

Reservations: Available year round through Bed & Breakfast of Philadelphia, page 223.

Rates: First-floor suite $65 single, $75 double. Third floor, $60 single, $65 double. $15 cot or futon.
♠ ♣ ✂ ✍

> From Washington, D.C.: *"Absolutely charming . . . friendly and interesting people—and good cooks too!"*

A visual treat. Everywhere you look there's something of interest—ethnic artwork, contemporary sculpture, a warehouse artifact, antiques, "a blend of different things we like that work with our lives." The added-on-to 1870s stone farmhouse has wide pine plank floors throughout. Books on art, nature, and architecture, and a huge Shakespeare collection, are in the spacious living room with fireplace stove. Outside, there's room to roam, a creek to think by, an apple tree, lots of birds and geese, blue heron, and sometimes—early in the morning—deer.

The host, a sculptor whose work draws upon organic influences—nature, bone, fossils, and shells—has a studio in the red Victorian barn. In addition, he has recently become a certified hypnotherapist. His wife is director of a foundation that issues arts and cultural grants.

In residence: One teenage daughter and a nine-year-old son. Two cats. One dog.

Foreign language spoken: Some French.

Bed and bath: First-floor suite has private entrance—large room with double bed, handmade quilt, private shower (tile stall with glass door) bath. Entire third floor is one large dormered treetop room with brass double bed, private tile tub and shower bath.

Breakfast: All healthy food. Fresh fruit. Homemade pancakes, muffins. Fresh eggs from free-range chickens and other products purchased at nearby farm market. In breakfast room at Mennonite table surrounded by oak bentwood chairs next to huge bay window overlooking bird feeder and sheep. Or on flagstone terrace under canopy.

Plus: Phone jacks in rooms. Chair swing. Hammocks. Transportation to/from Wings Field Commuter Airport.

Bed & Breakfast of Delaware Host #3

Chadds Ford, PA

Location: On four beautiful acres. On Route 52, 2 miles to Chadds Ford Winery or Longwood Gardens, 5 to Winterthur Museum. An hour to Lancaster County's Amish country or Philadelphia.

Reservations: Year round through Bed & Breakfast of Delaware, page 4.

Two-night minimum on holiday weekends.

Rates: For two or more nights, $75 per night for one couple; $110 per night for two couples traveling together. $5 surcharge for overnight stay.

♥ 🏠 ♣ 🗡

"For as long as I can remember—and I have lived here since I was six years old—the post-and-beam carriage house has been a guest house on the upper level. The bottom floor is still unfinished. Five years ago we redecorated, updated, and installed central air conditioning. My wife stenciled walls. Wall-to-wall carpeting was installed in the bedrooms, and we furnished with antiques and reproductions. It's sort of a magical, very private place where people can really visit, maybe have a reunion. Fresh flowers are always in several of the rooms. When I [the host is an engineer with Du Pont] bring breakfast with my wife's work-of-art fruit arrangements the night before, guests often ask about the history of the house and area, and, yes, for restaurant suggestions too. Sometimes we talk about world affairs. Often they tell me about their plans for the next morning. It's noon now and I can see that guests are still on the large glassed/screened porch enjoying themselves. They are welcome to wander on our four acres among beautiful gardens and stately trees—including one of the largest sycamores in the country. Our family, including the children and our two dogs, live in the main house, a Victorian adjacent to the carriage house."

Bed and bath: In the carriage house—a suite with one queen-bedded room and one room with two twin beds, one tub/shower bath.

Breakfast: Fresh fruit, yogurt, freshly baked goods. Hosts set table in carriage house.

Plus: Full kitchen with stove and microwave, dining room, sitting room. TV. Radio. Telephone.

KEY TO SYMBOLS
♥ Lots of honeymooners come here.
🏃 Families with children are very welcome. (Please see page xii.)
🏠 "Please emphasize that we are a private home, not an inn."
♣ Groups or private parties sometimes book the entire B&B.
♦ Travel agents' commission paid. (Please see page xii.)
🗡 Sorry, no guests' pets are allowed.
🚭 No smoking inside *or* no smoking at all, even on porches.

B&B at The Lighted Holly   215/444–9246
216 North Union Street, P.O. Box 885, Kennett Square, PA 19348

Hosts: Carolyn and Peter Zinner
Location: On Route 82 in this main street community, half a mile south of Route 1. Two miles south of Longwood Gardens, 5 miles south of the Brandywine River Museum, 7 miles north of Winterthur.

Open: Year round. Two-night minimum on holiday weekends.
Rates: $70 shared bath, $85 with private bath and fireplace, $125 with loft. $5 one-night surcharge. MC, Visa.
🏠 ♣ ✈ ⚓

Tradition reigns. In decor. In hospitality. And architecture. The Federal-style colonial brick townhouse, built between 1820 and 1840 (with two additions in the 1980s), was "all white with modern Swedish simplicity" when the Zinners first saw this "perfect home for the B&B we were looking for." They began the transformation by creating a two-level suite. By the time the first guests were welcomed in 1988, the entire house was redecorated with colonial print wallcoverings and antique and reproduction furnishings—with Oriental rugs on the first floor and carpeting in the bedrooms. There's a 19th-century cherry hutch in the dining room, and by the living room fireplace, a sofa and grandmother clock.

Peter is a photojournalist. Carolyn works for a hospital group information systems department. The B&B name? Holiday holly-patterned china is the B&B china. And year round, lights twinkle on the holly bush that grows in front of the house.

In residence: Two dogs—Jonathan, a terrier; Muffy, a Lhaso-poo.
Bed and bath: Three queen-bedded second-floor rooms; one is a suite with four-poster, working fireplace, and adjacent loft with antique double bed. Two rooms with beamed ceilings share a tub/shower bath.
Breakfast: 8–9. Fresh fruit, homemade breads and turnovers. Juice, coffee, tea. In fireplaced dining room at candlelit table set with holiday china, silver, and crystal.
Plus: Central air conditioning. Desk and phone jack in each room. Welcoming beverage. Goose down comforters. Fresh flowers. Snack-filled baskets.

Meadow Spring Farm   215/444–3903
201 East Street Road, Kennett Square, PA 19348

Hosts: Anne Hicks and daughter Debbie Axelrod
Location: On a 130-acre working farm. On Route 926, up a long lane with black and white cows (young stock) on one side and fields of corn and hay on the other. Five minutes

from Longwood Gardens and the Brandywine River Museum.
Open: Year round. Reservations required.
Rates: Single $55. Double, $65 shared bath, $75 private. $10 cot or crib.
♥ 🛏 🏠 ♣ ♦ ✈

Whether on Washington, D.C., TV, in the Philadelphia-area Bloomingdale's (for a "Meet-the-Hosts" program based on this book), in *Country Inns* magazine, or in the *New York Times*, this B&B and Anne are big hits. Since 1983,

(Please turn page.)

Meadow Spring Farm has been a perfect match for travelers who come for quiet (no sound of traffic); for the cows (about 200) and calves and sheep and lambs; for the chickens (guests may gather the eggs) and rabbits too. Guests love the perennial gardens, the in-ground swimming pool, and (in winter) the hot tub in the solarium. And they come for Anne, the hostess who, 45 years ago, arrived as a bride at this 1836 antiques-filled brick farmhouse. Now her almost-famous collections include cows, dolls, and Santas of cloth, porcelain, ceramic, and wood. Three sons have taken over the farming. B&B has become so busy that daughter Debbie left her full-time job to become cohostess.

"We've met museumgoers, honeymooners, entire families, skiers, canoers,—the greatest people from all over the world. What I love best is having guests return." They do. That's why reservations, especially on weekends, are usually booked weeks in advance.

In residence: Sparky, German shepherd, and Temba, a Lab, "greet guests and accompany you on paths around the farm." Visiting grandchildren are guides too.
Bed and bath: Seven rooms. In farmhouse, four second-floor rooms. One with canopied queen bed, working fireplace, private tub and shower bath. One with queen sleigh bed, fireplace, private bath. Room with two twin beds shares a bath with a single-bedded room. In separate building, private baths for room with twin beds and two queen-bedded rooms; first-floor room has small kitchen. Cot and crib available.
Breakfast: 7:30–9. Apple pancakes, fresh fruit, homemade breads as well as jams and jellies. Sausage, scrapple, or bacon; French toast or mushroom omelets. Homemade sticky buns on Sundays. In dining room, on glassed-in porch by the pool, or in your room.
Plus: Air-conditioned bedrooms with TVs and ceiling fans. Welcoming resfreshments include home-baked goods. Fresh flowers year round. Fresh fruit. Mints. Wood stove in kitchen. Fireplaced living room. Game room with pool table. Will meet guests at transportation points. Will plan everything from restaurant reservations to balloon rides. Babysitting. Kitchen and laundry privileges.

From Virginia: *"Homey, cozy atmosphere."* From Massachusetts: *"Immaculate . . . highest quality food, deliciously prepared and generous."* From Michigan: *"The house is filled with warmth."*

Scarlett House   215/444-9592
503 West State Street, Kennett Square, PA 19348-3298

Hosts: Susan Lalli-Ascosi and Andy Ascosi
Location: On main street of town, 3 miles south of Longwood Gardens. Short walk to shops and restaurants. Within 9 miles of Winterthur, Hegley, Brandywine Battlefield and River Museum. Thirty miles from Philadelphia and Lancaster.
Open: Year round. Two-day minimum on holiday weekends.
Rates: $65 shared bath, $85 private. $95 suite, double occupancy; $10 for third person in suite.
♥ ❖ ✈ ⊱

From New Jersey: *"Spectacular."* From Massachusetts: *"To top off the wonderful ambiance and accommodations, the innkeepers were warm, helpful, generous."* From New York: *"Nothing (here or abroad) compares to the service and hospitality . . . breakfast a culinary treat."* From Texas: *"Magnificent."* From New York: *"A romantic (not saccharine) Victorian atmosphere. . . . Captivating . . . beautifully decorated, elegant yet comfortable, not overdone . . . gas chandeliers that seem to have been made for the house . . . goody bag made us feel as if Grandmother had sent us off."*

The accolades are endless for this B&B, a classic American foursquare-style granite house built in 1910 with wraparound porch, chestnut woodwork, leaded glass windows and ornate fireplaces. The Ascosis, the first owners outside of the Scarlett family, began their "adventure," a three-year restoration phase, without plumbing! Now they host contented travelers including friends of a romance novelist who came with her husband for a weekend complete with flowers, champagne, chocolates, and notes pinned to the pillow. Now one parlor has red velvet settee and chairs, roses and lace; another, also fireplaced, has books (antiques, collectibles, Brandywine Valley) and a TV and VCR.

And to think "Susan's dream" all started in the 1970s with some antique hat pins and jewelry—and a memorable Nantucket B&B—before her 17 years in health care marketing. Andy is an engineer "who caught the Victorian bug. When we ran out of room, it was time to find a house of the period to go with our collection." Scarlett House opened in 1990.

In residence: In hosts' quarters, one-year-old Nicholas.

Bed and bath: Four second-floor rooms. Suite has ornately carved queen bed, sitting area with double sofa bed, private bath with glass-enclosed shower. Another room with carved high-headboard queen bed, private shower bath. One room with spindled oak queen bed and another with double four-poster bed share a hall tub/shower bath.

Breakfast: Usually 8–8:30. A buffet that may include mushroom-shaped chocolate chip scones (a specialty), mandarin orange muffins, poppyseed lemon bread. Fresh fruits. Freshly squeezed orange juice. Bread pudding, quiche, mushroom souffle, or apple crisp. Coffee with vanilla flavoring and a hint of chocolate. At candlelit table set with fine china, silver, and lace; on porch in summer.

Plus: Bedroom air conditioning and phone jacks. Afternoon tea or lemonade with fresh fruit, homemade cookies and pastries. Evening refreshments. Turndown service with fresh flower on pillow. Upright piano in music room. Large second-floor sitting area.

Looking for a B&B with a crib? Find a description with the ♣ symbol and then check under the "bed and bath" section.

Bed & Breakfast at Walnut Hill   215/444-3703

Kennett Square, PA
Mailing address: 214 Chandler's Mill Road, Avondale, PA 19311-9606

Hosts: Tom and Sandy Mills
Location: On a wooded site "along a crooked country road," facing a horse-filled meadow (that in the 1840s was site of a grist mill); other wildlife and a meandering creek also transit the meadow. Seven minutes from Longwood Gardens; 15–20 minutes from Winterthur, Hagley, and Brandywine River Museum. One hour west of Philadelphia's Center City; 40 minutes east of Lancaster; 25 minutes from Wilmington, Delaware.
Open: Year round. Two-day minimum on holiday weekends.
Rates: $60 single. $75 double.

Many guests want to live here forever! Antiques are imaginatively displayed and used in the 1844 mill house, which has been restored by the Millses since they came here as bride and groom three decades ago. Old barnboard siding is on some walls. A walk-in fireplace is in the beamed den. A buggy seat is now a coffee table; a washboard, a mirror; an ironing board, a flower stand. There are dried herbs; handcrafts; fresh flowers; family photographs; braided rugs; a formal living room; designer linens—and, available to guests year round, a hot tub.

Tom works for Du Pont. Sandy is a former Winterthur guide (for 10 years), caterer, and children's services social worker.

In residence: Devon, a yellow Labrador. One Persian and a tiger cat are usually outside.
Foreign languages spoken: Some French and Spanish.
Bed and bath: Three second-floor rooms. (Maximum of two booked unless guests are traveling together.) One shared tub and shower bath plus a half bath. One room has four-poster canopied double bed. One with two twin beds (and space for one extra bed). One room with an antique wicker single bed.
Breakfast: Usually 7–9. Guests' choice. Cottage cheese pancakes with hot blueberry sauce; French toast (plain or stuffed with peaches and cream); mushroom omelets; or frittatas. Homemade scones, muffins, rolls, and spreads. Served in front of bay window overlooking bird feeders, picturesque meadow, and stream.
Plus: Air-conditioned bedrooms. Afternoon or evening lemonade, tea, or cider with homemade sweets. Turndown service. Mints on pillow. Down comforters. Bathrobes. Library with cable TV.

> From California: *"Like visiting someone you knew in college . . . treated our four-year-old as if they were aunt and uncle . . . told us about covered bridges . . . went on to a more beautiful place, but we enjoyed Walnut Hill more."* From New York: *"A delightful couple who give you just the right amount of attention."* From Ohio: *"Wonderful sense of humor . . . shared recipes."* From Connecticut: *"Charming, as is the country setting."*

B&Bs offer the ultimate concierge service.

Cornerstone Bed and Breakfast   215/274–2143

RD 1, Box 155, Newark and Buttonwood Roads, Landenberg, PA 19350

Hosts: Linda Chamberlain and Marty Mulligan

Location: In the rolling hills of lovely chateau country. Very close to the Delaware line. Fifteen minutes to Longwood Gardens, the University ofDelaware, Brandywine River Museum. Twenty minutes to Winterthur and Amish country.

Open: Year round. Two-night minimum on weekends and holidays.

Rates: Double occupancy. $85 double bed. Queen $95; $110 with fireplace fall through spring.

♥ ❖ ◆ ✗ ⅙

Every four years, on Chester County Day, hundreds (1,800) stand in line here to tour the spacious rooms, which are filled with still-growing collections from all over the world—fine antiques, Persian and Chinese rugs, ticking clocks, and brasses.

Built between 1704 (the oldest part) and 1820 (the date on the cornerstone), with beautiful woodwork and elaborate mantels, the house was vacant in 1980 when Linda, a chemical company executive, bought it and fulfilled her childhood dream of living in a Chester County stone house. She gained vast experience as plasterer, painter, wallpaperer, and furniture restorer. Because she created a comfortable environment that is both elegant and casual, every day a guest asks if this is the family home.

She and Marty, an Eastman Kodak technical representative turned innkeeper (page 57), have expanded the beautiful perennial, herb, and rose gardens. And put exotic fish in the pond. They host guests (many give gift certificates to relatives) who enjoy the area's attractions, the walks here along the miles of carriage trails, the pool with Jacuzzi, and the pampering.

In residence: Ben, the official greeter, a golden retriever. Jake, the cat.

Foreign languages spoken: French and German.

Bed and bath: Four rooms, two suites, and one cottage, all with period antiques, all private baths. First floor—room with canopied queen bed, sitting room, shower bath. (All other baths have tub and shower.) On second floor—one double-bedded room; all others with queen canopies, two with working fireplace. Third-floor suite has king bed in one room, two double beds in the other. Just-completed cottage, overlooking swimming pool and fields, has two bedrooms, each with queen bed, and fireplaced living room.

Breakfast: 8–9. Juice, fresh fruit, croissants or homemade muffins, fresh toast. Egg entree, pancakes, or breakfast casserole. Special diets accommodated with advance notice.

Plus: Room air conditioners. Living room with two fireplaces. Large wicker-furnished porch. Coffee always on. Turned-down beds. Garden flowers. Plant-filled greenhouse. Bicycles to borrow.

---

*T*hink of bed and breakfast as a poeple-to-people concept.

Hamanassett   215/459-3000
P.O. Box 129, Lima, PA 19037-0129

Host: Mrs. Evelenc Dohan
Location: High on a hill on 36 acres, "a ten-minute walk to nowhere, with privacy, peace, seclusion, interrupted only by sound of birds." Seven miles to Chadds Ford. Within 20 minutes of fine dining; Longwood Gardens; and Winterthur, Nemours, Brandywine museums. A half hour from Philadelphia International Airport, 35 minutes to Center City Philadelphia.

Open: Year round. Two-night minimum September–December, May–June, and holiday weekends.
Rates: Double occupancy. $85 twin beds. $110–$210 suite (depending on number accommodated), $95 or $100 all other rooms. Singles, slightly less. $25 additional person.
♥ ⬛ ♣ ♦ ✗

Memorable. A half-mile-long horticultural extravaganza leading to an 1850 mansion (with 30-inch-thick stone walls), home to the Dohan family since 1870. Spacious and beautiful, with important heirloom antiques and collectibles, and intricate craftsmanship and architectural details throughout. Hospitality that is based on years of experience, stemming from the era when this was headquarters for the Lima Hunt, home to the Master of Hounds.

The greenhouse, filled with interesting and colorful flora from October to May, was built by Mrs. Dohan, a longtime Philadelphia Flower Show award winner, gourmet cook, and former English literature teacher. With a minimum of help, she maintains the entire house and has encouraged woodlands to minimize grounds maintenance.

Although many guests come for the area's attractions, a good number enjoy Hamanassett's formal gardens, fields, and country trails. Some come just for the experience of being here and meeting the energetic, friendly, gracious hostess. Travelers from all over the country wrote long, detailed letters that recall lively conversations, gourmet breakfasts, and the "relaxed and exquisite environment." It's the perfect setting for weddings (many are held here), for a Gallo wine television ad (the hostess participated), and successful murder mystery weekends.

Foreign language spoken: French—"un peu, tres peu."
Bed and bath: Six rooms, all with private full baths. On second floor, one with twin beds, one with four-poster queen, one with canopied king (with small refrigerator). On third floor (all air-conditioned), room with two double beds and sitting room with sofa bed; king with detached bath; suite for two to five persons with king-bedded room, room with canopied single, living room, two sofa beds, bath, small refrigerator.
Breakfast: 7:30–9:30 Monday–Saturday; 8–10 Sunday. Two fruits, juice, cereal, bacon and/or sausage and/or scrapple. Eggs cooked to order, French toast, blueberry pancakes, cheese omelet (house specialty). Homemade muffins, breads, croissants, and jams. Buffet in large dining room. Small groups sit in curve of French doors with view of lawns and woodlands.
Plus: In each room, fresh flowers arranged professionally by hostess, ice, fruit, TV. Library with over 2,000 volumes including current, classical, and first editions. Formal living room with Federal-era fireplace. Evening coffee or afternoon tea upon request.

Antique Row Bed & Breakfast   215/592-7802

341 South 12th Street   fax 215/592-9692
Philadelphia, PA 19107-5907

Host: Barbara Pope
Location: On "Antique Row"—with antiques and crafts shops—in Center City. Within 4 blocks of the Academy of Music, the University of the Arts, the Historical Society, three major hospitals, and new (under construction) Convention Center. Within walking distance of most cultural attractions, historic sites, "and the city's best jazz club." Two blocks from Hi-Speed Line to New Jersey's new aquarium. Near fine restaurants and inexpensive ethnic eateries.
Open: Year round.
Rates: Include tax. $55 double, $45 single. Suite $65 double, $55 single. Less for extended stays. $10 extra person in room. 🛏 ✣ ♦ 🍴

Although many guests come with an agenda, this is a good place for warm hospitality, for orientation to the city, and for suggestions such as a colonial garden, historic sites, major concerts, free performances, or "a superb collection of American art that can be absorbed in an afternoon."

Barbara has been hosting in her comfortably furnished 150-year-old townhouse for about 10 years. All guest rooms have shelves with take-away-if-you-haven't-finished-them books.

Bed and bath: Three traditionally furnished rooms, each with color TV. Three short flights to 15-foot-square double-bedded room that shares third-floor tub/shower bath with third-floor 15-foot-square double-bedded room. On first floor, two-level suite with private interior entrance off first-floor hall has queen bed, sofa bed in sitting room, private shower bath, and option of private kitchen reached via winding metal staircase. Rollaway available.
Breakfast: Menu and times are flexible. Usually 7–9 weekdays, 8–10 weekends. Juice or fruit, cereal, eggs, breakfast meats, toast, coffee, tea. Served in dining room furnished with an Oriental rug, 200-year-old Hepplewhite table, Victorian dining chairs, early American side table.
Plus: Fireplaced living room. Individual air-conditioning units. Down comforters.

> From Pennsylvania: *"An outstanding experience . . . very comfortable . . . very affordable . . . warm, friendly, helpful hostess who is knowledgeable about Philadelphia. Highly recommended!"*

Center City Retreat

Philadelphia, PA

Location: Residential neighborhood. Two blocks from the Italian Market and 2 blocks from Antique Row.
Reservations: Year round through Bed & Breakfast Connections, page 223.
Rates: $45 single, $55 double. $10 portacrib. 🛏 🛏 🍴 🚭

Books line the stairway to and an entire wall of the guests' floor. They reflect the interests—history, autobiographies, philosophy—and languages studied

(Please turn page.)

by the well-traveled hosts, who dub themselves "fans of Philadelphia." Together—he is a lawyer and she is a violin bowmaker, "possibly the country's only woman bowmaker"—they have a seven-person Afro-Brazilian band that has played in almost every area venue, from museums to Penn's Landing. Their 1850s townhouse is furnished with Grandfather's great antiques collection, which includes an Edison Victrola—"that should play as soon as I make some leather belts for it"—and about 100 records.

In residence: One two-year-old daughter. One Maine coon cat.
Foreign languages spoken: French, Portuguese, Bulgarian, Spanish.
Bed and bath: On guests' floor, the third—one L-shaped room with double bed, sitting area with sofa and desk, private (new) shower bath.
Breakfast: Flexible. Usually 8–9 weekdays, 8:30–10 weekends for cooked breakfast; self-serve cold breakfast if later. Fruit compote, French toast, and maybe one of 26 kinds of sausages—such as venison with juniper berries or pork with apple wine and cheese from nearby Italian Market.
Plus: Free off-street parking. Air conditioner, ceiling fan, and window fan in guests' room.

> From Illinois: *"Excellent hosts. . . . Interesting people. . . . Provided a lot of information about current events and happenings. . . . Accommodated personal breakfast preferences. Live in a wonderful location. . . . Very comfortable and well taken care of."*

Cromwell House
Philadelphia, PA

Location: On a quiet street with spring-flowering cherry and apple trees. A 5-minute walk from Benjamin Franklin Blvd., Philadelphia Museum of Art, Boat House Row, Logan Center. Two blocks to City Center. Convenient transportation to historic sites.

Reservations: Year round through Bed & Breakfast of Philadelphia, page 223.
Rates: $55 single, $65 double.
🛏 ✖ ✄

George Washington in full regalia greeted one late-arriving guest. Although I never had the opportunity to see him (the host) or the hostess attired in costume, I was delighted to describe my stay on a Philadelphia talk show. Although it was just a one-night stay, I felt richer for the warm experience.

The multifaceted hosts, parents of five grown children, have had many successful careers that have merged into their current work as theatrical producers. They do everything from writing to costuming, lighting to acting—for television and stage. The innovative productions often focus on history and involve the audience.

It is hard to believe that the hosts acquired their 1865 row house as a shell. Restored (by them) in full Victorian style, it has reproduced moldings, a formal parlor, a designer kitchen with solarium greenhouse, and an incredible south-facing library with central hearth and windows and plants on the end wall.

Foreign languages spoken: Some French and German.
Bed and bath: One very private third-floor room with twin beds. Victorian (Queen Anne) decor. Private full bath.
Breakfast: 7–9. Cereal, fruit, yogurt, muffins or sweet bread. Eggs or pancakes. Tea, coffee, juice. Served in dining room, in kitchen greenhouse, or outside in the city garden.
Plus: Central air conditioning. Ground-level parlor and powder room. Pickup available (extra charge) at Philadelphia International Airport, 30th Street train station, or bus station. Access to refrigerator. Suggestions for small museums, even the Rare Book Room in the library. The confirmed B&B hosts have been known to drive medical students to exams.

New Market Surprise
Philadelphia, PA

Location: In historic district, a mix of residential and commercial properties. On the southernmost point of Society Hill. Within walking distance of most historic sites, theater, many restaurants, shopping, Penn's Landing (three minutes' walk), convenient and good public transportation.
Reservations: Available year round through Bed & Breakfast of Philadelphia, page 223.
Rates: $60 single, $65 double.
♥ ⅋ ⅋ ✗ ⅋

Although it took more than a magic wand to change the abandoned shell into the warm and inviting private home, you almost have the feeling that the metamorphosis just happened naturally. The historically certified house, built in 1811, retains the original doors, pine floors, and fireplaces, as well as some chair rails and two narrow spiral staircases with pie-wedge-shaped treads. Contemporary furnishings, hand-painted Mexican tile in baths, and many plants and natural fibers give the home a very earthy look.

The hostess is a psychotherapist who is interested in food, arts, and social causes. When she restored the property acquired from the Redevelopment Authority, she took some photographs. They are shared with guests—as are many suggestions for things to do and places to go. Travelers from all over the world are grateful that a newspaper article (12 years ago, in the early days of B&B) mentioned the need for hosts in this area, now a tourist attraction in itself.

Bed and bath: Two double-bedded rooms, one on second floor and one on third (with working fireplace); each with private full bath.
Breakfast: Usually a full meal. May include oven-baked items such as souffle-like pancake topped with powdered sugar, lemon juice, and orange marmalade; or puffy French toast with bacon; or German apple pancake served with bacon or sausage. If it's a fix-your-own arrangement, homemade muffins are provided. Served in fireplaced kitchen that has exposed beams, a brick wall, and a greenhouse leading to garden.
Plus: Central air conditioning for first two floors. Window air conditioner in third-floor bedroom. Small walled garden. Metered street parking (or 24-hour lot, $10).

Shippen Way Inn

215/627–7266
416–418 Bainbridge Street, Philadelphia, PA 19147   **800/245–4873**

Hosts: Ann Foringer and Raymond Rhule
Location: In historic downtown district. With Famous Deli, a Thai restaurant, a French restaurant, and a popular pastry shop for neighbors. One block off South Street, known for its boutiques, ethnic restaurants, shops, pubs. Two blocks from Society Hill, 6 to Independence Hall, Liberty Bell, Visitor Center. Within walking distance of Penn's Landing and Hi-Speed water taxi to Camden's aquarium, and of bus for art museums and University of Pennsylvania.
Open: Year round.
Rates: $70–$80 double bed, $90 with fireplace. $90 twin beds. $90–$105 queen beds. Discounts for stays over three nights. Amex, MC, Visa.
♣ ♦ ✕

Surprise! Country ambiance in the city. A wrought iron gate leads to the courtyard, the connecting link to these two 18th-century houses. One is brick; the other, frame (unusual in Philadelphia). They were restored (the facade, shutter colors, and even type of mortar were approved by the Historic Commission) and renovated (gutted). Old beams were retained and added. Raymond worked on the exterior, which is complete with cedar-shake roof. Ann and her mother stenciled and decorated. They created a very comfortable, friendly environment, with country antiques and quilts, and with an open kitchen where guests can make a cup of tea and get hints for restaurants and places to see. Occasionally, Ann and Raymond's father, who lives in the restored blue-shuttered house next door, greets guests.

Raymond, resident innkeeper, paints with watercolors and oils. He and his sister Ann, full-time co-innkeeper who lives within walking distance, enjoy their role as "ambassadors for the city"—to friends and relatives of neighbors, and to guests from all over the world.

Foreign language spoken: "A little Spanish."
Bed and bath: Nine rooms (one with working fireplace) on three floors; size ranges from large to "tiny but cozy." All private shower baths. Some ground-floor rooms (two have private garden entrance); some on second floor are reached via steep spiral staircase; one is a third-floor dormer room. Twin, double, queen, four-posters (one with trundle bed) available.
Breakfast: 7:30–10. Freshly squeezed orange juice. Fruit. Homemade granola. Cereals. Baked goods. Buffet style in glass-enclosed breakfast room overlooking flower and herb gardens.
Plus: Central air conditioning. Ground-floor fireplaced sitting room. Private bedroom phones. TV in queen-bedded rooms. Afternoon wine and cheese in garden or by fireplace. Public parking nearby (some free, some charge). Suggestion for an Italian restaurant with opera performances.

From Massachusetts: *"It reminded us of Ireland!"*

---

*H*ospitality *is the keynote of B & B.*

Shirl's Shed

Huntington Valley, PA

Location: "Countrylike residential." On the edge of woods (with deer and turkeys on about 35 acres—"bring long sleeves and pants and hiking shoes"). No traffic sounds, "only birds." A half hour north of Philadelphia and south of New Hope. Within a couple of miles of several restaurants. Less than a mile to township park for picnicking and maintained walking trails.

Reservations: Available April through October through Bed & Breakfast of Philadelphia, page 223.

Rate: $90 per night.

♥ ✂ ⅏

> From Philadelphia: *"The most wonderful unique B&B ever stayed in . . . clean, warm, and comfortable, well stocked with food and very private . . . enjoyed watching two deer nibble on lawn while taking a shower in the greenhouse."* Another from the city: *"The hosts were very pleasant and most accommodating . . . the pool was lovely . . . we want to go back when we can use the Franklin stove."*

Your own hideaway was built by a horticulturist in 1950 as a gardener's shed and attached greenhouse. When the hosts bought the property, they converted this structure to a studio cottage so that their daughter, who lives in Spain, could have her private quarters when she visits. A black swimming pool that "looks like a pond" sits at the edge of the huge expanse of lawn and the woods. Old barn siding lines the insulated bedroom walls. Throw rugs are on the brick-patterned vinyl floor. You have TV, a refrigerator, a Franklin stove, peace and quiet, nature and privacy.

Bed and bath: One queen-bedded room (the potting shed) with armoire and sink, wicker chairs and glass-topped table. Attached bath (the greenhouse) with one window that opens; claw-foot tub with shower (sink is in bedroom) and curtains that cover the walls "just to the right height"; glass everywhere with views of sun, lawn and trees, moon and stars.

Breakfast: Whenever. Help yourself. Juice, fruit, cheese, jellies, butter, milk. Warm buns brought to your door. Electric teakettle for tea, coffee, instant hot cereal.

Plus: Firewood for stove. Wine. Sodas. Juices. Snack foods. Air conditioner and ceiling fan in bedroom.

The Barn at Gulph Mills

Radnor, PA

Location: Picturesque. On several acres overlooking greens and a pond. Close to many colleges, including Bryn Mawr, Haverford, Villanova. Four miles to Valley Forge National Park. Half hour from Center City Philadelphia.

Reservations: Year round through Bed & Breakfast Connections, page 223.

Rates: $85–95 per room. $25 rollaway.

♥ ♣ ♦ ✂ ⅏

(Please turn page.)

Dramatic. Luxurious. And welcoming. It's an 1802 (so the stone marker says) bank barn, made into a B&B in the late 1980s by the host, a designer and decorator of commercial spaces who has worked for Japanese architects in Japan. All sorts of interesting changes have been made to create unusual spaces, each with post-and-beam construction. One room is the old ice room, complete with wood walls. The deck, overlooking the rolling green and pond, is framed from old flooring. The dining room ceiling is wood. Wood from the stalls has become an extraordinary story-and-a-half staircase. There are lofty spaces. And a Japanese flavor with prints, scrolls, and porcelains. All combined with eclectic furnishings including English antiques. All very private. All remembered—by business travelers, parents of college students, wedding guests and honeymooners, Pakistani genetic biologists—the inspiration for the varied breakfast repertoire—and getaway Philadelphians too.

Foreign language spoken: Japanese.
Bed and bath: Three carpeted guest rooms, private baths. Large king-bedded room, full bath, sitting area with table and four chairs, small refrigerator. Cozy corner room with queen pencil-post bed, full bath, small refrigerator. Room with king sleigh bed, shower bath, sitting area. Rollaway available.
Breakfast: At 8. Hostess prepares and host serves cornbread waffles and sausage. Or lingonberry (berries from Scandinavia) pancakes with sour cream and fresh berries. Maybe grilled fish rice, miso soup, Japanese condiments. Or Pakistani/Indian steamed dumplings and a selection of curries. (Each one has a story.) In dining room, in fireplaced great room, or on deck.
Plus: In each guest room—private phone, air conditioner, individual heat thermostat. Fireplaced great room with 12-foot ceiling.

Amsterdam B&B   215/983–9620
P.O. Box 1139, Valley Forge PA 19482-1139   800/952–1580

Hosts: Pamela and Ino Vandersteur
Location: On two-lane Route 23, the road from Valley Forge National Park (6 miles from B&B) to Pennsylvania Dutch country (20 miles). Surrounded by farms. "Within 2 miles of several great restaurants." Forty-five minutes to historic Philadelphia and to Brandywine; 20 to King of Prussia Mall.
Open: Year round.
Rates: $65 shared bath, $75 private bath. Singles $10 less. MC, Visa.
♥ ⬛ ♣ ♦ ✳

People came from miles around to Pam's "nice little Indonesian tearoom" that seated 30 for dinner in this added-on-to 1860 general store with, in part, old 18-inch-thick stone walls. Shortly after she opened in 1989, guests who came for rijsttafel and other specialties asked to stay overnight. Thus was born the small European-style B&B. The combination was too successful! So now it's "just" a B&B, with a Jacuzzi for six, in the former greenhouse, available in the evening; with cooking influenced by Pam's training in Ino's native Holland; with Dutch tiles and warm colors; and with meticulous housekeeping.

To transform the building, a private residence when the Vandersteurs bought it, Ino took a three months' leave of absence from his pharmaceutical engineering position. Pam left her work in real estate and construction. They removed suspended ceilings, discovered original plaster under plastic brick walls, and found original latches and moldings too. The love story? Pam met Ino, who has been in this country for about 15 years, about 2 miles from here.

In residence: Two dogs in hosts' quarters, visited only by guest request. One Italian mastiff (very big) and one Boston terrier, "the size of a loaf of bread."
Foreign languages spoken: French, Dutch, German.
Breakfast: 7–8 continental; 8–9:30 choice of several entrees such as French toast, eggs any style, or the house specialty. Bacon or sausage. Fruit, orange juice, coffee, tea. "Can last for hours."
Bed and bath: Up a steep staircase, three air-conditioned second-floor rooms, new baths with European fixtures. One queen Danish bed, private tub and shower bath, TV, plus a deck. One room with queen bed, and sitting area with desk and sofa and one room with twin/king option with dressing room share (robes provided) a tub and shower bath.
Plus: Welcoming beverage. Wood-burning stove in living room. Big front porch. Guest refrigerator stocked with beverages. TVs available. Help-yourself coffee, tea, cocoa. Guest microwave. Patio. Badminton, Picnic table. Grill.

> From Pennsylvania: *"Amiable hosts . . . interesting conversations . . . deluxe accommodations with charm and character . . . fabulous food . . . even recommended tour of a fascinating artist's studio."*

The Great Valley House of Valley Forge

Box 110, RD 3   215/644–6759
Malvern, PA 19355   fax 215/644–7019

Host: Pattye Benson
Location: On 4 acres adjacent to 50 acres of woods with walking and jogging trails. A rural country setting, just off main road. Half a mile from Route 202, five from exit 24 (Valley Forge) of Pennsylvania Turnpike. Two miles to Valley Forge National Park; 6 minutes to King of Prussia Mall; 20 to Philadelphia.
Open: Year round. Two-night weekend minimum for room with private bath.
Rates: Double occupancy. $70 shared bath, $80 private. Singles $10 less. $10 third person in room.
♥ ♦ ⬤ ♣ ◆

"Did George Washington sleep here?" is one of the most frequently asked questions at this very popular antiques-filled B&B. It was established ten years ago in the state's second-oldest house, which has an "olde kitchen" (the original 1690 house) complete with walk-in fireplace, crane, and rare stone sink. Stone walls are 27 inches thick. Hinges and brackets are hand forged. A British gramophone is in the dining room. There's a vine-covered smokehouse. A tunnel that was part of the underground railroad. And lots of history shared by Pattye, a hostess with contagious enthusiasm, an interior designer/B&B instructor/National Trust for Historic Preservation presenter/quilter who has a master's degree in political science. Her husband Jeff, marketing director for a computer company, singlehandedly restored the

(Please turn page.)

"piece of American history" they found within five days after returning from living (and traveling in B&Bs) in England. This is a place that has been discovered by guests from all over the world, by business travelers who choose it over luxury hotels, by summer tourists who appreciate the pool, by families, and by honeymooners who know that Pattye rejoices in making a special breakfast for them.

In residence: Daughter Lyndsey, age nine. Whu Chi, a Shih Tzu.
Foreign languages spoken: French, German, and some Spanish.
Bed and bath: Three rooms. All hand stenciled, air-conditioned, with TV and radio, antique quilts. Entire third floor consists of two dormered rooms, each with a queen and a twin bed. One room has private en-suite bath with footed tub and hand-held shower. The other shares a shower bath with second-floor room that has a double bed, queen sofa bed, upright piano, and private phone. Rollaway and crib available.
Breakfast: Full 8–9:30. (Continental at other times.) Fruit. French toast, souffle, or quiche. Homemade breads and muffins. Freshly ground gourmet coffee. Served by fireplace in oft-photographed olde kitchen.
Plus: Fireplaces in kitchen and living and dining rooms. Guests have use of microwave, refrigerator, teakettle. Books and games. Down comforters. Turndown service. Picnic baskets ($15).

The Bankhouse Bed & Breakfast

875 Hillsdale Road, West Chester, PA 19382   215/344–7388

Hosts: Diana and Michael Bové
Location: On a country road, across from a 10-acre horse farm. One mile from town and restaurants. Five miles from U.S. Route 1; 3 from Route 202; 10 from Pennsylvania Turnpike; 8 miles to Longwood Gardens and Brandywine River Mu-
seum. Twenty minutes to Valley Forge National Park; 30 to Lancaster; 45 to downtown Philadelphia.
Open: Year round.
Rates: $85 private bath suite. $65 semiprivate. Corporate rates available.
🖤 ✖ ⅍

Just two guest rooms, yet close to a record number of guests' letters, with every one praising *everything*. A few excerpts:

> From Washington: *"The type of place that makes me want to put together another business trip to Philadelphia just so I can stay there."* From New York: *"Our first real B&B. Others had been more like small inns . . . lemonade and iced tea, carrots to feed the horses and donkey . . . spotless accommodations, a peaceful and historic setting."* From Illinois: *"Charming country decor and very comfortable. . . . The best breakfast I have ever had at a B&B."* From Maryland: *"Warm and cozy . . . with shiny wood floors and stenciling . . . felt pampered."* From Massachusetts: *" . . . invited our college daughter to have breakfast with us."* From Virginia: *"Health-conscious breakfast."* From Colorado: *" . . . a wealth of information on area, especially antiques shops and sightseeing."* From California: *"Greeted us with hot cider."* From New Hampshire: *"Thought of every detail."* From Maryland: *"A quaint old house built into the bank of a hill . . . delightful couple . . . interesting books and items by local artists and craftsmen."* From California:

"Enchanting . . . a view from balcony across a green hill with a pond and even a horse. . . . Good music with breakfast. . . . Diana is young and tireless and living her dream."

The Bovés opened in 1989 after spending 18 months renovating this 200-year-old farmhouse, after Diana had a wonderful time in Massachusetts as a substitute innkeeper, and after she decorated the Bankhouse with country antiques and folk art. Her newest interest is quilting. Previously, she was media department coordinator at the American College in Bryn Mawr, where Michael is a production engineer and professional voice talent.

Bed and bath: Entire second floor. One double-bedded room and one with twin beds share a very large full bath, a sitting room with book-filled wall, and a balcony. Private exterior entrance.

Breakfast: 8–9:30. Repertoire of 100+ muffin recipes plus many entrees such as German apple or whole wheat pancakes or French toast with hosts' own hot orange syrup. Freshly ground gourmet coffee or tea, juice, fresh fruit. In dining room overlooking horse farm and pond.

Plus: Central air conditioning. Sitting room with desk, private phone, ceiling fan, books, games. Fresh flowers. Flannel sheets. Homemade snacks.

Lenape Springs Farm   215/793–2266

580 West Creek Road, West Chester, PA
Mailing address: P.O. Box 176, Pocopson, PA 19366

Hosts: Bob and Sharon Currie
Location: Idyllic. Off the beaten path. On 32 acres along Brandywine Creek. Five miles northeast of Longwood Gardens; 4½ miles north of Chadds Ford; 10 miles north of Winterthur Museum. Near horseback riding, canoeing, antiquing, wine sampling. An hour to Philadelphia or Lancaster.

Open: Year round.
Rates: Double occupancy. $70 in carriage house. Third floor: $65 one room, $100 two rooms, $150 for three-room suite. $15 third person. Singles $5 less. Senior citizens, 10 percent less.
♥ ♯ ♥ ♣ ✗

An adventure awaits. And so it has been for the Curries, who bought this farm in 1977. Guests enjoy the restored three-storied 1847 stone "simple without ornaments" Quaker-built farmhouse; the adjoining carriage house; the deck with hot tub that faces the river and overlooks gardens and sweeping lawns; and the huge fireplaced (and air-conditioned) game room complete with pool table. When one guest asked about having a 1992 wedding here, Sharon was inspired to suggest that one gazebo be built in front and another down by a spring-fed stream. (They were in place for the wedding date.) Many guests appreciate the opportunity to take pretty walks; to tour the interesting early 1800s three-tiered bank barn; to talk with the owners of the boarded horses or with visiting blacksmiths or the veterinarian; and maybe to experience a truck or hayride with Bob, a Montana State University PhD

(Please turn page.)

chemical engineer, who grew up on a dairy farm in Montana. Here he raises cattle and grows winter hay.

"Now the farm is just about what we envisioned 15 years ago," say the Curries, warm hosts who share their home with travelers from all over the world.

In residence: Cats—Gizmo, Pretty Lee, Neutron. Dogs—Dutch, a mixed breed husky.
Foreign language spoken: Dutch. (The family spent seven years in Holland.)
Bed and bath: In main house—large second-floor room has queen bed, private shower bath. Third-floor suite with hall bath has one queen-bedded room and a larger room with two twins. In air-conditioned carriage house— two carpeted rooms, each with twin/king option. One with collection of bottles found on the farm, private full bath; other with Sharon's miniature doll collection, shower bath.
Breakfast: 6:30–9:30. Fresh fruit. Fresh mushrooms in Dijon sauce over poached eggs with English muffins; scrambled eggs with homemade muffins; Bob's buttermilk waffles on weekends and holidays. In dining room, in glassed alcove, or on deck.
Plus: Window fans in main house bedrooms. Tea, coffee, sodas. Hershey kisses at bedtime. Table and chairs under arbor overlooking lily pond with goldfish.

The Valentine
West Chester, PA

Location: Surprise! Just after many newer houses (the town) and before a 10-minute drive (the country) to Longwood Gardens. On two acres of woods, lawns, and magnificent trees and plantings including original Longwood Gardens' rhododendrons, which bloom in sequence from May until July.

Reservations: Year round through Guesthouses, page 224.
Rates: $95 private hall bath. $85 semiprivate bath. $110 with fireplace and attached private bath. $65 third-floor rooms, shared bath.
♥ ♣ ✯ ✂

"There's been a wedding here every weekend for the last two months," said the hostess as we talked about her restored and inviting three-storied 1860 brick house with cupola. The detail includes carved mahogany, walnut, and chestnut; tall ceilings with plaster ornamentation; exquisite ironwork from London; tall windows that open out to a loggia and antique fountains; and a historic gazebo by the creek. There's a blend of furnishings, many ferns and palms, Victorian settees in the sun room, and maybe live goldfish swimming in vases with fresh bouquets arranged by the hostess/decorator/special events coordinator, the one who found letters from the Civil War (read them at breakfast) in a cake tin (that somehow escaped the auction) when she moved here 10 years ago. This was the home of Du Pont's real estate—and Pennsylvania's first female—attorney, one of five daughters. (More discussion; pictures available.) The contemporary art on display, for sale here and in prestigious galleries nationwide, is the work of Harry Dunn, the area artist who designed the NBC peacock logo.

In residence: One five-pound peke-a-poo in hosts' quarters.

Bed and bath: Seven rooms. Second floor—one large air-conditioned room has antique brass double (feather) bed, working fireplace, private full bath. Room with brass double bed and one with large walnut double bed share large (new, but looks like it was always there) shower bath. Third floor—four antiques-furnished rooms, each with double bed, share original 1860 ceramic tile hall bath with claw-foot tub/shower bath.

Breakfast: Flexible. Usually presented at 9 on weekends. Fresh fruit or baked compote. Homemade bread, muffins, Danish, sticky buns. Croissant French toast; meat frittata and/or vegetable dish with homemade fresh salsa. Cooked cereal if you'd like. Juice, hot beverages. In fireplaced dining room. "Can last four hours on Sunday with people who never met before."

Plus: Fireplaced library. Wicker- and plant-filled wraparound porch. Evening sherry or brandy. Special occasions acknowledged.

From New York: *"We love the house and we love the hostess."*

Monument House

Dilworthtown, PA

Location: Rural. Overlooking rolling farmland. With monument to Lafayette by the tree where he was wounded. Within 10 minutes of Chadds Ford and not more than 20 minutes from any of the other Brandywine Valley attractions.

Reservations: Year round through Guesthouses, page 224.

Rates: $80 one room, private bath. $130 or $140 for entire floor ($130 three people, two rooms; $140 four people, two rooms). $25 rollaway. Singles $10 less.

♥ ♨ ⬥ ✕ ⚱

With 28 years' experience as Wedgwood's head designer in England, the host came to this country "by sheer chance" in 1979 to work for the Franklin Mint. Now he and his wife, freelance artists, design ceramics for major corporations; they also paint tile murals as private commissions. "Although we work alone in our separate (private) studios—his is up and mine is down—we switch and swap and help each other."

Since 1984 they have lived in this area. Their "comfortable, homely house, a home more than a house" has an extensive modern addition. The antiques-furnished guest rooms are in the original early 19th-century section. A wood-burning stove and TV are in a cozy living room. From the breakfast room you can see "lovely views right down to Shady Hollow, with corn or winter wheat and a farmhouse on the horizon at the far end."

In residence: One cat.

Bed and bath: For one party, the entire (top) second floor with two rooms. One with king/twin option and one with a double bed share one large shower (with seat) bath. Rollaway available.

(Please turn page.)

Breakfast: 8–9. "A proper breakfast." Fruit. Eggs and bacon, tomato, sausage. French bread, homemade fruit breads, English scones, or sweet rolls. Coffee or tea.

Plus: Central air conditioning, plus freestanding fans in guest rooms. Special occasions acknowledged.

From Virginia: *"Charming hosts. The breakfasts were magnificent! The house was delightful. A most enjoyable visit."*

Do you have to get up for breakfast?
There's no one rule. Check each description in this book for the various arrangements. More than one guest has been enticed by the aroma of fresh muffins. If you are on business or want to catch the morning ferry, eat-and-run is just fine. If, however, cuisine is a feature, plan on appearing at the specified time!

Vacationers (not skiers) find breakfast a very social time. One hostess says that even when guests say they want to be on the road early, they often linger over breakfast for hours. If hosts join you, please understand when they leave the table after a while.

Bucks County Reservation Services

Some Bucks County B&Bs are represented by:
  Amanda's Regional Reservation Service, page 258.
  Bed & Breakfast Adventures, page 54.
  Bed & Breakfast of Philadelphia, page 223.
  Bed & Breakfast Connections, page 223.
  Guesthouses, page 224.

KEY TO SYMBOLS
♥ Lots of honeymooners come here.
♣ Families with children are very welcome. (Please see page xii.)
♦ "Please emphasize that we are a private home, not an inn."
♣ Groups or private parties sometimes book the entire B&B.
♦ Travel agents' commission paid. (Please see page xii.)
✗ Sorry, no guests' pets are allowed.
✗ No smoking inside *or* no smoking at all, even on porches.

_____ Bucks County B&Bs _____

The Inn at Fordhook Farm   215/345–1766
105 New Britain Road, Doylestown, PA 18901   fax 215/345–1791

Hosts: Blanche Burpee Dohan and her husband, Michael; Elizabeth Romanella, resident innkeeper
Location: On 60 secluded acres of meadows and woodlands. Off Route 202, 1.5 miles east of Doylestown, "a town that is more like New England than some in New England." Twelve miles from New Hope. An hour from Philadelphia by train or car.

Open: Year round. Prefer two-night minimum on weekends; three nights on some holiday weekends.
Rates: Main house $93 semiprivate bath. $135 private bath. $20 third person. ($80–$90 corporate rate for singles, Sunday–Thursday.) Carriage house $175 (a couple) or $250 (two couples). Amex, MC, Visa.
♥ ❖ ♦ ✈ ✂

Imagine strolling on the grounds of W. Atlee Burpee's estate. Or sitting at his desk, where he wrote, by hand, the very first Burpee Seed Company catalog. Today the Burpees enjoy telling how the main house was used as a brooder house to raise game hens before it became the family residence. Now the spacious manor house is shared with romantics; with gardeners (new flowers and vegetables are introduced during open house in August); with business guests (small conference center available); with many who come to read by the fire, to walk through the woods and meadows (maps available), or to cross-country ski.

Members of the Burpee family are frequently in residence on weekends and during holidays. Blanche, a social worker who worked in adoptions and more recently was a financial consultant, and her brother Jonathan, customer services director for the Burpee Seed Company, tell Elizabeth, who was formerly with the Pennsylvania Academy of Fine Arts and New York Historical Society, that she now works *and* lives in a museum. It is filled with family heirlooms and photographs—each with a story. Among the eight other buildings on this National Register property is a carriage house with a B&B apartment that has a chestnut-paneled Great Room, magnificent vaulted ceiling, and Palladian windows. There's more, but you will just have to go to experience this national treasure.

In residence: Tammy, a shepherd/retriever, "greets guests, leads them on walks."
Foreign languages spoken: Michael Dohan speaks French, German, and some Russian. "Elizabeth Romanella can muster up a little Italian."
Bed and bath: Seven rooms. In carriage house suite, two rooms (king and queen beds) share full bath. In main house, five rooms, three with private baths. King/twin, queen, or double bed. Some four-poster, antique, and brass beds. Rooms range from huge master bedroom with working fireplace, private balcony, and large adjoining full bath to a cozy third-floor room under the eaves. Cot available.

Breakfast: 7:30–9:30 weekdays, 8:30–10 weekends. Fordhook (old fashioned oatmeal) pancakes, cheese omelets, cream cheese–stuffed French toast, smoked bacon, local sausage, poached pears with raspberry sauce, berries from the farm, homemade jams and freshly baked muffins. Served on heirloom china in dining room that has leaded bay windows, or occasionally on the huge tiled terrace under 200-year-old linden trees and overlooking acres of meadows. "Can last for hours."

Plus: Bedroom air conditioning. Afternoon refreshments; elaborate Saturday and holiday weekend teas with baked treats and watercress "from our stream" sandwiches. Tour of house. Large fireplaced living room. Fireplaced study/office with phone. Butler's pantry with refrigerator and teakettle. Picnicking on lawn. Badminton. Croquet. Free tickets to March Philadelphia Flower Show. Parting gift of Burpee seeds.

Maplewood Farm Bed & Breakfast

P.O. Box 239, 5090 Durham Road   215/766–0477
Gardenville, PA 18926-0239

Hosts: Cindy and Dennis Marquis
Location: On five acres along Route 413 with big old maple trees, pastures, a neighboring horse farm (lessons offered), a dairy farm, and a gentleman farm with sheep and goats. Five minutes to Point Pleasant (canoeing and tubing on Delaware River), 10 to Doylestown, 12 to Peddler's Village, 15 to New Hope.

Open: Year round. Two-night minimum on weekends; three over holidays.
Rates: Double occupancy. Weekends and holidays: shared bath $85; private bath $85 or $95 double bed, $100 queen bed. Suite $130. Midweek $15 less. $20 third person in room. $5 crib.
♥ ♣ ✈ ⚇

Sheep graze in the meadow. Guests are encouraged to gather fresh eggs from the henhouse. There's a nature walk down by the creek complete with a resident blue heron and, sometimes, deer. Guest rooms of this plaster-over-fieldstone farmhouse are decorated in country style, with colorful quilts, local antiques, and stenciled walls. Two walk-in fireplaces are in the 1792 summer kitchen/now living room. The second floor was built in 1826.

In 1990, following two years as Bucks County inn managers, Cindy and Dennis, at age 30, bought this property. It is now on the National Register, and the Philadelphia-area natives have become gardeners, sheep farmers, painters, and experts on area attractions as well as on cycling routes and historic covered bridges. Cindy, president of the Bed & Breakfast Inns of Bucks and Hunterdon Counties, is a former office manager of a marine construction company. Dennis, a trained biologist who worked in cardiovascular research, now works as a computer software engineer for Bristol-Myers Squibb. And, in season, he is an itinerant sheepshearer.

In residence: Stinky, their house cat. Champ, a yellow Labrador. Sally, a young black Lab.
Bed and bath: Seven cozy air-conditioned rooms with queen or double beds. Five with private bath. Room with queen bed and one with double bed share

(Please turn page.)

a hall tub/shower bath. Loft suite has exposed beams and natural oak and pine; living room with single pull-out couch, queen bed in loft above, private tub/ shower bath.

Breakfast: 8:30–10. Fresh fruits with yogurt and "our own homemade granola." French toast with pure maple syrup, omelets stuffed with fresh vegetables, or waffles with fresh blueberry topping.

Plus: Home-baked goods in afternoon. Guest refrigerator with cold beverages. California cream sherry for nightcap. By arrangement, hot-air balloon rides depart from the inn.

> From New York: *"Beautiful, charming, cozy, and quaint . . . friendly atmosphere . . . one of the most enjoyable getaways ever!"*

The Wedgwood Collection of Historic Inns
111 West Bridge Street, New Hope, PA 18938   215/862–2570

Hosts: Nadine Silnutzer and Carl Glassman
Location: Two acres of landscaped grounds on a main residential street in historic district. Two blocks to shops and restaurants. Wedgwood House (the one with a carriage on front lawn and a gazebo on the side) and Umpleby House are connected by brick walkways and gardens. Aaron Burr House is across the street and three houses toward town.

Open: Year round. Two-night minimum preferred for weekends, three nights for holidays.
Rates: Weekday/weekend $70/$90 double with semiprivate bath; $80/$115 double, $90/$135 queen or king with private bath; $110/$185 fireplaced suite. Singles $5 less. $20 rollaway. Corporate and long-term rates available.
♥ ♣ ♦ ✕ ✂

"Treat all guests as royalty," Carl advises his students (including many retirees). Now, 12 years after he and Dinie made their dream come true, the inn is a "collection" of three 19th-century houses, each with resident innkeepers who have been here for several years. All together, Wedgwood reflects the 1980s evolution of B&Bs in this country.

The story combines early (at age 30) career changes, historic preservation, community participation, and an interest in people, antiques, and entrepreneurship. When, in my first B&B book, I described the original (first) Wedgwood House, Carl was still working half time as a social think-tank researcher. Dinie had just left her work in gerontology. They restored the 1870 frame guest house and decorated with country pieces, Dinie's aunt's artwork, and a Wedgwood collection. Guests arranged—and many still do—to be married in the gazebo. Soon Dinie became antiques expert/interior and floral designer/baker; Carl, a full-time innkeeper and avocational historian. By 1985, when they purchased and restored the more formal but quite comfortable next-door 1833 stone Umpleby House, Carl, a management consultant by training, was known for his innkeeping seminars. An inn consultant, he became a licensed Realtor specializing in inns. A apprentice program was added. Saturday teatime with the hosts—and Carl's almond liqueur—became an established traditon. And so it has been, with latkes made from 50 pounds of grated potatoes at Chanukah time.

Aaron Burr, another frame Victorian, was restored in 1990, providing enough rooms and parlor space for family reunions, business meetings and corporate retreats. And in 1992 *How to Start & Run Your Own B&B Inn,* written by Ripley Hotch (The Inn on Montford, Asheville, North Carolina, page 191) and Carl, was published.

In residence: Jasper, a mature brown Lab mix.
Foreign languages spoken: French, Spanish, Dutch, and Hebrew.
Bed and bath: In each house, six rooms including one suite. Some with working fireplace. King, queen, double, and twin beds; private and two semiprivate baths. Rollaway available.
Breakfast: 8:30–10. Freshly squeezed orange juice, fresh fruit salad, home-baked muffins and sweet breads, hot croissants, homemade granola, yogurt, freshly brewed tea and coffee. Served in each house, or in your guest room upon request. Special Passover menu.
Plus: Bedroom air conditioners. Welcoming refreshments. Fresh flowers year round. Parlors with wood-burning stoves and games. Phones in Aaron Burr rooms; jacks in some others. "By luck" free horse-drawn carriage rides to and from town. (Can be booked for a fee.) Turned-down beds. Veranda. Hammocks. Pool and tennis club privileges, croquet and badminton. Inn-to-inn hiking and biking tours. Courtesy bus pickup from NYC.

> From New Jersey: *"Carl and Nadine love what they are doing and truly enjoy their guests."*

The Whitehall Inn   215/598–7945

RD 2, Box 250, 1370 Pineville Road, New Hope, PA 18938

Hosts: Mike and Suella Wass
Location: On 13 secluded acres. A working dressage horse farm with walking trails, gardens, fields, majestic chestnut and maple trees. Ten minutes southwest of New Hope, five from Peddler's Village.
Open: Year round. Two-night minimum on weekends, three nights on holiday weekends. Advance reservations required.

Rates: Include extraordinary afternoon tea. Double occupancy. Weekends, $130–$170 with private bath; $130–$170 with fireplace; $155–$170 with both. $130–$150 shared bath. Weekdays, $10 less. $20 per person for Chocolate or Strawberry Lovers' Concert Weekends with world-class musicians. Amex, CB, Diners, Discover, MC, Visa.
♥ ♦ ✗ ⅍

Style. With an afternoon tea not to be missed. With culinary talents acclaimed in major publications including *Gourmet, Food & Wine,* and the *New York Times,* and demonstrated in Bloomingdale's and Woodward & Lothrop's programs based on this book. With ultimate innkeepers who host many returnees (and romantics) in this 200-year-old stone manor house with a curved walnut staircase, wide pine floors, Oriental rugs, family heirlooms, and other fine antiques. And still, eight years since the two Oklahomans, a Sun Oil Company

(Please turn page.)

executive (Mike) and his speech therapist wife (Suella), created their fantasy inn, just six guest rooms.

Mike is the maitre d'/waiter/rose gardener who on his day off is career development instructor and doctoral student. Suella's creations are now the basis of a forthcoming cookbook.

In residence: Sarah, age 14, the cookie baker for an entire all-star baseball team including brother Todd, age 10. As this book went to press, Sarah was a multiple finalist in the nationwide King Arthur Flour Winterbake.
Bed and bath: On three floors, six rooms (four with working fireplaces) with queen or double bed. Four with private baths; three with tub and shower, one shower only. Two second-floor rooms share a full bath.
Breakfast: At 9. Their own blend of coffee; 30 teas. Suella's freshly baked coffee cake, yeast bread, and muffins. Freshly squeeed juice. An unending repertoire of appetizers and entrees; may be raspberries picked that morning with chantilly cream plus herbed cheddar cheese Dijon souffle. Or cheddar cheese and corn spoon bread followed by fruit/nut/cheese crepes. And Bucks County sausage. Served by candlelight on linen with European china and crystal, heirloom silver. Suella and Mike always join guests.
Plus: Pool. Tennis courts (racquets and balls provided). Carrots for feeding the horses. Bedroom and dining room air conditioners. Four p.m. tea with pastries and tea sandwiches. Evening wine or sherry. Spacious fireplaced parlor with pump organ and piano. In rooms—fresh fruit, flowers, imported English toiletries, Wass-made bath salts, velour robes. Turndown service with specialty chocolates.

> From Pennsylvania: *"We enjoyed everything—the beautiful bedroom, all the attention and goodies . . . breakfast, none to compare!! Your needlework, antiques, grounds. . . . A perfect 51st anniversary celebration."*

Ash Mill Farm   215/794–5373
P.O. Box 202, Holicong, PA 18928

Hosts: Patricia and Jim Auslander
Location: On 11 acres set back from Route 202. Less than a mile from Peddler's Village. Four miles from New Hope and Doylestown. Minutes to the Delaware River "in a Cotswold-like area where there's everything except downhill skiing!"
Open: Year round. Two-night weekend minimum; three on holiday weekends.

Rates: Double occupancy. Shared bath $75 and $85 midweek, $85 and $95 weekends. Private bath $90 and $95 midweek, $105 and $115 weekends. Suite $110 midweek, $125 weekends; $40 third person in suite. Amex, MC, Visa for reservations only.
♥ ♣ ♦ ✖ ✄

What's a Manhattan maritime litigation lawyer doing in the kitchen (many say he looks like a famous television chef); with "inherited" sheep; on a tractor/mower; and among acres of evergreens (grown for landscapers), wildflowers, and berries? What's it like for two bosses (Pat was in a major corporation) to run a small inn?

"We're having fun—and answering those questions all the time," say the Auslanders, who enrolled in an innkeeping seminar a few years ago. In 1989, when they bought this B&B with its wide central staircase, crown moldings, and stenciling, they furnished with colonial, Irish, and English antiques and Shaker reproductions. Since, *Victoria* magazine has taken photographs here, and the house has been used as a background setting for fashion catalogs. *Gourmet* has requested recipes. And Jim has become a restaurant critic for local newspapers.

In residence: Two dogs. (The Airedale is a great guide through the property.) Three cats. And those sheep.

Foreign languages spoken: "A smattering of French and Spanish."

Bed and bath: Six rooms. First-floor room has Queen pencil-post bed, private shower bath, air conditioning. Second floor: Corner room with queen canopied four-poster, two sitting areas, and air conditioning shares large tub and shower bath (robes provided) with cozy room that has double four-poster, ceiling fan. One room with double bed, private shower bath, ceiling fan. Another with canopied double bed, private shower bath, air conditioning. Third-floor suite has separate access to private shower bath from room with queen canopied bed and from adjacent sitting room with double sleep sofa.

Breakfast: 8:30–9:30. Herb-cheese omelet with fresh garden herbs, sour cream or blueberry pancakes, French toast made with homemade raisin cinnamon bread, ham strata, or eggs Benedict. Jim's muffins. Breakfast meats. Fresh fruit, caviar, coffee, teas. By dining room fireplace or on stone patio overlooking gardens and meadow.

Plus: Afternoon tea. (Could be onion soup and French bread in winter; lemonade with cookies, pear cakes, maybe strawberries and cream in summer.) Down comforters. Flannel sheets. Turndown service. Garden flowers. Nightcap by living room fireplace.

From New Hampshire: "*Relaxing . . . excellent cooking . . . beautiful home.*

Barley Sheaf Farm

215/794–5104
P.O. Box 10, Route 202, Holicong, PA 18928   fax 215/794–5565

Hosts: Ann and Don Mills, and Don Mills, Jr.

Location: Down a lane, far back from the road, on a 30-acre farm 10 minutes from New Hope; about an hour from Philadelphia.

Open: Year round except Christmas week. Two-night minimum on weekends; three nights on holiday weekends.

Rates: Double occupancy. $110–$145. Room with two queen beds, $135. Suite $155–$175. $17 additional person in appropriate rooms.

♥ ♨ ✳ ✖

Almost a legend. The first B&B in Bucks County. Established in 1979—after the Millses moved with three teenagers into the former home of noted

(Please turn page.)

playwright and drama critic George S. Kaufman, and after they had traveled B&B in England during Don's frequent trips as president of his New Jersey–based perfume company. Since, he has "retired" to full-time innkeeping and all the children have grown. And within the last few years, the Millses have extended their inn-decorating experience by licensing 14 lines including furniture, fabrics, wallcoverings, rugs, prints, and china.

Built in 1740 and expanded in stone in 1800, the gracious antiques-filled house is a designated national historic site with a peaceful, elegant, and warm ambiance. The inviting guest cottage, a former icehouse, has its own fire-placed sitting room. And the converted 1820 beamed barn was featured on "CBS This Morning" because it is now booked for small business meetings and conferences.

In residence: Sheep, constantly varying in number, who announce their presence. Winston, the cat. Lucy, the bassett hound.
Foreign language spoken: Ann speaks French.
Bed and bath: Ten air-conditioned rooms, each with private bath. Seven rooms in main house on second and third floors; three in cottage. Queen, double, or twin beds available. One room with two queen beds. One queen-bedded suite with fireplace overlooks pool and has adjoining room with trundle bed.
Breakfast: Seatings at 9 and 9:45. Full. Possibilities include apple crepes, souffle, sausage, honey from Barley Sheaf hives, breads, and the freshest of eggs. Served on brick-floored sun porch (wood stove used in winter) over-looking expansive lawns.
Plus: Swimming pool. Fireplaced living room. Potpourri.

The Bucksville House   215/847–8948

7501 Durham Road, Kintnersville, PA 18930

Hosts: Barbara and Joe Szollosi
Location: In pastoral countryside. Thirty minutes north of New Hope. On Route 412. One mile from Lake Nockamixon State Park with swim-ming, boating, fishing, hiking, and cross-country skiing.
Open: Year round. Daily July and

August. Weekends only September–June. Advance reservations re-quired. Two-night minimum pre-ferred; three nights on holiday weekends.
Rates: Rooms $85–115. Suite $125. Amex, MC, Visa.
♥ ✈ ✂

From New Jersey: *"One of Upper Bucks County's best-kept secrets. . . . After a delicious gourmet breakfast served in the gazebo, I took a stroll through the grape arbor and looked out onto the pond. . . . As a published romance author, I had been intrigued when Barbara and Joe shared so much of the house's colorful history with me the evening before. . . . As the delicious scent of ripening peaches filled the air, I knew without a doubt where I would set my next novel. . . . Best part . . . I'll get to go back."*

Maybe you'll meet that writer, who has researched the 18th-century guest list of the 1795 added-onto structure. The former wheelwright shop, hotel, speakeasy, tavern, and private home was standing vacant in 1984 when the two New Jersey teachers ended their search for an old house to renovate. Joe, a self-employed carpenter, and Barbara, who continues to teach, wove their magic and furnished with antiques, Joe's country reproductions, quilts and crocks, and Oriental rugs. Magazine photographers love the setting. Guests love it—and the hosts too.

In residence: "Muffy is our very friendly 16-pound calico cat."
Bed and bath: Four rooms and a suite; all with air conditioning and private baths. On first floor: handicapped-accessible room with double bed, private shower bath, ceiling fan, sofa, working fireplace. Three second-floor rooms: Two have canopied double bed and working fireplace, one has shower bath in room, the other a shower/tub bath next to room. Third room has double bed, ceiling fan, sofa, shower bath next to room. Third-floor suite—a double bed, sitting room with sofas, two ceiling fans.
Breakfast: 8:30–10. Fresh fruit cup, bran raisin nut waffles, and sausage; or fresh pineapple with kiwi, egg casserole, and ham. Homemade sticky buns. Juice, hot beverages, and homemade breads. In gazebo or in dining room that has 18-inch-thick stone walls and walk-in fireplace.
Plus: Tea, coffee, cider, and homemade cookies. Turndown service. Mints on pillow. TV room. Fireplaced living room. Coal stove in den. Old puzzles and board games. Tour of house. Deck. Screened gazebo. Yard and surrounding paths. Stocked fish pond.

> From Pennsylvania: *"Delightful, elegant, peaceful, hospitable, a gourmet's paradise . . . beautiful landscaping . . . restoration that is a labor of love . . . an out-of-the-way place but well worth the effort."*

Hollileif Bed & Breakfast Establishment
677 Durham Road, Wrightstown, PA 18940-9679   215/598–3100

Hosts: Ellen and Richard Butkus
Location: Parklike. On five acres with trees and flowers and a wooden bridge over a stream. Six miles west of New Hope, 5 south of Peddler's Village and north of Newtown. On Route 413. Half mile to fine restaurant.
Open: Year round. Two-night minimum on weekends; three nights on holiday weekends.

Rates: With fireplace, $120 October–April, $105 rest of year. $120 large room. $105 third-floor room. $110 queen bed (second floor). $100 with hall bath. $20 third person on futon. Senior citizens, 10 percent less. Corporate rates Monday–Thursday. Midweek rates (Monday–Thursday): $20 less. Amex ($5 surcharge), MC, Visa.
♥ ❖ ◆ ✗ ⅙

It's not the Caribbean, where the Butkuses were inspired to enter the hospitality field; but this plastered stone 1700s farmhouse with 40-foot holly trees at the entrance is closer to home for the native Pennsylvanians. Converted to a B&B in 1986 and purchased by Ellen and Richard four years

(Please turn page.)

later, it is decorated with country pieces, family artwork, and lots of lace and bows.

Ellen is a former social worker and contract negotiator. Richard is supervisor of a research and development machine shop at the Naval Air Development Center.

In residence: Two cats—"Furgy and Danielle enjoy guests' attention."
Foreign language spoken: A little Spanish.
Bed and bath: Two double-bedded rooms and three queen-bedded rooms on three floors. All private baths—four with shower; the one in hall (robes provided) has tub and shower. First-floor room has ceiling fan, and gas fireplace that works on propane with a thermostat. Third-floor room tucked under eaves.
Breakfast: 8:30–9:30; coffee and tea at 8. Frothy fruit juice mix. Fruit—maybe peaches in butterscotch brandy sauce. Muffins—zucchini date or peanut butter banana. Entree repertoire includes asparagus turkey omelet, French toast with homemade strawberry sauce, bacon cheese puff. Homemade granola. Recipes shared. Special diets accommodated. Served at individual long-skirted tables.
Plus: Central air conditioning in all common rooms and guest rooms. Fireplaced breakfast and living rooms. Arbor-covered patio overlooking garden. Afternoon beverages and home-baked items. Turndown service. Use of refrigerator. TV/VCR, stereo, board games, croquet, badminton, volleyball, horseshoes. Two double hammocks.

> From New Jersey: *"Know how to make people feel at home.... Richard's grounds work is miraculous."* From Texas: *"Helpful with historical points of interest."* From New York: *"Recommended restaurants, theater, made reservations ... morning newspaper ... immaculate ... innovative, well-prepared, elegantly served breakfast."*

Tattersall Inn   215/297–8233

P.O. Box 569, Cafferty and River Road, Point Pleasant, PA 18950-0569

Hosts: Herbert and Gerry Moss
Location: Quiet. On Route 32, surrounded by lawns, plantings, and century-old trees. Set a little above the village, 15 minutes north of New Hope. A few minutes' walk to tubing and canoeing on Delaware River, and to canal towpath.
Open: Year round. Two-night minimum on weekends. Three-night minimum on holiday weekends. Reservations required.
Rates: Double occupancy. $85 weekends and holidays. $99 two-room suite plus one large room with entry foyer. $10 less Monday–Thursday. $15 third person. Senior citizens 5 percent less weekends, 10 percent less midweek. Discover, MC, Visa.
♥ ✳ ◆ ✈

> From New York (among many): *"It is a full four-star—how about five—inn with low-keyed, warm, and helpful hosts.... Beautiful, homey, and romantic."*

Urbanites know they are "away" when they sit on the second-story porch and hear the nearby carillon through the tall spruce. Or when they have cheese and cider in the beamed-ceiling pub room with huge hearth. Or listen to Herb's vintage phonographs in the Victorian dining room. Two rooms date back to 1740. Additions made in the 1800s resulted in a fieldstone manor house with 18-inch-thick walls. Now restored, it is furnished with family antiques and Gerry's paintings and needlework. Until the Mosses took over the inn in 1985, Gerry was editor of RCA's technical abstracting service. Even today she says, "I still can't believe that we actually own Ralph Stover's house after all the wonderful times we had—while the children were growing up—exploring in the park (once part of the property) that was set up to honor him." Herb, a part-time consultant now, retired in 1988 from RCA, where he was a materials scientist.

In residence: Victoria, "a gentle cat not too sure of people."
Bed and bath: On second floor, six large air-conditioned rooms, all with queen beds and private baths. One suite with queen bed, sitting room with daybed, and an entry foyer. Cot available.
Breakfast: 8–10. Sometimes earlier, especially for 7 a.m. Tuesday flea market opening. Juice, croissants, whole wheat bread with raisins and/or walnuts, homemade muffins or cakes (maybe poppyseed or apple), jams, honey, milk, hot beverages. Selection of cereals. In candlelit Victorian dining room (hosts join guests), on one of the porches, or in your room.
Plus: Library. Old-fashioned pinball game. That wonderful antique phonograph collection. Jukebox. Upright piano. Chocolates. Apples. Book of guests' comments about area restaurants. Special occasions acknowledged.

Bridgeton House on the Delaware
P.O. Box 167, River Road, Upper Black Eddy, PA 18972   215/982–5856

Hosts: Beatrice and Charles Briggs
Location: On the Delaware River and along the river road. In a small historic village. A half block from canal towpath; 18 miles north of New Hope. Within walking distance of shops, restaurants, state park. New York City bus stops in Frenchtown, New Jersey (3½ miles south of inn).
Open: Year round. Reservations and two-night minimum weekend stays required April–December.

Rates: Double occupancy. Weekends $75–$85 village-side room, $105–$135 river-side room with private balcony, $135–$150 fireplaced suite, $185–$200 penthouse. Monday–Thursday $10–$35 less. Midweek hiking or biking inn-to-inn packages available. Credit cards for reservation guarantee only.
♥ ♣ ✕ ✂

A one-of-a-kind contemporary penthouse overlooks the river and tops this transformed 1836 Federal brick house, a photographer's delight, a getaway destination. Bea has decorated with country pieces; baskets; rag, braided, and Chinese rugs; dried flowers and plants; and lots of stenciling. There are French doors; private screened balconies; suites as well as smaller rooms. And the
(Please turn page.)

reason for it all: those water views, captured by the Briggses when they rescued the building in 1981. They found the original fireplace behind a closet, pine floors below 17 layers of linoleum. Charles, a master carpenter/professional restorer of 18th-century buildings/country furniture maker, made many moldings, and he even designed a lighting fixture. And for something completely different—to add to the wide range of accommodations, he, together with his brother Jon, added the dramatic cathedral-ceilinged third-floor penthouse in 1988. (Latest project is a getaway cottage next door with kitchen.)

Such changes to the building that was first a private residence, then a bakery, and then a general store! Before Bridgeton House, Bea and Charles had 10 years' experience in inns and restaurants. Now, as parents of two young children, they dovetail innkeeping with parenthood.

Bed and bath: Eleven air-conditioned rooms in the main building (three are fireplaced suites) with king, queen, or double beds; some four-posters, some canopied. All are air-conditioned; all have private baths. The penthouse with three large windows and contemporary furnishings has king-sized bed, a gas fireplace, a mahogany bath with oversized soaking tub, a separate shower, and a dressing room.

Breakfast: Weekdays 8:30–9:30; weekends until 10. Fresh or hot fruits, juices, homemade breads and pastries. Entree might be omelets, shirred eggs, or souffles. Eat by fireplace or riverside, or on the deck, porch, or terrace.

Plus: Afternoon tea and sherry. Fresh flowers, fruit basket, chocolates, and English toiletries in each room. Swimming or tubing off riverbank. Fishing. Sometimes hosts can meet guests who arrive by bus in Frenchtown, New Jersey, 3 miles away.

Woodhill Farms Inn

150 Glenwood Drive
Washington Crossing, PA 18977

215/493–1974
800/982–7619
fax 215/321–6487

Hosts: John and Donna Behun
Location: Secluded. On ten wooded acres. Five minutes from river with towpaths and bike rentals. Twenty minutes to Princeton University; 15 minutes south of New Hope. Two miles north of I–95.
Open: Year round. Two-night minimum on weekends.

Rates: Sunday–Thursday $60 single, $110 double. Weekends and holidays $75 single, $95 double. $15 cot; crib free. Reduced rates for two or more nights. Corporate and off-site conference rates available. MC, Visa.
♥ ♣ ♦ ✗

The only built-to-be-a-B&B (in 1978) in this historic area is unique for many reasons. Many well-traveled guests say that it reminds them of lodges in Germany and Switzerland. Contemporary in style, it has a large living room with beamed cathedral ceiling, floor-to-ceiling fireplace, indoor garden, and circular staircase to the second floor. Works (for sale) by local artists are on the walls. Furnishings in each very-private guest room vary—with rattan, brass, or a cherry four-poster. And on the grounds there are three new hiking trails (sorry you missed the blazing party) "where all you hear are birds."

In anticipation of John's retirement from Mobil Oil Corporation, the Behuns bought this B&B in 1985. Shortly after retirement, in 1992, he had the opportunity to return to Czechoslovakia for work with the World Environment Center and a reunion (what a story) with family members he hadn't seen since he was five years old.

In residence: Son David and his wife, Debbie.

Bed and bath: Six rooms on two levels with no two bedroom walls adjacent to one another. All private baths. King-bedded room with sunken tub bordered by indoor garden. One queen-bedded room has tub and shower; others have shower only. One room with double bed, shower bath. Rollaway and crib available.

Breakfast: Continental plus 7–9:30 Monday–Friday; full breakfast 8:30–9:45 weekends and holidays. Entree might be eggs Benedict with smoked turkey and hollandaise, blueberry pancakes, cheese strata with chives, almond raisin-filled baked apple.

Plus: Central air conditioning. Individual temperature controls. Wine, soft drinks, cheese, fruit, crackers, and nuts. Color television. Hair dryers. Complimentary champagne for special occasions. Kitchen privileges for long-term guests. Travel and relocation information from New York to Washington, D.C.

> From Florida: *"Charmingly decorated . . . elegantly prepared food."* From Pennsylvania: *"Stayed weekdays on business. Scenic, quiet . . . accommodating hosts. . . . Excellent value!"* From New Jersey: *"Our first B&B. Just what we hoped for . . . guests were of all ages . . . friendly atmosphere."* From Connecticut: *"Pristine . . . an entire wall turned into a semitropical garden. . . . Highly recommended."*

According to guests (many are preservationists and/or house restorers), there ought to be a medal for the meticulous work—everything from research to labor—done by B&B owners. Indeed, many have won preservation awards.

Lehigh Valley/Reading Area
Reservation Services

Some B&Bs in this area are represented by:
Bed and Breakfast Adventures, page 54.
Amanda's Regional Reservation Service, Ms. Orie Barr, 21 South Woodland
Avenue, East Brunswick, NJ 08816, 908/249–4944.

KEY TO SYMBOLS
♥ Lots of honeymooners come here.
♯ Families with children are very welcome. (Please see page xii.)
♠ "Please emphasize that we are a private home, not an inn."
♣ Groups or private parties sometimes book the entire B&B.
♦ Travel agents' commission paid. (Please see page xii.)
✗ Sorry, no guests' pets are allowed.
✂ No smoking inside *or* no smoking at all, even on porches.

__Lehigh Valley/Reading Area B&Bs__

Sycamore Inn Bed & Breakfast   215/966-5177

165 East Main Street, Macungie, PA 18062

Hosts: Mark and Randie Levisky
Location: On Route 100, 6 miles south of I–78. Two hours from New York City, one from Philadelphia and the Poconos. Ten minutes to Allentown (bus stops across from inn), to Doe Mountain ski area, and to Velodrome at Trexlertown; 45 to Reading outlets. Macungie Memorial Park is "our back yard."

Open: Year round. Two-night minimum for Antique Truck Show in June; three nights during Das Awksht Fescht and Wheels of Time show in August.
Rates: Double occupancy. $70–$80. $10 child over 12 with parent. MC, Visa.
♥ ❖ ✗

It's an old stone thick-walled farmhouse—two houses in one—with "kick-off-your-shoes" comfort. It's "Mark's dream"—inspired by New England B&B stays and his love of cooking. (Randie, too, is delighted with the outcome.)

The Leviskys moved here in 1988. By the time they opened as a B&B in 1992, father and son had removed the exterior stucco covering to expose the stone. All the floors were redone. A porch was enclosed with windows that open for fresh breezes. And the quiet back house became the inn, with a common room that features original plaster walls (freshly painted) and a stone walk-in fireplace. Guest rooms are furnished by theme—Victorian, primitive, oak, and "Gentleman's Room."

Mark, a private detective, took early retirement as a criminal investigator for the Pennsylvania State Police. Randie sells antiques right here, most frequently from the inn's furnishings.

In residence: "Two 'doorbells:' Sacha, a calm and gentle golden retriever. Niki is a friendly and excitable cocker spaniel." One teenage son.
Bed and bath: Five rooms. Two first-floor double-bedded rooms have private shower baths, private porch entrance. On second floor, two queen-bedded rooms share full Victorian bath with claw-footed tub/shower. One double-bedded room has private en-suite "outhouse" bath with Jacuzzi tub, shower, door with half moon, barn-wood walls, spider-and-fly stained glass.
Breakfast: 7–9. Fruit salad, juices, egg dishes, Levisky pancakes, Mom's Special apple dumplings, jams, muffins, and cereals. Early-bird coffee and tea. By common room fireplace or on enclosed porch.
Plus: Room air conditioning. Bedroom ceiling fans. Welcoming beverage. TV in common room. Mints on pillow. In park—pool, tennis courts, workout area, swings, basketball courts.

From Maryland: *"Warm, friendly atmosphere makes you feel as if you were staying with old friends . . . delicious food . . . loved the decor."*

The Enchanted Cottage   215/845–8845
Box 337, RD 4, Boyertown, PA 19512

Hosts: Peg and Richard Groff
Location: Secluded and private. Surrounded by acres of woods. In farm country with rolling hills. Four and a half miles west of Route 100; 15 minutes to Doe Mountain ski area, 16 miles east of Reading. Nine minutes' walk to a fine country res-taurant. Near antiques shops, country auctions, crafts and flea markets, historic sites, Reading outlets.
Open: Year round.
Rates: Double occupancy. $80. $10 less for each night after the second night. $15 extra bed.
♥ ⬛ ♦ ✈

"It's right out of a fairy tale!" exclaim many guests when they see the romantic stone and frame ivy-covered Cotswold-like cottage built by Richard with old materials and antique tools. It is—complete with brick walk outside. Inside there's a large beamed living room with flagstone floor, primitive antiques, a Franklin fireplace flanked by comfortable checkered-covered wing chairs, and a kitchenette. Upstairs, tucked under the eaves, there's an air-conditioned bedroom with quilt-covered cannon-ball pine bed and Laura Ashley bathroom.

Originally the cottage was built for grandchildren. But "we can't build as fast as our daughter creates grandchildren." In addition to house building—he made the main house and all the outbuildings—Richard constructs furniture and is involved with historic preservation. Peg, who used to work in the fashion industry in Manhattan, does tole and furniture painting. In addition, she is a volunteer Literacy Workshop teacher and has hosted and directed TV talk shows in Washington, D.C., and Reading, Pennsylvania.

The Groffs enjoy serving an elaborate breakfast in the main house. Their home for 30 years, it has a paneled, beamed, and fireplaced living room and— everywhere—primitives and artwork. "Fax? We don't even have a typewriter!" But they do have some guests who kiss them goodbye.

In residence: In the main house—three cats. "The Dolley Lama," a Himalayan; Rufus; and Obesa (Obie).
Bed and bath: The cottage is all yours. One bedroom with double bed. Private bath with antique claw-and-ball footed tub and hand-held shower. Rollaway.
Breakfast: 7:30–9:30. Fresh fruit. Popovers, homemade biscuits or muffins. Eggs Benedict or ham a la king on pastry shells; garnished with fruit or flowers. Freshly ground coffee. In dining room with wood stove or by garden. Hosts join guests.
Plus: Wine and cheese in cottage. Fresh flowers. Mints on pillow. Candy. Down comforters. Embroidered eyelet linen sheets. Dinner option ($20 per person by prearrangement). Picnic baskets prepared.

The place to stay has become the reason to go.

The Loom Room

RD 1, Box 1420, Leesport, PA 19533

215/926–3217

Hosts: Gene and Mary Smith
Location: Rural. Surrounded by two and a half acres of lawn, and flower and herb gardens. Two miles north of Reading Airport, just off Route 183 in Berks County. Within 25 minutes of antiques shops in Adamstown and Kutztown; 15 minutes to Reading outlets.

Open: Year round. Advance reservations requested.
Rates: Double occupancy. $45 shared bath, $50 private. $15 extra adult. Under age 15, free. Seventh night free.
♥ ♨ ♜ ✿ ✈ ✂

There's a wonderful story behind this B&B. Now the 1812 stone house with 2-foot-thick walls is "comfortable and antiquey" with open-beam ceilings, five working fireplaces, and country primitives everywhere. In 1975, when Mary and Gene, teachers and area residents "for years," were looking for a country cupboard, they chanced upon the auction of the neglected house. Two hours later they owned "the perfect place for a weaving studio and shop," a 10-room center hall colonial that had been a home, tavern, hotel, stagecoach stop, halfway house, general store, and post office. The "buy," which required all of Gene's building expertise, became the site of the Smiths' wedding—by the great summer kitchen walk-in fireplace. Gene opened a tool-sharpening business, and Mary established her enterprise for beautiful custom classic handwoven fashions (for men and women). The local conservancy awarded the Smiths a historical plaque. And then a 1985 B&B trip to Germany influenced the decision to add hosting to their activities.

This B&B has a very sharing style, with almost-famous after-dinner treats, with fireside conversations, and with tours of the reconstructed 1760 log house (another Gene job) where Mary weaves and displays the clothing she creates. And from the cupboard that *was* eventually found, for each female guest, the parting gift of a homemade sachet.

In residence: Mimi and Maytag, "guest-oriented" male tiger cats.
Bed and bath: Three second-floor rooms reached by "a stairway that is not steep at all." Two rooms, each with a double and a single bed, share a full bath. Private shower bath for room with a double bed, one twin bed, and a daybed. Rollaway and crib available.
Breakfast: Usually 8:30. (Preceded by a wake-up tray brought to your door with coffee or tea and juice.) French toast with homemade fruit sauce, local sausage or bacon, chipped beef on home fries. Homemade muffins, jams, and preserves. Coffee and teas. Served in kitchen, in dining room, or in Gene-built gazebo. Hosts join guests.
Plus: Air conditioning and ceiling fans in bedrooms. Evening dessert repertoire includes lemon meringue pie, Gene's "incredible sundaes and banana splits," Mary's apple dumplings or Tiramisu (complete with story of Italian chef in German restaurant, near Swiss border, who shared recipe).

---

*B*reakfast is where the magic happens.

The Pineapple Inn
439 Market Street, Lewisburg, PA 17837

717/524–6200

Hosts: Charles and Deborah North
Location: In the middle of the Susquehanna Valley in a Federal/ Victorian town. On a main street (Route 45) corner, 4 blocks from Route 15. A few blocks from Bucknell University. One hour east of State College and north of Harrisburg. Minutes from Woolrich and Christian Dior outlets, artists' studios, and Amish quilts for sale. Half hour from Lycoming College and Bloomsburg and Susquehanna universities.
Open: Year round. Two-day minimum stay required during area colleges' special events weekends and first December (Victorian Christmas Parade) weekend.
Rates: Single $49 weeknights, $59 weekends. Double $59 ($79 private bath). Suite $95. Amex, Carte Blanche, DC, Discover, MC, Visa.
♥ ♣ ✂

> From North Carolina: *"Furnished with prize antiques . . . in a jewel community. . . . A real homemade breakfast . . . a home away from home."* From Connecticut: *"Lovely . . . beautifully maintained. . . . Breakfast is delicious and charmingly served. . . . The best part is visiting with the Norths, who make everyone feel so welcome."*

The 1857 brick Federal home was lovingly restored by the previous owners before the Norths converted it to an inn in 1985. Since then they have continued the restoration. Deborah's natural flair for color and design comes through in the antiques-filled rooms. (Her degree is in Middle East archaeology, philosophy, and religion.) In the tall-ceilinged parlor, sometimes called a living museum, there's the only extant 1856 map of Union County, antique glass and china, a 1912 Steinway grand piano, and Victorian furnishings. Antiques in the guest rooms include armoires, brass beds, antique quilts, country pieces, and authentic furniture of the the Archbishop of Canterbury.

Guests can tell that Charles is doing just what he wants to do. Fatherhood encouraged his change from being convention director of the Hilton in Washington, D.C. (He was the one who handled the media the day President Reagan was shot while leaving the hotel.) Through 23 years of hotel and restaurant work, Charles dreamed of finding an undiscovered area filled with history, recreational opportunities, and distinctive shops. Here he is, wearing many hats, including those of B&B chef, area events coordinator, and museum board of directors member.

In residence: Occasionally you meet Marisa, Christopher, and Chad, active school-age children who lead the annual Victorian Christmas Parade with Charles, the official bell ringer.
Bed and bath: Six second-floor rooms, most with private full baths. Queen or double beds. Suite has a room with a queen, another with two twins.
Breakfast: 7–9. Features thick-sliced homemade Amish bread. Walnut Acres granolas (made and packaged nearby), Amish slab-cut bacon, country-fresh brown eggs, cinnamon stack muffins, cottage cheese pancakes (like those Charles served to Macy's shoppers in McLean, Virginia, during a B&B presentation), or French toast made with homemade bread.
Plus: Fully air conditioned. Complimentary tea, 4–6. Turned-down beds. Chocolates on pillows. Walking tour information of Lewisburg architecture. Cross-country skiing/hiking nearby.

Longswamp Bed and Breakfast

215/682-6197
RD 2, Box 26, Mertztown, PA 19539 fax 215/682-4854

Hosts: Elsa and Dean Dimick
Location: On five acres in a rural village, 15 minutes southwest of Allentown, east of Kutztown. Forty minutes to Reading outlets. Within eight minutes of Route 100, Doe Mountain ski area, horseback riding. Excellent restaurant nearby. An hour northeast of Lancaster.
Open: Year round.
Rates: $60 single, $70 double, $75 in cottage, Hideaway, and barn. $30 third person in room. No charge for babies. MC, Visa.
♥ ⁂ ✗ ✂

From Indiana: *"A very special place . . . every aspect of the home is a delight for the senses . . . rolling hills are compelling and beautiful . . . an orchard, herb and vegetable gardens, extensive flower beds, berry patches . . . all find their way into the kitchen and onto the table."* From Massachusetts: *"Extraordinarily comfortable home. . . . Tastefully appointed. . . . The Dimicks obviously enjoy their enterprise and making their guests feel welcome."*

With their five children no longer at home, Elsa, a caterer and psychiatric counselor, and her husband, an endocrinologist at Lehigh Valley Hospital Center, moved in 1983 from Allentown to this lovely 200-year-old Federal house "to have a whole new challenge." Grateful guests, including business travelers as well as vacationers, appreciate attention to detail. They relax by the fire. They enjoy the collections of books, magazines, records, and tapes. Some walk in the woods. "Most want to be part of what's going on. A few value privacy above all." Antiquers love the location—and so do sports-oriented visitors. From the Dimicks' point of view, "guests are terrific."

In residence: One loving black Lab. Several outdoor (only) cats.
Foreign language spoken: French.
Bed and bath: Ten rooms with Amish quilts and lovingly restored antiques. Six have private bath; four share two baths. In main house, six rooms on second and third floors with a queen-sized bed, a queen and a single, or a queen and a double. The cottage (1700s house that was part of Underground Railroad) has a large queen-bedded room with fireplace, an alcove with a single bed, private shower bath, and a living room with TV. Upstairs is a queen-bedded skylit room under the eaves, private shower bath. On the lower level level of cottage—The Hideaway, with a separate exterior entrance, has queen-bedded room, working fireplace, private shower bath. In part of the huge old stone barn—a recently completed suite has large queen-bedded room, private shower bath, living room with television and single daybed.
Breakfast: 8–10:30 Sundays. 6:30–10:30 other days. Bountiful and beautiful. Ever-changing repertoire includes fresh fruit combinations, whole-grain breads, muffins, interesting cereals, homemade granola. Dishes with polenta. French toast made with thick challah bread. By fireplace in summer kitchen overlooking lawns and fields.
Plus: Beverages before dinner. Bedroom ceiling fans. (All bedrooms air-conditioned in summer.) Second-floor veranda rockers. Potpourri. Current magazines. Shampoos, lotions. Basketball court in the barn. Bicycles (no charge). Use of refrigerator. Horseshoe pits. Bocci court.

Poconos B&Bs

The Beach Lake Hotel

717/729–8239
800/382–3897

Main Street and Church Road, P.O. Box 144
Beach Lake, PA 18405

Hosts: Erika and Roy Miller
Location: In a tiny country village off a main road "in the quiet part of the Poconos." Five miles to Delaware River for tubing, rafting, canoeing (pickup arranged). Three minutes' walk to Beach Lake for swimming, rowboating. Twenty minutes' drive to Lake Wallenpaupack, fishing, and ice skating. Near restored (suspension) Roebling Bridge; museums; train excursions; antiquing; ski resorts—Woodlock Pines, Mount Tone, Masthope; even a drive-in theater. 2½ hours from New York City.
Open: Year round. Two-night minimum on June–October weekends and all holiday weekends.
Rates: $95 per room. $75 for three-night reservations, Sunday–Thursday. MC, Visa.
♥ ❖ ♦ ✈

> Guests wrote: *"A fantasy fulfilled. . . . Recommended to us by friends who were impressed by the food and the decor. . . . Erika and Roy are a fountain of information on local folklore and roads away from the leaf peepers. . . . Old-fashioned country charm. . . . An elegant but laid-back kind of style. . . . Clean, clean, clean. . . . Had a field day in their filled-to-the-brim country gallery. . . . Loved this place so much we thought of keeping it a secret. . . . Reflects a lot of hard work and intelligent research by an interesting couple. . . . A sense of being transplanted back in time."*

Guests' enthusiasm is matched by the Millers, two former health administrators who have fulfilled their own fantasy of combining interests in cooking, interior design, antiques, restoration, music, and theater. They followed up on a 1986 *Country Living* magazine ad and fell in love with this place, which began around 1859 as a hotel and tavern. Through one year's work, they restored wainscoting, made the second-floor porch accessible to all, and added private baths. Throughout they have furnished with "for sale" antiques that represent many periods—an ambiance appreciated by lots of returnees and by *Travel & Leisure* too. Some guests ask, "Have you always lived here?" And some inquire about sources for floral reproduction Victorian wallcoverings and lace curtains. Raspberry bushes grow. So do fruit trees. And herbs. And the guest list.

In residence: In hosts' quarters, a Shih Tzu, "ten pounds of love!"
Foreign language spoken: Polish.
Bed and bath: Six rooms on second and third floors. All private baths; most are shower only, one has claw-foot tub. All double beds; two are canopied four-posters (if not sold), one requires a step stool.
Breakfast: 8–10. Entree might be apple pancakes and brandied grape sauce; eggs Benedict, eggs LeRoy (poached in artichoke bottoms and watercress hollandaise); mushroom-and-onion or cheese omelets. Homemade popovers, muffins, or coffee cakes and preserves. Juices. Hot beverages.

Plus: Air-conditioned bedrooms. Tea, wine, cheese, crackers. Fresh fruit in rooms. Bubble bath. TV in common room. Dinner ($20–$30) Thursday–Monday in dining room and gallery that seats forty.

From New York: *"Magical . . . like stepping back in time."*

Brookview Manor Bed & Breakfast Inn

RR 1, Box 365, Canadensis, PA 18325   717/595-2451

Hosts: Lee and Nancie Cabana
Location: On Route 447 and the Broadhead Creek, "in the heart of the Poconos." On four acres of lawns, gardens, tall hemlocks, "and trails that lead to a secret waterfall." About two hours from New York or Philadelphia. Minutes to Pocono Playhouse, Promised Land State Park, Alpine Mountain and Camelback ski areas, shopping and fine dining.
Open: Year round. Two-night minimum over holidays.
Rates: Double occupancy. Suites $105–$115 weekdays, $125–$145 weekends and holidays. Other rooms—$65–$90 weekdays. $85–$115 weekends and holidays. Amex, Discover, MC, Visa.
♥ ♣ ♦ ✖ ✌

When Nancie, a recreation therapist, and Lee, an American Red Cross director in Erie, Pennsylvania, decided to work together and be at home with Erin, they bought this manor house, a B&B since 1985, that had been built in 1911 as an opulent summer house. It has a light and airy feeling, with antiques and country furnishings; with views of mountains, woods, and stream from every window; with rockers and a swing for four on the wraparound porch. Wide open spaces include the front lawn, the delight of one amateur astronomer. And there have been so many requests for recipes that "a cookbook is in the works."

In residence: In hosts' quarters, Erin, age five.
Bed and bath: Eight rooms; all private baths. In main house (all tub/shower baths)—two queen-bedded suites; each with sitting room, one with an enclosed sun porch. One room with king bed. One with double bed, working fireplace. In carriage house—ground floor double-bedded room with private outside entrance and porch. On second floor—three-bedroom suite for families or couples traveling together; two rooms with double beds, one with two twins. Rollaway available.
Breakfast: 8:30–10. Juices. Fresh fruit. Homemade muffins. Hot entree could be cinnamon French toast or French toast a l'orange. Cereals including homemade granola. In sun porch, Fireplace Room, or Picture Window Room with stained glass. Can last for up to two hours.
Plus: Fireplace in living room, dining room, and den. Baby grand piano. Bedroom window fans. Fresh flowers. Refreshments at 5 p.m. Recreation room with darts, Ping-Pong and pool tables. Croquet, bocci, horseshoes, and badminton. Cookies and candies.

From New York: *"View of woods is hypnotizing. . . . The brook lulls you to sleep at night. . . . Lee and Nancie pampered us."* From Virginia: *"There was a feeling of privacy, and yet if you wanted to talk they were always available. . . . Enjoyed the book where guests recorded impressions of area restaurants."*

Academy Street Bed & Breakfast

528 Academy Street, Hawley, PA 18428   717/226–3430

Hosts: Judith and Sheldon Lazan
Location: In a quiet residential neighborhood. Five minutes from Lake Wallenpaupack. Near blueberry picking, playhouse, restaurants. Close to Route 6 and I–84. Two hours northwest of New York City.
Open: May–October, just weekends in spring and fall. Reservations preferred.
Rates: Include afternoon tea. $65–$70 double with shared bath, $75 double with private bath. $35 extra person in a room. MC, Visa.
♥ ♦ ✈

As Sheldon says, "The lake with swimming and boating is the big attraction here. At our home, it sometimes feels like a family reunion, when actually no one knew each other before." That's how it can be in the Italianate-style Victorian house that the Lazans bought in 1983 after having had a summer residence in Hawley for six years. The house was built in 1863 by Civil War Captain Joseph Atkinson, a lumberyard owner who used much premium oak and cherry throughout. Judith and Sheldon finished the restoration started by the previous owner, a commercial artist. The eclectic decor of the large, airy tall-windowed rooms is fresh and crisp with Victorian antiques, some wicker and pine pieces, vintage movie star photos, and fresh flowers and plants.

The Lazans, parents of three grown children, have lived in Brooklyn, Long Island, Cincinnati (where Judith had a restaurant), and New Jersey. A trip to Europe inspired Judith—"I love to fuss"—to become a full-time (seasonal) innkeeper. (And she does fuss—with breakfast, high tea, and bedtime treats too.) Sheldon, an engineer, weekend host, "and maintenance man," currently works as an engineering consultant.

Bed and bath: Seven air-conditioned rooms on first and second floors. Four with private bath; one with private half bath shares full hall bath with two other rooms. Queen, double, or twin beds. One with queen and a single. One with double and a single. Cots available.
Breakfast: 8–10:30. Buffet. Varied menu. Repertoire includes strawberry soup, baked eggs, amaretto pudding, quiche, French toast. Juices, fruit compote, homemade muffins, breads, croissants.
Plus: All rooms have cable TV. Amaretto coffee, tea, and cakes, 2–4 p.m. Lawn games. Off-street parking.

> From New York: *"Our first B&B experience was truly a pleasure . . . memorable hospitality."*

Can't find a listing for the community you are going to? Check with a reservation service described at the beginning of this chapter. Through the service, you may be placed (matched) with a welcoming B&B that is near your destination.

Roebling Inn on the Delaware   717/685-7900

Scenic Drive, P.O. Box 31, Lackawaxen, PA 18435-0031

Hosts: Donald (DJ) and JoAnn Jahn
Location: Facing the river in this quiet historic village. Within walking distance of National Park Service's Zane Grey Museum, Roebling's 1848 Delaware Aqueduct (restored) and Toll House (museum). Surrounded by big old trees. Five miles north of Barryville, New York; 15 miles west of Milford, Pennsylvania. Five minutes to Masthope Mountain; 30 to Tanglewood. Two hours from New York City.
Open: Year round. Two-night mini-

mum May–October weekends, three-night minimum on some major holidays.
Rates: Double occupancy. Weekdays $59 May–October, two-night special $99; $50 November–April. Weekends $65 November–March, $110 for two nights; $65 April–mid-May; $75 May 15–June; $85 July–Labor Day and October; $75 post Labor Day–September 30. $10 third adult. $5 child. Amex, MC, Visa.
♥ ♣ ♦ ✈

One of 10 "Weekend Therapy" places recommended by *New York* magazine is the fulfillment of DJ's dream. In 1987 the Jahns created the only B&B in town (it still is) when they converted the untouched-for-40-years Greek Revival house that was built as the home and office for the Delaware and Hudson Canal Company superintendent.

"We made it inviting and comfortable—with country pieces and some reproductions. Our guests are always telling us that they feel that they discovered a quaint charming nontouristy area with a beautiful landscape. A nostalgic train whistle may blow twice a day or night. There are two restaurants in town (one closes from December through March) and five more within 15 minutes. The nearest fast food place is 25 miles away. Just two hours from New York City and this is a different world! Honeymooners come. So do families. And groups that are cycling or canoeing from inn to inn. They attend summer stock, or take advantage of horseback riding, water sports, and, in the winter, skiing. And then there are those who get drawn into the simple pleasure of daydreaming from the front porch, where you can see upriver for about a mile."

As a teenager DJ worked in his family's New Jersey shore motels. Most recently he was general manager of upstate New York's (1886) Tuxedo Club, where the tuxedo originated.

In residence: Son Michael, "assistant innkeeper," age five. Kitty/Oshkosh, an outdoor cat.
Bed and bath: Five rooms; all with private bath and TV. Queen-bedded room on first floor. On second, one room with queen plus a daybed, one with two doubles, two queen-bedded rooms. Plus one cottage with double-bedded room, living room with double futon couch, bath, kitchen (breakfast optional).
Breakfast: 8–10:30. Hot dishes—eggs and bacon, cheese omelets, or pancakes—cooked to order, plus cold buffet. Orange juice, fresh fruit, cereals, English muffins, baked dish such as peach cobbler. At individual tables set with linen and silver in dining room with large floral wallcovering.

(Please turn page.)

Plus: Air conditioning and individual thermostat in each guest room. Comfortable guest living room. Beverages. Reservations made for canoeing, rafting, fly-fishing lessons. Directions to waterfalls. Eagles in winter.

Farmhouse Bed & Breakfast   717/839–0796
HCR 1, Box 6B, Mount Pocono, PA 18344-9701

Hosts: Jack and Donna Asure
Location: A quiet country road, 5 miles from two major highways. Minutes' drive to antiques shops and outlets; within walking distance of restaurants. Within 15 miles of ski areas. Ninety miles from New York City and Philadelphia.
Open: Year round. Two-night minimum on weekends and holidays.
Rates: Double $75 second-floor master suite, $85 first-floor parlor suite, $95 caretaker's cottage. Single $45/$55/$65. $25 extra person in room. Midweek, $10 less per night for stays over two nights. Discover, MC, Visa.
♥ ♦ ✗ ✄

"Many of our guests find that the pace here is nothing like what they are used to. Some curl up by the fire with a good book—and, when leaving, say they'll have to come back to see the attractions they saw in ads."

Once a strawberry farm, this was Jack's family home in the 1960s. In 1987, after Jack sold Memorytown USA, a honeymoon resort that had been established by his parents, the Asures restored this 1850 farmhouse—and the stone-walled icehouse—and filled them with family pieces and lots of collectibles.

Donna has experience in arts management. Jack, a hunter and fisherman, was a professional chef at his resort. Both hosts "love antiquing, flea marketing, and collecting everything!"

In residence: Keiko, "the B&B Princess," a long-haired gray indoor kitty. Roger and Jessica, backyard rabbits.
Bed and bath: A cottage and two main house suites, each with private phone line. Each suite has a queen bed, private shower bath, TV, compact refrigerator, front porch entrance. Large stone fireplace with first-floor suite; living room wood stove in second-floor suite. In cottage (original icehouse)—first-floor fireplace, refrigerator, shower bath, TV (second floor); small balcony leads to queen-bedded room "tucked into hillside" with ceiling fan.
Breakfast: 8–9:30. "Jack's outlandish cooking." Maybe raisin cinnamon bread coated with granola—cooked in omelet pan; an omelet with broccoli, cheese, and hollandaise sauce; or a blueberry-stuffed French toast croissant. (And still, special diets accommodated.) Juice. Homemade muffins or cake. Different menu daily as long as you are here. Served in country kitchen overlooking hill in back of property.
Plus: In farmhouse—private air-conditioning units for each room from spring to fall. Wood stove in common area. Evening refreshments. Secluded porch. Horseshoes. Lawn furniture. Special occasions acknowledged.

Excerpts from a *huge* stack of long enthusiastic letters—From New York: *"Real charm, warmth . . . cozy country atmosphere."* From Maryland: *"Inviting and homey appeal. . . . Set back from a winding two-lane road, surrounded by large trees and (acres of) carefully maintained grounds . . . a sense of seclusion and privacy."* From Pennysvlania: *"Jack and Donna provide a familylike atmosphere . . . also provide solitude."*

The Nethercott Inn   717/727–2211
P.O. Box 26, Main Street, Starrucca, PA 18462

Hosts: Ned and Ginny Nethercott
Location: In a tiny Endless Mountains borough with a population of about 150 people. Ten miles from the Starrucca Viaduct (150-year-old stone railroad bridge still in use); 35 from Binghamton, New York; 45 from Scranton, Pennsylvania; 19 to

Elk Mountain and Mount Tone ski areas; 10–15 minutes to cross-country skiing. Near streams for fishing.
Open: Year round.
Rates: For one or two guests—$65 per room. $15 extra bed. Amex, Discover, MC, Visa.
♥ 🏠 📬 ⁂ 🗡

The sign on the front lawn came with Ned and Ginny in 1986 when they moved from their ranch house B&B in California. "We love old houses, so when Ned retired from the Air Force, we searched for one in a quiet town. This Victorian—in what was once a thriving tannery and lumber community—seemed right for our dream of a B&B with an antiques shop."

For a hint of the complete renovation, see the before-and-after photo album. The house is carpeted throughout, and "furnishings are in the style of 1893 with hands-on antiques so you aren't afraid to touch anything. Our style of hosting means that all our guests are like family when they leave."

Newest project: Ginny's great-grandmother's diaries of 1898–1902, edited and published as *Klondike Tenderfoot* by Ginny and Ned in 1992. That spunky lady went to Alaska at age 40, bought two gold mines, worked in a millinery shop that is there to this day—and more. Inquire!

Bed and bath: Five second-floor rooms—all with mountain views. Four with queen beds. One with a queen bed plus adjoining room with two twins and a youth bed. Three rooms with tub/shower; two with stall shower.
Breakfast: 8–9:30. Fruit compote, orange juice, homemade sweet breads, egg souffle, special blend of decaf and regular coffees. In dining room on crystal and china.
Plus: Use of sleds. Wraparound veranda.

From the country: " Rural living is great. Did I tell you about the night the cows came? A farmer neighbor up the road had left a gate unlatched. About 10 p.m. I had 22 holsteins and one bull milling around the back yard, peering in the windows, mooing and munching! The guests loved it. (The garden didn't.)"

Pennsylvania Dutch Country
———— Reservation Services ————

Hershey Bed & Breakfast Reservation Service

P.O. Box 208, Hershey, PA 17033

Phone: 717/533–2928. Monday–Friday 10–4. Answering machine at other times.

Listings: Most are private homes; four are inns and four are farms. Located throughout southeastern Pennsylvania, including Hershey, Middletown, Harrisburg, Lancaster, Lebanon, New Cumberland, and Gettysburg. Send a self-addressed stamped envelope for a directory.

Reservations: Two-week advance notice preferred. Last-minute requests filled if possible.

Rates: $45–$50 single, $50–$90 double. Deposit required is 25 percent of total cost of stay. Refunds less $10 service charge made if cancellation is received at least 48 hours prior to arrival date. ♦

Renee Deutel knows her hosts and their homes—and she is fussy! She has places that are perfect for honeymooners, places where kids can milk a cow, places where you can gather your own eggs or just enjoy country living in an atmosphere of friendliness with easy access to many recreational facilities. She accommodates bridal parties, family reunions, and corporate retreats, and arranges "anything you need to make your trip special" including reservations for a memorable experience, a bountiful dinner at a long table in the Brethren home of the Meyer family.

Some B&Bs in Pennsylvania Dutch Country are also represented by:
Bed & Breakfast of Philadelphia, page 223.
Guesthouses, page 224.

KEY TO SYMBOLS
♥ Lots of honeymooners come here.
♯ Families with children are very welcome. (Please see page xii.)
◀ "Please emphasize that we are a private home, not an inn."
⁂ Groups or private parties sometimes book the entire B&B.
♦ Travel agents' commission paid. (Please see page xii.)
✶ Sorry, no guests' pets are allowed.
✕ No smoking inside *or* no smoking at all, even on porches.

Pennsylvania Dutch Country B&Bs

Adamstown Inn
62 West Main Street, P.O. Box 938
Adamstown, PA 19501-0938

215/484–0800
800/594–4808

Hosts: Tom and Wanda Berman
Location: In a small Dutch Country town (pop. 1,100) that is known for the 2,500 antiques dealers within a 3-mile radius. Ten minutes to "outlet capital" Reading, 20 to Lancaster. Within a half mile of one restaurant; many others minutes away.

Open: Year round. Two-day minimum on April–December weekends. **Rates:** Double occupancy. $65 double bed. $70 canopied queen. $85 queen bed, Jacuzzi. $95 king bed, Jacuzzi. MC, Visa.
♥ ♣ ♦ ✄

The innkeepers/restorers/antiques collectors have fans from all over the country, including some from New York who wrote: *"Spotless, inviting, homey, well cared for."* From Pennsylvania: *"Friendly, relaxed . . . felt pampered . . . good restaurant suggestions . . . convenient for antiquing."* From New Hampshire: *"Felt like we were visiting friends. . . . Our 81-year-old mother loved it as much as we did."* From Ohio: *"They were people I wish I could know better."* From Maryland: *"Had interesting information about the area, good bike-tour maps . . . new bathrooms . . . comfortable . . . lovely old-fashioned atmosphere."*

In 1989, after months of restoration (Wanda's brother helped), the Bermans opened this B&B, a large early 1800s yellow brick Victorian that had major 1920s additions—chestnut woodwork, leaded glass doors and windows, and a columned wraparound porch. They painted the exterior trim—with seven colors on the house, four on the garage. They furnished the fireplaced living room without clutter, with lots of comfortable seating, and with a working 1850 Estey pump organ, one of the many antiques refinished by Tom. Formerly a banker in Baltimore, now Tom is a Realtor and the inn's high-place painter. Wanda, a former mortgage banker, became the low-place painter, seamstress (41 window treatments), and baker. And for crafts shows, she makes folk art items, tole paintings, and dried flower arrangements (some blossoms are microwave dried) and wreaths.

In residence: Magic, a Brittany spaniel.
Foreign language spoken: A little German.
Bed and bath: Four second-floor rooms, all private baths. Master bedroom with king canopied bed, two-person Jacuzzi tub, shower. One queen-bedded room, two-person Jacuzzi. One room with canopied queen bed, shower bath. One double-bedded room (with seven windows overlooking garden), shower bath.
Breakfast: 7–9 coffee, tea, or hot chocolate brought to your room. Tom serves, 7:30–9:30, at dining room table set with antique china and crystal. Fresh fruit salad, juices, cheese plate or sausage balls, muffins, sweet breads, and cereal.

(Please turn page.)

Plus: Air-conditioned bedrooms. Afternoon or evening beverage. Bathrobes. Fresh fruit and flowers. Mints on pillows. Portable phone. Off-street parking.

Spring House
717/927–6906

Muddy Creek Forks, Airville, PA 17302

Host: Ray Constance Hearne
Location: Over a running spring in a tiny (population: 17) pre-Revolutionary village nominated for National Register. Very rural and scenic, off the beaten track (detailed directions are useful). Five miles from shops; 30 minutes southeast of York; 45 minutes southwest of Lancaster.

Open: Year round. Two-night weekend stays preferred except required for cottage.
Rates: Per room. $60 shared bath, $85 private bath. $95 cottage. $10 surcharge for one-night weekend stay.
♥ ♯ ♨ ♣ ◆ ✗ ⊱

> From Brazil: *"In this house I could enjoy deeply the serenity of Pennsylvania countryside, and from [Ray's] sensitivity I could also enjoy the rest of the world, especially through the Basque music and the frittatas."*

Almost a B&B pioneer! Since the spring of 1981 visitors have asked lots of questions about the plastered, whitewashed, and stenciled walls; floor cloths; country antiques, and Oriental rugs; pottery (some done by the hostess and fired in a kiln she made while a student at Antioch College); paintings (some her own) of local scenes; and herb garden too. She lives here "in the way I grew up—with wood heat, cookstoves, cool bedrooms, and good pure food and water." Ray, a dairy-farm girl who became a York County historic preservationist, turned B&B host after a 3½-month backpacking trip in England that followed 10 years of restoring this 18th-century stone house to its "simple strong character." Both *County Home* and *Country Decorating* (by *Woman's Day*) have featured this "genuine country inn."

In residence: Ulysses, "a cozy entertainng St. Bernard." Tachyon (Siamese), Tashi, and Tundrup, "purring companions."
Foreign language spoken: Spanish.
Bed and bath: Four rooms plus cottage. Large first-floor room with double bed, French stove, grand piano, private shower bath. On second floor, private shower bath for one large room with antique three-quarter bed and a double bed. Two double-bedded rooms, one with stove, share a bath with tub, no shower. Cottage, decorated in Japanese/French mode, has sleeping loft with queen-size futon; on first floor are shower bath, antique wood cookstove, daybed, antique clay tile floor.
Breakfast: By 9; hour arranged night before. Made with locally produced ingredients including organically grown wheat flour. Usually two main courses. Maybe wineberries on buttered buckwheat pancakes with maple syrup or honey from Ray's bees. Or a clafouti with ginger and pears; or a Basque piperade with peppers, onions, garlic, eggs, and smoked sausage. Jams and jellies (Ray makes her own pectin from green apples), and syrups from fruits she has picked and preserved. Served in dining room or on the porch.

Plus: Popcorn at just the right time. Local Amish cheese. Wine from award-winning winery 3 miles away. Porch swing. Feather beds, down puffs, and flannel sheets. Bicycle routes. Trout-stocked Muddy Creek. Swimming, canoeing, horseback riding, cross-country skiing. River trails and unused Ma and Pa railroad bed for hiking. Coming—8-mile scenic train trip on restored Maryland & Pennsylvania line.

Winding Glen Farm Tourist Home

107 Noble Road, Christiana, PA 17509   215/593–5535

Hosts: Bob and Minnie Metzler
Location: Very quiet. In a beautiful valley directly south of Christiana. Just down the road from a covered bridge. One mile from Route 41; 19 miles east of Lancaster.
Open: Year round.
Rates: $40 double. $9 child 6–12, $5 under age 6. Reservations required.
♯ ♦ ♣ ✈ ✄

"It's about 25 years since we started taking the overflow from motels. Then people started to come back and tell other people. Now we have guests who came as children and are bringing their own children. They really seem to like our farm life. Some just watch or try their hand at milking cows. Our thick-tired red Amish-made wagon that seats four children is very popular. Often I draw a map for touring the nearby Amish area; there's a grocery store, a hardware store, a bake shop, and one for antiques. Guests like to see the old mill where the miller, who turns on the old waterwheel, makes cornmeal, whole wheat flour, and pancake mix.

"We're Mennonites and we answer a lot of questions about our religion. We set up two projectors and show the slide show, 'Our Way of Life,' made by our married son Jerry, a woodworker, who lives next door. It is set to music and the narration talks about how we feel about things. It shows farm life in different seasons, our neighboring Amish, and some pictures from a trip Jerry took to Switzerland.

"I have quilts made by Mennonite ladies for sale. My husband hunts and fishes. Our 250-year-old farmhouse—with seven nonworking fireplaces—is homey and simply furnished with family antiques and pieces Jerry has made."

Bed and bath: Five rooms. Two shared baths, one with shower, one with tub, plus half bath on first floor. Four second-floor rooms; two with two double beds in each. One room with queen-sized bed and a single; another with a double bed. A third-floor room has two double beds and a single.
Breakfast: At 8:30. Full farm meal served family style. Three or four items such as pancakes made with whole grains and yogurt, home fries with cheese, zucchini rounds, oatmeal cake, scrapple, fruit salad, French toast, blueberry muffins.
Plus: Air conditioner in second-floor hall outside guest rooms; one on third floor. Porch.

If you have met one B&B host, you haven't met them all.

Churchtown Inn   215/445–7794

2100 Main Street, Churchtown, PA 17555

Hosts: Stuart and Hermine Smith, and Jim Kent

Location: On Route 23W with Amish buggies going by front door (and patio). Across from historic church. Views of hundreds of acres of farmland and Welsh Mountains in back. Five miles from Pennsylvania Turnpike; 20 miles east of Lancaster; 45 minutes from Philadelphia and Hershey. Two and a half hours from Manhattan and Washington, D.C.

Open: Year round. Two-night minimum on weekends, three on holiday weekends.

Rates: Double occupancy. $45 and $55 shared bath, $75–$95 private. Singles $5 less. $125 honeymoon suite in carriage house. Special holiday packages. MC, Visa.
♥ ♣ ♦ ✈

This inn is worth a cover feature. And that's exactly what I wrote for *Innsider* magazine after experiencing dinner at an Amish home and a musical reception back at the inn plus a treasure hunt "award ceremony" that included guests' tales of the day's discoveries (places and people).

It's no wonder that high season is year round at this B&B, recently named to the National Register of Historic Places. It has ambiance, art, European and American antiques, handmade quilts, comfort, its very own cookbook (and to think Stu took basic cooking lessons before opening), and innkeepers who are dubbed "favorite" in dozens of letters sent to me. As one Floridian wrote, "They have a special way of making guests feel like longtime friends."

After Stu and Jim restored this 18th-century fieldstone mansion in 1987, they saw the parking lot filled with Amish buggies during an opening held for the community. Subsequently some of those neighbors built additions to the inn: a lovely garden breakfast room, a carriage house/honeymoon suite with stone from a 1735 springhouse, and—for those special weekends—a ballroom.

For 20 years Stu directed singers—150 adults, 100 children, and two handbell choirs—in the northeast (in Carnegie Hall too) and in Europe. In New Jersey, Hermine, Stu's wife, was a health food retailer. Jim, who teaches ballroom dancing, was an accountant. Here they are active with the Lancaster Shelter for Women. At the inn they plan everything from carriage rides to murder mystery weekends, from formal Victorian balls to barbecues with accordion music.

Foreign languages spoken: Limited German and Italian.

Bed and bath: Eight queen-bedded rooms; all private baths except for two third-floor rooms that share a bath. One third-floor room has a queen and a single bed, cathedral ceiling, skylights, private full bath. In carriage house, first-floor honeymoon suite has elaborate shower bath.

Breakfast: At 9. Five-course meal beginning with freshly squeezed orange juice. Entree might be buttermilk pancakes with fruit, French toast made with Grand Marnier, Scottish oatmeal custard, or egg souffle. Homemade breads and jams. Coffee cake.

Plus: Air conditioning. Often, evening tea or wine in the Victorian parlor, maybe a sing-along with Stu at the antique grand piano and/or the sounds of antique organ, phonograph, and music boxes. Fresh flowers. Game room.

Den. Courtyard. Garden. Swing (what a view). Lavish Christmas decorations. By advance arrangement, Tuesday night or weekend dinner in Amish home ($12.50) where four daughters sing for guests.

The Columbian

360 Chestnut Street, Columbia, PA 17512

717/684–5869
800/422–5869

Hosts: Linda and John Straitiff
Location: "In a small friendly porch-sitting town." On a side street, on the last corner of the commercial district, with two neighboring "gorgeous restored mansions" in the other direction. Within walking distance of restaurants. Eight miles from Lancas- ter city line. About 20-minute drive to most Pennsylvania Dutch attractions.
Open: Year round.
Rates: Double occupancy, $60–$65; with fireplace or balcony $75. Discover, MC, Visa.
♣ ✖ ⅍

Everyone exclaims when they see the dramatic and beautiful staircase, its landing featuring an enormous stained glass window. And they find it hard to believe that the Straitiffs had to "play detective" in order to reassemble the stairway, which had been dismantled when the imposing brick Colonial Revival mansion was turned into apartments and a video store.

Most of the restoration work was done by Linda, a freelance writer and former Columbia high school teacher; John, an engineer "who can build or fix most anything—right now he's restoring a player piano"; and their teenage sons. They refinished and upholstered comfortable Victorian and English country pieces and opened in 1988. Some guests come for the clock museum (2 blocks away), which is the international headquarters for the National Association of Watch and Clock Collectors. Many come for sightseeing. And more than one returnee says that Linda's breakfast is the major draw.

In residence: Bear, "a rather large mix of golden retriever and Labrador, loves to meet guests who know of him."
Bed and bath: Five rooms. Each with sitting area and private shower bath; one has tub/shower combination. On first floor, queen-bedded room with working fireplace. On second, one suite with a queen-bedded room, a twin-bedded room, and a private porch. Other rooms have a queen or a queen and a twin bed. Rollaway available.
Breakfast: Flexible hours. Usually by 10. Half a grapefruit. Homemade granola. Quiche lorraine, waffles, egg casserole, blueberry or apple pancakes, or peaches and cream French toast. Fruit salad. Homemade breads and muffins. Juices, teas, coffee.
Plus: Central air conditioning in common rooms; individual unit in each guest room. Fireplaced living and dining rooms. Welcoming refreshments. Evening tea. Fresh fruit and flowers. All rooms have TV; some with ceiling fan too. Some have individual thermostat. Wraparound porches. Dinner reservations made at restaurants or in an Amish home. Suggestions, maps, directions for tourist attractions, shopping, and quiet activities too. Off-street parking. Transportation to/from Harrisburg airport or Lancaster train station.

(Please turn page.)

From Virginia: *"A dining experience."* From New Jersey: *"Greatest B&B we have come across."*

Clearview Farm Bed & Breakfast
355 Clearview Road, Ephrata, PA 17522   717/733–6333

Hosts: Glenn and Mildred Wissler
Location: A 200-acre farm in easy-to-find countryside. Three miles west of Ephrata; half mile off Route 322; 15 minutes from Pennsylvania Turnpike; 20 minutes to Lancaster and Reading outlets; 25 minutes to Hershey.

Open: Year round. Two-night minimum on holidays and during special events.
Rates: Per room. $69 shared bath. $89 private bath. $25 rollaway. MC, Visa
♥ ♣ ✗ ⚹

Whether guests come for the wide open farmland, for warm hospitality, and/or for attractions in the area, they are inspired to take a tour of this 1814 limestone farmhouse, which has been restored over a 34-year period by Mildred, the daughter of an antiques dealer, and Glenn, a farmer and (creative) master craftsman. There's an aptly named Garden Room. And a Royal Room. A Princess Room with a lace-covered four-poster. A wicker carriage with parasol and dolls. A sink set into an old bureau. A dining room with Victorian print paper and formal draperies. And an inviting living room that overlooks the manicured lawns and the pond with swans. Everywhere, you see Glenn's sense of color combined with Mildred's displays (lots of collectibles) and her wallpapering and sewing (all the curtains, drapes, and canopies)—a style of making things come together without a sense of clutter. Since 1989 this family home has been a B&B. "Our son is married. We were not ready to retire from farming and thought it would be fun—it is!—to share this large house that we continue to find treasures for."

Bed and bath: Five rooms, each with sitting area. On second floor—one with carved Victorian double bed, private bath with claw-foot tub and shower. Two queen-bedded rooms with marble-topped furniture share a hall tub/shower bath. On third floor—two with canopied queen bed, sink ensuite, private shower bath, exposed stone walls, hand-pegged beams. Rollaway available.
Breakfast: 8:30. Fresh fruit. Homemade muffins. Hot entree such as ham and cheese souffle, peaches and cream French toast, or Belgian waffles. At dining room table set with china, crystal, and fresh linens, or on screened and awninged porch.
Plus: Central air conditioning. Fresh flowers. Mints on pillows. Living room organ. Fireplace and wood stove in beamed den. Lawn furniture.

Many guests write: "I hesitate to rave too much for fear of finding no place at the inn next time I call."

Historic Smithton   717/733–6094
900 West Main Street, Ephrata, PA 17522

Host: Dorothy Graybill
Location: West side of Ephrata, overlooking Ephrata Cloister (five-minute walk). At beginning of residential section, on the corner (with traffic light) of West Main Street and South Academy Drive. Twenty-five-minute walk to town center.
Open: Year round. Reservations recommended. Two-night minimum stay for Saturday and holiday reservations.
Rates: $65–$85 Monday–Thursday. $95–$115 Friday–Sunday and holidays. $35 additional person over age twelve; 18 months to age 12, $20, under 18 months free. Singles $10 less. Suite $140 weekdays, $170 weekends and holidays.
♥ ⊁

Perfection, here art thou. Well, as close as it can be—in a stone center hall building that has been an inn since 1763. There's a country feel with a luxurious touch. Marvelous choice of colors. Antique pieces that are interesting to look at. Magnificent you-can-hardly-tell reproductions, patina and all, crafted by Allan Smith, Dorothy's partner. He also made the bath tiles.

Dorothy has worked along with him throughout the impeccable restoration of the inn, which was built like the Cloister buildings, of German architectural tradition. They began the restoration—which has included the stone walls around the inn—in 1979, the year a friend suggested that Dorothy change from retail store management to innkeeping. (The inn was reopened in 1982.) A craftswoman with a strong interest in folk arts, Dorothy is a director of a local art center. Guests learn about the area from a local resident: Dorothy is Pennsylvania Dutch and has lived within a mile of Smithton all her life.

In residence: Dorothy is often assisted by her brother, Donald.
Bed and bath: Seven rooms plus a suite. All with option of being lit entirely by candles. Each with private modern bath, small refrigerator, working fireplace, chamber music, antique or handmade reproduction furnishings. Canopied or four-poster king, queen, or double bed with handmade Pennsylvania Dutch quilt, upholstered chairs, writing desk. Two-floor suite has snack area, living room, queen bed, twin cupboard bed, whirlpool bath, and separate shower. Cot and antique cradle available.
Breakfast: Served at 8 and 9:15 in tavern room by the fire and Allan's gorgeous 6-foot pewter cupboard. Entree varies; maybe Pennsylvania Dutch waffles, whipped cream, and syrup. Orange juice, pastry, fresh fruit plate, hot beverage.
Plus: Air conditioning. In winter, feather beds available. Nightshirts made by the multifaceted innkeepers. Well-stocked library. Tavern/breakfast/dining room with tea, snacks (no charge). Gardens with fountain and outdoor furniture. Printed booklet of touring and shopping suggestions. Quilts for sale.

Unless otherwise stated, rates in this book are per room for two and include breakfast in addition to all the amenities in "Plus." As for taxes and gratuities, please see page xi.

The Osceola Mill House   717/768–3758

313 Osceola Mill Road, Gordonville, PA 17529

Hosts: Robin and Sterling Schoen

Location: Peaceful. On a bend in the road along the banks of Pequea Creek. About a mile north of Intercourse; 15 miles east of Lancaster.

Open: Year round except Christmas–New Year's. Two-night minimum on weekends.

Rates: $100 per room.

♥ ♣ ◆ ✈ ⚥

Found in 1989: A 225-year-old stone house, a B&B about to be featured in *Country Living*, that was as interesting as its location. In the heart of an Old Order Amish community without a power or telephone line in view. Approached via a little bridge over a creek with a gristmill on one side and the miller's house on the other.

Now, once again, after extensive Schoen research and many discoveries, there are 12-over-12 windows complete with 18th-century glass (and huge one-pane storm windows) overlooking the Amish fields "where work is the order of the day." The Victorian touches added over the years to the large Georgian-style house are gone. There's a beehive oven and four working fireplaces. And an 18th-century herb garden. And Williamsburg whitewash walls with period and local colors for accents. The 18th- and 19th-century antiques were moved from New Hampshire, where, in the 1980s, Robin had been an antiques dealer (fine furniture, prints, brass, and quilts) and interior designer.

Sterling, the gourmet cook, is a fly-fishing expert/former Philadelphia litigation lawyer who was a computer-related company administrator in New Hampshire. Here he is active in preserving this unique pocket of the country, where guests from all over the world take walks and meet Amish neighbors along the road, "where there's a glorious morning mist and spectacular sunsets."

In residence: One Newfoundland dog named Oliver.

Bed and bath: Four second-floor rooms share a tub bath plus the new shower bath just installed in the former nursery. One bath (private for one of the rooms) located downstairs. One room with high undressed canopy queen bed, working fireplace. One with pencil-post queen bed, working fireplace. Two with canopied queen bed. All with handmade quilts.

Breakfast: Usually 8:30. Specialties include German apple pancakes or French toast that some guests say are "alone worth the trip." Served in fireplaced keeping room or in dining room with those 12-over-12 windows.

Plus: Air-conditioned bedrooms, June–September. Directions to small step-back-in-time country stores. Heavy buggy traffic year round. Fascinating restoration stories. (The original door was nailed as a patch on a neighbor's barn.) Shared tips about 18th-century restoration and Pennsylvania antiquing.

*B*reakfast *is where the magic happens.*

Pinehurst Inn Hershey

50 Northeast Drive, Hershey, PA 17033

717/533–2603
800/743–9140
fax 717/534–2639

Hosts: Phyllis Long and family
Location: Surrounded by lawns, countryside, and (through the night) the sound of the passing train. Within a mile of the Sports Arena, Hersheypark, Chocolate World, Hershey Museum, Golf Courses, and Rose Garden. One hour's drive to Gettysburg and Lancaster.
Open: Year round.
Rates: Double occupancy. April 15–October 15, $54. Off-season $45. $5 more private bath. $5 extra person. MC, Visa.

♥ ♂ ◀ ⁂ ♦ ✗ ✄

During my three-day stay, I saw an amazing flexibility in this house and its Hershey-born hosts. It offers the perfect arrangement for just a few people around the fire or on the porch, or for a small conference (the reason I was there). The sprawling brick B&B was built by Mr. Hershey as a home—not a dormitory—for orphaned boys who attended the Milton Hershey School (which has a current coed enrollment of 1,500). There is a comfortable, welcoming many-windowed living room. The guest rooms have built-in bureaus and are decorated minimally as a reminder of their origin.

Phyllis, a substitute teacher at the school in the 1970s, lived here as a young child when her parents were Pinehurst house parents. "As a teenager I entertained some dates on the porch swing, the same one on which my mother read to her grandchildren. After our own four children grew up—in a Cape house right in town—we bought this property and established the B&B. In addition to tourists, we meet many visitors who come for the medical center; for weddings (right here sometimes); for theater, symphony, and the annual antique auto show. B&B really does bring the world to your doorstep."

In residence: Nickolas, a gentle Maine coon cat.
Bed and bath: Fifteen rooms on first and second floors. Three have private bath; 12 share five baths. Queen, double, or twin beds and rollaway.
Breakfast: Usually 8–9:30. Juice or fruit, homemade coffee cakes, teas, coffee. Cereal or scrambled eggs or pancakes.
Plus: Air conditioning. Bedroom ceiling fans. Chocolate kiss on each pillow. That swing is on the porch.

From New York: *"We like the stenciling that Phyllis has done . . . and the long tables at breakfast where she serves from a great choice."* From Massachusetts: *"Treated as visitors at a private home."* From Virginia: *"Great for 19 of us, ages 6 to 78, who gathered for a family reunion."* From Pennsylvania: *"Excellent hostess . . . attention to detail. . . . And there's nothing like sleeping on sheets that have that 'fresh air' aroma!"*

---

*O*ne out of five guests leaves with
the dream of opening a B&B.

Buona Notte Bed & Breakfast   717/295-2597

2020 Marietta Avenue, Lancaster, PA 17603

Hosts: Joe and Anna Predoti
Location: In the village of Rohrerstown, on a main road 2 miles west of Lancaster, 7 to 10 miles to most tourist attractions (east of Lancaster). Two miles from Franklin and Marshall College,

1½ from Wheatland. Near Park City shopping center.
Open: Year round. Two-night minimum on holiday weekends.
Rates: $50 private bath, $45 shared bath. $5 cot.
🔔 ⁂ 🐕 ⛌

Just what the Predotis think a B&B should be—"clean and comfortable, all redecorated and furnished with many older pieces bought at area sales. The turn-of-the-century brick house is just what we were looking for when we decided to move here from New Jersey in 1985. We wanted to be in the Lancaster area, but not on top of the tourist attractions."

In New Jersey Anna taught nurses how to use computers. Here Joe teaches elementary and secondary students. They offer a friendly, homey atmosphere, with suggestions for restaurants (the number one question) and information on the ways of the Amish and Mennonites (the next most frequently asked questions). Anna says "Hosting people from so many different places is fascinating. Sometimes it seems as if the world's problems are being solved around the breakfast table!"

Foreign languages spoken: Joe speaks Italian fluently, some French and Spanish.
Bed and bath: Three rooms. The one with private bath is on third floor, with a double bed and room for a cot. One double-bedded second-floor room and one third-floor room with two twin beds share a full bath.
Breakfast: 7:30–9. Fresh fruit, juice, homemade muffins, buns and rolls, homemade toast, jams, granola. Coffee, tea, milk. In tall-windowed country dining room.
Plus: Beverages. Air conditioning and ceiling fans in all bedrooms. Living room with ceiling fan and wood stove. Piano in dining room. Wraparound porch. Yard and picnic area.

Lincoln Haus Inn Bed & Breakfast

1687 Lincoln Highway East, Lancaster, PA 17602-2609   717/392-9412

Host: Mary K. Zook
Location: On main road, within walking distance of some restaurants. Bus and tourist trolley go by the house. Two miles off Route 30. Minutes to several colleges and many attractions. Five minutes to Pennsylvania Dutch Visitors Information Bureau.

Open: Year round. Two- or three-day minimum during holidays.
Rates: Double occupancy $45–$53 double, $65 suite. Singles $2 less. $10 rollaway. $5–$10 one-night surcharge. Off-season, 10 percent less, excluding holidays from December until March 15.
♥ 🔔 ⁂ ♦ 🐕 ⛌

From Pennsylvania: *"Staying with Mary is the next best thing to staying with family . . . have returned 'home' after a long working day to find Mary making applesauce from fruit of tree outside, or canning peaches, or pickling beets . . . foods that often turn up on the breakfast table. No shrinking violets at this table! Mary coaxes introductions and conversation. . . . House is set back from the highway behind a well-tended lawn complete with swing and shade trees. Inside and out, it is unmistakably the new identity of what was once an elegant private home, with handsome woodwork, pleasant rooms, and a now-modernized (but nonelectric) roomy kitchen."*

Mary, a Lancaster native and member of the Old Order Amish church, grew up without electricity. A B&B hostess since 1989, she lights the living room with gaslights—and, for safety reasons, provides electric lights in the bedrooms (which also have air conditioners). Often, guests ask her about Amish ways, about restaurant recommendations, about hidden places, and about having dinner (reservations made) with her Amish cousin or friends.

Foreign language spoken: German.
Bed and bath: Six rooms with a queen, a double or a double and a twin bed. All private baths; one with shower only, others with tub and shower. Suite has two double beds, double sofa bed, exposed beams, skylight, kitchenette. Rollaway and crib available. Across street—two apartments with option of breakfast provided.
Breakfast: Served family (Amish) style in dining room. Varies according to season. Breads. Pumpkin, raisin bran or whole wheat carrot muffins. Maybe zucchini pie, fresh fruit or home-canned peaches with mandarin oranges. Blueberry or clam and potato pancakes, also a very good quiche. Sausages, ring bologna or scrapple. Juice could be papaya/orange. Herbal teas, coffee blends.
Plus: "In cooler months, goodness of basement wood-burning stove can be smelled throughout the house."

O'Flaherty's Dingeldein House   717/293–1723

1105 East King Street, Lancaster, PA 17602   800/779–7765

Hosts: Jack and Sue Flatley
Location: On a main road. "Fifteen minutes from heart of Amish country; 10 from downtown, train and bus stations, discount shopping malls. Five minutes to a fine restaurant."
Open: Year round.

Rates: Double occupancy tax included; $63.60 twin or double bed, shared bath. $74.20 double or queen bed, private bath. $15 extra bed. No charge for playpen. Discover, MC, Visa.

♥ ♔ ♣ ✖ ✌

From New Jersey: *"Our first B&B. My husband was doubtful. We loved it so much that I took my mother the next time. My in-laws went for a weekend and now I can't wait to go again."* From Connecticut: *"Delicious food."* From California: *"They sent us to the best bargain shops and local attractions. . . . We often stay in family settings, but none as 'family friendly' as this."*

(Please turn page.)

Absolute naturals. Born innkeepers. The Flatleys got the idea "for our retirement" from a B&B trip in Ireland. In 1989 they bought this B&B, a traditionally furnished Dutch Colonial that was once the home of the Armstrong (floor tile) family and for 50 years was in the Leath (Strasburg Railroad and Museum) family. The colorful and profuse gardens are tended by Sue, who is also a fine craftsperson. Jack, formerly a manager with Boeing Helicopters, is co-chef and tour planner, the one who explored side roads and found Amish friends—a toymaker who lives on a farm and loves to meet guests; a cabinetmaker who shows you around a shop with air power, no electricity; and a family that may have you to dinner.

In residence: "Our Lhasa-poo, McTuffy, a great people dog."
Bed and bath: Four rooms. Private full baths for two third-floor rooms, one with queen and one with double bed. On second floor, room with double bed and one with two twins share a full bath. Rollaway available.
Breakfast: 8–10. Fresh fruit or poached pears in strawberry sauce, homemade breads and muffins. Heart-shaped blueberry pancakes, "world-renowned omelets," or quiche. "Specially brewed coffee."
Plus: Fully air-conditioned. Fireplaced living room and study. Afternoon beverages. Bicycle storage. Use of refrigerator. Porch swing, chairs, game table. Transportation to/from Lancaster airport, bus or train station. Custom-marked map of Amish country.

Patchwork Inn   717/293–9078
2319 Old Philadelphia Pike, Lancaster, PA 17602

Hosts: Lee and Anne Martin
Location: On a main road, adjacent to an Amish farm. Three miles east of Lancaster, near the village of Smoketown. Two miles from Bird-in-Hand farmers' market and craft shops.

Open: Year round. Two-night minimum on major holiday weekends.
Rates: $70 private bath, $60 shared. $80 suite. $15 per extra person in room. Discover, MC, Visa.
♥ ♣ ✈ ✂

From Michigan: *"Lee and Ann helped with off-the-beaten-path suggestions . . . inn is shiny clean and charming."* From New Jersey: *"We enjoyed our stay so much that the next time we brought six couples."* From Canada: *"A superb collection of books on the Amish and Mennonites and on quilting."* From New Jersey: *" . . . even told my wife about a remote Amish fabric store where she was finally able to find some specific quilting material. . . . Everybody wanted breakfast recipes."*

Hospitality is the feature of this updated and well-maintained 1800s farmhouse, where you'll find a collection of over 70 handmade quilts, country antiques, and old telephones (including a booth with working sign and fan).

It just so happened that B&B was taking hold in Lancaster when Lee was retiring in 1987 as a colonel from the Marine Corps. That's when he and his late wife, Joanne, opened the inn. They ran it together until she died in 1989.

Lee and Anne, married in 1991, have put their varied talents and antiques together. Anne, who has worked in high school media services, has a degree in foods and nutrition. In response to guests' requests, the Martins have produced a cookbook.

In residence: One 13-year-old cat, Precious, "seems to know who the cat lovers are."

Bed and bath: On second floor, three rooms and one suite, all with quilt-covered antique queen beds. One room has private full bath. Two rooms share one large full bath with double sinks. Suite has bedroom, living room with queen sofa bed, full bath, kitchen, and private entrance.

Breakfast: Usually 8:30. "Wholesome." Juice. Fruit. Breakfast pizza (recipe came from a guest) or Dutch babies. Homemade breads. Coffee and teas.

Plus: Air conditioning. Bedroom ceiling fans. Amish-made wood glider on front porch. Guest refrigerator. Flannel sheets in winter; line-dried sheets in summer. Bicycle storage and tour maps.

Bed & Breakfast of Delaware Host #31

Oxford, Pennsylvania

Location: A working dairy farm (95 cows) surrounded by Amish farms— and in back, a new 18-hole Scottish golf course. Within 20 minutes of Strasburg, Longwood Gardens, Winterthur Museum, Brandywine River Museum, Chadds Ford, Lancaster outlets. Within 10 minutes of fine dining, Herr's Potato Chips, Eldreth Pottery.

Reservations: Available year round through Bed & Breakfast of Delaware, page 4.

Rates: $50 single. $60 double. $15 third person in room. $5 surcharge for one-night stay.

♥ ❖ ♦ ✈

Welcome—in the herb garden with May wine made with sweet woodruff and fresh strawberries, or with sun tea with mint and lemon verbena; or in winter with hot cider by the working fireplace in the kitchen. Other herbs from the host's gardens flavor the full country breakfast featured at this B&B, which has been discovered by travelers from all over the world.

It's a restored 1793 brick farmhouse that was once a stagecoach stop, general store, and post office. Stucco, added in the early 1930s, was removed with hammer and chisel by the host—"yes, it was a big project"—in 1986. Furnished with many collectibles and antiques, the house is well located for exploring the area; for hearing the clip-clopping of Amish buggies; and, depending on the season, for seeing calves being born.

In residence: Two dogs. Numerous cats in the barn. Teenage daughter and 12-year-old son, "very busy with their own activities."

Bed and bath: On second floor, two (three available for one party) air-conditioned, antiques-furnished rooms. All double beds; one room has a double and a single. One pullout cot available. One shared tub/shower bath.

Breakfast: 8–9. Full country start to the day. Fresh fruit; home fries, sausage; apples sauteed in garlic, rosemary, and sage from the herb garden, with scrambled eggs and fresh dill. Blueberry muffins with lemon verbena and homemade sticky buns. In fireplaced breakfast room.

(Please turn page.)

Plus: Air-conditioned guest rooms. Welcoming beverage served in herb garden or in front of the fireplace. An old toolbox filled with brochures of attractions and guests' impressions.

The Apple Bin Inn
2835 Willow Street Pike, Willow Street, PA 17584

717/464–5881
800/338–4296

Hosts: Barry and Debbie Hershey
Location: On a main road, in center of village, near restaurants and shops. Two minutes to oldest house in Pennsylvania Dutch country. Four miles south of Lancaster. An hour north of Baltimore.

Open: Year round. Three-day minimum on holiday weekends.
Rates: Double occupancy. Shared bath $55; suite $65. Private bath $70. $15 additional person. Amex, MC, Visa.
♥ ♣ ✈ ⊱

"Take our county maps and get lost for an hour or two. That's what we tell our guests. And in minutes they are off the beaten track into beautiful countryside with farms and one-room schoolhouses. We know these roads from cycling." (When their children were younger, the Hersheys, Lancaster Bicycle Club members, took an 1,100-mile cycling trip to Florida.) "As area residents, we knew this 120-year-old house, a local landmark that was originally a grocery store and then a private residence with many additions built on through the years."

In 1986 the family started the B&B here. Now Barry makes apple checkerboards with three-dimensional apple playing pieces. Debbie quilts and cross-stitches. (And she has become proficient in sign language.) With a theme of "colonial charm and country flavor," the Hersheys have filled the house with folk art and crafts—and with contentment for both hosts and travelers.

In residence: Lauren, age 13. Two outdoor dogs, Cocoa and Buttons.
Bed and bath: Four double-bedded (pencil- or acorn-post) rooms. On first floor—private exterior entrance, cathedral ceiling, barn siding on walls, private shower bath. On second floor—room with pencil-post bed, wing chair, love seat, balcony overlooking yard, private tub and shower bath. Room with wicker and oak furnishings shares a bath with suite that has a sitting room. Cot available.
Breakfast: 8–9:30. Fresh fruits, homemade bread and muffins, egg casserole or German apple pancake, coffee, herbal tea. Plus a warm homemade dish. Served in country dining room or on one of two patios.
Plus: Air conditioning and color cable TV in each room. Evening refreshments. Dinner offered occasionally. Will meet guests at Lancaster airport, train, or bus. Piano in living room. Shaded patios. Hershey candy kisses. Secure bicycle storage. Custom packages for ice hockey games and dinner, for theater, and for walking or cycling tours. Picnic lunches prepared.

From Maryland: *"Beautiful . . . little touches in each room appreciated. . . . Food was great and the hospitality topped it. They helped us to find attractions and even a truly romantic anniversary restaurant."* From New Jersey: *"Cozy, comfortable, and clean. . . . Now I understand why B&Bs have become so popular."*

Swiss Woods Bed & Breakfast

717/627–3358
800/594–8018
fax 717/627–3483

500 Blantz Road
Lititz, PA 17543-9997

Hosts: Werner and Debrah Mosimann
Location: Off the beaten path, among rolling fields and country scenes. On the edge of woods that surround Speedwell Fordge Lake (hiking and fishing). Three miles north of Lititz and pretzel factory; 20 minutes to downtown Lancaster; 25 to Hershey.
Open: Year round. Two-night minimum on weekends; three nights on holidays. (January–March, Swiss fondue and raclette dinners by reservation only.)
Rates: Double occupancy. Downstairs $66 woodland view, $79 south-facing lakeview rooms. Suites $93 or $105 (with Jacuzzi). Ten percent less, January–March, Monday–Thursday. $15 extra person in room. Children under age one, free (crib available). MC, Visa.
♥ ♣ ♦ ✈ ⊬

From New Jersey: *"When you walk through the door, a sense of comfort and peace wraps around you. . . . An uncanny touch with detail that is surpassed only by warm kindness."* From Massachusetts: *"Suggested great bike routes . . . places to visit that weren't on tourist maps . . . rooms were light and airy . . . breakfasts spectacular."*

There are some weeks when I think that every Swiss Woods guest writes to me about their wonderful visit.

This is a Swiss-style house with natural woodwork and a contemporary country feeling—hosted by a Lancaster County native and her Swiss husband, whom she met in Austria while working with an interdenominational group.

Debrah explains, "Wherever we lived, it seemed that we had visitors who had come a long way. B&B seemed like something I could do at home. While still in Switzerland we drew our own plans for this house to be built—with Werner's help—on land that has been in my family."

Since opening in June 1986, they have added a huge beamed common room with a floor-to-ceiling stone fireplace at one end. They have planted thousands of daffodils (glorious in spring). Asparagus and red raspberries flourish. And the orchard produces peaches, nectarines, apples, walnuts, plums, cherries, and quinces that enhance breakfast for vacationers from all over the world.

In residence: In hosts' quarters—Mirjam Anne, age 11; Esther, age 10; Lukas, age 8; and Jason is 5. Two golden retrievers, Gretel and Heidi.
Foreign languages spoken: German and Swiss German.
Bed and bath: Seven rooms. On first floor, three queen-bedded rooms and one with two twins; each with private exterior entrance, sitting area, tub/shower bath. Two second-floor beamed cathedral-ceilinged rooms—each with a queen bed (one is a four-poster), balcony, private bath with Jacuzzi and hand-held shower. Second-floor suite with outside entrance; queen and one twin sleigh bed in one room, queen sofa bed in living room, large full bath, private deck with table and chairs. Crib available.

(Please turn page.)

Breakfast: 8:30–9:00. (Coffee available from 7:30 on.) Strawberry gratin or maybe a peach raspberry cream. Birchemuesli, an original Swiss recipe, is all-time favorite. Entrees might include cinnamon raisin French toast stuffed with wild berry cream cheese, granola apple pancakes, or egg sausage souffle. Homemade breads, buttermilk raised biscuits, chocolate chip/macadamia scones or sour cream bran muffins. Homemade jams such as pear-cranberry. Juice. Their own coffee blend. (Cookbook is coming.) In breakast room or on patio.

Plus: Central air conditioning. Cookie jar is always full. Instant hot water spigot in fully equipped guest kitchenette. Bedside Swiss chocolates. Goose-down covers. Binoculars. Bird book. Games and television. Coffee, tea, and sweets from 4 to 6 p.m. Gift shop with cowbells "depending on when we were last in Switzerland."

Herr Farmhouse Inn   717/653–9852

2256 Huber Drive, Manheim, PA 17545

Host: Barry A. Herr
Location: Pastoral. An 11-acre pocket with panoramic view of farmland, minutes from Routes 183 and 130, major highways just east of Mount Joy. Nine miles west of Lancaster.
Open: Year round.

Rates: Double occupancy. April–October $70 shared bath, $85 private bath, $95 suite. Ten percent less off-season for two-night stay (holidays excluded). $15 extra person in room. MC, Visa.

Now this wonderful limestone colonial, the fourth Herr restoration, is picture-perfect with chair rails, four-poster beds, Williamsburg colors, 22-inch-thick walls, and six working fireplaces. When Barry gives the guided tour requested by most guests, you hear about how he and his late wife found this gem—the oldest part dates back to 1737—which had not been remodeled. A tenant house for almost a hundred years, it had been vacant for at least seven when the Herrs returned to their native Lancaster County. Even though there was much to be done (see the before-and-after pictures), all the architectural details, including moldings, floors, and even the beehive oven, were intact. "It was a bit big for two people, so the B&B idea seemed just right."

The first Herr restoration was in 1969 in Connecticut, where Barry was in engineering and a building contractor. Here he cut cherry, walnut, and pear wood for the fireplaces. And he restored outbuildings that "should be good for another 50 years." Adding to the bucolic scene is the red (former dairy) barn; the chicken house, which is now a woodworking shop; two corncribs; and tobacco sheds (which are rented by a farmer who cures tobacco in them). The gazebo is used for picnic lunches. There are country roads for jogging. And, for every winter guest, a flannel nightshirt.

In residence: Clyde, "a friendly gray mostly-outside tiger cat."
Bed and bath: Three second-floor rooms plus a third-floor suite. Private full bath for room with canopied double bed and working fireplace. One room with canopied double bed and one with double rope bed (with working

fireplace) share a full bath. Up a steep stairway to suite with private full bath, two twin beds, sitting room with sofa bed. Rollaway available.

Breakfast: At 9. Fresh fruit, cereal, assorted breads, English muffins, home-made jelly, apple butter. Juice, coffee, tea, milk. In country kitchen with walk-in fireplace, in fireplaced dining room, or on sun porch.

Plus: Central air conditioning. Bedroom ceiling fans. Fireplaced common room. Game room with player piano. Wicker-furnished sun room. Lawn furniture, porch rockers, picnic table and grill. Indoor storage for bicycles.

The Noble House   717/426–4389
113 West Market Street, Marietta, PA 17547-1411

Hosts: Elissa and Paul Noble
Location: On main street of the historic district. "Some guests, too, fall under the charm of this town and spend hours walking around." Thirty minutes west of Lancaster and east of Hershey. Less than an hour from Baltimore, Maryland. Minutes to antiquing, outlet shopping, museums, theaters. Two blocks from trains (sound and nostalgia). A half block to Paul's toy train shop.
Open: Year round.
Rates: $55 per room. $75 efficiency apartment.
♦ ✈ ⅄

How often Elissa would say, "Some day we will find a little corner of the world to open a toy train shop for Paul and a B&B for me!" In 1992, two years after they found Marietta, the Nobles opened this B&B in an 1820 Federal brick townhouse that had been restored as an antiques and art gallery. It has 12-foot first-floor ceilings and huge windows, and it is furnished with a blend of pieces that date from the 1850s to the 1930s.

In Yorktown Heights, New York, Paul was an art director who also had a home-based Lionel train business. Elissa, who now teaches part time at a Waldorf School, was a child-care specialist.

In residence: Fred the dog. Crash Baby and Diesel, the cats.
Bed and bath: Two large second-floor carpeted rooms. One with king/twin option (and Elissa's antique doll collection) and one room with queen four-poster brass bed share (robes provided) a tub/shower bath. Crib available. Efficiency (self-serve breakfast or eat with hosts) has double bed, shower bath, dining area, kitchenette, cable TV; 1950s railroad sleeper car theme, patterned after Elissa's father's advertising campaign for Chesapeake and Ohio Railroad: "Sleep like a kitten, arrive fresh as a daisy."
Breakfast: 6–10. Wake-up basket muffins followed by meal in candlelit dining room or on porch. Fresh fruit and juice. Choice of egg dish or French toast. Home fries and breads. Freshly ground and locally roasted coffee.
Plus: Fireplaced living room with upright piano and color cable TV. Room air conditioners. Welcoming refreshments. Turndown service. Fresh flowers. Use of fitness center "down the street." Directions to shopping area with a 100-foot-long rocker-filled porch "where everyone sits."

(Please turn page.)

From Maryland: *"Charming, exquisite antiques, spotlessly kept. . . . Two break-fasts—first with morning paper . . . followed by brunch on antique china. . . . A lending library (really!) . . . congenial hosts."* From New York: *"Within walking distance of Susquehanna River . . . which at this point is wide, shallow, and picturesque . . . . I am British . . . felt transported to a genteel Victorian home in England."*

Vogt Farm Bed & Breakfast   717/653-4810
1225 Colebrook Road, Marietta, PA 17547

Hosts: Kathy and Keith Vogt
Location: On a quiet country road. A 30-acre farm with barns, a small pond with wild ducks (sometimes), cows in the pasture, and a garden. "Within 4 miles of all types of dining." Fifteen miles west of Lancaster.

Within 30 minutes of Harrisburg and Hershey.
Open: Year round.
Rates: $35 single, $55 for two; $10 each additional person in same room. ♦ ⬛ ✈ ⌿

From New York: *"Combination of good food, comfortable accommodations, and genuine warmth makes it our favorite B&B."*

"Our brick home was a real showplace, so we are told, when it was built in 1865. We like to say it is decorated in 'Early Vogt,' the kind of place where guests often gather in the kitchen. (One six-year-old, who had tested his parents' patience the day before, appeared while Kathy was making breakfast. 'Which of your children is most annoying?' he asked Kathy, who could follow his trend of thought. They had quite a conversation.)

"Through the years we have had guests from around the world. Now that the older kids are married, we have official empty (redecorated) rooms, some of which were featured in *Weekends* as well as *Country Decorating* magazine. When guests ask about our country elevator, I am happy to explain the process of storing corn, wheat, and soybeans in the big bins. . . . Kathy, an excellent cook [at ease with quantities—such as 1,800 ears of corn in one August day], quilter, family chauffeur, company gofer, emergency management coordinator at the farm, and wife, has lived within 5 miles of here all her life. I have my pilot's license and we have our own plane [for travels as far away as Prince Edward Island or Puerto Rico]. Our fun-loving family hosts with the motto, 'Backdoor guests are best.'"

In residence: Two teenage daughters, Jennie and Rebecca. Several outdoor barn cats. A small flock of sheep, a 4-H project.
Foreign language spoken: A little Spanish.
Bed and bath: Three second-floor rooms—with king/twins option, queen, or double bed—share a full bath (tub plus hand-held shower) and a half bath. Crib available.
Breakfast: At 8 on Sundays. Other days, 8:30. Early tea or coffee with wake-up call, if you'd like. Home-baked bread, rolls, coffee cakes, casseroles, and fruit. In large farm kitchen. Hosts join guests.

Plus: Bedroom air conditioners. Refreshing drink. Use of refrigerator. Living room with baby grand piano. Fireplaced basement family room with TV. Garden flowers. Maps. Tips, too, for things to see and do. Plush robes. Mints. Ice water in rooms.

Cedar Hill Farm   717/653–4655
305 Longenecker Road, Mount Joy, PA 17552-9300

Hosts: Russel and Gladys Swarr
Location: Rural and quiet. A 51-acre farm on a hill, across Chiques (pronounced "chickies") Creek via a steel bridge. Surrounded by meadows, trees, a martin house, even a dinner bell mounted on a tall post. One-quarter mile drive from Route 230. Midway (12 miles) between Lancaster and Hershey.
Open: Year round. Two-night minimum on holiday weekends.
Rates: $60–$65 double, $50 single. $20 additional adult in room. Amex, Discover, MC, Visa.
♥ ♫ ✿ ❋ ✖ ✂

What *Philadelphia* magazine dubbed "the creme de la Lancaster" for "weekend luxury" is a stone farmhouse, the birthplace of Russel, a third-generation farmer who now raises 56,000 chicks to laying age. The house's original 1817 side is simpler than the mid-1800s Victorian addition, which features a graceful winding stairway, high ceilings, and elaborate moldings. In 1987, when the Swarrs' son and daughter were grown, central air conditioning and private baths were added. A carved walnut bedroom suite with marble-topped dresser and washstand, made by Russel's cabinetmaker grandfather, provided pieces for two of the bedrooms. (The bed's footboard became the headboard for the other room.)

Gladys left her 17-year office job at NCR Corporation, worked with an interior designer to coordinate family heirlooms with period wallpapers and swags, and became a full-time innkeeper. The guest list includes a professional juggler who entertained on the lawn; newlyweds who arrived in gown and tux; guests in medieval outfits on their way to a Renaissance fair; a couple who drove from Nova Scotia for a puppy; government staffers; sightseers; and others who just want to relax—"warm, wonderful people who ask about farming, about the Amish and Mennonites, about the history of the house, and about our favorite road, where an Amish lady sells quilts in her home."

Bed and bath: Five second-floor rooms. All private baths. Queen bed (high headboard), tub and shower bath. Queen bed (high headboard), large sit-down shower, private wicker-furnished balcony. Double bed, shower bath. Two double beds, tub/shower bath. Twins/king option, claw-foot tub and shower bath. Rollaway and crib available.
Breakfast: 8–9. Homemade muffins, coffee cakes, and breads. Fresh fruit and cheeses. Individual cereal boxes with low-fat milk. Orange juice, coffee, decaf, tea, hot chocolate. In guests' favorite room, the kitchen with walk-in fireplace, huge beam, hanging herbs and baskets.
Plus: "I-could-sit-here-all-day" porches overlooking creek. Upright piano. Ice bucket. Use of refrigerator. Garden flowers. Separate guest entrance. TV room

(Please turn page.)

with stereo, VCR, and computer games. Sleds in winter. Croquet in summer. Hershey kisses.

From New Jersey: *"Decorated beautifully."* From Ohio: *"Perfect. Far exceeded our expectations."* From Pennsylvania: *"A quick escape by train from Philadelphia."*

The Country Stay   717/367-5167
2285 Bull Moose Road, Mount Joy, PA 17552-9767

Hosts: Lester and Darlene Landis
Location: Rural. "Where the silence and sounds of nature can be heard— the songs of birds, locusts, bullfrogs, and crickets." On a working farm. Minutes from Routes 743, 441, and 30. Within half an hour of Hershey, Lancaster, York, and Harrisburg. Within 15 minutes of fine dining and family restaurants.

Open: April–November. Two-night minimum for rooms on holiday weekends; two nights always for suite. Advance reservations required.
Rates: $55 single, $60 double, $110 suite. MC, Visa.
🐕 ✗ ⚕

From California, Georgia, Maryland, Virginia, Ohio, New York: *"Wonderfully decorated with antiques. . . . The grounds are as impressive as the inside. . . . Meticulously kept. . . . Took a midnight walk under a full harvest moon when rows of corn gleamed like silver . . . delicious food on a beautifully prepared table . . . served by mother and daughter in period dress . . . joined them for an evening bicycle ride . . . accompanied them to church on Sunday. . . . Traveled alone. Found warmth and friendship. . . . Les gave us tips on roads and eateries. . . . Shared facts about their home, their life, the area, things to see and do. . . . Shared information on quilts (my love) and sang around the [restored player] piano (my husband's a barbershopper). . . . We arrived as strangers and left feeling like family."*

Williamsburg and Victorian colors enhance the magnificent woodwork, the wide staircase to the second floor, the marble-topped furnishings, the comfortable living room chairs, the bay windows, and the high-headboard rope bed in this 1880 brick Victorian farmhouse, home to the Landis family for 23 years—and featured in both *Country Extra* and *Country Almanac*. Windows, each with a lighted candle, are decorated with graceful swags or ruffled curtains. In season, the window boxes overflow with blossoms. It's serene and welcoming. I, too, felt richer for my brief stop here.

In residence: Donavin, 20; Douglas, 16; Katie Joy, 8.
Bed and bath: One suite plus two rooms. First-floor Victorian suite with queen four-poster, sitting room, private bath. Private guest entrance to second-floor rooms—carpeted double-bedded room with handmade Amish quilt shares a full hallway bath with room that has queen canopied bed, Amish quilt. Extra mattresses available.
Breakfast: 8:15 Monday–Saturday; at 8 on Sundays. Fruit. Homemade breads, coffee cake, muffins or sticky buns, coffee, tea, juice.

Plus: Air conditioners and ceiling fans in bedrooms. Mints. Potpourri. Use of refrigerator. Porch rockers. Because guests asked, some of Darlene's handcrafts are for sale.

Hillside Farm Bed & Breakfast   717/653–6697
607 Eby Chiques Road, Mount Joy, PA 17552-0628

Hosts: Gary and Deb Lintner, nights and weekends; Gary's parents, Bob and Wilma, weekdays
Location: On two acres "in the middle of nowhere" surrounded by dairy farms. On a hill overlooking Chiques Creek, dam, and a mill house. Ten miles west of Lancaster; 35 east of Harrisburg.
Open: Year round.
Rates: Double occupancy. $62.50 private bath, $50 shared. $10 each additional person over age 10.
🛏 ❋ ◆ ✗ ⚡

Enter via the kitchen, the most popular gathering place in this 1863 red brick farmhouse. When the dairy went out of business in 1957, apartments went in. Since the Lintners opened as a B&B in 1989, they have continued to make changes, still decorating eclectically—with hundreds of milk bottles, ceramic and wooden cows, milk cans, and other country items. The stairwell features for-sale prints by a local artist.

Gary, a Lancaster County native, and Deb, "a transplant from Erie," work for the same construction company. He is project superintendent; she, an executive secretary.

In residence: In hosts' quarters—two indoor cats. Several outdoor barn cats.
Bed and bath: Five rooms. Third-floor carpeted loft has a double bed, two twin beds, space for rollaway, exposed beams, private shower bath. On second floor, one room with king/twins option shares a tub/shower bath (robes provided) with room that has queen four-poster. Two queen-bedded rooms; one with private shower/tub bath, and one with canopied bed, private shower bath.
Breakfast: At 8:30. Fruit cup or cobblers. Orange juice, coffee, decaf, tea, herbal tea, milk. Casserole, French toast, pancakes, or eggs. Ham, sausage, or bacon. Muffins or biscuits. Homemade jams and jellies. By candlelight; can last for hours.
Plus: Central air conditioning on second floor; window unit on third floor and ground level. Individual heat thermostats. Ceiling fans. (Note: Windows are to be kept closed at all times.) Guest refrigerator. Color TV/VCR in living room. Grand piano. Mints on pillow. Special occasions acknowledged. Fresh springwater in thermos pitcher. Suggested bicycling routes.

> From New York: *"The rooms are immaculate. The entire farm exuded warmth and real living . . . hearty, home-cooked food. . . . The Lintners went out of their way to make reservations for us. They called about artwork. They wrote to us with an answer about a quilt question. They are nice nice people who like people. I'm going back."*

Maple Lane Guest House   717/687-7479

505 Paradise Lane, Paradise, PA 17562

Hosts: Marion and Edwin Rohrer
Location: Pretty. Set back from the highway, surrounded by acres of lawn and rolling valley meadows with winding stream. One mile from Pennsylvania Railroad Museum of Strasburg.

Open: Year round. Two-night minimum on summer weekends.
Rates: Private bath $55 single, $65 double. Semiprivate bath $50 single, $58 double. $40–50 off-season. $8 cot. Crib, free.
♥ 🍴 ✥ ✗ ✄

> From Massachusetts: *"We have stayed at several farms in the Amish country and found this one to be by far the finest. Our beautiful accommodations included a bedroom hand stenciled by Mrs. Rohrer, with a handmade quilt and other home-made crafts. . . . Mr. Rohrer gave us a tour of the farm with a full explanation of the milking machinery."* From New York: *"Well away from traffic of other tourists and curiosity seekers . . . spotlessly clean . . . never-ending hospitality."* From Connecticut: *"Rooms were charming. . . . As we took our morning walk before breakfast, could see Amish children walking to school . . . could hear horses and buggies coming down the road. . . . The Rohrers made us feel like part of their family."*

This is home! Marion was born just a mile down the road in one direction; Ed, a mile in the other. They have been sharing their lifestyle with travelers for 25 years. Until 1980, when they built this colonial-style brick home, they lived next door in the 200-year-old fieldstone house that is now occupied by their married son (whom you are likely to meet when you tour the farm). This newer house is filled with family heirlooms and with Marion's hand-work, including quilting, painting, sewing, pierced lampshades, and counted cross-stitch—all pictured in a *Country Almanac* feature. For back roads, unad-vertised Amish shops, or covered bridge locations, you have the experts here.

Bed and bath: On second floor, four double-bedded rooms; two baths, which can be private depending on reservation arrangements. Cot and crib available.
Breakfast: 7:30–9. Juice, fresh fruits, several kinds of breakfast rolls, crack-ers, cheeses, cereal, homemade pecan rolls and/or cheese pastry, coffee, tea. A time when Marion answers a lot of questions.
Plus: Central air conditioning. TV in each guest room. Refrigerator. Organ in guests' Victorian parlor. Picnic table. Large front porch.

Limestone Inn   717/687-8392

33 East Main Street, Strasburg, PA 17579

Hosts: Janet and Dick Kennell
Location: In historic district on Route 896 "where the clatter of horses and buggies awakes you in the morning." Eight miles east and south of Lancaster city. Short walk to shops and walking tour of historic Stras-burg. Minutes' drive to Railroad Mu-

seum, antiques shops, outlet malls, Amish attractions, and quilt shop.
Open: Year round. Two-night mini-mum on weekends and holidays.
Rates: Double occupancy. $75 dou-ble bed, $85 queen. $95 with fire-place. All private baths. Amex.
♥ ✥ ✗

Shy? Not really, but Dick wasn't all that sure—in 1985—about B&B as the next step after retiring from 30 years as a forester with the federal government. For their fourteenth move—this time without six growing children—the grandparents of nine chose this handsome National Register 1786 limestone five-bay Georgian, considered one of Lancaster County's most important historic buildings. They restored and decorated with Williamsburg colors, primitive antiques, and period curtains. And they became co-chefs, who frequently wear colonial outfits during breakfast. Jan's dates back to her days as a costumed guide in Annapolis. Dick's brings out the actor in him—as well as his love of people.

In residence: Max and Betsy, "miniature schnauzers who love stroking."
Foreign languages spoken: A little French and German.
Bed and bath: Five rooms. Three queen-bedded rooms on second floor; two with private tub/shower bath; one with private shower bath and fireplace; rollaway available. Up steep staircase with display of Amish wall hangings are two third-floor double- or twin-bedded rooms "partially tucked under the roofline." From 1839 to 1860 they were Strasburg Academy dormitory rooms; now each has a private shower bath.
Breakfast: At 8:30. A five-course meal. Entree might be sourdough pancakes, French toast, or egg souffle. Bran and blueberry muffins.
Plus: Central air conditioning. Keeping room with fireplace flanked by wing chairs and spinning wheel. Family's player piano in living room. Individual thermostats in third-floor rooms only. Late-afternoon wine and cheese. Courtyard. Chocolates. Special occasions acknowledged. Suggestions for best buys, eating, biking. Ample bike storage. Dinner with Amish arranged with prior reservatons.

> From Maryland: *"The highlight of our vacation. . . . A beautifully restored distinguished-looking inn, but it was really Jan and Dick who made this B&B stand out."*

1854 House

717/252–4643
800/722–6395

811 Grand Manor Drive, Wrightsville, PA 17368-9802

Hosts: Roger and Amelia Healey
Location: "Off a cul-de-sac and back into the last century." On 22 acres of lawns and woodlands. One mile north of Route 30. Five-minute drive to Accomac Inn, award-winning restaurant. Two miles to public golf course. Eight miles east of York, 13 west of Lancaster.

Open: Year round. Two-night minimum preferred on holiday weekends.
Rates: Double occupancy. $65 double bed, $70 queen bed. Singles $5 less. Three-room suite (up to 6) $185. MC, Visa.
♠ ♣ ✈ ✂

Roger's dream, a "piece of country," is yours for as long as you are here. The B&B is a rejuvenated three-storied Georgian brick farmhouse filled with family antiques "from both sides." Some come from Roger's grandfather, who was an antiques dealer in New York City from 1895 until 1936. Since "finally finding" the farm in 1983, following 10 years in the defense industry and 22

(Please turn page.)

as an army officer (on several continents), Roger has become a restoration contractor. The Healeys also restored the summer kitchen, springhouse, and smokehouse. They dug a three-quarter-acre spring-fed pond (the children were ages 10 and 12 when the family moved here from the Washington, D.C., area). Now the pond is complete with dock, canoe, and stocked bass. And there are hiking and riding trails. (Bring your own horse—with advance notice please.)

Amelia, a former English teacher who has owned a needlework shop, is official chef and also irons all those antique table linens. And her enthusiasm for the area is contagious.

In residence: Seven cats; two are indoors, Buddy and Lena. In the barn, two horses that like to be fed.

Foreign languages spoken: Portuguese, Spanish, and some French.

Bed and bath: Four rooms. On second floor, queen-bedded room (Empire furnishings), ceiling fan, private hall bath with whirlpool tub and hand-held shower. Third floor—one room with double oak bed, private hall bath with footed tub and hand-held shower; one room with queen (padded headboard) bed, attached bath with whirlpool tub and shower. One room (booked only by same party that books any other room and shares its bath) with a day/trundle bed that converts from single to two twins or one king. This room also serves as a lounge with a TV and radio.

Breakfast: Flexible hours. Entree possibilities—pancakes, Southwestern eggs, eggnog French toast, or broccoli-cheese casserole. Juice, fresh fruit, homemade sweet bread, breakfast meat, "tons of coffee and tea." Family style at 1500s Spanish table set with china, crystal, sterling silver.

Plus: Central air conditioning. Welcoming refreshments. Turndown service. Mints on pillow. Springwater. Fresh flowers. Books. Games. Porch rockers. Seven-stall barn. And, in summer, fireflies.

From a father's account of a B&B stay: "Before falling asleep, my son read a few pages of a book he found downstairs in the living room. He put the book down on his chest, sighed, looked up at the ceiling and said, 'This is the life.'"

Central Pennsylvania Reservation
——————— Service ———————

Rest & Repast Bed & Breakfast
Reservation Service

P.O. Box 126, Pine Grove Mills, PA 16868

Phone: 814/238–1484, Monday–Friday 8:30–11:30 a.m. Answering machine at other times. Open peak Penn State weekends. Closed December 15–January 15.

Listings: 60. Four are inns. Four are cottages or guest houses on hosts' property. Most are private residences. Some available April–November only. Located in Centre, Blair, Huntington, Juniata, Union, and Clearfield counties—in and around Aaronsburg, Bellefonte, Boalsburg, Clearfield, Hartleton, State College, Spruce Creek, Tyrone (near famous Grier private girls' school).

Reservations: One week's advance notice usually needed. For big weekends, four months' advance notice recommended.

Rates: $35–$45 single, when available. $40–$70 double. Peak weekends $45–$75. $15 surcharge on peak weekends for one-night stay, where permitted. Family and weekly rates. Deposit of $25 per night required except for peak weekends, when $50 per room per night is required. All cancellations subject to $25 processing fee. Given at least 7 days' notice, balance of deposit is refunded; for football weekends, at least 14 days' notice required.

Linda Feltman and Brent Peters started the reservation service in 1982 to provide needed lodging during peak times in the Penn State area. Because travelers also come for history, culture, and recreation, the service has become active year round. More than 50 percent of the hosts have been on the roster for more than two years. "More than 90 percent attend our summer ice-cream social. They are a bunch of friendly folks, that's for sure!"

Plus: Some B&Bs available for up to 14 days. For short-term (4–20 days) housing in private apartments in hosts' homes, breakfast may or may not be included.

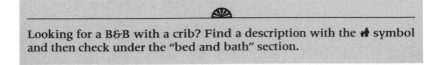

Looking for a B&B with a crib? Find a description with the ♣ symbol and then check under the "bed and bath" section.

Central and Western Pennsylvania
——————————— B&Bs ———————————

Ponda-Rowland Bed & Breakfast   717/639–3245
Beaumont, PA   fax 717/639–3245
Mailing address: RR 1, Box 349, Dallas, PA 18612-9604

Hosts: Jeanette and Cliff Rowland
Location: Serene. On a 30-acre wildlife sanctuary "where the pavement ends" in the Endless Mountain region. Four hours from Washington, D.C.; 3 from New York City, 2½ from Philadelphia. Ten minutes from Wilkes-Barre and Tunkhannock.
Open: Year round.

Rates: Double occupancy. $60 king or double bed. $70 king/two twins option. $30 one-night surcharge on holiday weekends and in October. No charge for crib or for one child under 10 in room; $10 for third adult or for child 10 or over in room. MC, Visa.

♥ ♠ ⊜ ⁂ ♦ ✈ ⁄

Found—by families, and by drummers who played from different points on the mountain. By artists, photographers, business travelers, antiquers, nature and animal lovers, a group on a yoga retreat, and romantics too. The Rowlands moved to this former dairy farm from New Jersey, where they had hosted paying guests in an 18-room antiques-filled house, in 1988. That's when Cliff retired from his positions in the U.S. Postal Service (preceded by many years in labor relations with Grace Line). Here, trails were cut. Next to one of the six ponds an open pavilion was built for skate changers and picnickers, and for swimmers who use the sandy beach, diving board, and slide. The "simple 150-year-old farmhouse" was changed by the Rowlands' son, a timber-frame builder, to a picture-perfect setting—with solid oak beams, some wood ceilings, and plank walls—for the museumlike collection of colonial antiques. Deer appear at dusk for feeding. There are mallards, great blue heron, doves, geese, feeding stations. A treasure.

In residence: Beau, a white German shepherd; Sam, a Labrador retriever. At last count—one cat, two sheep, one big turkey, a ferret, one potbellied pig, a few beef cattle, one rabbit, some chickens.
Bed and bath: Three second-floor carpeted rooms; all private shower baths. King bed, double, or large room with king/twins option plus a single bed. Crib available.
Breakfast: Guests' choice of hour. Eggs with bacon, sausage, or ham; or pan (corn) cakes—a specialty. Juices, fruit platter, toast, homemade and English muffins, jellies, coffee, tea, milk. Special diets and vegetarians accommodated. In candlelit dining room overlooking sanctuary.
Plus: Fireplaced great room. Bedroom ceiling fans. Refreshments. Dinner option for groups. Guest refrigerator. Beach towels. Binoculars. Toboggan. Volleyball. Horseshoes. Badminton. Cross-country skiing. Suggestions for unadvertised guided horseback mountain trail tours ($8 per hour) or Susquehanna River Valley air tour. Horse-drawn hayrides for families (no charge) "when weather is right." Explorers: bring boots or old shoes.

From Pennsylvania: " . . . *a place apart, created of warm hearts and gentle spirit. If there is a five-star B&B designation, we give Ponda-Rowland six!*" From New Jersey: "*Sensational . . . even an antique high chair for our little one, baby silverware, a special place mat. . . . Enjoyed canoeing on the pond and the nature walk where we encountered several deer.*" From New York: "*We went for one day and stayed for four. . . . Have been back two times within two months! . . . Rooms are lovely, food delightful, Rowlands are great, antiques a pleasure to peruse . . . plenty to do.*"

Shady Lane, A Bed & Breakfast Inn

Allegheny Avenue, P.O. Box 314   **717/525-3394**
Eagles Mere, PA 17731-0314

Hosts: Pat and Dennis Dougherty
Location: Surrounded by tall trees on a mountain top with a mesmerizing view of the Endless Mountains. A five-minute walk to swimming, boating, canoeing, and fishing on the gorgeous mile-long spring-fed lake (with groomed path around perimeter). Minutes' walk to craft and gift shops in small "village." All in a Victorian "town that time forgot," a resort town since the late 1800s, with summer theater and winter cross-country skiing, ice skating, and fa-mous toboggan slide. Forty-five minutes from I-80.
Open: Year round. Two-night minimum January 20–February 22 and on weekends June–October.
Rates: $65 double. $55 single. $100 quad in carriage house. $15 additional adult, $10 children. Ten percent less for senior citizens and AAA members, and for September–June midweek stays. Package rates for murder mystery weekends.
❖ ◆ ✻ ✂

From New York and Pennsylvania: "*A place where hospitality is the most important ingredient. . . . Comfortable rooms are very clean and cozy. . . . Breakfasts are great. . . . Best thing about Shady Lane is Pat and Dennis . . . helpful without being overwhelming. . . . Well cared-for property. . . . A quiet spot, well back from the road . . . no noise . . . just peace and quiet . . . a no-sign-of-civilization view.*"

"We came on a Memorial Day weekend in 1991, fell in love with the area, and stumbled upon Shady Lane, a spacious one-floor rancher, built in 1947 and completely redone in 1987. Within five months we sold our restaurant and home and moved here with the country comfortable furnishings that were waiting for that 'someday B&B,' a dream come true. Some guests who plan to do everything, do nothing—and can't believe how much they needed this!"

In residence: In hosts' quarters, Kelly, age 12.
Bed and bath: Seven rooms (with garden or mountain view) plus a carriage house (with mountain view); all private baths. Rooms with king or queen bed have shower bath; with double or twin beds (one has a daybed also), tub/shower bath. In carriage house—two bedrooms (double and twin beds), living room, kitchen, tub and shower bath.

(Please turn page.)

Breakfast: 7:30–9:30. (For early risers, self-serve coffee, fruit, cereal, and milk.) Juice, fresh fruit salad, homemade cakes or muffins, brewed coffee, selected teas, and a hot entree such as apple French toast or fluted sausage quiche. Special diets accommodated. In dining room with panoramic view.
Plus: Individual heat controls. Two sitting rooms (one with fireplace, books, games, television). Afternoon tea with cheese, fruit, and crackers. Guest refrigerator, hot pot. Mints on pillow. Volleyball, badminton, croquet, horseshoes. Chaise longues. Hammock under the trees. Lake privileges. Access to golf and tennis at Eagles Mere Country Club.

The Bechtel Mansion Inn
400 West King Street, East Berlin, PA 17316

717/259-7760
800/331-1108

Hosts: Charles and Mariam Bechtel; Ruth Spangler, innkeeper
Location: In Pennsylvania Dutch country. In the center of East Berlin on Route 234. Near fine restaurants, antiques shops, wineries, major weaving center. Eighteen miles east of Gettysburg; 40 west of Lancaster; 100 from Washington, D.C., and Philadelphia; 58 from Baltimore.
Open: Year round. Two-night mini-

mum on holiday weekends and all of October.
Rates: May 15–November 15 $65–$95 single, $75–$110 double. November 16–May 14 $55–$75 single, $72–$100 double. Suites $85–$95 single, $125–$135 double. $20 rollaway. All rates plus 5 percent service charge. Amex, Discover, MC, Visa.
♥ ♣ ♦ ✖ ✄

For honeymooners and anniversary couples, for architecture and history buffs, for arts and crafts–oriented travelers, and for skiers too, here's a magnificent 28-room 1897 Queen Anne Victorian that the Bechtels have restored and furnished with museum-quality antiques. The mansion has original etched glass windows, gold leaf wallpaper, brass chandeliers, beautiful woodwork, and handwoven Chinese carpets. On the National Register of Historic Places, it is also in a national historic district that includes 18th-century homes, a restored gristmill, an 18th-century school, an 1820 log house, and shops located in period buildings.

Charles's grandparents and great-grandparents were Virginia innkeepers. His father grew up in a Pennsylvania Dutch family here in East Berlin. Charles has led Smithsonian groups on walking tours and spearheaded the 40-mile Historic Conewago Tour, which includes German farmland, Victorian New Oxford, and early American East Berlin. Ruth, an area resident, is also quite knowledgeable about the Amish, Brethren, and local history.

The well-traveled Bechtels are weekend hosts. Charles is a Bell Atlantic manager. Mariam, a member of Senator Robert Dole's staff, is from Kansas.

Bed and bath: Eight rooms. Six with private full bath (some with shower, others with tub/shower); two with private half bath share a shower room. Private parlor in first- and second-floor suites. Other rooms are on second floor. Twin, double, and queen beds; rollaway and portacrib available.

Breakfast: 8:30–9:30. Fruit ambrosia, orange juice, coffee cake or home baked biscuits, muffins or breads, jams and jellies, coffee or tea. Served family style.
Plus: Air conditioning in all guest areas. Beverages. Porches. Living room with oak sliding shutters, bay window; walnut, oak, and mahogany furnishings. Breakfast room (original cooking kitchen) with exhibits by local artists. For sale in carriage house shop—German nutcrackers and smokers, handmade Amish-made children's and doll furniture.

Baladerry Inn   717/337–1342
40 Hospital Road, Gettysburg, PA 17325

Hosts: Tom and Caryl O'Gara
Location: On four secluded acres, at the edge of Gettysburg Battlefield National Park. Two miles south of the park's visitor center, restaurants, and town. Near golf courses, skiing, an-
tiquing, orchards, summer stock.
Open: Year round. Two-night minimum on holidays or special events.
Rates: Double occupancy. $70–95. Singles $10 less. MC, Visa.
♥ ❖ ◆ ✗

The 1812 brick house, a hospital during the Civil War, has some stenciled rooms and some that are wallpapered. Furnishings are traditional. The gathering place is the 1977 two- storied great room—with wood stove, library, piano, and dining area. On the grounds—complete with a succession of blooming trees, shrubs, and flowers—there's a gazebo and a tennis court. Tom, who worked in the insurance industry, and Caryl, who was with a New Jersey actuarial firm, are the parents of six grown children. With fond memories of their own B&B travels in Ireland, Europe, Canada, and the United States, they purchased this historic property, added tile baths, opened in 1992, and, just as this book went to press, were reflecting on a wonderful season in this "people business. Even when it rained, guests said they loved their stay here!" The name? Tom remembers his mother talking about her birthplace, Ballaghadereen, Ireland. "She always pronounced it 'Baladerry Inn!'"

Bed and bath: Five carpeted rooms, all private baths. On first floor, two queen-bedded rooms with shower baths. On second floor, two queen-bedded rooms; one with shower bath and one with shower and Jacuzzi tub; one room with two extra-long twin beds/king option, tub/shower bath across the hall.
Breakfast: 8–10. Juice. Fresh fruit. Hot and cold cereals. Entree possibilities—poached eggs with bacon or pancakes with sausage. Served at individual tables in great room or outdoors on brick terrace.
Plus: Fireplaced living room. Individual heat thermostats. Tennis racquets. Guest refrigerator. Fresh flowers. Spacious brick terrace with wisteria arbor.

Some executives who book a meeting at an inn return on a weekend for a getaway. Some on a getaway return with colleagues for a meeting.

The Brafferton Inn

717/337-3423

44 York Street, Gettysburg, PA 17325

Hosts: Mimi and Jim Agard
Location: In downtown Gettysburg, within walking distance of Battlefield, shops, restaurants, college, and theater. Fifteen minutes to Liberty ski area.

Open: Year round.
Rates: $80 shared bath, $95 private bath. $10 additional person. MC, Visa.
♣ ♦ ✄

A gem! You have to step into this building sandwiched between a stained glass shop and a bookstore to experience the warm hospitality in Gettysburg's first house, a B&B since 1985. Established by the Agards, it is on the National Register of Historic Places and has been featured in *Country Living*.

"Who has all the talent around here?" guests often ask. When Jim, chairman of the art department at Gettysburg College and restorer of seven Vermont houses, redid this 14-room stone house (which has a 7-room pre–Civil War clapboard addition), he applied magnificent copies of 18th-century stencils on whitewashed walls and decorated with country antiques, prints, samplers, and oil paintings. A potter made bowls for sinks. Guest rooms are separated from the main house by a glass-covered atrium. In the rear of the inn, near where Continental troops gathered, there's another Agard production, an intimate flower garden and deck.

Before moving to Gettysburg, Mimi was in public relations at CBS in New York City. Here she is unofficial tour guide to "wonderful people who come for the Battlefield and to hike, bike, and enjoy summer theater and area restaurants."

In residence: Two teenagers, Melissa and Brian. "A darling cream-color toy poodle," Quincy.
Bed and bath: Eleven air-conditioned rooms, eight with (nonworking) fireplaces. In 1860 addition—private baths for six first-floor rooms with a double or a double plus a twin daybed. In original 1786 house, two full baths shared by five second-floor rooms that have one double or two twin beds. Rollaways and crib.
Breakfast: 8–9. Seasonal fruit, juice, coffee, tea, and a warm dish such as peaches and cream French toast. Served in the dining room, which features a painted primitive mural of 18 Gettysburg buildings.
Plus: Player piano. Tour of house. Mints. Flowers. Tips on "how best to see the Battlefield." For area restaurants—menus on hand and reservations made. Lady Brafferton's tea—"best scones ever," truffles and tarts, finger sandwiches, home-brewed teas; three seatings on Monday, Wednesday, and Friday; $11 per person, $8 for B&B guests.

If you've been to one B&B, you haven't been to them all.

Keystone Inn
717/337–3888
231 Hanover Street, Gettysburg, PA 17325

Hosts: Wilmer and Doris Martin
Location: Residential. Two blocks to Battlefield, 5 to Lincoln Square. Nine miles to Ski Liberty.
Open: Year round. Two-night minimum on holidays and during special events.

Rates: Double occupancy. $59 shared bath; $75 private. Suite $100. Singles $5 less. $15 rollaway. Weekday package rates (four nights for price of three) available. MC, Visa.
♥ ♣ ☀ ✗ ✁

The three-story brick house was built in 1913 by a furniture maker, father of seven, with a wide, columned porch, much natural wood, and a grand chestnut staircase. Doris, who had worked in nursing for many years, thought it "cried B&B" in 1987, when Wilmer, an owner/operator of a farm in western New York for 20 years, accepted a job as crop farmer for a major operation here. The Martins converted the property back from five apartments, wallpapered, and furnished with family pieces with "home-away-from-home" ambiance. (Hence the room names such as *Grandpa's* or *Aunt Faye's*.) "Some fine antiques, but most are comfortable and practical." In 1991 they added a suite with complete kitchen and private phone. Now daughter Rita, who has worked at a Washington, D.C., B&B, has a part-time job right here.

Bed and bath: Five rooms. On third floor—room with king/twins option and room with queen brass bed each have private en-suite tub/shower bath. Two rooms, each with antique double bed, share hall bath with claw-footed tub and shower. On second floor—suite with antique queen hand-carved oak bed, full bath, living/dining room with queen sleep sofa, TV, private phone, full kitchen complete with popcorn popper and popcorn. Rollaway available.
Breakfast: 7–9:30. Choose from a full menu with juice, oatmeal or raisin muffins, entree—cinnamon apple or blueberry pancakes, waffles, French toast, creamed eggs and toast; scrapple, ham, bacon, or sausage. Coffee, tea, milk.
Plus: Central air conditioning. Upright piano. Afternoon coffee, tea, or lemonade. Wicker-furnished porch. Magazine and books. A before-and-after restoration photo album.

> From California (and echoed by many): *"Comfortable, clean (spotless) . . . like home. Delicious breakfasts. . . . Quiet . . . a perfect location for the Battlefield, the college, or the town."*

All the B&Bs with this ◀ symbol want you to know that they are a private home set up for paying guests and that they are not an inn. Although definitions vary, these private home B&Bs tend to have one to three guest rooms. For the owners, people who enjoy meeting people, B&B is usually a part-time occupation.

Goose Chase Bed & Breakfast   717/528–8877

200 Blueberry Road, Gardners, PA 17324

Hosts: Marsha and Rich Lucidi
Location: Serene. On 25 acres. Down a country lane. In orchard, antiquing, and flea market country. Within 15 minutes' drive of New Oxford (antiquing); one hour to Lancaster. Twelve miles north of Gettysburg.

Open: Year round. Two-night minimum on weekends.
Rates: Double occupancy. $69 shared bath, twins or king bed. Private bath $79 double bed, $89 queen with fireplace. MC, Visa.
♥ ⬛ ♣ ♦ ✈ ⚌

Idyllic outside—with extensive plantings, pond, stream, vegetable and herb gardens, pastures and nature trails. With blueberry bushes (pick-your-own arrangements) uncovered by the official gardener (Rich), who had looked in three states for property where he could grow grapes. Inside, the 1759 stone colonial house is Williamsburg perfect—with stenciling, deep windowsills, wide-plank floors, country antiques, handmade quilts, and a hostess who serves breakfast in colonial garb.

When a Realtor brought the Lucidis here, Marsha, who worked for a Washington, D.C., retailer, thought that the setting was just right for a B&B. They restored and opened in 1987. The match was so good that Rich built the guest house. And a pool was installed. Now there's also a patio with Adirondack chairs. Plus a deck with views. Murder mystery weekends are scheduled. And Rich, who retired in 1992 from teaching at the University of Maryland Dental School, is finding more underbrush to clear—while Marsha declares her second career "a joy."

In residence: Garrett and Morgan, chocolate-colored Labradors—"guides for short hike through woods to neighbor's apple orchard"—and six cats, three goats, and geese.
Bed and bath: Five rooms. In main house, first-floor room with antique (rope) double bed, private tub/shower bath. On second floor, room with two twin beds and another with a king bed share a hall shower bath. In guest house, two rooms; each has queen bed (one is four-poster, one is canopied), private full bath, working fireplace.
Breakfast: At 9. Fresh fruit. A hot entree such as Italian frittata. Honey butter and pumpkin muffins. Homemade breads, jams, and jellies.
Plus: Central air conditioning. "Tea, hot mulled cider, or our own wine with appetizers." Down comforters. Turndown service. Fireplaced living room. Library. Cross-country skiing on open fields.

A ccording to many hosts:
*"Guests come with plans and discover
the joys of hammock sitting."*

Beechmont Inn

315 Broadway, Hanover, PA 17331

717/632–3013
800/553–7009

Hosts: Monna and Terry Hormel; Susan Day, assistant innkeeper
Location: On a tree-lined residential street. Near intersection of Routes 194, 94, and 116; 15 minutes east of Gettysburg Battlefield; 45 from Baltimore. Near wineries, restaurants, farmers' market, state park, skiing, antiques shops, and outlet shopping. Two hours from Washington and Philadelphia.

Open: Year round. Two-night minimum on holidays.
Rates: Per room. $70–$85 with private bath. Suites $105 with kitchenette; $105 with fireplace; $125 with fireplace and whirlpool. Weekend packages (version with horse and carriage ride is very popular).
♥ ♣ ♦ ✈

All 16 rooms of this gracious Federal house, built by the Hershey family in 1834, were completely redecorated with Federal period colors and furnishings (some reproductions) when the Hormels decided to "create a memory that lingers pleasantly long after your stay has ended." Their attention to detail includes 18th-century books in the library and a collection of Civil War and local memorabilia. Romantics have inspired the addition of (gas) fireplaces and weekend packages. Gardens and even an old-fashioned glider swing are on the landscaped grounds. It's the kind of place that business guests return to as tourists.

Now that Terry's parents, who had several businesses in Hanover, have retired to the Southwest, Monna, a Hanover native who was a crafts and needlework buyer, is chief innkeeper. Terry, an adjunct professor (business management) at a local college and a former management consultant, is weekend chef. One of his antique Jaguar automobiles is usually in residence at the inn.

Foreign language spoken: "College French."
Bed and bath: Seven rooms (three are large queen-bedded suites) with queen or double bed; all private baths. Of the two first-floor suites, one has a fireplace; one, a fireplace and whirlpool. Second-floor rooms, including fireplaced suite with kitchenette and balcony, are reached by a wide spiral staircase. Extra bed in some rooms.
Breakfast: Memorable. Weekdays 7–9, weekends 8–9. Could be asparagus-and-ham crepes with Mornay sauce, sausage torte with corn custard, or herb cheese tarts with sweet potato souffle. Shirred eggs in bread basket. French country eggs. Freshly baked muffins or sweet breads. Spiced coffee, teas, juice, York County Fair prizewinning homemade granola. Desserts offered on weekends. In dining room, outside under the trumpet vine trellis, or in bed.
Plus: Air-conditioned guest and common rooms. Formal parlor and library. Wicker-furnished back porch. Vine-covered veranda. Flagstone patio with park bench under a 125-year-old magnolia tree. Off-street parking.

> Favorite quote from room diary: "*Well, I have no romance to report. (My sweetie at home will be happy about that!) I am a working girl used to boring hotels. I just came back from a relaxing evening on the porch petting the [outside] tabby cat. Thanks for making this a lovely 'working' vacation.*"

Conewago House
New Oxford, PA

Location: Gorgeous. On a ridge, on ½ mile of river frontage. Eight miles east of Gettysburg. Within 20 minutes of Ski Liberty and Ski Roundtop. Close to Caledonia State Park. "Great area for history, antiquing, the outdoors, Amish country." Fifty-eight miles from Baltimore harbor, 90 minutes from D.C. Beltway.
Reservations: Year round through Guesthouses, page 224. Two-night minimum for guest house accommodations.
Rates: $95. Second-floor riverview $115, third-floor suite $135; whole house $1,800 per week. Guest house $200 (two to four people), two-night minimum; $1,200 per week.
♥ ❖ ◀ ✕ ✄

One of a kind. When, in 1989, the prominent Baltimore architect finished redoing the National Register property, "B&B just seemed a natural outgrowth." Maples arch over the long driveway of this 1908 Arts and Crafts brown Shingle Style house. A wonderful Palladian window frames the stairway. In the stone-fireplaced living room, and in the dining room too, there is 6-foot-high wainscoting. Furnishings include pottery collections, antiques, some 1940s and '50s collectibles, and some ultramodern pieces. A large glass sun room looks onto the river. The entire tall-ceilinged guest house, formerly the stables, now has cedar walls, ceilings, and floors. Enormous glass garage doors give a view of the 50-by-25-foot brick swimming pool—what a setting—on a two-acre landscaped "island" surrounded by old sugar maples. From here you can see the rustic Adirondack-style gazebo up on a knoll. On most weekends the owner/architect is in residence and happy to give tours of his private museum, which has one of the country's largest collections of contemporary artist-designed furniture. If this all sounds familiar, you have been reading *Mid-Atlantic Country, Baltimore* magazine, the *Baltimore Sun*, or, most recently, *Country Home*.

In residence: Mighty Dog, a Jack Russell terrier. On weekends, Aalto, a cocker/Gordon setter mix. ("Everyone wants to buy one.")
Bed and bath: Three rooms and one suite in main house. Two bedrooms in guest house. Luxurious baths. Main house: on second floor, one huge riverview room (used to be two) with queen bed, elaborate bath with separate area for each fixture. Room with queen bed, full bath. Room with twin bed, shared full bath. Third-floor suite has queen-bedded room, large living room, bath with tub and shower. Guest house: two second-floor rooms, each with queen bed, large vanity. Downstairs, full bath, large dining room/sitting room, and small full kitchen.
Breakfast: Self-serve continental with bagels, muffins, breads, juices, cheeses, jams, coffee, tea.
Plus: Central air conditioning. Laundry in each building. Screened porch off huge kitchen of main house. Use of canoe and life vest. Ice skating when river freezes.

Hickory Bridge Farm

717/643-5261

96 Hickory Bridge Road, Orrtanna, PA 17353

Hosts: Nancy Jean Hammett and Mary Lynn Martin
Location: Quiet. On 100 acres in the Appalachian Mountain foothills. Apple blossoms, crops, trout fishing (bring license) in meandering stream right here. Eight miles west of Gettysburg, 60 to Baltimore. Five miles to Ski Liberty.
Open: Year round. Closed between Christmas and New Year's. Two-night minimum on weekends; exception when one-night opening is available one week prior to date requested. Reservations required.

(Restaurant open to the public on weekend evenings, to private groups weekdays.)
Rates: Monday–Thursday: $79 cottage; in farmhouse, $79 room with private bath, $110 (three people) or $135 (four people) two rooms with one bath; $150 (five people) or $195 (six people) three rooms with two baths. Weekends—$89 cottage; $89 one farmhouse room with private bath; $195 (five people) or $225 (six people) three rooms, two baths. Crib $10. MC, Visa.
♥ ♨ ♣ ✈

From Canada, from England, and "from all over," guests discover and return to this unique B&B, which evolved from Mrs. Hammett's research of the area a quarter century ago. When she found that a franchise was going to buy a local tavern located in a true country inn, an old stagecoach stop, the family bought, restored, and ran it. In 1977 they sold that property and bought Hickory Bridge—with B&B in the farmhouse (great for families) and in the cottages on the wooded hill. In the restaurant, located in the old barn across the street from the farmhouse, they displayed many farm-related antiques and began their tradition of all-you-can-eat farm-style meals with a set menu. Daughter Mary Lynn, restaurant manager, was in college then. Now her children have a steer as a 4-H project on the property. You'll probably meet her jeans-clad dad, whom Mary Lynn calls "a real country doctor." Nancy Jean continues to cook the breakfasts and greet "a long list of friends and friends of friends who feel like extended family."

Bed and bath: Seven air-conditioned rooms. In farmhouse, private shower bath for one room with queen bed. One room with queen and one with a double bed share a full bath. Four country-decorated cottages, each with a queen or two double beds, private shower bath, working Franklin fireplace.
Breakfast: 8:30–9. Farm style. Pancakes, sausage, eggs, bacon, homegrown fruits, homemade jams, apple butter, and potato bread. In farmhouse dining room or on deck.
Plus: Fireplaced farmhouse living room. Porches. Flowers. Mints. Use of bicycles. On the farm—covered bridge over stream; swing set; antique fire engine. Next to washhouse, a country store/museum that has jams and penny candy for sale, enormous collection of items—from boots and lace to tobacco bags and cash register—for display. Friday–Saturday dinner (starts at 5, last seating at 8; bring your own wine) $15.95 per person.

Curtinview
Howard, PA

Location: Secluded. On 20 wooded acres. Up a gravel lane, high on a hill overlooking historic village. Six miles north of Bellefonte. Within walking distance of Curtin Village. Two miles off I–80, exit 23, Mileburg. Twenty-five minutes to Penn State.
Reservations: Year round through

Rest & Repast, page 295. Two-night minimum on major events' weekends.
Rates: $55 per room. $15 one-night surcharge per room on peak weekends. $25 sofa bed if entire suite is booked by one party. $20 rollaway.
♥ 🛏 ♣ ✗ ✂

A complete turnabout by the couple who made mid-1980s headlines—"Operatic Soprano Gets Practice Raising Roof"—when they rebuilt a Bellefonte Victorian home that was, like this house, high on a hill. In 1989 the consulting engineer (who is also known for the award-winning 1947 Stimson fabric-covered plane that he restored) and his wife, a well-known performer/music teacher, built this brand-new log home. In 1990 they planted a vineyard here. Guests enjoy the wide front deck that overlooks the Allegheny foothills and Curtin Village, the community with a dominating mansion built by Richard Curtin of iron industry fame. In the evening you may see deer, bear, or other wildlife at this quiet getaway.

In residence: Two cats, Midnight and Tabatha.
Bed and bath: On private second-floor loft, two cathedral-ceilinged rooms—one with an antique spool double bed and one with two twin beds; a common sitting area with TV and, if entire suite booked by one party, a double sofa bed. One tub/shower bath. Rollaway available.
Breakfast: 7–9. Juice, fresh fruit, yogurt, cereal, muffins or French toast, coffee and tea.
Plus: Air conditioning and ceiling fans in guest rooms. Welcoming beverage. Hiking and cross-country skiing right here and/or in nearby state parklands.

Webb Farm Bed & Breakfast   717/725–3591
RR 1, Box 441, Spruce Run Road, Loganton, PA 17747

Hosts: Bud Webb and Sharon Maurer
Location: Quiet. Three miles from exit 27, I–80. On top of Central Pennsylvania mountains. "A great place for hunting." Within an hour's drive of Penn State, Williamsport (home of the Little League Museum), and

Woolrich Outlet Store. Fourteen miles to Ravensburg State Park.
Open: Year round.
Rates: Shared bath $45 double, $35 single. Private bath $65 double, $55 single. $10 crib.
🛏 ♣ ✗ ✂

"Bed and breakfast is something we had thought about. In 1991, with our children grown and married, we bought this large 1940s two-storied frame house that just seemed perfect. It's located on the Old Florida Fruit Farm, named for a man from Florida who planted 100 acres of apple trees over 100 years ago. It's surrounded by a white fence enclosing 1.6 acres. Outside the fence are fields of grain. We have a before-and-after photo album that shows what we did before opening here. Furnishings are nothing fancy, but they are comfortable. There's a double waterfall hidden atop the mountain about a half mile from here. And we tell guests about the covered bridge at Logan Mills."

Bud is a fertilizer dealer and farmer. Sharon is an office clerk and greenhouse operator.

Bed and bath: Four second-floor corner rooms overlook fields and old apple trees. Two rooms, each with a double bed, share a hall shower/tub bath. One room has king bed, private shower bath. One has a queen bed and a queen water bed, private shower bath. Crib available.
Breakfast: At 7. Orange or tomato juice. Fruit salad. Bananas and cold cereal. Fruit-of-the-season muffins. Freshly brewed coffee. Buffet style in dining room.
Plus: Window fans. Refreshments. Guest kitchenette. Large outdoor deck. Glasses, ice bucket, ice. Living room with television and VCR.

From Illinois: *"Warm hospitality . . . immaculately clean . . . nicely prepared and good food."* From Virginia: *"Location in mountains is beautiful. . . . We actually saw a group of deer just across the street from their home."* From Pennsylvania: *"Even in summer, we used a light sheet blanket. . . . Spring was beautiful with apple blossoms. . . . Enjoyed the countryside and walking along the country road."*

The Carriage House at Stonegate

RD 1, Box 11A   717/433–4340
Montoursville, PA 17754   fax 717/433–4563

Hosts: Harold and Dena Mesaris
Location: On 30 wooded acres along the banks of Mill Creek. On Route 87, a minute from I–180. Within 30 minutes of Lycoming, Bucknell, and Bloomsburg. Six miles east of Williamsport. Two miles from Williamsport/Lycoming County airport. Close to Crystal Lake Cross-Country Ski Center, hiking, fishing, and hunting.
Open: Year round.
Rates: $50 one room, $70 two rooms. $10 rollaway.
♥ ⭢ ⁂ ◆

From Virginia: *"Private, comfortable, and roomy. . . . Breakfast was great, the woods a mini adventure at every turn. . . . Gracious hosts who were helpful with information about the area."*

A haven at the end of the road—even in a winter's storm! Your own home away from home, a 1,400-square-foot getaway, is in a converted carriage

(Please turn page.)

house located just 30 yards from the main house, one of the oldest farmhouses in the lower Loyasock Creek Valley. Remodeled in 1985, the two-storied B&B has wide-board floors, hand-hewn beams, some country antiques, and some modern pieces. Harold and Dena usually book one party—could be a couple or up to 10 guests (for a wedding)—at a time.

If you'd like, there are opportunities to "meet the whole family"—Harold, a pilot and aircraft accident investigator; Dena, a teacher who is active in the community; their teenagers; and all the farm animals. For what Harold calls moderately difficult exercise, there are accessible old logging roads. For a little history, the hosts will tell you about the early valley settlement and direct you to the old family cemetery located about a quarter mile from the B&B. And a Harold-designed tour takes you to several state parks (one has 20 waterfalls) and three covered bridges.

In residence: In main house, teenagers—Allison, Meghan, Darcey, and Judd. One Newfoundland, several Persian cats, one sheep, two ducks, three geese, eight chickens—all with names.
Foreign languages spoken: Some Spanish and German.
Bed and bath: Two second-level rooms—one with a double bed and one with a four-poster queen bed—share a full and a half bath. Rollaway and crib available.
Breakfast: 7:30–10. Homemade muffins. French toast, cheese/bacon/potato quiche, or ham-and-cheese pudding. Fruit, juice, coffee, tea. Harold cooks breakfast and brings it to you in a basket.
Plus: On first floor, large sitting room with cable TV, dining area, fully equipped kitchen, refrigerator stocked with snacks. Window and floor fans in summer. Babysitting. Swing set. Electric blankets. Record for wildlife seen by early morning walkers: six turkeys and three deer.

The Bodine House   717/546–8949
307 South Main Street, Muncy, PA 17756

Hosts: David and Marie Louise Smith
Location: On a tree-lined street in a National Historic District, 3 blocks from center of Muncy. Ten minutes from I–80 and U.S. Route 15. Bucknell University and the city of Williamsport 15 minutes away. Within 30 minutes of sports, wineries, two state parks in Endless Mountains, summer theater.
Open: Year round.
Rates: Per room. $50 double bed, private hall bath. $60 canopied double bed, private bath. $65 two single beds, private bath, fireplace. Singles $5 less. $15 rollaway.
✶ ⅋

From Maryland: *"Beautifully kept and elegant home in a lovely small town. Even though it rained most of the hours we were there, we enjoyed walking in the rain and coming back to the candlelit sitting room for refreshments."*

Colonial Homes, in a glorious four-page spread, pictured this restored Federal townhouse, which was occupied by the same family for about 165 years. It has been home to the Smiths since they moved from Washington, D.C., for a quieter pace. They had always admired this small town as they drove through on their way to visit relatives. When they moved here 15 years ago, they furnished with 18th- and 19th-century antiques. The fireplaced living room, lit by candles and furnished as a typical Philadelphia townhouse in Marie Louise's home city, includes a baby grand piano that has been enjoyed by several talented guests. A portrait, painted by a German itinerant artist, is of the hostess's great-great-grandmother at about age 90. A dining room bureau was David's great-grandmother's.

In Washington, David was a marketing manager; here he is host/chef/gift and picture-framing shop owner. Marie Louise is business manager in a physician's office.

Bed and bath: Four second-floor rooms, each with individual heat control and air conditioner. Two rooms with canopied double bed, private bath (one with tub and shower, one with shower). One with two single beds, working fireplace, private bath with shower. One with double bed, private full hall bath.
Breakfast: 7:30–8:30. Hot and cold cereal, bacon and eggs, toast, muffins, coffee, tea, milk, juices. Served by candlelight; in winter, by the dining room fireplace.
Plus: Refreshments 5–7 p.m. Line-dried sheets. Free use of bicycles. Brick garden patio. Second-floor study/library. Off-street parking.

General Potter Farm
Potters Mills, PA

Location: Set way back from road. On pretty acreage (for walks) with Sinking Creek at the bottom of the property. Thirteen miles east of Penn State University. Near Amish country, caves, museums, and state recreational areas. Coming soon—an entrance via a less-traveled road, over a stream and through the woods.

Reservations: Year round through Rest & Repast, page 295. Two-night minimum on major events' weekends.
Rates: Double occupancy. Shared bath $55–65 double. Private bath $65–75 double. One-night surcharge on peak weekends $15.
♥ ⁂ ✄ ⚍

The search for an old house ended in 1990 with this B&B, which had been restored in part by previous owners. It's a 17-room red brick farmhouse—the oldest part was built in 1820—that is on the National Register of Historic Places. A large fireplaced living room overlooks the pasture, where the boarded horses—eight are draft, two are thoroughbreds—add to the scene.

What a combination! The host's (three-generation) furniture store, which sells reproductions, has decorators who assisted with the selection of paint and wallcoverings for the guest rooms. Because the hostess's father, an antiques dealer, imports English scrubbed pine (farm) pieces, some here may change from time to time. Others are accent pieces in the host's store, located in an 1880s barn in State College.

(Please turn page.)

By the time you read this, perhaps the first floor will have been redecorated and the major landscaping plan with plants, fencing, walkways and herb garden will be well under way. And maybe you'll meet some former guests who couldn't get a booking but wanted come by to visit the folks who love sharing their country home.

In residence: In hosts' quarters, two preschoolers, one golden retriever, and one black Lab. In the barn, two cats.
Bed and bath: Three second-floor rooms. One with two antique twin beds shares shower bath with room that has queen sleigh bed. Room with queen pencil-post bed has private en-suite shower/bath.
Breakfast: Usually 8–9:30. Fruit, juice, baked goods, yogurt and granola, coffee and tea. Plus, on weekends, stuffed French toast, Belgian waffles, quiche, or strata. In fireplaced formal dining room or on deck overlooking creek.
Plus: Homemade cookies for evening snacks.

The John Thompson House B&B

Stormstown, PA

Location: On 26 scenic acres with cornfield, paths, woods, pond. At the foot of Bald Eagle Mountain. In the village of Stormstown, on a road shared by farm equipment. Eight miles west of Penn State.
Reservations: Year round through Rest & Repast, page 295. Two-night minimum on major events' weekends.
Rates: $50–60 shared bath, $55–75 private bath. $15 one-night surcharge on peak weekends.
♥ ♨ ✿ ✈ ⚟

"In 1990 we left our jobs in the human resources department of a company. My husband was in the training and development department (he consults now), and I was in recruiting and employee services. We moved from the Philadelphia area to this 1817 Georgian stucco house with random-width pine floors, 9-over-6 bubble glass windows, and all this glorious land complete with a meandering stream. We painted, replastered, and added a bath. Furnishings include some reproductions, anything we happen to find that we like, and antiques including a lock display case (everyone asks about it) that is filled with redware. There's a welcoming electric candle in every front window. Oil lamps are in all the rooms. Beyond B&B, we weren't sure what we would do, but we have become small-scale farmers with organic tomatoes, pumpkins, and herbs. Depending on the season, some guests wiggle toes in the pond or cross-country ski (we do too) on the trails. Some accompany our son to the pond while he points out the fish and blue heron or talks about the woodchuck seen yesterday. We're meeting many who come for Penn State events—and business travelers too."

Guests leave this B&B with the feeling that they have visited with friends.

In residence: Son Doug, "our official guide." Herman, a friendly chocolate Lab; Shakespeare, "a recluse of a cat."
Foreign language spoken: Some Spanish. "Please speak slowly."

Bed and bath: Three second-floor rooms. Master bedroom with double bed with feather bed, private tub and shower bath. At other end of hallway, one room with a double bed with feather bed and a queen sofa bed and a room with two twin beds share a bath that has separate shower and an unusual tub—"even shower lovers use it"—with an oil light on one wide rim.

Breakfast: At guests' convenience. (Caution: Those who sleep on feather beds tend to oversleep.) Juice, fruit, homemade muffins or banana bread, pancakes with apple cider syrup and sausage or omelet, coffee or tea. In spacious dining room or on screened deck with view of meadows and stream.

Plus: Fruit basket. Fresh flowers. Forgotten items. Screened porch with view of meadows and stream. Volleyball and croquet.

From Pennsylvania: *"Beautiful people. . . . Everything was perfect. . . . Take a walk in the field and woods before breakfast. It's great!"*

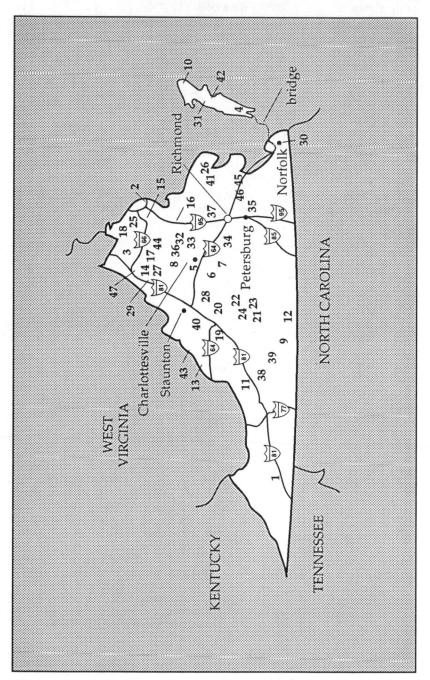

The numbers on this map indicate the locations of B&Bs described in detail in this chapter.

VIRGINIA

1 **Abingdon**
   Summerfield Inn, *317*
2 **Arlington**
   Memory House, *318*
3 **Boyce**
   The River House, *319*
4 **Cape Charles**
   Nottingham Ridge, *320*
   Pickett's Harbor, *321*
   Sea Gate Bed & Breakfast, *322*
5 **Charlottesville**
   Alderman House, *323*
   Bollingwood, *323*
   The Inn at Monticello, *324*
   Recoletta, *325*
   Sunnyfields, *325*
6 **Charlottesville: North Garden**
   Ammonett Farm, *326*
   Ingleside, *327*
7 **Charlottesville: Scottsville**
   Chester, *328*
   High Meadows Vineyard &
   Mountain Sunset Inn, *329*
8 **Charlottesville: Stanardsville**
   Edgewood Farm Bed &
   Breakfast, *330*
9 **Chatham**
   House of Laird, *331*
10 **Chincoteague**
   The Watson House, *332*
11 **Christiansburg**
   The Oaks Bed & Breakfast
   Country Inn, *333*
12 **Cluster Springs**
   Oak Grove Plantation, *334*
13 **Covington**
   Milton Hall Bed and Breakfast
   Inn, *335*
14 **Edinburg**
   Mary's Country Inn, *336*
15 **Fairfax**
   The Bailiwick Inn, *337*
16 **Fredericksburg**
   La Vista Plantation, *338*
17 **Front Royal**
   Chester House Inn, *339*

18 **Leesburg: Lincoln**
   Springdale Country Inn, *340*
19 **Lexington**
   Llewellyn Lodge, *341*
20 **Lexington: Raphine**
   Oak Spring Farm and
   Vineyard, *342*
21 **Lynchburg**
   Langhorne Manor, *344*
   Lynchburg Mansion Inn Bed
   and Breakfast, *345*
   The Madison House Bed &
   Breakfast, *346*
22 **Lynchburg: Amherst**
   Dulwich Manor Bed &
   Breakfast, *347*
23 **Lynchburg: Madison Heights**
   Winridge Bed & Breakfast, *348*
24 **Lynchburg: Monroe**
   "St. Moor" House, *349*
25 **Middleburg**
   Middleburg Country Inn, *350*
26 **Mollusk**
   Greenvale Manor Waterfront
   Inn, *351*
27 **Mount Jackson**
   Widow Kip's Shenandoah
   Inn, *352*
28 **Nellysford**
   The Acorn Inn, Inc., *353*
   The Meander Inn, *354*
29 **New Market**
   A Touch of Country, *355*
30 **Norfolk**
   Page House Inn, *356*
31 **Onancock**
   The Spinning Wheel Bed and
   Breakfast, *357*
32 **Orange**
   Hidden Inn, *358*
   The Holladay House, *359*
33 **Orange: Gordonsville**
   Sleepy Hollow Farm B&B, *360*
34 **Palmyra**
   Danscot House, *361*
35 **Petersburg**
   The High Street Inn, *362*

36 **Pratts**
Colvin Hall Bed and
Breakfast, *363*
37 **Richmond**
The Emmanuel Hutzler
House, *364*
Summerhouse, *365*
University of Richmond area
B&B, *366*
The William Catlin House
Inn, *366*
38 **Roanoke**
Mary Bladon House, *367*
39 **Smith Mountain Lake**
The Manor at Taylor's
Store, *368*
40 **Staunton**
Ashton Country House, *369*
Frederick House, *370*
The Sampson Eagon Inn, *371*
Thornrose House at Gypsy
Hill, *372*
41 **Urbanna**
The Duck Farm Inn, *373*
42 **Wachapreague**
The Burton House, *374*

43 **Warm Springs**
Anderson Cottage Bed &
Breakfast, *375*
44 **Washington**
Caledonia Farm, *376*
The Foster-Harris House, *377*
Sycamore Hill House &
Gardens, *378*
45 **Williamsburg**
Colonial Capital Bed &
Breakfast, *379*
Legacy of Williamsburg Inn, *381*
Liberty Rose B&B, *382*
Newport House, *383*
Williamsburg Cottage #10, *384*
Williamsburg Manor Bed and
Breakfast, *384*
Williamsburg Sampler Bed and
Breakfast, *385*
46 **Williamsburg: Charles City**
Edgewood Plantation, *386*
North Bend Plantation B&B, *387*
47 **Woodstock**
The Country Fare, *388*

_____Virginia Reservation Services_____

Bensonhouse

2036 Monument Avenue, Richmond, VA 23220

Phone: 804/353–6900. Monday–Friday 10–6. Weekend hours vary.

Listings: 20 hosted private residences. Some inns. Most are within 10 minutes of Richmond's sites and attractions. A few are in Petersburg, Williamsburg, Fredericksburg, and on the Eastern Shore of Virginia. Almost all have private baths. Most are air-conditioned and are located in or near historic areas. Directory ($3) with SASE.

Reservations: Prefer two to three weeks' advance notice but will accommodate last-minute requests if possible.

Rates: $55–$115 single. $60–$135 double. Some hosts offer discounts for families. Deposit of 50 percent of total stay required. Deposit, less $20, refunded if seven days' notice of cancellation is provided; no refund with shorter notice. Amex, Discover, MC, Visa; cash or checks preferred. ◆

As a businesswoman who travels frequently, Lyn Benson appreciates unique accommodations with hosts who are sensitive to guests' needs. Through her well-established and respected service she makes a special effort to match guest to host as well as home "to maximize the B&B experience."

Plus: Fully furnished unhosted self-contained apartments, carriage houses, and homes for relocating executives. Leased for a month to several months at a time.

Guesthouses

P.O. Box 5737, Charlottesville, VA 22905

Phone: 804/979–7264. Monday–Friday 12–5; emergency call forwarding on weekends. Closed weekends, major holidays, and Christmas week.

Fax: 804/293–7791, 12–5 weekdays.

Listings: 60 regular hosts. More than 150 for major University of Virginia weekends. Almost all listings are hosted private residences. Six are inns. Directory is $1.

Reservations: Two weeks' advance notice preferred.

Rates: $48–$100 single, $52–$200 double. $4 surcharge for one-night weekend stay in spring and fall. Some weekly rates available. Deposit of 25 percent of total fee plus state and local tax required. With seven days' advance notice of cancellation, deposit less $15 service fee refunded. Amex, MC, Visa for deposits only. ◆

Originally established for America's bicentennial year, Mary Hill Caperton's service has many experienced hosts in the Charlottesville/Albemarle County area. Most are within 20–30 minutes of Monticello, Ash Lawn, and University of Virginia. The wide range of rates includes luxurious estates, antebellum homes, and modest comfortable residences. Some homes are on the National Register and have been on the annual "Historic Garden Week in Virginia" tour.

Plus: Short-term (one week to three months) housing available in apartments or efficiency suites and in guest cottages with host nearby.

Princely Bed & Breakfast, Ltd.

819 Prince Street, Alexandria, VA 22314

Phone: 703/683–2159. Monday–Friday 10–6.

Listings: 30. Mostly hosted private residences. A few unhosted apartments.

Reservations: One week's advance notice and two-day minimum stay preferred.

Rates: $80–$90 per room. $10 surcharge for a one-night stay. Monthly rates available. Deposit required is equal to one night's stay. With more than seven days' notice of cancellation, full refund will be made, minus $20 service charge. ◆ ✻

"Deluxe accommodations and beautifully served breakfasts" have been offered by E. J. Mansmann's Alexandria hosts since he established the service in 1981 on retiring from the State Department. All have private baths and air conditioning. Most hosts live in Old Town in historically significant and antiques-furnished houses (many are part of benefit tours) near fast, frequent transportation to Washington, D.C. The oldest house owned by a host was built in 1750. (Alexandria is 8 miles from George Washington's Mount Vernon.) One 1820 house is in the cobblestoned Captain's Row block.

Plus: Some hosts take guests sightseeing.

KEY TO SYMBOLS
♥ Lots of honeymooners come here.
⚐ Families with children are very welcome. (Please see page xii.)
☛ "Please emphasize that we are a private home, not an inn."
❖ Groups or private parties sometimes book the entire B&B.
◆ Travel agents' commission paid. (Please see page xii.)
✻ Sorry, no guests' pets are allowed.
✔ No smoking inside *or* no smoking at all, even on porches.

Virginia B&Bs

Summerfield Inn   703/628–5905
101 West Valley Street, Abingdon, VA 24201

Hosts: Champe and Don Hyatt
Location: In historic district of a town with "five excellent restaurants" and mountain views. One block from Barter Theatre, the country's oldest continuously running repertory theater. Near Virginia Creeper hiking and biking trail; 20 minutes from Appalachian Trail. One hour west of Blue Ridge Parkway, two from Roanoke. One-half mile from I–81, exit 17.
Open: March–December. Reservations recommended April–October; required other months. Two-night minimum on special weekends.
Rates: $55–$60 single; $65–$75 double. Ten percent discount on stays of three or more nights. Amex, MC, Visa.
♥ ❖ ◆ ✈

> From half a dozen states: *"Elegant . . . charming . . . hospitable hosts. . . . A pleasant experience for a woman traveling alone. . . . The stay was the highlight of our trip. . . . A marvelous blend of yesterday and today. . . . Breathtaking antiques. . . . Breakfast served with china, sterling, and crystal. . . . A jewel!"*

Those comments hint at the praise heaped on the home environment created by the Hyatts, hosts who enjoyed B&Bs during their own travels in California. They thought about Don's retirement from dentistry and bought a grand 1920s house in Abingdon, the town where Champe's parents lived for 25 years while her father was manager and president of the Martha Washington Inn. After extensive renovations the Hyatts opened in 1987, with color schemes—soft pinks and greens—chosen from a living room portrait of their children, who are now grown. The paneled dining room with Oriental decor, the tall king four-poster, and the wraparound veranda with welcoming flags and popular porch rockers became part of a glorious *Virginia Southwest* magazine feature. A jewel indeed.

In residence: "Pepper, our resident miniature schnauzer, the perfect pet, has been called 'the little square dog.'"
Bed and bath: Four spacious second-floor rooms, all with fans on 10-foot ceilings, private full baths (robes provided for those that are unattached). King, double, or twin beds.
Breakfast: 7–9:30. Juice, fruit, muffins or pastries, coffee, milk. In elegant dining room or on porch.
Plus: Sun room with plenty of plants, wicker furnishings. Guest pantry with refrigerator, ice, juice, soft drinks, setups. Phone jacks in rooms.

> From Marilou Awiakta, Cherokee/Appalachian poet: *"A road-weary poet looks for a place with good vibes. Warm, quiet, private, hospitable—and interesting. Hosts Champe and Don Hyatt create the vibes. Summerfield Inn is the place."*

Memory House

703/534-4607

6404 North Washington Boulevard, Arlington, VA 22205-1954

Hosts: John and Marlys McGrath
Location: A corner lot in a residential neighborhood on Route 237. Ten-minute drive to Arlington Cemetery and Washington, D.C. One block from the East Falls Church subway station. Three blocks from Route 29 and I-66, exit 69. Within 9 blocks of shops and restaurants; 4 to bike trails.
Open: Year round. Usually, two-night minimum on weekends.
Rates: $65-$70 single. $70-$75 double. $10 children; $5 infants (bring portacrib).
♥ ⛵ ♦ ✈ ⚂

A 1985 *Washington Post Home* magazine cover feature told the seven-year restoration story of this 1899 house, which has been on house tours for the Smithsonian Institution Associates and the Christian Assembly Center building fund. In 1986 a *Post* feature on Memory House inspired the McGraths to host. (It was a natural for Marlys, whose parents had a resort.) Among their memorable guests: Californians who were snowed in for four days—and eventually moved nearby.

Outside, the McGraths painted in six tones, and they replaced (a traffic-stopping procedure) the decorative iron cresting atop the highest peak. Inside, the parlor and dining rooms walls were painted and stenciled. Many of the antiques were restored by Marlys, who has made good use of her seventh-grade carpentry instruction (in Iowa) as well as other courses in interior design, upholstery, chair caning, and picture framing. Six-foot-five John, who owns a men's hair styling salon, did all the prizewinning needlepoint. The newel post came from a similiar house that was torn down. The Victorian powder room has a door from Washington's Dodge Hotel. And everywhere there arc lots of collectibles.

In residence: Megan, age 16.
Bed and bath: Two rooms with air conditioners and TV (black and white). Small cot for child. First floor—in back, beyond the dining room—room with double bed, private half bath, plus hall bath with claw-foot tub. Second-floor guest room has twin beds, sink in room, shared hall tub bath. Attachment for shampooing available.
Breakfast: At 7:30, 8, or 8:30. Expanded continental. In dining room set with hand-crocheted tablecloths and John's mother's antique Wedgwood china and Depression-era glassware.
Plus: Welcoming beverage. In parlor, a restored antique Reed organ and a Hammond electric organ. Robes. Fresh flowers. Wicker-furnished porch. By arrangement, pickup for arriving guests at subway.

> From California: *"Warm and welcoming . . . enjoyed handiwork, antiques, breakfasts. . . . Made us feel right at home."*

Unless otherwise stated, rates in this book are per room for two and include breakfast in addition to all the amenities in "Plus." As for taxes and gratuities, please see page xi.

The River House

Route 2, Box 135, Boyce, VA 22620

703/837–1476
fax 703/837–2399

Hosts: Cornelia and Don Niemann
Location: On corner of Route 50 and Shenandoah River; on 17 acres, 100 yards from 2-mile-long walking and cycling dirt road that borders the Shenandoah River. Three miles to Appalachian Trail; 14 east of I–81 and Winchester; 16 west of Middleburg; 67 to Washington, D.C.
Open: Year round. Two-night minimum on holiday weekends.

Rates: Ground floor: $90 queen, $100 king/twins. Second floor: $80 double bed, small bath; $85 king/twins, shower bath; $95 double, tub/shower bath. Saturday night–only reservations, 25 percent surcharge. Scheduled "Enter Laughing" and murder mystery weekend packages include superb dinner. $15 rollaway or crib. MC, Visa.
♥ ♯ ♯ ♣ ♦ ✄

Now the Niemanns are known nationwide for their winter "Enter Laughing" play-reading weekends for closet thespians. Manhattanites who met on stage ("Don was a fabulous actor"), they have lived for 25 years in their seven-fireplaced fieldstone house. A B&B since 1985, it was a military hospital during the Civil War and a popular restaurant in the 1940s. "We've given it five major overhaulings, and we have furnished with a personal flair in stage-set style with Chinese, French Provincial, some so-called treasures, and some beautiful and unusual pieces, including a 150-year-old cathedral chime clock that belonged to Don's grandfather."

Cornelia, a fireball who calls herself "a woman of an uncertain age," is a former professional actress/teacher of French ("my first language")/community theater director. She shares recipes—with the caveat that she never measures. Don (just as lovable), a former radio announcer who became an independent school headmaster at age 28, is now headmaster emeritus of the country day school he founded in 1982, a year after he had a serious automobile accident.

Foreign languages spoken: French (fluently) and Spanish.
Bed and bath: Five large air-conditioned rooms, all with private baths *and* working fireplaces. On 1780 ground floor (former slave quarters) with private exterior entrance, two rooms with shower baths "just outside the door." One with a queen and a double sofa bed; other with walk-in fireplace, king/twins option, and double sofa bed. Stair lift available to rooms on 1820 second floor. One large double-bedded room has en-suite tub/shower bath. Room with king/twins option, shower bath/dressing room is connected to double-bedded room that has very small shower bath. Rollaways and cribs.
Breakfast: Four-course brunch at 10 in dining room. (Continental self-serve available for early risers.) Juice, fruit, meat, egg dish, two vegetables, hot breads. Hot beverages. Special diets accommodated. Menu never repeated, regardless of length of stay. Family style on antique linens. Up to two hours, "maybe more!"

(Please turn page.)

Plus: Fruit and mineral water in rooms. Snacks in stocked kitchenettes on each floor. Fireplaced living and dining rooms. Piano. Bathrobes. Huge collection of plays. Activity and restaurant suggestions. Cycling maps. Games. Books. Grandchildren's swings, sandbox, toys. Private phones. Fax and copier available.

> From Virginia: *"Don and Cornelia are the most charming couple we have ever met . . . a relaxing visit in the countryside. . . . We hiked . . . visited caverns. . . . The food is excellent and the atmosphere is very romantic."*

Nottingham Ridge   804/331–1010
P.O. Box 97B, Cape Charles, VA 23310   804/442–5011

Hosts: Bonnie Nottingham and M. S. Scott
Location: Secluded. High on a hill, at the end of a pretty winding lane through woods and farmland. With fox and deer and, in the pond, beavers. Four miles north of Bay Bridge Tunnel, halfway between (one hour from) Williamsburg and Chincotea-gue, just off state highway 13. Near winery. Ten minutes to golf course, tennis courts, charter fishing boats.
Open: Year round. Two-night minimum on weekends April–October.
Rates: $50–$60 single. $75–$90 double. $20 extra person. Family rates available.
♥ ♨ ☙ ♣ ✄ ✔

> Excerpts from many guests' letters: *"A quiet place with a beautiful view of the bay, in lovely pine woods, well off the beaten track . . . I travel all over the world and would rate this B&B the best . . . a beautifully appointed, comfortable home. . . charming hostess and unbelievable breakfasts. . . . Shared flavor of the community, information about local activities and eating places. . . . A short walk over the dunes to secluded private beach. . . . Breathtaking sunsets."*

A whole different world. Still, virtually undeveloped. No wonder many guests, enchanted with this unique spot, ask if there might be nearby property for sale.

In 1975, when the family was younger, the Nottinghams had the two-storied brick colonial house with raised panels and heavy woodwork built by a local craftsman. It's warm and cozy, with antiques, reproductions, and collectibles. A welcoming fire glows in the family room during chilly months. "Guests sigh—winter or summer—when they arrive at what they call their 'retreat.'" As guests attest, Bonnie, who loves to cook, knows the art of hospitality. Cohost Scotty's family has lived in the area for several generations; he loves the outdoors and local history.

In residence: Mutt, a bird dog.
Bed and bath: Three rooms with private baths. One first-floor room with private entrance, queen-size canopied bed, full bath, bay view. Upstairs, two rooms with queen-size beds; one with full bath and bay view, the other with shower bath. Rollaway and sleeping bag available.
Breakfast: 6–9. Maybe Virginia baked ham, sweet potato biscuit, bacon quiche, waffles, homemade bread and (sometimes hot) jam. In country kitchen or on porch.

Plus: Central air conditioning. Evening wine and cheese. Fireplaced family room. Acres of private beach. Suggestions for Eastern Shore back roads, the state wildlife refuge, a walking tour, or harbor cruises.

Pickett's Harbor   804/331–2212
Box 97AA, 28288 Goffigon Lane, Cape Charles, VA 23310

Hosts: Sara and Cooke Goffigon
Location: Rural. On 27 Chesapeake Bay acres of private beach directly across from Virginia Beach. Four miles north of the Chesapeake Bay Bridge Tunnel. Two miles from Route 13 on Virginia's Eastern Shore.

Open: Year round. Best times to call are 6–7:30 a.m. and 5–10 p.m. Two-night minimum during holidays.
Rates: $65 single. $85 double ($95 one-night weekend stay for two). $25 cot.
♥ ⚓ ♣ ⚴

A real find: on a secluded and marvelous wide private beach "for family, guests, seagulls, brown pelicans, and sandpipers" with spectacular sunsets. A colonial home that has a kitchen with cupboards, doors, and floor made from old barn lumber. It's decorated with antiques, reproductions, and country pieces, and in season there are wildflower arrangements in every room.

Cooke, an avocational pilot who "retired from the ABC Commission and manicures the yard," and Sara, a secondary school teacher, built the home on family land. (Sara grew up on the farm, just a half mile away down a country lane.) Now that all five Goffigon children are grown and gone, the world comes to this wonderful doorstep. Guests come for a retreat, for auctions, for nearby nature tours. Some come to beachcomb (acres), to swim, to fish, or to crab (a skill Sara has taught to many, including an anthropologist who was with a camel caravan in the Sudan for about a decade). Others come to research old homes or to take day trips to Norfolk, Williamsburg, or Virginia Beach. *Mid-Atlantic Country* came in the winter and produced a glorious five-page spread.

Bed and bath: Six rooms, all with views of Chesapeake Bay. First-floor queen-bedded room shares a full bath. On second floor, two cozy dormer rooms—one with a double bed, the other with a three-quarter bed—share a full bath. Queen-bedded room has private shower bath. Double-bedded room and one with queen share a full bath and a dressing room. Cot and sleeping bags available.
Breakfast: 6–9. Juice or fresh fruit, sweet potato biscuits, popovers, rolls, cinnamon buns, bran muffins, ham, sausage, cheese-egg-sausage casserole, scrapple, eggs, and, in season, fish. In the kitchen, in Williamsburg-style dining room, or on the porch overlooking bay.
Plus: Central air conditioning. Fireplaced living room. Dining room with open fireplace. Ceiling fan in bedrooms and on porch. Beverages. Use of refrigerator. Dinner sometimes available by advance arrangement. Paths through woods "where deer, squirrel, quail, foxes, and rabbits roam freely."

Sea Gate Bed & Breakfast   804/331-2206

9 Tazewell Avenue, Cape Charles, VA 23310-1345

Hosts: Chris Bannon and Jim Wells
Location: Two houses from the beach in a small (pop. 1,500) Eastern Shore Victorian town, a designated historic district. Within walking distance of shops, restaurants, golf course, dock (from which to fish and crab), marina, fishing charters. Five miles north of state park. Ten miles north of Chesapeake Bay Bridge and Tunnel, and from Federal Wildlife Preserve; 35 northeast of Virginia Beach and Norfolk; 35 south of Tangier Island ferry.
Open: Year round. Two-night minimum on holiday weekends.
Rates: Per room. Queen bed with private bath $75; private half bath $65 or $70 (with porch). King bed $60.
♥ ⊶ ♣ ♦ ✕

> From Maryland: *"An opportunity to 'step back in time' to a lifestyle that many of us have lost touch with."* From Virginia: *"Enchanting ... gracious home, lovely breakfast, enthusiastic conversation, masters at what they do."*

That has been the reaction from the day the hosts opened in what they call Camelot, "the perfect place to live, where the beach is never crowded, where it's quaint and quiet, true no-glitz 1950 Americana." Reporters who come on assignment return for their own getaway. The *Los Angeles Times* has covered Sea Gate. So have *International Getaways* and *The Washingtonian*. Several guests have returned to buy property in the recently rediscovered—it's becoming gentrified—waterfront town.

The restored/rebuilt/redesigned (with new bathrooms, porches, and stairway too) 1910 house is furnished eclectically with a blend of French, English, and American antiques together with some Persian and Chinese rugs. The exceptional rag-rolled (faux finish) and raised relief painting was done by Jim, an interior designer, a Manhattanite who searched the entire East Coast for a shore location for what was to be a personal getaway. Since he and Chris, a manager of conference centers and small retreat houses, opened in 1988, they have become very involved in the community. In summer, breezes come on cue. Year round, there are sunsets too.

In residence: Albert, the cat.
Bed and bath: Four second-floor rooms, all with custom handmade quilts, color TV. Private full bath for room with queen antique brass bed, semiprivate enclosed porch overlooking bay. Three rooms share a shower bath: one has private half bath, four-poster queen bed, semiprivate enclosed porch with bay view; another has private half bath, queen bed; one has king bed and a sink.
Breakfast: Usually 8–10. Maybe French toast made with homemade bread or European-style scrambled eggs. Bacon, sausage, or ham. Fresh fruit, cottage cheese, cereals, juices, hot beverages. Served in kitchen, in dining room with gas burning fireplace, or on year-round enclosed or screened breakfast porch.
Plus: Afternoon tea. Central air conditioning (seldom needed). Ceiling fans. Fireplaced living room. Fresh flowers. Beach towels. Outdoor hot and cold shower. Use of bicycles. No parking problems. Pickup service arranged from marina.

Alderman House

Charlottesville, VA

Location: Just a mile from the university, with no other house in sight.
Reservations: Year round except December 15–February 1 through Guesthouses, page 315.

Rates: Per room. $72–80. $4 one-night surcharge spring and fall weekends.

Elegance. Southern hospitality. And history. The *Washington Post* and *Country* magazine have featured this formal Georgian house, which was built in the early 1900s as the retirement home of the first University of Virginia president. It is now the residence of a gracious hostess and her physician husband, parents of a grown family. Seminar leaders, international visitors, and students' parents are among those who have appreciated their hospitality, the flower-filled brick-walled terrace, and a delightful balcony with pink awnings, lounge chairs, and hanging plants.

In residence: One grown daughter. One black poodle.
Bed and bath: Two second-floor rooms, each with private full bath. One with canopied double four-poster bed. One with twin beds.
Breakfast: 7:30–9:30. Cheese souffle. English muffins, homemade preserves, fresh fruit, coffee or tea. Served in crystal-chandeliered dining room or on the terrace.
Plus: Central air conditioning. Today's papers. Beverages.

From California: *"Wonderful hosts and house. Superb!"*

Bollingwood

Charlottesville, VA

Location: In a convenient neighborhood, within walking distance of the university.
Reservations: Year round through Guesthouses, page 315.

Rates: $68 per room. $4 one-night surcharge on spring and fall weekends.

The fence-enclosed city gardens and slate terrace of this handsome colonial have been featured during Historic Garden Week. Built in 1927 with many windows, the house is furnished with antiques throughout.

Word has it that Albemarle County natives are rare in Charlottesville. Here you have one, a woman returned after living in New Orleans, New York, and Washington, D.C. She has experience as a stockbroker and as a presidential personnel staffer. Several of her guests have been journalists who wrote articles about area gardens, starting right here.

In residence: Bear, a very friendly terrier who loves guests.
Bed and bath: Two second-floor rooms, each with private full bath. One with two twin beds. Another room with a canopied double and, in a connected room, a three-quarter bed.

(Please turn page.)

Breakfast: Flexible hours. Homemade breads and muffins. Raisin bread French toast. Served in formal dining room or on terrace.
Plus: Bedroom air conditioners and ceiling fans. Tea or wine. Tour of house. TV. Fireplace in lovely living room. Extensive library/sun room.

> From Washington, D.C.: *"Wonderful time. Excellent breakfast. Great house. Comfortable bed. Great dog."*

The Inn at Monticello

804/979–3593

Route 19, Box 112, Charlottesville, VA 22902   fax 804/296–1344

Hosts: Carol and Larry Engel
Location: On expansive grounds with bubbling brook and mountain views. Ten-minute drive to University of Virginia and historic Charlottesville district. Two miles to Monticello and the Michie Tavern (old homestead).
Open: Year round. Two-night minimum at holidays, graduation time, September 15–November 15.

Rates: Double occupancy. Queen beds: canopied $130 weekends and holidays, $120 Sunday–Thursday; or four-poster $125 weekends and holidays, $115 Sunday–Thursday. Double beds $115 weekends, $105 Sunday–Thursday; with fireplace $130 weekends, $120 Sunday–Thursday. $10 singles. $25 third person in room. MC, Visa.
♥ ♦ ✻ ✄

> From England: *"It was our first experience of the States and we were lucky to start at the inn . . . everyone felt as if they were honored guests . . . beautiful rooms with selected antique furniture . . . breakfast, artistically presented, outside in the sunshine . . . grounds offered especial delight. . . . It would be possible to sit all day watching the variety of wildlife, basking in the hammock, reading or rocking on the veranda until the evening drink with the hosts and a discussion of restaurants, booked by Carol, who has an extensive knowledge of food and a perception of what each guest might like best. . . . We did sample other B&Bs in America but voted Inn at Monticello the best."*

Overnight innkeepers—almost. The Engels opened in this 1850 manor house in 1989, six months after they had been guests from South Dakota at a Virginia B&B. They decorated with an uncluttered look, mostly with colonial colors and furnishings and traditional print fabrics. Carol is a part-time college student majoring in historic preservation. Larry, a former golf bag manufacturer, is a golf club distributor.

In residence: Alex Adams, assistant innkeeper. "And our daughter, Alicia, helps at the inn. Putnam is our pet poodle."
Bed and bath: Five rooms, all private full (tub/shower) baths. Two first-floor rooms (can be a suite) with queen arched canopy beds. Wide staircase to second floor, which has two double-bedded rooms, one with a working fireplace. Another fireplaced room with four-poster queen bed and bath "two steps down the hall" (robes provided). Rollaway available.
Breakfast: 8:30 or 9:30. Orange yogurt pancakes topped with fresh fruit, bacon-crab quiche, spinach frittata, pecan waffles, or apple pancakes. Fresh fruit. Bacon, ham, or sausage. Homemade baked goods. Juice, coffee, tea. At kitchen harvest table overlooking grounds or on terrace.

Plus: Central air conditioning. Common room with fireplace at each end. Beverages. Fresh flowers. Turndown service. Down comforters. Croquet court. Double-wide hammock. Wine tasting weekends. Picnic lunches arranged. "For meanderers, directions to a quaint little town about 15 miles away."

Recoletta

Charlottesville, VA

Location: Within walking distance of University of Virginia, restaurants, theaters, and shops. Ten-minute bus ride to downtown.
Reservations: Year round through Guesthouses, page 315.

Rates: $68 single or double. $4 one-night surcharge on spring and fall weekends.

By the time most guests rise for breakfast, this hostess has probably walked many laps around the university track. Guests feel very much at home in this Mediterranean-style villa built with flair and imagination, with a red tile roof and a walled garden complete with pools. The comfortable and rather elegant living room filled with books gives the feeling of an Italian library. There are American antiques and many from Central America as well as from Europe. The effervescent and welcoming hostess, an administrator in education, is active in the Society for the Prevention of Cruelty to Animals. (For an epitaph, she once chose "Born a dog, died a gentleman.") Many seasoned travelers write that this is their favorite B&B.

In residence: One cat.
Bed and bath: One second-floor room with brass double bed, adjoining private tub/shower bath.
Breakfast: Until 9:30. Juice, fruit, eggs, bacon or sausage, muffins, gourmet jams, yogurt, cereals, coffee, tea.
Plus: Bedroom air conditioner and fan. Beverages. Fireplaced living room.

From Boston, Massachusetts: *"One of the very best places we have ever stayed."*

Sunnyfields

Charlottesville, VA

Location: Can barely be seen from the road (Route 53), 1 mile southeast of Thomas Jefferson's Monticello and north of James Monroe's Ash Lawn–Highland; 10 minutes to Charlottesville. On 10 acres surrounded by meadows and ash and magnolia trees on preserved countryside. Minutes from winery (tasting tours).

Thirty minutes to Blue Ridge Parkway and Shenandoah Valley.
Reservations: Year round through Guesthouses, page 315.
Rates: $80 per room. $72 if bath is shared. Singles $25 less. $4 one-night surcharge on fall and spring weekends.

(Please turn page.)

Enter through the black iron gate and drive up the half-mile tree-lined lane to this 1830 brick manor house built by William B. Phillips, Thomas Jefferson's master builder, who was also the principal brickmason for the University of Virginia's Rotunda. Changes through the years brought a widow's walk on the roof, columns in place of walls in some of the spacious rooms, and early 20th-century mantels on enlarged fireplaces. Eclectic furnishings include some antiques dating back to 1686 as well as contemporary paintings. From the screened porch you have views of the vineyards that were originally owned by the vintner Thomas Jefferson brought here from Italy—the native country of the host, a painter and potter who exhibits in New York galleries. And what about travelers, who have been staying here since 1989? "They usually come to visit historic places and are on a busy schedule, but sometimes they just decide to relax right here."

Foreign languages spoken: French, Italian, and German.
Bed and bath: Four rooms on air-conditioned second floor. Antique double bed, fireplace, adjoining tub/shower bath. Queen bed, fireplace, adjoining (new) shower bath. Room with four-poster, fireplace, ceiling fan shares adjoining tub/shower bath if other members of same party also book room with two twin beds and ceiling fan.
Breakfast: 8–10. Toasted fresh breads, croissants, butter, preserves, honey, juices, milk, cereal, tea or coffee. Served on screened porch or by country kitchen fireplace. In bedrooms upon request.
Plus: Working fireplaces in library, kitchen, and living and dining rooms. Fresh flowers. Beverages. Pool. Tour of host's studio.

> From Virginia: *"Accommodations were clean and attractive... entire environment quite pleasing ... host is a first-rate goodwill ambassador for state of Virginia."*

Ammonett Farm
North Garden, VA

Location: Pastoral. On a small farm with beautiful views. Twenty minutes south of University of Virginia, 30 to Wintergreen ski resort.
Reservations: Year round through Guesthouses, page 315.

Rates: $60 single. $68 double. $4 one-night surcharge on spring and fall weekends.

"I might be feeding a calf or two when you arrive. We serve home-cooked homegrown foods in our green room, so called because it was added to the house for lots of plants—and people."

It's a century-old, meticulously restored farmhouse. Home to the host family for over a decade, it is filled with family pieces and a country feel. "Some guests feed the calves. Others just relax. This is a very low-key place."

In residence: One young adult. Inside, a cockatiel. Outside, cats, dogs, rabbits, a small herd of beef cattle.

Bed and bath: Three second-floor rooms. One double-bedded with private full bath. One with a double and one with two twins share a full bath. Rollaway and crib available.

Breakfast: Flexible hours. Home style. Fruit or juice, homemade bread and jelly, eggs and bacon; cereal. Hostess joins guests.

Plus: Tea or wine. Bedroom window fans. Tour of house and farm. Hiking on more than 50 acres of woodlands and pasture.

Ingleside

North Garden, VA

Location: "Away." On a hill overlooking grazing animals, sweeping fields, valleys, woods, and steep mountains. A working farm on 1,250 acres. Twenty miles south of Charlottesville.

Reservations: Year round through Guesthouses, page 315.

Rates: $68 per night. $4 surcharge on spring and fall weekends.

♥ ⌫ ♦ ✕ ✄

Turn off the main road for a mile of paved road and another that is unpaved onto the half-mile-long gravel road. Drive "straight up" to this early Victorian house, which was built by the hostess's great-great-grandfather with big square rooms, 10-foot ceilings, and huge windows. Most guests seem to gravitate to the recently added big country kitchen with, of course, those views. They enjoy meeting the well-traveled hosts—a British-born landscape architect and his wife—who maintain a breeding herd of cattle. At last count they had about 60 cows and calves. In addition, the hosts speak of their "retirement home for horses." You'll see about 25 equines that are "cared for and loved." Although some Charlottesville-oriented guests come just to stay out of the city, many enjoy the walks (short or hours long) through open fields, along a stream, or down into and up out of the valleys. (Bring hiking boots.) Some "discover" foundations of old cabins or a family cemetery. And they comment: "Wonderful people . . . an exceptional B&B experience. . . . We want to return."

In residence: Outside dogs—"a mixture and two basset hounds who love to escort guests on walks."

Bed and bath: One first-floor double-bedded room with working fireplace, adjoining tub/shower bath.

Breakfast: Flexible hours. Juice. Fruit course. Cereals including various granolas. Pancakes or sweet rolls and homemade breads. In fireplaced dining room.

Plus: Window air conditioner. Tennis court. In October, sight of newborn calves in addition to spectacular foliage.

If you have met one B&B host, you haven't met them all.

Chester   804/286–3960

James River Road, Route 4, Box 57, Scottsville, VA 24590

Hosts: Gordon Anderson and Richard Shaffer
Location: On a seven-acre estate with more than 50 varieties of trees (including Virginia's largest recorded white pine) and shrubs, each identified with botanical and common name. Just off Route 20. Within half an hour of Monticello, Ash Lawn, Charlottesville; 45 minutes from Skyline Drive.

Open: Year round. Two-day minimum during UVA graduation and parents' weekends, July 4, and December 22–January 2.
Rates: Per room. $100 private bath. $65 shared bath; $75 with fireplace. $85 queen-bedded room with adjoining sitting room. $30 sofa bed (one or two people).
♥ ⛵ ⋆⋆⋆ ♦

> From New Hampshire: *"Memorable and elegant meals . . . tastefully decorated . . . spotless . . . the most comfortable mattress you can imagine . . . lingered over specially brewed coffee . . . hosts joined us for drinks on the front porch . . . suggested routes . . . marked maps."* From Illinois: *"The conversation was animated to put it mildly. . . . Grounds bring one back to a more leisurely lifestyle. . . . A single overnight yielded more relaxation than the time invested would warrant."*

Gordon was a Wall Street investment banker for 23 years and Dick a legal administrator in Manhattan before they spent a year restoring the gracious 1847 Greek Revival frame house built by a landscape architect from England. Shortly after opening in 1986, this B&B was acclaimed by James Yenckel in the *Washington Post,* and the hosts have appeared twice in Woodward & Lothrop's cooking demonstrations given by *Bed & Breakfast in the Mid-Atlantic States* innkeepers. Featured on Historic Garden Week in 1991, Chester has a columned portico, four porches, eight wood-burning fireplaces, expansive lawns, and large stands of English boxwood. Many of the furnishings were acquired during the hosts' own extensive travels. (The innkeepers also have an antiques shop in Scottsville.) This is "home" with Oriental rugs, comfortable chairs, traditional pieces, classical music, and artwork.

In residence: "We breed and show borzoi (Russian wolfhounds) who love people and often are visited by guests." Johnny Weismuller and Esther Williams are outside cats.
Bed and bath: Five rooms; all with heated towel racks. Private full bath for first-floor room that has four-poster double bed, wood-burning fireplace. On second floor, suite with queen four-poster bed, pedestal sink, wood-burning fireplace, sitting room with double sofa bed shares a tub-and-shower bath with room that has a double bed, pedestal sink, wood-burning fireplace. Guests in room with king bed and wood-burning fireplace walk through library to tub-and-shower bath shared with smaller room that has a double bed.
Breakfast: 7–9:30. Fresh fruit. Eggs (maybe sherried) or omelets, or Swedish oven pancakes; local sausage or bacon. Homemade breads. Cereals. Juices. Coffees, teas. Served with fine china, crystal, and silver on large screened porch or by dining room fireplace.
Plus: Central air conditioning. Beverages. Flowers. Bicycles. Library with satellite TV, stereo, books. Croquet. Laundry room with ironing facilities. Tour

of house, kennels, greenhouse. Picnic baskets prepared. Sociable dinner party ($24 per person includes wine; advance reservation required) at table set with fine china, sterling silver, and Waterford crystal; hosts join guests. Take-home recipe booklets. Cigarettes provided in living room. "Guests' dogs allowed in our kennel."

High Meadows Vineyard & Mountain Sunset Inn
804/286–2218
800/232–1832
Route 4, Box 6, Scottsville, VA 24590

Hosts: Peter Sushka and Mary Jae Abbitt
Location: Pastoral. On 50 acres along Constitution Highway (address of presidential homes), 15 minutes to Monticello and Ash Lawn; 20 minutes from Charlottesville. Two and a half hours from Washington, D.C.
Open: Year round. Two-day minimum on weekends and holidays in

April, May, and September through November.
Rates: Per room. Sunday–Friday $85–$145. Saturday (includes dinner for two) $70 more. $15 extra person. Senior citizens, 10 percent less. MC, Visa.
♥ ♣ ♦ ✁

Food. Antiques. Charm. Three historic National Register buildings. With a Pinot noir grape vineyard planted in 1985. With daily evening wine tastings and the option of the evening meal. There are nature trails, gorgeous gardens with antique roses, a gazebo by the pond, and an antique London taxi waiting to carry guests to local sites. All of this was preceded by four years of living in England while Peter was a Navy submarine officer. Then, as retirement years approached, there were three years of commuting from Washington jobs to restore "the dream," two interconnected houses—a Federal brick structure built in 1832 and an 1883 late Victorian stucco-over-brick. In 1991 Peter and Mary acquired a Queen Anne manor house on adjacent acreage with spectacular mountain views.

In residence: Kali, a golden retriever, and Snickers, a dachshund.
Foreign language spoken: French.
Bed and bath: Twelve air-conditioned rooms (five are suites) and a two-room cottage. Some rooms with fireplaces; all with antiques—country, Victorian, and elegant. Rooms have king, queen, queen and a double, or a double and a twin bed. Locations range from garden level to second floor up a steep staircase. All with private baths; variations include shower bath with seat, Jacuzzi for two, whirlpool, deep tub for two, tub and shower, or shower without tub. Call for complete descriptions!
Breakfast: At 9. Freshly squeezed juice, homemade muffins and toast, fruits, baked egg and meat dishes, coffee, tea. Served in fireplaced dining room or on terrace.
Plus: Four common rooms. Five porches. Welcoming beverage. Fresh flowers. Fruit. Candy. Decanter of port or sherry in guests' rooms. Guest refrigerator. Croquet. Horseshoes. Peter is chef for Saturday candlelit six-course meal with wine. Friday three-course meals ($40 per couple) by request. Sunday–

(Please turn page.)

Thursday gourmet picnic supper basket ($40–$50 per couple); eat in dining room, by fireplace, or on the grounds.

> Guests wrote: *"We always have a hint of hesitation when we plan to return, wondering how it can be so special again. And it always is."*

Edgewood Farm Bed & Breakfast

RR 2, Box 303, Stanardsville, VA 22973-9405   804/985–3782

Hosts: Eleanor and Norman Schwartz
Location: Off the beaten track on a 130-acre farm with woods (hiking), a river, streams, many birds. Five miles from town. Twenty-five miles north of Charlottesville; 15 to Swift Run Gap entrance of Shenandoah National Park/Appalachian Trail. Within 20 minutes of crafts shops, antiquing, wineries, pick-your-own strawberries, apple orchard and cider mill. Two hours from Washington, D.C., or Richmond, Virginia.
Open: Year round except Christmas, Easter, and Thanksgiving.
Rates: Double occupancy. Shared bath $55 double bed, $65 queen bed. Private bath and queen bed $75. Singles $5 less. Rollaway $15. MC, Visa.
♥ 🏠 🛥 ♣ ♦ 🐾 ⚲

> From many Virginians: *"Greeted with sparkling cider, fruit, and cheese. . . . Beautiful mountain views from all the rooms. . . . Gone to great lengths to establish elegance, a sense of authenticity, and comfort. . . . Grounds, too, are beautifully maintained. . . . What makes it a special place are the people who run it. . . . Breakfast is sumptuous. . . . Have spent our vacations bicycle touring . . . stayed at many B&Bs. . . . Among the very best."* From California: *"Memorable."*

In 1986, the first B&B guests were members of one of the many families who had owned this 1790 Virginia colonial farmhouse with 1860 addition. Since, the Schwartzes have heard others share some oral history about the property and the plantation overseer's house. The extensive restoration took place with the help of a historic preservationist and a professional decorator. Furnishings are period antiques—"some from our home state of Texas"—and reproductions. Every room has a working fireplace. Norman, a retired air force officer, and Bob Cary, a son-in-law, have established a nursery here with the state's largest selection of herbs and unusual perennials. In 1994 they plan to offer pick-your-own flowers for drying plus wreath-making supplies. Eleanor was a writer/editor with the air force at the Pentagon. She dovetails the completion of her civil service career (as a personnel specialist in Charlottesville) with greeting delighted guests.

In residence: "Buddy, our sweet farm dog, will love you to death if you let him. Garfield is our cat."
Bed and bath: Three second-floor rooms. One with queen Victorian. One with four-poster. Steep staircase leads to one with double brass-and-iron bed. Two full baths; can be private or shared depending on number of rooms booked. Rollaway and crib available.
Breakfast: 6:30–10. Early coffee in kitchen or, by request, at your door (complete with a flower). Entree in dining room set with china, silver, and

fresh flowers might be breakfast casserole with ham or sausage, eggs, cheese, cream sauce. Four or five homemade sweet breads, muffins, or coffee cakes. Juice, fruit, hot beverages. "Constantly trying new recipes. Cookbook is planned."

Plus: Central air conditioning. Bedroom ceiling fans. Complimentary Virginia-made goats' milk toiletries. Morning newspapers. Horseshoes. Croquet. Maybe a Carolina wren nesting in front porch grapevine heart wreath. Patio. Transportation to/from Charlottesville Amtrak station and/or Shenandoah National Park. Picnic baskets, $25 for two. Dinner by advance notice, $25 for two.

House of Laird   804/432–2523
335 South Main Street, Chatham, VA 24531-1131

Hosts: Ed and Cecil Laird
Location: On a street lined with other big old lovely homes. Two-minute walk to bucolic village. "Five minutes to just about every place, including Chatham Hall School for Girls, Hargrave Military School, excellent restaurant." One hour to Appomattox, 45 minutes to Blue Ridge Parkway, 20 to Danville (last Confederate capital). Two hours south of Charlottesville and north of Raleigh-Durham, North Carolina.
Open: Year round.
Rates: Per room. $38 year round except weekends, when the rate is $57. New library suite, $78. MC, Visa.
■ ⁂ ◆ ✗ ✂

> From Virginia: *"The quintessential experience. . . . Exquisite. . . . Detail includes heated towel bars and plush robes. . . . In a small town rich in history and architectural heritage. . . . The crowning touch is breakfast."*

A best-kept secret, maybe. Affordable luxury, surely. And romantic. Professionally decorated in 1988 with fine antiques, Oriental rugs, and imported wallcoverings and fabrics, the century-old Greek Revival with original moldings and glass had been in one family until the Lairds bought it "to create a personalized B&B"—after seeing a *Country Living* ad, and after they found Chatham on the map! The magnificent floor-to-ceiling dining room mirror is reputed to have been in Washington, D.C.'s Willard Hotel (Abraham Lincoln's era). The handsome 1830 Empire four-poster has been in Cecil's family "for years." The teddy bear collection started during the hosts' mid-1980s courtship. Kentucky-born Cecil was in banking in Richmond when her neighbor introduced her to his college roommate, Georgia-born Ed, who was in real estate in California. Here, "in this one-traffic-light town," two happy people "host [pamper] wonderful [and contented] travelers from near and far."

In residence: Tonk, a Siamese/Burmese cat, in hosts' quarters.
Bed and bath: Three rooms and library suite with (new) private adjoining baths. First floor—handicapped-accessible suite with queen tester bed, a queen Murphy bed, working fireplace, bath with tub and hand-held shower. Second floor—three rooms (two with queen beds, one with two twin canopied beds) with shower baths.

(Please turn page.)

Breakfast: Early coffee or tea outside your door. Continental at 7, full at 8:30. Breakfast roulade, quiche, sausage, crepes, fresh fruit. "Ed's smoothie," a fruit drink. Freshly baked breads and muffins. In formal dining room with cloth napkins, antique china, and period silver.
Plus: Working fireplaces in guests' sitting room and library suite. Central air conditioning. Beverages and snacks. Fresh fruit and flowers. Turndown service. Cable TV in each room. Schedule for recommended antique auction one hour away. Upon departure, "a care package."

The Watson House   804/336–1564
4240 Main Street, P.O. Box 402, Chincoteague, VA 23336

Hosts: Tom and Jacqueline Derrickson; David and Jo Anne Snead
Location: On a corner of Main Street, across the street from Chincoteague Bay, ¼ mile from the heart of town. One mile to the Chincoteague National Wildlife Refuge, 2 to beach.
Open: March–November. Two-night minimum most weekends; three on holiday weekends.
Rates: Per room. Double bed $69–$89 weekends, $59–$75 midweek. Larger double room $85–$95 weekends, $75–$85 midweek. Queen $89–$99 weekends, $79–$89 midweek. MC, Visa.
♥ ♣ ✈ ⅛

"This B&B was my father's idea. He's always wanted one, and wanted it to be here on the island where we've always lived. In 1991 he, together with my husband, put a bid on this turn-of-the-century house, and then they told my mother and me about their plan. It was fun to redo the entire place and to add the friendly and welcoming wraparound porch complete with ginger-bread, inspired by Cape May B&Bs. Half of the Victorian and country furnishings came from local residents who wanted us to have Chincoteague pieces. The other half we bought at auctions. Since opening in 1992 it seems that we have become known for our food—both breakfast and teatime."

Jackie used to work for NASA. She and husband Tom, an electronic technician, take turns as hosts along with co-chef Jo Anne (Jackie's mom) and David (Jackie's Dad), a plumber.

Bed and bath: Six rooms; one on first floor, five on second. All attached private baths; one has claw-foot tub and shower, rest have shower without tub. Queen iron-and-brass beds or double high-back oak beds. Two rooms have sitting rooms. Rollaway available.
Breakfast: 8–9:30. Buffet includes French toast or egg-and-meat casserole, hot or cold fruit dish, homemade pastries/breads/muffins, cold cereals. In dining room or on side porch.
Plus: Air conditioning. Bedroom ceiling fans. Individual thermostats. Teatime with cakes and cookies at 4 p.m. Complimentary use of bicycles, beach towels, and beach chairs. Fresh flowers on special occasions.

---

*One out of five guests leaves with
the dream of opening a B&B.*

The Oaks Bed & Breakfast Country Inn

311 East Main, Christiansburg, VA 24073   703/381–1500

Hosts: Margaret and Tom Ray
Location: On grounds with massive oak trees. In historic district, 3 blocks from downtown. Two miles from I–81, 8 from Virginia Tech and Radford University; 26 from Blue Ridge Parkway and Roanoke; 28 to winery, ½ to antiques shops, and 12 to hiking. Short drive to restaurants, including European cuisine at a mountain vineyard, family-style Cajun food, and Southern home cooking.

Open: Year round. Designated minimum stays for university special events' weekends.
Rates: Double occupancy. $95–$110 Sunday–Thursday, $105–$120 Friday and Saturday. Singles $10 less. Corporate rate Sunday–Thursday, $75 per room. Amex, Discover, MC, Visa.
♥ ❖ ♦ ✗ ✓

"One man who composed an original song for his wife played it for her on our piano on their first anniversary. Lots of business travelers come. Others who are gung ho to hike sometimes choose to read a good book on our wraparound porch. And from the original builder's two surviving daughters—they're almost 90—we get hugs and encouragement along with tales of this 1889 yellow Victorian occupied by their family until 1982. We lived in Royal Oak, Michigan, for 28 years before moving to Washington, D.C., for 8 years. In 1989 we created this B&B and named it after the majestic 300-year-old white oaks."

Margaret, a former corporate executive who had her own public relations agency, is a fine seamstress and cook. Tom is a multifaceted architect. Just two weeks after the Rays arrived here, Hurricane Hugo claimed two of the ancient oaks. The remaining seven are now part of a fascinating restoration program.

In 1992, The Oaks made *Country Inns* magazine's "top twelve" list. The grand staircase has been discovered by a bridal photographer. Contemporary and antique furnishings blend in an elegant ambiance. Fireplaces are in two parlors, the dining room, and the wicker- and teak-furnished sun room. French doors open onto a large terrace by a perennial garden, a gazebo, and a fish pond with fountain.

In residence: Miss Lulu, "a spirited Scottie, our social director." Sidney, "a beautiful fat and lazy Persian."
Bed and bath: Five air-conditioned rooms, private baths. First floor: very quiet room with canopied queen bed, tub and shower bath. Second floor: canopied king, gas fireplace (due soon), refrigerator, his and her baths with claw-foot tub. Five-windowed turreted room with queen bed, gas log fireplace, refrigerator, bath with dressing area, Jacuzzi for two, shower. Canopied queen, fireplace with gas logs, refrigerator, private tub and shower hall bath. Third floor: king canopied bed, tall ceiling with skylight, gas log fireplace, shower bath, TV.
Breakfast: A hallmark. Flexible weekday hours. Weekends, at 9. Perhaps curried eggs with Shitake mushrooms in white wine sauce or apricot-walnut pancakes with ice cream and orange syrup. Fresh breads and fruit. Tom's

(Please turn page.)

almost-famous coffee. French service in candlelit dining room with antique china, sterling silver, linen napkins.
Plus: In all bedrooms—ceiling fans, private phones, turndown service. Beverages. TV and VCR in sun room. Library. Games. Garden. Rockers on wraparound porch. Sun deck. Festive month-long Victorian Christmas celebration.

Oak Grove Plantation   804/575–7137

Highway 658, Cluster Springs, VA   (winter) 703/527–6958
Mailing address: P.O. Box 45, Cluster Springs, VA 24535

Host: Pickett Craddock
Location: On a 400-acre tree farm with great hiking, biking, and bird-watching. Five miles south of South Boston, Virginia. Antiquing locally. Thirty minutes from Buggs Island Lake (fishing, boating, swimming, quilt store, 18th-century mansion) and Danville, Virginia (where you tour last capital of Confederacy and Victorian homes on Millionaires' Row). One hour north of Durham, North Carolina.

Open: Daily Memorial Day weekend through Labor Day and on weekends and during special events in May and September.
Rates: Per room. $50 double, $45 single. $5 children over six. Three-day midweek family packages: ($250 for two adults and one child, $275 with two children; includes three breakfasts, two dinners, two days with four hours of supervised activities for one or more children.
🏠 🛏 ♣ ♦ ✗

> From New York: *"A strong sense of another time . . . walked for hours through woods and meadows . . . service on family china was gracious and elegant."* From Washington, D.C.: *"Picked us up at train station . . . delicious home-cooked breakfast and special vegetarian dinner . . . played croquet on front lawn . . . a gracious hostess who knew when to be affable and when to allow privacy."* From North Carolina: *"Comfortable bringing our two-year-old . . . wonderful food, charming rooms."*

You, too, can discover this off-the-beaten-path haven—thanks to Pickett's desire to share the Classical Revival house built by her great-great-grandfather on a tobacco plantation. Three-foot-high wainscoting carved with stars and bars, floor-to-ceiling parlor windows, an antique box grand piano, and a Korean Buddha are all part of the family history—and occasional house tours. Adults unwind. Kids climb magnolia and oak trees. From a trestle they count the boxcars of a passing train. And they find turtles and frogs in the creek.

Pickett, a Washington, D.C., preschool director and caterer, has hosted since 1987. She continued her B&B dream—still with grace—through one summer with a broken leg, the result of an accident when she and husband Mike Doan, an editor for *Kiplinger Washington Newsletter*, went to Honduras to meet newborn Sara.

In residence: Daughter Sara is three. "Tara is our people-loving dalmatian."
Foreign language spoken: Spanish.

Bed and bath: Two second-floor air-conditioned rooms share a new crystal-chandeliered full bath that has a private porch. Additional bath with tub is on first floor; robes provided. Room with working fireplace has canopied double four-poster bed made for Pickett when she was seven. Other room has king/twins option. One crib and sleeping bags for children available.
Breakfast: At guests' convenience. An egg dish, waffles, or pancakes. Bacon or sausage. Fresh fruit. Homemade breads. In bay-windowed dining room that has Victorian floral print wallpaper.
Plus: A calendar of area events. Glassed-in sun porch. Iced tea or lemonade whenever. Individual heat thermostats. Fresh flowers. Kitchen and laundry facilities. Use of two adult bicycles, baby jogger, backpack. Babysitting. High chair, swings, games. Dinner, $12 per person, by reservation. No television. Line-dried sheets.

Milton Hall Bed and Breakfast Inn

207 Thorny Lane, Covington, VA 24426-9803   703/965–0196

Hosts: John and Vera Eckert
Location: A rural mountain setting. On 44 acres next to George Washington National Forest. In Callaghan, 5 miles west of Covington. One mile from I–64, exit 10. With "sweeping lawns" much as they were when the house was built. Thirty minutes south of The Homestead in Hot Springs, 20 minutes east of The Greenbrier Hotel in White Sulphur Springs, West Virginia.
Open: Year round.
Rates: Double occupancy. $140 suite. $95 master bedroom. $85 queen bed. $75 double bed. MC, Visa. ♥ ♣ ♦

Come to breakfast when you want. Unwind. And beware: Many who come with plans to attend theater, go horseback riding, or visit the baths in Warm Springs "do" as little as possible. As John, the retired naval officer who was for nine years a computer corporation analyst and manager, says, "Our guests enjoy the scenery, good restaurants, small villages, the hike from our back door into the national forest, and comfortable fireplaced rooms."

The rather imposing brick exterior with gables, buttressed porch towers, and Gothic trimming gives way to a plainer interior, as intended by one of England's oldest families when they built the house in 1874. The Eckerts decorated the Virginia Historic Landmark, which is also on the National Register, with muted bird- and floral-patterned wallpapers, with reproductions and some antiques. Their player piano, purchased in England, has been restored. Tea at four is very English. Before B&B, Vera, as a Washington, D.C., sales associate, specialized in fine English china. Here, the Eckerts' hospitality is influenced by their 26 years of travel with the United States Navy.

In residence: Heather, 18. Sassy, a 7-year-old Brittany.
Bed and bath: Six rooms, all with four-poster beds, private baths, working fireplaces. First-floor suite has two rooms with fireplaces—one queen-bedded room and a parlor with queen sofa bed—both with French doors leading to garden; shower bath. On second floor—master bedroom with queen four-poster, sitting area with sleep sofa, antique tub/shower bath. One queen with

(Please turn page.)

shower only. One queen with antique tub/shower bath. One queen with modern tub and shower. One antique double four-poster, private bath suite at opposite end of hall with whirlpool tub, exercise bike.

Breakfast: At guests' convenience. Juice, fresh fruit, local meat or fish (sausage, bacon, rainbow trout), baked cheese grits or sliced baby red potatoes browned in butter, fresh-baked biscuits or muffins, milk and cereal, coffee or tea. In fireplaced dining room overlooking gardens.

Plus: Air-conditioned bedrooms. Fireplaced living room with TV and that 1916 player piano. Welcoming beverages. Turndown service. Bedtime snack. Flannel sheets. Fresh flowers. Unlimited firewood. Use of bicycles. Picnic baskets ($6 per person) and suggestions for picnic sites. With advance arrangement, informal country supper ($8.50 per person) or full dinner ($20 with wine). Croquet. Option of TV in room.

Mary's Country Inn   703/984–8286
218 South Main Street, Route 2, Box 4, Edinburg, VA 22824

Hosts: Mary and Jim Clark
Location: On spacious grounds in the Shenandoah Valley, just off Route 81. Next to the historic Edinburg mill (now a restaurant). Near "easy access to an absolutely awesome view of the Seven Bends of the Shenandoah."

Open: Year round except January. Two-night minimum in October.
Rates: $70 double, shared bath. $75 double, private bath. $85 suite. $55 single. $10 rollaway. No charge for portacrib.
♥ ♂ ♣ ♦ ✖

"Down-to-earth, country comfortable without airs" is the feeling enjoyed by guests (many returnees) who come for hiking, fishing, or hunting in the George Washington National Forest. Some come for the caverns, museums, antiquing, or vineyards, or for "solitude and inspiration." Always, visitors are welcomed into the Clarks' studio. Jim, a retired engineer, made the stained glass windows and transoms here. Mary is a photgrapher and artist who teaches at Shenandoah University.

The 1850 miller's house had several additions, including the massive Jeffersonian French doors leading to a wraparound porch in 1890. A miller's residence until 1982, when it became an inn with the Clarks doing just about all the conversion work. Their works, along with local crafts, antiques and collectibles, are displayed throughout.

Bed and bath: Five second-floor rooms, all with sitting areas. Suite has a double bed in one room, a single bed in the other, private bath with claw-foot tub. One room with extra-long double bed, large bath with claw-foot tub. If more than one of the three double-bedded rooms is booked, they share a full bath; many times arrangements are made for that bath to be private. Rollaways and portacrib available.

Breakfast: 8–10. Fresh fruit, cereals, homemade muffins or fruit breads, sweet rolls, biscuits, eggs, sausage/bacon, juices, coffee, tea, milk. Served buffet style in dining room, on wraparound porch overlooking the green, or on patio.

Plus: Bedroom air conditioning and ceiling fans. Beverages. Wood stove in common room. Vintage carriages on lawn or in carriage house. Swing, wicker chairs on wraparound porch. Flower and vegetable garden. Bikes for rent.

From Virginia: *"Homey atmosphere, delicious food, many suggestions of exciting things to do followed by their eagerness to hear of our day's outing over a hot beverage (on a cold November day!) and home-baked goodies. We left feeling like part of a wonderful family. . . . Antique coaches* [on lawn or in carriage house], *lawn concerts, historic Edinburg town festival, and a bubbling creek nearby with ducks and fish. Mary and Jim will help you to enjoy it all."*

The Bailiwick Inn

703/691–2266
4023 Chain Bridge Road, Fairfax, VA 22030
800/366–7666
fax 703/934–2112

Hosts: Anne and Ray Smith
Location: On main street of historic district (self-guided walking tour available). Across from courthouse of 1800. Minutes' walk to George Mason University campus (jogging territory for some). Close to Routes 123 and 236. One block to bus to 20-minute Metrorail ride into Washington, D.C. Within 25 minutes of countryside, 20 to Civil War battlefield, 30 from National and Dulles airports.

Open: Year round.
Rates: Double occupancy. Garden level $105. First- and second-floor rooms $130; $165 with fireplace. Suite $225. Ten percent discount for families, senior citizens, business travelers. Murder mystery and winemaker weekend packages. Amex, MC, Visa.
♥ ♣ ♦ ✈ ✄

From Massachusetts: *"One of the most beautifully decorated B&Bs I have ever seen . . . delicious breakfasts . . . afternoon tea with scrumptious pastries. . . . Anne and Ray Smith and all the staff are every bit as wonderful. . . . My nights at impersonal hotels are over."*

Other guests concur. So do wedding parties, executive meeting planners, and romantics who appreciate this award-winning historic showplace, which was featured in *Country Inns* and *Mid-Atlantic Country*. The entire restoration and renovation of the 19th-century Federal brick house took place within six months in 1989, including extensive research conducted on every detail, from authentic colors to elaborate Gothic Revival dentil crown moldings to the Virginians for whom each room was named. Six decorators furnished with antiques and reproductions—Chippendale, Sheraton, and Duncan Phyfe; with damasks, velvets, woven silks, and period wallcoverings. Some rooms are similiar to those you may see in George Washington's Mount Vernon. Some window treatments are copied from Thomas Jefferson's designs.

The inn, named for bailiwick's oldest meaning, "area around the court," was created by Anne, a former Virginia school speech pathologist, and Ray, a developer/former Cosmos Club chef. They are gardeners and gourmet cooks "who enjoy visiting with people." In 1992 they added a restaurant, open for dinner Tuesday–Sunday.

(Please turn page.)

Foreign languages spoken: French and some Spanish.
Bed and bath: Fourteen large rooms with private baths; four with working fireplaces. Private entrance to two garden-level rooms; one is handicapped-accessible. Feather beds on beds in all rooms. All baths en suite except one hall bath (robes provided). Two baths with two-person Jacuzzis and hand-held showers; rest have shower only. All queen four-poster beds except one second-floor room with twin beds and the third-floor suite that has king bed, sitting room, Jacuzzi bath.
Breakfast: 7:30–9 weekdays; 8:30–10 weekends. Juice in crystal goblets, fruit, muffins, hot beverage. Main course might be "Robert E. Lee eggs"—English muffin, poached egg, mushroom sauce, Virginia ham. Served on Wedgwood china in dining room or in brick-walled colonial garden with fountain.
Plus: Central air conditioning. Two fireplaced and book-lined parlors. Tea at 4 p.m. Turndown service with chocolates on goose-down pillows. Guest refrigerator. Classical music. Babysitting. Picnic baskets arranged. Their own cookbook. Phone jacks. Access to computer and fax.

La Vista Plantation

703/898–8444
fax 703/898–1041

4420 Guinea Station Road
Fredericksburg, VA 22408-9341

Hosts: Michele and Edward Schiesser
Location: Surrounded by farm fields, herb and vegetable gardens, pond for fishing, woods with paths for walks, cycling, bird-watching. Eight miles south of Fredericksburg, just off Route 1. Five miles from I–95. On the East Coast bicycle trail. Near Civil War battlefields, antiques shops, pick-your-own farms. An hour to Monticello and Mount Vernon.
Open: Year round.
Rates: $65 single. $85 double. Children 12 and under, free. Additional person $5 ages 12–17; $10 age 18 and older. Seventh night free. MC, Visa.
♥ ♯ ♦ ✖ ✁

From Massachusetts: *"A warm welcome. Plenty of space and privacy. Lovely antiques and artworks. Morning brought the rooster's crow, sunlight streaming in from all sides, and a delicious hot breakfast. . . . A feeling for the period of the lovely house."* From Texas: *"Marvelous."* From Virginia: *"Truly made us feel at home. . . . Wished we could have stayed longer."*

Romantics wrote about sitting by the fire. Some guests see their first lightning bugs here. They enjoy the opportunity to gather eggs and explore 10 acres. Business guests, too, appreciate hearing some history and anecdotes about the 1838 Greek Revival manor house, which was occupied by both armies during the Civil War. Since 1983, when the Schiessers moved from the Victorian house they renovated in Maryland, this has been a restoration-in-progress for Mickey, a former junior high school teacher, and Ed, chief of exhibits and design at the Hirshhorn Museum.

They made the sunny English basement (with cathedral-type windows) into one of the area's first B&Bs by updating the former winter kitchen and furnishing the spacious rooms with antiques, Ed's limestone sculptures, and many books. This arrangement of a home-within-a-home provides as much privacy or company as you wish. The more formal first-floor guest room has wide heart pine floors, Empire furniture, and an antique clock collection.

In residence: William, age 13; Julia, 11. Emily, "beautiful, well-behaved, quiet English setter." Chickens and rabbits.

Bed and bath: Rooms on two floors. A four-room ground-level suite with private shower bath, double bed in huge room, living room with queen-sized sofa bed, fireplace, large fireplaced kitchen, two private entrances. On first floor, a huge fireplaced room with king four-poster bed, large private full bath. Crib available.

Breakfast: 7–9:30. Danish with coffee or tea, La Vista's fresh brown farm eggs, toast, bacon, homemade jams from fruit trees here, orange juice, milk. Varied menu for extended stays. Served in main-floor dining room or in guests' rooms.

Plus: Central air conditioning (window unit in suite). In-room TV, radio, phone. Beverages. Fresh flowers. Plenty of wood in hearths. Flannel sheets. The family's living room. Today's newspaper. Use of two bicycles, rowboat, and fishing tackle. Option of dinner (no charge) to those arriving on bicycles. Babysitting if arranged in advance. In December, pick-your-own Christmas trees.

Chester House Inn

703/635–3937
800/621–0441

43 Chester Street, Front Royal, VA 22630

Hosts: Bill and Ann Wilson
Location: On two acres in historic residential district. One block from renovated Main Street with its old-time general store, and antiques and craft shops; summer evening concerts at village common gazebo. Within minutes of Shenandoah National Park; Skyline Drive and caverns; George Washington National Forest; winery tours; recreational activities including horseback riding, canoeing, fishing, golf. Three miles south of I–66, exit 6; 70 miles west of Washington, D.C.

Open: Year round. Two-night minimum on some September, October, and holiday weekends.
Rates: Double occupancy. Shared bath $60 double bed, $75 king or two twins. Private half bath $85. Private full bath $105. Two-bedroom suite $170; if rooms rented separately (shared bath), $80 queen, $90 king. Twenty percent business travelers' discount, Sunday–Thursday. Amex, MC, Visa.
♥ ♣ ♦ ✂

From Maryland: *"A relaxed and gracious home away from home."* From Bangladesh five-star hotel assistant manager: *"Enjoyed a lot as member of group study exchange team by Rotary Foundation and appreciated hospitality which I have never seen for my last ten years in the industry."*

The simple bronze "Chester House" plaque on the wrought iron fence symbolizes the Wilsons' low-key approach to B&B, Bill's seventh career. He has worked in labor relations and as a stockbroker, manufacturer, conference center manager, and educational administrator. A chance conversation, a

(Please turn page.)

single B&B stay, and timing led to innkeeping in 1989. Bill, the chef, a New Englander by birth, and Ann, a former veterinary technician who is now official gardener, were enthusiastic Front Royal residents when they moved to "Ann's dream," this stately 1905 Georgian mansion that was always a private home.

Distinctive dentil molding is in the living room. Furnishings are antique and traditional. The extensive gardens include a formal boxwood maze, a fountain, wisteria arbors, shade trees, and benches. Small groups and non-profit community organizations also enjoy the opportunity to have fund-raisers and small dinner parties here.

In residence: Hickory and Spice are English springer spaniels.
Bed and bath: Six second-floor rooms, varying in size. Master bedroom has waist-high queen four-poster, private full bath, and sitting room. Two-bedroom suite has one room with king bed, another with queen; one full bath shared if rooms reserved individually. Room with antique double spool bed and corner room with king/twins option share a full bath. Corner room with high pencil-post queen bed, private half bath, shared shower.
Breakfast: 8–10. Freshly squeezed orange juice or apple cider. Homemade popovers or muffins. Fresh fruit. Cold cereals. Hot beverages. In formal dining room at table set with silver and crystal. Can last up to two hours.
Plus: Central air conditioning. Living room with upright piano. Complimentary beverages. Guest refrigerator. Turndown service. Mints on pillow. Fresh flowers. Bathrobes. Board games and cards. Badminton. Champagne tray for special occasions.

Springdale Country Inn

Route 722, Lincoln, VA 22078

703/338–1833
800/388–1832
fax 703/338–1839

Hosts: Nancy and Roger Fones
Location: On a main artery surrounded by farmland in historic district. On six acres with terraced gardens; brook; jogging paths; original spring-, smoke-, and henhouses still here. Minutes to country store. Two miles to antiquing, restaurants, cycling trail; 5 to golf and vineyard towns. Ten miles west of Leesburg, 45 west of Washington, D.C., 18 from Dulles airport, 20 to Harpers Ferry.

Open: Year round.
Rates: Per room (vary according to private baths and working fireplaces). $95–$125. $200 three-room Victorian Suite (up to six people). Group ($35.50 and up for 25 or more), corporate, and government rates and packages available. Diners, Discover, MC, Visa.
♥ ♦ ♣ ♦ ✕

"Little Girls' School Would Make Great B&B" read the newspaper advertisement photograph caption. Fast forward through five years of restoration/discovery, zoning hearings, research, and refurbishing, and you arrive at a 28-room Federal frame building "all back to the way it was in the 1830s." What was the East Coast's first boarding school for girls, and later a Civil War hospital as well as a stop on the Underground Railroad, now has period wallcoverings; authentic antiques; refinished wide-board floors "without carpets, because they didn't have them in the old days"; and a (hidden) sprinkler system too. The Foneses show guests the dining room lamp under which Sam Rayburn and Lyndon Johnson played poker with their weekend retreat host, Dr. Walter Splawn, the then head of the Interstate Commerce Commission. To 200-year-old recipes, Nancy, who has developed an in-house catering company, adds native herbs and wildflowers that she has planted here. Weddings (inside or out), family reunions, and business meetings utilize the open spaces and formal ballroom (with piano). Many cycling groups use the inn as a base for trips. "Interluders find us on weekends."

Nancy was with Scholastic publications as a software trainer; Roger, a lawyer with the U.S. Justice Department.

Bed and bath: Eight rooms (two can be a suite) with double or twin beds; three with working fireplace. Six full unattached baths; three are private (one has whirlpool tub), three are shared. One room on first floor with Murphy bed is handicapped-accessible. All rooms have desks and sofas. Third-floor room has office space and equipment; TV and private phone may be arranged. Trundle beds available.
Breakfast: 7–noon. Homemade granola bars, Scottish shortbreads, Bavarian "quark" (a compote with yogurt and fruit), deep-dish apple pancakes, country baked eggs, frittata, pecan waffles, mini–eggs Benedict, country puff pastries. Eat in dining room, on sun porch, or in room.
Plus: Central air conditioning. Fireplaced parlor and living and dining rooms. Five p.m. tea or wine and cheese hour. Complimentary recipe booklets. Oversized towels. Guest refrigerator. Homemade sweets. Overhead projector. VCR. Slide projector. Parking for 60 cars.

Llewellyn Lodge   703/463–3235
603 South Main Street, Lexington, VA 24450   800/882–1145

Hosts: Ellen and John Roberts
Location: In a lovely old residential neighborhood of this historic Shenandoah Valley community, "a New England town in Virginia." Ten minutes' walk to downtown historic area. Five-minute drive to Virginia Military Institute; three to Washington & Lee University or Virginia Horse Center.

Open: Year round.
Rates: Queen $65, $70, or $75. Two double beds $70 (for two); $15 additional person. Twin beds $70. King with TV $80. Singles $10 less. Amex, MC, Visa.
♥ ♣ ♦ ✗

Ellen says, "I've been in the hospitality business for 25 years, working in New York City for Pan Am and Finnair, and in Washington, D.C., with Finnair, Washington Circle Inn, and Fourways Restaurant. From all my worldwide travels, I fell in love with the concept of B&B, and in 1985 bought this half-century-old brick colonial. I added some new plumbing and closets and furnished with antiques and period pieces, and with things I collected from different parts of the world. In 1989 I married John, a native who knows the area well. Because he is in the building supply business, some guests who move here find that he is helpful with contractors!

(Please turn page.)

"Interesting people travel to B&Bs. Some guests are Civil War buffs. Some come for Garden Week, the Quilt Show, or the universities." And many write to me about "friendly hosts who make you feel at home."

Bed and bath: Six rooms, all private baths; three shower, three with tub and shower. Five second-floor rooms—king with sitting area and TV, three with queen beds, one with two double brass beds. First-floor room has two four-poster twin beds.
Breakfast: 8–9:30. Juice. Farm-fresh eggs with ham and sausage or bacon; French toast; or Belgian waffles. Homemade muffins or biscuits with home-made jellies. Garnished with fruit of the season. Hot beverages. Served in dining room.
Plus: Central air conditioning. Bedroom ceiling fans. Beverages and canapes. Fresh summer flowers. TV and telephone room. Will meet guests at the Greyhound bus stop.

> From Maryland: *"Hospitality is fantastic; the house is a home; the rooms are appointed quite nicely; the breakfast is a gourmet's delight and tailored to each guest; the price for all of this is quite reasonable. What more could one ask?"*

Oak Spring Farm and Vineyard   703/377–2398

Route 1, Box 356, Raphine, VA 24472

Hosts: Jim and Pat Tichenor
Location: Pastoral. A 40-acre farm with extensive lawns, an orchard, 5 acres of vineyards, hay and alfalfa fields, perennial gardens, woods and streams, and many original outbuildings. Fourteen miles north of Lexington, 20 south of Staunton. Three miles north of I–81 exit 200 (Fairfield).
Open: Year round.
Rates: Double occupancy. $63 double or twin beds, $73 queen. Singles $10 less. $15 extra person. MC, Visa.
♣ ✳ ✂

> From Pennsylvnaia: *"Every room is decorated in exquisite taste. . . . Charming hosts with interesting stories about their world travels and lots of information about local points of interest."* From Virginia: *"Hosts [who are] sensitive to your own privacy. . . . Cows and donkeys graze in the field, and geese in the nearby stream all blend into a restful farm setting, a welcome change from urban life."*

The Tichenors restored the 1826 Federal brick house in 1989, after having been hosts for four years in a Lexington Victorian house they had restored following Jim's retirement as a colonel. Here they have hung the paintings of old houses they have lived in on several continents; furnished with antiques from all over the world; and become grape growers.

Your house tour comes complete with some history, restoration discoveries, plans for an archaeological dig right here, and maybe a ghost story too. On walks through the woods you may feel "as if you're on top of the world." Miniature horses, burros, and a dwarf cow are in the pasture and barn rented by the Natural Bridge Petting Zoo. There's a springhouse still very much in use, and on the columned porch, a swing.

Foreign languages spoken: Some French and German.

Bed & bath: Three large second-floor rooms with private baths. One with a queen bed and a twin bed, en-suite tub and shower bath. Room with two Art Deco twin beds, en-suite tub/shower bath. Double bed with bath just outside room (shutters enclose path from room to bath); antique claw-foot tub positioned "so you can sit with a glass of wine or whatever and enjoy the view with complete privacy"; separate shower.

Breakfast: 8–9:30. "Something different every day." Freshly squeezed orange juice. Fresh fruit from orchard in season, fruit compotes or fruit soup. Apple spice bread, blueberry muffins, southern biscuits, "sinful but delicious" toast made from croissants. Jams and wine grape jelly. Special diets accommodated. In dining room with farm views.

Plus: Central air conditioning. Fireplaced living room. Before-dinner beverages. Down comforters. Turndown service. Handmade chocolates on pillow.

From Bernice's mailbag: "And then there was the classmate from 1935, whom I hadn't seen in 50 years, who read about us in your book. He's been here twice."

Lynchburg

This is a rediscovered city—the visitors' center is open seven days a week from 9 to 5—with two symphonies, theater, five historic districts, seven hills, one of the country's oldest farmers' markets, superb restaurants, and five colleges. Within the last few years prospective innkeepers (and others) have found Lynchburg and restored architectural treasures that were built by 19th-century residents who were successful in tobacco, cotton, iron, or flour.

B&B owners share their enthusiasm about this community "without smog or traffic problems." They direct guests to museums, including poet Anne Spencer's home and Poplar Forest, Thomas Jefferson's retreat. They share information about walking, driving, or biking tours; outlet shops; recreational sites. Fifteen minutes to the west, there's the Blue Ridge Parkway; Appomattox National Park is 15 minutes to the east. Within 45 minutes—Wintergreen ski resort, Smith Mountain Lake, Natural Bridge, Crabtree Falls, the Appalachian Trail.

Langhorne Manor

804/846–4667
800/851–1466
(guest line) 804/845–8419

313 Washington Street
Lynchburg, VA 24504-4619

Hosts: Jaime and Jaynee Acevedo
Location: In a quiet downtown neighborhood of large older homes on historic Diamond Hill. Two blocks from Visitors' Information Center, three from Lynchburg Expressway.
Open: Year round. Two-night mininum for college graduations and parents' weekends.

Rates: Double occupancy. $70 shower bath. $80 or $85 full bath. $95 suite. $15 extra person. $50–$75 business accounts. Package rates include area dining, theaters, museums, massage. Inquire about catering services and dinners for four or more. Amex, MC, Visa.

"We know it's old (1850s with major changes in 1909). We know it's big (27 rooms plus a carriage house). We think it's wonderful (grand antebellum architecture). And we are told it is magnificent!" Horseshoe-shaped exterior steps lead to a crystal-chandeliered and columned entranceway. Eclectic antique furnishings include matched Louis XIV gilt parlor pieces.

In 1987 a National Trust for Historic Preservation advertisement brought the Acevedos to the then-vacant mansion that had been converted in the 1930s to thirteen apartments. Restoration—"it's ongoing"—began with help from neighbors. Jaynee made most of the window treatments "with yard upon yard of moire, damask, tapestry, and lace." Jaynee and Jaime met while working for the same Washington, D.C., catering company. Since greeting their first guests in 1990, the historic preservationists have become very involved in the community, opened an art gallery in their enormous second-floor hall, and established a small catering business for corporate clients. Jaime's Colombian heritage influences the interesting menus and is seen in many ancestral traditions shared with guests and neighbors.

In residence: Jimmy, age eight. William, age four. Arizona is a long-haired cat.

Foreign language spoken: Jaime speaks Spanish.

Bed and bath: Four very large second-floor (19 steps from first floor) rooms with air conditioning and ceiling fans. All private baths. Three double-bedded rooms; one with shower bath, two with full bath. Suite has two double beds, sitting room, TV, full bath.

Breakfast: Usually 8:30–9; coffee earlier. Among favorites "rarely made with recipes"—gingerbread waffles/lemon ice cream; cottage cheese pancakes/sauteed fruit and yogurt; egg-and-spinach roulade; garlic potatoes; Virginia ham; fruit strudels; muffins (eggnog, spiced pear, lemon parsley, zucchini basil); scones. In oak-paneled candlelit dining room with classical music in background.

Plus: Evening beverages—hot butterscotch, spiced chocolate, panella (Spanish raw sugar and lime drink), teas. Cookies baked by the boys. Mixers and bar fruits. Babysitting. Turndown service. Off-street parking. Take-away and "getting lost" maps. Area brochure collection. Books to borrow.

> From Texas: *"Most creative and delicious breakfasts I've ever had . . . immaculate, wonderful accommodations . . . perfect proprietors . . . they enjoy what they do and make everyone feel at home in their home."*

Lynchburg Mansion Inn Bed and Breakfast

804/528–5400
405 Madison Street, Lynchburg, VA 24504-2435   800/352–1199

Hosts: Bob and Mauranna Sherman
Location: In residential National Register district with other restored mansions (tours arranged). On street with turn-of-the-century brick and Belgian block.

Open: Year round.
Rates: $84 single, $89 double. $129 suite. $20 third person. Amex, MC, Visa.
♣ ♦ ✄ ✂

Drive through the gates of the 6-foot iron fence that surrounds the stucco Spanish Georgian mansion and carriage house. Continue under the columned porte cochere. When you enter the 50-foot grand hall—pictured in *Country Inns* magazine and viewed by thousands during Historic Garden Week—you see magnificent cherry woodwork everywhere, photos from the original owner's family, and a three-storied spindled staircase. Decor is classic, elegant, and comfortable. All hardware is copper. Doorknobs are cut glass. The 105-foot wicker- and plant-filled wraparound veranda, truly an outdoor living space, is terra-cotta tiled. Azaleas, hydrangeas, boxwood, hollies, flowering trees, and wisteria too, have been planted on the grounds, which were once known for their elaborate gardens.

The Shermans, Realtors in northern Virginia for over 20 years, wanted "a grand old home and a change of place and activity. We knew nothing about Lynchburg when we saw the *Washington Post* ad for this house (which had those cherry columns hidden behind sheet rock). Now we have the joy of seeing brides toss bouquets from the Juliet balcony. Guests unwind, explore

(Please turn page.)

this luxurious B&B, sip iced tea or hot chocolate, and enjoy the city's history and culture."

In residence: In hosts' quarters—two miniature schnauzers.
Bed and bath: Four rooms with private en-suite tub/shower baths. First-floor suite has private veranda entrance, king-bedded room, solarium with queen sleep sofa, space for three-quarter rollaway, working fireplace; solarium with refrigerator (with beverages), popcorn maker. On second floor, one room has king four-poster with steps on both sides, 16 pillows, lots of lace, working fireplace, large original tub in bath. Country French room has queen four-poster, armoire, desk. The Nantucket king-bedded room has shells "and gifts from friends who know we love the water."
Breakfast: Upstairs, early coffee and juice on a silver tray. Flexible hours for meal. Orange juice and ice water in crystal. Hot or cold fruit dishes. Peach French toast, quiche, sausage-and-egg casserole or Belgian waffles with country ham. Butter shaped in roses and leaves on crushed ice. All presented in formal dining room with silver, antique china, background music.
Plus: Central two-zone air conditioning. Fireplaced living room with piano. Fireplaced library with period books. Turndown service. Beverages, goodies, and fruit always available. Many amenities, including room phones; clock radio; color TV with remote control, free HBO, ESPN, and other channels; potpourri in lace; morning newspaper at your door. Parking on premises. Hot tub planned.

From Texas: *"Five-star accommodations."*

The Madison House Bed & Breakfast
413 Madison Steeet, Lynchburg, VA 24504   804/528–1503

Hosts: Irene and Dale Smith
Location: On a tree-lined brick street in residential historic district with several restored mansions (tours arranged).
Open: Year round. Two-night minimum on weekends in May and October.

Rates: $60 single. $70 double. $80 with screened veranda. $95 suite. Holiday specials include dinner. Extended-stay and midweek discounts. MC, Visa.

The award-winning exterior restoration of the oldest house on the block features elaborate gingerbread and a cast iron front porch. Two crystal chandeliers are in the grand front hall, which has original walnut fretwork and a large floral print wallpaper. There's an antique (working) pump organ, an 1890s camera complete with its original bellows and tripod, and a stained glass peacock window in one parlor. Many portraits hang in the other parlor. All the comfortably sized rooms have original woodwork and period furnishings. Irene has collected Victorian costumes. Dale, a Civil War buff, has accumulated quite a library.

Always a private home, this 1880 wood frame house, an example of Italianate and Eastlake Victorian architecture, became a B&B when the Smiths wanted a lifestyle change. Before opening here in 1990, they personally "did everything but the wiring and plumbing." (Glass globes from an 1896 chandelier were sitting intact in the basement!) In Washington, D.C, Irene was an executive with the federal government. Now she's a full-time inn-keeper who delights in serving high tea at four, by the fire in winter. Dale, a former television news anchor in Vermont, is communications director for a medical assocation.

In residence: One small dog in hosts' quarters.
Bed and bath: Four large second-floor rooms with queen or king bed (one is canopied). All private full baths; two are original large 1895 tile rooms. One room has private wicker-furnished screened porch; another can be a suite with adjoining sitting room, large-screen TV with HBO.
Breakfast: Usually at 8:30. French toast, eggs Benedict, quiche, or eggs any style. Homemade breads and muffins, sausage or other breakfast meat, spoon bread, Dale's potatoes. Fresh fruit, tea, juice, "the best cinnamon coffee." In fireplaced dining room at antique English table set with Grandmother's silver and Wedgwood china. Can last for up to two hours.
Plus: Central air conditioning. Phone in each guest room. In portrait parlor, antique phone that works. Hair dryers. Fresh flowers. Pickup and drop-off at transportation points.

Dulwich Manor Bed & Breakfast   804/946–7207
Route 5, Box 173-A, Amherst, VA 24521

Hosts: Bob and Judy Reilly
Location: At the end of a winding country lane. On 85 acres of wood-land and meadows with mountain views and lots of wildlife. Fifteen miles north of Lynchburg, 3 from Sweet Briar College; 22 from Blue Ridge Parkway; 20 to spectacular Crabtree Falls, 45 to Natural Bridge, 25 to Wintergreen ski resort.

Open: Year round.
Rates: Double occupancy. $65 shared bath. $75 private bath and working fireplace. $85 with Jacuzzi. Honeymoon packages available. Third person in room: $20 adult, $5 under age 12, $10 ages 12–17.
♥ ♯ ♣ ♦ ✗

A perfect match. Guests agree with the hosts, who, in 1988, ended their year-long search for a new lifestyle away from the metropolitan New York area. (Bob was an actor and Judy worked in public relations and advertising.) The Reillys bought this imposing 22-room English-style brick manor house with a columned veranda, a third-floor ballroom, a large oak central staircase, five acres of lawn, and, in the spring, "a sea of lace from dogwoods." They did all the papering and painting and furnished with antiques, reproductions, and Judy's dried arrangements. They added baths (more coming) and a screened gazebo with hot tub.

The multifaceted hosts—they are the official gardeners/wedding coordi-nators/historic preservationists too—love sharing "this absolutely lush coun-tryside, which is relatively undiscovered, with guests who want to come back just to relax."

(Please turn page.)

In residence: Two dogs—one mixed breed and one cocker spaniel. Two lap cats—not allowed in guests' areas.

Bed and bath: Six air-conditioned rooms; two also have ceiling fans. On third floor, a "treehouse room" with antique double bed, country furnishings, private shower bath. On second floor, five very large queen-bedded rooms. One with canopied bed, large bath with whirlpool tub and separate shower. Two rooms—one with private shower bath, one with private tub/shower bath—have working fireplaces and window seats. One with Shaker-style canopied bed shares a full bath with room that has a queen and a twin bed. Rollaway, crib, and high chair available.

Breakfast: 8:30–9:30 weekends; weekday time set by guests. Main dish may be cheese-and-egg souffle, baked stuffed French toast, blueberry or apple pancakes. Side dish may be corn or apple fritters, potato pancakes, quiche. Bacon, ham, or sausage. Fruit in season. Orange juice, fresh-brewed teas, and coffees (decaf).

Plus: Parlor with fireplace, upright piano. Study with fireplace, TV. Refreshments. Robes. Hammock. Badminton. Double swing. Fresh flowers. Transportation to/from bus, train, or airport. Planned tour routes. Reservations for horseback riding and restaurants.

> From New Jersey, Maryland, North Carolina, Virginia, Florida, California, Massachusetts: Plaudits about everything from decor to food, from accommodations to hospitality. *"The best."*

Winridge Bed & Breakfast   804/384–7220
Route 1, Box 362, Madison Heights, VA 24572-9781

Hosts: LoisAnn and Ed Pfister
Location: On 14 acres—3 are lawn—with panoramic views of Blue Ridge Mountains. Six miles north of Lynchburg, 14 east of Blue Ridge Parkway.

Open: Year round.
Rates: Per room. $59 shared bath; $69 private. Family rate—second room is 50 percent less for under age 18.

> From Virginia, Pennsylvania, Florida, California, North Carolina, Massachusetts, Indiana, Minnesota: *"Unique blend of elegance from a bygone era and the warmth of a modern-day family. . . . great suggestions for places to eat and visit. . . . Lovely and relaxing . . . even provided a crib and toys for our eight-month-old. . . . Able to conduct my business during the day and actually look forward to return to my evening 'digs.' . . . Simple elegance. . . . Breakfasts are beautiful and delicious. . . . The bed was so-o-o comfortable that we came home and bought a similar mattress. . . . Meticulously clean . . . chocolates before bedtime. . . . The house is absolutely grand. . . . Out in the country. Nice and quiet. . . . You would have thought we were friends for years. . . . Wish we could have stayed longer."*

Those excerpts are from dozens of ecstatic letters written to me. A family atmosphere is exactly what the Pfisters had in mind when they decided to move from the Lynchburg house that they had restored to this 1910 white frame Southern colonial with mesmerizing view from its full-width second-story porch. Restoration here included four new 20-foot Corinthian columns. Ed, a Marriott Corporation general manager who plays percussion with the Lynchburg Symphony, planted perennial gardens. LoisAnn retired from her 10-year catering position "to be home with our daughters, to cook, and to meet people." It's a perfect blend.

In residence: Frances, age seven; Elizabeth, age five. Outdoors—horses Blaze and Chrissy; Charlie, a German shepherd; four cats; Bitzie, a Bernese mountain dog.
Bed and bath: Three second-floor rooms. One with queen four-poster, three large bay windows, private shower bath. Room with queen bed and another with two twins share a full bath with footed tub and brass/porcelain shower.
Breakfast: 6:30–8:30. Fresh fruit. Juice. Oven-baked French toast with pecan topping, bacon-and-cheese frittata, or stuffed French toast with fresh blueberry sauce. Strawberry cream cheese Danish, blueberry patch muffins, or coffee cakes. Hot beverages. Served in dining room with tall bay windows.
Plus: Air conditioning. Bedroom ceiling fans. Individual thermostats. Fireplaced library and living room. Cranberry cooler or mint tea. Homemade treats. Turndown service. Line-dried sheets. Books. Games. Swing. Hammock. Picnic table. Bluebird houses. Pick-your-own strawberries for snacks or picnics. Gather chestnuts to take home.

"St. Moor" House

804/929–8228

Route 1, Box 136, Monroe, VA 24574

Hosts: John and Jean Camm
Location: Serene. Surrounded by acres with pastures (cows and horses), woods, two-acre pond. Facing High Peak Mountain. Adjacent to peach and apple orchards. Eight minutes' drive to Sweet Briar College; 15 from Blue Ridge Parkway,

Otter Creek exit; 35 to Appomattox. Just off Route 29, 8 miles south of Amherst, 7 north of Lynchburg.
Open: Year round.
Rates: Shared bath $46 single, $59 double. Private bath, $65 for room.
♥ ♯ ◀ ✗ ⅍

This is worth going out of your way for. The contemporary post-and-beam house with walls of windows was built in 1975 with 1800s hand-hewn chestnut beam posts. Some of those posts frame the living room floor-to-cathedral-ceiling fireplace constructed of more than five thousand 1790-era handmade bricks. Trees on the property provided lumber for the exterior. Throughout there are comfortable antiques and Oriental rugs.

As for the enthusiastic hosts: John and his family are the sixth generation to live on the land his great-great-grandfather patented over 200 years ago. A retired educator who now maintains the land, John is known to "spin a few yarns" about current local efforts to recreate the bateaux that once river-shipped tobacco to Richmond. Jean, a war bride who knew B&B in her native England, is a retired teacher who refinishes antiques and works with historical and environmental groups.

In residence: Samson, a black Lab, and Chipper, a golden retriever, "will keep you company, if invited."

(Please turn page.)

Bed and bath: Three antiques-furnished double-bedded rooms with views of countryside. On first floor, two adjoining rooms share full bath. Second-floor room has private full bath, private balcony.
Breakfast: Usually 8:30-9. Low-cholesterol option offered. Homemade quiche, sausage/ham/cheese/egg casseroles. Hot breads, sweet rolls. Fresh fruit from neighbor's orchards. Juice, coffee, tea. Served on English china and linens in dining area or on sun porch.
Plus: Central air conditioning. Deck with those views. Hints for antiquing and sightseeing.

From Maryland: *"Combination of modern architecture and antiques; best of both worlds . . . wonderful hot breads, exquisite silver and china, flowers, cookies at night, good magazines tucked beside bed, and best of all, talk, old-fashioned adult conversation on every topic in the world."* From Washington, D.C.: *"We're bird-watchers who enjoyed the pond and adjacent fields . . . long stretches of hilly backcountry roads for running. . . . Neighbors all waved as I went by!"* From Indiana: *"When we visit our son at college, Jean always has a snack waiting for us when we return 'home.'"*

Middleburg Country Inn

109 East Washington Street, Middleburg, VA 22117

703/687–6082
800/262–6082
fax 703/687–5603

Hosts: John and Susan Pettibone
Location: On Route 50, the main street of a historic one-light town (population: 550) in fox hunting country. On landscaped grounds with apple and quince trees. Separated from Episcopal Church (open to public; needlepoint kneelers go back to 1825) by two period houses. Walk to shops, galleries, restaurants. Forty miles west of Washington D.C.; 50 to Skyline Drive. Two miles to three wineries that offer tours. Ten-minute drive to Oatlands, National Trust mansion with formal gardens.
Open: Year round.
Rates: Double occupancy. $75 Sunday–Thursday (corporate rates available). $95 Friday–Saturday; $135 Saturday only. $10 extra person. No charge for children. Amex, Discover, MC, Visa.
♥ ♨ ♣ ♦ ✗

Welcome! Upon arrival, you will be served a pot of tea and cookies in your room. And an invitation to make yourself at home, to help yourself to soft drinks and snacks in the kitchen, and (spring through fall) to take a buggy ride to the nearby horse and cattle farm that has been in John's family for three generations.

Susan learned the art of innkeeping from her mother, who was still running a North Carolina inn—in Nag's Head—at age 90. Together, in the late 1980s, Susan and John planned and directed the two-year conversion of this red brick building, a parsonage for 150 years. They tunneled through one 18-inch brick wall (guests love to hear "what was"); opened and refurbished fireplaces; furnished with antiques and favorite family pieces and yards and yards of fabric; and built a rear balcony that offers a wonderful view of the countryside—and sunsets too. Since opening in 1988, the inn has become popular with tourists (lots of international travelers) and business guests as well as wedding planners and family reunions. Before becoming full-time innkeeper, John was a Washington, D.C., brokerage firm manager. The Pettibones' three college-age children assist during school vacations.

Foreign languages spoken: French, Spanish, and "Southern English."
Bed and bath: Eight rooms on three floors, all with canopied beds—king, queen, double, or two double beds—working fireplaces, private (all new) full baths, cable TV, VCR (lending library of movies right here). Two rooms have kitchenettes. Some have pull-out sofas. Cots and cribs available.
Breakfast: 8:30–11. "A brunch prepared by John." Waffles, pancakes (plain, blueberry, or apple spice), scrambled or poached eggs, locally made sausage that is "talk of the guests." Almost-famous glazed coffee cake served warm. Homemade breads, muffins, jams, jellies, and apple butter. Hot beverages. In dining room at table for eight or at small tables with umbrellas on open veranda overlooking old cemetery, countryside, and mountains.
Plus: Central air conditioning. Fireplaced living room. Organ in lobby. Homemade brownies, cakes, cookies, or pie. Babysitting. Horseshoe pit. Off-street parking. Transportation to/from Dulles International Airport.

Greenvale Manor Waterfront Inn 804/462–5995

Route 354, Box 70, Mollusk, VA 22517

Hosts: Pam and Walt Smith
Location: On a 13-acre private peninsula on Rappahannock River and Greenvale Creek. On private mile-long catalpa tree–lined road, 1 mile from Route 354, a country road. Good seafood restaurants within 5 to 25 minutes. Near antiquing, historic sites, quiet fishing villages, golf courses, boats for rent. Two and a half hours from Washington, D.C.,

and Norfolk; 90 minutes to Richmond, Williamsburg, and Fredericksburg.
Open: Year round. Two-night minimum on holiday and May–Labor Day weekends.
Rates: Per room. $65 English basement, $75 first floor, $95 second-floor suites. $85 guest house suites. MC, Visa.
♥ ✳ ◆ ✈

> From England: *"Beautiful house, home cooking, and wonderful people. I'm in heaven."* From Virginia: *"Tranquil takes on a new meaning."* From Connecticut: *"I could not have asked for more romantic accommodations."*

A quiet getaway. Discovered by *Condé Nast Traveler, The Washingtonian, Baltimore* magazine, and *Mid-Atlantic Country*, it's a beautifully restored (by the Smiths) 1840 plantation house that has 1960s added-on wings and guest houses. Furnishings include antiques, reproductions, Walt's grandfather's oil paintings, and Pam's grandmother's quilts. There's a fireplaced den for reading. A 60-foot-wide screened veranda faces spacious croquet and badminton lawns—with ospreys and heron on the water beyond. A secluded dock for fishing and crabbing. A sandy beach and a pool. Bicycles to borrow. Sunsets. Sometimes, summer Saturday night crabfests right here.

In 1987 Pam was a personnel manager; Walt, a marketing consultant. "We were not looking for an inn when we saw this in the rain and fog and loved it. . . . Long story. After six trips from Connecticut, we saved Greenvale from the auction block." Now Pam, a full-time innkeeper, and Walt, a Realtor, host guests, including many returnees who come for peace, privacy, and hospitality.

In residence: Three cats, Annie, Pia, and Remington. Two goats, Sandstone and Huckleberry.
Bed and bath: Four rooms; two are suites. Plus two suites in one guest house. (Another guest house available for longer-term rental.) In manor house—two large second-floor suites, each with king four-poster bed, working fireplace, sitting room, shower bath. First-floor room with queen bed, shower only bath. Private and cozy queen-bedded "English basement" room (only room without water view), shower bath. In B&B guest house—suite with queen bed, tub/shower bath; suite with queen bed, tub/shower bath, deck overlooking water.
Breakfast: 8:30–9:30. (Coffee at 8:00.) Juices. Fresh fruit. Egg dishes, pancakes, or French toast. Homemade muffins. In formal dining room or on that marvelous screened veranda.
Plus: Central air conditioning. Fireplaced living room with piano. Fireplaced and paneled den with TV. Late-afternoon tea, soft drinks.

Widow Kip's Shenandoah Inn   703/477–2400
Route 1, Box 117, Mount Jackson, VA 22842   fax 703/477–2400

Hosts: Betty and Bob Luse
Location: Rural setting. Shenandoah River is 50 yards from house which is visible from I–81. Short walk to village center with four antiques shops. Four fine restaurants within 10 miles. Two hours from Washington, D.C.

Open: Year round.
Rates: In main house—$55 single, $65 or $70 double. Courtyard efficiency cottages—$75 and $85. $12 per extra person. MC, Visa.
♥ ♦ ♦ ♣ ♦

The restored 1830 home, once part of a 300-acre farm, has picture-perfect guest rooms—featured in *Country Inns*—with wonderful wallcoverings in shades of burgundy, mauves, yellow, Wiliamsburg blue, or peach and green. Guests come for all the area offers—hiking, canoeing, downhill skiing, golf, antiquing, caverns, and restaurants. And they enjoy the pool right here.

This is not a coast-to-coast-search or even a lifelong-dream story. It all began with a "You'd make great B&B hosts" comment from the Luses' daughter-in-law in Virginia. It continues with Bob, retired from the world of marketing in Manhattan, seeing a *New York Times* ad about this B&B for sale. One trip is all it took. By Christmas 1991 the Luses—Betty had extensive organizing and hostessing experience—were instant innkeepers, starting the moment they moved their Victorian furnishings into this B&B, which was established by the previous owner. Now their "forest" (it will be) of 800 newly planted trees is growing. The Shenandoah Valley Music Guild has come here for tea. The hosts, who are very active in the community, "go and see and do and eat in the restaurants of this wonderful area. B&B is like having company

24 hours a day and we love it." The feeling is mutual: Guests comment on the hospitality—and they wish Betty would write a cookbook.

In residence: Cali, a calico cat.
Bed and bath: Seven air-conditioned rooms with private baths. In main house—working fireplace in each guest room. First-floor room has 8-foot-high Lincoln double bed, shower bath. Four second-floor rooms, one with canopied double, tub and shower bath; one canopied queen, shower bath; two double-bedded rooms, shower bath. In one cottage is a double-bedded room, sitting room with trundle bed for two, cable TV, tub and shower bath, kitchenette. Second cottage has a double-bedded room, shower bath, cable TV, shower bath.
Breakfast: At 8 and at 9 (can last for a couple of hours). Stuffed French toast is a favorite. Shenandoah apple juice, homemade sausage patties, homemade muffins and breads. Fruit. Hot beverages. In Victorian dining room.
Plus: Fireplaced living room with VCR, classic old movies, game board, books. Welcoming beverages. Picnic table area with gas grill. Bicycles (no charge).

The Acorn Inn, Inc.   804/361–9357
P.O. Box 431, Nellysford, VA 22958

Hosts: Kathy Plunket Versluys and Martin Versluys
Location: Rustic, rural, peaceful. In orchard and vineyard country in Blue Ridge Mountains' foothills. On Route 634—12 miles from Wintergreen resort's ski slopes; 2½ miles to golf course, deli, restaurants; 30 miles southwest of Charlottesville.
Open: Year round. Two-night mini-

mum in October and some holiday weekends.
Rates: In barn—$47 double, $39 single. Double occupancy in farmhouse (available seasonally) $55, $10 third person. Cottage $95 for two, $10 additional person over age 16. MC, Visa.
♥ ♦ ♣ ✈ ✁

The original horse stall doors are still used —now for each of the guest rooms in the converted one-story barn. The hosts, two world travelers, have created a clean, warm, comfortable, and affordable European-style place to stay. In 1991 they added a solar water heating system and a skylit "uncommon room" with a huge locally made wood-burning soapstone fireplace and bake-oven. (Cookies often made here on chilly weekends.)

Martin, a carpenter and conservationist, formerly did microfiche work for a Dutch publisher. A native of Holland, he has bicycled through almost 100 countries. Before settling down here in 1987, Martin and Kathy, a photographer and wood-block printmaker, lived in South America for four years. Their own residence, a renovated 1937 farmhouse, is 100 yards from the inn.

In residence: Klaas, age four, rides in trailer on parents' tandem.
Foreign languages spoken: Dutch, German, Spanish, and Portuguese.
Bed and bath: Ten carpeted rooms, each about 12 feet square, with double bed, wardrobe, chair and desk, 5-foot-high screened window, individually controlled baseboard electric heat. Two baths, one for men and one for

(Please turn page.)

women, each with two sinks, two toilets separated by shuttered doors, and handicapped-accessible showers. Cottage with one bedroom, living room with TV, bath, kitchen, sleeps four or five. In January, February, May, October, and by special arrangement—two farmhouse queen-bedded rooms share a tub/shower bath.

Breakfast: Usually 8–9. Orange juice, fresh fruit, homemade whole wheat breads, sweet loaves, cream cheese, butter and jams, fruit cobbler in season. Buffet style.

Plus: Central air conditioning. Color TV. Sauna. Hot beverages always available. Microwave and toaster. Refrigerator space. Outdoor table and gas barbecue. Laundry facilities.

From North Carolina, New York, Maryland, Virginia, Washington, D.C.: *"Congenial innkeepers who specialize in the art of conversation. . . . Impressive collection of their own photographs and woodcuts. . . . The Acorn created our adventure. . . . A hybrid of a pension and a hostel. . . . Helped them make cider on an antique press. . . . Treated us like family."*

The Meander Inn

804/361-1121
fax 804/361-1380

P.O. Box 443, Routes 612 and 613
Nellysford, VA 22958

Hosts: Kathy and Rick Cornelius
Location: Secluded. Thirty minutes south of Charlottesville. A 50-acre working farm off a dirt road, just across a trestle bridge. On a granite knoll with panoramic views of Blue Ridge Mountains and Wintergreen. Half a mile off Highway 151. Within 10 minutes of wineries, Wintergreen ski resort, championship golf courses, tennis, horseback riding, and Appalachian Trail.

Open: Year round. Two-night minimum on special events' weekends and holidays.
Rates: Per room. Monday–Wednesday $70 private bath, $60 private hall bath. Thursday–Sunday $90 private bath, $80 private hall bath. Weekend rates apply during holidays and in October. MC, Visa.
♥ ♣ ♦ ✗ ✄

"Many of our guests, who come to focus on Monticello and other historic sites, stay in the country. They visit the small wineries, hike to Crabtree Falls, go horseback riding, and attend crafts or antiques shows. Or they stay right here, rock on the porch, watch the horses in the pastures, and allow Waylon to escort them to the river to fish or to look at the beaver dam. After skiing, they sip wine in the outdoor hot tub and then enjoy a gourmet meal at the nearby Stoney Creek Cafe."

This B&B sort of started with the player piano that the Corneliuses restored when they were living in Washington, D.C. Rick was the U.S. Navy's environmental attorney, and Kathy, a Paul McCartney fan, was in sales with AT&T. Subsequently they spent all of 1987 restoring this 1913 Victorian farmhouse—"perfect for the piano and people too"—and filled it with comfortable antiques and reproductions. Here they keep chickens, raise hay, and board 10 horses (not for public riding). Kathy is full-time innkeeper. Rick is president of an environmental consulting firm.

In residence: "Waylon, our rottweiler, loves to play tug-of-war with his rope and guests." Four outdoor cats. "Oscar is the great blue heron who lives on our stretch of the Rockfish River."
Foreign languages spoken: French and some Spanish.
Bed and bath: Five second-floor rooms accessed by front and back stairs. Four with queen beds (two are four-posters), private full baths; one queen room with private hall shower bath. Rollaway available.
Breakfast: Until 10. Eggs (gather your own, if you'd like) served in vegetable frittata, sausage and grits casserole, or pear pancakes. Blueberry or raspberry (freshly picked) strudel, muffins, or sweet breads. Breakfast meats, fresh or baked fruits, coffee, and juice. In dining room or on deck overlooking the river.
Plus: Central air conditioning on first level; bedrooms have separate units. Bedroom ceiling fans. Ornate wood stove in living room. Refreshments. Robes provided for outdoor hot tub open until 11 p.m. (River) swimming hole right here.

From Delaware: *"Rick and Kathy will feed your body in the morning while the Meander Inn (if you let it) nourishes your soul."*

A Touch of Country   703/740–8030
9329 Congress Street, New Market, VA 22844

Hosts: Dawn Kasow and Jean Schoellig
Location: On main street (Route 11) in a small town (population: 1,400), ¼ mile off I–81. Two hours from Washington, D.C. Thirty minutes to Skyline Drive, 15 to Luray Caverns. Across from two churches. Within walking distance of restaurants and shops.

Open: Year round. Two-night minimum on holiday and October weekends.
Rates: Double occupancy. Hallway bath 60. En-suite bath $65 double, $70 queen. Singles $10 less. Ten percent discount for entire house. MC, Visa.
🏠 ✳ ♦ ✗ ✁

From Washington, D.C.: *"Comfortably furnished . . . everything is immaculate . . . floor plan and arrangement of house enables maximum privacy . . . breakfast is a high point . . . generous and attractive portions of healthy fare . . . a wealth of information on local points of interest and history . . . a friendly and warm setting."*

The 1870s frame house was, except during its 1920s days as a tourist house, a private residence. In 1988 Jean and Dawn restored it and furnished with collectibles and some antiques. In Washington, D.C., Jean was a registered nurse and educator; Dawn was in pharmaceutical sales and education. Here they host guests who come for hiking (several special overlooks and mountain paths recommended), the Skyline Drive, antiquing, and caverns. Jean dovetails hosting with nursing; Dawn cooks at a local restaurant.

(Please turn page.)

In residence: Four dogs—two Labradors and two cocker spaniels—live in their own outdoor houses.

Bed and bath: Six air-conditioned rooms; all private shower baths. In main house—four rooms with ceiling fan and adjoining baths. Three with queen bed; one room with a double and a twin bed, paneling from old church parsonage. Carriage house has two double-bedded rooms, en-suite baths. Rollaway available.

Breakfast: 8–9:30. Fruits, eggs, breakfast meats, pancakes, French toast, breads, muffins. In dining room at three tables set for four.

Plus: Wood stove in family and living rooms. Air-conditioned family room with TV, VCR, CD, tape player. Tea and sodas. Use of refrigerator. Alpenglo sparkling cider in bedrooms. Porch swings.

Page House Inn   804/625–5033

323 Fairfax Avenue, Norfolk, VA 23507-2215

Hosts: Stephanie and Ezio DiBelardino

Location: "In Norfolk's secret garden, the old-fashioned tree-lined Ghent Historic District, a neighborhood filled with history and culture." A block from Chrysler Museum with renowned glass collection. Short walk to financial district, Waterside, Sentara Norfolk General Hospital, Eastern Virginia Medical School.

Open: Year round. Two-night minimum for Harborfest, first week in June.

Rates: Double occupancy. $75–$85 twin or double bed. $95 queen canopy with fireplace and whirlpool, $105 with fireplace, whirlpool for two. $125–$135 suites with wet bar. Singles $5 less. $25 third person.
♥ ♣ ♦ ✗ ✂

From New York: *"Not only a beautiful work of art but an exquisite experience."*

Some other guests speak of the "drawing room atmosphere created by the Perle Mesta of Norfolk" in this Georgian Revival built in 1898 with Flemish bond–pattern brickwork and a colonnaded front porch. It was scheduled for demolition in 1990 before being rebuilt by contractor Ezio DiBelardino, a Renaissance man who, like the original builder, Herman Page, immigrated to this country. Following an intense series of zoning hearings (a saga in itself), the DiBelardinos opened as a B&B in 1991. Today the elegant, comfortable, award-winning house symbolizes the impact that B&Bs have had on historic preservation and the hospitality industry. It is filled with wonderful artwork; 19th- and early 20th-century antiques and reproductions; Staffordshire china; 51 new handmade solid oak paneled doors; a monumental three-storied staircase; handmade oak Venetian blinds; and Page family mementos, including the family Bible and an 1863 lineage chart that dates back to A.D. 1237.

And there's Stephanie. A former chemical corporation executive, she, together with craftsman Ezio, is hailed by major media personalities and other travelers from all over the world; by in-vitro patients who were B&B guests in the previous Norfolk DiBelardino home; by Herman Page descendants; and by 1,000-plus local residents who toured the house for the benefit of the Children's Hospital.

In residence: Tootsie and Charlie, two Boston terriers.
Foreign languages spoken: "Fluent Italian, limited Spanish."
Bed and bath: Six rooms—three can be suites with living room and wet bar; all private baths. On second floor, queen-bedded rooms with working fire-places; two have canopied bed, whirlpool bath. On third floor, skylit rooms. Room with two twin beds, oversized shower in bath. Double sleigh bed, claw-foot tub and hand-held shower. Large twin-bedded room with deep-soaking tub in bath. Each floor has a common sitting area with views of the turn-of-the-century row houses.
Breakfast: 7–9. Continental plus. "According to guests' requests and chef's whim; includes best cappuccino in town!" Fresh fruits. Freshly baked hard rolls, muffins, or scones. In formal dining room at table set with starched linens, fine china, crystal. (Continental menu for room service.)
Plus: Central air conditioning. Fireplaced living room. Private phones in rooms. Tea or cappuccino. Soft drinks in guest refrigerator. Turndown service; mints or cookies. Fresh fruit and flowers, hospitality baskets.

The Spinning Wheel Bed and Breakfast

31 North Street, Onancock, VA 23417   804/787–7311
Winter contact: 509 South Fairfax Street   (winter) 703/684–0067
Alexandria, VA 22314

Hosts: David and Karen Tweedie
Location: On residential block on main street in historic 1680 water-front town. One block to town hall, bakery, three restaurants, gazebo in old town square, and historic museum open to public. Short walk to wharf in deep-water harbor (come by boat) or to ferry to Tangier Island. One mile from Route 13.
Open: May–October (weekends only in spring and fall). Two-night minimum on weekends.
Rates: Double occupancy. $75 third-floor rooms. $85 first- and second-floor rooms. $15 rollaway. MC, Visa.

❖ ◆ ✗

"Yes, bid on tandems! Some day we're going to have a B&B." The Tweedies' "some day" happened in 1993, when they opened the first B&B in Onancock, the "charming nonresort-like" town they fell in love with during "an adventure—a trip where we stay at B&Bs and explore unfamiliar areas."

David thinks Onancock looks the way Long Island did when he grew up there. For Karen it is reminiscent of New England, where she learned how to spin on an antique wheel. Now she has a collection—some are 250 years old—displayed throughout this 1890s folk Victorian. Over a five-year period the house has been impeccably restored by Karen, an elementary school teacher of the deaf, and David, a speech pathologist and audiologist who teaches graduate courses at Gallaudet University in Washington, D.C., along with professional tradespeople. The Tweedies have also restored their exten-sive and still-growing antiques collection. "We're auction hounds!" All the pine floors are refinished. New baths—some with Karen's own random

(Please turn page.)

pattern for tiles—are done. Old hardware and fixtures, bought at auction, are on the third-floor custom-made reproduction doors. In preparation for the grand opening, David took a gourmet cooking course. Karen modeled the quilts for the queen beds after traditional patterns in her collection.

Foreign language spoken: Karen and David know American Sign Language.

Bed and bath: Five rooms with antique brass or iron beds modified for queen mattresses; all new attached private shower baths. The three third-floor rooms have cathedral ceilings and share a deck. Rollaway available.

Breakfast: 8:30–10. Eggs Benedict, crepes, or omelet. Fruit. Homemade muffins or rolls. Hot beverages. For breakfast in bed—"a continental picnic."

Plus: Air conditioning. Bedroom ceiling fans on first and second floors. Ornate 1800s parlor stove for chilly evenings. Wine and hors d'oeuvres upon arrival. Turndown service. Mints on pillow. Bathrobes. Fresh flowers. Tandem and 10-speed bikes.

Hidden Inn

249 Caroline Street, Orange, VA 22960

703/672–3625
fax 703/672–5029

Hosts: Barbara and Ray Lonick
Location: A surprise. At the intersection of Routes 15 and 20, turn into the unpaved drive to a pocket of seven acres of lawn and trees. Four miles from Montpelier. Within 15 miles of three wineries and two battlefields; 30 miles northeast of Charlottesville, 90 minutes from Washington, D.C.

Open: Year round. Two-night minimum on weekends.
Rates: $79–$119 double, $59–$79 single. $139–$159 suite. $20 rollaway. Dinner option $29 per person. Winery, wedding, and honeymoon packages available. MC, Visa.
♥ ❖ ♦ ✄ ⚹

An amazing transformation. My husband and I stayed here when it was decorated in country style. When the Lonicks bought the Victorian farmhouse in 1986, they redecorated the spacious public areas with beautiful reproduction Victorian gas chandeliers, Oriental rugs, and formal swags. The dining room is picture perfect. (*Forbes* magazine thought so too—when they covered a cycling group that stayed here.) The large fireplaced living room has comfortable seating. Jacuzzis and fireplaces are added features now that a guest house, a carriage house, and a cottage have been renovated. Guests requested recipes so often that Barbara wrote a 50-page cookbook.

Before becoming fun-loving hosts, the Lonicks lived in Washington, D.C., and San Francisco while Ray was a Xerox sales executive. Their four-year search for a new career and place brought them to this area, which they knew from driving their daughter to Sweet Briar College. Now they host many who come for romantic getaways, many returnees, and many who like good food.

In residence: "Duke, a lovable Chinese pug. Outdoor cats patrol the grounds."
Foreign language spoken: Spanish.

Bed and bath: Ten rooms. Five in main house (first and second floors). Total of five—two with working fireplace—in three other buildings; one with screened porch, one with private deck, one with private veranda. All private baths; oversized Jacuzzi tubs, tub/shower units, or shower only. King/twins, queen, or double beds; some four-posters, some canopied or brass; handmade quilts (some by Barbara). Cottage has skylights, double-sized Jacuzzi tubs, color TV.

Breakfast: 8–10; other times for business travelers. Juice, cereal (oatmeal in winter), homemade muffins and biscuits, fresh fruit with yogurt and granola, cheese eggs, maple-flavored sausage, pumpkin pancakes. "Our own special coffee."

Plus: Air conditioners in all bedrooms, ceiling fans in some. Electronic piano in main living room. Tea (included in rate) at 4 p.m. with cookies or homemade breads. Wicker-furnished wraparound porch. Guest refrigerators. Bath sheets. For late arrivals, candlelight picnic basket ($39) with champagne or wine. With advance notice, dinner option Tuesday–Saturday.

The Holladay House

155 West Main Street, Orange, VA 22960-1528

703/672–4893
800/358–4422
fax 703/672–3028

Hosts: Pete and Phebe Holladay

Location: On a block of older homes—next door to Pete's Uncle Billy's house—with lovely gardens and treed yards. Across from gas station in this friendly historic town. Minutes' walk to James Madison Museum, church where General Robert E. Lee worshiped, historical society, cafe and market in an old firehouse. Four miles east of Montpelier. "Our countryside has rich farmlands, pick-your-own orchards, interesting little shops, and vineyards to tour." Ninety minutes from Washington, D.C., and Richmond, Virginia; 30 from Charlottesville.

Open: Year round. Two-night minimum on October weekends.

Rates: $75 semiprivate bath. $95–$120 private bath. $15 rollaway. $185 two-room suite with kitchenette. Midweek ski rates available. MC, Visa.

♥ ♨ ✿ ⚓ ♦ ✈ ⚒

If your idea of B&B is "a sense of place," you have come to the right place. Doctor Holladay, Pete's grandfather, bought this 1830 Federal house in 1899 and added to it as the family grew. In 1989, after Phebe and Pete restored the house—they even removed paint from the exterior brick—they received a beautification award. Phebe, an elementary school art teacher, chose all the wonderful room tones of peach, blue, rose, and green. For all to see, at the top of the stairs, she placed a magnificent silk and velvet quilt made with intricate patches, each signed by friends and relatives of Pete's great-grandmother. Pete, a born innkeeper (complete with beard), "placed other family heirlooms where Phebe told me to"—and changed careers. Formerly he was a college business manager. Now he is also a part-time real estate agent—and president of the superb state association of bed and breakfasts.

(Please turn page.)

In residence: Zachery Lee Taylor and Tigger Two are "two yellow tabbies kept in hosts' quarters, although some guests encourage them to break the rules."

Bed and bath: On three levels, four large rooms and one two room suite, each with sitting area. One room with queen four-poster shares a large full hall bath with smaller (but popular) room with double rope bed (chamber pot and washstand are part of decor). Queen-bedded room has Victorian furnishings, adjoining large full bath. Another queen-bedded room has adjoining private shower bath. Ground-level suite (great for families or two couples traveling together) has one room with a double bed and a single bed, sitting area, and kitchenette; large full bath connects to room with double bed. Rollaway available.

Breakfast: Anytime before 10. Pete's almost-famous biscuits, muffins, and scones. Juice, fresh fruit, fried apples, eggs. Usually brought to your room; if you prefer, served in dining room.

Plus: Guest rooms have air conditioners (some have ceiling or window fans and phone jacks too); TV in some. Mints. Some rooms have guest refrigerator. Bathrobes. Fresh garden flowers. Side porch with swing. Back deck.

Sleepy Hollow Farm B&B   703/832–5555
16280 Blue Ridge Turnpike, Gordonsville, VA 22942   fax 703/832–2515

Hosts: Beverley Allison and Dorsey Allison Comer

Location: In historic rural district, on U.S. Route 231. Three miles north of Gordonsville; 9 miles southwest of Orange; six to Montpelier; 25 to Skyline Drive; 60 from Richmond; 90 from Washington, D.C. Near horseback riding and horse stabling (at neighboring farm), golf, wineries, antiquing, fishing, crafts, hiking, gardens, old Indian digs.

Open: Year round. Two-night minimum most weekends in April, May, June, October, and November.

Rates: Main house $60–$95 double, $50–$75 single; $125 quad suite, $15 fifth person. Cottage $85–$95 double, $75 single; $120–$130 two couples; $225 four couples. MC, Visa.
♥ ♨ ⁂ ♦

Set in a peaceful hollow, the (constantly) added-on-to 18th-century house (bricked over in the 1940s) is surrounded by a pond used for swimming and fishing; a gazebo; barn; croquet lawn and playing field; stream; and herb gardens used for cooking and garnishing. The Blue Ridge Mountains form the backdrop for cattle on a neighbor's pasture.

Since Beverley began hosting in 1984, she has made some interesting changes with the help of her builder son. Now adjoining the gracious antiques-filled beamed and fireplaced dining room is a glass-enclosed terrace, filled with light, plants, and an enchanting dollhouse too. The cottage, finished in antique pine and old chestnut wood, has country charm.   A former ABC news journalist and missionary in Central and South America, Beverley is a writer, a graphic designer, the chairman of a missionary organization for Honduras, and a fabulous cook who sets a very attractive table. In addition, as parents will tell you, she has a special way with kids.

Guests also receive a warm welcome from daughter Dorsey, one of five siblings who grew up here.

In residence: Three dogs: "Brew is old, dignified, gentle. Sheila is a good Aussie. Bartles, a Border terrier, suffers from terminal cuteness." Two cats. "And one grandchild is on the payroll."

Foreign languages spoken: Spanish and French.

Bed and bath: Six rooms, each quite different; all private baths. In main house on first floor, room with antique double four-poster canopied bed (pictured in *New York Times*), dressing room, private tub/shower bath; another with antique queen bed, working fireplace, Jacuzzi bath. On second floor, smallish double-bedded room with private hall tub/shower bath. Suite of two connecting rooms (one beyond the other), one with a double and a single; other with two twin beds; tub bath tucked under eaves. In cottage—one two-storied suite has kitchen, great room with wood stove and queen sofa bed, upstairs double-bedded room and new shower bath. Other suite has fireplaced sitting room, double sofa bed, upstairs double-bedded room, new shower bath. Rollaway and crib available.

Breakfast: Usually 7:30–9:30. Farm-fresh eggs (Dorsey raises chickens), local bacon and sausage. Fried apples. Home-baked breads and biscuits. Hot and cold cereals. Fruit cobbler, sausage/cheese/herb pies, or cheese grits.

Plus: Central air conditioning. Welcoming refreshments. Fresh fruit and flowers. Turndown service. Mints. Phone jacks. TV in some rooms. Guest refrigerator. Swings. Sandbox. Babysitting.

> From Virginia: *"Beverley Allison is genuinely interested in people. The house and grounds say 'welcome!' . . . full of beautiful old furniture and pictures . . . could easily be Grandmother's house."*

Danscot House   804/589–1977
P.O. Box 157, Palmyra, VA 22963

Hosts: Connie and Sven Pedersen

Location: Set way back from Route 15 on 100 acres of woods for hiking, pond and open pasture. Bordered by a bird sanctuary, by Rivanna River to the north, and by Raccoon Creek to the South. One mile south of Palmyra, 9 miles south of I–64. Twenty minutes to Monticello; 30 to Charlottesville, 60 to Richmond. Within 25 minutes of several vineyards.

Open: Year round. Two-night minimum on Fork Union Military Academy's Parents Day (October) and Graduation Day (May).

Rates: Double occupancy. Shared bath $50; $60 with fireplace. Private bath $70 with fireplace. $10 rollaway.

♥ ⬛ ♣ ♦ ✈ ✂

Guests seem as interested in the Pedersens' 18 years in East Africa as they are in this historic 1777 farmhouse, which has served as a tavern (overnight guests came on horseback), a courthouse, and a jail. Now it is furnished with European antiques and African art. Often, foreign travelers are greeted with the flag of their home country flying from the pole. Sven, from Denmark, and Connie, from Scotland, both grew up in families that were in the hotel and

(Please turn page.)

restaurant business. They met and married in Tanganyika, now Tanzania, East Africa, and their three children were born in Kenya, not far from the equator.

From 1974 until Sven retired from his corporate position in 1989, the hosts lived in Long Island, where Connie was a Realtor. After purchasing this bucolic property, they "rearranged" the interior, added decks and baths, and welcomed their first guests in 1991.

In residence: MacAllister ("Mac"), a Yorkie terrier, and Penny, a mutt.
Foreign languages spoken: Danish, German, and Swahili. "Norwegian and Swedish understood."
Bed and bath: Three second-floor rooms. One room with queen four-poster bed has working fireplace, private tub/shower bath. Another large fireplaced room has two twin beds; shares a shower bath with smaller room that has two twin beds. Rollaway available.
Breakfast: Usually at 9. Full English menu. Eggs any style, bacon, cereals, fruits, juices, fresh bread from local Mennonite bakery. In fireplaced dining room.
Plus: Central air conditioning. Bedroom ceiling fans. Fireplaced living room. Guests' library/TV room with veranda overlooking garden and pond. Turn-down service. Mints on pillow. Fresh flowers. Guest refrigerator. Make-your-own tea and coffee arrangements in each guest room. Suggestions include "must-see Monticello" along with Palmyra's stone jail museum, built in 1828 "when the prison and courthouse on our farm became obsolete."

The High Street Inn   804/733–0505
405 High Street, Petersburg, VA 23803

Hosts: Candace Noé and Carol Pond
Location: "Just off I–95" in historic district with homes built from 1735 to 1900. On a street studied by architecture students. Two blocks from museums, shops and restaurants. Thirty minutes from downtown Richmond or James River planta-tions. Within an hour of Williamsburg and Busch Gardens.
Open: Year round.
Rates: Double $50–$55 shared bath, $60–$70 private. Suite $80. Singles $5 less. Rollaway $10. MC, Visa.
♥ ♨ ♦ ✈

> From Pennsylvania: *"We came across it by accident but have been back many times. . . . Our son and his bride spent the first night of their honeymoon there, due to our singing its praises. . . . Very helpful innkeepers."* From Ohio: *"A treasure."* From Virginia: *"Impeccable. . . . Exquisite in every detail from the lace curtains to the furnishings. . . . A warm welcome."*

Each high-ceilinged guest room reflects a different period, from Empire to Eastlake. There are still some gas/electric fixtures and original beveled mirrors. Since opening as a B&B in 1986, the 18-room yellow brick 1891 Queen Anne house fronted by an iron fence has been on a Historic Garden Week in Virginia tour and the Noés have received a Historic Petersburg Foundation Preservation-Restoration Design Award.

When the Noé family grew, they moved across the street, and Carol, an area native, brought to innkeeping her knowledge of history along with a love of people and old houses. "Often guests who say they want to leave early decide to enjoy their stay and a leisurely breakfast." Guests meet Candace on the mornings that Carol attends college courses, "now that my children have finished their degrees!"

Bed and bath: Five second-floor rooms. All baths have shower and claw-footed tub. Private baths for suite with queen-sized bed and sitting room, room with double bed and balcony, and room with two twin beds. Two double-bedded rooms share a bath. Rollaway and crib available.
Breakfast: 8–9:30. Juice, fresh fruit, croissants, home-baked muffins, Virginia ham biscuits, coffee or tea. Served in dining room.
Plus: Bedroom air conditioners. Refreshment bar. Parlor with a playable melodeon. Tour of house. VCR with classic and foreign films. Stereo. Books and games. Off-street parking.

Colvin Hall Bed and Breakfast   703/948–6211
HCR 03, Box 30G, Route 230 East, Pratts, VA 22731-9801

Hosts: Dave and Sue Rossell
Location: Quiet. In the Central Piedmont region, near wineries (five within 20-mile radius), antiques shops, Civil War battlefields. Ten minutes to Montpelier. One mile east of Route 29. Twenty minutes south of Culpeper, 25 north of Charlottes-ville and east of Skyline Drive/Shenandoah National Park. Ninety minutes from Richmond, Virginia, or Washington, D.C.
Open: Year round.
Rates: $60 twin beds. $85 queen or king bed. MC, Visa.
🛥 ❀ ✈ ✄

From Maryland: *"A fascinating place with interesting nooks and corners . . . queen bedroom with loft and fireplace, quilts, lots of special touches. . . . Far enough to get away from it all but also near to my favorite hiking spots. . . . We were so excited by the scenery that we hiked all the way to the highest waterfall . . . mulled cider and homemade coffee cake in our room, several morning newspapers, delicious breakfast prepared to suit my impossible special diet . . . but most of all warm and congenial company."*

Drive through the red gates to 7½ acres of open pasture and woods, to this tin-roofed center hall 1870 house that was added to around 1900. In the 1980s, when the Rossells restored and updated the cozy country retreat (see the fascinating before-and-after photo album), they decorated with a country flavor, with crafts, quilts, and bing cherry reds and slate blues. They retained the original heart pine floors and wainscoting. In back they added a tier of decks including one around an above-ground swimming pool. Since opening in 1989, they have been recommended in the *New York Times*. Sue is an elementary school teacher. Dave is a university administrator. Guests—including romantics—can tell that they enjoy sharing their home.

In residence: Four cats—Corky, Spunky, Sylvia, Patches.

(Please turn page.)

Bed and bath: Three second-floor rooms. Large one with canopied queen bed, vaulted ceiling, working stone fireplace, private hall shower/tub bath just outside the room. Another large room has king bed with antique walnut headboard, original tiled working fireplace flanked by wing chairs, with private shower bath. Room with king/twins option (access to sitting room with a daybed and color remote cable TV) shares first-floor shower bath with hosts. Rollaway available.

Breakfast: Usually 8:30–9:30. Blueberry, peach, pumpkin, or whole wheat pancakes with Vermont maple syrup and link sausages; stuffed French toast and grits with bacon or sausage; or bacon/ham or sausage strata. Fruit dish. Homemade breads or biscuits. Coffees, teas, and juices. Served in "bountiful amounts" on china in dining room; or served on wicker-furnished sun porch or on deck under umbrella.

Plus: Central air conditioning. Fireplaced living room. Beverages. Fresh flowers. Flannel sheets. Down comforters. Horseshoe pits.

The Emmanuel Hutzler House   804/355–4885

2036 Monument Avenue, Richmond, VA 23220   804/353–6900

Hosts: Lyn M. Benson and John Richardson

Location: In middle of 1⅓-mile-long historic district of boulevard with grassy median in middle, imposing bronze statues of Confederate heroes, and architecturally diverse mansions on both sides. Ten minutes to downtown financial district or West End. Within walking distance of restaurants. One and a half miles from I–64 and I–95.

Open: Year round.

Rates: $89–$125. $10 rollaway. Corporate midweek discounts. Amex, Discover, MC, Visa.

♥ ⁂ ♦ ✈ ⊁

The grand Italian Renaissance home was totally restored in the late 1980s by Lyn, a former social worker and volunteer coordinator for the state of Virginia, and John, her partner, who manages corporate apartments. The two-and-a-half-year project has resulted in a warm, welcoming "old Richmond" ambiance with the original mahogany and oak paneling, marble fireplace, interior columns, and coffered beamed ceiling on the first floor. Upstairs, rebuilt rooms feature added architectural details such as old moldings and fireplace mantels. Throughout, there are antiques and reproductions and Lyn's collections of miniature antique furniture and oil-on-board folk art paintings by a Virginia artist. The hosts are well versed in the history of the house. And about the famous boulevard and its other houses too. And in the art of hospitality: Lyn's bed and breakfast reservation service, page 315, is one of the oldest in the country.

In residence: TC, "a handsome 20-pound gray striped tabby cat."

Bed and bath: Four second-floor queen-bedded rooms; two with a four-poster. All with coordinated fabrics and wallcoverings. All adjoining private tiled shower and tub baths; one with separate dressing area and one with double sinks, 4-by-6 Jacuzzi tub, separate shower.

Breakfast: Usually 8–9:30. (Earlier for business guests.) French toast, scrambled eggs, or egg casserole with mushroom sauce. Juice, fresh fruit, cereals, hot beverages. Served in formal dining room.
Plus: Central air conditioning. In-room telephone and cable television. Lighted off-street parking.

From Washington: *"Our third B&B on this trip. The nicest bath, the coziest bedroom, and the best host and hostess. Thoroughly enjoyed the visit and the house."*

Summerhouse
Richmond, VA

Location: On historic Monument Avenue. Two-block walk to 15-minute bus ride to center city. Forty-five minutes to Williamsburg.
Reservations: Year round through Bensonhouse, page 315.
Rates: Second floor $95 single, $105 double. Third floor $85–$95 per room. Honeymoon or anniversary package includes hospitality basket, fruit and cheese tray, fresh flowers, and, if you'd like, breakfast in bed.
♥ ☕ ♣ ♦ ✖ ✄

Featured in *Southern Living,* on a Christmas tour, and on a Virginia garden tour, this 1909 Greek Revival house is richly appointed with Oriental rugs, French crystal chandeliers, and oil paintings. The hosts, antiques collectors, began in 1987 by gutting a burned-out residence and finished with the installation of recessed lighting and authentically reproduced millwork. Still—after renovating six houses—their enthusiasm is high. Still, after many years of hosting, they they find bed and breakfast guests "absolutely wonderful."

In residence: A five-pound dog who barks only when you knock at the door.
Bed and bath: Two rooms maximum booked at a time; shared bath arranged only for members of same party. All rooms are carpeted. On third floor—one full bath; room with two twin four-poster beds; another with queen bed, wet bar, and refrigerator. Second floor has queen bed, full bath, optional adjoining suite with working fireplace. Rollaway available.
Breakfast: 7–9:30. Fresh juice, muffins, butter, coffee, tea. Served on silver trays with starched napkins, sterling flatware, silver coffee service, fresh flowers.
Plus: Central air conditioning. Beverages. Cable TV in each room. Tour of house. Fireplaced living room.

From Washington, D.C.: *"We were thrilled with our first bed and breakfast experience! . . . Absolutely lovely. . . . We felt we had spent a delightful weekend with friends."*

---

*G*uests arrive as strangers, leave as friends.

University of Richmond Area B&B
Richmond, VA

Location: Quiet. In a wooded, quiet residential cul-de-sac near the University of Richmond.
Reservations: Year round through Bensonhouse, page 315.

Rates: $60 single, $68 double. $15 rollaway for child.
◀ ✖ ⅄

Four out of five guests—or so it seems—have a mutual friend or acquaintance with this well-traveled host, an avid gardener and bridge player who has been to France, Russia, China, Japan, and Europe. Now that the family is grown and gone, the energetic host welcomes Richmond visitors to this immaculate, eclectically furnished old frame house.

Bed and bath: With garden entrance—one large room with two twin beds, en-suite tub/shower bath.
Breakfast: 7:30–9. Juice, fruit, cereal. Bacon and eggs or, by request, a substitute. Hot beverages.
Plus: Central air conditioning. Antiques-furnished living room. Lots of books. Use of patio off garden.

> From Georgia: *"We had a wonderful experience here. Our hostess was delightful, warm and most hospitable. Happy to recommend the same to everyone."*

The William Catlin House Inn   804/780–3746
2304 East Broad Street, Richmond, VA 23223

Hosts: Bob and Josie Martin
Location: In the city in a restored historic neighborhood with brick sidewalks, residences (one converted to a restaurant), offices in row houses across the street, and—a block away—St. John's Church, where in 1775 Patrick Henry gave his "Give me liberty or give me death" speech.

A few blocks—half a mile—to downtown shops and restaurants. And one-half mile from Route 95.
Open: Year round.
Rates: (Taxes included.) Private bath $89.50 double, $72.50 single. Shared bath $70 double. $140 suite. Discover, MC, Visa.
♥ ◀ ♣ ♦ ✖

Empire furnishings and Oriental rugs are in most rooms of this restored 1845 house. "And someday it will be all Empire," says Josie, who together with Bob, an antiques buff, looked at properties "all over—including Kentucky, Mississippi, Alabama, South Carolina, and New York"—before deciding that this well-established B&B, featured in *Southern Living* and *Colonial Homes,* was in the right history-filled location for their desired lifestyle change. In Pennsylvania they lived in an old country farmhouse. Bob was a newspaper photographer, Josie a police dispatcher. Here they greet guests from all over the world. They offer a wake-up call with coffee or tea before breakfast; also lots of sightseeing tips, antiquing information, and maps.

Bed and bath: Five rooms. On second floor—queen canopied beds and working fireplaces. Two rooms with private full baths; two share bath. Ground-floor suite with exterior entrance has one room with two twin beds and one with a double four-poster, working fireplace, shower/tub bath, and patio.

Breakfast: 7–9. Juice and/or fresh fruit. French toast with fried apples, bacon and eggs, pancakes and sausage. Served by candlelight in crystal-chandeliered dining room.

Plus: Central air conditioning. Fireplaced living room and dining room. Guest refrigerator. Sherry. Transportation from airport, bus, or train station.

The Mary Bladon House   703/344–5361

381 Washington Avenue, S.W., Roanoke, VA 24016-4303

Hosts: Bill and Sheri Bestpitch
Location: On a corner in a National Register historic district with other Victorian homes. Just outside and within walking distance of downtown business district. Twelve blocks from restored Farmers' Market and "Center in the Square" arts and entertainment complex. Five minutes from Blue Ridge Parkway, 10 south of I–81.
Open: Year round.
Rates: $60 single. $75 double. $110 suite for one or two; $10 each additional person. For business travelers and for five or more consecutive nights, 20 percent less. MC, Visa.
♥ ⚔ ⁂ ◆ ✕ ⚰

From Canada: *"On three-week trip . . . one of the best B&Bs we found."* From Scotland: *"Very attractive . . . friendly, welcoming proprietors."* From North Carolina: *"Took a personal interest in seeing that we enjoyed our entire visit."* From Illinois: *"Charming, clean, and very comfortable . . . food was homemade and well presented. . . . Our favorite spot was the swing on the Victorian porch."* From Virginia: *"Total experience was great."* From Australia: *"When I arrived home* [from a worldwide cycling tour], *there in the mail was my lost T-shirt I had left at Bladon House. Now that's what I call service!"*

Bill was a state agency administrator (now he's a program development planner) and Sheri an accountant when, in 1990, they changed careers by buying this established Victorian B&B. It is furnished with a blend of fanciful Victorian and simpler Eastlake pieces.

Foreign language spoken: German.
Bed and bath: Two rooms plus a two-room suite. Rockers and easy chairs in all bedrooms. One upstairs room and one downstairs with access to wraparound front porch each have a double bed and private shower bath. Second-floor suite (good for families) has private balcony, full bath, eat-in kitchen, three-quarter rollaway bed, a double bed in two bedrooms, each with ceiling fan. Crib available.
Breakfast: Anytime until 9:30. Cook's choice of pancakes, waffles, French toast, or eggs; bacon, ham, or sausage; home fries or grits; fresh fruit, juice, coffee, tea. Hot and cold cereals available.

(Please turn page.)

Plus: Window air conditioners throughout. Victorian-furnished parlor with Victorian playing cards on writing table. Late-afternoon tea with homemade cookies. Down comforters. Flannel sheets. Guest refrigerator. Fresh flowers. Transportation from local airport. Cordless phone available. TV by request. Dinner, theater, and concert reservations made. Dinner by advance reservation ($20 per person) for four or more.

The Manor at Taylor's Store

Route 1, Box 533, Smith Mountain Lake, VA 24184

703/721–3951
800/248–6267

Hosts: Lee and Mary Lynn Tucker
Location: On 120 Piedmont region acres with magnificent mountain views, six private spring-fed ponds, trails. Five minutes from restaurants and recreational facilities of Smith Mountain Lake; 20 minutes to Blue Ridge Parkway and Roanoke.
Open: Year round. April–October, two-night minimum with Saturday night stay.
Rates: Per room. Private bath $75, $80, $90, and $100. Semiprivate bath $80. Ten percent less for business travelers and innkeepers. MC, Visa.
♥ ♨ ♣ ♦ ✖ ⌿

It's romantic. And historic. And the perfect setting for frequent hot-air balloon launchings. This is a place to get away from it all. Or find plenty to do.

The easy-to-be-with Tuckers added a sun room, a lattice-enclosed hot tub, an exercise room, and a slate-floored Great Room with billiard table and large-screen TV to the circa 1820 Federal-style colonial mansion that they, as newlyweds in the mid-1980s, restored and furnished with lovely antiques. Mary Lynn, a former registered nurse specializing in nutrition, thinks of renovating as "having a three-dimensional canvas to paint on." (Subsequently, she became the first president of the Bed & Breakfast Association of Virginia, a model organization.) Lee is a pathologist, a vintager (chardonnay and gewurztraminer grapes are maturing in the vineyard), and, at times, a bricklayer too.

In residence: Outdoors—Saint George and Basil, Newfoundlands; three cats; two Arabian horses and one quarter horse. Ducks and geese at the ponds.
Foreign language spoken: A little German.
Bed and bath: Six rooms (plus three-bedroom cottage for families or groups). On garden level with private exterior entrance—double bed, shower bath, private indoor wicker-furnished sitting porch. Main-level room has two canopied double beds, working fireplace, tub and shower bath. On second floor—queen canopied bed, bath, and dressing room with sunken bath for two. Victorian room with double bed, shower bath. Colonial room with queen canopied bed, French doors to balcony shares large tub and shower bath with queen canopied bed that also has French doors to balcony.
Breakfast: Time arranged with guests. Heart-healthy menu. Baked pancakes, waffles, muffins, quiches, souffles. In formal fireplaced dining room with picture window overlooking mountains (and, sometimes, a hot-air balloon launch) or in plant-filled sun room.

Plus: Central air conditioning. Beverages and cookies. Guest kitchen. Five working fireplaces in common rooms. Baby grand piano and Stanford White tall clock in parlor. Library. Movies. Terry robes. Newly planted formal colonial garden. Right here—canoeing, fishing, hiking, swimming, cross-country skiing, ice skating. And—someday—an archaeological dig on site.

From North Carolina: *"Elegant charm. . . . Having stayed in inns and B&B in North America and Europe, we would give this outstanding B&B and its hosts the highest rating."*

Ashton Country House

703/885–7819
1205 Middlebrook Avenue, Staunton, VA 24401-4546   800/296–7819

Hosts: Sheila Kennedy and Stan Polanski
Location: Peaceful. Set way back from secondary road on 24 acres with lots of trees and Lewis Creek in front. In back—a bank barn, pastureland, and a hill from which there's a great view of mountains (Alleghenies and Blue Ridge) and spires of Staunton.

Open: Daily in summer; on weekends and holidays year round. Two-night minimum July 4, Memorial Day, late-September weekends, and all October weekends.
Rates: Double occupancy. $80 master room; $20 adjacent room with single sleigh bed. Other rooms $65 double, $60 single.
♥ 🖼 ✳

From Florida: *Great food, a lovely house and, best of all, super people."* From New York: *"Truly a gem. Comfortable yet grand at the same time. . . . Gourmet breakfast served with fine china and silver. When Stan played the piano* [Porter, Gershwin, and Ellington selections] *during coffee, we felt as if we were in a movie."* From North Carolina: *"Exactly what we had pictured a B&B to be . . . attention to detail in each room. . . . First evening ended up in the kitchen while Sheila was cooking . . . one by one other guests joined us—probably drawn by the aroma. . . . We're already planning our next stay."*

That's just the B&B style Sheila, a sixth-grade teacher and graduate of the New York Restaurant School, dreamed about "all through my thirties—with a vow to open by age 40!" When she and husband Stan, a professional musician and a computer programmer, "discovered" Staunton in 1987, they bought this spacious pillared 1860 Greek Revival with brick walls inside and out (privacy ensured) and four porches (hear birds, cows, the creek). Before opening in 1990, they decorated with yellows, roses, and creamy greens; used pattern-on-pattern concepts; and furnished with a blend of antiques, many oil lamps "for an old-timey smell," and lots of rocking chairs. And in 1991 *Bon Appétit* included the B&B in a Shenandoah Valley feature.

In residence: All outdoors—Cyrus and Joey, the goats, who take walks with guests; Jasper Angus White (Jaws), a West Highland white terrier; 14 cats, all named.
Bed and bath: Four second-floor rooms (one has adjoining single) with nonworking fireplaces. Queen or double bed; some canopied. Private baths with shower stalls for two (little seat in each corner) and heat lamps.

(Please turn page.)

Breakfast: Flexible timing. Usually one serving. Orange juice, spiced coffee, teas, freshly baked muffins, fresh fruit, compote, baked egg dish with bacon or sausage, home fries, pancakes. In fireplaced dining room with rose-colored ceiling. (Can last for a very long time on winter Sundays!)

Plus: Fireplaced living room with 1930 Knabe grand piano. Ceiling fans in bedrooms (on 11-foot ceilings). For late-afternoon arrivals, tea with scones and cookies, lemonade, coffee, mineral water. Flannel or all-cotton sheets. Chocolates. Recipes shared. Maps for hiking, biking, antiquing, dining.

Frederick House

703/885–4220
800/334–5575

Frederick and New Streets, P.O. Box 1387
Staunton, VA 24401

Hosts: Joe and Evy Harman
Location: In downtown historic Staunton, across from Mary Baldwin College. Within walking distance of Woodrow Wilson Birthplace and refurbished Amtrak train station. Near Skyline Drive, Blue Ridge Parkway, and Museum of American Frontier Culture.

Open: Year round.
Rates: Double occupancy. $85 suite, $75 large room, $50 small room, $20 extra person. Amex, DC, Discover, MC, Visa.
♥ ⚔ ⚜ ♦ ✶ ⚲

> From New York: *"Akin to staying at the home of a good friend or doting relative! . . . More reasonable than places with half the amenities or hospitality."* From Maine: *"The combination of Joe Harman, a super-accommodating innkeeper, and the warm and immaculate, relaxing and luxurious accommodations really helped me unwind."* From Pennsylvania: *"A delight. Antique furnishings, hardwood floors, Oriental rugs. . . . Breakfast was stupendous."*

The feeling is mutual: Joe Harman loves doing what he does here in the town where he grew up. In Washington, D.C., he was a banker, Evy an auditor. In 1983 they became award-winning restorers after supervising a crew that converted three adjoining houses, built in 1810, 1850, and 1910, into the inn. In time they bought one neighboring building and then another. So now there are five on the same block. Between two there's a courtyard with fragrant garden that brings a lavender aroma to the inn, a lovely place furnished with antiques and period pieces.

The hosts also have a jewelry store (Evy's work), and they operate a farm. Joe is the full-time innkeeper who tells guests about restaurants, a walking tour (right here) of the historic area, mountain hiking trails, or back roads for cycling or driving.

Bed and bath: Fourteen rooms—six suites and eight rooms, each with private bath and entrance. King, queen, double, and twin-sized beds. Cots and crib available.

Breakfast: Usually 8–10:30. Choose from long menu including apple raisin quiche, ham-and-cheese pie, granola with yogurt and fruit, homemade waffles. Special diets accommodated. Juice, fresh fruit, homemade bread, coffee and tea. Evy is chef. Classical or mountain (dulcimer) music plays. Guests tend to linger here in the just-for-guests Chumley's Tearoom.

Plus: Each room has TV, AM/FM radio, phone, air conditioning, ceiling fan, terry robes. Extra charge for exercise facilities and indoor swimming pool (both at athletic club next door), and for laundry facilities or babysitting.

The Sampson Eagon Inn

238 East Beverly Street, Staunton, VA 24401

703/886–8200
800/597–9722
fax 703/886–8200

Hosts: Frank and Laura Mattingly
Location: Bordered by wrought iron fence in a neighborhood of beautifully preserved mid- to late-19th century residences. One block from Woodrow Wilson Birthplace and Mary Baldwin College; 2 from downtown shops and restaurants. Four miles from I–81/I–64. Forty minutes west of Charlottesville.

Open: Year round. Two-day minimum on fourth weekend in May, July 3–4, and October weekends.
Rates: $75 double. $65 single. Suites $85 double, $75 single. $15 daybed in suites. Corporate rates and AARP, senior citizen, and off-season discounts available.
✿ ◆ ✈ ⊬

From Virginia: *"Everything exquisitely attended to—from the restoration, furnishings, and landscaping, to the elegant but very relaxed and delicious breakfast."* From California: *"The owners have thought of everything—and they are extremely helpful and friendly."*

The Mattinglys, Renaissance folks indeed, combined all their interests when they spent 18 months restoring their elegant in-town residence. "Pick a period" Laura says of the restoration. "This Greek Revival (circa 1840) mansion has Italianate, Victorian, and Colonial Revival elements in its five later remodelings and additions." In 1992, a year after opening, they were awarded the Historic Staunton Foundation Preservation Award.

For 20 years Frank was a hospital administrator in the Washington, D.C., area. Then he started a company to preserve old buildings. "His specialties of paint finishes and plaster came in handy when he decided to become an innkeeper." Laura was an art college administrator, with the Corcoran Gallery in Washington. And together, the avid gardeners had a part-time antiques business. Now Frank has a part-time business in old-house restoration including log houses.

The gracious setting is enhanced by antique furnishings—mostly Federal and Empire—from their personal collection. The attention to detail is based on their own B&B experiences.

(Please turn page.)

Bed and bath: Four air-conditioned rooms, each with canopied queen bed, private attached modern bath, TV with VCR. One large first-floor bedroom with sitting area and sit-down shower (with hand-held shower head). On second floor—three rooms (two are suites with sitting room and daybed) with tub/shower bath.

Breakfast: Usually 8–9. (Early coffee on porch or in library.) Fresh fruit, fresh orange juice, homemade breads, hot beverages. Main-course favorites include Grand Marnier souffle pancakes; Kahlua/pecan waffles with strawberry sauce or real maple syrup; omelets with fresh mushrooms, cheese, and herbs from garden. Bacon or sausage. Low-cholesterol diets accommodated. In formal dining room with English bone china, sterling, and cut crystal.

Plus: Formal living room. Beverages upon arrival or on return from dinner. Turndown service. Bedside Belgian chocolates. Basket of personal items. Movies for VCRs. Guest refrigerator. Portable guest phone. On-site parking.

Thornrose House at Gypsy Hill   703/885–7026
531 Thornrose Avenue, Staunton, VA 24401

Hosts: Suzanne and Otis Huston
Location: On spacious grounds across from Gypsy Hill Park with its swimming pool, 18-hole golf course ($10), lighted tennis courts, jogging paths, gazebo with summer band concerts. Six blocks from Staunton's walking tour.

Open: Year round. Three-day minimum Fourth of July weekend; two days on October weekends.
Rates: Double occupancy. $55 double bed, $60 queen bed, $70 king bed. Singles $10 less. $10 rollaway.
♦ ♣ ⚤ ✕

> From Maryland: *"Picked for proximity to golf course, not knowing what to expect . . . decorated beautifully . . . white-glove clean . . . fell so in love with one of the wallpaper borders that we are putting it in our home . . . a five-star breakfast . . . all the special touches are reflective of its innkeepers . . . provide restaurant menus, give suggestions from own dining experiences, sightseeing tips complete with directions. . . . Our stay was everything we hoped it would be and more."*

"After our own B&B trips in New England, we talked about doing this in Virginia, so when Otis took early retirement from Du Pont, we drove 2,200 miles all over this state looking at many wonderful properties. We fell in love with Staunton, small-town America with wonderful Victorian architecture—very different from other places we have lived in. Everyone—from neighbors to tradespeople—was so helpful and welcoming! Guests, too, get a good sense of this warm community when they take the self-guided tour and have chance conversations with 80-year-olds who talk about the old days. There's a lot to see and do in this area, yet some guests just want to sit on the porch and unwind."

In 1992, when the Hustons bought this B&B, a two-storied modified Georgian brick house, they redecorated with light colors, establishing a rose theme throughout the house "to create a homey Victorian feeling."

Suzanne has worked in newspaper production, as a teacher, and as a historical-site docent "all over." The Hustons' own travels have taken them to Canada, Mexico, Europe, and Japan.

In residence: During college vacations, one daughter. Two cats reside in hosts' quarters, sometimes visit cat lovers.

Bed and bath: Five second-floor rooms with antique or period pieces. King, queen, or double bed. All private baths with tub and/or shower.

Breakfast: 8–9:30. House specialty is Otis's birchermuesli—oats, raisins, fresh fruit, whipped cream, and nuts. Heart-healthy hot entree. In fireplaced dining room or on veranda.

Plus: Four bedrooms are air-conditioned; one room has ceiling fan. Fireplaced parlor with grand piano and television. Tea or lemonade with homemade snacks at 4 p.m. Turndown service. Wicker-furnished veranda. Garden-in-process has pergolas in place.

The Duck Farm Inn   804/758–5685
P.O. Box 787, Route 227, Urbanna, VA 23175

Host: Ms. Fleming Godden
Location: Secluded. On 12 acres of woods and fields on the Rappahannock River (2 miles wide at this point). Off a private unpaved lane, a mile and a half from historic harbor town with its marinas (day slips available, and boats can be chartered); shops; antiques stores; award-winning restaurant; annual oyster festival. Forty-five minutes to Williamsburg, 60 to Richmond, 2½ hours from Washington, D.C.
Open: Year round.
Rates: Double occupancy. $75 private bath; $65 shared. Singles $15 less. $15 third person. $10 child with parent. Cash or check deposit required.

♥ ⬛ ❖ ◆ ✖ ✄

Drive across plantation fields and over a dam and you come to this contemporary two-storied brick home built on a hillside in 1965. Its sliding glass doors provide views of the expansive lawns—bordered by marsh and woods—that lead to the private beach. Once part of a 150-acre duck farm, the largest of its kind east of the Mississippi, the house was purchased by Fleming in 1989 when her daughters suggested the B&B idea to her.

With their help she decorated the entire 6,000 square feet, furnishing with old and new, with antiques and modern art, and with various window treatments. Fleming majored in clothing and design at Carnegie Mellon University and is a former artist and fashion model who had her own modeling school in Fort Lauderdale, Florida. Here she maintains this enormous property,

(Please turn page.)

cooks the breakfast (rave reviews), and meets "wonderful people, including many who are surprised to find such a beautiful and quiet spot. They come for a romantic getaway, to look for boat slips or retirement real estate, or just to read and relax."

In residence: Two dalmatians, Oliver Twist and Lady Domino. Trouble and Bisquet are cats.

Bed and bath: On two floors—six rooms; four overlook lawn and river. Two queen-bedded riverfront rooms, private custom-tiled shower/tub baths, sliding glass doors to wraparound deck. Two king/twins rooms share a shower/tub bath. On ground floor, two riverfront queen-bedded rooms with large connecting bath that has double sinks and shower/tub. Rollaway available.

Breakfast: 8–9:30. Juice. Fruit. Homemade jumbo blueberry or cinnamon muffins. Crepes, pancakes, or scrambled eggs with cheddar cheese and homegrown tomatoes. Hot beverages. In fireplaced dining room (with large Depression glass display) overlooking the deck and river, or on deck.

Plus: Central air conditioning and heat (three-zone heat pump). Ceiling fans in three bedrooms. Sliding glass doors in fireplaced and paneled lounge/bar/game room and in library/TV room. Guest refrigerator, ice machine, and microwave in bar. Bathrobes. Lacy sheets. Intercom system with radio in all rooms. Beach umbrellas, cushioned lounges, floats, and large tubes. Use of paddleboat for three and canoe. Small coolers.

The Burton House   804/787–4560
11 Brooklyn Street, Wachapreague, VA 23480

Hosts: Pat, Tom, and (son) Mike Hart
Location: One block to waterfront with rental and fishing boats, and restaurant. On an undeveloped peninsula that overlooks Barrier Islands. On a corner adjoining grounds of Volunteer Fireman's Carnival (held two weeks in July) with ferris wheel and merry-go-round. Forty-five-minute drive to Chincoteague Island.
Open: Year round. Two-night minimum weekends May–September.
Rates: Double occupancy. Private half bath $55 single, $65 double. Private full bath $65 single, $75 double. MC, Visa.

♥ ⬛ ❖ ◆ ✳ ⅍

"There are 300 year-round residents in this town, where we have lived 'forever.' Our son, Mike, works for the post office and loves his flower gardens and the yard. Tom and I love fishing, outdoor life, and antiques. From B&B articles in magazines, we got 'the bug' in 1986 and completely restored the century-old place that's always been called 'The Burton House.'

    "We repaired and refinished locally found furniture—brass beds, rockers, china cabinets, you name it. [Other pieces can be purchased in their small antique shop.] Tom is a carpenter whose pride and joy is the screened gazebo made with posts and trim from a 1902 hotel. It provided a great background for a cover photo of us used on an AT&T promotion piece. In 1991 we bought (and saved in time to open in the summer of 1992) the next-door house, which had not been lived in for 27 years. Now it's Hart's Harbor House, our home with four uncovered and working fireplaces (especially appreciated by winter guests) and with enormous guest rooms. The yard extends to some rental cabins and a 14-boat–slip marina."

Townspeople and guests alike are amazed and pleased.

Bed and bath: Ten rooms. On three floors in Burton House—seven rooms with queen, double, two twins, or a double and a daybed. Private full bath for first-floor double-bedded room. Six rooms, each with a private half bath, each share a shower bath or a shower/tub bath with one other room. (Exception: three third-floor rooms share one shower bath.) Hart's Harbor House has three second-floor rooms. Private skylit baths with tub and shower for the two queen-bedded rooms. Private shower bath for room with double bed and "best view."

Breakfast: Until 10. Locally made sausages. Juice, fruit, bacon, eggs, muffins or biscuits, coffee. Sometimes waffles, Latvian pancakes, or French toast. Served family style in the Burton House dining room or gazebo porch.

Plus: Afternoon refreshments. Central air conditioning plus individual units and ceiling fans in bedrooms. Large deck next to gazebo. Bicycles (no charge).

Anderson Cottage Bed & Breakfast

Old Germantown Road   703/839–2975
Warm Springs, VA 24484-0176   fax 703/839–3058

Host: Jean Randolph Bruns
Location: In a mountain valley village, west of Shenandoah Valley. On two acres (one is lawn) with gardens and mature plantings. With stream from (96°F) Warm Spring Pools, half a mile away, flowing through property. Two excellent restaurants nearby. Five miles to Hot Springs and renowned Homestead Hotel.
Open: Main house, March–November. Cottage, year round.
Rates: Main house $55 or $65 per room, $70 or $75 suite. Cottage $110 single or double occupancy.
🛥 ⚶ ♦ ✂

> From England: *"A living museum . . . if you encourage her to talk about the house, you have a privileged view back in time, through the eyes and memories of a witty, articulate chronicler and protector of a lost American tradition. We had meant to stay a night, stayed for three, and would have moved in permanently if life had allowed!"* From Virginia: *"Gives you space to be alone and be yourself, yet your needs are always met quietly and quickly. This is a place to come if you enjoy peace and quiet and genuineness. If you want frilly lace, Godiva on your pillow, and television in your room, go elsewhere. But if the old summer places intrigue you, explore here."* Also from Virginia: *"I love the little hallways and old wood floors,*

(Please turn page.)

the pretty wildflowers in front of the house, breakfast near the fireplace on a chilly morning."

Jean usually describes it as "a quiet place with plenty to do." What began in the 18th century as a four-room log tavern "rambles without one right angle or straight line." An inn for 80 years until the 1950s, it has been in Jean's family for over 100 years, and her permanent residence since 1981. She is a former journalist/medical center public relations director/Realtor who is active as a library trustee, as a Meals-on-Wheels driver, and with Amnesty International. She reads (extensive library right here), gardens, and refinishes furniture. When Homestead Hotel guests tour the small museum room here, she is official guide. Her guests poke around this old house, read on the porch, wade in the creek, take the warm baths, hike, explore—and write lyrical letters to me. This B&B makes me feel good all over.

Bed and bath: Four rooms plus a cottage. First-floor suite has private entrance, queen-bedded room, fireplaced parlor, tub/shower bath. On second floor—suite with queen-bedded room, parlor with twin bed, old-fashioned tub in bath. One large queen-bedded room with claw-footed tub bath. Very large room with a double and a twin bed, beamed ceiling, working fireplace, shared bath. Family-friendly cottage has one queen-bedded room, another with two twins, one tub/shower bath and one with shower only, living room with windows on three sides, fireplaced dining room/kitchen.

Breakfast: About 9. Cheese strata and apples; buttermilk pancakes with maple syrup and sausage or bacon; or turkey hash, basil tomatoes, wheat rolls, peach preserves. Juice, fruit, coffee, tea.

Plus: Fireplaced parlor and dining room. Extensive library. Upright piano. Croquet. Badminton. Suggestions for one day; other days; eating out; driving tours with hand-drawn maps and stops at an Arabian horse farm, old family cemeteries, hiking trails. "Creek shoes" for wading. "Forgot a sweater? I have a collection of old ones in assorted sizes and colors."

Caledonia Farm   703/675–3693
Route 1, Box 2080, Flint Hill, VA 22627

Host: Phil Irwin
Location: Four miles north of Washington and "the number one–rated restaurant in North America and four far more affordable great evening dining options." On a "never-to-be-divided" 52-acre cattle farm bordered by stone fences. On Route 628, near Skyline Drive. Sixty-eight miles southwest of Washington, D.C.

Open: Year round. Two-night minimum on holiday weekends and the entire month of October.
Rates: $80 main house room, semi-private bath. $140 suite. Fifty percent surcharge for Saturday one-night stays. Discover, MC, Visa.
♥ 🛏 ❖ ♦ ✈ ✂

Phil, a retired Voice of America broadcaster who has visited hundreds of B&Bs throughout North America and Europe, raises beef cattle. His Federal-style manor house, built in 1812 and restored in 1965, is on the National Register of Historic Places. It has 2-foot-thick stone walls, individual heat and air conditioning, heart pine floors, working fireplaces in each room—and all that acreage and those mountain views. Take a house tour and you'll hear about its history and about the family cemetery. And Phil is prepared with suggestions for walking (here, if you'd like—on the grounds) or mountain climbing (right behind the farm) to 3,300 feet. He offers the treat of a hayride to a clearing in the adjacent Shenandoah National Park. He and his wife, Florence, sometimes host small conferences, and they participate in movable feasts with other B&Bs in the area.

In residence: "One gregarious outside cat." Beef cattle herd.
Foreign languages spoken: (Minimal) German and Danish.
Bed and bath: Two suites and two rooms, all with working fireplaces, individual heat control, air conditioning. On main-house second floor, two double-bedded rooms share a full bath. Converted 1807 summer kitchen (connected by portico to main house) has double-bedded room and full bath upstairs, and a living room with huge original cooking fireplace on the first floor. Handicapped-accessible room available by reservation.
Breakfast: On the hour (arranged night before), 7–11. Choose from menu that includes fruit, eggs, smoked salmon, omelets, grits, and eggs Benedict. Served by candlelight and with "unannounced extras."
Plus: Antiques-filled gathering room. Patio and three porches with spectacular views. Cycling routes (bicycles provided). Directions to nearby stables, wineries, caves, antiquing, scenic drives. Hayride ($10/person). Reservations arranged for horse-drawn carriage rides, balloon ascensions, special photography, conferencing, battlefield tours.

The Foster-Harris House

703/675–3757

Main Street, P.O. Box 333, Washington, VA 22747   800/666–0153

Host: Phyllis Marriott
Location: With mountain views from 40 acres to one side and behind; private home on other side. In a town (pop. 250) that is 6 blocks long and 2 blocks wide, with two art galleries and three crafts shops in old houses and a bookstore in an old cabin. Three blocks from The Inn at Little Washington and minutes from two

other fine restaurants. Near antiquing, hiking, horseback riding. Fifteen minutes from Skyline Drive; 65 miles west of Washington, D.C.
Open: Year round.
Rates: Sunday–Thursday, $85 queen bed, $80 double bed. Friday and Saturday, $105 queen, $100 double. Discover, MC, Visa.
♥ ❖ ◆ ✗ ⅄

With experience in foods (Washington, D.C., Capitol Hill gourmet deli owner and caterer) and real estate, Phyllis pursued her B&B idea and found this turn-of-the-century house, which was established as the area's first B&B in

(Please turn page.)

1983 by an owner who left a legacy of perennial flower beds and a long list of returnees. The cows "over the hill" still moo in the morning. (Some guests ask if it's a recording.) Decor is country style. And many guests rave about breakfast.

In residence: Lulu, a friendly mixed breed, part Lab, "loved by everyone."
Bed and bath: Four second-floor rooms, all private baths. One with queen bed, wood-burning stove, private hall bath with oval whirlpool tub with shower. Two with queen bed, each with en-suite tub/shower bath. Smaller double-bedded room with tub/shower bath.
Breakfast: At 9 or 9:30. Juice, fruit, breads or muffins, an egg dish or baked French toast, breakfast meat, hot beverages. Served in dining room by fireplace wood stove.
Plus: Central air conditioning. Late-afternoon beverages and cookies. Popular front porch with swing. Fireplaced parlor. Down comforters. Restaurant reservations made.

Sycamore Hill House & Gardens   703/675-3046
Route 1, Box 978, Washington, VA 22747

Hosts: Kerri and Stephen Wagner
Location: Spectacular. On top of Menefee Mountain on 52 undeveloped acres of woodlands and meadows. "At end of mile-long, romantic winding road." Twelve miles from Skyline Drive and Shenandoah National Park. Sixty-six miles west of Washington, D.C.

Open: Year round. Two-day minimum October weekends and holidays.
Rates: Per room. $100 full bath. $115 shower bath. $130 full bath with double sinks. Less for stays of more than four days, except April–June and September 15–Thanksgiving. MC, Visa.
♥ ⬛ ✣ ◆ ✈ ⚥

"How did you ever find this place?" ask first-timers as they arrive. The mountain's only structure, this contemporary (1967) stone home features a round glass center with a 65-foot veranda. Here, at seemingly the top of the world, is the mesmerizing panoramic view filled with layers of other mountaintops that prompted Kerri to leave her 15-year position as agricultural lobbyist in Washington, D.C. What a setting for Stephen, a freelance commercial illustrator, to create works seen in major publications such as *National Geographic* and Time-Life books. And all because two people followed their curiosity when chancing upon a "For Sale" sign during a drive in the countryside.

Since buying the house in 1987 from the original owners, the Wagners have refurbished inside and out. Decor includes Oriental rugs, traditional and modern furnishings, originals of Stephen's works, window treatments framing views, and—everywhere—plants, trees, and flowers. On the property, which has become a certified National Wildlife habitat, are Kerri's organic herb and vegetable gardens, appreciated by local restaurants; annual and perennial flower beds; thousands of spring bulbs and hundreds of dogwoods and redbuds; and hummingbirds, bluebirds, white-tailed deer, maybe red fox or wild turkey. And more views.

In residence: Mollie Bean, a 40-pound fluffy white miniature sheep dog. The cat is named Miss Kitty.

Bed and bath: Three rooms, each with queen bed, private bath. Master Bedroom has pine four-poster, dressing room, full bath with double sink. Peach Room has brass bed, shower bath. White Wicker Room has full bath just across the hall.

Breakfast: At 9; flexible when house is not full. Repertoire includes home-baked cranberry braided bread baked apples; cinnamon apple puff; yeast breads; rolls, coffee cake. French toast; omelets; souffles; shrimp-and-cheese strata. Breakfast meats, fresh fruits, local cider, freshly squeezed orange juice. Fresh trout on occasion. In formal dining room with classical music and floor-to-ceiling view of mountains.

Plus: Central air conditioning. Ceiling fans. Stereo and piano in living room, which has tiled fireplace flanked by bentwood chairs. Home-baked cookies and brandy in bedrooms. Special occasions acknowledged. Down comforters. Flannel sheets. Turndown service. Mints on pillow. Bird books and binoculars. A printed list of birds and seasonal flowers.

Colonial Capital Bed & Breakfast   804/229–0233
501 Richmond Road, Williamsburg, VA 23185   800/776–0570

Hosts: Barbara and Phil Craig
Location: Residential. Across the street from stadium of College of William and Mary and its Alumni House. Three blocks from historic area. Five-minute drive to Colonial Parkway entrance.
Open: Year round. Two-night minimum on Easter, Valentine's Day, and Presidents' Day weekends and on April–December weekends.

Rates: April–December—$70 single, $90 double, $125 triple in suite ($20 each additional person), $100 for room with king/twin option. January–March except Easter weekend — $56 single, $72 double, $100 triple in suite ($16 additional person), $80 king/twin option. Honeymoon packages available. MC, Visa.
♥ ♣ ♦ ♣ ♦ ✈

From Illinois: *"Twelve of us who enjoyed a family reunion feel we've found our home away from home . . . hosts epitomize warm hospitality, thoughtfulness, and graciousness . . . charming coordinated early American decor . . . complimentary toiletries . . . excellent restaurant suggestions. . . . As the wife of a former resort innkeeper, I am keenly aware of comforts and amenities provided and, of greater importance, of the personality of a place. This B&B is outstanding."* From Florida: *"Prepared a separate breakfast to accommodate my wife, who is a vegetarian."* From Pennsylvania: *"Even met our plane."*

(Please turn page.)

Williamsburg accents combined with antiques acquired over a 30-year period are throughout this Colonial Revival house, which was built in 1926 as a tourist home. When Phil and Barbara, native Virginians, bought it in 1988, they returned from North Carolina to redo the entire place as a B&B. "Our inspiration came from trips to England and Scotland," says Barbara, former associate director of admissions at Meredith College. Phil was vice president of a securities corporation. Guests' long letters written to me confirm that the hosts mean it when they say, "We're here to spoil you."

In residence: Well-trained Ginny (Virginia Lee), a golden retriever, does not enter the parlor, dining room, or sleeping areas.

Bed and bath: Five rooms, all canopied beds; private baths, some with sink in room. On second floor—two with antique double bed; one with shower bath, one with shower and claw-foot tub. One with queen bed, full hall 1920s tub/shower bath (robes provided). Room with four-poster twin/king option. Narrow steep steps to third floor, which has room with dormered windows on three sides, a double bed, private tub/shower bath; if coupled with room (with TV/VCR) across the hall, this becomes a suite that sleeps five with a bath and a half (robes provided). Rollaway available.

Breakfast: Usually 8:30. Repertoire includes baked French toast with caramelized topping, strawberries, and sour cream; Virginia ham-and-cheese souffle; yeast-based waffles. Fresh fruits, specialty teas and coffees, juices. In dining room or adjoining solarium.

Plus: Bikes (no charge). Zoned central air conditioning. Living room with Oriental rugs and fireplace flanked by wing chairs. Welcoming refreshments include tea, local wines, Virginia peanuts. Turndown service. Mints on pillow. Screened porch and patio overlooking fenced yard. Off-street parking. Central ticketing service for Colonial Williamsburg, Busch Gardens, Jamestown.

Do you have to get up for breakfast?
There's no one rule. Check each description in this book for the various arrangements. More than one guest has been enticed by the aroma of fresh muffins. If you are on business or want to catch the morning ferry, eat-and-run is just fine. If, however, cuisine is a feature, plan on appearing at the specified time!
Vacationers (not skiers) find breakfast a very social time. One hostess says that even when guests say they want to be on the road early, they often linger over breakfast for hours. If hosts join you, please understand when they leave the table after a while.

Legacy of Williamsburg Inn
930 Jamestown Road, Williamsburg, VA 23185

804/220–0524
800/962–4722
fax 804/220–2211

Hosts: Mary Ann and Ed Lucas
Location: On a heavily wooded lot with English gardens in front; wonderful view of pine, holly, and dogwood trees from back deck. Across the street from wooded acreage owned by the College of William and Mary. Ten-minute walk from historic area.
Open: Year round.
Rates: Per room, $80–$85. Suite $125–$130. MC, Visa.
♥ ✲ ✖ ✔

Eighteenth-century ambiance everywhere. With authentic colors and fabrics. A fireplaced library with many books on antiques and Colonial Williamsburg. Eighteenth-century games in a fireplaced tavern/game room modeled after the Weatherburn Tavern in Colonial Williamburg. A billiards room with a billiards table made in England and an English dart board. A keeping room where candlelit breakfasts are served by the fireplace. One trip to Colonial Williamsburg in 1985 convinced the Lucases, dealers in 18th-century furnishings, that they should go back to Ohio, sell the farm, and move to Virginia. Earlier, Mary Ann and Ed had designed, built, and managed a restaurant; they also raised race horses. Here they bought a clapboard and many-dormered house that was built in 1976 and remodeled it into this B&B. Mary Ann is a full-time innkeeper "still very much in love with people and 18th-century decor." Ed is vice president of sales for a commercial refrigeration company. Together they enjoy "sharing our antiques and favorite eating places, biking routes, and wonderful walks."

In residence: Hannah, a yellow Labrador, lives outdoors, "loves to shake hands with guests."
Bed and bath: Four rooms; each with canopied and curtained queen or double bed. Two are suites with working fireplaces. Suites have shower/tub baths and other rooms have showers only.
Breakfast: At 8. (Coffee at 7:45.) House specialty—hotcakes with apple topping. Or Belgian waffles, omelets, quiche, homemade peach cobblers, biscuits and gravy. By fire or in gazebo. Can last for two hours; some call it an "all-day breakfast."
Plus: Central air conditioning. Wine and fresh fruit in each room; plus, in suites, wine, cheese, and crackers. Turndown service. Chocolates. Robes. Treetop (built up high) gazebo "in middle of bird sanctuary with deer too."

> From Georgia: *"Authentic in every detail save the very fine and modern bath. . . . Mary Ann had book lights for reading, plush bathrobes, bikes, umbrellas, iron. . . every extra imaginable."* From Maryland: *"Friendly and open hosts. . . . Elaborate and delicious breakfasts. . . . Enthusiasm for their beautifully decorated home is evident . . . candles and music too . . . an unforgettable experience."*

Liberty Rose B&B   804/253-1260

1022 Jamestown Road, Williamsburg, VA 23185

Hosts: Brad and Sandra Hirz
Location: One mile from restored area. On a hilltop acre of old trees.
Open: Year round. Two-night minimum on major event weekends.

Rates: $95 Savannah Lace. $135 Magnolias Peach; $40 third person. $155 Rose Victoria. $165 Suite Williamsburg.
♥ ♦ ✈ ✁

Intentionally romantic. With yards and yards of custom-colored vintage reproduction fabrics—silks, jacquards, and cut velvets; with gorgeous wallcoverings; seven trees at Christmas; and—everywhere— collectibles, quilts, and refinished antiques, all placed with a strong sense of display and color, comfort, and fun too. (All are pictured in a detailed brochure.)

The enthusiastic hosts do everything themselves and are happy to share decorating ideas, resources, and bargains. (A catalog is planned.) The Hirzes do such a good job of hosting that 6 out of 10 of their guests leave with the dream of opening a B&B. While they lived on the West Coast, Brad was in farming, Sandi in interior design. In 1986 they both came to Williamsburg and fell in love while doing the first restoration on this 1922 dormered clapboard house. Since, they've added architectural accents, exquisite bed coverings, reporcelained claw-footed tubs, and the ultimate touch of a take-home long-stemmed silk rose.

In residence: Mister Goose, "our gorgeous outdoor kitty."
Bed and bath: Four queen-bedded rooms, one with adjoining twin room. "Savannah Lace" has tub bath, TV. "Magnolias Peach"—lace-canopied bed, TV/VCR in armoire, black marble shower bath; adjoining room with antique twin feather bed. "Rose Victoria" with French canopied bed, elaborate bed curtains, TV/VCR, long down sofa, full bath with Victorian wall from turn-of-century house, floor from 1740s plantation. "Suite Williamsburg"—huge carved four-poster with elaborate coverings, working fireplace, six windows, TV/VCR in dollhouse, French sofa, chandeliered bath with black Italian tile shower, claw-footed tub.
Breakfast: 8:30. Repertoire of both hosts includes waffles, hotcakes, or stuffed French toast. Bacon, sausage, or Virginia baked ham. Homemade croissants filled with eggs, bacon, cheese, tomato, and spices. Coffee, tea, juice, fresh fruit, homemade muffins, scones. Served on glass-enclosed parlor porch.
Plus: Central air conditioning. Baby grand piano in the fireplaced living room. Chocolate chip cookies. Soft drinks always available. Refrigerator space. Gold flashlights by the bed. Bubble bath. Robes. Antique sleigh for picture taking. "A tiny but irresistible gift shop with many of our guests' handmade specialties."

Is B&B like a hotel?
How many times have you hugged the doorman?

Newport House   804/229–1775

710 South Henry Street, Williamsburg, VA 23185-4113

Hosts: John and Cathy Millar
Location: In residential neighborhood. Set back about 50 feet from
Route 132. A five-minute walk to
historic area and Colonial Williamsburg.

Open: Year round. Two-night minimum on some holiday weekends.
Rates: Per room, $105–$110 first
night, $95–$100 each additional
night. $20 third person in room.
♥ ♣ ◆ ✖ ✔

> From Virginia: *"A treasure in every sense of the word. . . . The result is delightful
> visit with old friends. . . . Close to restored area but far from the madding crowd."*
> From Maryland: *"Combines 20th-century comfort with 18th-century elegance
> and taste."*

Historical stories at breakfast. Colonial country dancing in the ballroom
(beginners and observers welcome) on Tuesday evenings. Eighteenth-century recipes. A hammock between two pecan trees. Hints about a quiet
saltwater beach, historic plantations, a ferry ride. Antiques for sale. A rabbit
that captivates guests. Even colonial clothing to rent for dinner at a tavern!

In 1988 the Millars, descendants of 18th-century Williamsburg area residents, built this authentic reproduction of a Newport, Rhode Island, house
designed in 1756 by Peter Harrison, "an architect who is primarily responsible
for our speaking English rather than French today." (Ask them to tell you the
story.) Siding is wood carved to resemble stone.

John, a college teacher/former museum director/former captain of an historic
full-rigged ship, has written a dozen books on historical topics. Cathy, a practicing
registered nurse when the Millars lived in Rhode Island, is an inn-
keeper/mom/beekeeper/gardener who sews 18th-century clothing. Their entire
home is furnished in English and American period antiques and reproductions.

In residence: Son Ian, born April 1991. Sassafras, a house-trained Dutch
rabbit.
Foreign language spoken: French.
Bed and bath: Two second-floor rooms (overlooking gardens), each with
one extra-long queen four-poster canopy bed plus one single four-poster
canopy bed, attached private shower bath. Rollaway and crib available.
Breakfast: Usually 8–9. Johnnycakes, muffins, waffles, eggs, casseroles. Fruit
compote or baked apples. Coffee. Tea made from their own herbs. Honey
from garden. In formal dining room.
Plus: Central air conditioning. Individual thermostats. Fireplaced living
room. Harpsichord (guests may play) in ballroom. Babysitting. Rides to/from
transportation points. Nonallergenic comforters. Off-street parking. Some
Thursdays, Scottish country dancing.

Innkeeping may be America's most envied profession. As one host
mused, "Where else can you get a job where, every day, someone tells
you how wonderful you are?"

Williamsburg Cottage #10

Williamsburg, VA

Location: Secluded. Behind the main house. In a neighborhood with well-spaced houses and quiet winding wooded lanes. Adjacent to the College of William and Mary. Within a mile of Colonial Williamsburg.
Reservations: Year round through Bensonhouse, page 315. Two-night minimum on all holidays and weekends except nonholiday weekends in January, February, March.
Rates: $105–125 for one or two. $10 extra person.
♥ ♨ ♣ ♦ ✗ ⅙

Your very own private getaway—all 1,300 square feet—with colonial furnishings and gas log fireplace in the living room, Oriental rugs on hardwood floors, a small kitchen, and patio with wrought iron chairs. Built as a guest house in the 1930s, this brick-with-clapboard dormered cottage complete with an herb garden in front is, once again, for guests. The hosts, in residence in the main house, are happy to provide you with any information—and/or to let you enjoy your secluded retreat.

Bed and bath: One second-floor room with brass queen bed, tiled tub/shower bath. On first floor—queen-sized sleep sofa, half bath. Gas fireplace, small kitchen.
Breakfast: Help yourself to juice, muffins, and hot beverage provided in the small Pullman kitchen.
Plus: Central air conditioning.

From Florida: *"The most perfect place. . . . Lovely decor, wonderful fireplace, beautiful surroundings, and absolute privacy. Less than a mile from Colonial Williamsburg. A relaxing, romantic retreat."*

Williamsburg Manor Bed and Breakfast

600 Richmond Road, Williamsburg, VA 23185   804/220–8011
                                        800/422–8011

Hosts: Laura and Michael Macknight
Location: Between a church and Alumni House of College of William and Mary. Three blocks to historic area.
Open: Year round. Two-night minimum on weekends.
Rates: $90 per room.
♥ ♣ ⁂ ✗ ⅙

Your place at the breakfast table is always set and waiting—with 15-inch Villeroy and Boch plates, stemmed goblets for juice, and poufed and pressed napkins too. It's at the 12-foot-long table in the fireplaced dining room that was "switched" with the living room when newlyweds Laura and Michael redid the entire brick colonial house. Originally built for professors, it became a guest house in the 1930s and was most recently a rooming house for students. Friends of the Macknights took care of new ceilings. Laura's mom (from Williamsburg Sampler, page 385) made new crown moldings and frames for pictures and helped with decorating—with hunter greens, deep burgundys, swags and jabots, Oriental rugs, and Waverly prints. Dad, too, "helped a lot" with what he calls "a wonderful big dollhouse." Auction finds and family treasures are throughout. Since opening in the fall of 1992, Laura is no longer working as a catering director, but Michael has continued as a chef at a local restaurant. Now the young couple—still in their twenties—do catering together. And a cookbook is in the works.

In residence: Zeus, an outdoor golden retriever.
Bed and bath: Five rooms, all private en-suite baths. One on first floor with queen four-poster, shower bath. On second floor—one queen four-poster, tub/shower bath; one canopied double, shower bath; one queen bed has connecting bath shared (with same party only) with room with two twin beds.
Breakfast: At 8:30. Eggs in pastry with roasted tomatoes, chives, and Swiss cheese; Surry sausage hash; or malted waffles with homemade syrups and preserves. Fresh fruit; freshly baked muffins, breads, or rolls. Special diets accommodated.
Plus: Central air conditioning. Bedroom ceiling fans. Guest refrigerator. Cable TV in each room. Off-street parking. Picnic baskets $15. Dinner by reservation; $45 per person.

Williamsburg Sampler Bed and Breakfast
922 Jamestown Road, Williamsburg, VA 23185-3917   804/253–0398
                                                        800/722–1169

Hosts: Helen and Ike Sisane
Location: Across from the College of William and Mary. Less than a mile to Colonial Williamsburg. Three miles from I-64, 2 to business district, 1 to restaurants.

Open: Year round. Two-night minimum on weekends.
Rates: Per room $85–$95; two persons maximum per room.
♥ ⛵ ♣ ♦ ✗ ✄

The sampler collection began when Dag Hammarskjold, then secretary general of the United Nations, gave a sampler to the Sisanes as a wedding gift. After Helen left her United Nations position as postal administrator, she became a Realtor and interior designer and continued collecting embroidered and cross-stitched American samplers as well as pewter, antiques and reproductions. Now she is an accomplished woodworker who makes furniture and, occasionally, a picket fence—and maybe, by the time you arrive, moldings where Ike thinks they belong. "She can do all those things so well!"

In 1984 Ike, a federal government administrator, and Helen were looking for a home near historic Williamsburg, and they bought this 18th-century brick plantation-style Colonial mansion within 15 minutes of viewing it. Built in 1975 (ask Ike about the fascinating site research/archaeological process), it was designed inside and out with early 18th-century architectural authenticity, with crown and dentil moldings and pegged hardwood planked floors. In 1988 Ike's opportunity to be a policy administrator in Europe prompted the idea of B&B with Helen as hostess—as a way to keep this unusual property. He returned in 18 months to innkeeping, "a job I really love."

(Please turn page.)

In 1990 the Sisanes built a replica of Colonial Williamsburg's 18th-century Coke-Garrett Carriage House as a woodworking studio for Helen. And in 1992 the enthusiastic innkeepers helped the younger Sisane generation to launch a B&B (See page 384).

In residence: In hosts' quarters—Toby, a friendly Yorkshire terrier.
Bed and bath: Four second-floor rooms, each with king or queen rice-carved four-poster bed. All with private shower baths, wing chairs, concealed TV.
Breakfast: At 8:30. The "skip lunch" kind. Juice, coffee, sweet cake, muffins, fruit cup. Waffles, French toast, quiche or Western eggs with potatoes, sausage. Served in dining room that has a pump organ, one of those acquired treasures that comes complete with a story collectors love to hear.
Plus: Central air conditioning. Bedroom ceiling fans. Fireplaced great room. Back porch overlooking wooded grounds. "If you'd like, a little tour of the carriage house workshop." Candy. Fruit bowl. Special occasions acknowledged. Off-street parking. Transportation to/from airport, train, or bus station.

> From Iowa: *"We enjoyed our stay at Williamsburg Sampler as much as we enjoyed the city itself."* From Virginia: *"Excellent hospitality. Very clean. Helpful with touring. Beautiful furnishings."*

Edgewood Plantation

4800 John Tyler Memorial Highway
Charles City, VA 23030

804/829–2962
800/296–3343

Hosts: Julian and Dot Boulware
Location: Set back from Route 5 (which has a cycling path) with its 3 miles of plantations, including Shirley, Evelynton, Berkely, and Sherwood Forest, open to the public. Adjoining fish hatchery has walking trails and lake for fishing. Short drive to "two fantastic restaurants—one in a coach house, another in an old farm." One and a half miles from James River, 28 west of Williamsburg, 24 east of Richmond.
Open: Year round.
Rates: Shared bath $110, $118 with sink in room. Private bath $138 first floor, $155 second floor and cottage. MC, Visa.
♥ ◢ ♣ ♦ ✣

Canopied beds, armoires, settees, marble-topped tables, an 1840 square piano, Persian rugs, vintage clothing, ruffles, hatboxes filled with antebellum millinery, books, jewelry, dolls, china, folk art, huge gold leaf–framed mirrors . . . a formal parlor and dining room, a country kitchen with baskets and folk art. The 30-year collection—featured in several magazines, including *Country Home* and *Early American Life*—is arranged throughout the Gothic Revival house on property that was once part of Berkely Plantation. Restoration began when the Boulangers bought it in 1978. That's when Julian removed a plaster wall and found a kitchen fireplace just where Dot wanted one. Neighbors stopped by to advise and to reminisce about the plantation's history and earlier appearance. By 1982 Dot, in Victorian dress, began conducting tours of the 11 rooms and the three-story freestanding winding staircase that brides love. Elaborate Christmas decor, with 17 trees, became a tradition. And the Boulwares added a hot tub, swimming pool, and gazebo. As for B&B,

begun in 1984, Julian is one of those won-over husbands. Now he dovetails hosting with working for Phillip Morris "so that we can support our passion for antiques!"

Bed and bath: Eight rooms. In main house, second floor—four rooms with working fireplaces. One with canopied king bed, love-story-based window etching, small private shower bath. One with canopied queen bed, small private shower bath. Two rooms, one with canopied queen and one with queen Victorian high-headboard beds, each with a sink in room, share a claw-footed tub bath. Third floor, "perfect for two couples or a group"—two large rooms, each with two double beds and a sofa, separated by a sitting room; shared full bath. In cottage with country decor, first floor—1820 walnut queen four-poster, sitting area, TV hidden in a dollhouse, full bath. Second floor—rose-covered vine-canopied queen bed, sitting room, kitchen area, full bath.Trundle available.

Breakfast: 8–9:30. Fruit. French toast and bacon, biscuit and eggs, or sausage and gravy over biscuit and fresh apples. Bacon and home-fried potatoes. Coffee and tea. By country kitchen fireplace, in formal dining room by candlelight, or on wicker-furnished veranda.

Plus: Central air conditioning. Welcoming refreshments. Turndown service with rose and sachet. Hiking trails. Creek for fishing. Antiques and gift shops here. Golf and tennis at nearby country club.

North Bend Plantation B&B   804/829–5176

12200 Weyanoke Road, Charles City, VA 23030-0128

Hosts: George and Ridgely Copland
Location: Quiet. Thirty minutes west of Colonial Williamsburg, in Virginia plantation country. Three miles off Route 5, overlooking George's 250 acres of corn, wheat, soybean, and barley fields, part of 850-acre property that has 28 acres along the river.
Open: Year round.
Rates: Double occupancy. $95 or $105.
♥ ⬛ ♣ ♦ ✈ ⅙

"George has lived all his life in this Greek Revival house built in 1819 [and enlarged in 1853] for his great-great-aunt Sarah Harrison, sister of the ninth president. Many of the antiques in the large open rooms are original to this Virginia historic landmark, which is named for its location on the James River. It is 2 miles by foot, on our tandem, or by car along a colonial road with much wildlife to be seen. Paths in the woods lead to Civil War trenches and a Revolutionary graveyard. Many guests enjoy the billiard table bought by George's grandmother in 1916. Some play the piano and others gather round to sing! They appreciate the rare book library. And from our sun porch there's a magnificent vista with deer, geese, and llamas. Benches are under the magnolia tree. It really is beautiful here. Our pool, too, is enjoyed by guests who come with a heavy agenda. Many come back for the peacefulness, to 'do' this wonderful plantation area, or to witness the pageantry of the fox hunts that take place at North Bend in November, December, or January.

(Please turn page.)

And to think that, in 1984, a friend had to talk us into hosting! B&B brings the world to us."

Ridgely, a registered nurse who is a nurse practitioner, has lived here for 34 years.

Foreign languages spoken: "A little French and German."
Bed and bath: Four second-floor rooms (two beds are canopied); all with private baths, armoires, Laura Ashley linens, and Waverly prints. Three (two are 20 by 20 feet) with queen beds and shower baths; one has a connecting double-bedded room. One room with double sleigh bed has hall bath "right beside entrance door" that features the original deep long tub put in by George's grandfather in 1916.
Breakfast: Country style. All you can eat. "Until 9:30. If you come down at that hour, ring the old farm bell and George will come up from the barn." Fruit. Orange juice. Bacon, ham, or sausage. Eggs to order. Biscuits, home-made jelly. George's acclaimed waffles. "Used to serve in dining room; guests requested huge country kitchen—to be with George!"
Plus: Fireplace in each room. Air conditioning. (All bedrooms also have ceiling fans.) Afternoon or evening tea, coffee, or lemonade. Robes. Garden flowers. Turndown service. Use of refrigerator. Down comforters. Croquet. Volleyball. Horseshoes. Badminton. Swimming pool.

From Washington: *"To be able to write at the desk used by General Sheridan— what a thrill."* From several Virginians: *"A real home. A real working farm with very hospitable folks. . . . It was terrifc. And far from traffic. Real peace. . . . Made history come alive. . . . Made our honeymoon special. . . . A truly perfect way to heighten our experience with the grandeur of Colonial Williamsburg. . . . It was like staying with old friends!"*

The Country Fare   703/459-4828
402 North Main Street, Woodstock, VA 22664-1802

Host: Bette Hallgren
Location: In Shenandoah Valley within walking distance of village and hiking path that leads to a summit view of the Seven Bends of the Shenandoah River. Near Belle Grove, the National Trust plantation; caverns; Bryce Mountain; wineries; 90 minutes from Washington, D.C.

Open: Year round. Two-night minimum on October weekends.
Rates: Double occupancy. Private bath $65. Shared bath $55 queen bed, $45 double bed. $20 third person in room. Visa.

From Maryland: *"Thank heavens for the preservation of solitude and charm along the main thoroughfare in the small town of Woodstock. What a contrast from metropolitan Washington area! . . . Pure relaxation. . . . Warm and cheerful breakfast. . . . A short walk to a quiet shopping center, a local movie theater, and the Springhouse Restaurant. . . . We think of Bette Hallgren's antiques-filled rooms as a reflection of the tranquil days of milk delivery and neighborliness."*

One of the oldest homes in the Shenandoah Valley, the restored 1772 log and brick house has stenciled bedrooms, Williamsburg colors and wallpapers, inside window shutters, and four fireplaces. In 1985 Bette, grandmother of four, moved here from Massachusetts, where she had a career in management for a library subscription agency. The B&B is furnished with Grandmother's antiques. Here Bette provides biking and hiking maps; crafts ideas and supply sources; an upstairs sitting porch with old-fashioned swing and rockers; and, in the living room, a stone fireplace, books, and magazines.

Bed and bath: Three second-floor rooms. The one with adjoining private shower bath has a double bed. Another double-bedded room shares a full bath (with footed tub) with queen-bedded room. Rollaways, portacrib, and air mattresses ("kids love these!") available.

Breakfast: 8–9. Continental plus. Homemade breads (poppyseed, pumpkin, zucchini), fresh fruit in season, juices, beverages, "plus Grandmother's treats and surprises." Served in candlelit dining room with sterling, crystal, china; in season by wood-burning stove.

Plus: Bedroom air conditioners and ceiling fans. Fireplaced common room with reading material. Fresh flowers in season. Large brick patio. Hiking and biking maps. Off-street parking.

KEY TO SYMBOLS
♥ Lots of honeymooners come here.
♠ Families with children are very welcome. (Please see page xii.)
♦ "Please emphasize that we are a private home, not an inn."
♣ Groups or private parties sometimes book the entire B&B.
♦ Travel agents' commission paid. (Please see page xii.)
✖ Sorry, no guests' pets are allowed.
⚡ No smoking inside *or* no smoking at all, even on porches.

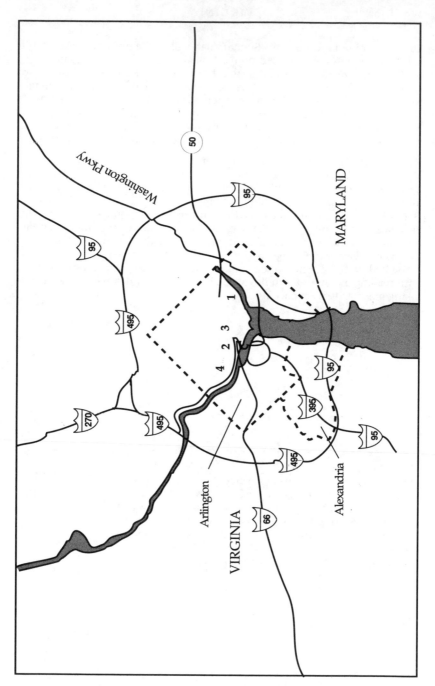

The numbers on this map indicate the locations of B&Bs described in detail in this chapter.

WASHINGTON, D.C.

1 Capitol Hill
  Bed & Breakfast Accommoda-
    tions, Ltd. Host #137, *395*
  Bed & Breakfast Accommoda-
    tions, Ltd. Host #145, *396*
  Bed & Breakfast Accommoda-
    tions, Ltd. Host #170, *396*
  The Bed & Breakfast
    League/Sweet Dreams &
    Toast Host #5, *397*
2 Dupont Circle
  Bed & Breakfast Accommoda-
    tions, Ltd. Host #125, *398*
  Swann Bed & Breakfast, *398*
3 Logan Circle
  Bed & Breakfast Accommoda-
    tions, Ltd. Host #100, *399*

4 Northwest
  Bed & Breakfast Accommoda-
    tions, Ltd. Host #128, *400*
  The Bed & Breakfast
    League/Sweet Dreams &
    Toast Host #1, *400*
  The Bed & Breakfast
    League/Sweet Dreams &
    Toast Host #2, *401*
  The Bed & Breakfast
    League/ Sweet Dreams &
    Toast Host #3, *401*
  Inver House, *402*
  Kalorama Guest House at
    Woodley Park, *403*

Washington, D.C.

Where do you want to be?

The following descriptions of Washington's B&B locations have been provided by Bed & Breakfast Accommodations, Ltd. and The Bed & Breakfast League/Sweet Dreams & Toast reservation services, described on pages 393 and 394.

Capitol Hill: A historic district that includes a wonderful residential area as well as the U.S. Capitol, Library of Congress, and U.S. Supreme Court. Many B&B homes are within walking distance of the east end of the Mall.

Cleveland Park: A historic district in Northwest Washington distinguished by its large number of Victorian summer homes—many on spacious lots with gardens—now converted to year-round use. Site of Washington National Cathedral and embassy residences.

Dupont Circle: Just north of the downtown business district in the hub of activities. A popular in-town residential area.

Logan Circle: Once home to the gentry, Logan Circle fell into neglect during the 1950s. Since the 1970s there has been a renaissance, with many Victorian houses restored.

Northwest: Lovely homes on broad lawns away from the hustle-bustle of downtown, but still close in.

According to guests (many are preservationists and/or house restorers), there ought to be a medal for the meticulous work—everything from research to labor—done by B&B owners. Indeed, many have won preservation awards.

Washington, D.C.,
Reservation Services

Bed & Breakfast Accommodations, Ltd.

P.O. Box 12011, Washington, DC 20005

Phone: 202/328–3510

Fax: 202/332–3885.

Listings: 85 including private homes, guesthouses, apartments (three-night minimum), and inns (one has a restaurant). Most are in and around Washington; a few are in nearby suburbs such as Alexandria, Fairfax, and Crystal City in Virginia, and Takoma Park, Bethesda, and College Park in Maryland. All Washington accommodations are accessible to public transportation; many are in historic homes decorated with antiques. All are air conditioned.

Reservations: One month's advance notice recommended. Two-night minimum for advance private home reservations; one night available in inns or on a last-minute basis in private homes.

Rates: $45–$150 single; $55–$225 double. Family and seasonal weekly rates available. Apartments recommended for families; $15 each additional person. $50 deposit required; balance due two weeks prior to arrival. $10 one-night surcharge. If cancellation is received with three full business days' notice (seven for holiday reservations), there is a $15 charge; less notice, two nights' charge. Amex, Diners, MC, Visa. ♦

By demand, this well-established and well-run service has grown to include more than bed and breakfasts. The staff books travelers in accommodations—many but not all are in historic properties—that range in style from budget to luxurious, and in size from 2 to 55 rooms.

The Bed & Breakfast League/
Sweet Dreams & Toast

P.O. Box 9490, Washington, DC 20016–9490

Phone: 202/363–7767, Monday–Thursday 9–5; Friday 9–1. Closed for two weeks at Christmas, and all federal holidays.

Listings: 85. Mostly hosted private residences. Ten unhosted apartments. All are in Washington, D.C. Many are in historic districts; all are within walking distance of public transportation. All are air conditioned. Many have private baths. All serve at least a continental breakfast. Short-term (over three weeks) hosted and unhosted housing available.

Reservations: Two-day minimum stay. At least 24 hours' notice required; two weeks preferred.

Rates: $40–$125 single. $50–$140 double. $10 one-night surcharge. $10 booking fee per reservation. $25 deposit per room. Deposit is not refundable; balance paid is refunded if cancellation is telephoned to the office more than eight days in advance of arrival; if later, rate for one night plus booking fee charged. Amex, MC, Visa; 5 percent service charge.

Founded in 1976 and directed by Millie Groobey since 1985, this is one of the oldest B&B reservation services in the country. The philosophy behind host selection is that location must be in a safe and convenient area, within walking distance of public transportation, and that all hosts are gracious and welcoming to travelers. (It is true! I have used the service several times.)

Both Virginia and Maryland offer B&B accommodations with interesting hosts who live very close to Washington, D.C., and good public transportation.

In nearby Maryland:

Chevy Chase, Chevy Chase Bed & Breakfast, page 32
Olney, The Thoroughbred Bed & Breakfast, page 42
Silver Spring, Bed and Breakfast of Maryland Host #185, page 46

In nearby Virginia:

Arlington, Memory House, page 318
Fairfax, The Bailiwick Inn, page 337

In Alexandria many hosts are represented by:

Alexandria, Princely Bed & Breakfast, Ltd., page 316

Washington, D.C., B&Bs

Bed & Breakfast Accommodations, Ltd. Host #137

Washington, DC

Location: On Capitol Hill, 7 blocks behind the Capitol. Within walking distance of Supreme Court and Library of Congress. Three blocks to buses. Ten-minute walk to Eastern Market subway stop and Union Station (shops, cinemas, restaurants, Amtrak, subway).

Reservations: Year round through Bed & Breakfast Accommodations, Ltd., page 393.
Rates: $60–$65 single, $70–$75 double. $10 one-night surcharge.
♥ ♦ ✖ ✗

Featured on several house tours as well as in the *Washington Post,* this 1902 house was restored by the host, a fashion designer who came to Washington from New York and Boston.

You enter through antique leaded glass double doors to a property noted for its chestnut paneling and decorative moldings. The dining room is hexagonal; one bedroom, octagonal. Two of the five original gas fireplaces have been converted to burn wood.

Bed and bath: Two second-floor double-bedded guest rooms share a full bath.
Breakfast: At 8:30. Continental; sometimes with homemade bread.
Plus: Central air conditioning. Private phone and color TV in each room. Double porches overlooking a brick patio surrounded by greenery and flowers.

From California: *"Extremely gracious host who made me feel very comfortable . . . allowed me to 'fit' into the city."*

KEY TO SYMBOLS
♥ Lots of honeymooners come here.
✚ Families with children are very welcome. (Please see page xii.)
◼ "Please emphasize that we are a private home, not an inn."
✢ Groups or private parties sometimes book the entire B&B.
♦ Travel agents' commission paid. (Please see page xii.)
✖ Sorry, no guests' pets are allowed.
✗ No smoking inside *or* no smoking at all, even on porches.

Bed & Breakfast Accommodations, Ltd. Host #145

Washington, DC

Location: A tree-lined street of historic homes on Capitol Hill. Ten blocks east of the Capitol, Supreme Court, Library of Congress. One-half block to bus; five-minute walk to subway. Within walking distance of outdoor Eastern Market, restaurants, boutiques.

Reservations: Year round through Bed & Breakfast Accommodations, Ltd., page 393.
Rates: $60–$70 single, $70–$80 double, $15 twin rollaway. $10 surcharge for one-night stay. Apartment $75 single, $85 double, $15 third person.
♯ ⊯ ◆ ✖

Preservationists hail this 1891 house as the earliest and finest local example of Colonial Revival architecture and interior design. Guests hail it as a wonderful B&B. (It is not forgotten by the saleswoman from Milwaukee and the Oregon forester who met here and married a year later.)

The hostess, who is knowledgeable about Washington's political, social, and cultural scenes, is responsible for decorating the 13-foot-ceilinged rooms with period furniture and artworks. Since "growing up in Montana and living in all major areas of the country including Alaska," she has restored other properties in Washington, has become a management consultant, and is a partner in a catering firm.

In residence: Two cats, "super intelligent" Dosha and Muffin.
Bed and bath: Four rooms on second and third floors. One with twin beds (room for a rollaway) shares a full bath with king-bedded room. Two double-bedded rooms (one has a private half bath) share a full bath. One-bedroom apartment, separate entrance, has double-bedded room, sleep sofa in living room, rollaway bed, kitchen, washer/dryer.
Breakfast: 7:30–9:30. Fresh fruit, juice, milk, hot or cold cereal. Muffins, croissants, scones or bagels. Gourmet coffees and teas (regular or decaf). Served in formal chandeliered dining room with silver, crystal, and china; on patio in good weather.
Plus: Central air conditioning. Private phone and color TV in each room. Library with current periodicals and several thousand volumes.

Bed & Breakfast Accommodations, Ltd. Host #170

Washington, DC

Location: On Capitol Hill, facing Pennsylvania Avenue. Five blocks from the Capitol, Library of Congress, botanical gardens, Mall. Bus stop in front of house; 1 block to subway. Close to shops, restaurants, Sunday flea and farmers' markets.

Reservations: Year round through Bed & Breakfast Accommodations, Ltd., page 393.
Rates: $60–$70 single, $70–$80 double. $10 one-night surcharge.
⊯ ◆ ✖ ✂

There's a Florida room (where breakfast is served), a more formal Florentine room, and a garden. The guest room that faces the park on Washington's major avenue is decorated with rococo Victorian antiques. The New England guest room has the original tin ceiling, chestnut wood paneling, and country and Shaker antiques. Most of the original architectural details have been preserved in this carefully restored, air-conditioned Victorian townhouse.

One of the well-traveled hosts, a hotel reservation manager, is a native Washingtonian; the other, a multilingual court reporter, was born and raised in Pennsylvania Dutch country.

Foreign languages spoken: Spanish, Italian, Russian, and a little German.
Bed and bath: One large (Victorian) double-bedded room and one (New England) with a queen bed share a full bath.
Breakfast: 7:30–9:30. Fresh fruit, juice, specialty breads, croissants, muffins, coffee and tea.

From Massachusetts: *"We loved it. Great breakfast. . . . Offered great recommendations on sites and restaurants."* From California: *"A beautiful environment . . . hospitable surroundings."*

The Bed & Breakfast League/ Sweet Dreams & Toast Host #5
Washington, DC

Location: Capitol Hill, 8 blocks (about 20 minutes' walk) east of U.S. Capitol. On a quiet street, 1½ blocks from Pennsylvania Avenue; 3 to Eastern Market subway stop.
Reservations: Year round, two-night minimum, through The Bed & Breakfast League/Sweet Dreams & Toast, page 393.
Rates: $60–$75 single, $70–$85 double.
♥ ➤ ✗ ✂

The Southern-born hosts offer Southern hospitality—and plenty of privacy—in this freshly decorated Victorian townhouse. The guest suite has a comfortable sofa and chairs, some antiques, and a convenient kitchen. The hostess is a Capitol Children's Museum staffer; her husband is a federal agency psychologist.

Bed and bath: First-floor guest suite with private entrance. Bedroom/sitting room with queen bed, private tub/shower bath, kitchen, private deck.
Breakfast: Continental. Help yourself from stocked refrigerator.
Plus: Central air conditioning. Color and cable TV and private phone line in suite.

Unless otherwise stated, rates in this book are per room for two and include breakfast in addition to all the amenities in "Plus." As for taxes and gratuities, please see page xi.

Bed & Breakfast Accommodations, Ltd. Host #125
Washington, DC

Location: In Kalorama Heights, a residential neighborhood of Victorian townhouses and a wide variety of cuisines. Six blocks to Adams Morgan and to Dupont Circle subway stop on red line. One and a half miles north of White House. Ten-minute walk to business district, five-minute walk to Washington Hilton, 15 to Omni Shoreham.

Reservations: Year round through Bed & Breakfast Accommodations, Ltd., page 393.

Rates: $60–$70 single, $70–$80 double. $10 one-night surcharge.
◖ ◆ ✈ ⅄

Why B&B? "After reading one too many stories about people who left anonymous unfulfilling jobs to open an inn, I decided to host *now!*"

That was about eight years ago, after the host moved from Oklahoma, restored the Victorian, and completed a quest for antiques to blend with Oriental pieces and contemporary art. "It's an unusual house; it has Victorian bay windows in back that catch the light and sun, and a Mediterranean-style front. This is an old and fascinating area with interesting places such as a combination cafe/bookstore with good titles, great music (live on weekends), and marvelous places for desserts. Or try a small shirtsleeve-style neighborhood restaurant with refreshingly good South American dishes prepared by its Salvadorean owners at incredible prices."

The host is a former history professor who owned a Union Station shop featuring folk art of several Latin American countries.

In residence: One affectionate Burmese cat, Pasha, "which loosely translates to 'Heat Cat' in Turkish."
Bed and bath: Five rooms, some with decorative fireplaces. Four second-floor queen-bedded rooms (one has additional twin bed) share two baths—one with tub and shower ring, one with full bath. On third floor, two-room suite with king bed and sleep sofa adjoins a private full bath.
Breakfast: 8 weekdays, 9 weekends. Continental.
Plus: Central air conditioning. Three fireplaced public rooms. Plenty of books. Television and telephone in room upon request. Two parking places, $5 each.

> From Texas: *"A real treat."* From New York: *"A comfortable bed, a good breakfast and a delightful host. Who could ask for more?"*

Swann Bed & Breakfast
Washington, DC

Location: Dupont Circle. Near downtown Washington. Within walking distance of Dupont Circle subway stop, art galleries, several small museums, Washington Hilton Hotel, "and more restaurants than you could eat in if you stayed for two months."

Reservations: Year round, two-night minimum, through The Bed & Breakfast League/Sweet Dreams & Toast, page 393.

Rates: $40–$50 single, $45–$60 double.
◖ ✈ ⅄

This location appeals to many conventiongoers and business travelers who appreciate the hospitality of the host, a former antiques dealer who is associated with an antiques lighting shop. The Victorian townhouse is filled with many wonderful Victorian and Chinese pieces.

Bed and bath: Four rooms share two tub/shower baths. On second floor, one room with double bed, one with one twin. On third floor, one room with double bed, one with twin.

Breakfast: A cooked breakfast is served in the kitchen or dining room.

Plus: Central air conditioning.

> From Connecticut: *"Beautifully decorated . . . clean and comfortable . . . lovely, quiet, aesthetically pleasing neighborhood."* From South Carolina: *"Overwhelmingly kind and witty host."*

Bed & Breakfast Accommodations, Ltd. Host #100

Washington, DC

Location: Adjoins Logan Circle historic district. Ten blocks northeast of White House; 10-minute walk to subway stop.

Reservations: Year round through Bed & Breakfast Accommodations, Ltd., page 393.

Rates: $60–$70 single, $70–$80 double. $5 crib. $10 surcharge for one-night stay. Apartment $75 single, $85 double.

A house tour favorite, most recently part of "Christmas at the Smithsonian," this restored century-old Victorian has for 17 years (18 months for the woodwork) been an avocation for the hosts. Furnished with many antiques, the house provides a wonderful setting for weddings and local theater group cast parties too. The latticed porch was pictured in Manhattan's Bloomingdale's photo essay based on this book.

The host, a lawyer, is a partner in a real estate development and syndication firm. The hostess has studied interior design and for the last decade has been very involved with the bed and breakfast movement in Washington.

Bed and bath: Five rooms share three baths. Second-floor room with canopied queen bed. On third floor, two double-bedded rooms; one with queen bed and queen sleep sofa; one with a queen and a twin bed. Apartment with queen bed and sleep sofa, laundry facilities.

Breakfast: At 8 on weekdays, 9 on weekends. Juice, coffee or tea, and a choice of two items—muffins, croissants, raisin toast, bagels. Sometimes, German pancakes or homemade waffles. Served in dining room under Victorian chandelier.

Plus: Central air conditioning. Area-controlled heating. Private phone and color TV in guest rooms. Parking ($5) if reserved in advance. Player piano. A Barbie-doll collection for young guests to play with.

> From England: *"A stunning home, but the hospitality is what endears this B&B to us."* From North Carolina: *"Accommodating to the extent of lending me a bike lock so I could travel by bike."* From Alabama: *"Greeted me with a cup of tea. Made me feel like a welcome friend."*

Bed & Breakfast Accommodations, Ltd. Host #128
Washington, DC

Location: The Woodley/Cleveland Park area. Across the street from the National Cathedral. Three blocks from Embassy Row and the Naval Observatory; 15-minute walk to subway and Sheraton and Shoreham hotels. Many restaurants on nearby Connecticut and Wisconsin avenues.

Reservations: Year round through Bed & Breakfast Accommodations, Ltd., page 393.
Rates: $60–$65 single, $65–$75 double. $10 one-night surcharge.
🛏 ♦ ✈ ✄

The Georgian-style house, built by a famous Washington builder, Harry Wardman, in 1924, has a spacious fireplaced living room on the first floor, a library with TV and VCR on the second. The antiques and art have been collected by the host, who has lived in California, Europe, and Asia. For the past 15 years, she has been a Washingtonian involved in civic organizations.

Bed and bath: Four rooms. On second floor, one double-bedded room and one with two twin beds share a full hall bath. On third floor, one room with two twin beds and one with a canopied queen bed share a large full bath.
Breakfast: 7:30–9:30. Fresh fruit, waffles, muffins. In formal fireplaced dining room.
Plus: Central air conditioning. Porch. Garden. Off-street parking.

Guests wrote: *"Incredible B&B. . . . Breakfast was wonderful . . . superb . . . fantastic."*

The Bed & Breakfast League/ Sweet Dreams & Toast Host #1
Washington, DC

Location: Cleveland Park. A quiet "close-in" section of Northwest Washington. Six blocks north of the Washington National Cathedral. Ten-minute walk to Cleveland Park Metro stop. One block to crosstown bus.

Reservations: Year round, two-night minimum, through The Bed & Breakfast League/Sweet Dreams & Toast, page 393.
Rates: $45–$65 single, $65–$75 double.
🛏 ✈

The welcoming host, a native New Englander who has lived in Washington for 25 years, had a career in public health nursing before becoming immersed in tourism. Some guests follow suggestions for a walking tour of this neighborhood, which was designed in the 1880s to be an out-of-town summer resort. Others may be given a night driving tour of the lighted federal buildings and monuments. Throughout the large Cape Cod–style home, there are family antiques including rocking chairs and a rope bed.

Bed and bath: Three rooms. Master bedroom has double bed and private attached bath with tub and shower. Second bedroom has one twin bed, desk, and private or shared hall bath with tub and shower. Third bedroom has one double bed and private or shared hall bath.

Breakfast: Flexible hour. Continental. In formal dining room with flower-filled bay window overlooking the spacious yard.

The Bed & Breakfast League/ Sweet Dreams & Toast Host #2

Washington, DC

Location: North Cleveland Park. In a quiet "close-in" section of Northwest Washington. Near the Washington National Cathedral, American University, the new embassy district, and Metro.

Reservations: Year round, two-night minimum, through The Bed &

Breakfast League/ Sweet Dreams & Toast, page 393.

Rates: $40–$70 single, $60–$80 double.

🛏 ✖ ✂

> From Ontario, Canada: *"Beautiful furnishings. Clean, quiet, safe location. Great breakfast with lots of coffee, fruit, and a variety of breads. Especially liked the strawberry muffins and homemade preserves. Firm beds. Very considerate and informative host."*

Antique furnishings, prints, and Oriental rugs give this home a warm ambiance. The host worked for several government agencies before owning and operating a small people-oriented business.

In residence: Two memorable and popular dogs—a standard poodle and a "zany but beautiful and well-behaved" five-year-old that came from the animal shelter.

Bed and bath: Three second-floor rooms. One with two twin beds and private attached bath with shower. Two other rooms have one double bed each and may share (or one may have as private) a private tub/shower bath.

Plus: Air conditioning. Off-street parking for guests' cars. TV and phone in guest rooms.

The Bed & Breakfast League/ Sweet Dreams & Toast Host #3

Washington, DC

Location: In a quiet, uncongested neighborhood near a major street (MacArthur Boulevard). Ten-minute drive to American University, Georgetown, and to two subway stops that have inexpensive parking. Within walking distance of restaurants, C&O Canal, and to canal towpath for walking, jogging, and cycling.

Reservations: Year round, two-night minimum, through The Bed & Breakfast League/Sweet Dreams & Toast, page 393.

Rates: $50–$65 single, $60–$75 double.

🛏 ✖ ✂

(Please turn page.)

There's a welcoming, relaxed feeling in this quarter-century-old multilevel house built on a hillside. The living room has big comfortable sofas and thick carpeting. Throughout, there are fiber artworks done by the hostess in her home studio, and by other artists. Her husband is a budget analyst for a government agency. Guests comment on the hospitality, the friendliness of the experienced hosts, and the fact that table linens and settings change daily.

Bed and bath: One room with queen bed, private en-suite tub/shower bath. One room with two twin beds, private hall bath with tub and shower.
Breakfast: Continental.
Plus: Central air conditioning. Color TV in each bedroom. Two decks bordered by treed hillside. Parking available on driveway or street.

Inver House
Washington, DC

Location: A quiet neighborhood in Northwest Washington, near the zoo. One block off Cleveland Avenue; 15-minute walk to Woodley Park/Zoo subway stop. Within walking distance of shops, restaurants, the Omni Shoreham and Washington Sheraton hotels; 25 minutes' walk to the National Cathedral.
Reservations: Year round, two-night minimum, through The Bed & Breakfast League/Sweet Dreams & Toast, page 393.
Rates: Vary according to room and bath arrangements: Summer $65–$105 single; $75–$115 double. Rest of year $75–$130 single, $85–$140 double.
📧 ❄️ ✈️

This secluded neighborhood, home to several ambassadors, is tucked in between several major streets. After staying here once, many B&B travelers return to this elegant 1920s detached single-family house, which is filled with magnificent antique rugs and furnishings, porcelain, and artwork. The host is a consultant on environmental issues.

Bed and bath: Three second-floor rooms, accessible by elevator. One with king bed, sitting area, private deck, private en-suite large shower bath. One room with queen bed and one with king bed have a connecting tub/shower bath.
Breakfast: Continental, maybe buffet style on weekends, in formal dining room.
Plus: Central air conditioning. Off-street parking. Color cable TV and private phones in rooms. Fine linens. Use of living room, study, sun porch, and a very pretty yard. Limousine service (additional charge) available by prior arrangement.

All the B&Bs with this 📧 symbol want you to know that they are a private home set up for paying guests and that they are not an inn. Although definitions vary, these private home B&Bs tend to have one to three guest rooms. For the owners, people who enjoy meeting people, B&B is usually a part-time occupation.

Kalorama Guest House at Woodley Park

202/328–0860
fax 301/951–3827

2700 Cathedral Avenue, NW, Washington, DC 20008

Host: Richard L. Fenstemaker; assistants: Mike Gallagher and Mary Ann Eitler
Location: Residential. Quiet. Downtown in embassy district. A few blocks from the National Zoo and Woodley Park subway station. One block off Connecticut Avenue at the corner of Cathedral and 27th Street.

Open: Year round. Two-night minimum on most weekends March–June, September, and October.
Rates: $40–$60 single with shared bath, $45–$65 double with shared bath. $50–$80 single with private bath, $55–$85 double with private bath. Suite $85 single, $10 each additional person. Amex, MC, Visa.
♦ ✖

Personalized hospitality (noncorporate life) was the main attraction of B&B for Richard, a former assistant manager of a 500-room Sheraton Hotel who sometimes gives innkeeping seminars.

Here, guests often comment on the relaxing and warm environment filled with period furnishings and brass beds, Oriental rugs, artwork, and live potted palms. Refinished pedal sewing machines are used as desks. Many rooms have original mantels.

Richard explains: "The area was developed in 1912 for government workers' single-family homes. As a corner house, my house, one of the largest, was valued at $12,000 when the others cost $9,000. It was a rooming house when I took it over and put a lot of myself into it. In addition to many business travelers and tourists, we host friends and relatives of neighbors. One couple who stayed with us three years ago, before they went to Poland in the foreign service, returned last month for a few weeks while they looked for a Washington apartment."

In residence: Freckles, "a friendly cocker spaniel whom guests love."
Bed and bath: Eleven rooms. Seven with private baths. "Each room is different in size and shape, although the furnishings are consistently antique." One two-room suite has a double bed and a sofa bed. Other rooms have double, twin, or queen-sized beds.
Breakfast: 7:30–10:30 weekdays. 8–11 weekends. Freshly baked croissants (delivered daily by a local baker), English muffins, toast, coffee, tea, butter and jam. In the lower-level breakfast room or on small porch.
Plus: Sherry (5–9 p.m.) by the fireplace. Air conditioning in bedrooms and parlor. Coffee is on throughout the day. Candy and flowers in each room. Laundry facilities. Parking ($5 per night). Free use of phone for local calls. Suggestions for favorite restaurants and relatively unknown walking tours of historic buildings.

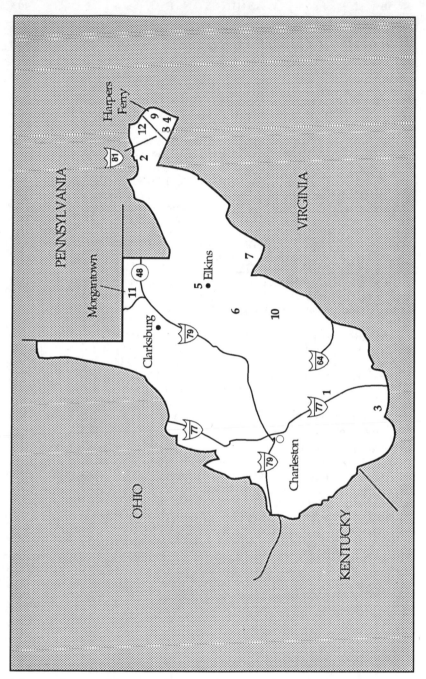

The numbers on this map indicate the locations of B&Bs described in detail in this chapter.

WEST VIRGINIA

1 Beckley: Prosperity
   Prosperity Farmhouse Bed &
   Breakfast, *406*
2 Berkeley Springs
   Highlawn Inn, *407*
3 Bramwell
   Three Oaks and A Quilt, *408*
4 Charles Town
   Gilbert House B&B of
   Middleway, *409*
   Hillbrook Inn, *410*
5 Elkins
   The Retreat at Buffalo Run, *411*
6 Elkins: Huttonsville
   Hutton House Bed &
   Breakfast, *412*

7 Franklin
   McCoy's Mill B&B, *413*
8 Gerrardstown
   Gerrardstown's Prospect Hill
   Bed & Breakfast, *414*
9 Harpers Ferry
   Fillmore Street Bed &
   Breakfast, *415*
10 Hillsboro
   The Current, *416*
11 Morgantown
   Maxwell Bed & Breakfast, *417*
12 Shepherdstown
   Thomas Shepherd Inn, *418*

West Virginia B&Bs

Prosperity Farmhouse Bed & Breakfast

Box 393, Prosperity, WV 25909   304/255-4245

Hosts: Tara and John Wooton
Location: On 80-acre cattle farm off a country road. Near WV White Water Rafting Company, Winterplace ski area, Prosperity Speedway. Five minutes from shopping mall, theaters, restaurants, bowling alleys, parks. In a town not included on many maps; take exit 48 on I–77, North Beckley. Six miles from I–64 and I–77 and near I–79. Fifty miles southeast of Charleston.
Open: May–October.
Rates: $35 single. $40 double. $5 additional person. Children under age 12 free.
🛉 🛥

What was a granary for 100 years has become a very private B&B—a perfect arrangement for two couples traveling together or for families—on the grounds of (just 10 yards from) the hosts' century-old farmhouse. For the conversion, barn wood was installed on the inside walls. Floors and ceilings are original. There are crisp white curtains, Laura Ashley fabrics, some antiques, and local crafts.

Tara, a teacher, is delighted with the outcome—and with hosting. "Many come for white-water rafting. We had one family reunion here. And some travelers find us a perfect stopover, as we are four hours from Cincinnati, Charlotte, Pittsburgh, and Raleigh. Sometimes they join us for fishing, basketball, haying, gardening—or walking on the dirt road that leads up to a knoll where there used to be a school. Children love the pond, which is full of frogs, turtles, and fish. . . . John, a lawyer and lifelong resident of the area, is a great storyteller, local historian, and very likable guy! . . . We love to share this unpopulated beautiful area."

In residence: In hosts' quarters, Jody, age 12; Clint, age 10. Two golden retrievers. Cows and chickens.
Bed and bath: In this totally private house—two sleeping areas. Beds for six people. One shower bath. First floor has queen sleep sofa, kitchenette. In large upstairs room, canopied double bed and two trundles that can be a king; ceiling fan. Advance reservations required for crib or rollaway.
Breakfast: Flexible hours. Fruit (some homegrown). Juice. Waffles, crepes, or pancakes with ham or bacon. Homemade muffins. Served in farmhouse, on deck, or in B&B kitchen. Self-serve in your own house is an option.
Plus: New in-ground (20-by-4-foot) pool. Private deck. Mints. Tour of farm.

Unless otherwise stated, rates in this book are per room for two and include breakfast in addition to all the amenities in "Plus." As for taxes and gratuities, please see page xi.

Highlawn Inn   304/258–5700

304 Market Street, Berkeley Springs, WV 25411

Hosts: Sandra Kauffman and Timothy Miller

Location: On a quiet side street. At the top of a steep hill, 3 blocks from center of town known for its mineral baths, antiques and crafts shops, and 18-hole championship golf course. Two hours from Washington, D.C.

Open: Year round. Reservations required. Two-night minimum on most weekends.

Rates: $70–$80 per room. $95 suite. Aunt Pearl's: $90 large room with view of ridge; $95 room with private lattice-enclosed porch with glider, chair, plants; $100 room with private exterior entrance, sitting area; $105 huge first-floor room. Memorial Day through October, Saturday night candlelight six-course dinner party, $35 per person includes complimentary bottle of award-winning West Virginia wine.

♥ ❖ ✈

"We'd like to choose our next-time room now," say many guests as they leave this inn, which has almost become a legend in its nine-year history.

On her way to becoming an innkeeper/historic preservationist/chef par excellence, Sandy was an urban law firm legal administrator (manager of 60 staff members), president of the Association of Legal Administrators, and an antiques dealer. Since restoring the 1890s house, she and Tim, the conference and wedding specialist, have restored an adjacent Victorian home (Aunt Pearl's) and connected it to Highlawn with a stairway and lighted walkway. The rooms, with names such as Lovers' Loft and Ridgeview, are decorated with Victorian wallpapers, a green and rose color theme, and white iron-and-brass beds.

The Murder Mystery Weekends, November–April, are so popular that reservations are made weeks and even months in advance. Also in demand: holiday and Saturday night (May–October) dinners that feature local ingredients, Sandy's own herbs, and reduced salt, fat, and sugar recipes.

Many Washingtonians met Sandy when she gave a cooking demonstration in Woodward & Lothrop's main store. Recent press coverage includes a lovely spread in *Southern Living.*

In residence: "Jackie, a special kitty who adopted our inn and loves naps in the hallway. Several friendly porch cats for petting."

Bed and bath: Ten rooms. In *Highlawn,* five second-floor rooms plus a first-floor suite with private entrance and porch. All private baths, all but one with claw-foot tub and shower. Beds are double or king/twin options of brass, carved walnut, or white iron-and-brass. In *Aunt Pearl's,* four queen-bedded rooms, private en-suite baths—two tub and shower, two shower only.

Breakfast: 8:30–10. "Unforgettable." Could be freshly squeezed orange juice, egg-and-cheese casserole, locally produced country sausage and bacon, grits, homemade jams to top "mile high" biscuits, hot glazed cinnamon rolls, honey orange pastry made with local wildflower honey, prizewinning locally made apple butter. Fresh herb dishes in season; always a vegetarian dish. Sandy's own coffee blend.

(Please turn page.)

Plus: Air conditioning and color TV in rooms. Rockers and swing on verandas. Large lawn. English soaps. Mineral water. Coffees, teas.

> From Virginia: *"Enchanting. . . . An oasis. Original Victorian elegance recreated. Antique furnishings . . . luxurious linens, quiet and restful atmosphere. We really felt pampered. . . . The innkeeper has a rare talent for making each visit a memorable one."*

Three Oaks and A Quilt   304/248–8316
Duhring Avenue, P.O. Box 84, Bramwell, WV 24715

Host: "B.J." Kahle
Location: Off the beaten path. In a town of about 1,000 people. Eight miles north of Bluefield, West Virginia. In a residential section atop a hill across from the Thomas Mansion "Carriage House."

Open: Year round.
Rates: $55 double. $5 less for single occupancy. Discounts for stays of three or more nights.
♥ ◂ ✕ ⅄

"Most people come here to see the coal operators' mansions in this town, which is on the National Register of Historic Places. They fall in love with the area and want to return. One is quickly renewed in the restful, relaxing atmosphere. My grandfather bought this house in 1904 and it has remained in the family ever since. I restored it, using and reusing everything possible. The oaks are to keep you cool; the quilts are to keep you warm."

A magnificent "Whig Rose" appliqued quilt, one of B.J.'s collection (of four dozen), is hanging on the front porch wall. Inside, the homestead is freshly painted and papered.

Mother of three grown children, B.J. has taught in five states.

Bed and bath: Three second-floor rooms. Two shared baths, one with tub, the other with shower. Two rooms with double beds (one is grandparents' cherry bed, the other a Henry Ford four-poster pencil bed). One room with twin beds. Handmade quilts, traditional patterns, on every bed.
Breakfast: Weekdays at 7; flexible on weekends. Juice, casseroles, cinnamon rolls, Christmas Eve Plum Pudding Bread, quick breads, glazed apples, hot beverages. Menu varies according to guests' tastes and B.J.'s schedule. Served in the dining room amidst a quilt collection.
Plus: Late-afternoon beverages. Bedroom fans. Mints. Fresh flowers. Thick towels. When time permits, tour of area.

> From Florida: *". . . A return to genteel hospitality . . . in a 19th-century town so well preserved that it lacks a gas station on Main Street . . . everything in apple-pie order . . . intangible comforts of a welcoming front porch with a swing, a formal 19th-century dining room, and kitchen conversations."* From Mississippi: *"Special insight into the town's past and present . . . it's not just a comfortable place to stay at a great price; it's an experience."*

The place to stay has become the reason to go.

Gilbert House B&B of Middleway

P.O. Box 1104, Charles Town, WV 25414   304/725–0637

Hosts: Bernie and Jean Reid Heiler
Location: In the National Register village of Middleway, with 18th-century architecture, footbridge by mill, gazebo, old cemeteries. Surrounded by church yards and fronted by old flagstone sidewalk. Five minutes to Charles Town and I–81, 15 to Harpers Ferry, 30 to Antietam Battlefield.
Open: Year round. Two-night minimum preferred on weekends. Reservations required.
Rates: $90 third-floor room. $110 or $130 second-floor suites. $20 one-night surcharge for Saturday night stay only. Reduced rates Monday–Thursday ($10 less the first night, $20 each additional night). Amex, MC, Visa.

♥ ⬛ ⁂ ♦ ✗ ⚯

Thanks to the Heilers' restoration, the village has a historic B&B with 20th-century comforts. Following major structural work, the early Georgian stone colonial has been furnished with Oriental rugs, great master artworks, fine antiques, and interesting pieces collected during the hosts' worldwide travels.

Jean, an artist/calligrapher/financial analyst and one of the first female Harvard Business School graduates, was president of an investment firm. Bernie, a petroleum engineer, commutes from Harpers Ferry to Washington on the train. They were Boston based for 20 years before launching their new lifestyle in 1984. Here, Jean has played the role of contractor and foreman for the 18th-century-style log house rebuilt on the property. She has helped the village to become quietly rediscovered and worked to save Charles Town's Old Opera House. Both hosts are active with Washington's Shakespeare Theatre.

Foreign languages spoken: Spanish and German.
Bed and bath: Three rooms—with two more under restoration. On third floor (with sound of rain on tin roof): 18th-century high double bed, en-suite shower/tub bath. On second floor: one large room, Lincoln (double) bed plus a single bed, working fireplace, two sitting areas, tub/shower bath. Champagne in bridal suite with huge living room, 18th-century bed (adapted to queen size) with curtains, working fireplace, en-suite bath with claw-foot tub, hand-held shower.
Breakfast: At 9. (Coffee ready earlier.) Freshly squeezed orange juice, fresh fruit, Bernie's bread or Jean's muffins. Quiche with asparagus or spinach, or French toast. Homemade jelly or Jamaican marmalade. Maybe steak and eggs. Cakes and pies. Freshly ground coffee. Special diets accommodated. In main room, in dining room, or on porch.
Plus: Air-conditioned bedrooms. Welcoming refreshments. Fresh flowers. Candy. Fresh fruit. Chinese sandalwood and English Pears soaps. Fireplaces. Piano. Library.

> From Maryland: *"Made for a romantic getaway . . . gracious hosts full of interesting stories and bits of regional history . . . breakfasts were feasts . . . good advice on restaurants and sightseeing."*

Hillbrook Inn   304/725-4223

Route 2, Box 152, Charles Town, WV 25414-9635

Host: Gretchen Carroll
Location: It's there, "farther down the drive than you think possible," 5 miles west of town, an hour from D.C. Beltway, off a winding country road, on 17 acres. Surrounded by miles of peach orchards, a thoroughbred farm, and hundreds of acres of Angus. In the crook of Bullskin Run, with "wildly angled roofs" reflected in the duck pond.
Open: Thursday–Sunday year round (closed first two weeks in April and last two weeks of August), "with good food, drink, and music in the Tavern."
Rates: Per person based on double occupancy; include seven-course dinner and wine. $165 small room, $180 large room, $190 with fireplace/balcony/porch. Specials January–March.
♥ ✣ ♦ ✗

This award-winning inn is noted for its setting, its decor, its cuisine—and Gretchen, the innkeeper, who still remembers when the property was just her Sunday drive destination inspired by a *Washington Post* photograph. That was in 1984, when she was Georgetown University's director of study abroad and the founding director of the International Student Exchange Program—following a Foreign Service–oriented life with her father and her husband.

Gretchen fell in love with the one-room-wide, half-timbered Tudor manor house that cascades down 15 levels (no two rooms are on the same level) and transformed it into "a feast for the senses." It has an English country house ambiance with collections of antiques—"all are used; we're not a museum,"—and polished floors, lots of old wood and brass, Oriental rugs, and more than 2,000 window panes. There are no secrets: personally and in a printed guide Gretchen directs guests to auctions and shops, the source of many of the inn's furnishings. And some guests hire her to decorate their homes in Hillbrook style.

Maybe by the time you read this, there will be a new old-looking gatehouse complex with half a dozen more "ultimate" guest rooms, a meeting space adaptable for indoor weddings, and a boathouse over the pond.

Foreign language spoken: French.
Bed and bath: Only five rooms, each with antique double bed and feather bed, sitting area, air conditioning, ceiling fan, views. Each unique (working fireplace, wood stove, porch, or location); fully described when you call. All private baths; one with tub and shower, some with hand-held shower.
Breakfast: 8:30–10. Chef Christine's menus include French toast with warm cranberry orange syrup or pecan pancakes with apricot ginger butter, apple brandy syrup, and a dollop of sour cream. Served by Gretchen on glassed-in porch.
Plus: Fireplace at each end of 20-foot-high living room. Library. Down comforters. Beribboned chocolates. "Lots of places to just be." Small tables and chairs on Bridge of Sighs over stream. Hammock. Terrace with fountain. Perennial gardens. Picnic baskets prepared. Fresh Bullskin Run springwater from original springhouse on property.

The Retreat at Buffalo Run   304/636-2960
214 Harpertown Road, Elkins, WV 26241-9662

Hosts: Bertha and Earl Rhoad (year round); Kathleen Rhoad (summers and holidays)
Location: On five acres of wooded grounds. Three blocks from Davis and Elkins College. One mile from downtown Elkins. Between Canaan Valley/Timberline and Snowshoe/Siler Creek ski areas. Near a cranberry wilderness; white-water outfitters; caves and caverns for spelunking; the Augusta Heritage Arts Workshops. Four hours west of Washington, D.C.
Open: Year round.
Rates: $37 single. $48 double. $10 extra person in room.
♥ ♨ ⚑ ❊ ♦ ✗

The wraparound porch has swing and rocking chairs. Hummingbirds are at the feeders. Tall shade trees, evergreens, rhododendron groves, and a hammock are on the grounds of the turn-of-the-century house that Kathleen "just knew" would be the right place (and new career) for her semiretired parents. Within half an hour of the Realtor's showing, the Rhoads made an offer. They redecorated and furnished with homey antiques, art, and contemporary pieces.

Kathleen, a college career counselor in Chicago, in Washington, D.C., and now at a Florida community college, had dreams of becoming a foreign Service Officer. Here she skis, hikes, goes antiquing, floats down Cheat River in inner tubes—and hosts! Her parents, avid bird-watchers and gardeners, met as teenagers in Hershey, Pennsylvania. Cook and seamstress Bert is a member of West Virginian Scenic Trails Hiking Club. In Florida, Kathleen is a member of Rare Fruits Club. Earl, most recently a Sweetheart Cups training director, was a printer and small-town newspaper publisher. They all concur: "For us, B&B in this wonderful old house was meant to be."

Bed and bath: Six rooms on second and third floors share three tub/shower baths plus a half bath. Queen or double beds; one room has two double beds, two have extra-long queen beds. Rollaways available.
Breakfast: At guests' convenience. Fresh fruit. Homemade muffins. Entree possibilities: Dutch babies; Swedish pancakes; blackberry custard; overnight French toast with calamondin marmalade. Selected from Kathleen's cookbook collection or from Bertha's recipes inspired by home territory, Pennsylvania's Lancaster County.
Plus: Afternoon beverages. Piano. Cordless phone. Guest refrigerator. TV. Games. Coloring books for children.

From Michigan: *"Superior because of personal care and attention to detail . . . I would go back for the breakfasts alone. . . . The most important element of the Retreat's charm is human. The combination of two generations of hosts who take an interest in their guests, without intruding on their privacy."* From Virginia: *"All sorts of information was computerized and available as a handout. . . . My son called them Grandma and Grandpa by the time we left."*

To tip or not? (Please turn to page xi.)

Hutton House Bed & Breakfast   304/335–6701
Route 219/250, Huttonsville, WV 26273   800/234 6701

Hosts: Dean Ahren and Loretta Murray

Location: High on a hill on Route 219/250, overlooking "tiny Huttonsville" (pop. 250), Tygart Valley, Laurel Mountains. Within 45 minutes of Snowshoe ski resort, Cass Scenic Railroad, National Radio Observatory; 17 miles south of Elkins. "Near great home cooking as well as four-star dining."

Open: Year round. Two-night minimum on holiday weekends and October Forest Festival.

Rates: $50–$55 shared bath, $65–$80 private. Singles $5 less. $10 extra adult in room, $5 ages 5–9. Ten percent less for senior citizens. Discover, MC, Visa.

♥ ⅰ ❖ ♦ ⅍

From Australians living in Washington, D.C.: *"We stayed with our three children, aged 9 to 21 months. They can't wait to visit again."* From Ohio: *"They made us feel so welcome that we never wanted to leave."* From Virginia: *"Spacious enough to offer complete privacy, but also a warm, homey atmosphere."* From Pennsylvania: *"Wonderful, creative cook . . . incredible array of baked goods . . . lacy curtains . . . rich woods that glow . . . knickknacks . . . huge soft towels . . . hints for our four days . . . most of all, sitting on that glorious porch and reading, looking at the sunset, talking, even singing old folk songs . . . left feeling pampered, rested and full."*

Help yourself to coffee in the kitchen. "Hang out" at the bar-type counter while breakfast is being prepared. Maybe have muffins in the dining room and move on to the wraparound porch for the main course. Copy and exchange recipes. Play bumper pool, badminton, or croquet. Sit in the porch swing that hangs from a tree. Bring up some subject and maybe, later, find a book about it on your pillow. Be prepared for flexible, happy, sharing hosts—who, while on their honeymoon five years ago, followed a garage sale sign and came upon this turreted National Register Queen Anne Victorian, vacant then, with winding staircase that inspired the next-day deposit.

They opened as a summer B&B for three years, while Loretta continued in Philadelphia as a physical education teacher ("some qualifications for this!") and Dean as a contractor. In 1991 they became full-time innkeepers (and Dean, a real estate developer) who are active in the community.

In residence: Three outdoor cats—Mica, Yip, and Stinky.

Bed and bath: Seven rooms. Four on second floor, three on third. King/twins (shared bath), queen (private bath), queen and one or two twins (shared bath), double bed with Jacuzzi bath, or double bed with private bath, turret sitting room. Crib available.

Breakfast: Flexible hours. Repertoire includes creme brulee with raspberries, zucchini frittata, stuffed Italian sausage, pineapple sorbet with kiwi, lemon pancakes, stuffed French toast, turkey ham with green pepper, whole-grain pancakes with maple syrup made right here. Special diets accommodated.

Plus: Dinner by reservation. Spontaneity. "Lots of laughs."

McCoy's Mill B&B

304/358–7893

Thorn Creek Road, Box 610, Franklin, WV 26807

Hosts: Glen and Iris Hofecker
Location: At the foot of mountains, where Thorn Creek rushes into the headwaters of the south branch of the Potomac River. Just off Route 220; waterwheel visible. Three miles south of Franklin.

Open: Year round. Two-night minimum on September and October weekends.
Rates: $50 single, $60 double. Less for three or more nights.
♥ 🖤 ⁂ ✈

> Guests wrote: *"A fantastic experience. . . . A combination of a step back into history, into a mill that is being restored; a memorable evening and morning visiting with fascinating folks; a stick-to-the-ribs breakfast with the best homemade apple butter we've ever had. . . . Sleeping next to the sound of a rushing stream. Waking up to one of the most picturesque scenes in West Virginia. What more could one ask for?"*

And all because of the great flood of 1985. Glen, a cabinetmaker who reproduces clocks and Chippendale furniture—mostly Newport style—had restored a 1756 mill in Virginia. While working with the West Virginia flood disaster relief, he found McCoy's Mill, the state's oldest (1757) landmark, and felt it would be a great place to share with others via B&B. What the Hofeckers have created is "an escape, a place where guests never seem to be in a hurry," a friendly, comfortable B&B with a bedroom that has been pictured in *Mid-Atlantic Country.*

The present mill of post-and-beam construction was built in 1848. The adjoining miller's house was built in 1909. Glen has created a small hydroelectric plant that uses the mill and mill wheel to produce electricity for heat and lighting in the B&B and shop. Latest project: a new workshop, a wonderful log cabin with the stone fireplace that remained, all by itself, from miller's original house.

In residence: A Yorkie, Tinker, "terribly bright, terribly human" (the Yarmouth Port, Mass., *Register*); "adorable . . . goodwill ambassador" (Maryland guests).
Bed and bath: With view of creek, dam, or river—three large second-floor rooms (several horizontally paneled walls) with private tub/shower baths. Two with queen-size beds. One with two double four-poster beds. Rollaway and crib available.
Breakfast: 7–9. Full country breakfast could include sausage, biscuits, and gravy; pancakes; or French toast with cinnamon apples. Juice. Fruit. Homemade breads. Glen and Iris join guests on deck overlooking waterwheel or in country kitchen.
Plus: Fully equipped guest kitchen ($30 charge for cooking). Tour of house and mill. Barbecue. Picnic tables. Fishing on premises; some fishing equipment available.

B&Bs offer the ultimate concierge service.

Gerrardstown's Prospect Hill Bed & Breakfast

304/229–3346

P.O. Box 135, Gerrardstown, WV 25420

Hosts: Hazel and Charles Hudock
Location: Secluded. On a 225-acre working farm. At the foot of North Mountain. Four miles from I-81. About a 90-minute drive from Washington, D.C. Near Harpers Ferry, Antietam, Gettysburg, and Winchester.

Open: Year round. Two-night minimum preferred. (Arrival time 3–10; departure by 11.)
Rates: Per room, $85; $95 Saturday night only. Cottage, $95 for two; $20 each additional person. MC, Visa.
♥ ❖ ✖

"A discovery," say first-time guests, who drive between the stone pillars, cross over the stone bridge, and pass ducks and geese before arriving at the Georgian mansion. The grand main hall has a graceful open stairway with a three-storied mural of early colonial life. Built between 1789 and 1802 by a businessman who outfitted wagon trains going west, the elegant residence was restored in 1978 when the Hudocks decided to come for what B&B guests seek: peace and quiet. With five children grown—now visiting grandchildren come—"B&B just sort of happened."

The house is on the Register of Historic Places and is filled with antiques collected through the Hudocks' 28 years of traveling when Charlie was a meteorologist with the U.S. Navy. (He delights in seeing guests guess the origin of some items.) It's the kind of place where you can be very private or "wander into the kitchen for tea and talk." Or spend time with Charlie, who loves to share his extensive collection of books and photographs. Or go for long walks through the woods. Discover herb, vegetable, and fruit gardens. Enjoy the scene of cows and calves.

In residence: Charlie smokes a pipe. Kersey, a large long-legged mixed pup. Elmo, a "Morris-like" cat. Ducks and geese.
Bed and bath: Two large mansion rooms, each with a private full bath, working fireplace, and sofa and comfortable chairs. One with a double bed; the other, a queen-sized. In a Flemish brick cottage, former servants' quarters, down the hill where stream can be heard—one second-floor room with double bed plus a queen foldout sofa in the keeping room, shower bath, kitchenette, living room, working fireplace, and dining area.
Breakfast: 8–9. Juice, fruit, baked omelet or apple pancakes with sour cream and maple syrup, homemade biscuits, jams and syrups. In formal dining room with china, silver, and crystal. Cottage guests, too, eat breakfast in main house.
Plus: Tea or wine. Tour of house. Ponds for fishing (release catch) and ice skating. Country roads for cycling.

> From Missouri: " . . . *Every small detail attended to . . . beds turned down . . . homemade cookies and tea in the afternoon . . . a historic and lovely house with great people.*"

---

*G*uests arrive as strangers, leave as friends.

Fillmore Street Bed & Breakfast   304/535–2619

Fillmore Street, Box 34   (answering service) **410/321–5634**
Harpers Ferry, WV 25425-0034

Hosts: Alden and James Addy
Location: On a quiet side street in the historic area. Within walking distance of all historic attractions.
Open: Year round. Closed Thanksgiving, Christmas, and New Year's.
Rates: Per room. $72 full bath, $65 shower bath.
♥ ✈

> From Delaware: *"Cozy but elegant . . . peaceful."* From D.C.: *"Everything from the wicker furniture on the porch to the matching bed and dresser makes you feel at home. . . . A perfect introduction to B&B for my 65-year-old mother."* From Maryland: *"Superb host and hostess. I especially loved breakfast—served by the most charming butler, waiter, PhD!"*

No longer a well-kept secret, the antiques-filled Victorian with blue/green shutters and white picket fence has been home to two educators for 20 years. "We do B&B, as we have for 9 years—for fun and to make practical use of our house, which is in a wonderful area. Although most guests come to visit the Harpers Ferry National Historic Park, many come, particularly in winter, for a getaway from urban areas."

The Addys often share their interest in history, antiques, art, theater, and gardening. Fillmore Street is definitely a B&B where the hospitality is remembered at least as much as the country Victorian decor.

Bed and bath: On second floor, two air-conditioned rooms. Each has a queen bed, private adjoining bath. One bath with tub and shower; the other, shower only.
Breakfast: Continental (brought to guests' rooms) 8:30–10:30. Full at 9 in dining room. Juice. Fresh fruit. Sausages, herbed scrambled eggs with mushroom and/or tomato garnish, buttered rosemary potatoes, spiced applesauce, muffins and homemade preserves; or baked stuffed eggs, omelets, or baked eggs au gratin; muffin, cheese and bread souffle, steamed buttered apples, apple-rum cake or pie, or orange-cinnamon French toast. Vegetarian diets accommodated. Everything prepared without salt and with natural ingredients.
Plus: As a Pennsylvania guest wrote, "The finest details to the letter." Fresh flowers. Chocolates. Mints. Beverages. Turndown service. Fireplaced dining room. Guests' upstairs sitting room with library. As the Addys say, "Guests are free to tour the house." Garden. In-room television. Extensive sightseeing material. Will meet guests at Harpers Ferry train station.

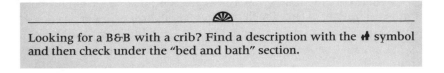

Looking for a B&B with a crib? Find a description with the ♯ symbol and then check under the "bed and bath" section.

The Current

304/653–4722

HC 64, Box 135, Hillsboro, WV 24946

Hosts: Leslee McCarty and John Walkup
Location: In the Allegheny Mountains, within sight of the Greenbrier River. Five miles from the Pearl S. Buck Birthplace. Near cross-country skiing and hiking in Cranberry Wilderness, Droop Mountain, and Watoga state parks.
Open: Year round. Two-night minimum on holiday weekends.
Rates: $40 single, $50 double. $10 extra person.
♥ 🏠 ⁂ ⊱

After pedaling along the incredibly beautiful Greenbrier River Trail on our first mountain-bike B&B-to-B&B trip, we approached The Current to find a hot tub on the near side, a Morgan horse farm across the way, and beyond, the spire of a white church against a mountain backdrop. The whole visit was a wonderful introduction to West Virginian hospitality.

Leslee and John had just purchased the church. Now they are in the process of restoring it for meetings—and maybe even for more guest rooms. Their 1905 farmhouse, owned by one family until 1985, has refinished woodwork. The furnishings and collections, arranged with flair, include John's great-grandfather's walnut and cherry bed with 6-foot headboard; Leslee's grandmother's quilts; Raggedy Ann and Andy dolls; and West Virginia crafts and photographs.

The easy-to-be-with hosts met while organizing a local festival for world hunger. Since their marriage they have continued to work on benefit events, a land trust for the Greenbrier River (work on the trail is scheduled for completion by 1993), and individual people-to-people projects too. John, a native who can trace his family's arrival in Greenbrier Valley back to about 1760, is a photographer and guitar player and runs a cattle farm that you are likely to pass "15 miles down the river." Leslee, a community activist, is a substitute teacher. (She was a hit for a Woodward & Lothrop cooking demonstration, representing B&Bs in this book.)

We left—well fed—with "don't miss" suggestions and fond memories.

In residence: Leslee's parents, retired teachers and avid golfers, are first-floor suite summer residents. Squeaky, a German shepherd. Ashley, a lovable mixed shepherd. Four outdoor cats, all named "Kitty."
Foreign languages spoken: Spanish fluently. German haltingly.
Bed and bath: Four spacious double-bedded rooms. First-floor suite has TV, private tub/shower bath. Three second-floor rooms share upstairs half bath and a first-floor tub/shower bath. Enclosed porch has two "especially nice for kids" daybeds. Rollaway bed.
Breakfast: 8–9. Freshly baked bread, homemade jelly, omelet or cottage cheese pancakes with strawberries, cereal, juice, fruit. Served in dining room with wood stove or in large fireplaced country kitchen.

Plus: Beverages. Deck (for stargazing too). Hot tub. Wood stove makes for skiers' "hangout" dining room. Wildflower arrangements. Canoe and bicycle rentals arranged. Dinner (semivegetarian available) for guests ($10 per person) traveling the Greenbrier River Trail. Babysitting. Kitchen and laundry privileges.

Maxwell Bed & Breakfast   304/594-3041
Route 12, Box 197, Morgantown, WV 26505-8615

Hosts: Pat Keith and Emma B. Maxwell
Location: Quiet. At Ridge Way Farm, surrounded by woods and fields overlooking Cheat Lake. Two miles from U.S. 68, exit 10. Eight miles east of Morgantown and West Virginia University. Two miles to Lakeview Resort and restaurants.
Open: Year round. "Best to call in evening."
Rates: $30 single. $40 double; $55 with bed nook. Suite (both rooms) $80.

If meeting people is what B&B is all about, you've come to the right place, an organic farm where Pat, a former social worker and just-retired rural mail carrier, raises Scotch Highland cattle and tends the vegetable garden and fruit orchards. Emma Maxwell, her mother (a winter Arizona resident), is a retired social worker who, at age 69, put a pack on her back for a worldwide trip. She rode elephants and camels, took canoe and rapids trips, stayed in African villages . . . and visited 137 countries before returning home in 1980. Now "88 years young," she speaks of being semiretired.

To the 1895 house that "no longer looks old and is not antiques-filled unless you count mother and daughter" the do-it-yourselfers have added a solar room with rocking chairs from which you might see white-tailed deer and wild turkey.

In residence: Two dogs, Kate and Allie, "trained staff members who greet guests politely." Two cats, Grey Kat (travels with Emma in winter) and Miss Pansy.
Bed and bath: In second-floor guest area, two cozy rooms, each with king bed, two chairs, desk. Common sitting room with TV, and a bed nook—an alcove with twin bed. One bath with wall-hung, hand-held shower.
Breakfast: 6–9. Full farm breakfast varies. Juice, cereal, warm muffins. French toast; pancakes; potatoes, bacon or sausage, eggs. In season, figs, raspberries, or strawberries from the garden. Homemade applesauce, jams and jellies. Herbal teas. Choice of coffees always includes freshly ground organically grown coffee from Peru and Mexico. Special diets accommodated.
Plus: Many ceiling fans. Hosts provide four-wheel drive up the hill during winter snows. It is worth staying here just to be on mailing list for annual seasonal newsletter.

(Please turn page.)

From West Virginia (echoed in a huge stack of letters): *"Stayed while job interviewing. Pat and Emma are part of the reason our current address is Morgantown. Delightful people—warm, friendly, and funny. They are living what to us 'burned-out city folk' seemed a dream—a small farm that leans toward self-sufficiency—and they make it seem so easy. Orchard, pond, flowers—and a raised-bed vegetable garden that any gardener would drool over. And then there's their food. . . . "*

Thomas Shepherd Inn   304/876–3715
300 West German Street, P.O. Box 1162, Shepherdstown, WV 25443

Host: Margaret Perry
Location: Residential. At crossroads of Routes 45, 230, and 34. Minutes' walk to shops and restaurants. With landscaped yard—in the state's oldest community, which has a college-town aura, a 1738 gristmill, and not a single stoplight. Within walking distance of Chesapeake and Ohio Canal towpath (halfway mark for cyclists from Georgetown to Cumberland). Eight miles to Harpers Ferry, 4 to Antietam Battlefield. Ninety minutes from Washington, D.C., and Baltimore. Near antiquing, rafting, tubing.
Open: Year round. Two-night minimum on weekends and holidays.
Rates: $85 weekday, $95 weekend. $10 surcharge for one-night weekend stay. $20 extra person. Business rates Sunday–Thursdays except holidays—$65 one night, $55 per night for two or more nights. Five percent discount for AARP members and senior citizens. Amex, Discover, MC, Visa (plus 5 percent surcharge).
♥ ♞ ❊ ✖ ✄

"Sour cream pancakes with blueberries or maybe strawberry sauce. Nectarines poached in white wine and ginger with creme fraiche. Stuffed French toast with apricot raisin sauce. Omelets with garden nasturtium and chive fillings. Blueberry orange soup from a guest's recipe. Sausage ricotta pancake. Austrian plum cake. Poppyseed muffins. My own peach preserves. . . . "

In the morning Margaret decides what she'll make for your breakfast, the feature of her inn. Innkeeping followed years of restoring and selling houses. When Margaret moved from Connecticut to Washington, she became a full-time culinary student at L'Academie de Cuisine, worked with caterers, and then decided to "create her own internship." In 1989 she bought this stately 1868 Federal (painted) brick house, which had been meticulously restored as a B&B by a former Foreign Service officer and his wife. They filled it with antiques and items collected from around the world. Margaret added many indoor plants and a garden of herbs and edible flowers.

In residence: Walter and Veronica, Lhasa apsos "who stay in their apartment unless asked to visit."
Bed and bath: Six rooms, all private baths. Double, queen, or a double and a twin bed; some canopied, four-posters, and sleighs. Four shower baths en suite; one hall tub/shower bath; one claw-footed tub bath. Rollaway available.

Breakfast: Usually at 8:30 or 9:30. A daily creation. Served family style in two dining rooms.

Plus: Fireplaced living room. Central air conditioning. Guest cordless phone. TV in library. Fresh flowers. Complimentary beverages. Sometimes, spontaneous treats. Treetop porch. Margaret's own potpourri. Picnic baskets ($12) with advance notice.

KEY TO SYMBOLS

♥ Lots of honeymooners come here.
♯ Families with children are very welcome. (Please see page xii.)
▰ "Please emphasize that we are a private home, not an inn."
❖ Groups or private parties sometimes book the entire B&B.
♦ Travel agents' commission paid. (Please see page xii.)
✖ Sorry, no guests' pets are allowed.
✄ No smoking inside *or* no smoking at all, even on porches.

INDEX

DELAWARE

Reservation services, 4
Laurel, Spring Garden Bed & Breakfast Inn, 5
Lewes, Bed & Breakfast of Delaware Host #35, 6
New Castle, Bed & Breakfast of Delaware Host #32, 7
Odessa, Bed & Breakfast of Delaware Host #34, 7
Wilmington, The Boulevard Bed & Breakfast, 8

MARYLAND

Reservation services, 12
Annapolis
    Amanda's Host #112, 14
    Amanda's Host #259, 14
    Bed and Breakfast of Maryland Host #129, 15
    Bed and Breakfast of Maryland Host #139, 16
    College House Suites, 17
    The William Page Inn, 18
Annapolis: Edgewater, Riverwatch Bed & Breakfast, 19
Baltimore
    Amanda's Host #110, 20
    Amanda's Host #201, 20
    Celie's Waterfront Bed & Breakfast, 21
    Mr. Mole Bed & Breakfast, 22
Baltimore: Fallston, Broom Hall Bed & Breakfast, 23
Baltimore: Lutherville, Twin Gates B&B Inn, 24
Baltimore: Stevenson, Gramercy Bed & Breakfast, 25
Berlin, Holland House B&B, 26
Burtonsville, Bed and Breakfast of Maryland Host #189, 27
Cambridge, Glasgow Inn Bed & Breakfast, 28

Chesapeake City
    Inn at the Canal, 29
    Two Rivers Farm, 30
Chestertown, Brampton, 31
Chevy Chase, Chevy Chase Bed & Breakfast, 32
Easton, Amanda's Host #137, 33
Frederick, Middle Plantation Inn, 33
Hagerstown
    Beaver Creek House Bed & Breakfast, 34
    Lewrene Farm B&B, 35
    Sunday's Bed & Breakfast, 36
Havre de Grace, Bed & Breakfast of Delaware Host #36, 37
Monkton, Amanda's Host #209, 38
New Market, National Pike Inn, 39
North East, The Mill House Bed & Breakfast, 40
Oakland, The Oak & Apple, 41
Olney, The Thoroughbred Bed & Breakfast, 42
Princess Anne, Elmwood c. 1770 B&B, 43
St. Michaels, Parsonage Inn, 44
Sharpsburg, The Inn at Antietam, 45
Silver Spring, Bed & Breakfast of Maryland Host #185, 46
Smithsburg, Blue Bear Bed & Breakfast, 46
Snow Hill
    Chanceford Hall Bed & Breakfast Inn, 47
    The River House Inn, 48
Taneytown
    Antrim 1844, 49
    Glenburn, 50
Vienna, Tavern House, 51

NEW JERSEY

Reservation services, 54
Alloway, Josiah Reeve House, 56
Avon-by-the-Sea, Cashelmara Inn, 57

Bay Head
  Bay Head Gables, 58
  Conover's Bay Head Inn, 59
Beach Haven, Pierrot by the Sea, 60
Cape May
  The Abbey Bed and Breakfast, 61
  Abigail Adams' Bed & Breakfast
    by the Sea, 62
  The Albert Stevens Inn, 63
  Barnard-Good House, 64
  The Brass Bed Inn, 65
  Captain Mey's Inn, 66
  COLVMNS by the Sea, 67
  The Duke of Windsor, 68
  The Gingerbread House, 69
  The Humphrey Hughes House, 70
  The Mainstay Inn & Cottage, 71
  Manor House, 72
  The Mason Cottage, 73
  The Queen Victoria, 74
  The Wooden Rabbit, 75
  Woodleigh House, 76
Clinton, Leigh Way Bed and Break-
  fast Inn, 77
Flemington
  The Cabbage Rose Inn, 78
  Jerica Hill Inn, 79
Lyndhurst, The Jeremiah H. Yere-
  ance House, 80
North Wildwood, Bed & Breakfast
  Adventures Host #479, 81
Ocean City
  BarnaGate Bed & Breakfast, 82
  New Brighton Inn, 83
  Northwood Inn Bed & Breakfast,
    84
  Top o' the Waves, 85
Princeton, Red Maple Farm, 86
Spring Lake
  Ashling Cottage, 87
  Sea Crest by the Sea, 88
Stanhope, The Whistling Swan Inn,
  89
Stewartsville, The Stewart Inn, 90
Woodbine, The Henry Ludlam Inn,
  91

NEW YORK

Reservation services, 96, 102–
  105, 142, 153, 159, 180
Albany, The American Country Col-
  lection Host #097, 143
Altamont, Appel Inn, 143
Avoca, Patchwork Peace Bed &
  Breakfast, 160
Bainbridge, Berry Hill Farm B&B,
  124
Bolton Landing, Hilltop Cottage
  B&B, 144
Branchport, Four Seasons Bed &
  Breakfast, 161
Brooklyn, Bed & Breakfast on the
  Park, 107
Burdett, The Red House Country
  Inn, 162
Canandaigua: Rushville, Lakeview
  Farm Bed n' Breakfast, 163
Cazenovia, The American Country
  Collection Host #162, 164
Chautauqua, Plumbush at Chautau-
  qua, 181
Chautauqua: Westfield
  Westfield House, 182
  The William Seward Inn, 183
Cooperstown
  Creekside Bed & Breakfast, 125
  The Inn at Brook Willow, 126
  Litco Farms Bed & Breakfast, 127
  Thistlebrook, 128
Cooperstown: Richfield Springs,
  Summerwood, 129
Corning
  1865 White Birch B&B, 164
  Rosewood Inn, 165
Croton-on-Hudson, Alexander
  Hamilton House, 108
Deposit, The White Pillars Inn, 135
Dolgeville, Adrianna Bed & Break-
  fast, 130
East Hampton
  Centennial House, 97
  Mill House Inn, 98
Elmira: Chemung, Halcyon Place
  Bed & Breakfast, 166
Ghent, The American Country Col-
  lection Host #082, 112

Goshen: Campbell Hall, Tara Farm Bed & Breakfast, 113
Guilford, The Village Green Bed & Breakfast, 131
Hammondsport
The Blushing Rosé B&B, 167
The Bowman House, a bed and breakfast, 168
Hampton Bays, House on the Water, 99
High Falls, Captain Schoonmaker's Bed & Breakfast, 114
Ilion, Chesham Place, 132
Ithaca
Buttermilk Falls Bed & Breakfast, 169
Hanshaw House B&B, 170
Rose Inn, 171
Ithaca: Alpine, The Fountainebleau Inn, 172
Ithaca: Groton, Gale House Bed & Breakfast, 173
Jeffersonville, The Griffin House Bed & Breakfast, 136
Katonah, The American Country Collection Host #155, 115
Keene Valley, Trail's End, 154
Kingston, Rondout Bed & Breakfast, 116
Lake George: Lake Luzerne, The Lamplight Inn Bed & Breakfast, 145
Lake Placid, Stagecoach Inn, 155
Long Eddy, The Rolling Marble Guest House, 137
Lowville, Hinchings Pond B&B Inn, 156
Middletown/Goshen: Slate Hill, The American Country Collection Host #064, 117
New Berlin, Sunrise Farm, 133
New Paltz, Ujjala's Bed & Breakfast, 118
New Paltz: Clintondale, Orchard House, 119
New Paltz: Wallkill, Audrey's Farmhouse B&B, 120
New York
Abode Bed & Breakfast Host #77, 109

Urban Ventures Host #HAR111, 109
Urban Ventures Host #CON200, 110
Niagara Falls: Lewiston, The Cameo Inns, 184
Penn Yan, The Wagener Estate Bed & Breakfast, 174
Queensbury, Crislip's Bed & Breakfast, 157
Rhinebeck, Village Victorian Inn, 121
Rhinebeck: Stanfordville, The Lakehouse Inn . . . On Golden Pond, 121
Rochester, 428 Mt. Vernon—a bed and breakfast inn, 177
Rochester: Fairport, Woods-Edge Bed & Breakfast, 178
Rochester: Mumford, Genesee Country Inn, 179
Saranac Lake, Adirondack Bed & Breakfasts Host #10, 157
Saratoga Springs
Saratoga Bed and Breakfast, 146
The Six Sisters Bed and Breakfast, 147
Union Gables, 148
The Westchester House B&B, 149
Saratoga Springs: Schuylerville, The Inn on Bacon Hill, 150
Schenectady, The Widow Kendall House, 151
Southampton, The Old Post House Inn, 100
Stamford: Hobart, Breezy Acres Farm Bed & Breakfast, 133
Stillwater, The American Country Collection Host #005, 152
Syracuse, The Russell-Farrenkopf House, 175
Tannersville, The Eggery Inn, 138
Watkins Glen: Rock Stream, Reading House, 176
West Shokan, Haus Elissa Bed & Breakfast, 139
Westhampton Beach, Seafield House, 101
Woodstock: Chichester, Maplewood Bed & Breakfast, 139

Woodstock: Mt. Tremper, Mount Tremper Inn, 140

NORTH CAROLINA

Asheville
   Applewood Manor, 188
   Black Walnut Inn, 189
   Cairn Brae, 190
   The Inn on Montford, 191
Banner Elk, The Banner Elk Inn B&B, 192
Beauford, Pecan Tree Inn, 193
Black Mountain, Bed and Breakfast Over Yonder, 194
Charlotte
   The Homeplace Bed & Breakfast, 195
   The Inn on Providence, 196
Clyde, Windsong: A Mountain Inn (and llama farm), 197
Durham
   Arrowhead Inn, c. 1775, 198
   Old North Durham Inn, 199
Durham: Hillsborough, The Hillsborough House Inn, 200
Franklin, Buttonwood Inn, 201
Hatteras, Outer Banks Bed & Breakfast, 202
Henderson, La Grange Plantation Inn, 203
Hendersonville, The Waverly Inn, 204
Hiddenite, Hidden Crystal Inn, 205
Kill Devil Hills, The Figurehead, 206
Lake Lure, The Lodge on Lake Lure, 206
Mount Airy, Pine Ridge Inn, 207
Murphy, Huntington Hall Bed & Breakfast, 208
New Bern
   The Aerie, 209
   Harmony House Inn, 210
Rutherfordton, Pinebrae Manor, 211
Salisbury
   The 1868 Stewart-Marsh House, 212
   Rowan Oak House, 213

Statesville, Aunt Mae's Bed & Breakfast, 214
Sugar Grove, Rivendell Lodge, 215
Tarboro, Little Warren Bed and Breakfast, 216
Wilson, Miss Betty's Bed & Breakfast Inn, 217
Winston-Salem, Lady Anne's Victorian Bed & Breakfast, 218

PENNSYLVANIA

Reservation services, 223-224, 258, 270, 295
Adamstown, Adamstown Inn, 271
Airville, Spring House, 272
Allentown: Macungie, Sycamore Inn Bed & Breakfast, 259
Beach Lake, The Beach Lake Hotel, 264
Beaumont, Ponda-Rowland Bed & Breakfast, 296
Blue Bell, Blue Heron B&B, 225
Boyertown, The Enchanted Cottage, 260
Canadensis, Brookview Manor Bed & Breakfast Inn, 265
Chadds Ford, Bed & Breakfast of Delaware Host #3, 226
Christiana, Winding Glen Farm Tourist Home, 273
Churchtown, Churchtown Inn, 274
Columbia, The Columbian, 275
Doylestown, The Inn at Fordhook Farm, 246
Eagles Mere, Shady Lane, A Bed & Breakfast Inn, 297
East Berlin, The Bechtel Mansion Inn, 298
Ephrata
   Clearview Farm Bed & Breakfast, 276
   Historic Smithton, 277
Gardenville, Maplewood Farm Bed & Breakfast, 247
Gettysburg
   Baladerry Inn, 299
   The Brafferton Inn, 300
   Keystone Inn, 301

Gettysburg: Gardners, Goose Chase
  Bed & Breakfast, 302
Gettysburg: Hanover, Beechmont
  Inn, 303
Gettysburg: New Oxford, Con-
  ewago House, 304
Gettysburg: Orrtanna, Hickory
  Bridge Farm, 305
Gordonville, The Osceola Mill
  House, 278
Hawley, Academy Street Bed &
  Breakfast, 266
Hershey, Pinehurst Inn Hershey,
  279
Howard, Curtinview, 306
Kennett Square
  B&B at The Lighted Holly, 227
  Meadow Spring Farm, 227
  Scarlett House, 228
Kennett Square: Avondale, Bed &
  Breakfast at Walnut Hill, 230
Lackawaxen, Roebling Inn on the
  Delaware, 267
Lancaster
  Buona Notte Bed & Breakfast,
    280
  Lincoln Haus Inn Bed & Break-
    fast, 280
  O'Flaherty's Dingeldein House,
    281
  Patchwork Inn, 282
Lancaster: Oxford, Bed & Breakfast
  of Delaware Host #31, 283
Lancaster: Willow Street, The
  Apple Bin Inn, 284
Landenberg, Cornerstone Bed and
  Breakfast, 231
Leesport, The Loom Room, 261
Lewisburg, The Pineapple Inn, 262
Lima, Hamanassett, 232
Lititz, Swiss Woods Bed & Break-
  fast, 285
Loganton, Webb Farm Bed &
  Breakfast, 306
Manheim, Herr Farmhouse Inn,
  286
Marietta
  The Noble House, 287
  Vogt Farm Bed & Breakfast, 288

Mertztown, Longswamp Bed and
  Breakfast, 263
Montoursville, The Carriage House
  at Stonegate, 307
Mount Joy
  Cedar Hill Farm, 289
  The Country Stay, 290
  Hillside Farm Bed & Breakfast,
    291
Mount Pocono, Farmhouse Bed &
  Breakfast, 268
Muncy, The Bodine House, 308
New Hope
  The Wedgwood Collection of His-
    toric Inns, 248
  The Whitehall Inn, 249
New Hope: Holicong
  Ash Mill Farm, 250
  Barley Sheaf Farm, 251
New Hope: Kintnersville, The Buck-
  sville House, 252
New Hope: Wrightstown, Hollileif
  Bed & Breakfast Establishment,
  253
Paradise, Maple Lane Guest House,
  292
Philadelphia
  Antique Row Bed & Breakfast,
    233
  Center City Retreat, 233
  Cromwell House, 234
  New Market Surprise, 235
  Shippen Way Inn, 236
Philadelphia: Huntington Valley,
  Shirl's Shed, 237
Point Pleasant, Tattersall Inn, 254
Potters Mills, General Potter Farm,
  309
Radnor, The Barn at Gulph Mills,
  238
Starrucca, The Nethercott Inn, 269
Stormstown, The John Thompson
  House B&B, 310
Strasburg, Limestone Inn, 292
Upper Black Eddy, Bridgeton
  House on the Delaware, 255
Valley Forge, Amsterdam B&B, 238
Valley Forge: Malvern, The Great
  Valley House of Valley Forge, 239

Washington Crossing, Woodhill
   Farms Inn, 256
West Chester
   The Bankhouse Bed & Breakfast,
   240
   Lenape Springs Farm, 241
   The Valentine, 242
West Chester: Dilworthtown, Mon-
   ument House, 243
Wrightsville, 1854 House, 293

VIRGINIA

Reservation services, 315
Abingdon, Summerfield Inn, 317
Arlington, Memory House, 318
Boyce, The River House, 319
Cape Charles
   Nottingham Ridge, 320
   Pickett's Harbor, 321
   Sea Gate Bed & Breakfast, 322
Charlottesville
   Alderman House, 323
   Bollingwood, 323
   The Inn at Monticello, 324
   Recoletta, 325
   Sunnyfields, 325
Charlottesville: North Garden
   Ammonett Farm, 326
   Ingleside, 327
Charlottesville: Scottsville
   Chester, 328
   High Meadows Vineyard &
   Mountain Sunset Inn, 329
Charlottesville: Stanardsville, Edge-
   wood Farm Bed & Breakfast, 330
Chatham, House of Laird, 331
Chincoteague, The Watson House,
   332
Christiansburg, The Oaks Bed &
   Breakfast Country Inn, 333
Cluster Springs, Oak Grove Planta-
   tion, 334
Covington, Milton Hall Bed and
   Breakfast Inn, 335
Edinburg, Mary's Country Inn, 336
Fairfax, The Bailiwick Inn, 337
Fredericksburg, La Vista Plantation,
   338

Front Royal, Chester House Inn,
   339
Leesburg: Lincoln, Springdale
   Country Inn, 340
Lexington, Llewellyn Lodge, 341
Lexington: Raphine, Oak Spring
   Farm and Vineyard, 342
Lynchburg
   Langhorne Manor, 344
   Lynchburg Mansion Inn Bed and
   Breakfast, 345
   The Madison House Bed & Break-
   fast, 346
Lynchburg: Amherst, Dulwich
   Manor Bed & Breakfast, 347
Lynchburg: Madison Heights,
   Winridge Bed & Breakfast, 348
Lynchburg: Monroe, "St. Moor"
   House, 349
Middleburg, Middleburg Country
   Inn, 350
Mollusk, Greenvale Manor Water-
   front Inn, 351
Mount Jackson, Widow Kip's Shen-
   andoah Inn, 352
Nellysford
   The Acorn Inn, Inc., 353
   The Meander Inn, 354
New Market, A Touch of Country,
   355
Norfolk, Page House Inn, 356
Onancock, The Spinning Wheel
   Bed and Breakfast, 357
Orange
   Hidden Inn, 358
   The Holladay House, 359
Orange: Gordonsville, Sleepy Hol-
   low Farm B&B, 360
Palmyra, Danscot House, 361
Petersburg, The High Street Inn,
   362
Pratts, Colvin Hall Bed and Break-
   fast, 363
Richmond
   The Emmanuel Hutzler House,
   364
   Summerhouse, 365
   University of Richmond area
   B&B, 366
   The William Catlin House Inn, 366

Roanoke, Mary Bladon House, 367
Smith Mountain Lake, The Manor
    at Taylor's Store, 368
Staunton
    Ashton Country House, 369
    Frederick House, 370
    The Sampson Eagon Inn, 371
    Thornrose House at Gypsy Hill,
    372
Urbanna, The Duck Farm Inn, 373
Wachapreague, The Burton House,
374
Warm Springs, Anderson Cottage
    Bed & Breakfast, 375
Washington
    Caledonia Farm, 376
    The Foster-Harris House, 377
    Sycamore Hill House & Gardens,
    378
Williamsburg
    Colonial Capital Bed & Breakfast,
    379
    Legacy of Williamsburg Inn, 381
    Liberty Rose B&B, 382
    Newport House, 383
    Williamsburg Cottage #10, 384
    Williamsburg Manor Bed and
    Breakfast, 384
    Williamsburg Sampler Bed and
    Breakfast, 385
Williamsburg: Charles City
    Edgewood Plantation, 386
    North Bend Plantation B&B, 387
Woodstock, The Country Fare,
388

WASHINGTON, D.C.

Reservation services, 393
Capitol Hill
    Bed & Breakfast Accommoda-
    tions, Ltd. Host #137, 395
    Bed & Breakfast Accommoda-
    tions, Ltd. Host #145, 396
    Bed & Breakfast Accommoda-
    tions, Ltd. Host #170, 396
    The Bed & Breakfast
    League/Sweet Dreams & Toast
    Host #5, 397

Dupont Circle
    Bed & Breakfast Accommoda-
    tions, Ltd. Host #125, 398
    Swann Bed & Breakfast, 398
Logan Circle, Bed & Breakfast Ac-
    commodations, Ltd. Host #100,
    399
Northwest
    Bed & Breakfast Accommoda-
    tions, Ltd. Host #128, 400
    The Bed & Breakfast
    League/Sweet Dreams & Toast
    Host #1, 400
    The Bed & Breakfast
    League/Sweet Dreams & Toast
    Host #2, 401
    The Bed & Breakfast
    League/Sweet Dreams & Toast
    Host #3, 401
    Inver House, 402
    Kalorama Guest House at
    Woodley Park, 403

WEST VIRGINIA

Beckley: Prosperity, Prosperity
    Farmhouse Bed & Breakfast, 406
Berkeley Springs, Highlawn Inn,
407
Bramwell, Three Oaks and A Quilt,
408
Charles Town
    Gilbert House B&B of Middle-
    way, 409
    Hillbrook Inn, 410
Elkins, The Retreat at Buffalo Run,
411
Elkins: Huttonsville, Hutton House
    Bed & Breakfast, 412
Franklin, McCoy's Mill B&B, 413
Gerrardstown, Gerrardstown's Pros-
    pect Hill Bed & Breakfast, 414
Harpers Ferry, Fillmore Street Bed
    & Breakfast, 415
Hillsboro, The Current, 416
Morgantown, Maxwell Bed &
    Breakfast, 417
Shepherdstown, Thomas Shepherd
    Inn, 418

ABOUT THE AUTHOR

Bernice Chesler, "America's bed and breakfast ambassador," has appeared on dozens of television and radio programs including "CBS This Morning," CNN, and NPR's "Morning Edition." She is known for her personalized approach and attention to detail. Guests from all over the world write to her about their B&B experiences. She shares their impressions—and her own, gathered through hundreds of stays and extensive interviews—in her books; in Meet-the-Hosts programs conducted at such major retailers as Bloomingdale's, L.L. Bean, Filene's, and Abraham & Straus; in workshops; and in lectures at bed and breakfast conferences from Maine to California.

Recipient of the nation's first B&B Achievement Award and first B&B Reservation Service Award, the author has written for 'GBH, Yankee, Country Almanac, Family Circle, and Innsider magazines and for the Boston Globe and the Washington Post.

BBB—Before Bed and Breakfast—Ms. Chesler conducted thousands of interviews throughout the country for documentary films seen on national public television. As publications coordinator for the Emmy Award–winning television program "ZOOM," produced at WGBH, Boston, she edited twelve books emanating from the series. She is also the author of the classic guide In and Out of Boston with (or without) Children.